T5-CCN-051

SOCIAL
PSYCHOLOGY

SOCIAL PSYCHOLOGY

Jeffrey H. Goldstein

Temple University

Academic Press

A Subsidiary of Harcourt Brace Jovanovich, Publishers

New York / London / Toronto / Sydney / San Francisco

Cover and chapter opening art by Cathy Hull.

Copyright ©1980, by Academic Press, Inc.
All rights reserved.

No part of this publication may be reproduced or
transmitted in any form or by any means, electronic
or mechanical, including photocopy, recording,
or any information storage and retrieval system,
without permission in writing from the publisher.

Academic Press, Inc.
111 Fifth Avenue, New York, New York 10003

United Kingdom Edition published by
Academic Press, Inc. (London) Ltd.
24/28 Oval Road, London NW1

ISBN: 0-12-287050-6
Library of Congress Catalog Card Number: 78-64447

Printed in the United States of America

TO THE STUDENT

Social psychology has always lived in a divided house. The first two American textbooks of social psychology, both published in 1908, indicated even then a disagreement over subject matter, method, and philosophy. In its early days as a separate intellectual discipline it was generally true that there were as many different social psychologies as there were social psychologists. Today that is less true, although there is by no means a single social psychology in which there is universal agreement on subject, method, or theory. This makes it difficult for you "to learn social psychology," but it is, nonetheless, a healthy state of affairs. A field in which everyone agrees on all issues is one in which stagnation can easily occur. It is important for social psychologists to question what they and other social psychologists do, how they do it, and for what reasons. Only in this way can new methods, theories, and subject matter be developed. If learning is to have any meaning, it is as important for the student of social psychology to question the teacher as for the teacher to question the student. Precisely because social psychology consists of such a diversity of theories, methods, and topics, it is important to recognize their limitations, as well as their merits.

As a social psychologist, I have my own beliefs and feelings about the proper study of social behavior. One of the themes of this book is that social behavior is motivated largely by peoples' needs to find meaning and order in their lives. Attitudes are formed and changed, people are helped and harmed, and attachments are begun and terminated, when they provide order and "make sense" to a person. But behavior is not always logical. It makes sense to the people engaged in it, and so we speak of psycho-logic. No less than others, my behavior, too, is motivated by a need to find order, meaning, and organization in experience. Finding such meaning often involves distortions and biases, an emphasis on some facts at the expense of others. This book is motivated primarily by my own needs to make sense out of social psychology. I can only hope that it provides some meaningful organization to you as well.

In looking for patterns and structure in social psychology, I have undoubtedly ignored some information and focused on other information. Chapters 1 and 2 indicate that all observations are biased—purely objective observation is a myth. If you think that I am correct about some interpretation or idea, it is as likely to be because you share some of my biases and assumptions as because I have struck the truth. Of course, if you think some of my notions are ridiculous, it may only mean that you do not share my biases. In either case, you should know that the behavior of social psychologists is caused by the same factors and operates on the same principles as the behavior of those who form the subjects of their study.

If it is true that all observation is biased in some way, then perhaps I should share some of my biases with you, so that you can interpret what appears in the following pages in light of these biases. Perhaps the overriding principle that influences my views of social behavior is a particular theoretical orientation I hold, and which is shared by a great many other social psychologists. I consider myself to be a cognitive social psychologist, meaning that I assume human beings to be qualitatively different from other species of organism, and see them as the initiators of behavior, rather than only as responders, and believe that peoples' views of their environment are more important than the objective environment in determining behavior. These issues are discussed fully in Chapter 1.

I have therefore set fairly modest goals for this book. I would like to present some of the fundamental issues that underlie much work in contemporary social psychology, to give the reader a sense of the history of social psychological ideas. In other words, I would like the reader to learn to appreciate how social psychologists think about and see issues of human social behavior. Second, it is important to know some of the hallmarks of social psychological research and theory, and to this end, a number of classical studies are presented. While many of these are now questionable on methodological grounds and seem hopelessly out of date, they often marked turning points in the development of the field. Knowing something about social psychology's past will help you to understand its present and predict its future. Third, I want to familiarize you with what I see as the most interesting and most important concerns of present-day social psychology. Not all of social psychology today seems either interesting or important, at least to me. Therefore, current theory and research presented in this book will be chosen selectively. Finally, I would like to present some approaches to the applications of social psychology to real-world problems, pointing out both the benefits and potential costs of letting social psychologists have some say in policy formation.

There is considerable emphasis on social psychology's past and its future. This is largely because I believe social psychology to be going through a transition phase wherein new directions are being charted. But it is difficult to present what now appears to be chaos in a meaningful way for students. By focusing on the past it is easier, perhaps, to make sense out of the present. So it is not my intention to bring the reader up to date on all theory and research in contemporary social psychology. Nor do I wish to review research that is not rooted in theory, unless that research is historically important or is applicable to some real-world problem. I have tried to keep the mention of names of social psychologists in the text to a minimum. References are usually placed in parentheses so that you may follow up ideas of interest. Names are selectively placed in the body of the text, however, and those that appear with some frequency are considered important in the history of social psychology.

In order to provide a broader context within which to view social psychological theory and research, I have included a half-dozen interviews with prominent social psychologists. In these interviews, issues related to the development and application of ideas are discussed. Editorial asides and comments about social psychology are presented in the Time Outs. These are designed both to make your reading more enjoyable and to lead you to think more critically about what you have read. Sometimes, in the main text itself, but especially in the Time Outs, humor has been injected, usually to make a point (even if the point is only that social psychology is but one way of examining human behavior, not the only way, or always the best way). I have had a good deal of fun in writing this book, along with a few agonizing struggles, and I can only hope that you are able to experience some of the spirit of the first, while minimizing the second. Social psychology as a profession is both hard work and a lot of fun. Studying it should be no less challenging and no less enjoyable.

TO THE
INSTRUCTOR

Whether or not one agrees with Gergen that social psychologists are capable only of studying historical, time-bound phenomena in a largely descriptive fashion, there can be little doubt that, historically, changes in the content of social psychology have occurred quite rapidly. With the advent of World War II, for example, social psychologists turned their attention toward the war effort; as a result an enormous amount of research was done on leadership, group productivity, attitudes, and propaganda. The Kitty Genovese slaying in 1964 led to a now vast quantity of research findings on helping and bystander intervention. Times change, and social psychologists' concerns change with them. Perhaps these changes are good for the field, and perhaps they represent attempts to accommodate fluctuations in prevailing social, economic, and political conditions. Change is healthy: the evolution of surface topics of social psychological concern has broadened the field, attracted new students with fresh ideas, and has been a mechanism functioning to prevent stagnation.

The following list of topics contrasts the primary concerns of social psychologists in the 1950s and the 1970s, as suggested by the indexes of social psychology textbooks written during these periods.

1950s	1970s
dogmatism	aggression
emotion	altruism
group pressure	attribution
leadership	conformity

morale and productivity	environmental psychology
person perception	ethical issues in research
propaganda	interpersonal attraction
rigidity, authoritarianism	obedience to authority
social norms	role-playing
values	social power

What have these nearly two dozen topics in common? What in the social psychology of the 1950s could enable one to predict the social psychology of the 1970s and 1980s? Perhaps there are no common themes, no continuity from one generation of social psychologists to the next. Conceivably, as Gergen maintains, social psychology is merely experimental history—social psychologists simply explore in their laboratories topics that interest them as private citizens of a particular culture at a particular time.

I do not believe this is the case. There are commonalities, albeit sometimes subtle and latent, between many of today's social psychologists and those of the past. This is not to say that Auguste Comte, Kurt Lewin, or George Herbert Mead would embrace what appears in the *Journal of Personality and Social Psychology* as their field of interest. Nor do I suggest that they would even recognize it as social psychology. But in one sense, these men are responsible for much of what appears in today's journals and textbooks. It is this commonality and continuity I would like to explore further in this book.

The examination of nearly any aspect of social behavior from a particular frame of reference is social psychology. What Comte, Lewin, and Mead have in common with Asch, Festinger, Newcomb, Schachter, Sherif, and Zajonc is not a surface topic of common interest, but a way of examining behavior and a set of objectives which lead to that examination. If social psychologists were merely scientists researching particular topics, it would be more convenient to conceive of aggressionists, groupists, or attributionists, than to consider them under one heading. Social psychology is a perspective on or philosophy of human interaction. It is not about attitudes; it is not about aggression; it is not even about social interaction. It is a *process* and as such is not *about* anything. The "real" social psychology must often be gleaned from between the lines of our journals and books. But it is there, and it is worthwhile to try to uncover it.

My purpose in this book is simply to present what I perceive as the essence of social psychology—that is, to indicate a particular way of seeing social relations and, to a degree, to suggest some implications of that way of seeing.

I recognize that intructors and students are often at cross-purposes in basic courses. Students want to learn something about themselves in the world as it is and instructors often want them to learn only about social psychology as it is. To paraphrase Kurt Lewin, nothing is more relevant to the world as it is than a relatively enduring way of perceiving that world. Therefore, this book begins with a fairly abstract and general discussion of philosophical, theoretical, and methodological issues in social psychology.

Emphasis throughout the book has been placed on the intellectual development of ideas, beginning often with the earliest psychological research on a topic, and showing how failures to replicate this research and subsequent interaction effects have led to qualifications of those initial findings. So, in a sense, most topics are presented first as main effects and later as interaction effects. There is also a good deal of emphasis placed on the cultural, historical, and social relativism of knowledge. Therefore, cross-cultural research is discussed whenever it is relevant in order to indicate some of the limitations that must be recognized before generalizing too broadly. Social psychology is a vast territory (though some of my colleagues believe it to be only half that). I have, therefore, found it necessary to restrict the discussion of some topics so that other, more recent interests could be included. The last two chapters are on applications of social psychology to real-world concerns. Chapter 13 discusses a variety of issues now coming into prominence. Among these are the social psychology of sports, jury proceedings, mental illness, science, and social psychology itself.

I have tried to strike a balance between the older, classical studies of social psychology and the more up-to-date developments in the field. "Truth is timeless, certainly, and one doesn't have to be up to date to be right," Saul Bellow has written. I have tried to emphasize studies that have stood the test of time.

ACKNOWLEDGMENTS

Intellectual debts are the most difficult ones to repay. To two sets of teachers I owe special thanks: my parents and my grandmother, through whose gentleness, kindness, and humor, I am more receptive to other people and their ideas than I would otherwise have been. As well, I am indebted to Marshall Walker, Professor of Physics at the University of Connecticut, and Ralph Rosnow, then at Boston University and now a friend and colleague at Temple University, who awakened my interest in science. This book is dedicated to them, and to Carolyn.

Numerous friends and colleagues have read portions, and, in several instances, all of the manuscript. Their suggestions and criticisms have greatly improved the quality of this book. William Ickes, of the University of Wisconsin, and David Lundgren, of the University of Cincinnati, who kindly commented on the entire manuscript, made a significant contribution. The insights of James H. Bryan, of Northwestern University; Don Carlston, of the University of Iowa; Roger Davis, of Temple University; Peter Gumpert, of the University of Massachusetts–Boston; George Levinger, of the University of Massachusetts–Amherst; and Zick Rubin, of Brandeis University, who read various portions of the manuscript, were invaluable. Conversations with John D. Edwards, David Kipnis, and Edna and Uriel Foa led to many changes in the tone or emphasis of several chapters. Seymor Feshbach, Ken Gergen, Jim Jones, George Levinger, Marianne LaFrance, and Clara Mayo were kind enough not only to permit my interviews with them to appear in this book, but to offer helpful advice on editorial matters as well. I am very grateful to them for their assistance.

Finally, students in a number of classes at Temple University have suffered through the reading of poorly typed and primitive drafts of this book. Although many students offered helpful comments, I am particularly grateful to Maria Ippolito, Elizabeth Lasz, Roslyn Kravitz, and Rick Reichert for their suggestions.

December 1979   *Jeffrey H. Goldstein*

CONTENTS

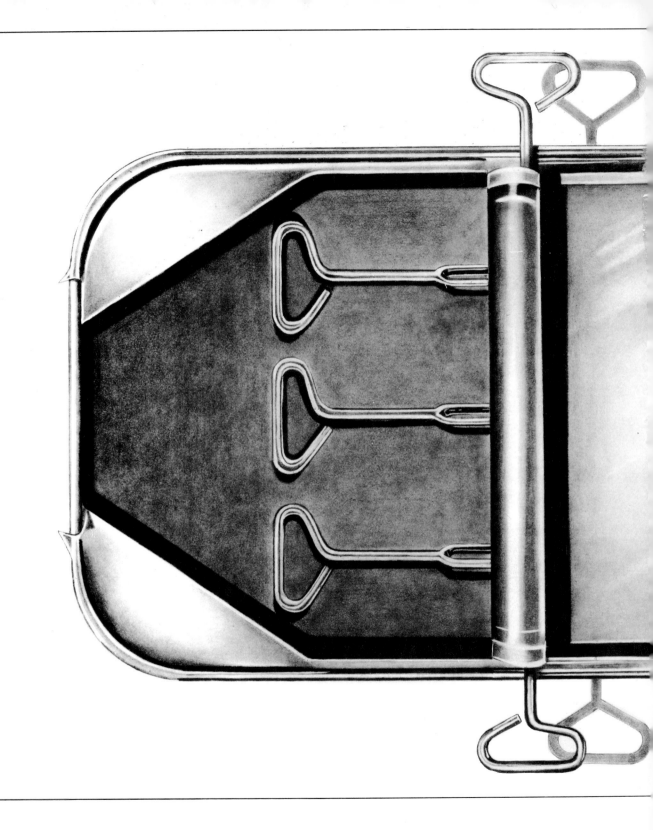

Cathy Hull

1
SOCIAL PSYCHOLOGY: PHILOSOPHICAL AND THEORETICAL ISSUES

My grandmother does not know what I do for a living. I don't hide my profession from her, but it's difficult to explain what a social psychologist does. I have a brother who is a physician. If he is a doctor, then despite my PhD, I must be something else. My Uncle Frank is a clinical psychologist in private practice. Since I do not treat patients, I must not be a psychologist. How, then, can I call myself a doctor and a psychologist, but not have a medical degree and never treat patients?

Social psychology has been defined as the study of social behavior, the study of how people organize and respond to their social experience, the study of people in groups, the study of interaction, and the study of the effects of one person on others (see G.W. Allport, 1968). It seems that social psychologists cannot agree on a very precise definition of their profession. And little wonder: Social psychologists work in a variety of settings, from universities to hospitals and psychiatric facilities, from Madison Avenue to the Pentagon. Their activities are almost as varied. They help to design buildings, construct training and development programs, and conduct research on a wide variety of topics, including attitudes and persuasion, the effects of pornography, childhood socialization, and urban riots. Yet despite the apparent diversity of the field, there are some common elements in what social psychologists do.

In general, social psychology is primarily concerned with human interaction, that is, with the effects that one or more persons have on one or more other people. The effects people have on one another are not limited to face-to-face situations. Social psychologists often examine the effects of indirect, impersonal, or "general" others. For example, we might easily study the effects of architectural design on an individual's mood or behavior. Such research would not involve how one person directly affects another, but would explore how the products of one person's behavior affect another's behavior. So, we can broadly define social psychology as *the study of how one person's behavior, or the results of that behavior, affect other people's behavior, or the results of their behavior.*

If we use this as our working definition, we soon find that almost everything people do falls within the scope of social psychology. Psychologists normally slice up the study of behavior into smaller, more manageable units, which correspond to various branches of the field: experimental psychology, physiological psychology, clinical psychology, developmental psychology, and so on. There are over 30 divisions of the American Psychological Association, and each represents a more or less different way of viewing human behavior. Using our broad definition of social psychology, all these branches of psychology, with the possible exception of physiological psychology, can fall within its domain. For example, learning, which is usually studied by experimental psychologists, is defined as a change in behavior. What causes a change in behavior? Usually, it is the behavior of another person. So, strictly speaking, learning falls within the province of social psychology. Developmental psychology is concerned with the effects of parental behaviors on child development. Because it clearly involves the effects of people's behavior on others, it, too, is encompassed by social psychology. Much of abnormal psychology is assumed to arise either from past experiences with others or from inconsistent or "improper" rewards and punishments received from others. In this sense, much of clinical psychology also falls under the heading of social psychology. Even in clinical settings, where psychotherapists work with one or more patients, one person's behavior clearly influences another's.

As we will see, social psychologists have branched out into what is generally considered the territory of other social scientists. In many cases it will not be clear whether a theory or research article was written by a social psychologist, a developmental psychologist, an experimental psychologist, or a clinical psychologist. For our purposes—learning about social behavior—it is of little importance where that learning comes from or who produces it. To study any behavior, however, some approaches, or levels of analysis, are more appropriate than others.

LEVELS OF ANALYSIS

All of psychology is concerned with human behavior. Most human behaviors can be analyzed on at least four levels: the biological, physiological, psychological, and social. As an example, let us examine a single act of violence in which one person strikes another. On the biological level, this behavior might be explained by arguing that human beings have evolved from lower species that are aggressive. Thus, our biological heritage prompts an act of violence.

On the physiological level, the event can be explained with reference to the bodily processes of the aggressor. In a moment of anger, certain hormones may have been released that acted upon specific areas of the brain, resulting in motor movements we call aggression.

We could also describe and explain the aggressive act psychologically by referring to the aggressor's perception of the victim and of himself, his early childhood experiences, and his learning of aggressive behavior from parents or peers.

Social explanations of the incident might refer to the society in which the aggressor lived. Perhaps it is one in which violence is condoned. Perhaps, hitting someone is not considered aggressive in this society. Or perhaps the aggressive act has something to do with the relationship between the aggressor and the victim.

Which of these possible types of explanation is correct? Is one of

You might explain this moment as an example of socially acceptable violence, or a healthy channeling of innate or learned aggressive tendencies. But think how your explanation of this scene would differ if these people were wearing jeans and the one on the left was clutching a pigskin wallet.

them more correct than the others? It is safe to say that all four levels of analysis are scientifically legitimate, and that no one of them is inherently better than any other.

All these influences operate on most human behaviors. It is generally accepted that we have evolved from biologically inferior species (that is, having simpler brains and nervous systems), and so some of our behavior may be traced to these biological origins. It is also true that any behavior requires some changes in physiology. Sometimes these are quite subtle, as when we are sitting quietly, thinking about something, and the changes are hormonal and biochemical changes in the nervous system. Other behaviors require a complex coordination and interplay of brain chemistry, muscular movement, and changes in the level of activation of the central and the autonomic nervous systems. But every human act can be analyzed in physiological terms.

Many behaviors, however, cannot be fully explained biologically or physiologically. Psychosomatic illness, for example, is defined as a physical symptom that does not have a physiological cause. Ulcers and twitches are often thought to be psychosomatic. We must refer to psychological factors to explain such symptoms. Likewise, to *predict* who will act aggressively, when, and against whom, biology and physiology are insufficient. Although they are useful in under-standing *how* a person responds in some situations, biological and physiological explanations may not enable us to predict *what* the person's response will be. In order to make predictions about a person's behavior, we often need to know how a person views a situation, and *what* (as opposed to *how*) that person thinks and feels. What a person thinks and feels is a psychological matter that may also involve social factors. For instance, people living in the same community often hold similar political views. So, there is a complex interplay between psychological and social factors. Social psychology is concerned with both the psychological and social causes of behavior.

As we move from biological to social levels of analysis (see Figure 1.1), several important issues arise. First, it is always possible to see some biological factors in any physiological process. Likewise, it is always possible to see some physiological processes in any psychological activity. Finally, psychological processes can be recognized in any social situation. In short, the lower levels of analysis in Figure 1.1 are always present to some extent in the higher levels. The crucial question confronting the student of human behavior is: How important are such lower levels in explaining and predicting higher levels of behavior? The biologist, for example, would argue that there are biological bases for much social behavior. Animals often have social organizations, methods of communication, and social interaction. Biologists often point to the similarities between animal and human behavior and imply that the former adequately explain the latter. (E.O. Wilson, 1975; Wispé & Thompson, 1976). The social psychologist would probably answer that the similarities between animal and human behavior are interesting but coincidental.

Whenever we study physiological, psychological, or social processes, there is always the possibility that the biological level is

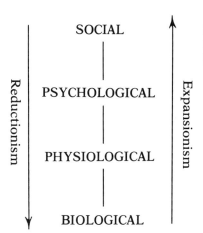

Figure 1.1.
Levels of analysis of human behavior.

applicable. Most scientists reject the notion that biology explains all physiology, or that physiology explains all psychology, or psychology all social activity. Discussing issues on too low a level is referred to as *reductionism*. We may also make the opposite error, what might be called *expansionism*: explaining a lower level with an irrelevant higher level. Some sociologists, for instance, attempt to explain crime solely with reference to social variables such as social class. But crime involves psychological processes—the decision to engage in criminal activity, the motive for this behavior, the criminal act itself. These are psychological processes that cannot adequately be explained or predicted only with reference to social class.

SOME BASIC ASSUMPTIONS
OF SOCIAL PSYCHOLOGY

Any attempt to understand, predict, explain, or control behavior rests on a number of assumptions. Merely by having enrolled for a course in social psychology, you have implicitly assumed the following: that human behavior can be studied (in other words, that it is understandable or explainable); that behavior is caused and not random, meaningless, or idiosyncratic; and that the causes of behavior can be known. All these assumptions are necessary for a study of psychology. If behavior is random, meaningless, and without causes, then it doesn't make any sense to study it, because there is really nothing to study.

These assumptions are premises that we accept as true before studying behavior. Although most of these assumptions are not easily tested or otherwise provable, they are worth examining, for each has implications for how and what we, as students of psychology, can learn.

Human behavior can be one of two things: it can be random, with no underlying causes, or it can be caused, in which case behavior is the result of particular antecedent conditions and events. If everyone's behavior is purely accidental or coincidental, then studying behavior can lead only to erroneous conclusions or to the conclusion that behaviors occur in no regular, orderly fashion.

No one seriously entertains the notion that behavior is without causes, that it occurs for no particular reasons. Certainly no psychologist could believe that behavior is without causes, and cannot be studied meaningfully, because that is what psychologists spend much of their time doing. Because it appears to us that behavior is orderly and is caused, it makes sense to proceed on the assumption that behavior is not random.

Once behavior is assumed to be caused and to operate according to certain principles, everyone studying behavior makes the further assumption that it is possible to discover those principles. If the causes of behavior cannot be discovered, it doesn't make much sense to devote our time to the study of behavior because we will learn nothing as a result. Most psychologists assume that it is possible to learn why people act as they do.

It is probably impossible to prove that the causes of behavior can be fully understood. About the only way we can tell whether we understand a person's behavior is to try to predict what that person will do in the future. If our prediction is accurate, that is a good indication that the causes of behavior are understood.

Psychologists make a number of other assumptions about behavior. We will discuss these assumptions as the need arises, because most of them are associated with particular theories of behavior and not all psychologists make the same additional assumptions (Lana, 1969). It is important to recognize, though, that psychology is based on assumptions about behavior that are ultimately untestable. Some or all of these assumptions may be incorrect. At the moment, we have no way of knowing.

SOCIAL PSYCHOLOGY AS A SCIENCE

Most definitions of social psychology involve the word *study*. Our working definition is "the study of how one person's behavior affects

To make good music requires control, precision, and a willingness to experiment. But this seemingly scientific approach does not transform musicians into scientists.

other people's behavior." *Study* generally means something quite specific, a scientifically conducted, empirical piece of research. In other words, this definition implies that social psychology is a science. Before you argue that social psychology is about as scientific as selling used cars, think about what the word *science* means.

Ask ten people at random what a scientist is and you will probably get such answers as "A scientist is someone, such as a physicist or a chemist, who studies the laws of nature," and "A scientist is someone who discovers facts about the physical world." These popular views restrict science to the study of the physical universe and conceive of it as somehow concerned with "truth" or with "laws" about the universe. If pressed further, people will often tell you that scientists do research and that the purpose of this research is to discover the "secrets of nature."

This view of the scientist and the scientific enterprise is much too limited. If we were to define science as studying, through research, the laws of nature, or as hard factual knowledge about the universe, we would have to exclude most of the sciences from our conception of science. Astronomers, whom most people consider scientists of the first order, do not do experiments on the planets or stars. Meteorologists often do small-scale research on weather patterns, but they have a dismal record of predicting changes in the weather. Obviously, then, experimentation and precision are poor indicators of whether an activity is scientific. Carpentry and musical composition are two very demanding and precise fields, but neither can claim to be a science.

If experimentation and precision do not identify a science, how is science to be defined? Science is a *process* that uses particular means to achieve particular goals, that is, *a field of study that employs research in order to build and test theories of some aspect of the universe*. This definition has two important components. The first is that it includes research, but research alone does not make an enterprise scientific. It is scientific only if the purpose of that research is the testing or building of theory. The combination of these two elements marks a field as a science. Note that this definition does not say whether the research is practical, factual, or precise. A field of study is scientific only if it attempts to produce theories that are testable by empirical means. In this way, science can be seen as a process rather than a product. It involves doing something (research) for a particular reason (theory).

A science is thus one way of studying various aspects of the universe; it is not the only way and, in many cases, it may not be the best way. It often has proved to be the best way of learning the nature of *things*, and most psychologists assume that the best way to learn about *human behavior* is by using scientific methods and goals. This means that most psychologists do research in order to develop and test theories about human behavior. By doing empirical research that is related to some theory, psychologists are scientists. This should not be interpreted to mean that psychology is as precise as physics or chemistry; in most cases, it is not. But psychologists are engaged in a particular kind of process—doing research to build and test theories—that places them in the same category as physicists, astronomers, meteorologists, and chemists. Psychologists are distinguished from other scientists not by a lesser degree of precision in their measurements and predictions, but by the different subject matter that they study.

Of course, not all psychologists are scientists. A psychologist is a scientist only if she or he conducts empirical investigations designed to develop or test theory. While much of this book discusses scientific social psychology, we will nevertheless discuss some ideas and research that stem from a nonscientific approach. Chapters 12 and 13 are devoted exclusively to practical aspects of social psychology.

THE GOALS OF SOCIAL PSYCHOLOGY

It is generally agreed that social psychology has two primary goals: the understanding of social behavior, *theory building*, and the prediction of future behavior, *theory testing*. While a number of means for achieving these goals are discussed in Chapter 2, something needs to be said about the goals themselves.

All social psychologists are interested to some degree in understanding social behavior. Understanding, once achieved, can then be applied in a variety of ways: to change the social order, to solve social problems, and to build theories of behavior. One of the basic problems in the study of knowledge is how a person knows when something is understood. What does it mean to understand something? If someone asks you, "Do you understand what I mean?" how can you be certain that you haven't misinterpreted that person's statement or position? In general, when such a question is asked, the responses of most people indicate that they think they know what the speaker means. In other words, they have a *feeling* of understanding. If we are speaking of social behavior, how can we know when we understand why people do certain things?

A BRIEF EXCURSION INTO PHYSICS

In the second century A.D., Ptolemy proposed a system of the universe in which the earth was a stationary planet at the center of the heavens. The sun and the heavens revolved around the earth in

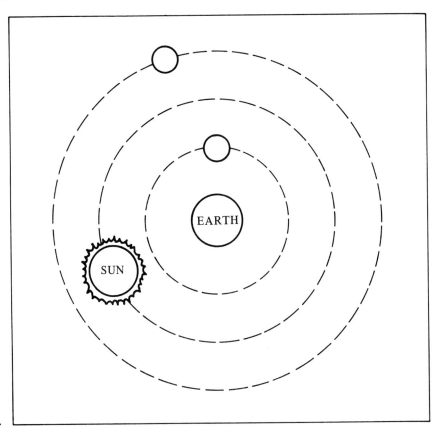

Figure 1.2.
Geocentric view of the universe with circular orbits.

circular orbits (see Figure 1.2). For at least thirteen centuries, the Ptolemaic view of the heavens was universally accepted. People believed they had a complete and perfect understanding of the changing seasons and the alternation of day and night because they "knew" that the sun revolved around the earth. Yet we know today that their understanding was incorrect.

The system that replaced Ptolemy's was the heliocentric theory. Copernicus (1473–1543) proposed that the planets revolved around the sun and that they did so in orbits that were circular (Figure 1.3). Not only was this proposal revolutionary—in both senses of the word—but it was rejected by almost everyone at the time. In the sixteenth century, Galileo (1564–1642), with the aid of his telescopes, was able to provide observations that supported Copernicus' theory. As a result, Galileo was charged with heresy and his books were officially banned for over two hundred years. When it finally won acceptance in the seventeenth century, Copernicus' heliocentric theory increased human understanding of the operation of the universe.

But it, too, was incorrect. We now know that the planetary orbits are not circular but elliptical, a notion proposed as early as the sixteenth century by Johannes Kepler (1571–1630). Our changing views of the universe did not end with Galileo, Copernicus, and Kepler, but continued into the nineteenth and twentieth centuries. Einstein's theory of general relativity, for example, has radically altered our ways of viewing such basic physical dimensions as space and time. Some of Einstein's theoretical positions have recently been challenged, so we still do not understand the construction of the universe in any absolute fashion.

If people could so readily "understand" the operations of the solar system on the basis of theories that now seem clearly incorrect, how can social psychologists be certain that we understand something so much more subtle, like human behavior? The answer is that we cannot be certain, even if our "knowledge" makes sense to us, just as the Ptolemaic system made so much sense to so many people for so long.

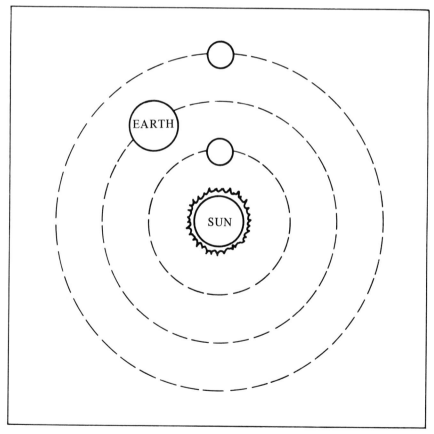

Figure 1.3.
Heliocentric view of the universe with circular orbits.

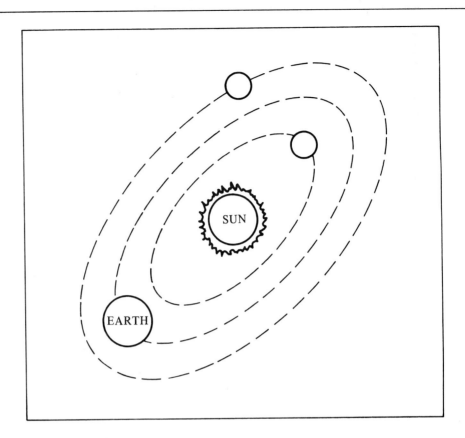

Figure 1.4.
Heliocentric view of the universe with elliptical orbits.

UNDERSTANDING HUMAN EMOTION: AN EXAMPLE FROM PSYCHOLOGY

There are many examples of understanding based on incorrect theories in the psychological as well as the physical sciences. A theory of human emotions that was widely accepted for nearly 2000 years was the *theory of humors,* first proposed by Hippocrates (ca. 460–366 B.C.), and elaborated upon by Galen in the third century A.D. Recognizing a strong relationship between the operation of the body and emotional temperament, the humoral theory proposed that our character and moods were determined by four bodily secretions, called humors: blood, produced by the liver; phlegm, from the lungs; yellow bile, known as choler, produced by the gallbladder; and black bile, known as melancholia, produced by the spleen. The proportions of these four humors were said to determine personality and temperament. Even today, the residues of the theory can be found in our language—people are often described as "phlegmatic" or "melancholic." The humoral theory was a great aid to understanding human behavior for seventeen centuries—until advances in physiology proved it incapable of explaining personality and mood (Cashdan, 1972).

How much of what we understand today is based on incorrect theory? Probably a great deal. Theories in modern physics and astronomy are considerably more precise and sophisticated than earlier theories. But they are not without their critics, who may, in time, prove correct. If that happens, today's theories will have to be discarded and replaced with even better ones.

These examples raise a number of fundamental questions about understanding, and they carry with them the need for caution in drawing conclusions. Understanding has most often proved to be based on incomplete or inaccurate information. If understanding is one of the goals of social psychology and if we accept that nothing can be understood for certain, where does that leave us? Frankly, in a rather paradoxical position. Wishing to understand social behavior, we must recognize that any understanding we attain may be incorrect or incomplete. We therefore must content ourselves with *relative understanding*, understanding that is more complete and more accurate than that which came before.

Theories are artificial devices constructed to aid understanding. One theory may be able to explain more facets of behavior or predict some behavior more accurately than another. Therefore, that theory offers a better explanation than the other, but we cannot consider it to be a complete explanation. Theories are constructed to be discarded when their usefulness has been outlived; they are constructed to be replaced by more useful theories.

Theories do not necessarily discuss tangible, observable phenomena. Theories may consist of *hypothetical constructs*, nonobservable entities inferred from observable phenomena. For example, the concept of attitude in social psychology is an important component of many theories. Attitudes are thought to be internal and not directly observable. Various procedures can be used to *infer* a person's attitude toward some object; while this lends credence to the belief that attitudes are real, it does not prove their existence. Theories are not true-to-life descriptions of real-world phenomena, they are, instead, artificial *models* of the world. This is true of any scientific theory, not just psychological theories.

In physics, for example, one current theory holds that there are subatomic particles, "quarks," which have fractional electrical charges of + or $-1/3$ or $2/3$. The quark theory of Murray Gell-Mann hypothesizes that neutrons, which have no electrical charge, simply consist of two quarks with a $-1/3$ charge and one quark with a $+2/3$ charge. Do quarks actually exist? Has anyone ever seen a quark? No, but there is *evidence* that quarks exist. At least there is evidence that the concept of a quark is useful in helping to explain the behavior of small particles. Since quarks are assumed to combine, the question of how they are held together arises. One theory says that they are held together by a property known as "gluon." Does gluon exist? No one knows. But it makes no difference whether gluons or quarks exist. For the moment they are useful concepts, and so we will use them. So it is with many psychological concepts. Attitudes, beliefs, attribution, values, learning, personality—all these are hypothetical constructs that may help us to understand and predict certain facets of behavior. They are useful, and as long as they remain so, they will continue to be used.

THEORIES IN SOCIAL PSYCHOLOGY

A *theory* is a set of statements about some aspect of a phenomenon. In psychology, it is an explanation of some behavior or set of behaviors. Occasionally, theories are defined as being well supported by research (English & English, 1958), but this is not a necessary condition of theory.

There are two types of criteria by which theories are evaluated: necessary aspects and desirable aspects (Shaw & Costanzo, 1970). It is necessary for a theory to be internally consistent (not to contradict itself); to be testable; to deal with some real aspect of behavior; and to state clearly the behavior(s) with which it deals. It is desirable for a theory to be unambiguous and to state how its concepts can be measured and observed.

One criterion often overlooked in psychology is that theories, if they are false, must be capable of being proved false. The concept of *falsifiability* states that tests are capable of demonstrating the invalidity of a theory if the theory is not true (Popper, 1959). A theory should be stated so that clear evidence can be gathered to support *or* refute it.

A theory that explains too much is no better than one that explains too little. For example, suppose a theory states that frustration causes aggression. A researcher conducts an experiment only to find that frustration brought about depression. If the theory can also be interpreted to explain both sets of results (that frustration leads to depression as well as aggression), then the experiment can be viewed only as supportive of the theory. If we cannot imagine any possible results that would disprove the theory, then it is not falsifiable and is scientifically worthless.

Every theory has some probability of being untrue. We can never accept a theory as final or absolute. A theory that states that the sun revolves around the earth can be shown to be false. We use the criterion of falsifiability because *theories can never be proved true,* but sometimes can be shown to be false.

Theories also vary in their degree of *heuristic value,* that is, in

Theories often begin with observation. A clever social psychologist could glean a wealth of information by observing this group's responses to the passing parade.

how much research they generate. The more research generated by a theory, the greater its heuristic value. Research generation is valuable because results may occur that open still other avenues of investigation. Unexpected or serendipitous results often prompt researchers and theorists to examine behavior that otherwise would have been ignored.

WHERE DO THEORIES COME FROM?

There are essentially two bases for theories: Theories begin with some observations or research and build upon these, or they begin with some basic notion or scheme arrived at in the absence of research (Shaw & Costanzo, 1970). In either case, theories must be tested after being formulated. Social scientists are often accused of being armchair theorists, developing theories that are unrelated to reality. There is nothing wrong with this approach to theory development so long as the scientist is willing to evaluate the theory on the basis of empirical research. Whether or not theories begin in observations, their value is determined by their ability to predict correctly the outcome of empirical observations. (These issues are treated more fully in Chapter 2.)

Human social behavior is an extraordinarily complex subject. It is far more difficult to arrive at workable theories of social behavior than to formulate theories about the behavior of inanimate objects. For one thing, human beings can be influenced by the very theories designed to explain their behavior. This is the problem of *reflexivity:* People can intentionally act to disconfirm a theory. Therefore, social theorists encounter difficulties that do not hinder physical theorists. In recent years, reflexivity has become a matter of concern among social psychologists, and there has been considerable debate about the nature of social psychological theory (Gergen, 1973b; M. Manis, 1976; McGuire, 1976; Schlenker, 1974, 1977; see also interview with Gergen, Chapter 13).

While there are dozens of theories in social psychology, there are only a few different theoretical *approaches* to the study of social behavior, with each approach containing many theories. There are, after all, just so many different assumptions we can make about human behavior, and only so many ways of explaining a single action.

Different theoretical approaches look at social behavior in slightly different ways. A particular approach comprises theories that share the same set of assumptions about human nature. Because these assumptions are not always specified by the theorist, it seems best to discuss them separately here.

In contemporary social psychology there are two dominant approaches to the explanation of social behavior, the *behaviorist approach* and the *cognitive approach*. Most current social psychological theories fit conveniently into one of these two categories. Other theoretical approaches that will also be discussed, either because they are historically important or because they are becoming more prominent, are symbolic interactionism, psychoanalytic theories, and what I will call the structuralist approach.

BEHAVIORISM IN SOCIAL PSYCHOLOGY

Contemporary behaviorist theories are sometimes referred to as *learning theories*, because they assume that all behaviors, with the exception of instincts, are the result of learning. In order to see how this position evolved, we will begin with a brief discussion of empiricist philosophy and work forward to the present.

The *British empiricists*, including Isaac Newton (1642–1727), John Locke (1632–1704), and David Hume (1711–1776), were concerned with the issue of knowledge and its certainty. How, they asked, could someone know something for certain? The cornerstone of Locke's analysis was borrowed from Aristotle, the notion that at birth the human mind was a *tabula rasa*, literally, a blank slate. If mature humans had mental characteristics, it was assumed that these were *acquired* during their lifetime through experience; that is, they were learned. For the empiricists, experience was the only path to knowledge. Ideas cannot produce knowledge because they, too, are products of experience. In psychological terms, this means that personality, behavior, and temperament are all determined by sensory experiences. Thoughts and feelings, rather than being viewed as causes of behavior, were viewed as the effects of past behavior.

One of the difficulties with this view of behavior is that it fails to provide a satisfactory explanation of human motivation. A good psychological theory explains why behavior occurs. A prominent philosophical explanation for human action, proposed by Thomas Hobbes (1588–1679) and Jeremy Bentham (1748–1832), was referred to as utilitarianism or *hedonism*. The essential characteristics of hedonism are that people are motivated by self-interest and a desire to maximize pleasure and minimize pain.

If we combine the essential features of empiricism with the motivational force proposed by Hobbes and Bentham, then we have a psychological theory of behavior quite similar to what psychologists referred to early in the twentieth century as behaviorism.

John B. Watson (1878–1958) is generally credited with originating the approach known as *behaviorism*, though a similar approach had been suggested in Russia by Bekhterev (1857–1927). Watson attempted to make psychology, which at the beginning of the twentieth century was generally considered to be the study of consciousness or mind, into a more scientifically respectable discipline. He proposed that, because the mind could not be observed or measured directly, psychologists should devote their attention to the study of behavior, which could be observed and measured.

R.L. Thorndike (1913) had proposed the *law of effect* at the turn of the century. It states in quasi-scientific terms that any behavior followed by pleasure will be "stamped in" (learned), and any behavior followed by pain will be "stamped out" (not repeated). Watson (1913, 1919) added a change in terminology and emphasis and made this the foundation of his approach to psychology. We have, then, a general approach to the study and explanation of behavior that emphasizes the importance of rewards (pleasure) and punishments (pain), which are assumed to be the major causes of behavior.

Behaviorists, from Thorndike and Watson to the present, share several basic assumptions: Organisms are born without social or psychological traits; behavior, with the exception of instincts, is the result of experience or of particular kinds of experience; and behavior is motivated by a need to maximize pleasure and minimize pain.

These behaviorist/empiricist ideas persist today in a variety of learning theories. Coupled with developments in nineteenth-century biology, they stress the continuity between one species of organism

Behaviorists maintain that behavior is the result of experience and is motivated by a need to maximize pleasure and minimize pain. This young man has discovered that touching a ticklish spot produces pleasure.

and another (e.g., E. O. Wilson, 1975). It is permissible, and even desirable, for behaviorists to study the behavior of nonhuman organisms in order to learn something about human behavior. There is also the assumption that organisms, including humans, are infinitely pliable. Watson once remarked:

Give me a dozen healthy infants, well-formed, and my own specified world to bring them up in and I'll guarantee to take any one at random and train him to become any type of specialist I might select—doctor, lawyer, artist, merchant-chief and, yes, even beggar-man and thief, regardless of his talents, penchants, tendencies, abilities, vocations, and race of his ancestors. (J.B. Watson, 1934, p. 104)

The primary type of learning theory in the 1920s came from Russia, where Sechenov (1829–1905) and Pavlov (1849–1936) had developed the concept of conditioned reflexes. We now refer to this type of learning as *classical conditioning*. It involves the pairing of a neutral stimulus (conditioned stimulus) with some stimulus (unconditioned stimulus) that naturally elicits a particular behavior (unconditioned response). After repeated pairings the neutral stimulus will come to elicit the response by itself (conditioned response). This is discussed further in Chapter 3.

In the 1930s and 1940s, elaborations of behaviorism were made primarily by B. F. Skinner and Clark Hull. Skinner, the most prominent American behaviorist, developed two important concepts that considerably extended Watson's views. One is referred to as *operant conditioning*, in which a response is quickly followed by a reward or punishment. Rather than pairing a neutral stimulus with an unconditioned stimulus, as in classical conditioning, a response is strengthened or weakened by the reinforcement that follows it. Skinner theorized that complex behaviors could be conditioned by the process of *shaping*, in which partial responses are reinforced and then combined to form a complex response. Skinner also proposed that reinforcements need not follow each response or partial response in order to have an effect on behavior. Various *schedules of reinforcement* can be used to shape behavior, from continuous to partial reinforcement (Ferster & Skinner, 1957).

Clark Hull (1884–1952) and his students provided an explanation for the effects of reinforcements on behavior by proposing that rewards "stamped in" behavior because they returned the organism to a state of equilibrium or *homeostasis* (Cannon, 1932). Rewards are reinforcing, in other words, because they reduce biological drives.

Social Learning Theories   Two learning theories employed by social psychologists are less extreme in their assumptions than most behaviorist theories. The social learning theories of Julian B. Rotter (1954) and Albert Bandura (1965b, 1973) stress the importance of social situations and the role of cognitive processes in learning.

J. B. Rotter is a clinical psychologist who, in 1954, proposed a theory of personality derived from the learning theory of C. L. Hull (1952). Rotter does not stress overt behavior nearly so much as more traditional learning theorists. He instead focuses on *behavior potential*, which may consist of emotions and cognitions (J. B. Rotter & Hochreich, 1975). Rather than emphasizing the importance of reinforcements, Rotter stresses the role of the individual's *expectancy* of receiving reinforcements. Of course, past reinforcements in a particular situation influence the individual's expectations of receiving reinforcement in a similar situation in the future, but it is expectancy that influences behavior at any given moment.

Not all reinforcements are equally effective. Ten dollars may have a greater *reinforcement value* to someone who is penniless than to someone who is wealthy. Rotter's social learning theory places considerable emphasis on how an individual perceives a particular situation. This is a major characteristic of cognitive and symbolic interactionist theories and is rarely stressed in behaviorist theories.

Perhaps the most frequently researched aspect of Rotter's theory is the notion of expectancy. J. B. Rotter (1966) developed a scale to measure the generalized expectancies that people may have. People

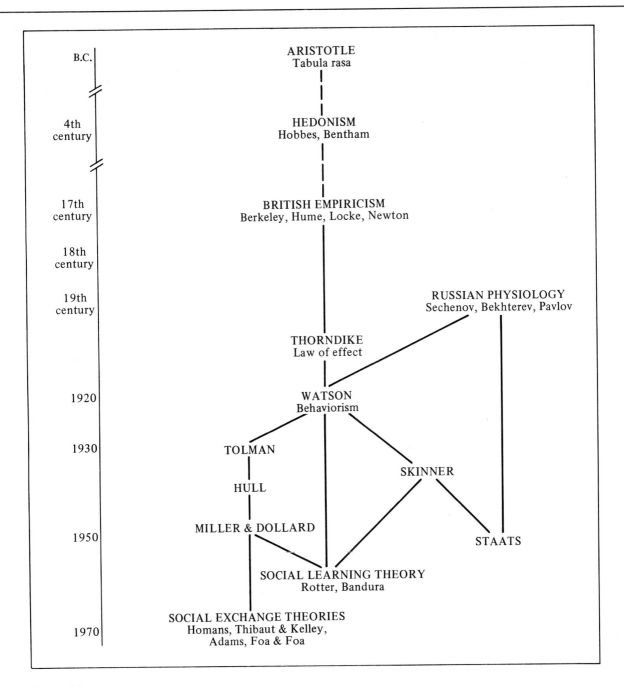

Figure 1.5.
Development of behaviorism in social psychology.

differ in the extent to which they believe that they control their own fate. Some believe they have personal control over their lives, that they can plan and initiate strategies that will bring them rewards. These people are characterized as having an *internal control of reinforcement expectancy.* Others seem to believe that no matter what they do, they are still at the mercy of fate, chance, luck, or external forces beyond their control. These people are characterized as having an *external control of reinforcement expectancy.* Rotter's internal–external control scale has been used in numerous studies in social and personality psychology (Garfield, 1978; Hamsher, Geller, & Rotter, 1968; Rotter, Chance, & Phares, 1972).

Albert Bandura's social learning theory is "social" for a different reason. Whereas Rotter emphasizes past social experiences and expectations of reinforcement in a given situation, Bandura stresses the fact that learning itself is a social process.

Most learning theories emphasize the importance of reinforcement. Bandura (1965b) instead suggests that learning takes place in the absence of reinforcement. He makes an important distinction, made earlier by E. C. Tolman (1932), between *learning* and *performance.* For instance, learning to drive a car involves the acquisition of certain behaviors: knowledge of the gas pedal, the brake, the gearshift, and the ignition. Being able to get into a car and drive it requires previous learning. But many people who have learned to drive do not do so; they have learned a response but do not perform it. Learning is the acquisition of new potential behaviors; performance is choosing to engage in a learned behavior.

Bandura has questioned the importance of rewards and punishments in learning. For example, in order to explain how a two-year-old child is able to speak English, a traditional behaviorist would have to argue that words, which were previously meaningless, were paired with symbols or objects that had meaning for the child (classical conditioning). Skinner (1957) has argued that the child utters meaningless sounds and the parents selectively reinforce meaningful utterances (such as "da da"), gradually shaping the child's verbal behavior until the child speaks the language of its parents. Bandura replies that such shaping would take years, and cannot account for the fact that children utter sentences that they have never heard before.

Bandura suggests that learning occurs by *imitation* or *observational learning.* Children are exposed to the language of their parents and siblings and they imitate often-heard sounds. The ability to imitate the responses of others accounts for learning. Rewards and punishments are seen as important determinants, not of learning, but of performance. For example, if a child is rewarded for speaking often or for talking about her feelings, then she is likely to do this frequently. But if she is punished, she will refrain from speaking out, even though she has the capacity to do so if she chooses. In short, the choice of which behavior to engage in is determined by reinforcement; the ability to engage in behaviors is determined by imitation and the modeling of other people's behaviors.

Social Exchange Theories A group of behaviorist theories has been developed to account for the behavior of two people interacting with each other, or *dyads*. These theories often use simple economic terms, such as *cost* instead of punishment, but they are basically operant conditioning models.

Exchange theories view human interaction as an exchange of social, psychological, or material resources. They predict that interaction will be continued if it is sufficiently profitable to both parties; it will be discontinued if one or both parties believe it is not rewarding enough.

There are four basic social exchange theories in social psychology: Homans' theory of elementary social behavior (1961); the social exchange theory of John Thibaut and Harold H. Kelley (1959, 1978); equity theory, first proposed by J. Stacy Adams (1963, 1965) and elaborated upon by Walster and Walster (1978); and the resource exchange theory of Uriel Foa and Edna Foa (1974).

Homans' theory of elementary social behavior conceived social behavior in dyads largely in economic terms. What one person gives to another is considered a *cost* to the giver; what is favorably received from another is a *reward*. Subtracting a person's costs from rewards yields the *profits* of the exchange. It is important to recognize that one person's costs do not necessarily equal another's rewards, so that it is possible for both parties in an exchange to profit or to

Social exchange theories attempt to explain why two people interact with each other—and why they sometimes stop interacting.

experience a net loss. The values of rewards and costs also change over the course of protracted interactions. An important concept in Homans' theory is *distributive justice,* the idea that "a man in an exchange relation with another will expect that the rewards of each man be proportional to his costs—the greater the rewards, the greater the costs—and that the net rewards, or profits, of each man be proportional to his investments—the greater the investments, the greater the profit" (1961, p. 75).

Like Homans', *Thibaut and Kelley's (1959) social exchange theory* assumes that interaction between individuals can be evaluated in terms of the rewards and costs to each participant. Thibaut and Kelley introduced two important social psychological concepts, *comparison level* and *comparison level for alternatives*. If the profit from an exchange is below some acceptable level, the comparison level, then the interaction will be terminated. Our expectations about an exchange, are part of the comparison level. But Thibaut and Kelley also recognize that unprofitable exchanges often continue for long periods of time. For example, why do people continue to date others who are not particularly attractive to them? To account for such unrewarding exchanges, Thibaut and Kelley suggest that people attempt to determine the relative costs and rewards from other, alternative relationships. Would some other relationship be more profitable? These considerations are part of the comparison level for alternatives. A relationship will be continued if the profits from it are greater than those from other possible relationships.

J. Stacy *Adams' equity theory* (1965) elaborates upon Homans' notion of distributive justice and states it in more precise terms. In particular, a person compares the ratio of inputs to outcomes for himself and others. Equity is the extent to which you perceive your relative outcomes in a situation to be proportional to your inputs, in comparison to the perceived inputs and outcomes of others. If they are proportional, then a state of equity is said to exist. If not, then inequity exists and you will attempt to change the situation to bring about equity.

Imagine a worker in a factory, Annie Orfanitis, with a BA in English, who is hired at $3 an hour to put widgets into phlanges. She is dexterous and efficient at her job, though she considers it boring. Across the table from her is a high-school dropout, Maisy Day, who has been with the company for several years, and whose job it is to take widgets out of phlanges. Maisy earns $6 an hour and she is not nearly as efficient as Annie. Annie sees her inputs as her education and skills and her effort expended on a boring task; her outcomes are equal to $3 an hour. She perceives Maisy's inputs to be much less than her own—little education and little skill—and her outcomes to be greater, $6 an hour. This perceived state of inequity will cause Annie to attempt to bring about equity. She could do this either by asking for a raise, so that her outcomes would increase, or she might decrease her inputs by decreasing the speed at which she works. In either case, the relative imbalance between her input/outcome ratio and Maisy's will diminish, thereby reducing inequity. Note that inequity results when outcomes are too high, as well as when they are too low. So, someone who perceives herself to be overpaid will also experience inequity and will attempt to restore equity, perhaps by increasing inputs.

The precise nature of what is exchanged in interpersonal encounters has not been clearly specified by most exchange theorists. *Foa and Foa's theory of resource exchange* discusses the nature of the resources that are exchanged between people during interaction. They propose that there are six classes of resources that may be exchanged, and that they can be ordered along two dimensions, concreteness and particularism (see Figure 1.6).

In the optimum type of exchange, a person gives the most abundant resource for one that is wanted. The most satisfying types of exchange involve those in which resources adjacent to one another are exchanged. When distant resources are exchanged, for example, information for love, the exchange is less satisfying than the exchange of information for money. One feature of resource exchange theory is the assumption that the six resource classes are basic, unlearned structures used universally in interpersonal exchanges.

Critique of the Behaviorist Approach Many of the behaviorists' assumptions are not directly testable. For example, we do not know whether humans are qualitatively different from other species, nor do we have any way of finding out. Likewise, there is no way to find out whether there are psychological or social predispositions in humans at birth.

The idea of initiative or creativity is also a problem for behaviorists. For example, operant learning theorists assume that responses are made, then reinforced, then repeated. But where do these initial responses come from? Skinner's answer (1957) is that they are random. The young child in his crib makes random sounds: "ga ga, goo goo, da da." At "da da," mother perks up, smiles at her child, and reports with pride that her son said "da da." While it is plausible that such responses occur randomly, it is not an idea that can be easily tested. Why does the child make any sounds? Behaviorists are not able to answer this. The issue is whether responses, prior to being shaped, are random, unmotivated, meaningless behaviors or whether they are in some sense meaningful.

What of behavior that does not seem to be motivated by rewards? Recently a young Japanese man sailed from Japan to California in a 25-foot sloop. When asked why he undertook his four-month solo voyage, he replied, "Mostly because it excited me." Here is an

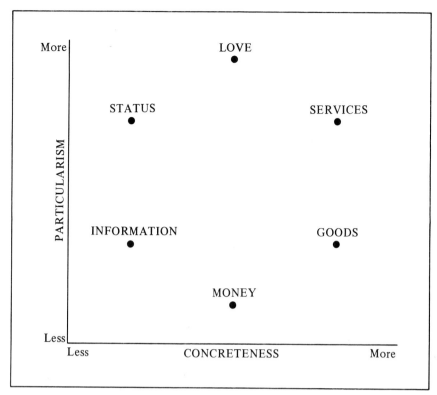

More ┤   LOVE
     │   ●

            STATUS   SERVICES
             ●   ●

P
A
R
T
I
C
U   INFORMATION   GOODS
L   ●   ●
A
R
I
S
M
                  MONEY
                   ●

Less ┤
     Less   CONCRETENESS   More

Figure 1.6.
The cognitive structure of resource classes. (From Foa & Foa, Societal structures of the mind, 1974, p. 82.)

example of behavior that, from all appearances, was not motivated by rewards or the expectation of rewards, nor by imitation. It seems to have been self-motivated (Berlyne, 1960). Behaviorists find it difficult to account for such behaviors (Skinner, 1974, 1977).

Behaviorists see individuals as responsive organisms. Their behavior is a response to reinforcements existing in present or past environments. External events are seen as the causes of behavior. Feelings, plans, and thoughts are not the causes of behavior but the results of past experience.

Many terms used by learning theorists are ambiguous. They state that learning occurs when a positive reinforcement is presented following a response. A positive reinforcement is defined as any stimulus that increases the probability of a response. Despite Skinner's statements to the contrary, such definitions are circular, or tautological (Braginsky & Braginsky, 1974). Is a cigarette a positive reinforcement? The only way to find out is to do a study in which a cigarette is given following some response. If the behavior is repeated, then we can say that a cigarette is a positive reinforcement. Such a situation makes the very foundations of operant notions untestable; there is no way to define reinforcement independent of its effects. If a reinforcement is a reinforcement only when it works as predicted, then the theory can never be falsified. Stimuli, then, do not have reinforcing properties. The reinforcement value of a stimulus depends on its perceived value to the recipient. If a person does not smoke, then a cigarette is not a reinforcement. Even to a smoker, a cigarette will act as a positive reinforcement only when the person wants one. So, rewards and punishments do not exist in any absolute sense; stimuli are reinforcing only if they are perceived to be by their recipients.

Behaviorism not only drove psychology out of its mind, but failed in other respects to add scientific respectability to psychology. Watson and Bekhterev wanted to make psychology a more objective science than it was at the beginning of this century. They proposed that this could be accomplished by focusing on behavior rather than on the mind. The assumption that the study of behavior in animals as well as in humans could add to our knowledge of human behavior is largely untestable. While I would not want to take a drug that had not first been tested on animals, I would hesitate to conclude that humans cannot sing just because animals cannot. There seem to be limits to the kinds of things we can learn about human behavior from the study of animal behavior. Precisely what these limits are, no one knows. Though behaviorist theories seem perfectly adequate to account for some types of learning, it is questionable whether they can adequately explain all types of human behavior.

THE COGNITIVE APPROACH

Perhaps the most common approach to theory in social psychology is the cognitive approach. There are no fewer than a dozen different cognitive theories dealing with social behavior. All cognitive theories make common assumptions about human nature and the causes of behavior. While it is possible to trace this approach back to the work of Plato, I will take as a historical starting point the group of philosophers known as the rationalists.

The *rationalist philosophers*, who include René Descartes (1596–1650) and Immanuel Kant (1724–1804), were, like the empiricists, interested in knowledge that could be accepted with certainty. The rationalists questioned whether the physical senses, through direct experience, were capable of providing unquestionable truth. The senses as a means of acquiring knowledge were questioned because they were often fallible in providing information about the external world.

Both Descartes and Kant concluded that the mind was a primary instrument of knowledge. The mind interprets sensory experience, often constructing it independently of reality, as in a dream. The capacity for active, rational thought became the single most important route to knowledge. Thought was the one trait that distinguished humans from other species.

The mind is also active: It creates, organizes, interprets, distorts, and seeks meaning. If there is a motivational basis to rationalism, as hedonism served as the motivation for empiricists, it is this active tendency of the mind to interpret and organize experience.

The basis for most current cognitive theories in social psychology is the work done by Gestalt psychologists at the beginning of the twentieth century. The Gestalt psychologists were a group of German psychologists who made a conscious effort to provide an alternative approach to the psychology then prevalent in Western Europe. Most of the research and theory at the turn of the century were concerned with subjectively perceived changes in external stimuli, such as changes in the brightness of a light or the loudness of a sound. The Gestalt psychologists argued that this stress on stimulus–response connections overlooked the fact that humans do not respond automatically to stimuli in their environment, but are *active organisms* who interpret and even distort their environment before responding to it. They argued that the proper study of psychology was a study of the active organism rather than of the environment.

The earliest Gestalt psychologists, such as Alexius Meinong, Christian von Ehrenfels, Wolfgang Köhler, Max Wertheimer, and Kurt Koffka, studied perception because that is where they could most easily demonstrate the shortcomings of stimulus–response psychology. They used the term *Gestalt*, which roughly means "pattern" or "configuration," to emphasize the fact that people organize their perceptions into meaningful units. Their earliest research was designed to show that stimuli are not simply perceived and responded to, but are organized, interpreted, and evaluated prior to responding. For example, the notion that a stimulus was always perceived the same was questioned by demonstrating that a stimulus, such as "1" could be seen as the number one, as in *1, 2, 3*, or as the letter el, as

Figure 1.7.
Closure. Although the pictures are constructed of a number of irregular black shapes, distinct figures are perceived.

in *l m n o p*. When shown a 350-degree arc, nearly everyone asked to describe it called it a circle. This tendency to simplify and complete incomplete stimulus patterns is called *closure*. (See Figure 1.7.)

In a series of perceptual studies, the Gestalt psychologists demonstrated three basic principles: Perception is active; people do not respond to what is "out there" in the environment, but they interpret, organize, and otherwise make maximum sense of the environment; and there is a tendency for the organism to simplify perception. All these principles are consistent with the major concepts of rationalist philosophy, particularly the emphasis on the organism as active, rather than merely a passive responder to environmental stimuli; the notion that the mind is a filter through which experience passes; and that experience is somehow changed in the process.

While Gestalt psychologists were interested mainly in perception, a number of social psychologists adopted their ideas and applied them to social behavior. Among them are Solomon Asch, Kurt Lewin, and Fritz Heider (see Heider, 1973).

Beginning in the 1940s, Solomon Asch began to apply Gestalt notions to the study of social behavior. Asch (1946) formulated social Gestalt research in impression formation and group judgments (Deutsch & Krauss, 1965). Underlying this research was the assumption that experience is not perceived in an arbitrary fashion but is organized so as to be meaningful. Asch's pioneering studies are discussed in Chapters 4 and 10.

Probably no figure in the history of social psychology is more revered than Kurt Lewin (1890–1947). Cognitively oriented social psychologists owe many of their concepts, approaches to research and theory, and training to him.

Like other Gestalt psychologists, Lewin (1936) believed that people perceive and respond to stimuli in terms of their total environmental context and that a person's behavior likewise must be viewed in some context. He borrowed the concept of *field* from physics to refer to the totality of forces influencing a person at any given moment. Physicists viewed the behavior of an object as the result of a number of simultaneously acting fields of force, which could be described by means of vector analysis and topological mathematics (see Figure 1.8).

A single act of human behavior was seen by Lewin, not as a response to a simple stimulus, but as the product of different forces acting simultaneously upon the person. According to Lewin, behavior is *multiply determined*. It is always the product of a number of different forces acting, sometimes complementarily and sometimes competitively, on the person.

Lewin referred to all the psychological forces acting upon a person as the *life space*. Life space includes an individual's goals and needs, all the factors that the person is conscious of at a given moment,

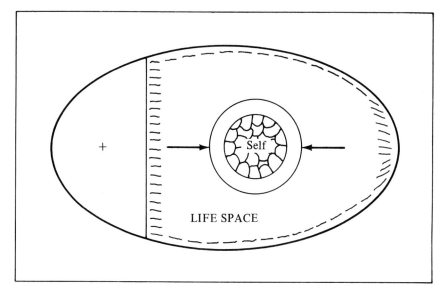

Figure 1.8.
Lewin's topological representation. + = positive goal region. The self is seen as part of the psychological environment. Various cognitions are represented as portions of the self and are influenced by forces (vectors, represented by arrows) from the psychological environment. (Adapted from Lewin, A dynamic theory of personality, p. 266. Copyright © 1935. Used with permission of McGraw-Hill Book Company.)

and self-awareness. The person, in other words, is also a psychological object in his environment to which he can respond. Behavior was said to be a function of the life space: the person and his psychological environment: $B = f(P,E)$.

The function of theory, Lewin said, is to point the way to new knowledge. Experiments can only yield a jumble of ambiguous facts and numbers unless they are made sensible by the presence of theory. The proper purpose of research is to test theory. Lewin also believed, however, that theory and research could combine to provide powerful explanations of social problems. His concept of *action research* embodies his belief that properly conducted experiments, those designed to test theories, could teach us more about the solution to social problems than any other approach. Research could be conducted in real settings, or experimental situations could be created that duplicated certain critical features of real settings (Lewin, Lippitt, & White, 1939).

Lewin's field theory led to the formulation of a number of topics for social psychological study. Lewin is credited with the concept of *group dynamics*. Like Gestalt psychologists, Lewin viewed the individual members of a group not as isolated individuals but as parts of a complex, interdependent organization. A group is more than the sum of its individual members. A group possesses dynamic properties that individuals do not possess. These notions gave rise to what is now referred to as *sensitivity training* or *T groups*. In 1946, Lewin was asked by the Connecticut Interracial Commission to train leaders for community programs designed to combat racial and religious prejudice. The purpose of these training sessions was to make people more aware of the feelings and thoughts of others and to use the cohesiveness of the group setting to assist in gaining these insights. As a result of his success with these groups, a permanent center for sensitivity training, the National Training Laboratories, was established in Bethel, Maine, in 1947.

Lewin's concept of *tension* was important as a motivating force of human behavior. Tension is created whenever a psychological need exists; the tension is reduced when that need has been satisfied. Among the implications of this is that unfinished tasks leave the person in a state of tension, because the goal of completion has not been reached. The tension that exists when a task is not completed should make itself felt in a number of ways—by influencing memory and perception, and by creating a need to complete the task (Zeigarnik, 1927).

Lewin's concept of psychological tension became a central point of numerous theories, known as *cognitive consistency* theories. The essence of these theories is that individuals have a need to maximize meaning in their perceptions, feelings, cognitions, and experiences. When meaning or organization is not optimal, then a state of psychological tension exists that motivates the person to attempt to reduce tension. This can be done by bringing about maximum organization or meaning. The idea of cognitive consistency was first proposed by another Gestalt psychologist, Fritz Heider, and later expanded into cognitive dissonance theory by Leon Festinger (1957).

Fritz Heider is one of the most important figures in modern social psychology. His theories are based on rationalist philosophy and Gestalt psychology and are found in his influential book, *The psychology of interpersonal relations* (1958). Heider believed that in order to understand the behavior of others, it is necessary to understand how they see themselves and their social world. Rather than impose the psychologist's abstract concepts on people's behavior, he attempted to analyze the commonsense psychology that most people themselves use to explain their behavior. Thus, the technical terms of Heider's theories are common concepts that people report as being important to them.

Two aspects of his theory in particular have caught the imagination of social psychologists: cognitive balance and causal attribution. In discussing the ways in which people form sentiments toward other people and toward objects, Heider assumed that there is a need to simplify and organize our perceptions and cognitions. What could be simpler than a world in which everyone we like shares our sentiments? Because this is the simplest and the most "meaningful" world, there is assumed to be an internal drive toward this state of maximum simplicity, which Heider called *cognitive balance*.

Heider developed a simple graphic way of demonstrating sentimental attachments between two people. From the point of view of a particular person (P), who confronts another person (O), we can represent their sentiments toward some object or issue (X) by the use of arithmetic signs. A positive sentiment or attitude is represented by a plus (+) and a negative sentiment by a minus (−). In Figure 1.9, Person does not like Socialism (X), but Other does. What will Person's feelings toward Other be? According to Heider, the world would be maximally simple if everyone we liked agreed with us. Those who disagree with us create uncomfortable psychological tension, and so we tend not to like such people. Thus, the theory would predict that Person would not like Other.

As proposed by Heider, balance theory has a number of limitations. It conceives of sentiments as either positive or negative, without room for weak or strong sentiments or for neutral sentiments. Balance theory is limited to situations in which two people hold sentiments toward the same object. (See Figure 1.9.)

Heider was perhaps the first psychologist to study how people perceive the causes of their own and others' behavior. If someone hurts your feelings, it matters a great deal whether you think that person hurt you deliberately or accidentally. How we perceive the causes of behavior influences how we react to other people, how we may go about changing their behavior, and even how we feel about ourselves. Heider assumed that because people have a need to make sense of experience, they will attempt to determine the reasons others behave as they do. We can attribute the cause of any single behavior to some characteristic of the actor, to some characteristic of the actor's environment, or to a combination of these two factors. *Attribution theory* and some of its many implications are discussed in Chapter 4.

Critique of the Cognitive Approach   Cognitive theories are difficult to test directly. For example, Lewin proposed that people may complete an interrupted task because of psychological tension. There is, however, no way to measure this tension directly; it must be inferred

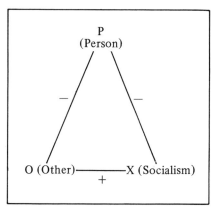

Figure 1.9.
Heider's cognitive balance model.

from observations. Likewise, Heider assumes that there is a need to maintain cognitive balance and that imbalance produces a tension-like drive state. There is no way to determine whether such states exist except by reference to behaviors presumably caused by these internal cognitive states. The greatest problem with most cognitive theories is a methodological one: We cannot measure directly the very concepts that are most basic to the theories. It is possible in some indirect way to determine certain properties of people's cognitive systems (e.g., Osgood, Suci, & Tannenbaum, 1957; Zajonc, 1960), but most of the important theoretical concepts of cognitive theories remain beyond the reach of current research methods. Cognitive theories are thus placed in somewhat the same position as Sherlock Holmes in trying to determine the causes of a particular crime. They attempt to eliminate all the noncognitive explanations and assume that whatever remains, even if it is unmeasured, must be the cause.

Cognitive theories can explain certain behaviors that are problematic for behaviorists: creativity, curiosity, and self-initiated behavior are all seen as manifestations of the inherent need to make sense of experience. There can be little doubt, either, that Lewin's notion that behavior is multiply determined is accurate. The concept of the human organism as qualitatively distinct from other species, as an active, initiating being, is intuitively appealing to many people. But the methodological difficulties presented by cognitive theories are serious ones that, in some instances, make the theories nonfalsifiable and untestable.

SYMBOLIC INTERACTIONISM

Most theoretical approaches in social psychology emphasize the behavior of an individual in a social context; the focus is on the behavior of a single person. Symbolic interactionism places primary emphasis on the mutual interaction that occurs in social situations.

George Herbert Mead stands out as the foremost symbolic interactionism theorist. Though he himself published no books on symbolic interactionism during his lifetime, after his death in 1931 his lectures and notes were edited and published by his students (Mead, 1934, 1964).

Symbolic interactionism constitutes a theoretical perspective designed to explain the development of personality, or *self*, behavioral *acts*, which occur through communication, and social behavior. It assumes that humans are qualitatively different from other species because we have the ability to communicate through symbolic language. It is language that enables people to interact effectively. Through language we can agree upon the meaning of events, communicate about intentions and objects, and cooperatively solve

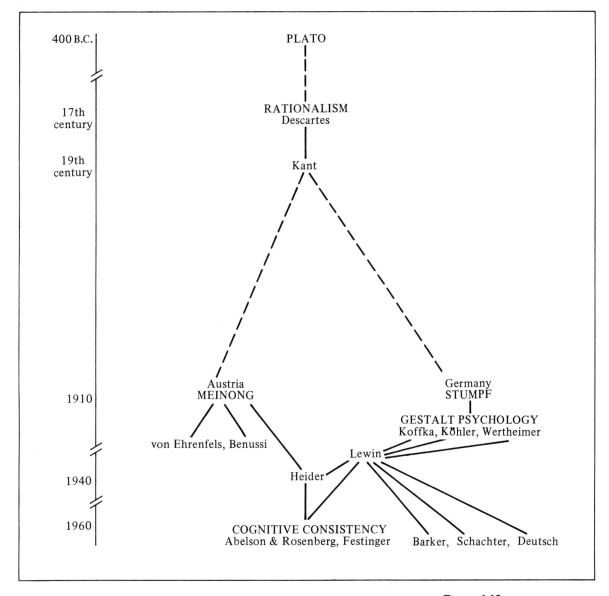

Figure 1.10.
Development of the cognitive approach in social psychology.

problems. In order to engage in social interaction, we must master language, have a concept of ourselves, and have a view of the expectations of other people (see Chapter 3).

There is a close connection between cognitive theories and symbolic interactionism. Mead states that humans "respond to events and objects in terms of meanings they have attributed to them." If two people respond in a similar way to a particular situation, it is because they have a *shared meaning* of that situation. For Mead, the essence of social behavior is the social act, in which two or more individuals must take each other into account in satisfying their impulses. Because individuals do not live in isolation, there can be no understanding of behavior without an understanding of interaction.

Behavior is created by interaction rather than merely occurring during the course of interaction. We can never understand human behavior by studying the individual in isolation; we can never predict human behavior by apprehending all of the psychological qualities of an individual. For behavior is a function of the interaction itself and not merely of those qualities which individuals bring into the interaction (Lauer & Handel, 1977, p. 43).

There is less research by social psychologists from a symbolic interactionist perspective than from a cognitive and behaviorist perspective (see Lauer & Handel, 1977; J. G. Manis & Meltzer, 1967). Nevertheless, many of Mead's ideas have found their way into the vocabulary of social psychology: definition of the situation, role-taking, self, and generalized other are all terms commonly used today. This is not to say that no research is undertaken from a symbolic interactionist perspective (e.g., C. N. Alexander & Weil, 1969; Backman, Secord, & Pierce, 1963; D. M. Kipnis, 1961; M. H. Kuhn & McPartland, 1954; M. Manis, 1955). Perhaps the greatest contribution of the symbolic interactionist perspective is its use and development by a variety of role and self theorists. These theorists have elaborated upon Mead's basically sociological ideas and applied them to a wide variety of psychological situations, including psychotherapy (Rogers, 1951), personality (Gordon & Gergen, 1968), and social interaction (Garfinkel, 1967; Goffman, 1959, 1974).

PSYCHOANALYTIC THEORIES IN SOCIAL PSYCHOLOGY

No field of psychology has remained uninfluenced by the work of Sigmund Freud (1856–1939). His ideas have been so pervasive in twentieth-century Western thought that students, fresh to psychology, are often as well versed in psychoanalytic concepts as their professors. We should note at the outset that it is incorrect to speak of *a* Freudian theory or of psychoanalytic theory as a single, unified set of propositions. In fact, there are several different psychoanalytic theories, dealing with different aspects of behavior or with similar behaviors at different times. There are basically three Freudian theories of importance to social psychology: the theory of personality structure, the process of psychosexual development, and psychoanalytic views of society. Though all of these theories are interrelated in various ways, they can be specified and evaluated independently.

The first two, concerned with personality, are discussed in Chapter 3, and Freudian views of society are discussed in Chapters 8 and 10.

A group of psychiatrists who trained with Freud and who are referred to as *neo-Freudians* have often written of social psychological matters. Most prominent among them are Alfred Adler, Karen Horney, and Harry Stack Sullivan. While none proposed specific social psychological theories, all contributed particular concepts and ideas that social psychologists have found useful.

STRUCTURALISM

Unlike behaviorist and cognitive theories, structuralism is characterized more by a goal and a shared set of assumptions than by a particular explanation of behavior. It may even be appropriate to speak of structuralism as a movement within the social sciences, because it is taking hold in a variety of disciplines. In anthropology, the structuralist point of view is most strongly represented by Claude Lévi-Strauss (Gardner, 1973); in sociology, by the work of T. Parsons and Bales (1955); in linguistics by Noam Chomsky (1957); and in psychology, by Freud, Lewin, Piaget, George A. Kelly, and Foa and Foa. It has even been applied to the analysis of musical composition by Leonard Bernstein (1976).

Because structuralism is not a well-integrated, unified theory of human action, it is difficult to state without ambiguity just what is meant by the term *structure*. Each theory defines structure in a somewhat different fashion. With the help of a few examples, it should be possible at least to demonstrate how structuralists go about structuralizing.

Imagine two casual acquaintances walking toward each other on the street. As they meet, Alex says hello to Barney:

ALEX: Hi, Barney, how are you?
BARNEY: Fine, and you?
ALEX: I'm fine. Nice to see you.
BARNEY: Nice seeing you. 'Bye.
ALEX: 'Bye.

This is a simple, common bit of social interaction. How would social psychologists describe and explain this simple example? A behaviorist might note that people are often reinforced by others when they stop to say hello and therefore Alex initiates the conversation because of stimuli associated with previous rewards. A cognitive psychologist might state that both Alex and Barney have certain expectations about this type of situation and, so as not to violate those expectations, engage in this interaction. A psychoanalyst might interpret the exchange as a way of expressing instinctive,

Hi, how are you?
Fine, and you?
Just fine. Take it easy.
You too.

To a structuralist, this converstion has little to do with health. Instead, it is a form of mutual acknowledgment.

psychic energy. A symbolic interactionist would make reference to the expectations that Alex and Barney have about the behavior of the other. To a structuralist, what appears on the surface is not nearly so important as what lies beneath. When Alex inquires after Barney's health, he is not really interested in Barney's physical state. Asking "How are you?" has little, if anything, to do with health. If our structuralist were knowledgeable about the culture, he or she would note that what is really going on in this case is more accurately described by the following conversation:

ALEX: You're Barney; I've seen you before. I recognize you and I want you to know that.
BARNEY: I, too, know who you are, and I know that you know who I am.
ALEX: Since we've just acknowledged each other, perhaps it's time to move on.
BARNEY: Yes, I'm busy, too. I expect we'll see each other again.

What seem to be simple statements about each other's health turn out to be something quite different: an interaction whose purpose is mutual recognition and acknowledgment. Structuralists would attempt to determine both the deeper meanings that underlie surface behavior and whether these deeper meanings or structures are universal.

Structuralists share five general assumptions:

1. Behavior is representative of underlying structures.
2. To understand behavior fully we must also know what structures influence the behavior.
3. Structures are unlearned, universal determinants of behavior.
4. Structures often operate unconsciously.
5. It is possible, through systematic observation, to determine the structures underlying behavior.

Structuralism is new to social psychology, and because of its unfamiliarity and relative ambiguity, it has not been subjected to much empirical testing. Some studies in social psychology have been undertaken from a structuralist position, most notably those by Uriel Foa and his colleagues (Foa, 1971; Foa & Foa, 1974; Foa, Megonigal, & Greipp, 1976; Foa & Turner, 1970). Structuralism seems to hold promise because it is a broad theoretical approach rather than a specific and narrow theory. But its very breadth raises questions of falsifiability and, as a general approach, it may not be adequately testable.

Summary

Social psychology is concerned with the direct or indirect effects of one or more persons' behavior on one or more other persons. The study of such behavior can be approached on at least four levels: biological, physiological, psychological, and social. Social psychology emphasizes the psychological and social levels of analysis.

Most social psychologists engage in the empirical study of social behavior. This means that they are interested in building and testing general theories of behavior. Theories are always to be considered tentative, and always have some probability of being false. The goal of theory is to aid understanding and to focus research. The components of theories need not consist of real entities, but may include hypothetical constructs.

In approaching social behavior scientifically, the social psychologist makes a number of assumptions about behavior that are not testable. Among these are that behavior is caused and meaningful, and that it is possible to discover these causes through scientific means.

Theories can be grouped into a number of general approaches.

Table 1.1.
Some Characteristics of Different Theoretical Approaches

Approach	Temporal Emphasis	Animal Studies	Focus on:	Falsifiability	Heuristic Value
Behaviorist	Past, present	Appropriate	Conscious organism, physical environment	Low	High
Cognitive	Present	Inappropriate	Conscious person, psychological environment	Moderate	High
Symbolic interactionist	Present, future	Inappropriate	Conscious person, psychological environment	Low	Low
Psychoanalytic	Past	Inappropriate	Unconscious	Low	Moderate
Structuralist	Past, present	Inappropriate	Unconscious	Low–moderate	Low–moderate

Five such approaches have been discussed: behaviorist, cognitive, symbolic interactionist, psychoanalytic, and structuralist. Each approach makes somewhat different assumptions about human nature and therefore emphasizes different determinants of behavior (see Table 1.1).

Identifying a specific theory as belonging to one of these five general approaches provides valuable information about the assumptions made by the theory, its historical roots, the kinds of behavior it emphasizes, and the particular types of variables it assumes cause behavior.

Behaviorist theories assume that behavior is a result of experience, particularly experiences that result in rewards and punishments, and place emphasis on past reinforcement and the anticipation of reinforcement.

Cognitive theories assume that humans are motivated to seek order and meaning in their lives. Animals are not assumed to share this trait with humans. Cognitive theorists place relatively little emphasis on past experience and a maximum emphasis on the immediate situation as a cause of behavior. Behavior is assumed to be caused by subjective assessments of a situation rather than by objective features of the environment.

Symbolic interactionism stresses the interaction between participants in a social situation. Of particular importance in determining social behavior is the shared meaning of a situation with others, which comes about through communication.

Psychoanalytic theories place maximum emphasis on past experiences, particularly early childhood experiences. Behavior at any moment is largely a result of unconscious motives and mechanisms, though these are particularly difficult to study scientifically.

Structuralism is perhaps the broadest of the five theoretical approaches. It represents a general goal rather than a particular theory, and as such is difficult to test. Structuralists see all behavior as the result of underlying entities that must be inferred from behavior.

Without question, the behaviorist and cognitive approaches have been, and still are, dominant in social psychology. Both present problems to researchers. Behaviorism often does not include precise and falsifiable statements, and cognitive properties must often be inferred. Because no single theoretical approach is easily testable, they all co-exist, if not peacefully, then more or less independently. A social psychologist's choice of theoretical approach is probably dictated as much by personal as by scientific considerations. Those who wish to make social psychology as scientific as possible often choose behaviorism because it permits the most rigorous types of research design. Those with a more humanistic bent are apt to be cognitive theorists because of the emphasis on rational thought and on the distinction between human and animal natures. Those impressed with the ability of psychoanalytic theories to explain even the most complex behavior often approach things from a Freudian perspective. At the moment, there is no scientifically acceptable way to demonstrate the undisputed superiority of one approach over another. Each has its own disadvantages and strengths. As we will see in subsequent chapters, different approaches sometimes lead to different predictions or explanations of behavior in a particular situation. More often, however, the different theoretical approaches merely emphasize different behaviors or different aspects of behavior, and thus complement rather than compete with one another.

Can all theories be reduced to a single, scientifically acceptable theory? Some psychologists have argued that differences between theories result from semantic confusion rather than disagreements over basic phenomena. They have proposed that if the theories were stated in clear language, perhaps in the language of symbolic logic or mathematics, they would always complement one another. No doubt there is some truth to this argument, but there are some basic, irreconcilable differences between theoretical approaches that no language can resolve. At the moment, these basic disagreements exist on a philosophical level and there is no way to settle these issues empirically. It is conceivable that future advances in research methodology will resolve some of these arguments, but for the moment, the student of social psychology must live with the knowledge that some of these approaches make faulty assumptions about human nature—without knowing which. It has proved valuable in psychology to have a number of competing approaches to behavior. Because of this competition, researchers are more careful to design their studies so as to rule out some of the competing theoretical explanations and lively debate is apt to result when those from different theoretical schools get together to discuss social behavior.

Suggested Readings

*Braginsky, B., & Braginsky, D. *Mainstream psychology*. New York: Holt, 1974. A critique of radical behaviorism, humanistic psychology, and a call for cognitive theories and action research.

Capra, F. *The tao of physics*. New York: Bantam, 1977.

Dubin, R. *Theory building*. New York: Free Press, 1969. A text on the nature and development of theories in the social sciences.

*Gardner, H. *Quest for mind*. New York: Knopf, 1973. An excellent introduction to the structuralist movement, with emphasis on Lévi-Strauss and Piaget.

*Available in paperbound editions.

*Gardner, M. *Fads and fallacies in the name of science*. New York: Dutton, 1956. An analysis of pseudo-science, written with wit and style. A terrific way to learn about the philosophy of science.

*Koestler, A. *The ghost in the machine*. New York: Macmillan, 1968. An intelligent criticism of behaviorism.

*Skinner, B. F. *About behaviorism*. New York: Random House, 1974. In which Skinner answers his critics.

*Walker, M. *The nature of scientific thought*. Englewood Cliffs, N. J.: Prentice-Hall, 1963. Philosophy of science from a physicist's point of view.

Some Pertinent Journals

(Because there are so many different psychology journals that now specialize in particular topics, a few journals that deal in the subject matter of each chapter will be listed along with the suggested readings. The student will be able to find the latest theorizing and research in current issues of these journals.)

Journal for the Theory of Social Behavior

Journal of the History of the Behavioral Sciences

Psychological Review

The Sociologist of Science (A newsletter published by the Dept. of Sociology, Cornell University, Ithaca, N. Y. 14853)

cathy Hull

2
THE TESTING OF THEORIES: RESEARCH METHODS IN SOCIAL PSYCHOLOGY

SOME NOTES ON THE TESTING OF THEORIES

Why is it, you wonder, that every time you take a course in a subject that promises to be exciting, they throw a section on research methods at you? They do it in political science and economics, and in sociology and history. In psychology, they make a fetish of it.

There is good reason to emphasize research methods. Nearly everything that we know as social psychologists comes from research done by social psychologists. Therefore, if we are to understand how social psychologists explain aggression, attraction, and altruism, we have to appreciate how they go about accumulating knowledge. Furthermore, understanding how research is done will enable you to evaluate more critically the ideas that social psychologists propose. And it is research, after all, that distinguishes social psychology from earlier philosophical attempts to explain social behavior. Social psychology not only proposes explanations, it tests them. Support for a theoretical explanation comes from objective, empirical observation, not from history or argument or personal belief. Scientific beliefs stand or fall on the amount of research that supports them. If a theory has little or no research evidence to support it, then it must be considered a weak explanation. Once research has provided support for a theory, then a social psychologist can have added confidence in that explanation.

Is this young aggressor responding to his own feelings of frustration? This is one theory that social psychologists have been studying for years. The problem is that theories are so difficult to prove. (It's also difficult to fit two on a tricycle.)

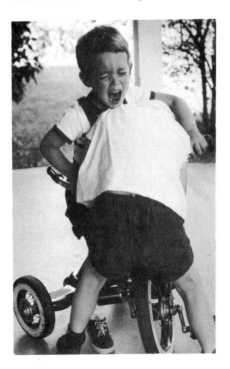

Let us take a fairly simple example. Suppose you are interested in why one person attacks another. As we shall see in Chapter 8, many theories of human aggression have been proposed through the years. In your search for an answer to the question of why aggression occurs, suppose you happen to come across the book by Dollard, Doob, Miller, Mowrer, and Sears (1939) entitled *Frustration and aggression*. On reading this slim volume, you find that the authors propose that aggression occurs when people are frustrated. You now have a tentative or possible answer to your question.

If you found this a convincing argument, and if you were a philosopher instead of a scientific social psychologist, your search would end. But since you are a scientist, this is not the point at which you end your search, it is the point at which you begin. You ask, "Does frustration cause aggression?" The theory tells you that it does, but should you believe it? If so, on what basis? The theory may convince you, but how could you prove to a skeptic that frustration causes aggression? Clearly we need some specific criteria in order to accept a theory as "true" in any sense. The most convincing kind of evidence is objective evidence—that is, evidence that can be produced by anyone who is interested in the question. If a skeptic doubts the value of the theory, then he or she should be able to carry out observations in order to determine whether the theory is a good one.

The scientific social psychologist plays the role of the skeptic. After reading a theory, the social psychologist asks what sort of test would prove—or disprove—the theory. It is the function of research to provide such a test.

Even a fairly simple theory is not easy to test. The more complex a theory is, the more ambiguous and complicated the answers to our questions will be. For this reason, social psychologists tend to ask precise and limited questions about behavior. Instead of asking, "Are people aggressive by nature?," social psychologists ask, "Will people aggress against others when they are frustrated?" The second question is more limited and, therefore, easier to answer by means of research.

TESTING THEORIES VERSUS
TESTING HYPOTHESES

Suppose that you decide to conduct research in order to test the frustration–aggression theory. There are a number of ways to do this. You may decide that the best way is to frustrate some people (referred to as the *experimental group*) and not frustrate others (referred to as the *control group*), and then measure aggression in both groups. The theory states that the frustrated people will be more aggressive than the nonfrustrated people. For your research, you decide that you can frustrate people by depriving them of food for several hours. Therefore, you have your experimental and control groups fill out forms for several hours, but you provide lunch only for your control group. Then you give all your participants a written test, such as the Buss–Durkee Hostility Inventory (Buss & Durkee, 1957), to measure their aggression.

Just as the theory predicted, your frustrated people are more aggressive than your nonfrustrated people, as measured by the Buss–Durkee Inventory. Have you made a complete and adequate test of the theory? Unfortunately, you have not. The theory states simply that "Frustration causes aggression." What you have done is deprive some people of food and then measure their aggression with a paper-and-pencil test. You may indeed have produced in your experimental group a kind of frustration that comes from not being able to eat when hungry. You may also have measured some kind of aggressiveness with the Buss–Durkee Inventory. But have you tested the theoretical statement, "Frustration causes aggression"? No, because you cannot produce "frustration" *in the abstract;* you can only produce a single instance of a specific frustration. You cannot measure "aggression" in the abstract either, but only a specific instance or type of aggression. And you certainly cannot measure the concept of "cause" directly. Theories are always abstract and general; they refer to broad classes of behavior and general states that cannot be produced, observed, or measured. In short, theories can never be tested completely and directly because they always refer to general time periods, actions, states, and events. Research, on the other hand, must deal with specific and limited actions, states, and events at a given time. So we must infer specific, representative examples from theories and then test specific examples by doing research on them. These specific examples are referred to as *hypotheses*. A hypothesis is a statement, logically derived from a theory, that is representative of that theory. Research is a means of determining whether a particular hypothesis is true or false.

If research is consistent with a hypothesis, we can state that the results *support* the theory, but no results can *prove* a theory. If people deprived of food score higher on the Buss–Durkee Inventory than those not deprived of food, you can only say that your experiment supports the frustration–aggression theory.

There is another reason why supportive results do not prove a theory. *People are much too complex for a single change in their environment to produce only a single change in their psychological and physiological states.* Whenever we do one thing to people, such as deprive them of food, we may also do other things to them. Any one state that a person may experience probably reflects a number of different influences. Depriving people of food may change their physiology, their thoughts, their attitudes, their feelings, and their perceptions. And any one of these changes may cause an increase in aggression. So, even if our research provides support for a theory, it cannot prove that the theory is true.

What if your research *failed* to show that the people deprived of food were more aggressive? What if both groups were equally aggressive, or if the group that was not deprived of food was more aggressive than the group that was deprived? Would this disprove the theory? Disconfirming results are always difficult to interpret and they have caused much consternation in social psychology (A. G. Greenwald, 1976). Results that were not predicted by the theory may mean that the theory is false. They may also mean that the researcher, by depriving people of food, did not produce frustration at all, but some other behavioral or emotional state. Finally, it is possible that the Buss–Durkee Inventory does not measure aggression, but some other type of behavior. What we can say about nonpredicted results is that the theory receives no support from the research and is therefore open to question. In most such cases, the research will be *replicated*, or repeated, using different or better procedures in order to test the theory further. If the results still fail to support the theory, then there is a good chance that the theory is false.

THE NATURE OF HYPOTHESES

Hypotheses can be derived from theories in a number of ways, all of which require that the hypothesis be either explicitly stated by the theory or implicit within it. In the case of our example, our hypothesis, "frustration causes aggression," is identical to a statement in the theory itself. But this hypothesis is quite broad and requires refinement before it can be used as a specific prediction for research. We would have to determine which people to use in our research, what we mean by frustration, and precisely what is meant by aggression. In such a case, we would have a broad theory, the frustration–aggression theory, from which we derived an abstract or general hypothesis, "frustration causes aggression," which then requires translation into specific, observable terms, perhaps "when nursery school children are deprived of food, they will punch a doll when given an opportunity to do so." In this case, we have two different hypotheses, one stated in broad, theoretical terms and one stated in specific, operational terms. Our research tests the specific hypothesis, which then tells us whether the theoretical hypothesis is supported. If the theoretical hypothesis is supported, then we can say that the theory from which it was derived is also supported.

It is possible to view a hypothesis as a *prediction*. The frustration–aggression theory leads to the prediction that frustrated people

A GLOSSARY OF TECHNICAL TERMS*

In the left-hand column are terms commonly found in research reports and technical works in psychology. The right-hand column provides the meaning of the terms.

"It has long been known that ..."

I haven't bothered to look it up.

"While it has not been possible to provide definite answers to these questions ..."

The experiments didn't work out, but I figured I could at least get a publication out of it.

" ... handled with extreme care throughout the experiments."

... not dropped on the floor.

"It is clear that much additional work will be required before a complete understanding ..."

I don't understand it.

"It is hoped that this work will stimulate further work in the field."

This paper isn't very good, but neither is any of the others on this miserable subject.

"The agreement with the predicted curve is ... excellent."
     ... good."
     ... satisfactory."
     ... fair."

... fair.
... poor.
... doubtful.
... imaginary.

" ... of great theoretical and practical importance."

... interesting to me.

*From Good (1965, pp. 52–53). These definitions were adapted from McClimont (1958) and Grahamjun (1957).

will be aggressive. This is a prediction about the outcome of research. Hypotheses, in other words, lead us to expect certain results from our research. We must determine whether the hypothesis, and the theory from which it came, successfully predicted the outcome of research.

COMPONENTS OF HYPOTHESES

Hypotheses derived from theories vary in their degree of generality. They may also vary in the degree to which they predict different kinds of relationships between variables. Two basic types of prediction may exist in hypotheses: *causal* predictions and *correlational* predictions. The frustration–aggression theory, for example, states quite clearly that frustration *causes* aggression. The theory could just as easily have stated that frustration is positively related to aggression, meaning that people who are highly frustrated would also be highly aggressive. In this second form, the theory does not deal with the cause of aggression. Instead, it states only that frustra-

"Three of the samples were chosen for detailed study."	The results on the others didn't make sense and were ignored.
"These results will be reported at a later date."	I might possibly get around to this sometime.
"Typical results are shown."	The best results are shown.
"It is suggested ..." "It may be that ..."	I think.
"The most reliable results are those of Jones."	He was a student of mine.
"It is generally believed that ..."	A couple of other people think so, too.
"It might be argued that ..."	I have such a good answer to this objection that I shall now raise it.
"Well known."	(i) I happen to know it. (ii) Well known to some of us.
"Obvious, of course."	(i) I was not the first to think of it; (ii) I also thought of it independently, I think.

tion and aggression are related to each other in some way. If a theory specifically states that a certain variable causes another, then the best research strategy is to expose some people to the causal variable in order to see whether the predicted effect occurs. If the theory states only that two variables tend to occur together, a researcher can simply measure each variable and determine whether they are related as predicted.

Causal hypotheses have two components: a cause, which is called an *independent variable*, and an effect, which is called a *dependent variable*. In our example, the theory contains the causal hypothesis that frustration causes aggression. In this hypothesis, frustration is the independent variable that is predicted to cause a change in the dependent variable, aggression. Some theories also discuss reasons why particular independent variables cause particular dependent variable changes. A theory may say that frustration causes aggression because frustration makes people emotionally aroused and the emotional arousal leads to an increase in aggression. This gives us a third variable, emotional arousal, which presumably intervenes between the independent variable of frustration and the dependent variable of aggression. In this case, we would call emotional arousal an *intervening variable*.

If a hypothesis is correlational rather than causal, we can predict that as the level of one variable changes, there will be a change in the level of another variable. Here is a correlational hypothesis derived from the frustration–aggression theory: People who are highly frustrated are also highly aggressive. This hypothesis says nothing about frustration causing aggression; it states only that the two things tend to vary together. As one variable changes, the other will also change. For correlational hypotheses, it is inappropriate to speak of variables as either independent or dependent. These terms are reserved for discussing causal hypotheses.

TESTING HYPOTHESES: METHODS OF INQUIRY

Let us use the frustration–aggression theory to show the various ways in which a hypothesis may be tested. Suppose that we want to determine whether frustration causes aggression, as the theory predicts. The first decision to make is whether to test the theory by attempting to produce frustration in the research subjects or by measuring frustration. All the different types of research that social psychologists conduct fall into these two basic categories of experimental research and correlational research.

MANIPULATING VERSUS MEASURING VARIABLES

Our reading of the frustration–aggression theory can lead us to the hypothesis that people who are highly frustrated will be highly aggressive. Thus, we can test this hypothesis in two stages. First, we can measure the extent to which people are frustrated, perhaps by using the Rosenzweig Picture-Frustration Test (Rosenzweig, 1946). Then, we can measure how aggressive they are, perhaps by using the Buss–Durkee Hostility Inventory. The theory predicts that people who are most frustrated ought to score the highest on the aggression measure. This study is a *correlational study* because it seeks to determine the relationship between two variables, frustration and aggression.

An equally logical hypothesis that can be derived from the theory states that frustration causes aggression. In order to test this hypothesis, we can frustrate some people and not others and then measure aggression in both groups. In this study, which would be classified as an *experimental study*, we actually manipulate the variable of frustration by making some of the research participants frustrated. If the theory is correct, this frustration will cause an increase in aggression. There are several important differences be-

Table 2.1.
Hypothetical Data from
Correlational Study

Person	Frustration Score	Aggression Score
1	5	7
2	5	8
3	6	9
4	3	5
5	2	3
6	2	5
7	1	4
8	8	7
9	6	7
10	5	6
11	9	9
12	8	10
13	3	4
14	6	6
15	3	1
16	8	6
17	2	3
18	8	9
19	6	6
20	4	5

tween experimental studies, in which variables are manipulated by the researcher, and correlational studies, in which no variables are manipulated. These differences are discussed in detail in the following sections. But we should emphasize at the outset that one important difference is the degree of control exercised by the researcher. This is a crucial feature of research, because increased control helps to make research results less ambiguous.

CORRELATIONAL RESEARCH

Let's pursue the hypothesis that there should be a relationship between the extent of a person's frustration and the level of that person's aggressiveness. You can test it by measuring both variables in a group of people. Suppose that your professor lets you administer the Rosenzweig Frustration Test and the Buss–Durkee Inventory to her class of 20 students. Each student completes both tests and you now have 20 pairs of scores, which can be organized as in Table 2.1. Given these data, how can you determine whether there is any relationship between the frustration scores and the aggression scores? The theory predicts such a relationship. It also predicts that as a person's frustration score increases, so should that person's aggression score. The relationship, in other words, is a positive one: the value of one variable increases as the value of the other increases. This can be determined quite easily by computing one of the several statistical measures of association known as *correlation coefficients*. In this example, the scores on each test can vary considerably, and each student's score is independent of others' scores. For these reasons, the Pearson product–moment coefficient of correlation is computed. This statistic gives you two important pieces of information. It yields a number, ranging from 0 to 1, and an arithmetic sign of either − or +. The number, which is usually a decimal, tells you the *strength* of the relationship between the two variables. The closer the correlation coefficient is to 1.0, the stronger the relationship between the variables. The sign tells you whether the *direction* of the relationship is positive or negative. If it is positive, the subjects' scores on the aggression variable will be higher if their scores on the frustration measure are higher. Negative coefficients mean that as the scores on one variable increase, the scores on the other decrease (see Figure 2.1).

Most statistical measures of relationship yield coefficients that can range from −1 through 0 to +1. Thus, if we see two different correlation coefficients of −.75 and +.75, we should recognize that the relationships that exist between the variables measured are equally strong, but that the direction of the relationships is different.

Assume that you conduct the frustration–aggression study by measuring each of these variables in a class of 20 people and that you obtain the data presented in Table 2.1. Computing a Pearson product–moment correlation yields a coefficient of +.80. This indicates that there is a fairly strong positive relationship between frustration and aggression in this study. A correlation as strong as +.80 would not occur by chance as often as 1 in 100 times.

The results of this study clearly are consistent with the frustration–aggression theory, though, as we have seen, consistent results do not prove that a theory is true. But do these results actually support the frustration–aggression theory? Are there any *alternative explanations* for the results?

Any correlational study has at least two explanations aside from the explanation provided by the theory being tested. Recall that the theory states that frustration *causes* aggression. Can we conclude from our study that it does? It is quite possible that aggression causes frustration, rather than the other way around. For example, we can argue that in our society, highly aggressive people find it frustrating to express their aggression because of the laws and penalties prohibiting aggression. Thus, it is reasonable to explain the relationship between frustration and aggression by saying that aggression causes people to become frustrated.

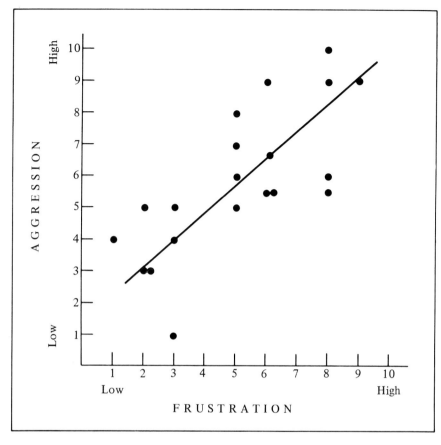

Figure 2.1.
Frustration and aggression.

It is also possible to explain the results as due to some other variable that was not considered in the research. Both frustration and aggression may be caused by some third variable, such as social class. People without much money, for example, may be highly frustrated because they are unable to obtain things they need or want. They live in poor neighborhoods where they probably are exposed to street crime and violence and may themselves become aggressive as a result. Thus, the correlation between frustration and aggression may be explained by the fact that poverty makes people both frustrated and aggressive. In this explanation, frustration does not cause aggression, nor does aggression cause frustration; poverty, which was not measured in the study, causes both frustration and aggression.

Correlations tell us only that a certain relationship exists between variables; they provide us with no information about causality. If we are testing a theory which states that one variable is the cause of another, then correlational research will not give us a satisfactory test of that theory. Even though the results of a correlational study may be consistent with the predictions made by the theory, the results are open to too many alternative explanations to increase our confidence in the theory. We should emphasize that while correlational studies have their weaknesses, the psychologist may have no recourse but to conduct correlational research. It is often impossible to manipulate important variables of interest to psychologists. If we were interested in gender, race, social class, age, personality characteristics, or nationality as variables, we could not make some people males or Orientals, or wealthy, old, or neurotic, in order to conduct an experiment. We would have to be content with correlating these variables with some other variables of interest.

Types of Correlational Research   Correlational studies are not limited to paper-and-pencil tests in classrooms or research laboratories. They do not even require living people. Correlational research can be done in a wide variety of settings, using a wide variety of measures. We might decide to test the frustration–aggression theory by observing people dealing with real-life frustrations, if we could find a way to measure their aggressiveness. For example, we could observe people's reactions to a stalled elevator, a traffic jam, a stuck door, or a long line at the supermarket. All these situations fit the theory's definition of frustration as some interference with ongoing, goal-directed activity. If the theory is correct, then people who encounter these frustrations will become more aggressive. We could observe this by seeing whether they honk their horns, begin to curse, or otherwise show their anger (e.g., Doob & Gross, 1968). These field studies would be considered correlational rather than experimental, because the researcher does not have control over the independent variable of frustration and cannot determine which people will be frustrated or when.

Will these drivers show their frustration by honking their horns and cursing, or will they merely hold their heads? Since this is New York City, they will probably do all three.

It is possible to conduct important psychological research using historical records, official statistics, census data, and other sources of *data archives*. Among the types of data that have been used in psychological research are statistics from professional sports (e.g., Gamson & Scotch, 1964; Goldstein, 1979b; Grusky, 1963; Mosteller, 1979), high school yearbooks (Barthell & Holmes, 1968), data from fund-raising organizations and hospital records (Winston, 1932), and political bumper stickers (Wrightsman, 1969). An excellent summary of research employing these and similar unobtrusive measures and data archives has been presented by Webb, Campbell, Schwartz, and Sechrest (1966).

The U.S. government and the United Nations are excellent sources of data for psychologists. One study was conducted using data from official statistics kept by the U.N. Feierabend and Feierabend (1966) studied the relationship between various types of frustration, such as having little food to eat, few medical doctors, and crowded housing conditions, and aggression as measured by records of military and police activity. We will discuss this archival study in greater detail in Chapter 8.

Despite some of the weaknesses of correlational studies, namely, the lack of control exercised by the researcher, the susceptibility of results to alternative explanations, and the studies' inability to test causal hypotheses adequately, they have important merits. Correlational studies may be conducted in natural settings, with a wide variety of people serving as research subjects, and may be conducted on historical and other data archives that preclude the possibility of various types of bias. For theories in which traits of a person (such as age, sex, social class, race, and nationality) are important variables, correlational research is frequently the only type available to the investigator.

EXPERIMENTAL RESEARCH

Social psychologists generally attempt to conduct experimental rather than correlational research for two reasons: Experiments can provide causal information and there tend to be fewer alternative explanations for their results. True experiments must have one or more independent variables that are intentionally manipulated by the experimenter, and subjects who are randomly assigned to the various groups in the experiment.

Let's return to our example of frustration–aggression theory. If you conduct an experimental test of the theory, you intentionally frustrate some people, the *experimental group,* and not others, the *control group.* In short, you manipulate the independent variable of frustration. This may be accomplished by giving the experimental group an impossible task, or by preventing them from eating for several hours. The dependent variable of aggression is measured in both groups. Let us assume that the frustrated subjects are more aggressive after being frustrated than the control group. Does this indicate that frustration causes aggression? It does only if the two groups of subjects were about equal in aggressiveness to begin with, and if they were about equal in all other respects. How can we be sure of this equality? The preferred procedure is random assignment of each participant to the experimental or control group. Several methods can be used, but the most common is a random numbers table.

If there is a sufficient number of people (more than 30), and if they are randomly assigned to the groups in the experiment, then we can assume that the two groups are *equivalent in all respects*. Note that randomization does not ensure that the groups are *identical;* however, it tends to make them statistically equivalent. If we randomly assign 40 people to an experimental or a control group, we may find that the average age of the experimental group is 19 years, 7 months, and that of the control group 19 years, 5 months. These differences fall within the range of chance, and so while the two groups are not identical, neither are they very different from each other. If a difference exists after an independent variable has been manipulated, that difference can be attributed with some confidence to the manipulation of the independent variable.

It is possible to have more than one experimental or control group in a true experiment. We may, for our example, have three groups: one that is not frustrated, one that is moderately frustrated, and one that is highly frustrated. Or, we could investigate independent variables in addition to frustration. We may divide subjects randomly into those who are frustrated and those who are not, and divide each of these groups randomly into those who are given an opportunity to retaliate against their frustrator and those who are not. In such an experiment, wherein two or more independent variables are manipulated and studied simultaneously, the research design is called a *factorial design.* Factorial designs are valuable techniques of experimental research, for they permit the experimenter to assess the effects of variables alone and in combination with one another. A single variable often has little effect on a dependent variable; but when it is combined with a particular level of some other variable, it may have a striking effect. Such a finding is referred to in statistical terms as an *interaction effect.* If variable X and variable Y are found to interact with each other, that means that a particular combination of XY has effects that neither X nor Y has alone.

How does an experimenter know, after manipulating one or more independent variables, that they actually have the intended effect? In our example, how do you know, after making experimental subjects go without food, that they are actually frustrated? The experimenter must determine whether, in fact, the manipulation of the independent variable caused the intended state to appear in experimental subjects. This is usually determined by a *manipulation check,* most often a question or series of questions designed to determine whether the manipulation actually "took." In our hypothetical experiment, it would be reasonable to ask participants whether they felt frustrated. Those in the experimental group should, of course, report feeling more frustrated than those in the control group. If this is the case, the experimenter is then in a better position to say that the independent variable of frustration has been successfully manipulated.

Unlike correlational research, experimental studies are less ambiguous in their implications. You could not argue convincingly that aggression caused frustration, since it is clear in our experiment that frustration preceded aggression. It is also unlikely that frustration and aggression were both caused by some third factor, since the experimenter actually produced the frustration. In sum, many of the alternative explanations of results that plague correlational research are inapplicable to experimental research. The confidence that you have in the theory should be considerably greater following supportive experimental results than following supportive correlational studies.

Obviously, experiments have their limitations. Most experiments are conducted in research laboratories. There the experimenter has considerable control over conditions and variables that may influence the results. The experimenter can manipulate one or more variables, while ensuring that other variables remain constant; subjects can be randomly assigned to groups; and the experimenter can create a situation for the subjects that sets limits on what they perceive, feel, or are permitted to do. Nevertheless, the weaknesses of experimental methods become apparent when we consider the artificiality of most experimental settings and the limitations on time and place imposed by laboratory research.

In a fairly typical experiment on aggression, for example, college students report to a research laboratory, are met by the experimenter, introduced to another subject, and then exposed to some independent variable manipulation designed to make them angry or frustrated (see Chapter 8). This often involves giving the subjects a test that is impossible to complete and then telling them that other students completed the test quickly and accurately. This experimentally induced failure often makes subjects frustrated, and manipulation checks bear this out. The subjects then have an opportunity to administer shocks of varying intensity to another student as part of a learning task. The intensity of the shocks administered is an index of aggressiveness, and constitutes the dependent variable.

In many experiments using this general procedure, frustrated subjects are reported to be more aggressive than nonfrustrated subjects. These results clearly support the frustration–aggression theory, and there are few alternative ways of explaining such findings. But can such studies be generalized beyond the laboratory, to people other than college students, and to other types of frustration and other types of aggressive behavior? In short, while it is fairly clear that the experiment provides an adequate test of the hypothesis, it is unclear how much we can generalize from this experiment to other situations.

Psychologists speak of these two issues as internal and external validity. *Internal validity* is the extent to which an experiment provides an accurate test of the hypothesis. *External validity* is the extent to which the results of an experiment can be generalized to additional situations, times, and people.

The first concern of a researcher is to find out whether a particular hypothesis derived from a particular theory is true or false. Thus, the researcher's main interest is in internal validity. In our example, the researcher wants to know: "Does frustration cause aggression?" Research is designed to answer this question. If the research can provide a relatively unambiguous answer, then an additional concern becomes relevant—generality. Once internal validity is achieved, the researcher may then want to know: "Do all types of frustration cause aggression? Does frustration cause aggression all the time, or only some of the time? Does frustration cause aggression in all people—students and nonstudents; males and females; old and young; Americans and non-Americans?" These are questions about the external validity of the research.

The internal validity of experimental research tends to be higher than that of correlational research because there are fewer possible ways to interpret the results of an experiment. However, the external validity of experimental research is frequently low because experiments often involve a limited amount of time, a restricted sample of participants, and an artificial setting in a research laboratory.

Social psychologists have recently sought to improve the external validity of their research. They have attempted to combine the best features of correlational studies with the best features of experimental studies so that internal validity will be satisfactorily high and external validity will also increase. In the last decade, social psychologists have begun to conduct much of their research outside the laboratory with subjects other than college students. They have attempted to do this while still retaining some control over independent variables and randomization.

Experimenter Effects   I do not mean to imply that experiments always have low external validity or that they always have high internal validity. Rosenthal and Rosnow (1969) raised serious ques-

Experiments that are carried out in artificial settings may have very little external validity. This student is trying to complete an impossible test. Will her eventual frustration lead to aggression? If so, can we be sure that she will react like this in another setting?

tions about the internal validity of much experimental research in social psychology. They suggested that experimenters often communicated, perhaps unconsciously, what it was they expected subjects to do. Such *experimenter expectancy effects* diminish the internal validity of research because subjects behave as they believe the experimenter wishes them to. Likewise, subjects who volunteer to participate in experiments may differ from people who prefer not to participate (Rosnow & Rosenthal, 1976; see also Kruglanski, 1975), and this can seriously diminish the external validity of the findings. Rosenthal and Rosnow suggest that experimental studies may not provide adequate tests of hypotheses because of these experimenter expectancy effects. Of course, expectancy effects could be reduced by employing an experimenter who is unaware of the hypotheses under study. And with sufficient planning, experiments can be conducted outside the laboratory. While there are relatively few

Table 2.2.
Characteristics of Different Research Methods

Method	Control by Researcher	Internal Validity	External Validity	Possibility of Experimenter Bias
Correlational study	Low–moderate	Moderate	Moderate	Moderate
Experiment	High	High	Low–moderate	Moderate–high
Quasi experiment	Moderate	Moderate–high	High	Moderate
Field experiment	High	High	High	Low
Observational study	Low	Low	Moderate	Moderate
Case study	Low	Low	Low	High

experimental field studies in social psychology (T. D. Cook & Diamond, 1976; Riecken & Boruch, 1974), their tendency to have both high internal validity and high external validity makes them powerful scientific tools (see Table 2.2).

EXPERIMENTAL FIELD STUDIES

Conducting true experiments in field settings requires that the experimenter manipulate one or more independent variables and that research participants be randomly assigned to the experimental and control groups. Such experiments usually require the researcher to create a situation in the field to which some people will be exposed. This has been done in factories, where changes in job requirements were instituted (Coch & French, 1948/1952); in organizations, where changes in the physical plant were made (Roethlisberger & Dickson, 1939); and at a summer camp, where cooperative and competitive tasks were manipulated (M. Sherif, 1958). Field researchers also have set up "street situations" by blocking roads or sidewalks, or by exposing randomly selected pedestrians to an independent variable such as an emergency, a staged robbery, or an accident.

Field experiments can be done on a very large scale. For example, the U.S. Office of Economic Opportunity studied the effects of a guaranteed minimum income on a sample of several hundred families (Kershaw, 1972). The hypothesis was that providing families with a guaranteed minimum income would improve living conditions and health, as well as alter spending patterns, feelings of self-esteem, and work habits.

Families that qualified for welfare in New Jersey and parts of Pennsylvania constituted the population of subjects for the experiment. Families participating in the three-year experiment were randomly assigned to one of five groups: a control group that was not provided with a guaranteed income, but which continued to receive welfare payments, and four experimental groups that were guaranteed different annual incomes, ranging from $2000 to about $5000 after taxes. These amounts (increased for dependents) represent the minimum amount of tax-free money that a family of four would receive. Thus, if a father who worked during the year and had earnings of $3500 were in the experimental group receiving a minimum income of $5000, he would be given an additional $1500 by the government. The dependent variables in the experiment included frequent interviews with each family, and work, medical, and bank records.

As it turned out, providing families with guaranteed minimum incomes had little effect on their economic, medical, social, or psychological characteristics. But our purpose here is simply to show that it is possible to conduct large-scale experiments in non-laboratory settings where independent variables are experimentally manipulated and subjects are randomly assigned to groups.

QUASI EXPERIMENTS

Quasi experiments are much more common in social psychology than true experiments conducted in field settings. A quasi experiment has one of the two characteristics of a true experiment: either one or more independent variables is manipulated, or subjects are randomly assigned to groups (Campbell & Stanley, 1966). In a typical quasi experiment, some independent variable is manipulated in a real-life setting. For example, in a study by Staub (1974), people walking near Harvard Square in Cambridge, Massachusetts, saw a man who appeared to be in pain fall to the sidewalk. Some of the witnesses saw him clutch his chest, complain of heart pains, and fall to the ground. Others witnessed him grab his knee, complain of pain in his leg, and fall to the pavement. These staged events constituted the manipulation of the independent variable of "type of emergency." While Staub could vary the type of pain supposedly experienced by the man, he could not assign some passersby to witness the heart-attack victim and some to see the victim with the bad knee. In other words, random assignment of subjects to groups was not possible. The dependent variable in this study was the speed with which witnesses helped the victim.

Quasi experiments are invaluable tools in social psychological research because of their obvious relevance to real social events, situations, and people. In other words, they have a tendency toward high external validity. But because random assignment is not possible, internal validity tends to suffer. The failure to assign subjects randomly to groups does not permit the researcher to assume that all groups of subjects are statistically equivalent.

For example, it is conceivable that all those who were on the streets of Cambridge while the man was suffering an apparent heart attack were different in some ways from those who were on the streets while the man complained of his knee. Suppose the first incident occurred at 11:30 AM, and the second at 12:15 PM. We could argue that people who are on the streets at the earlier time are wealthier, have more leisure time, or are less likely to be in a hurry than those on the streets at the later time. This may be because many workers cannot go to lunch until noon, and are required to be back at work by 1:00 PM. Those with higher status jobs, and those with no jobs, are free to stroll around before noon. Hence, if the heart-attack victim drew more helpers than the knee-injured victim, the results might be explained by the fact that those who helped the heart-attack victim did so because they had more free time.

Although this is not a very plausible interpretation, the fact that subjects were not randomly assigned to groups does not permit us to rule it out. Whenever two or more groups are involved in the same study, unless they have been randomly constituted, there is always the possibility that they differ in one or more respects that influence the results. Quasi experiments, then, sacrifice some internal validity for the sake of increased external validity.

Quasi experiments can occur without the intentional intervention of a researcher; Campbell (1969) has called these *natural experiments*. In a natural experiment, an event occurs which is then studied by the social psychologist. For example, states may pass laws that lessen the penalty for drug use, or decrease the speed limit, or permit capital punishment. The researcher can then study the effects of these laws by comparing behavior in those states that have enacted such laws with behavior in states that have not. While people cannot be randomly assigned to states, the new laws act essentially as "naturally manipulated" independent variables. In such quasi experiments, researchers must recognize that modest changes in behavior, say a slight increase or decrease in drug overdoses or traffic fatalities or homicides, may be part of a long-term trend and may not have been caused by the enactment of the new law. The statistical analyses required for such natural experiments must take into account these long-term trends (Campbell, 1972a; Cook & Campbell, 1979).

CROSS-CULTURAL RESEARCH

Social psychologists frequently study large-scale social variables such as child-rearing techniques, political ideology, exposure to mass media, and the economic system. Since any single culture tends to have a narrow range of these variables, it is often desirable to study their effects by examining behavior in different countries or in different cultures.

For example, most children in Western cultures are reared by their biological parents. If you want to test a theory that predicts that the child–caretaker relationship is an important determinant of adult behavior, then it would not be feasible to conduct such a test only in Western cultures, where there is so little variation in such relationships. Methodologically, it would be preferable to study children in cultures where there is great variability in responsibility for child-rearing, in order to examine such effects on later behavior (Whiting & Child, 1953).

Since so much social psychological research is conducted in the United States, Canada, and Western Europe, it is possible to criticize that research as being too limited in scope (e.g., Faucheux, 1976; Israel & Tajfel, 1972). For example, if we find that frustration causes

These Chinese-American boys, growing up in the U.S., must deal with two different cultural influences. Social psychologists often study such groups but rarely make real cross-cultural studies—comparing child-rearing practices in the U.S. and China, for example.

aggression in Western countries, such as the United States and France, can we therefore conclude that it also does in Russia, Bolivia, and Turkey? Because the external validity of studies conducted on a limited population is at least questionable, it is often desirable to replicate research in other cultures.

Often research originally conducted with American, British, or Canadian subjects is repeated in another Western country, such as Germany, France, or Sweden. This is actually a *cross-national* replication rather than a truly *cross-cultural* replication, as Western countries share a common core culture. In many cross-national and cross-cultural replications, the results obtained in the initial study are duplicated in other countries or cultures (e.g., Castell & Goldstein, 1977; Mantell, 1971; Shaw, Briscoe, & Garcia-Esteve, 1968; Sommer, 1968). Such similarity in findings is perhaps less instructive than differences that may be found between countries or cultures (e.g., Kelley, Shure, Deutsch, Faucheux, Lanzetta, Moscovici, Nuttin, Rabbie, & Thibaut, 1970; McGinnies & Ward, 1974; Milgram, 1961; Sanada & Norbeck, 1975; Goldstein, Silverman, & Anderson, Note 1).

One source of data exists for the express purpose of conducting cross-cultural research, the Human Relations Area Files (HRAF). The HRAF consists of the collected writings, analyses, and observations of over 500 different societies studied by anthropologists, sociologists, missionaries, psychologists, and others (Murdoch, Ford, Hudson, Kennedy, Simmons, & Whiting, 1950). While the primary focus of the HRAF is on society as a unit, the files contain a great deal of information useful to the social psychologist. In one study, described in detail in Chapter 8, the generality of a theory of human aggression was tested by examining the data from over 80 different societies (Watson, 1973).

Because the researcher has no control over which people are citizens of which countries (random assignment of subjects to countries or cultures is not possible), cross-cultural research is always correlational. This makes national or cultural differences particularly difficult to interpret. As a hypothetical example, suppose a researcher attempts to replicate an American frustration–aggression experiment in Senegal, West Africa, but fails to find a difference between a frustrated and a nonfrustrated group of subjects. If the experiment is internally valid, then obviously there is some difference between the two cultures, and so we can say that the frustration–aggression theory applies to Americans but not to Senegalese.

The problem arises in trying to explain why the theory is inapplicable to the Senegalese. What is the difference between the two cultures that explains the difference in response to frustration? Because the research subjects were not randomly assigned to be Americans or Senegalese, there may be a variety of subtle and not so subtle differences between them that can account for differences in results. It is difficult, however, to determine precisely what the differences are. Thus, while cross-cultural research is often valuable in setting limits to the external validity of theories, it is difficult to interpret. Nevertheless, it is frequently used to test the generality of theories (Brislin, Lonner, & Thorndike, 1973).

OBSERVATIONAL RESEARCH AND CASE STUDIES

While the vast majority of social psychological research involves correlational studies, experiments, and quasi experiments, there are other valuable techniques available to the researcher. These techniques include various kinds of observational studies and case studies.

Observational studies involve neither the manipulation of variables, the random assignment of participants to groups, nor the direct measurement of variables. Instead, they require the researcher to note behavior in some systematic fashion in a natural setting. Observational studies are generally of two types: *nonparticipant observation* and *participant observation*. A nonparticipant observational study was conducted by Fine (1977) on certain behaviors of Little League baseball teams. Fine recorded the boys' use of obscenities when speaking to one another, and the circumstances under which obscenities were spoken. These bits of information were then analyzed by comparing the number of obscenities uttered in the company of other males, of females, in mixed company, and the circumstances surrounding the boys' obscene speech.

Participant observation requires that the researcher be an active member of the group under study. In 1956, three social psychologists, Leon Festinger, Henry Riecken, and Stanley Schachter, joined a group whose leader, Mrs. Keech, had predicted the destruction of the earth at a particular date and time. The social psychologists presented themselves as believers in her ability to communicate with inhabitants of another planet, Clarion. Mrs. Keech claimed to have been forewarned by Clarionites and she urged Earthlings to join with her in being saved by a flying saucer that would take the faithful from the Earth just before it was destroyed by flood and earthquake. The social psychologists joined the group in order to observe how and to what extent members would support one another in the face of an unfulfilled prophecy. They found that after the predicted date of destruction passed, rather than acknowledge that a mistake had been made, the group actually took credit for preventing doomsday and began to recruit new members. While the results of this study are difficult to quantify and analyze in statistical terms, they provide some important theoretical insights into group dynamics, social relationships, and persuasion.

Social psychologists occasionally study a few isolated individuals in order to test or develop theories of some aspect of behavior. These studies are referred to as *case studies*. Case studies provide the basis for psychoanalytic theory and are frequently presented as supporting research for it (Freud, 1963a, 1963b). In an early social psychological study on the nature of social attitudes, M. Brewster Smith, Jerome S. Bruner, and Robert W. White (1956) closely explored ten individuals' attitudes toward Russia. The men in their study were not chosen to be representative of all men, because the researchers were primarily interested in examining how attitudes form, how they are supported, and how they alter our way of viewing the world. Rather than providing a test of a theory, such case studies more often serve to generate theoretical ideas. Because the individuals under study are seldom representative of any larger population, case studies provide a means of examining some aspects of behavior in depth and arriving at hypotheses. The hypotheses can then be tested by more conventional methods.

MEASUREMENT IN SOCIAL PSYCHOLOGY

Comparisons form the very foundation of research. A researcher attempts to test a hypothesis by comparing two or more individuals or groups of individuals, or by comparing the same individuals at two or more different times. Statistical analyses of data are efficient methods for determining the extent to which differences occurred by chance.

It is important to recognize that statistics form an integral part of scientific research procedures in social psychology. It is not enough for the researcher simply to look at the results of a study and conclude that there is or isn't a relationship between variables or that an independent variable caused a change in a dependent variable. The researcher must demonstrate that the relationships or changes that occurred in her or his research are large enough to be meaningful. If the changes or relationships are greater than might be expected by chance, the odds are high that the differences are due to the independent variable.

Because measuring instruments in psychology are not perfectly reliable, some variation in scores will occur for no apparent reason. For example, if you take the College Entrance Examination Boards on two different occasions, it is unlikely that your scores for quantitative and verbal abilities will be identical both times. Even if you learn or forget nothing between the two tests, you can expect some slight variation in scores. Psychological researchers must recognize that such variations in scores occur, and must then determine how much of the variation is due to this random fluctuation and how much to some real, meaningful change. Statistics enable researchers to estimate these effects.

If you compare two randomly constituted groups, you are likely to find some minor difference between them on any possible measure. For example, if you give IQ tests to two random groups, the mean score of one group may be 110.8 and that of the other 112.1. Such slight differences are to be expected purely on the basis of chance. If statistical tests indicate that the difference is too large to be attributed to chance, then the difference is assumed to have been caused by some variable to which one group was exposed but not the other. In experiments, this is the independent variable.

The researcher must test hypotheses against error due to unreliable tests and measurements, and variations that naturally occur between people. For correlational studies, the researcher must determine how much of the relationship that exists between two variables is random error and how much signifies a meaningful relationship. The most common statistical tests for determining such relationships are *coefficients of correlation*. There are two major correlation coefficients used by social psychologists; each is applicable to a different type of data. If you are dealing with tests that yield one of several possible scores for each subject, and if each of these scores consists of an equal unit, then the data are analyzed by the *Pearson product–moment coefficient of correlation*, or *r*. For example, if you are studying the relationship between a person's age and IQ, then the Pearson r would be used since age is a variable whose units are all equal (1 year is always 365.25 days), and IQ tests yield a standard unit. But if you are interested in relative scores, such as class standing (1st, 2nd, 3rd, and so on) and age, one of these variables is only a rank ordering. In such cases, the most appropriate type of correlation to compute is a *Spearman rank-order coefficient of correlation*, symbolized by the Greek letter rho, ρ. If you are studying the relationship between two variables that have only nominal values, such as gender (male, female) and political party affiliation (Democratic, Republican, Socialist, Independent), then the appropriate statistical test is a *chi square*, χ^2.

These are but three of the many ways to determine relationships between variables but they are the ones most commonly used in social psychological research on correlational hypotheses. Statistical tests are presented in terms of chance probabilities, expressed as $p < .05$, or $p < .01$, and so on. The first figure indicates that the results of a study would occur by chance less than 5 times out of 100, meaning that 95 times out of 100 such results would not occur by chance. In the second figure, the results would occur by chance only 1 out of 100 times. Thus, over 99 times out of 100, results such as these are caused by nonrandom, nonerror factors.

In experimental studies, two or more groups are usually compared. In our frustration–aggression example, the researcher measures aggression for both the experimental and the control groups. The question is then the statistical one of determining whether such an observed difference can be accounted for solely on the basis of chance.

If only two groups are used in an experiment, the most common statistical test to determine whether there is a meaningful difference between them involves comparing the mean aggression scores of the two groups using a t test. The t test takes into consideration not only the mean score for each group, but also the extent to which each of the members of each group differed from the mean; in other words, the *variance* is also taken into account. If more than two groups participate in the experiment, a test called an *analysis of variance* will be used. There are many kinds of analyses of variance, depending upon the particular design of the experiment, but all of them yield a number, symbolized by F, which can be used to determine the likelihood that the results were caused only by chance. When a t or an F is computed, the researcher looks in a statistical table to determine the number of times out of 100 that such a number would occur by chance. Just as correlation coefficients and χ^2s are expressed in terms of probabilities, so, too, are t and F values. If the results of an experiment are not likely to have been caused by chance, then they are likely to have been caused by some factor, presumably the independent variable. When the probability of the results obtained is less than .05, the researcher usually refers to the results as *statistically significant*. This implies that the results were unlikely to have occurred by chance.

NON-HYPOTHESIS-TESTING RESEARCH

I have suggested that the goal of most social psychologists is to develop and test theories of social behavior. While this is the most efficient use of research, it is possible to conduct research that has little if any relationship to theories of social behavior. In social psychology, research is often conducted for three reasons that are only indirectly related to theory: to generate hypotheses, to study some observed aspect of reality more closely, and to elaborate upon previous research findings.

HYPOTHESIS-GENERATING RESEARCH

Very often, behaviors that may be of interest to the social psychologist will have been ignored or overlooked by existing theories. For example, a social psychologist who is interested in the phenomenon

Social psychologists are rarely on hand to observe people's reactions to real-life emergencies. Therefore, researchers must simulate emergency situations in order to test bystander intervention.

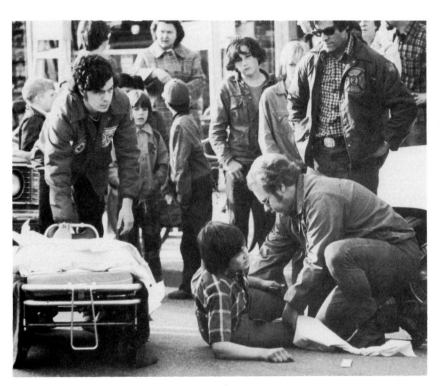

of wife-battering will have a difficult time finding a theory that attempts to explain such behavior. In such cases, research may be conducted to provide some tentative explanations of the phenomenon, which can then be tested in the form of theoretical hypotheses. The researcher may begin by interviewing husbands and wives who have been involved in cases of abuse, comparing their attitudes, feelings, and experiences with those of nonabusive couples. The data from such a study may then be used to formulate hypotheses that can be tested more clearly and directly in subsequent research. The conclusions of such exploratory studies are only inferences from the data and the data do not in any way prove that those conclusions are true.

RESEARCH INITIATED BY REAL EVENTS

There are numerous real-life situations that might be of interest to social psychologists, but no good theoretical explanation of them is available. In such cases, the researcher may attempt to reproduce the event in the laboratory in order to arrive at some sort of tentative explanation for it. In attempting to reconstruct a natural event in the unnatural environment of the laboratory, the researcher is merely trying to *simulate* the natural event—to capture it in miniature in order to study it more closely. Social psychologists, for example, are often interested in wars and natural catastrophes such as floods and earthquakes. To study such events, they may set up experimental situations in which people compete against others or cope with a simulated mini-disaster (see Chapter 9; Kelley, Condry, Dahlke, & Hill, 1965; A. L. Klein, 1976; Mintz, 1951). Such simulations have one or more characteristics in common with real events, but they are at best only weak imitations.

One well-known example of research instigated by an actual event is the series of studies conducted by Latané and Darley (1970). This research, discussed in detail in Chapter 7, was initiated by the slaying of a woman that was witnessed by at least 38 people, none of whom went to her aid. In the absence of any theoretical explanations for this failure of bystanders to intervene, Latané and Darley conducted studies that attempted to simulate various aspects of emergency situations, both in the laboratory and in quasi-experimental field studies.

RESEARCH ON RESEARCH

A common type of research in social psychology seeks to elaborate, clarify, or refine the results of previous research. For example, Latané and Darley noted that bystanders offered help less often when they were in a group than when they were alone. Subsequent research by other psychologists has attempted to refine these observations by varying the type of emergency and the characteristics of the bystanders (e.g., Clark & Word, 1974; Piliavin, Rodin, & Piliavin, 1969; Wilson, 1976).

THE RELATIONSHIP BETWEEN THEORY AND METHOD

As we saw in Chapter 1, theories differ both in their fundamental assumptions about human nature and in the terms they use to explain behavior. Behaviorist theories emphasize observable, measurable aspects of gross motor behavior. Cognitive and symbolic interactionist theories emphasize the internal and structural aspects of human interaction. Psychoanalytic theory stresses the importance of unconscious motives. Clearly, some research methods are more applicable to some of these theoretical approaches than others.

When behaviorists conduct experimental research, the dependent variables usually consist of observable behaviors. Cognitive and symbolic interactionist theorists attempt to measure not only behavior, but also the psychological processes that give rise to that behavior. When cognitive theories are tested in experimental research, there is often a need to correlate various aspects of cognitive organization and cognitive processes with behavioral dependent measures (e.g., Zajonc, 1960). Hence, more correlational and quasi-experimental research is conducted by cognitively oriented theorists than by behaviorists. Symbolic interactionists must often determine how a person perceives the environment and his or her place in it in order to test theories; they generally use participant observation and correlational studies (e.g., H. S. Becker, 1963; R. S. Brooks, 1963/ 1967). Because psychoanalytic theory emphasizes the role of past experience in an individual's life and the importance of unconscious drives and wishes, psychoanalysts frequently employ case studies as the preferred method of research (e.g., A. Freud & Dann, 1951). Psychoanalytic theory has also generated a number of research tools designed to provide insight into unconscious motives, and these *projective tests* are used almost exclusively by analytically oriented researchers.

Theories set limits on the kinds of research that can be used to provide satisfactory tests of those theories. Thus, a behaviorist approaches research on aggression quite differently than a cognitive theorist or a psychoanalyst. The theory leads the researcher to look at, and look for, particular relationships and causes. The behaviorist observes or manipulates certain environmental factors and then observes aggressive behavior as a dependent variable. The cognitive theorist also observes environmental factors and aggressive behavior, but attempts to determine how the subjects viewed their actions and how they perceived the environment at that moment. Psychoanalytic theorists are not so concerned with the immediate environment or with the individual's perception of it, but rely more on a knowledge of the individual's past experiences with aggression and with conscious and unconscious feelings about aggression.

Rather than providing contradictory results, different approaches to the topic are likely to produce complementary results that focus on different levels or different aspects of the same behavior. Contradictions stemming from different theories and from different types of research do arise, often because of a difference in emphasis or interpretation (e.g., Hovland, 1959; Platt, 1964).

WHY OBSERVATIONS CANNOT EXIST WITHOUT THEORIES

"If social psychologists are interested in some problem, such as aggression, why don't they drop all the verbiage and methodology and simply go ahead and study it? Why not just observe who is aggressive and when, and then come up with the explanation? That certainly seems like a more objective way to learn about behavior than thinking up an explanation and then testing it. Having a hypothesis before observing behavior seems less objective because it gives the researcher a built-in bias."

I have heard this argument many times, not only from students but from colleagues as well. I think it stems from what might be called the *fallacy of "pure" observation*. It is not possible to be a "pure observer" without any biases, hunches, or hypotheses. Suppose that you want to observe human aggression and abstract from your observations an explanation for aggressive behavior. You want to be purely objective in your observations. But which people will you observe? Children? adults? males? females? whites? blacks? Orientals? And when will you observe them? In the morning? afternoon? Where? At home? school? work? during play? And how will you record your observations? You will have to deal with these and other questions before beginning your observations.

Suppose you decide to observe children and adults, of both sexes, in Pennsylvania. And suppose, further, that you decide to observe people in department stores and supermarkets, and that you decide to count the number of times one person pushes another. By choosing these people and these behaviors to observe, you have eliminated all other people and all other behaviors. On what grounds? Most likely, you have some reasons for your choices, such as the belief that adults and children are equally aggressive, but that males are more aggressive than females. In short, you are testing a hypothesis: Males are more aggressive than females, regardless of age. So you are not entering into this study without expectations. These expectations or predictions are precisely what we mean by hypotheses. Intellectually, it is more honest to state your hypotheses ahead of time than to deny that any expectations are guiding your observations.

Another problem is that observation is always less than perfectly objective. When your instructor looks out over the classroom, he or she may see a particular student, all the others fading into a blur in the background. Or a particular pattern of colors may be clear, with yellow and blue and red sweaters standing out against a sea of muted shades. What we observe is a function of past experience, expectation, and attention; it is rarely a complete and accurate perception of what exists in the environment. As we shall see in Chapter 4, the idea that we can observe the environment accurately and totally objectively is an illusion.

HAVE I GOT A THEORY FOR YOU! *POST HOC* EXPLANATIONS

Research methods were designed to provide the researcher with an answer to a question, which is stated in the form of a hypothetical prediction. The researcher asks, "Does frustration cause aggression?" and a well-designed study is capable of providing a yes or no answer to the question. The research is not capable of giving any answer other than a relative yes or no; it cannot tell us, "Here is what causes aggression," or "Some factor other than frustration causes aggression." It can only provide us with a probability estimate in answer to a specifically stated hypothesis.

Imagine that a social psychologist, Minnie Morse, decides to deprive one group of people of food for several hours and not to deprive a second group, which will be given potato chips and Coke. She then administers the Buss–Durkee Hostility Inventory to both groups. Suppose that she finds the deprived group scores higher on the inventory than the nondeprived group.

	No food	Potato chips, Coke
Hostility score	15	4

Minnie may conclude from this experiment that eating potato chips and drinking Coke decrease aggression. Or that depriving people of potato chips and Coke causes aggression. This makes sense since potato chips and Coke taste good and therefore people who consume them feel good and become nonaggressive. In either case, she may advocate that the government save the world from warfare

Looking at this picture, you might assume these are happy patriots celebrating July 4. In fact, they are angry demonstrators at a protest march. A single observation often gives us a misleading perception of an event.

by shipping potato chips and Coke to all bellicose nations.

Suppose, though, that Minnie's results look like this:

	No Food	Potato chips, Coke
Hostility score	4	15

In this case, Minnie may conclude that eating potato chips and drinking Coke cause aggression. This makes sense because potato chips and Coke may increase your blood-sugar level, which could cause an increase in aggression. She cleverly advocates that the government prohibit the shipment of potato chips and Coke to all unfriendly nations.

The point of this exercise is to indicate that *any* nonrandom results from any study can be interpreted in *some* way. If the researcher waits until the results are in before stating what those results mean, then there is no chance that the results will fail to have some meaning. They will always support the researcher's explanation since the explanation was proposed *post hoc* (after the collection of data).

ETHICAL PRINCIPLES IN
THE CONDUCT OF
RESEARCH WITH HUMAN
PARTICIPANTS*

The ethical principles below were recommended by the Ad Hoc Committee on Ethical Standards in Psychological Research of the American Psychological Association.

1. In planning a study the investigator has the personal responsibility to make a careful evaluation of its ethical acceptability, taking into account these Principles for research with human beings. To the extent that this appraisal, weighing scientific and humane values, suggests a deviation from any Principle, the investigator incurs an increasingly serious obligation to seek ethical advice and to observe more stringent safeguards to protect the rights of the human research participant.

2. Responsibility for the establishment and maintenance of acceptable ethical practice in research always remains with the individual investigator....

3. Ethical practice requires the investigator to inform the participant of all features of the research that reasonably might be expected to influence willingness to participate and to explain all other aspects of the research about which the participant inquires....

4. Openness and honesty are essential characteristics of the relationship between investigator and research participant. When the methodological requirements of a study necessitate concealment or deception, the investigator is required to ensure the participant's understanding of the reasons for this action and to restore the quality of the relationship with the investigator.

Post hoc explanations of research results are a misuse of research procedure. The purpose of research is to provide a yes or no answer to a specific question. If that question is posed only after data collection, the research will never say no.

Note that in our example Minnie Morse never considered that depriving people of food caused frustration. Had she been familiar with frustration–aggression theory, she would have known that such a deprivation can, among other things, cause frustration. If a theoretical hypothesis is not stated beforehand, the data are open to too many different possible interpretations. The manipulation of food deprivation may be seen as frustrating, or as changing blood-sugar levels, or as making people feel good. Food deprivation can influence all these things, and more. A theoretical hypothesis helps us to interpret our research operations and guides us in checking our manipulations in order to ensure that we have produced the intended state in research participants.

Post hoc explanations of results can often be used as hypotheses to be tested in future research. Minnie Morse may say that, on the basis of her study, she believes that making people feel good decreases aggression. She may then test this hypothesis in another study

5. Ethical research practice requires the investigator to respect the individual's freedom to decline to participate in research or to discontinue participation at any time. . . .

6. Ethically acceptable research begins with the establishment of a clear and fair agreement between the investigator and the research participant that clarifies the responsibilities of each. The investigator has the obligation to honor all promises and commitments included in that agreement.

7. The ethical investigator protects participants from physical and mental discomfort, harm, and danger. . . . A research procedure may not be used if it is likely to cause serious and lasting harm to participants.

8. After the data are collected, ethical practice requires the investigator to provide the participant with a full clarification of the nature of the study and to remove any misconceptions that may have arisen. . . .

9. Where research procedures may result in undesirable consequences for the participant, the investigator has the responsibility to detect and remove or correct these consequences, including, where relevant, long-term aftereffects.

10. Information obtained about the research participants during the course of an investigation is confidential. . . .

*From American Psychological Association (1973, pp. 1–2).

where she manipulates the independent variable of mood. But *post hoc* explanations in and of themselves are meaningless. The results of a study do not provide support for a *post hoc* explanation.

SOME ETHICAL CONSIDERATIONS

In recent years, social psychologists have become increasingly concerned with the ethical aspects of research on human subjects. Beginning perhaps with experiments on obedience to authority (see Chapter 8), several issues have arisen that deserve the attention of researchers.

Until the war in Vietnam, behavioral researchers tended to believe that conducting scientific research was necessarily a valuable enterprise, potentially beneficial to humankind. After all, social psychologists rendered important services to the government during World War II (Boring, 1944) and, later, to industry. Science as a positive value was pervasive in twentieth-century Western culture, and it took a series of events in physics and later in psychology to call this value into question (see Roszak, 1969). For years, sociologists and others had the cooperation of minorities in the United States for the conduct of their research. Though that research was supposed to benefit the minorities, it was rarely used to their advantage. In the 1960s, a research project in Chile, known as "Camelot," sponsored by the U.S. government, was found to be less concerned with science than with surveillance (Horowitz, 1967). Finally, questions raised by psychologists about the ethics of deceiving subjects and exposing them to potential harm or distress led to a widespread debate among researchers that is still going on (Armistead, 1974; Baumrind, 1964; Gergen, 1973a; Wilson & Donnerstein, 1976).

Cook (1976) has noted ten ethical issues involved in social psychological research:

1. Research involving people without their knowledge or consent.
2. Coercing people to participate in research.
3. Withholding from participants the true nature of the research.
4. Deceiving research participants.
5. Leading participants to commit acts that diminish their self-respect.
6. Violating participants' rights to self-determination, as in changing their behavior or opinions.
7. Exposing participants to stress.
8. Invading the privacy of participants.
9. Withholding benefits from subjects in control groups.
10. Failing to treat participants fairly and to show them consideration and respect.

Of course, all these issues are not involved in every social psychological study, and many of them can be avoided by the careful investigator. Nevertheless, observing people without their knowledge and consent, and withholding information from participants and misleading them about the nature of the research are common techniques in social psychological research. To deal with such ethical problems, the American Psychological Association has drafted a code of ethics for researchers, portions of which appear in "Ethical Principles in the Conduct of Research with Human Participants," page 74.

Most discussions of ethical problems in research conclude with the statement that each researcher must weigh the potential risks versus the potential benefits of a study, and then proceed only if the benefits seem to outweigh the risks. That is a reasonable conclusion to draw, though additional safeguards for the protection of research participants seem warranted. The most common safeguard is a review committee that judges the benefits and risks of a proposed study before allowing the researcher to begin it.

The types of topics that social psychologists study may, in part, be responsible for the ethical dilemmas in which they often find themselves. Much social psychological research is concerned with control and manipulation of people rather than independent variables. It is even possible to characterize some social psychological research as totalitarian. A person may be influenced to act violently or be persuaded that his or her attitudes are wrong (see Argyris, 1975). Of course, it is both theoretically and practically important to permit researchers to study such behaviors as persuasion, aggression, obedience, and conformity, provided participants are not unduly subjected to potentially damaging experiences. These are important topics and psychologists have the right to confront them in their theories and research. There is, however, another side to life, which social psychology has virtually ignored. There has been relatively little theory and research on joy, happiness, cooperation, sharing, entertainment, and leisure. The study of such "positive behaviors," if I may call them that, seems to require different research methods than the study of more negative aspects of behavior. (While it is possible to think of a way to conduct laboratory experiments on joy, it seems more plausible to conduct observational studies and case studies on joyous experience.) If researchers are concerned with antisocial and manipulative behaviors, they are more likely to employ manipulative and antisocial strategies in their research.

Theories, because they are general and abstract, cannot be tested **Summary** directly. In order to test a theory, a hypothesis is logically inferred from a theory and evaluated by means of research. Hypotheses may be correlational or causal. For correlational hypotheses, the relationship between two or more variables is examined, and may be estimated by a variety of statistical tests. Among these tests are the Pearson product–moment correlation, the Spearman rank-order correlation, and the chi-square statistic. Causal hypotheses are generally tested in experimental studies in which one or more independent variables are manipulated and their effects on dependent variables are measured.

For a study to be a true experiment, research participants must be randomly assigned to the groups under study and the experimenter must intentionally manipulate at least one independent variable. When only one of these two characteristics is present, the study is defined as a quasi experiment. Correlational, experimental, and quasi-experimental studies can be conducted either in the laboratory or in field settings. Correlational research is more versatile than experimental research because it may make use of data archives and qualitative data. Cross-cultural studies are correlational. Other types of research employed by social psychologists include observational studies and case studies. Experimental studies provide less ambiguous tests of hypotheses than other types of research and have higher internal validity. Field studies tend to have higher external validity than laboratory studies because they are conducted under more realistic conditions.

Research may be initiated for hypothesis-testing as well as for hypothesis-generating. Research can also be used to examine real-life events and to elaborate on previous research.

In most cases, data from research are analyzed statistically. The use of statistics enables the researcher to determine what proportion of the results can be attributed to random error and chance. Results are considered statistically significant only if they are not due to chance.

The kind of theory you are interested in testing will determine, in part, the kind of methods you use in research. Behaviorists are most apt to use experimental procedures, while cognitive and symbolic interactionist theorists more often employ correlational methods. Psychoanalytic theorists rely heavily on case studies.

Theories and hypotheses guide the researcher and provide important information about what variables to examine, control, and measure. A hypothesis must be posed before data collection because *post hoc* explanations cannot be supported by data collected prior to their formulation. All observations are biased, but proposing a hypothesis before data collection is probably less biased than proposing it *post hoc*.

Concern over the welfare of research participants has led to the formulation of a code of ethics for psychological research. Ethical problems can often be minimized by careful planning. Ethical problems are sometimes inherent in the types of behavior social psychologists choose to study.

Suggested Readings

*Golden, M. P. (Ed.). *The research experience*. Itasca, Ill.: F. E. Peacock, 1976.

*Huff, D. *How to lie with statistics*. New York: Norton, 1954.

*Mayo, C. & LaFrance, M. *Evaluating research in social psychology: A guide for the consumer*. Belmont, Calif.: Wadsworth, 1977.

*Tanur, J. M., Mosteller, F., Kruskal, W. H., Link, R. F., Peters, R. S., & Rising, G. R. (Eds.). *Statistics: A guide to the unknown*. San Francisco: Holden-Day, 1972.

*Available in paperback edition.

*Webb, E. J., Campbell, D. T., Schwartz, R. D., & Sechrest, L. *Unobtrusive measures: Nonreactive research in the social sciences.* Chicago: Rand McNally, 1966.

Psychological Bulletin
Personality and Social Psychology Bulletin
Behavioral Science
Sociological Methodology

Pertinent Journals

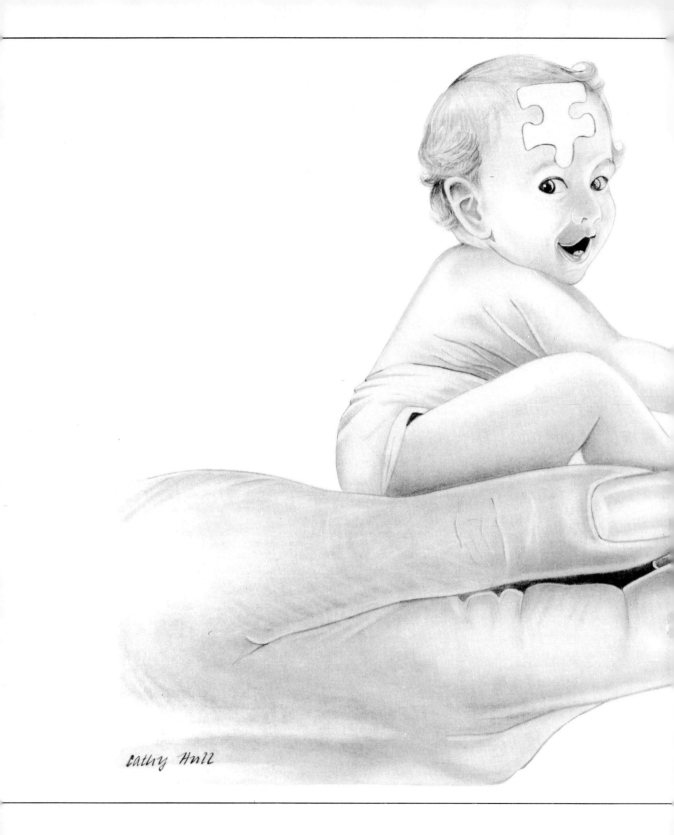

cathy Hull

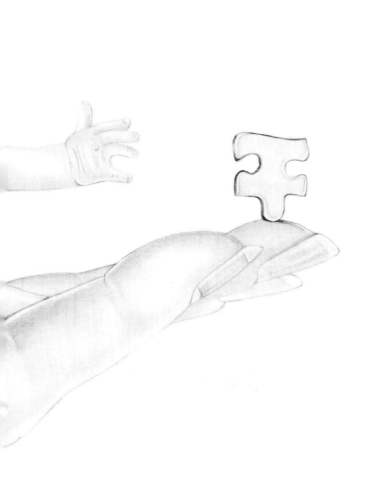

3
SOCIALIZATION: THE DEVELOPMENT OF SOCIAL BEHAVIOR

An infant enters the world without knowledge of rules, roles, or relationships among people. Between infancy and adolescence, society's basic expectations and limitations are imparted to the child in a complex series of processes generally referred to as socialization. Think of the enormous number of social principles that young children must learn in order to become effective, cooperative members of society. They must learn about relationships in families; about proper and expected behavior toward peers, relatives, teachers, and strangers; and about playing and working cooperatively. Children also must learn something of the social, moral, and legal sanctions associated with various behaviors. And they must acquire a general knowledge of the economic and political systems so that these institutions will be perpetuated from one generation to the next. All this is learned in addition to acquiring basic motor and intellectual skills. While socialization is a process that continues throughout life, we assimilate most of these social skills in an impressively brief span of time.

Socialization means the acquisition of skills and traits that enable you to function effectively with other members of your society. Socialization is not something that merely "happens" to a person during infancy or childhood. Most attitudes, values, beliefs, and skills undergo a kind of psychological maturation that is part of the socialization process. For example, political socialization does not end when a child's political beliefs first take shape. Instead, there is a long-term process of refining, elaborating, and testing these beliefs throughout the person's life.

Young children hold a number of basic beliefs about the political system that seem primitive and simplistic to adults. A study of American grade school children found that many of them have only a vague, but favorable, conception of government (Hess, 1969). Almost all the young children, for example, agreed that "the American flag is the best flag in the world" and that "America is the best country in the world." One child was asked what the government is:

"The Government is like the President, but he isn't actually a President. . . . Maybe he makes the laws of the country. Maybe he tells the numbers on the license plates. . . . I heard on the radio that he's in charge of the income tax. He can higher it or lower it."

"What does he spend the money on?"

"How should I know? Like the Government doesn't know what we spend our money on. He spends it for food, clothing, things for his wife, and that sort of thing." (Hess, 1969, p. 26)

(Come to think of it, what *does* the government spend the money on?)

These children in the second or third grade have already acquired a variety of attitudes and beliefs about political institutions. Yet,

this clearly is not the end of the political socialization process. Older children learn to make a distinction between the individuals who hold offices and the offices themselves. They become aware of the system of checks and balances; of the interrelationships among various branches of government; of the relative weakness and strength of political institutions. This process ends neither in adolescence nor in adulthood, but probably continues to change for many years. *Because socialization is an ongoing process, you are almost never what you once were and not quite what you are to become.* Attitudes, values, beliefs, and skills undergo almost constant modification, refinement, and testing. Because the rate of change of these characteristics may vary, there is rarely a one-to-one correspondence between any of these variables and a person's behavior. In other words, attitudes and values may not predict behavior perfectly because they are in a state of transition, and a person may act on past attitudes or present attitudes, or even try new ones. If we recognize that most psychological entities, like attitudes and values, are in a state of flux, then it is easier to understand why these entities may not always enable us to predict behavior.

The political socialization of these children is just beginning. Although they already agree that "the American flag is the best flag," they will refine and test this belief as they grow older.

WHAT'S IN A NAME*

A couple might have no difficulty at all in deciding to have a child; it's the name that gives them the problem. They'll spend days, weeks, even years mulling over names, accepting, then rejecting, sometimes right up until a child is born and after.

So difficult is this decision that children have been born without given names, and it is not unknown for parents to change a child's name a few weeks after the birth, because they are still having trouble with the sound of it.

Names do matter to people. And in recent years psychologists have been stirring up even more interest in them, with research indicating that undesirable names (in minds of classmates or teachers) may be a handicap, while desirable names may be helpful. The names, the psychologists say, are linked to the way children are viewed by others and the way they view themselves.

Dr. John McDavid and his colleagues at Georgia State University first got interested in the subject when they realized that the most popular children in the classroom they were studying were also the ones with the commonest names.

Not only did having a desirable name such as John, Michael, or Sally seem related to how well liked one was, but Dr. McDavid with his co-researcher, Dr. Herbert Harari, later concluded that it was linked to the teacher's grading.

Essays from hypothetical children named Elmer or Bertha were graded lower by teachers than the same essays when they bore popular names.

Dr. S. Gray Garwood . . . followed up on the earlier research with a study of how children with desirable and undesirable names perceived themselves. He used only boys' names because the ones for girls go in and out of fashion too quickly, while the popularity of

THE AGENTS OF SOCIALIZATION

It is often said that "society" teaches its values, beliefs, and attitudes during the socialization process. Of course, that is imprecise because "society" is an abstraction. It is individual members of a society who are responsible for passing on the culture to children, and most studies have focused on the three chief agents of socialization: parents, teachers, and associates or peers. (It is easy to remember these because their first letters form the acronym PTA.) Since no two parents, teachers, or peers are alike, every child is exposed to different aspects of the total culture.

Parents are the primary socialization agents. During the first two years of a child's life, they are responsible for most of the child's boys' names remains relatively constant over the years. (Others have observed that there has been some change in boys' names recently with Jason, Mark and Brian becoming very popular.) The desirable names in this study, conducted in Atlanta, were Craig, Gregory, James, Jeffrey, John, Jonathan, Patrick, Richard and Thomas. The undesirable names were Bernard, Curtis, Daryl, Arnold, Horace, Jerome, Maurice, Roderick and Samuel.

Dr. Garwood found that the boys with desirable names generally thought of themselves in a more positive way than the others. They had higher aspirations, too.

Also looking at the name issue is Dr. Thomas Busse, an educational psychologist at Temple University who had studied more than 2000 children's names. . . .

The boys who tended to have the highest IQs regardless of their parents' level of education, or their ethnic background, tended to bear names such as David, Michael, Paul, John, Gary, James, Richard, Scott and Steven.

The most desirable girls' names and the girls reputed to be the brightest were Susan, Linda, Barbara, Carol, Cindy and Diane. . . .

All of the researchers warn against getting carried away with the name game. It's important, they say, for parents and teachers to realize that a name brings to a child a set of biases from other people. But a name, which can vary in desirability from one group to another, is just a single factor in how a child is viewed, and it is tightly intertwined with others, such as appearance and economic level. Also, they point out, the research only indicates what happens on the average. Some children with the strangest names do think well of themselves and prosper. Unusual names can be handy in politics, for instance, helping a candidate stand out. . . .

*Richard Flaste, *The New York Times*, 4 February 1977, p. A12.
*Flaste (1977).

experiences. Later, siblings begin to influence the child by providing other experiences and other people for comparison. They also help the child learn how to interact with age-mates. Teachers then begin to exert an influence on the child and, with school- and playmates, become largely responsible for socialization until early adolescence.

Children learn quite different things, through different techniques and different agents of socialization, at different ages. Parents and teachers not only use highly explicit and intentional methods of instruction, they also influence the child through more indirect and subtle means, such as their own behavioral demonstrations. Peers influence one another primarily through interaction, particularly during play. And, of course, children are also motivated to learn things on their own.

RECIPROCITY AND SOCIALIZATION

We have noted that socialization is not a process that ends at any particular age. It is equally important to remember that whenever one person influences another, the influencer is also affected to some extent. Just as parents influence their children, children influence their parents. When parents teach their children skills, values, and behaviors, their own skills, values, and behaviors are changed in the process (Bell & Harper, 1977). In this way, behavior develops and changes throughout life. When a couple has a child, their behavior changes and they acquire social roles and develop skills they did not have previously. In traditional studies of socialization, the focus was on the effects of the parents' behavior on the child. Only now are psychologists beginning to explore the ways in which the child's behavior affects the parents.

AGE-DEPENDENT DEVELOPMENT

Many psychologists who study socialization tend to emphasize the chronological age at which children first manifest certain skills or beliefs. This comes, in part, from the findings of Jean Piaget, the noted Swiss biologist, who observed that children tend to develop certain cognitive abilities at certain ages (e.g., Piaget, 1932/1950, 1954). From my perspective, the amount of experience that a child has had interacting with others, what might be called the child's *interactional age*, is more important (Denzin, 1975). By interacting with others, children not only have direct experiences that lead to social and emotional growth, they also acquire expectations of how their own development should progress. Expectations exert a strong influence on child development. Both the child's and the parents' expectations will determine, in large part, what a child will attempt to do or learn. For example, if a culture expects children to walk at age three, that is most likely when parents will teach them to walk, despite the fact that middle-class American children learn to walk a year or more earlier (Kagan & Klein, 1973).

THE NATURE–NURTURE DEBATE

It is in discussing the topic of socialization that the nature–nurture debate generally arises. This controversy deals with the question of whether a person's behavior in later life is determined primarily by genetic inheritance (nature) or by experience and learning (nurture). The debate has been recurrent in psychology and every so often, like the flu, it comes back in a slightly different strain.

Most recently, the nature–nurture debate has raged over the issues of race and intelligence, and over the origins of social behavior. Are differences in IQ test scores that may exist between races due to inheritance or to learning and cultural factors? Are patterns of social behavior, such as altruism or violence, genetically determined, or are they the result of past experiences?

These questions are, for all practical purposes, unanswerable. In fact, nature *versus* nurture is a false dichotomy. It is not a question of one or the other, but of the interaction between the two (e.g., Dworkin, Burke, Maher, & Gottesman, 1976; Matheny & Dolan, 1975). Genetic constitution sets upper and lower limits on the individual's rate and course of development, but learning experiences determine where the person will fall within this constitutionally determined range. It is methodologically impossible (and ethically undesirable) to determine precisely what proportion of a human being's behavior is caused by inheritance and what proportion by environment. It seems safe to assume that the range for any group of individuals is sufficiently broad for experience to have a major effect on later behavior.

In order to demonstrate the breadth of this range, a number of cross-cultural studies are discussed in this and subsequent chapters. My purpose in stressing cultural diversity is to show that human behavior is not nearly so homogeneous as many would have us believe. Many people have argued that one or another form of human social behavior is genetically based. One reason this belief persists is that the world really is becoming increasingly homogeneous owing to the spread of mass media, rapid means of transportation, multinational corporations, and so on. Many of the tribal cultures of only

You may not be able to speak the language or understand the customs, but you'll feel right at home as soon as you spot the Pepsi-Cola sign.

a few decades ago have disappeared or been assimilated into larger, Westernized cultures. There are probably few people in the world today who have not tasted Coca-Cola or seen a Hollywood movie. This increased cultural homogeneity fosters the illusion that human behavior is similar throughout the world because of biological determinism. The disappearance of pre-industrial cultures makes it more difficult for the full range of human potential to be observed. This, in turn, leads people to assume that humans act pretty much the same everywhere because of "human nature." But the fact that people once acted radically different from the way they do today suggests that experience and environment strongly influence behavior.

THEORIES AND PROCESSES OF SOCIALIZATION

Infants and young children develop so many skills and traits in such a short period of time that it would be astonishing if all this development took place through only one mechanism. As it happens, a number of different processes assist this rapid psychological and social growth. These processes are rarely independent of one another, and often interact in complex ways. For example, many physiological changes occur during infancy and early childhood, and these changes are accompanied by a rapid increase in cognitive complexity and ability. How cognitive development is influenced by physiological factors, and in turn influences social development, is largely uncharted territory. We will review a number of basic socialization processes. All these processes are inextricably linked to other changes that occur during socialization, including physical maturation, psychological development, and changes in the child's social environment.

PSYCHOANALYTIC THEORY

According to Freud (1920/1970), humans are born with a set of instincts that supplies the energy for all subsequent behavior and development. Although he first proposed only a single source of instinctive motivation, Freud later modified his views to include two sources of energy: life instincts (called *libido* or *eros*) and destructive instincts *(thanatos)*. These sources of energy are part and parcel of being human, and they are referred to collectively as the *id*. Since the id operates unconsciously, people are unaware that these instincts exert any influence on their behavior.

Because the id is unconscious, it makes no distinction between reality and fantasy. It is able to satisfy its aggressive and sexual impulses either by fantasizing about them or by acting upon them. Satisfaction through fantasy is known as *primary process* thinking. Freud thought that the life or "sexual" instincts and the destructive or "aggressive" instincts continually built up to higher and higher levels until they were satisfied either through behavior or primary process thought, such as dreams.

But man does not live by dreams of bread alone. The organism must find a way to satisfy its instincts in a realistic fashion. To do this, it borrows some energy from the id to form the *ego*, which deals with reality on a conscious level. The ego includes the self, memories, feelings, thoughts, perceptions, and beliefs.

While the ego is capable of satisfying id impulses, such as the impulse to eat or to sleep, these drives must be satisfied in a socially acceptable way. Therefore, the ego gives up some of its energy to form the *superego*, whose primary purpose is the regulation of the ego's behavior. The superego, which is sometimes equated with the conscience, consists of the internalized values of society. That is, the superego comes to view behavior according to the parents' values, and these parental values are usually consistent with the dominant values of society. The ego is capable of satisfying the id's desire for food, but it is the superego that directs the ego's eating toward objects that the society considers appropriate. For instance, it is possible to satisfy the hunger drive by devouring another person, but the superego guides the hungry person to seek food that is socially acceptable, such as beef. The superego, like the id, is unconscious, so we are unable to recognize its precise demands upon the ego.

Because the ego is so important for the satisfaction of instinctive id impulses, a person often seeks to protect the ego from threatening thoughts and perceptions. This protection involves what Freud referred to as *ego defense mechanisms*. These are all psychological devices that deny, distort, or deal selectively with various aspects of reality. For example, the defense mechanism of *repression*, which Freud saw as the most important one in neuroses, involves the selective forgetting of threatening experiences or thoughts. When an event is repressed, it is no longer conscious, and so the ego does not have to deal with it. Other defense mechanisms include reaction formation, denial, projection, and rationalization, and are discussed in later chapters.

Psychosexual Stages of Development   Freud proposed five stages of human development from infancy to adolescence: the oral, anal, phallic, latency, and genital stages. Freud and later psychoanalysts developed their ideas about the first three stages most fully, and these are generally regarded as more crucial to later adult behavior than the subsequent stages.

For each stage, there is a particular bodily zone, referred to as an *erogenous zone*, through which the sexual instincts (libido) obtain gratification. During the *oral stage*, which lasts from birth to about

Freud might say that these two boys apparently have resolved the crisis of the phallic stage by adopting typically masculine traits. What would he say if he learned that these two are also co-chairmen of the school bake sale?

eight months of age, the erogenous zone is the mouth, and gratification is achieved primarily by sucking. During the *anal stage*, which is generally from eight months to two years of age, the erogenous zone is the anus. In the *phallic stage*, from the third to the sixth year, the genital organs are the primary erogenous zone. There is no particular erogenous zone in the *latency* period, a period of sexual dormancy that lasts from about age 5 to 12. During the *genital stage*, which is post-puberty, the individual becomes a mature, social being.

During each psychosexual stage of development, there is a particular threat or frustration that must be coped with in some fashion. If the frustration is not worked through in a satisfactory way, the person may become *fixated* at a particular stage, and as an adult may display characteristics typical of that stage. For example, during the oral stage, the individual must learn to cope with the fact that its mother is not continuously available to satisfy the infant's needs. Individuals who become fixated at the oral stage may later display such traits as passivity or withdrawal, or may indulge in behaviors that attempt to compensate for the loss of the mother's breast, such as overeating. The frustrations encountered in the anal stage are toilet training and the accompanying demands for self-control. Fixation at the anal stage may result in such character traits as disorderliness, irresponsibility, dirtiness, or the opposite extremes of punctuality, orderliness, and the tendency to hoard or collect things.

The phallic stage presents the child with the most complex and significant frustration. Depending upon the child's ability or inability to cope with this frustration, a variety of personality characteristics may result. For boys, the crisis of the phallic stage is the *Oedipus complex*. While Freud did not name the comparable crisis for girls, it is often referred to as the *Electra complex*. The question with which Freud deals is how boys come to identify with their fathers and develop characteristically masculine traits, and how girls come to identify with their mothers and develop feminine traits. Before the phallic stage, children of both sexes identify primarily with the mother. According to Freud, boys find libidinal pleasure in masturbation, and the object of libidinal energy is the mother. The boy wishes to possess his mother, but finds that her attentions are devoted not only to him but also to his father. The boy comes to fear castration from his father, a fear that he represses. Along with this castration anxiety comes the repression of the desire to possess the mother. As a result of this repression, the boy comes to identify with the father so that he may vicariously possess his mother. For girls, the process is even more intricate. Girls are said to possess "penis envy" upon discovering that a male has a penis. Because the little girl unconsciously wishes to have a penis, she comes to desire her father, who possesses this organ, and resent her mother, who is a rival for her father's attention. In order to possess her father vicariously, she identifies with her mother.

Psychoanalytic theory proposes that the ways in which these conflicts are resolved will influence later adult personality and behavior. Many psychoanalysts place particular emphasis on the Oedipus and Electra complexes in explaining and treating neurotic disorders. Many of these ideas have been challenged on a number of grounds, from their lack of testability to their rather blatant sexism (Chesler, 1972).

Although the psychoanalytic theories of personality structure and psychosexual development may be seen as two distinct theories, Freud saw complex interrelationships between them. As some of the energy from the id evolves into an ego and superego, psychosexual development also occurs. For example, the superego is seen as developing during the phallic stage, and the ways in which the Oedipus and Electra complexes are resolved by children will influence the development of their superegos. When a child identifies with a parent, there is a tendency to internalize many of that parent's social and moral views. Of course, which parent the child identifies with depends on the resolution of the Oedipus or Electra complex.

Because the development of attitudes, values, and morality is embodied in the concept of the superego, it is this personality structure that is central to the socialization process. Once the superego has developed, the child is "a society in miniature"—that is, the child's values and moral code usually reflect society's values and ethics.

Freud wrote extensively about the development of society and culture as well as of personality (1921/1945, 1913/1952, 1930/1962). He saw many social institutions and customs, particularly in "primitive" societies, as manifestations of the Oepidus complex. Primitive taboos and the worship of totems were seen as indications of sons' desires to band together and slay the father. Group formation and cohesion were viewed as parts of a defense mechanism that directs hostility toward the father. Then, through reaction formation, which involves denying an unconscious motive and acting on its opposite, the group comes to identify strongly with the group leader.

Freud assumed that his theories were universal, even though he developed them from a narrow sample of European patients. To test Freud's assumption, psychoanalytic theories have been subjected to a good deal of cross-cultural research. These studies have produced some evidence that the stages of psychosexual development are universal (Whiting, 1969), that dreams are attempts to resolve psychic conflicts (Lee, 1958), and that defense mechanisms are widely evident (Wright, 1956). But considerable evidence suggests that perhaps the most basic concept, the Oedipus complex, is not universal at all (Malinowski, 1937; A. Parsons, 1964). This implies that socialization and personality development are more heavily dependent on social and cultural institutions than Freud believed. To illustrate how psychoanalytic theories have been used in cross-cultural socialization research, we will look at a study on psychosexual development.

Male Initiation Ceremonies Different societies use various means to mark adulthood and increase a person's identification with the values and behaviors of same-sex adults. In our society, a number of minor events, rather than a single dramatic ceremony, mark a young man's transition from childhood to adulthood: his voice begins to change and he begins to shave; he goes to high school and learns to drive a car; he is given full legal status as an adult at age 18. Other societies mark the transition more abruptly, often in a rite of passage. For example, the Thonga of South Africa have an elaborate ceremony that every boy must go through in order to become a man (Junod, 1927; Whiting, Kluckhohn, & Anthony, 1965). When a boy is between 10 and 16 years of age, he is sent by his parents to a "circumcision school," which is held every few years. With his peers, he is subjected to severe hazing by adults and is made to undergo a series of trials, including being beaten with clubs, having his clothes taken from him, and having his hair cut. "He is next met by a man covered with lion manes and is seated upon a stone facing this 'lion man.' Someone then strikes him from behind and when he turns his head to see who has struck him, his foreskin is seized and in two movements cut off by the 'lion man'" (Whiting et al., 1965, p. 283). He is then isolated for about three months and forbidden contact with women. (If a woman should glance at him during this time, she is killed.) During this initiation, the boy undergoes beatings, exposure to cold, thirst, and eating of unsavory foods, punishment, and the threat of death. Although this initiation is extremely severe, many other societies have rites of passage that include painful hazing, genital operations, seclusion from women, and tests of endurance and manliness.

According to Whiting and colleagues (1965), such male initiation rites serve to break the boy's dependency on his mother and increase his identification with adult males in the society. They hypothesize that in societies where boys show excessive dependency on their mothers, initiation ceremonies would be more likely to occur. Among the Kwoma of New Guinea, for instance, the infant sleeps in the same bed as his mother for two or three years, while the father sleeps isolated from wife and child and abstains from sexual intercourse with her during this time. After weaning, the child is suddenly provided with his own bed, and the father resumes sleeping with the mother. Whiting and associates hypothesize that "it is this series of events that makes it necessary, when the boy reaches adolescence, for the society to have an initiation rite of the type we have already described. It is necessary (1) to put a final stop to his wish to return to his mother's arms and lap, (2) to prevent an open revolt against his father who has displaced him from his mother's bed, and (3) to ensure identification with the adult males of the society" (p. 286).

This hypothesis is obviously derived from the notion of the Oedipus complex, but it is not a rigid statement of the Oedipal theme. It does not assume, as Freud did, that the Oedipus complex is universal, but that it varies in importance from one society to another. In examining 56 societies for both mother–son dependency and the presence of adult initiation ceremonies for males, Whiting and colleagues found strong support for their hypothesis. Male initiation rites are most likely to occur in societies where sons are highly dependent on their mothers.

Psychoanalytic theory has had a profound impact on our views of child development and the relationship of the individual to society. Nevertheless, it is difficult to test many psychoanalytic ideas, and we are left primarily with clinical case studies as a means of validating the theory. Despite the lack of clear-cut evidence for many Freudian concepts, there is widespread agreement about three of them: (1) children adopt many of their parents' values and norms during the first several years of life; (2) early childhood traumas often leave their mark on later personality and behavior; (3) many of the motivations for behavior lie outside the realm of consciousness.

LEARNING: CLASSICAL AND OPERANT CONDITIONING

The infant's world is, to quote William James, "a blooming, buzzing, confusion!" Adult speech makes no sense, the physical environment is an undifferentiated mass of shapes and shadings, and objects that cannot be digested remain mysteries. During the first two years of life, meaning becomes attached to speech, to the environment and its physical properties, and even to the complex relationships among people and objects. Much of this learning involves a relatively simple process of assigning labels to things and investing those labels with some primitive emotional connotations, usually "good" or "bad." This is accomplished most often through classical conditioning, in which the child learns to associate emotional meaning with words and later to associate words with objects.

A study of classical conditioning by C.K. Staats and Staats (1957) clearly demonstrates how initially neutral words can acquire emotional connotations. Three-letter nonsense syllables such as *XEH* and *YOF* were presented to college students on a screen. While memorizing these syllables, they were also to learn other words, which were either emotionally positive (such as "beauty," "sweet," and "friend") or negative ("thief," "ugly," and "evil"). Each time one of the nonsense syllables appeared, it was paired with either a positive or a negative word. Other nonsense syllables were interspersed, paired with neutral words. After seeing each nonsense syllable 18 times, the students were asked to indicate how favorable or unfavorable each was on a 7-point rating scale, where 7 was most favorable. In the first experiment, when *XEH* was paired with positive words, it was rated 4.8; when it was paired with negative words, 3.1. The syllable *YOF* was rated 2.4 when paired with negative words and 4.7 when paired with positive words. Thus, previously neutral words acquired emotional meaning via this classical conditioning procedure.

Many of the objects in a young child's world are meaningless or emotionally neutral. These objects, which are initially neutral, acquire meaning by classical conditioning—by repeated pairings with words or behaviors. Mother and father take on positive emotional meaning for the infant because they are repeatedly associated with affection, nurturance, and comfort. Behaviors that are then associated with mother and father also acquire positive meaning and value for the child. These formerly neutral figures can then be combined with other neutral objects so that they, too, have meaning for the infant. A previously neutral object that acquires meaning is a *conditioned stimulus.* If this conditioned stimulus is then paired with another neutral object so that the latter also acquires meaning, the process is referred to as *higher order conditioning.*

A second kind of learning is referred to as *instrumental* or *operant conditioning.* Operant conditioning may also lead to the development of meaning and value by providing rewards or punishments following some verbal or overt behavior. If a child expresses a positive feeling for reading, and is then rewarded for this expression, that should tend to strengthen favorable attitudes toward reading. Attitudes, beliefs, and verbal behavior may be conditioned not only by tangible rewards and punishments, but also by words and gestures. We tend to think of rewards and punishments as tangible objects, such as candy or physical punishment. But reinforcements can be more subtle. A smile or frown, a "thank you," or a handshake may

Rewards aren't always tangible. A subtle smile or a juicy kiss can reinforce and condition behavior just as easily as a piece of candy.

all be reinforcements that strengthen or weaken our behavior.

Many subtle behaviors, such as facial expressions and posture, may be influenced by reinforcements. We can even use gestures and sounds to condition other gestures and sounds. In *verbal operant conditioning*, subtle reinforcements are given for certain verbal responses. If someone expresses an unfavorable attitude toward the government, and you nod your head in approval, smile, or say "mm-hmm," that may strengthen that person's attitude against the government. There is considerable research to demonstrate the effectiveness of such techniques, although the precise mechanisms by which verbal operant conditioning and the classical conditioning of attitudes operate are not entirely clear (Goldstein, Rosnow, Goodstadt, & Suls, 1972; Insko & Cialdini, 1971; Zanna, Kiesler, & Pilkonis, 1970).

LEARNING: IMITATION AND MODELING

"Like father, like son" is the folk version of Bandura's (1965b) social learning theory. It is this theory of modeling and imitation (reviewed in Chapter 1) that most adequately explains the striking similarities between children and their parents on such diverse issues as political affiliation (Hyman, 1959), political ideology (Kraut & Lewis, 1975), the helping of others (Rushton, 1975), and personality traits such as Machiavellianism (Kraut & Price, 1976).

Children are encouraged to imitate behaviors of parents and older siblings, particularly those of same-sex models (Grusec & Brinker, 1972). According to the theory, children are apt to learn the distinctive behaviors that they observe, and are likely to perform those behaviors that are positively reinforced. Reinforcement, either to the model or to the observer, is assumed to play a role only in performance, and not in actual learning.

While there is a correlation between the attitudes, values, and behaviors of parents and those of their children, children are not carbon copies of their parents. This is partly because their responses do not exactly mimic their parents', and partly because parental tendencies to reward and punish responses are not always consistent. Parents may occasionally reward aggressive behavior, for example, even though they more often punish it. These inconsistencies in reinforcement may lead to erratic behavior in children, to anxiety, or to consistently antisocial behavior (Aronfreed, 1968). If children believe that reinforcements are totally independent of their behavior, they may show signs of depression and *learned helplessness* (Dweck & Reppucci, 1973; Seligman, 1975). Learned helplessness arises when repeated punishments cannot be avoided. Following unavoidable punishment, animals and people seem unable to learn appropriate avoidance responses. For example, dogs given inescapable shocks subsequently fail to learn a simple response that will prevent the shocks. Seligman and his colleagues (D.C. Klein, Fencil-Morse, & Seligman, 1976) suggest that this sort of reinforcement schedule also causes depression in humans.

Several theories of imitation and modeling exist. These theories differ in predicting which model a child is most likely to imitate. We know from research that same-sex models are more apt to be imitated (Grusec & Brinker, 1972). Is a person who receives rewards more likely to be imitated than one who controls the distribution of rewards? Bandura, Ross, and Ross (1963) found that children are more likely to imitate the behavior of the model who controls the rewards than that of the model who receives the rewards.

Because social learning theory is most often employed by social psychologists in the study of helping and aggression, it is discussed in greater detail in Chapters 7 and 8. It is important to note here that much of what children learn from their parents is not through deliberate training but rather through imitating the actions of their parents. It is often the case that children are more likely to do what their parents do than what their parents say they should do.

SOME COMMENTS ON PSYCHOANALYTIC AND LEARNING THEORIES

Reinforcement learning theories and psychoanalytic theories share several assumptions. Both assume that developing behaviors, such as achievement motivation, dependency needs, and attachment to parents, are derived from primary biological drives and the social contact required for drive satisfaction (S. Cohen, 1976). In other words, all later behavior is assumed to stem either directly or indirectly from basic biological instincts. Learning and psychoanalytic theories also tend to view socialization as a process that disrupts the biologically determined course of "natural growth." This view is widespread in Western culture. The belief that abiding by a general social–moral–legal code is in some ways inconsistent with inherent nature underlies a good deal of faddism in clinical psychology and psychotherapy. Freud said that many neurotics are simply oversocialized; they have internalized society's rules so thoroughly that their basic id impulses have no means of realistic release. Other psychologists, most notably O. H. Mowrer (1961), see neuroses as a result of undersocialization; neurotic individuals have not internalized strongly enough the standards, values, and ethics of society.

In the psychoanalytic view especially, spontaneous, impulsive, and intuitive responses are considered more "natural" than thoughtful, reflective, controlled actions. A good deal of humanistic or "third-force" psychology adheres to this view. Many of the "touchy feely" psychological exercises developed over the past decade reflect the assumption that to think before acting is antithetical to human nature. Braginsky and Braginsky (1974) note that the encounter movement is "a convenient psychic whorehouse for the purchase of a gamut of well-advertised 'goodies': authenticity, freedom, wholeness, flexibility, community, love, joy," and that these groups "simplify, distort, and coarsen our sensibilities. Manipulative gimmicks, simplistic lexicon, and psychic striptease replace the intelligent, sensitive struggle of man attempting to come to terms with himself, with others, and with the world" (pp. 85–86; see also Koch, 1971).

Other views of socialization do not suggest that individual needs are incompatible with the needs of the larger society. For example, role theory and social learning theory do not imply that the individual is a beast who must be controlled and tamed to become a useful member of society. Rather, they hold that the society channels individual behavior into socially productive routes without suppressing or inhibiting individual growth and development. In these views, socialization may be seen as the road that guides an individual on a self-initiated journey, rather than as an obstacle placed in the individual's path to fulfillment. The fuel that impels this journey is often the need to explore the environment and to obtain a sense of mastery or competence over it.

EXPLORATORY BEHAVIOR, CURIOSITY, AND THE CONCEPT OF COMPETENCE

People often go out of their way to experience new and novel sensations. Unless we assume they have a need for novelty or an innate sense of curiosity, it is difficult to explain such behavior. Radical behaviorists assume that behavior is motivated primarily by a need to maximize positive reinforcement and to reduce internal drive states. But humans and other animals often behave in ways that seem to *increase* drive states (Berlyne, 1960). For example, avoiding unfamiliar objects and environments seems a logical way to minimize fear arousal. From a learning theory perspective, strange objects should not be attractive because they have no drive-reducing or reinforcing property. However, organisms often approach novel objects rather than avoid them. Animals appear to go out of their way to interact with these presumably fear-arousing objects, and novel and unfamiliar objects can often lead to the same kinds of behaviors as positive reinforcements. Berlyne (1960, 1972) suggests that unfamiliar objects, events, and people lead to slight increases in physiological arousal (called *arousal boosts*) that are in themselves

These two boys may be somewhat frightened by this big roaring machine, but their curiosity certainly hasn't been dampened. In fact, they seem to be enjoying what Berlyne calls arousal boosts.

pleasurable. It seems, then, that drive reduction does not underlie all behavior and that arousal may be a source of motivation. R. W. White (1959) proposes that exploratory behavior and curiosity are motivated by a need to develop a sense of mastery over the environment. Overcoming fear of the unknown, for example, may increase feelings of mastery or competence. The need to approach novel objects, to try new things, to visit unexplored territories, and to learn unfamiliar material may be deeply rooted in the need for a sense of accomplishment, competence, or mastery.

These concepts of a need for stimulation and for a sense of competence are vital to human development. If one adopts a strictly behaviorist view of socialization, one would have to ascribe the origin of any new behavior to one of three sources: (1) genetic, biological, or instinctive drives; (2) a random act that received some sort of reinforcement; (3) an earlier learned series of actions that is elicited by a new situation. For example, according to the strict behaviorist interpretation, a child who begins to play with blocks either is demonstrating a biologically based behavior, is anticipating rewards, or is generalizing previously learned playing responses. The idea of competence or curiosity suggests another plausible explanation for novel behavior: the child begins to play with blocks because of a need to overcome an initial fear of these unfamiliar objects, or because of a need to experience a sense of mastery over this aspect of the environment. While it is often difficult to determine which of these ways of interpreting novel behavior is most correct (Emmerich, 1977), it is safe to say that curiosity and the need to master the environment are important sources of motivation in children and adults (e.g., Hay, 1977).

Intrinsic and Extrinsic Incentives   What effects do external rewards and punishments have on children and adults who have some predisposition to explore and master their environment? There is considerable evidence that when external justification is provided for tasks that already interest a person, those extrinsic incentives undermine both performance of the task and later interest in the task (Condry, 1977; Deci, 1975).

Suppose that a group of children plays a weekly pick-up game of baseball. There may be few external rewards for these games; the children play because it is fun. Now let us assume that some of the parents get together and decide to offer a reward, a trip to a major-league baseball game, to the best team. The children now play less for the inherent fun of the game than for the extrinsic incentive of going to a big-league game. They are apt to perceive their weekly games as more of a chore than previously and some of their interest in the game will be undermined (R. Anderson, Manoogian, & Reznick, 1976; Lepper, Greene, & Nisbett, 1973). On the other hand, intrinsic interest in an activity may be increased by providing rewards and encouragement that, alone, would be insufficient incentive to engage in the activity. In this situation, the participants must supply some of the motivation themselves (Goldstein & Bredemeier, 1977).

SYMBOLIC INTERACTIONIST
THEORIES OF SOCIALIZATION

Symbolic interactionism theories describe socialization as a lifelong process that operates whenever one person interacts with another (Lauer & Handel, 1977). In this view, each person learns the rules and social roles of society through the socialization process. By interacting with others, the person learns the social meaning of behaviors, objects, and ideas. Most of this learning comes about through language, according to George Herbert Mead (1934), one of the early leading symbolic interactionism theorists.

According to these theories, the individual is born with no awareness of being a distinct entity. The ability to manipulate abstract symbols, particularly in the form of a spoken language, enables the biological organism to develop into a social organism. Only when a person has a sense of self—when he or she can refer to the self as an object in the same way that others can be referred to—can the individual engage in meaningful social interaction.

For Mead, as for William James (1890) before him, the self develops through interaction with others. If people treat someone in a particularly friendly way and act as if she is intelligent, then she will develop a definition of herself as friendly and intelligent. This concept was referred to as the *looking-glass self* by Charles H. Cooley (1902); we view ourselves from the perspective of other people. In order to see ourselves from another's viewpont, we must view the world through his or her eyes. We must learn to take the positions of others; in Mead's term, *take the role of the other.* Role-taking

During the play stage, children try out the roles of others around them. As they play dress-up or talk to an imaginary playmate, they learn more about the social roles of others—and their own social roles as well.

becomes a necessary ability for the development of self. Furthermore, in order to take a role, we need a language, which gives us the ability to communicate about people and objects.

The development of self, or personality, follows an invariant sequence of stages. During the first, *preparatory stage,* the infant's behavior is generally a meaningless imitation of others. Children do not understand the reasons for their own behavior. By imitating others, they gradually learn to take the role of others. This is accomplished more fully in the second stage of development, the *play stage.* During this period, children play the roles of *significant others* around them: mother, teacher, postman, doctor, and so on. They learn to treat themselves from the point of view of specific others. They may, for example, admonish themselves from the point of view of their mother by saying, "You shouldn't do that. Wait till your father gets home." By engaging in such role-taking behavior, children begin to respond to themselves as objects with social meaning.

During the *game stage,* the completion of the self occurs. "In time, the child finds himself in situations wherein he must take a number of roles simultaneously. That is, he must respond to the expectations of several people at the same time. This sort of situation is exemplified by the game of baseball. . . . Each player must visualize the intentions and expectations of several other players. In such situations the child must take the roles of groups of individuals" (Meltzer, 1967, p. 11). During the course of such interactions, children build up a *generalized other* point of view; they view themselves from the perspective of large numbers of people, or "society."

Mead distinguishes two aspects of the self: the "I" and the "me." These are somewhat analogous to Freud's notions of the id and the superego. The *I* consists of the impulsive tendencies of the individual, while the *me* is, like the superego, "a society in miniature." The closest Mead came to Freud's concept of ego was in his conception of *mind.* Mind consists of cognitive processes, plans for action, and conversations within ourselves between the *I* and the *me.* Mind is not an entity, as ego was to Freud, but a process.

Behavior in any situation requires that the individuals present arrive at some meaning or definition of that situation, and of themselves within it. This requires role-taking, in which each individual anticipates the responses and behaviors of the others. In this sense, behavior in a situation is determined by the individuals' expectations of the behavior of others. Expectations about the future determine behavior in the present.

During the course of interaction, each person communicates a definition of the situation to others by his or her behavior. It may become apparent to some participants that their definitions differ widely. By means of a series of communications and behavioral acts, a commonly shared definition emerges. When a consensus has been reached, each person can carry out his or her plans and strategies of action.

Not much research in social psychology has been undertaken from the symbolic interactionist framework, but many of the concepts are supported by research from cognitive and other perspectives. For example, symbolic interactionism stresses the notion that objects acquire meaning through interpersonal interaction, and that the meaning of a given object is probably widely shared in a social community. Jahoda and Harrison (1975) interviewed 30 Catholic and Protestant boys aged 6 and 30 aged 10 in Belfast, and a comparable sample of boys in Edinburgh. One of the tasks given to the children was to imagine that they found an object on the street. They were to identify the object and say what they would do with it. The objects were a pack of cigarettes, a letter, a milk bottle, and a parcel. Table 3.1 shows the number of children of each age perceiving the object as threatening, such as a bomb. The "meaning" of such objects is certainly different in violence-torn Belfast than it is in peaceful Edinburgh.

We have reviewed several of the major theoretical processes of socialization. In order to illustrate these fundamental mechanisms and to introduce some of the important topics dealt with in later chapters, a number of specific areas of socialization are discussed below.

Because they almost always study adults, social psychologists have paid relatively little attention to the origins of most social behaviors. For example, while they have conducted considerable research and developed a handful of theories on helping and charity, social psychologists have paid scant attention to the social-developmental origins of prosocial behavior in children. The same may be

Table 3.1.
Frequency of Perceiving One or More Common Objects as "Bombs"

	Bombs	Not Bombs
Age 6		
Belfast	9	21
Edinburgh	1	29
Age 10		
Belfast	24	6
Edinburgh	2	28

From Jahoda and Harrison (1975, p. 12).

said of most of the topics discussed in later chapters of this book: attribution, social perception, persuasion, attraction, aggression, group formation, and intergroup relations. These undoubtedly originate in early childhood experience and growth. While developmental issues are often ignored by social psychologists, it is important to understand that a developmental perspective requires one to view these issues as dynamic. Also, studying the origins of behavior may tell us something important about its change and future course.

SEX ROLES AND SYMBOLIC INTERACTIONISM

Just as neutral objects may acquire meaning through interaction and communication, so, too, may the self acquire meaning, according to symbolic interactionism. The expectations of our parents, social stereotypes, and our own behavior combine to determine whether we are thought to be "masculine" or "feminine." There is little doubt that parents in contemporary Western societies treat boys and girls differently from infancy on (Best, Williams, Cloud, Davis, Robertson, Edwards, Giles, & Fowles, 1977; Gurwitz & Dodge, 1975; Maccoby & Jacklin, 1974; Rothbart & Maccoby, 1966). The society at large also holds different expectations about appropriate male and female behavior, and these stereotypic perceptions are reinforced by stories, films, magazines, newspapers, and television. Males traditionally are presented as high achievers, strong, unemotional, dominant, while females are depicted as unassertive, passive, emotional, and weak. It is not at all surprising that young children internalize the meanings attributed to gender by parents, peers, and the general community (Weitz, 1977). Sex differences, when they are not biologically determined, are the result of the different meanings assigned to "male" and "female" in a society (H. Barry, Bacon, & Child, 1957). The same kinds of stereotypes and the same social support systems for stereotypic behavior exist with respect to race and other traits, as we shall see in Chapter 10.

DIFFERENTIATION, GENERALIZATION, AND ATTITUDES

Many psychological phenomena may be seen as the means by which people simplify experience to achieve a sense of competence. However, we must distinguish between simplifying and oversimplifying. The perceptions and beliefs of children frequently amuse adults because children tend to oversimplify. As children mature socially, they make more and more refined judgments about the environment.

This young barber has not let social stereotypes cramp her style. Even a symbolic interactionist could hardly depict her as unassertive, passive, or weak.

For example, as their cognitive abilities develop, children learn to categorize objects and events into ever more complex and abstract sets of categories (Bruner, Goodnow, & Austin, 1956). Developing children also make increasingly refined and complex judgments about morality (Kohlberg, 1963), perception (Foa & Foa, 1974), political attitudes (Hess, 1969), and social relations (Mead, 1934). While socialization itself is a process of *differentiation*, developing more and more refined categories and beliefs, a process of *generalization* also emerges (Foa & Foa, 1974). In generalization, different objects may be responded to in similar ways. Differentiation requires the individual to develop new categories for judging the environment; generalization requires only that two or more objects be placed in the same category. The relationship between differentiation and generalization may be clarified by an example.

The child first learns to interact differently with father and mother; later on he realizes that these two interactions have some common elements which differentiate them from interactions with siblings. Thus father–mother generalization, expressed by the term "parent," is based on the new differentiation between parents and siblings. To discover that two classes of social events have common features it is first necessary to recognize them as different and then to contrast them with a third class without the features. (Foa & Foa, 1974, p. 27)

In a cross-cultural study of differentiation of family roles, Foa, Triandis, and Katz (1966) found that the child first learns to differentiate between the self and others. This is followed by differentiation of sex, and later by differentiation of generation, with parents seen as a "different" generation and siblings as the "same." This order of differentiation has been found to hold universally across cultures.

Differentiation of objects and events in the environment is not a purely cognitive activity; it also involves emotional differentiation. Children not only learn to differentiate younger same-sex people from older same-sex people, they are also likely to associate positive or negative emotions with these categorizations. Consistently favorable or unfavorable responses to a class of objects are defined as *attitudes*.

Though there are many theories about the development of attitudes (Ostrom, 1968), there is fairly widespread agreement that attitudes are ways of organizing and making sense of experience. They enable a person to respond to an object as a member of a class of objects. Thus, attitudes serve an economical purpose, enabling a person to make evaluative judgments of objects without having to appraise each object in detail.

Without guiding attitudes the individual is confused and baffled. Some kind of preparation is essential before he can make a satisfactory observation, pass suitable judgment, or make any but the most primitive reflex type of response. Attitudes determine for each individual what he will see and hear, what he will think and what he will do. To borrow a phrase from William James, they "engender meaning upon the world"; they draw lines about, and segregate, an otherwise chaotic environment; they are our methods for finding our way about in an ambiguous universe. (G.W. Allport, 1968, pp. 61–62)

Attitudes develop from experience. This includes the unpleasant experience of punishment, the pleasurable experience of reward, and the association of objects and concepts with certain emotions. It also includes the observation of others' behavior, which leads the observer to internalize inferred attitudes. The agents of socialization are the sources of most of our attitudes. We learn attitudes through the processes of classical and operant conditioning and through social learning and modeling by parents, teachers, and peers. We also acquire attitudes by self-observation, by observing how we behave in given situations (Bem, 1972).

Because the function of attitudes is to simplify the environment, they must make sense to the individual. Archie Bunker's attitudes toward minorities help him maintain what is, to him, a meaningful view of the world. His attitudes may not strike an observer as logical; they are psycho-logical, that is, they make sense to their possessor.

If attitudes are favorable or unfavorable response tendencies, then they should help to predict an individual's responses to a given class of objects. This is not always the case. Numerous studies have failed to find high correlations between measures of attitudes and overt behavior (e.g., Dillehay, 1973; Kutner, Wilkins, & Yarrow, 1952; LaPiere, 1934; Wicker, 1969), though some have identified a positive relationship (Calder & Ross, 1973; Goodmonson & Glaudin, 1971).

There are a number of reasons why overt behavior may be inconsistent with an individual's measured attitudes. First, attitudes, like most other traits, are not permanent fixtures, but constantly evolve. Depending on the situation, the person may act on past or present attitudes, or even develop a new attitude for the occasion. Second, our measurements of both attitudes and behavior leave something to be desired, and we cannot expect to find high correlations between two fairly unreliable measures. Third, the behavioral response tendencies that are part of attitudes must be distinguished from overt behavior. While you may have a negative attitude toward strawberries (that is, a response tendency to avoid eating strawberries), you may eat strawberries under certain circumstances, such as when you are a guest at someone's home and are offered strawberries for dessert. There are, in other words, other determinants of behavior besides attitudes, and often these determinants override attitudes. Fourth, several different attitudes may be evoked by a given situation, not all of them consistent with one another. Finally, there may be the appearance of inconsistency where none actually exists. For example, a person may not act on his attitudes. Tom may have a favorable attitude toward kidney transplants, yet not be a kidney donor. This is not necessarily inconsistent; it may be that the probability of expressing the attitude is greater than the probability of expressing the behavior.

CHARITY BEGINS AT HOME: THE DEVELOPMENT OF PROSOCIAL BEHAVIOR

In recent years, social psychologists have become increasingly interested in studying positive forms of social behavior, such as cooperation, charity, and help-giving. In Chapter 7, we will review prosocial behaviors in adults, but for now, we will explore only the origins of the tendency to help or ignore others in need.

As a general rule, cooperative and prosocial behaviors increase with age (Barnes, 1971; H. Cook & Stingle, 1974; Gottschaldt & Frauhauf-Ziegler, 1958). Children's play most clearly reflects the nature of this development, from solitary play in two- to three-year-olds, to partial cooperation at around age five, to complex group participation at about seven years of age.

While children may not be as sensitive to features of the environment as older people, their cooperative behavior is tempered by the reward structure of the situation. When rewards are sufficient to go around, four-year-olds are more apt to cooperate than when only one of them may receive a reward or when rewards are limited (Nelson & Madsen, 1969). And when they have had a recent experi-

Cooperative and prosocial behaviors appear to be developing nicely in this group of 11- and 12-year-olds.

ence with success, children are more apt to be charitable than when they recently have experienced failure (Isen, Horn, & Rosenhan, 1973).

Of course, it is not age per se that determines the level of positive social behavior, but some concomitant of age. Both the symbolic interactionist George Herbert Mead (1934) and the developmental biologist Jean Piaget (1932/1950) state that cooperative behavior requires the ability to view a situation from the perspective of the other person.

According to Piagetian theory, cooperative and altruistic behaviors represent a late phase in a natural progression of moral stages (Kohlberg, 1963; Piaget, 1932/1950). Thus, moral development depends on discrete changes in cognitive abilities and perceptions of the social and physical environment. At the earliest, most primitive level of moral thought, children do not recognize rules for evaluating their own or another's actions. At the next level, rules are seen as absolute and morally correct because they are given by an authority. Something is considered right because "it is right." At a later stage of moral judgment, children recognize that the rules are merely arbitrarily agreed-upon conventions. Finally, children recognize that rules may be changed. While many developmentalists see these stages as fixed and immutable, that view is not always consistent with either logic (Kurtines & Greif, 1974; Sampson, 1978) or research evidence (Bethlehem, 1973; Schaie & Parham, 1974).

A number of studies, based loosely on social learning theory, suggest that it is possible to increase children's levels of moral judgment or charitable behavior by providing them with explicit training in morality (Schleifer & Douglas, 1973) or with adult models who act in a charitable manner (M.L. Hoffman, 1975; Rushton, 1975). M.L. Hoffman (1975), for example, found that altruistic behavior in ten-year-olds is positively related to having an altruistic parent, usually of the same sex, who encourages the child to take the role of the victim when disciplining the child. That is, discipline involves focusing the child's attention on apology to the victim and reparation of damage.

IS ALTRUISM AN INSTINCT?

There is fairly convincing evidence that altruistic behaviors may exist in a variety of species (Krebs, 1971; E.O. Wilson, 1975). Rats, primates, and insects have been observed to perform actions that benefit other members of their group. Campbell (1965) and others have argued that cooperative behaviors are genetically programmed into various species. Is *Homo sapiens* among these?

In 1965, Donald Campbell argued that there is an inherent altruism in humans that perpetuates the survival of the species. There is some evidence to suggest that acts of helping fellow humans are deeply rooted human behaviors. Studies by R.F. Weiss, Boyer, Lombardo, and Stich (1973) have demonstrated that performing altruistic acts can serve as reinforcement to people in an instrumental learning task.

In 1972, Campbell reassessed his earlier position (1972b). He still believes altruism is inherited, but he now conceives it to be socially rather than genetically inherited. He revised his thinking primarily on logical grounds.

Let us suppose that mutations have produced a heterogeneity within a social group so that there are some individuals with genes predisposing a self-sacrificial (altruistic) bravery which furthers group survival, and others with genes predisposing a self-saving (nonaltruistic) cowardice. Let us suppose that due to the presence of the bravery genes in some individuals, the group as a whole survives better. This increases the average reproductive opportunity of both the brave and the cowardly among the group members. The net gain for the brave is reduced to some degree because of the costs of risks they incur. The net gain for the cowardly has no such subtraction. Thus while all gain, the cowardly gain more, and their genes will gradually become more frequent as a result. There is no way in which the altruistic genetic tendencies could increase relative to the cowardly, to say nothing of becoming predominant, if there is a self-sacrificial component to the bravery. (p. 25)

In other words, if altruism involves risk to the altruist, the proportion of altruists compared to nonaltruists will steadily diminish and we will ultimately have a society with no gene pool for altruism. In the case of social insects, such as ants, bees, and termites, this problem does not arise because neither the cowardly nor the heroic produce offspring; they are both sterile. Only the queens and the drones have offspring. It is thus highly improbable that altruism is genetically determined in humans, even though there appears to be a genetic basis for it among certain other species.

Along with our genetic heritage, we humans also "inherit" a social culture. Many have argued that these two inherited dispositions—the genetic and the social—are at odds. This belief is apparent in the theories of Marx, Hobbes, and Freud, among others. Campbell argues that altruism is a product of our social–cultural evolution that runs counter to our genetic evolution. Altruism is a result of social learning, and as such has become a built-in part of our social, cultural, and legal structures. There is no genetic basis for altruism in humans, but there is a powerful sociocultural force for altruistic acts. Altruism strengthens our social bonds and increases the likelihood that our social institutions will survive.

LEARNING TO BE AGGRESSIVE

An act of violence is usually the result of a conflict. Of course, some people are compelled to aggress because of a genetic or physiological abnormality, such as a brain tumor; others, classified as "sociopaths," aggress because they do not understand or do not care about the consequences of their actions. But aggression is usually the result of a conflict between two independent and mutually inconsistent tendencies: the tendency to aggress against someone and the tendency not to aggress. When the pro-aggression tendencies outweigh the anti-aggression tendencies, aggressive behavior occurs. When the anti-aggression tendencies predominate, then no aggression ensues. The issue of defining aggression is dealt with in considerably more detail in Chapter 8; here, we will use a common definition: *Aggression is the intentional injury of another individual.*

Both pro- and anti-aggression tendencies may be divided into long-term and short-term or situational factors. Long-term tendencies are relatively enduring personality characteristics of an individual, such as norms, attitudes, and values relating to aggression, prior experiences with aggression, and the knowledge and ability to use aggressive and nonaggressive strategies in interpersonal disputes. In any specific situation, other elements may also facilitate or inhibit aggressive behavior.

The primary source of enduring factors relevant to aggression is the socialization process. During socialization, the child acquires a set of values, norms, attitudes, beliefs, and expectations about aggressive behavior. These long-term norms are usually acquired through the processes of imitation and modeling, and classical and operant conditioning. No two individuals are likely to share precisely the same norms about the appropriateness, means, or desirability of aggression. But large social groups, such as whole cultures or subcultures, are likely to have many aggression norms in common (e.g., Wolfgang & Ferracuti, 1967). For example, most Americans learn that aggression is desirable when used in defense of self or country.

Once acquired by an individual, these long-term norms are relatively stable. One reason social norms persist is that individuals tend to associate with others who share these norms. Another is that the norms are likely to be integrated into a person's cognitive framework and influence perception and the interpretation of experience (Blumenthal, Kahn, Andrews, & Head, 1972). Basic norms, values, attitudes, beliefs, and expectations become the bulwark of subsequent beliefs and experiences. Table 3.2 shows some of the long-term factors associated with aggression and nonaggression.

Even the most violent individual is not perpetually violent, and even the most passive among us can be incited to aggression under certain circumstances. Circumstances that facilitate aggression are called situational aggression factors. Among such factors are those that diminish normal inhibitions against aggressing, such as familiar environments and the presence of aggressive weapons (see Goldstein, 1975). Any factor that momentarily lowers tendencies to aggress or raises restraints against aggressing is a situational anti-aggression factor. The fact that personal, long-term traits interact with immediate, situational traits is referred to as a *person-by-situation interaction*. Psychologists have traditionally discussed personality as the primary cause of behavior. Only recently have they recognized that the immediate situation directly influences behavior and, perhaps more importantly, combines with personality to influence behavior.

As people learn which situations, targets, and means are appropriate for aggression, they also learn which situations, targets, and means are inappropriate. In our society, we tend to learn that certain people are inappropriate targets of violence, such as women, young children, and the elderly. We learn which specific behaviors are permissible in a fight and which are taboo. We also learn which situations are "aggressible" and which are not. Fighting is more apt to occur in a barroom or an alley than in a church or a theater. People also learn positive forms of social behavior that are incompatible with aggression, such as altruism.

How do these factors combine to determine aggression? The probability of aggressive behavior is assumed to be determined by

Table 3.2.
Factors Associated with Aggression and Nonaggression

	Short-Term	Long-Term

Aggression	*Characteristics of the actor:*
	   Immediately prior aggressive acts
	   Loss of cognitive control of behavior
	   Low identifiability
	   Moderate amount of alcohol ingestion
	   Moderate emotional arousal
	 Consequences of actor's behavior:
	   Cognitive justification for aggression
	   Devaluation of victim
	 Environmental factors:
	   Abundant opportunities for aggression
	   Availability of a weapon
	   Familiar environment
	   Familiar or similar target
	   Recent exposure to violence
		Characteristics of the actor:
		   Deindividuation
		   Impulsivity
		   Low level of moral judgment
		   Negative labels for targets
		   Positive labels for aggression
		 Consequences of actor's behavior:
		   Rewards for aggression
		 Parental characteristics:
		   Aggressive models, unpunished
		   High punitiveness
		 Environmental factors:
		   Aggressible situations
		   Exposure to aggression in others

	Short-Term	Long-Term

Nonaggression	*Characteristics of the actor:*
	   Aggression anxiety, guilt
	   Arousal of pleasant emotions
	   Fear of punishment
	   High identifiability
	   Immediately prior nonaggressive acts
	 Environmental factors:
	   Presence of authority figure (for
	   those low in moral judgment)
	   Unfamiliar environment
		Characteristics of the actor:
		   Ability to delay gratification
		   Ability to take role of others
		   High level of moral judgment
		   Inclusive concept of "we"
		   Individuation
		   Negative labels for aggression
		   Positive regard for others
		 Consequences of actor's behavior:
		   Rewards for nonaggression
		 Parental characteristics:
		   Affection, control, nurturance
		   Nonaggressive models
		 Environmental factors:
		   Nonaggressible situations

Note: The characteristics of the actor listed under short-term factors are temporary or transient states, most often induced by the physical or social environment, rather than enduring traits of the actor. From Goldstein (1975, pp. 104–105).

the ratio of pro-aggression elements, both long-term and situational, to anti-aggression elements. Each factor in the model may be perceived as more or less important by different people or by the same person at different times. Thus, aggressive conflict is assumed to be based not only on the sum of pro- and anti-aggression factors, but also on their relative importance to the individual (see Figure 3.1).

Thinking of aggression in terms of conflict has several implica-

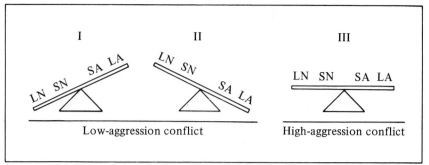

Figure 3.1.

Aggression conflict. In I, the short-term and long-term aggression factors are outweighed by the short-term and long-term nonaggression factors, so nonaggressive behavior will result. In II, the aggression factors outweigh the nonaggression factors, so aggression will result. In III, they are about equal, so it is unclear which type of behavior will ultimately be expressed. In the last condition, the individual will have to evaluate closely each element in the situation before deciding which behavior to engage in. (LN = long-term nonaggression factors; SN = short-term nonaggression factors; SA = short-term pro-aggression factors; LA = long-term pro-aggression factors.) [From J.H. Goldstein, Aggression and crimes of violence. (New York: Oxford Univ. Press, 1975, p. 88)]

tions. First, any act of aggression is the result of a fairly large number of different variables. Second, the contribution of any single variable, such as frustration, will depend on the number and type of other elements present, both as part of the individual's personality and as part of the immediate environment. Third, in treating aggression as the result of a cognitive conflict, we may expect aggressive behavior to have cognitive consequences, such as a reduction of conflict or a reevaluation of the situation. Fourth, since the number of elements in conflict may vary from person to person or situation to situation, the length of time it takes to aggress and the intensity of the aggression may also vary. The more conflict present, the longer it will take to decide whether to act aggressively. Although few studies have measured the time it takes to respond aggressively, some evidence suggests that it takes longer in high-conflict situations than in low-conflict situations (Goldstein, 1975). In addition, when conflict is high, there are more cognitive consequences of aggression, such as the justification of aggressive behavior, the devaluation of the victim, and a change in the perceived intensity of the aggressive behaviors.

While this view of aggression is fairly general, it does enable us to survey, within a single model, a variety of causes of aggression: social learning and imitation, frustration, anger, the immediate social situation, personality, and learning. These issues are discussed more fully in Chapter 10.

THE ORIGINS OF
SOCIABILITY

Plato believed humans to be political animals who gathered in public for purposes of social interaction. We recognize some animal species as social and others as nonsocial (or, more accurately, we place species on a continuum from relatively nonsocial to highly social). Clearly, humans are among the most social of species.

Developmental psychologists are grappling with the origins and the precise nature of this sociability. Mother–infant interaction is seen as the genesis of later sociability, though this simple dyadic (two-person) unit itself is highly complex. The infant's attachment to and dependency on the mother provide the first social interaction. Mother–infant interactions are not static, but change over time as the infant develops (Cairns, 1972). Social psychologists have paid scant attention to human sociability, except to notice such fairly superficial changes as the age at which children first respond to another's race or physical attractiveness (e.g., Langlois & Stephan, 1977), or their ability to remember certain physical or social characteristics of another person (e.g., Diamond & Carey, 1977).

Developmental research on basic social psychological processes is rare. One example of such research is a study by Peevers and Secord (1973) of the concepts used by people of varying ages to describe others. Subjects ranging from kindergarten children to college students were asked to describe three friends and one disliked peer. These verbal responses were then categorized and factor-analyzed to determine the underlying dimensions of person descriptions. As expected, the complexity and differentiation of descriptions increased with age. Peevers and Secord also reported that, with age, people see others as more individual and can differentiate them from the physical and social environment to a greater extent. In short, others are perceived more in terms of their unique personal traits as the judge's age increases.

In view of the relative scarcity of developmental social psychological research, we must rely on accounts by others of the origins of social behavior. Not surprisingly, Freud, Piaget, Mead, and the major personality and developmental theorists have dealt with this issue. We know from developmental research that depriving children of social interaction only serves to make social behavior more attractive (Eisenberger, 1970; Gewirtz & Baer, 1958), and we know from studies done on other species that the quality rather than the quantity of social interaction is most important for later development (Harlow, 1958). Most questions from a social psychological perspective about the development of social interaction must await further research.

Socialization is the series of processes by which an infant becomes
a fully functioning social adult. During infancy and early childhood,
the person acquires an extraordinary array of social, cognitive, and
motor skills. While these continue to develop throughout the person's
life, the first two or three years see the most social and physical
development. Given the enormous amount of learning that occurs,
it is not surprising that there are a number of different processes by
which this learning takes place. These include the development of
personality through critical incidents in the child's life (according to
psychoanalytic theory), and the acquisition of specific behaviors
through operant conditioning, classical conditioning, and social
learning (imitation and modeling). There are also internal sources of
motivation that impel a person to explore the social and physical
environment so as to master it and develop a sense of competence.
Symbolic interactionism sees social interaction as the cause of
personality rather than an effect of personality and prior learning.
It is through interacting with others, particularly once the child has
learned to speak, that a sense of self develops and the individual is
able to view himself through the eyes of others. Through this
perspective-taking, the individual becomes a full-fledged member of
society.

Although developmental issues are often ignored by social psychologists, some work has been done on the origins of attitudes,
prosocial behavior, and aggression. In most instances, the processes
by which these behavioral dispositions are acquired from parents,
teachers, and associates are classical and operant conditioning and
imitation and modeling.

Summary

Goslin, D. *Handbook of socialization theory and research.* Chicago:
  Rand McNally, 1969.
*Maccoby, E. E., Jacklin, C. N. *The psychology of sex differences.*
  Stanford, Calif: Stanford University Press, 1974.
*Weitz, S. *Sex roles.* London and New York: Oxford University Press,
  1978.

Suggested Readings

Child Development
Developmental Psychology
Journal of Experimental Child Psychology
Sex Roles

Pertinent Journals

*Available in paperback edition.

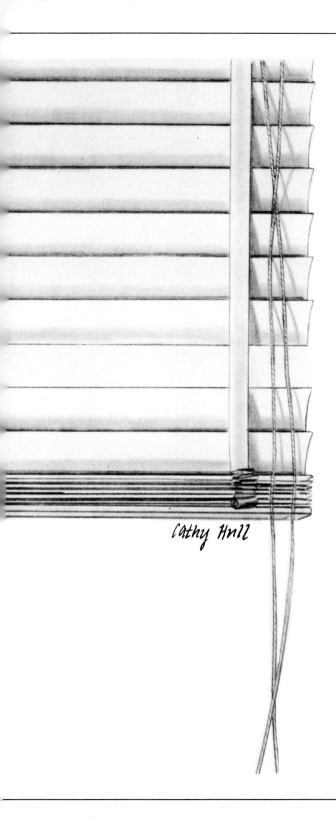

Cathy Hull

4
SOCIAL PERCEPTION AND ATTRIBUTION

OBJECT PERCEPTION AND
PERSON PERCEPTION

OBJECT PERCEPTION
LANGUAGE AND PERCEPTION/PAST
EXPERIENCE, EXPECTATION, AND
PERCEPTION/SOME GESTALT
PRINCIPLES OF PERCEPTION

PERSON PERCEPTION
ACCURACY IN PERSON PERCEPTION/
IMPRESSION FORMATION

ATTRIBUTION

SUMMARY

SUGGESTED READINGS

We do not see all there is to see or hear all there is to hear. Our eyes and ears respond to a limited range of light and sound waves. Our bodies are comfortable in a very narrow range of temperatures. In fact, our entire sensory apparatus seems designed to limit stimulation and to restrict our range of experiences. Our sensory organs simplify the physical environment, just as our cognitive apparatus helps us simplify and organize our social environment and experiences.

If there is an overriding theme to this book, it is the cognitive/rationalist idea that people need to make sense of their experience. As we have seen, much of our behavior can be explained as techniques for understanding the world and our place in it. You may enroll in a psychology course, for example, because of a desire to make the behavior of others and of yourself more understandable. Psychologists are fortunate because their profession is the preoccupation of people in general—trying to make sense of what does not always seem sensible. This chapter will emphasize two areas: object perception and person perception. We will see how people's perceptions of the physical world (object perception) and the social world (person perception) are determined largely by their need to discover, or impose, order and consistency on experience.

OBJECT PERCEPTION AND PERSON PERCEPTION

We all live in a single world that we share with over four billion other people, and yet each of us lives in a separate subjective world. It is often startling to encounter someone whose view of the world is very different from our own. Talking to someone from a different social class or another culture can dramatize how very differently the same events may be perceived. I doubt that each individual has a totally idiosyncratic way of thinking about everyday events, but there are certainly a great many distinct points of view. Communists and capitalists hold different views of human nature, variously interpret the same historical events, and perceive the behaviors and motivations of individuals in contrary ways. New Englanders and southerners, males and females, blacks and whites, Asians and Europeans, teachers and students, children and adults, and other groups of people with different experiences, needs, and expectations are apt to perceive events in quite dissimilar ways.

Perceiving physical objects is a slightly less complicated process than perceiving other people. The perception of other people often involves their intentions, feelings, expectations, and behaviors, as well as their interactions with the perceiver. When we view and evaluate a physical object, whether it is natural, as a tree, or fabricated, as a painting, we do not need to deal with any psycho-

We tend to assume that we are seeing what is really there when we look at an object, but even this kind of perception is colored by individual experiences and expectations. This man's view of this sculpture is different from ours, both literally and psychologically.

logical qualities of the object, such as its goals and desires. If a physical object moves in space, we do not have to ask whether the object desired or was motivated to move. We can explain and predict such a movement solely by reference to physical forces—gravity, wind resistance, and other fields of force. If a person is the object of perception, and that person "moves," that is, engages in some behavior, we must evaluate the internal, personal forces acting on the person, such as wishes, desires, and needs, as well as the physical or environmental forces, such as whether the person was coerced to do something. We will begin with a discussion of object perception, both because it is somewhat simpler to deal with and because many of the processes involved also operate in person perception.

OBJECT PERCEPTION

Whether we are dealing with object or with person perception it is not a pure process of seeing what is really there. Psychologists and physiologists agree that *perception is always selective.* Human beings have a limited sensory capacity—we can see only a fraction of what is present, hear only a limited range of sounds, and feel only rather coarse changes in contour or temperature. We are further limited by our psychological needs, expectations, and experiences. Regardless of how we perceive an object in the physical world, our perception of it is selective in the sense that our sensory organs are incapable of receiving and interpreting all its physical characteristics, and our cognitive apparatus would be incapable of handling all that information even if our sense organs were not.

Object perception is also selective in another way. The same

HOW TO KNOW WHERE YOU ARE

As Caesar's and his slayers' versions
Of his true worth did not accord,
As Cypriotes fell out with Persians
And Greek disputed Greek with sword,
As Jason differed with Medea
And Bonaparte with Talleyrand,
The forms of onomatopoeia
Do not agree from land to land.

In Oshkosh, Hollywood, and Nutley
The sound of breaking plates is "crash!";
In Helsinki, it changes subtly
To *"krats!,"* suggesting scratch and gnash;
A tingletangle *"kling!"* is Denmark's;
In Rome, a raucous *"patatrac!"*;
In China, a cartoonist's pen marks
"Hua-la-la!" for cracking crock.

In Portugal, when platters shatter
And scatter all about a room,
They smack of elephantine clatter
Or bongo drums: *"catrapuz-boom!"*
In Budapest, extremist factions,
Surmounting politics, concur
That dishes fracture into fractions
With double sibilants: *"chir-churr!"*

So if, one dawn, a clap of thunder
Awakes you on a quick world tour,
And, half asleep and dazed, you wonder
What country you are in, procure
The plates you bought as gifts for givers
And let one fly until it breaks,
Then, as it shivers into slivers,
Note carefully the sound it makes.

William Walden, *Atlantic*, November 1974, p. 87.

---

object has different meanings for different people, and the meaning attached to an object influences the way it is perceived and responded to. A classic experiment by Bruner and Goodman (1947) illustrates this point. Ten-year-old children were asked to estimate the size of various coins. Bruner and Goodman found, particularly among children from poorer families, that the sizes of coins were overestimated, especially quarters and half-dollars. The more valuable the object was to the children, the greater its size was estimated to be (see also Hitchcock, Munroe, & Munroe, 1976; Levine, Chein, & Murphy, 1942; Tajfel, 1957). As this study demonstrates, the subjective importance of an object influences perceptions of it.

The importance attached to objects influences not only perceptions of them, but also the ways in which information about these objects is inferred, stored, and recalled. Most particularly, there is a close link between language and perception. Our experience with objects influences our vocabulary related to them, and vocabulary pertinent to objects influences our perception of the objects.

LANGUAGE AND PERCEPTION

The links between language, thought, and behavior are complex and only imperfectly understood. An early twentieth-century theory of language and experience was proposed by Benjamin Lee Whorf (1897–1941). The two primary hypotheses of Whorf's analysis of language are: (1) all thought is dependent on language; and (2) the structure of language influences the manner in which the environment is perceived and understood (Chase, 1956). Language, according to Whorf, sets limits on what we *can* experience and think. Today, a somewhat weaker version of the Whorfian theory is commonly accepted (Cole & Schribner, 1974; Slobin, 1971). This modified theory suggests that language simply makes it easier to experience those events for which we have an adequate vocabulary. While we do not, for example, have a single word for a color between red and orange, we can still perceive such a color, though not as readily as if a word designating that precise color existed in the language (see Brown & Lenneberg, 1954). It is certainly easier to recognize objects and events for which a vocabulary is available, and it is easier to classify and remember linguistically codable phenomena.

One implication of the Whorfian hypotheses is that people who speak different languages have different views of the world. Whorf's (1956) most quoted example is the fact that Eskimos have many words for different kinds of snow while most Americans (with the exception of skiers) do not distinguish between different kinds of snow and do not have the vocabulary to make such distinctions easily. To most of us, snow is snow.

Experts in many areas develop specialized vocabularies that enable them to make fine distinctions unrecognizable to the lay person. What you call an "old book" a book collector might call an "incunabulum," meaning a book printed in the fifteenth century. Whether the vocabulary preceded the distinctions, or the distinctions gave rise to a specialized vocabulary, is irrelevant to our purposes. What is important is that language, once acquired, makes it easier to perceive certain kinds of distinctions.

PAST EXPERIENCE, EXPECTATION, AND PERCEPTION

Perhaps the most consistent influence on perception is past experience. Familiarity with objects makes them easier to recognize; they seem to stand out from their environment. Look at one of your old class pictures and you will have no trouble spotting your face in the crowd. An experimental demonstration of the effects of past experience on perception was published by Leeper in 1935. He used an ambiguous picture in which either an attractive young woman or an old woman can be seen (see Figure 4.1). Different subjects in his study were shown redrawn figures that emphasized either the young or the old woman. Then the ambiguous picture was presented. Participants who had been shown the young woman saw only the young woman in the ambiguous drawing, while those who had been shown the old woman saw only her image in the drawing.

A cross-cultural study of a similar nature was conducted by Bagby

Figure 4.1.
Ambiguous figure. Is this a picture of a young or old woman?

(1957). Mexicans and Americans who had been matched for age, sex, education, and social class were shown pairs of photographs. One photograph in each pair depicted a typical Mexican scene, such as a bullfight, and the other depicted an American scene, such as a baseball game. A special slide viewer briefly presented one photo to each eye. This situation is called *binocular rivalry;* two images are presented to the brain, but most subjects report seeing only one image. Which image would be seen? The results indicate the importance of past experience in perception: 74 percent of the Mexican subjects saw only the slides depicting typical Mexican scenes, while over 84 percent of the American subjects saw only the slides depicting American themes. These differences strongly suggest that past experience with an object or event makes it more salient and easily perceived.

SOME GESTALT PRINCIPLES OF
PERCEPTION

Until the 1920s, much psychological research on perception dealt with slight changes in an external stimulus and how readily noticeable such changes were to respondents. This research stressed stimulus–response connections in perception, correlating changes in stimuli with changes in responses.

The early Gestalt psychologists argued against this simple S–R position (see Chapter 1). Köhler, Koffka, and Wertheimer, among others, stressed the idea that people interpret, organize, and assess stimuli before they are fully perceived. In particular, the Gestalt psychologists proposed that stimuli are perceived in terms of the perceiver's past experiences, needs, and expectations, and also the context in which they are presented.

When we listen to Beethoven's Fifth Symphony, for example, it is not three G's and an E^b that we hear in the first movement, but the relationship between notes. If this theme were transposed to another key and we heard three F$^\sharp$s and a D, it would sound the same to anyone except those with perfect pitch. We do not hear particular sound frequencies when we listen to music, but rather the relationships between frequencies.

Likewise, we perceive many objects primarily in terms of their relationships to other objects in the environment. Max Wertheimer (1923) proposed a number of perceptual principles. Among these principles are:

(1) *Common fate.* Objects that share a common trait, for example, movement, are perceived together.

(2) *Similarity.* Objects that are similar are grouped together, as in **--**--**--**--. Thus, in this array of asterisks and dashes, we perceive pairs of asterisks and pairs of dashes and not simply a single unit consisting of sixteen parts.

(3) *Proximity.* Objects close to one another in time or space are perceived together. For example, *abcd efgh* and *abc de fgh*. In the first series *d* and *e* are seen as belonging to two different units, while in the second array *de* forms a unit.

(4) *Common boundary.* Elements are perceived together if they are connected in some physical way; (XX) (XX) becomes two pairs of X's because they are enclosed in pairs.

(5) *Good form.* Elements that are balanced, symmetrical, or complete are more readily perceived than complex or random elements.

(6) *Expectation or set.* Objects that we expect to encounter are more readily perceived.

To these principles we can add two more that stem from Gestalt psychology:

(7) *Figure–ground.* Certain aspects of a complex stimulus stand out and the remaining elements recede into the background. This is evident in many of the drawings of M. C. Escher and in the prints of Victor Vasarely, and in a good many jokes

and riddles. "How do you get four elephants into a Volkswagen?" "Two in the front seat, two in the back." There is a sudden switch from the dimension of size to the element of number. Size is the prominent feature of the question (figure) and number is not (background). Upon hearing the answer, a person must switch figure and ground.

(8) *Assimilation–contrast.* Objects close to a person's own predilections or experiences are perceived to be closer than they actually are, while those at variance with past experiences or expectations seem to be farther away than they are in reality. For example, a gray object against a white background seems darker than the same object against a black background. This is because the object is contrasted to the background. Likewise, red and orange will seem similar if they are presented along with a blue object.

Once some object is familiar to us, we tend to maintain our original perception of it. For example, when we stand in front of a closed door, it appears rectangular in shape. When we open the door, it actually looks like a trapezoid, but we still perceive it as a rectangle This phenomenon is referred to as *perceptual constancy.* We "know" that doors are rectangular, and so we interpret a trapezoidal visual image as though it were a rectangle. Of course, this is a functional way of perceiving the environment; the door is the same shape whether it is open or closed. Cross-cultural research has shown that people who live in cultures with no right angles are less susceptible to optical illusions based on angularity. Evidently, they do not develop perceptual constancy about such unfamiliar objects as rectangular doors (Segall, Campbell, & Herskovits, 1966).

We are neither physically nor mentally capable of perceiving objects in all their real-life complexity. Of course, this presents problems to social psychologists as researchers, because research is a process of drawing conclusions from observation. If observation is less than perfectly objective, then research is always ambiguous to some degree. It also means that people are incapable of describing any object or situation completely or "objectively." So if you encounter someone whose view of the world is radically different from your own, you may take comfort in the knowledge that the other person's view is as incomplete and nonobjective as yours.

PERSON PERCEPTION

If object perception is subjective and laden with ambiguity, person perception is even more complex. For all practical purposes, we perceive people as having free will; they can, ought, want, and need to behave in certain ways, all of which play some role in our perceptions of them.

Social psychological theory and research on person perception fall conveniently into three categories: (1) the accuracy of person perception; (2) evaluative impression formation; and (3) attribution. The first category, accuracy of person perception, concerns the ability to make accurate judgments of fairly objective traits of other people, such as their emotional states at a particular time, their ethnicity, their intelligence, and their personality. Evaluative impression formation deals with how we arrive at our own feelings about other people. Most research in this area concerns one person's liking for another on the basis of a limited amount of information. Attribution theory involves how we explain the causes of behavior.

ACCURACY IN PERSON PERCEPTION

Person perception research began with Charles Darwin's influential book, *The expression of the emotions in man and animals* (1872). Darwin argued that certain expressions were associated with emotions evolved from earlier, functional behaviors. Laughter, for example, may have derived from the feeling of triumph that followed the defeat of an enemy (Rapp, 1951). Following Darwin's observations, psychologists assumed that certain characteristic expressions and gestures always accompanied a particular emotional state. Various researchers thus began studies designed to determine how readily recognizable particular emotional states are.

Darwin and many psychologists (e.g., F. H. Allport, 1924) writing in the early twentieth century included photographs and drawings of men and women experiencing certain emotions. In subsequent research, subjects were asked to identify the emotion expressed in each picture (Feleky, 1914; Woodworth, 1938). This research led to inconsistent and inconclusive findings. Participants in the early studies often confused certain emotions, such as love, happiness, and mirth.

Woodworth (1938) and Schlosberg (1952) believed that these easily confused emotions were in some fundamental sense more similar to one another than emotions such as surprise and contempt, which were rarely confused. Therefore, they began to study the underlying structures of emotional states rather than the recognition of emotional states. Schlosberg suggested that two dimensions lie behind all emotions: unpleasantness–pleasantness and rejection–attention. Any emotion can be characterized, he proposed, by these two properties. More recently, other researchers have attempted to determine empirically what the dimensions underlying emotions are. Osgood,

AN INTERVIEW WITH
MARIANNE LA FRANCE
AND CLARA MAYO

Marianne La France is assistant professor of psychology at Boston College. She received her PhD from Boston University, where Clara Mayo is professor of psychology and co-director of the Center for Women's Development. Mayo received her PhD from Clark University. La France and Mayo are the authors of *Moving bodies: Nonverbal communication in social relationships,* and *Evaluating research in social psychology: A guide to the consumer.*

JHG: How did you become interested in collaborating on the topic of nonverbal communication?

MLF: In undergraduate work in Canada, my first social psychology course introduced me to the field of human nonverbal communication. It was exciting to me and fit my perceptions of the way the world worked. But there was little research then. I came to Boston University as a graduate student and walked into Clara's office and said, "You're interested in person perception—and I think nonverbal communication belongs in your ball park." Tell Jeff what your first reaction was.

CM: I said yes, I'm interested in person perception, but I had been working for some fifteen years on the cognitive aspects of impression formation and all I knew about nonverbal communication was body language, which struck me as simpleminded. That people who sit with their arms and legs crossed are not to be approached seemed to me to be a tiny part of a complex issue.

MLF: We used to have raging battles over the importance of nonverbal versus verbal communication.

CM: I think ours is a particularly productive collaboration because it is open to conflict—we often approach a new problem from very different points of view and we argue it out intensively. I think much collaborative research begins with agreement. Ours was a kind of collision. Here I was doing the verbal–cognitive side of impression formation and Marianne argued for the behavioral–nonverbal side. My question was, "How do people think about others?" and Marianne's reaction was, "But first you have to know what they do."

MLF: Our work on racial differences in gaze began when I was learning to use slow-motion film analysis to code body movement. One film I was analyzing was of a conversation between a black man and a white man. In coding their body movement, I sensed that something was wrong in their conversation. At first, my reaction was that there was some subtle racism going on. Then, it seemed the black man was not looking enough at the white. This led us to the idea that the pattern of looking among blacks was different from the pattern of looking among whites.

CM: And that's when my own interest was stirred because I have a long-standing concern with racism, and it seemed that cultural differences between blacks and whites might be contributing to tension in interracial encounters. This possibility made research in nonverbal communication seem potentially useful.

MLF: The first study involved two filmed conversations. We analyzed the film frame by frame (there are about 15,000 frames of film in two five-minute conversations). In this and a subsequent field study, we found that blacks look less while listening than do whites.

JHG: When you use the term *nonverbal communication* are you referring to the whole range of topics studied by social and clinical psychologists—personal space, population density, architectural design, body language—or something more specific?

CM: Usually nonverbal communication includes facial expression, gaze direction, interpersonal distance, touch, paralinguistics, body movement, and posture. Some people include the environmental elements as well.

MLF: What we are particularly interested in are the nonverbal behaviors that are patterned and rule-regulated and that help create, maintain, and sustain human relationships. It's not just a matter of presenting a single nonverbal cue—somebody smiling, somebody frowning— and asking what do judges think of it? In learning a language, one also learns a whole host of nonverbal routines that are important for regulating human interaction. Various people would argue that the distinction needs to be made between nonverbal *behavior* and nonverbal *communication*. Nonverbal behavior can be unique to a given individual, can be specific to a given time and place, can lead to impressions without being in any

way related to communication processes. Nonverbal communication should be reserved for behaviors whose meaning is widely shared. Nonverbal communication is especially exciting to me because it is interdisciplinary and methodologically diverse. There are philosophers, psychiatrists, linguists, anthropologists, social psychologists, people in a wide variety of social science disciplines doing this stuff. The research methods are also broad-ranging. There are the people who lock themselves away to analyze a single film; there are experimental studies, there are naturalistic observations, there are paper-and-pencil formats.

CM: In our book, we tried to present an integrative picture of the nonverbal field. The book grew out of our natural inclination to people-watch. As social psychologists, we get to people-watch professionally as well as recreationally.

JHG: How has familiarizing yourself with the topic changed the kind of people-watching you do? Is it like becoming a bird watcher, where suddenly you see birds everywhere that you hadn't noticed before?

CM: Doing research on nonverbal behavior made me more aware of the nonverbal things that people share, the things that bring them together in interaction.

JHG: What people say is often assumed to be less genuine than their nonverbal behavior. Yet you say in *Moving bodies* that one should not make that generalization. *(Continued)*

MLF: There is some intriguing research on "leakage and deception cues." There are clearly times when people are deceiving themselves or others about their psychological state, when they are very depressed or very angry and for a variety of reasons cannot admit it to themselves or others and it bounces out nonverbally. But I think that is a relatively rare occurrence.

JHF: You're saying that most of the time there is congruence between verbal and nonverbal behaviors?

MLF: Yes, we need that congruence. The system hangs together; redundancy is part of the nature of human communication.

JHG: There are considerable sex differences in nonverbal communication. Would you summarize these?

MLF: Sex differences have been found in every aspect of nonverbal communication. The differences are in line with the sex-role literature that says that men are more assertive and dominant. The nonverbal cues convey that—men interrupt more, take more personal space, take more "air time" in conversations by more talk and more pausing. Women, on the other hand, tend to be more interpersonally concerned and they show it by being more facially expressive, more sensitive to others' nonverbal cues, and more nonverbally responsive.

JHG: These are behaviors consistent with cultural sex-role stereotypes. Would you expect changes in nonverbal communication as sex roles change?

MLF: We recently completed a study in which we took four gender-related nonverbal behaviors—smiling and gazing (feminine behaviors) and interrupting and filled pausing (masculine behaviors). We selected masculine males, feminine females and androgynous males and females on the basis of the Bem Sex Role Inventory. We videotaped them talking in same-sex pairs. The general question was: Do androgynous people show less sex-typed behavior or more cross-gender behavior than traditional males and females? In general, we found that androgynous people demonstrate more cross-gender behavior as well as some lessening of typical masculine and feminine behavior. Androgynous males gaze and smile more than masculine males; androgynous women interrupt and fill pauses more than feminine females. Androgynous males show less pausing than masculine males and androgynous females smile less than feminine females, showing that both androgynous groups curtail the extremes shown by their sex-typed counterparts.

JHG: What are the obvious gaps in our knowledge of nonverbal behavior? What needs to be done in the area?

CM: In general, we know very little about how the nonverbal cues combine, how the nonverbal system works as a whole. More specifically, there is more to be learned about cultural nonverbal patterns. We are only beginning to know what nonverbal behavior is near universal and what behavior is culture specific. Another neglected area is the role of nonverbal cues in social influence such as persuasion, teaching, therapy, and advertising.

JHG: But advertising people have some notions about nonverbal characteristics of credible communicators. They use models who don't blink for 60 seconds. Their eyes must be filthy by the time they finish making a commercial.

MLF: They do have some ideas, but we don't know yet how the whole communication system works. Credibility involves not just eyes, but facial expression and vocal tone and body posture. All these cues comment on the "truth" or falsity of other cues. One blink does not a liar make.

Suci, and Tannenbaum (1957) have proposed three dimensions on which emotions (and other phenomena, such as the meaning of words) differ. These dimensions are pleasant–unpleasant, or the *evaluative* dimension; active–passive, or the *activity* dimension; and strong–weak, or the *potency* dimension. Any emotion can be represented as a point in this three-dimensional space, and one emotion differs from another in terms of one or more of these three attributes.

This shift from recognition of emotions to a focus on the dimensions of emotion was accompanied by criticism of the methodology involved in the recognition studies. Researchers pointed out that the accuracy of emotional perception depends heavily on the specific kinds of judgments the subjects are asked to make (Frijda, 1969; Tagiuri, 1969).

Recently, other researchers have focused on the accuracy problem, most notably Paul Ekman and his colleagues (Ekman & Friesen, 1974; Ekman, Sorenson, & Friesen, 1969). They found that if the research is adequately designed, people in different cultures generally agree in their identification of emotions from photographs.

There has been considerable research exploring the accuracy of perception of personality traits. Here, however, the methodological problems are even more restrictive (Bender & Hastorf, 1953; Cronbach, 1955; Estes, 1938; Vernon, 1933). The problems concern the number of personality traits involved in the judgment task, how they are presented to research subjects, and what sorts of judgments subjects are required to make. Hastorf, Schneider, and Polefka (1970) summarize some of these problems:

If A rates B's hostility, we must have some measure of how hostile B is before we can determine A's accuracy. Vernon used test scores, Estes used the evaluations of trained clinicians, and Dymond employed the stimulus person's own self-rating. There are other possibilities. . . . Standard tests and behavior measures also pose problems, and indeed we could probably get only fair agreement that any given criterion for accuracy is an appropriate one. (p. 29)

Since the mid-1950s, research on the accuracy of person perception has declined. Today, the concern is less with accuracy than with the nature of the judgment process (Bieri, 1966). As social psychologists, we should emphasize how people perceive their environment rather than the accuracy of their perceptions.

IMPRESSION FORMATION

Recently, interest has focused on the kinds of perceptions people have about others, the information they use in forming these judgments, and the kinds of processes they assume operate in other people's personalities. These topics are generally discussed together under the heading of impression formation.

The Gestalt Approach of Solomon Asch   In the 1940s, Solomon Asch (1946) conducted what has become a landmark study in social psychology, opening up the area of research known as impression formation. He was concerned with the question of how we form unified impressions of other people. There are two possibilities, according to Asch (1952). One is *summative formulation,* in which our view of a person is the sum of all those characteristics that we have observed. "According to this assumption, to know a person is simply to know a number of facts about him. If we represent the various qualities of a person by the letters *a, b, c, d,* and *e,* the full impression may be expressed as: Impression = a + b + c + d + e" (p. 207). Thus, our impression of a person whom we observed to be friendly, kind, helpful and intelligent would somehow reflect the sum of those traits. Asch suggested the *Gestalt formulation* as the second possibility. In this view, traits are evaluated in terms of other traits and can interact with one another, each influencing the relative importance or meaning of the others.

In Asch's (1946) research, a list of characteristics was read to each of two groups of college students. One group was told that a person was "intelligent, skillful, industrious, warm, determined, practical, and cautious." The second group was told that a person was "intelligent, skillful, industrious, cold, determined, practical, and cautious." Both groups received identical descriptions, except that the word *cold* was substituted for *warm* for the second group.

The students were then given a checklist containing other attributes and asked to indicate which ones applied to the person described. Asch found that the variation of one trait in the description, warm–cold, led to differences in the impressions formed of the person. Table 4.1 summarizes some of these differences on the adjective checklist. Asch argued that the warm–cold variable represented a central trait in impression formation, one that influenced the quality of the overall impression to a great extent. Not all traits have this apparent capacity. Asch replicated the experiment, but instead of varying warm–cold, he varied polite–blunt. This variation had no such influence on the overall impressions formed, and was thus termed a *peripheral trait*.

The concept of central and peripheral traits has been criticized on a number of grounds, particularly on the ground that certain traits are more highly correlated with the adjectives in the checklist than others. (S. Rosenberg, Nelson, & Vivekananthan, 1968; Warr & Knapper, 1968; Wishner, 1960; Zanna & Hamilton, 1972). The study nevertheless demonstrates that the meaning of a particular characteristic of a person may change depending on its context—a notion taken directly from Gestalt studies of object perception. Thus, a person who is described as "intelligent and cold" may have a different sort of intelligence than one described as "intelligent and warm." The first description implies a kind of calculated, methodical intelligence, while the second implies a commonsense and creative intelligence.

While Asch's research dealt only with people's perceptions of a hypothetical person, Harold Kelley (1950) studied impressions of a real person. Prior to hearing a lecturer, two classes of students were read a brief introductory speech in which the lecturer was described

Table 4.1.
Percent of Subjects Choosing Each Adjective

Adjective	Warm (n=90) %	Cold (n=76) %
Generous	91	8
Wise	65	25
Good-natured	94	17
Happy	90	34
Humorous	77	13
Sociable	91	38
Popular	84	28
Important	88	99
Humane	86	31
Restrained	77	89
Altruistic	69	18
Imaginative	51	19

Note: n = number of subjects in each group. From Asch (1952, adapted from Table I, p. 209).

as "a rather cold [or very warm] person, industrious, critical, practical, and determined." Following the lecture, students wrote impressions of him in the form of essays. Two results stand out. First, as reported by Asch (1946), there were more favorable impressions of the lecturer when he was described as "warm" rather than "cold." Second, judgments of him were altered by prior information. Students who had formed a preliminary impression of the lecturer from the introductory speech tended to evaluate his actual behavior in light of this early impression. This happened even though the lecturer gave the identical, memorized talk on both occasions. In general, later information about a person is viewed in the context of early information.

One important discovery from these early impression-formation studies is that impressions of others tend to be uniform, consistent, and integrated. The student subjects in these studies formed rounded impressions of others on the basis of limited amounts of information. When forming impressions of others, people tend to round out incomplete information, to fill in gaps, to go beyond the information given in arriving at a single, relatively unambiguous picture of the person. In Asch's words, "It is hard not to see the person as a unit."

Asch proposed two different principles of impression formation from simple adjective descriptions: summation and Gestalt. In the 1960s, these opposing principles of information integration again found their way into the research literature under the heading "adding versus averaging."

Adding versus Averaging in Impression Formation   In most of the early impression-formation studies, subjects were given varying lists of adjectives. Asch initially used seven adjectives for each group, varying only "warm" or "cold." What happens to our impression of another person when the number of adjectives is increased or decreased? Does adding a mildly positive trait to a list of highly positive traits increase or decrease the overall favorability of the impression? This is one of the central issues in the controversy known as adding versus averaging. The issue is whether people integrate adjectival information by somehow arriving at an average of all the traits presented, or whether each additional adjective contributes an equal amount of information to the overall impression.

Asch's Gestalt formulation implies that some kind of averaging process occurs, although he suggests a more complex process than simple averaging. He argues that the actual favorableness of a trait such as "intelligence" changes when it is accompanied by "warm" or "cold." Asch's formulation is a kind of weighted average in which each adjective is given a weight determined, in part, by the adjectives that accompany it.

The averaging model, which is an extension of Asch's Gestalt principle, has been most clearly developed by N. H. Anderson (1965, 1971). The summation principle, also referred to as the additive principle, has been revived by a number of social psychologists, most notably Martin Fishbein and his colleages (Fishbein, 1963; Fishbein & Ajzen, 1975). A number of researchers have attempted to determine which of these two formulations most clearly accounts for one person's overall impression of another person.

In what was proposed as a crucial test of the two formulations, N. H. Anderson (1965) varied the favorability of each adjective presented to subjects and also the number of adjectives presented. One group, for example, might be presented with only two highly favorable adjectives describing a hypothetical person: "intelligent, friendly." Another group might receive four highly favorable traits: "intelligent, friendly, kind, strong." Some groups were given unfavorable traits or a combination of favorable and unfavorable traits. Anderson reports that the results of his study, in which each subject was asked to form a single impression of the likability of the person, were inconclusive. Certain results supported the averaging model, others were more consistent with the summation model.

As interpreted by Fishbein and Ajzen (1975), the reason so many studies fail to support one or the other formulation is that they do not take account of several important variables. First is the possibility that some traits are discounted by subjects. For example, if you heard a person described as "friendly, warm, kind, good-natured, outgoing, and a bully," you would probably find the last trait inconsistent with the preceding traits and therefore give it less weight. Second, some information presented in the form of adjectives is redundant and so may have little influence on an overall impression. For example, "bright, intelligent, smart, scholarly and witty" may imply only a single characteristic of the person rather than five distinct traits. Finally, Fishbein and Ajzen propose that subjects assign a probability weight to each trait, that is, they decide some traits are more likely to belong to the person than others. Probability weighting is a sophisticated way of saying that certain traits are more or less discounted.

The area as a whole is extraordinarily complex, owing at least as much to methodological problems as to the complexities of theory. Because adjectives will be more or less correlated with each other, methodological problems arise over the relationship between traits in a stimulus list and those on the dependent measure, usually an adjective checklist. What at first appeared to Asch to be a central trait, "warm–cold," and a peripheral trait, "polite–blunt," turn out on closer examination to be differentially correlated with the adjectives on the checklist.

Studies in these areas are more than exercises in mathematics and methods. Despite their complexity, they may provide us with important knowledge about the utilization of information, the storage and cognitive manipulation of information, and the interactions of social judgment and perception.

Implicit Theories of Personality   One of the clearest implications of the early work on impression formation, particularly that of Asch and Kelley, is that people often seem to have some sense of what traits belong with certain other traits. When a hypothetical person is described as intelligent, friendly, warm, and unpretentious, a great many middle-class Americans will assume that the person is also easygoing and likable. The fact that these latter traits are *assumed* to belong with the former traits is an indication that people have their own *implicit theories of personality*, in which several traits are seen as clustering together. To put it in statistical terms, implicit theories of personality indicate that most people believe certain characteristics of a person are highly correlated with other characteristics. Of course, not everyone's implicit theory of personality is the same. Presumably, each individual's theory reflects that person's past experience with others (see Schneider, 1973).

The concept of implicit theories of personality may explain why we go beyond the given information to form integrated impressions of others. Many people's implicit personality theories assume that if a person possesses a number of positive traits, then that person will also possess other positive traits. This is called the *halo effect* (Thorndike, 1920). It is evident not only in impression formation, in which a healthy and wealthy person is also assumed to be wise, but in a good deal of personality research as well (Wiggins, 1973). The halo effect has been found to occur most powerfully when it is important to form an impression of another and when the subject must be relatively certain of his or her judgment (O'Neal, 1971; O'Neal & Mills, 1969).

Cross-Cultural Research on Implicit Theories of Personality   Implicit theories of personality may consist of various components, one of which is an individual's expectations about the makeup of others' personalities. Expectations, as we have seen, tend to make certain events, objects, or traits more salient and distinctive to a person. An experiment by Bruner and Perlmutter (1957), conducted in the United States, France, and Germany, makes the point that distinctive stimuli are readily noticed and form the basis for impressions. Bruner and Perlmutter argue that our impressions of others are more likely to be based on attributes that are distinctive than on attributes that all or many people have in common. Thus, if you are confronted with three physicists, one of whom is American, one German, and one French, your impressions of them are more apt to be based on their nationality than on their profession.

Bruner and Perlmutter also hypothesize that great familiarity with a particular attribute makes it less likely that impressions will be based on that attribute. To use their example, if you know Americans better than Frenchmen or Germans, the first impression you form of an American will be less determined by nationality than will your first impression of a Frenchman or a German. Presumably this happens because the greater our familiarity with an attribute, the more aware we are of the inappropriateness of stereotypes. Knowing a good deal about Americans makes simple statements about them seem like overgeneralizations.

In their research, Bruner and Perlmutter presented college students in France, Germany, and the United States with descriptions of French, German, and American businessmen and college professors. The nationalities and professions were varied so that students were given all possible combinations. After a brief description of nationality and occupation was read, students rated each person on an adjective checklist. As hypothesized, when the students were presented with three businessmen or three professors whose nationality varied, nationality became the predominant basis for their impressions. Also as predicted, students in each country were more likely to use nationality as a basis for impressions when the stimulus person was a foreigner than when he was a compatriot.

Some researchers have proposed that there may be a universal way of conceiving of personality (Norman, 1963; Passini & Norman, 1966; Stricker, Jacobs, & Kogan, 1974). They suggest that each culture has words in its language to describe personality in terms of

Because this piano player seems so friendly, warm, and likeable, many people will assume he is also intelligent and easy-going. Most of us follow implicit theories of personality like this, without being aware that we have such theories in mind.

five basic factors: extroversion, agreeableness, conscientiousness, emotional stability, and culture. While there is no evidence that such concepts are absent from any language, research with Filipino subjects indicates that only the first three factors are commonly used by Filipinos. Guthrie and Bennett (1971) suggest that

Americans and Filipinos will make different estimates of the probability of occurrence of certain behavior having observed other behavior. For example, noting that someone is hypochondriacal, an American expects that he will be anxious. Our data suggests that these two behavior manifestations are independent of one another in the implicit theory of Filipinos. . . . [T]he Filipinos make inferences and hold expectations that Americans do not hold. (p. 312)

Further Evidence on the Role of Past Experience and Expectation in Impression Formation Past experience is a powerful determinant of how something is perceived. The Bagby experiment on binocular rivalry and the study by Leeper with ambiguous pictures demonstrate that past experiences lead us to hold certain expectations that influence perception. To demonstrate the role of past experience and expectation in the perception of human traits, we will look at a classic study.

In 1951, Dartmouth lost an important football game to Princeton in Princeton's Palmer Stadium. It was a particularly rough game, in which Princeton's All-American quarterback received a broken nose in the second quarter and a Dartmouth player suffered a broken leg in the third quarter. The game was hotly debated for weeks on both campuses.

Albert Hastorf and Hadley Cantril (1954) administered questionnaires to Princeton and Dartmouth students a week after the game and also showed the same motion picture of the game to a sample of undergraduate students at each school. While watching the film, the students were to note any infractions of the rules they saw. The study found consistent and clear differences between the Princeton and Dartmouth students in their perceptions of the game. While the Dartmouth students were aware that the press had charged Dartmouth with trying to "get" the Princeton quarterback, only 10 percent of the Dartmouth students believed those charges as compared to 55 percent of the Princeton students. When Dartmouth students watched the film of the game, they noted an average of 4.3 infractions against the Dartmouth team and 4.4 against Princeton. When Princeton students viewed the same film, they noted 9.8 infractions against Dartmouth and only 4.2 against Princeton. Hastorf and Cantril note of their results:

. . . the data here indicate that there is no such "thing" as a "game" existing "out there" in its own right which people merely "observe."

The "game" "exists" for a person and is experienced by him only in so far as certain happenings have significance in terms of his purpose. Out of all the occurences going on in the environment, a person selects those that have some significance for him. . . . (p. 132)

Comparable differences in the perception and interpretation of other sporting events have been noted by Mann (1974) and Zillmann, Bryant, and Sapolsky (1979).

Expectations may influence not only our perceptions of others but also our behavior toward them. In a controversial study published in 1968 by Rosenthal and Jacobson, teachers' expectations about the potential intellectual growth of their students were experimentally manipulated. A random 20 percent of pupils in an elementary school were selected. Teachers were then informed that, on the basis of tests, it was predicted that these students would show a marked increase in IQ during the school year. At the year's end, the students identified as potential bloomers did indeed do better than their classmates, particularly in the first through third grades.

Rosenthal and Jacobson (1968), arguing from the basis of Robert K. Merton's (1948) notion of *self-fulfilling prophecy*, believed that the teachers' expectations about these randomly selected pupils somehow changed their behavior toward them, with the result that the teachers' expectations were confirmed.

Some attempts to replicate these findings have been unsuccessful (Clairborn, 1969; Fielder, Cohen, & Finney, 1971), and the Rosenthal and Jacobson study has been criticized on methodological grounds (Elashoff & Snow, 1970). However, more recent studies by Seaver (1973) and Rubovits and Maehr (1971) have supported the teacher-expectancy effect. Seaver reasoned that teachers who had taught the older siblings of students would have certain expectations about

If these students do well in school, their teacher will expect their younger brothers and sisters to do just as well in their turn.

those students. For example, if a teacher found John Dimitri in her class just a year or two after having John's older brother as a student, she would have some expectations about John's potential, based on the performance of his brother. If John's brother was a good student, she would expect John to be a good student; if John's brother was a poor student, she would expect John to be a poor student. By examining the school records of students whose older siblings either did or did not have the same teachers, Seaver found strong support for the expectancy effect. Those students whose older siblings performed well in school also performed well if they had the same teachers. Those whose older siblings did not do well performed poorly if they had the same teachers.

ATTRIBUTION

As you read the pages on perception, you may have noticed the absence of certain themes. In particular, social psychologists who have studied our perception of people and events have emphasized the personalities of observers or the observed, but have often ignored environmental features of social perception. Within the past decade this imbalance has been redressed by research on attribution.

Attribution assumes that people have a need not only to make sense of experience but also to determine the causes of events. Theories and research on attribution will be presented chronologically so you can see how social psychological theory has changed and become more refined over time.

Heider's Notions of Attribution   Though Heider (1958) also analyzed attributions of impersonal events (Bassili, 1976; Heider & Simmel, 1944), he was concerned primarily with our perception of social behaviors. In analyzing some social event, Heider suggests that we first attempt to determine what caused it. Any action of another person may be seen as the result of *environmental* or *personal* influences, or a combination of the two.

As an illustration of these perceived causes, assume that you are playing golf with Arnold Palmer and O. J. Simpson. On the first hole, Palmer gets a hole-in-one; so does Simpson. You take two strokes to complete the hole. When Palmer gets a hole-in-one, you may say to yourself that he is the most skillful golfer in the world. He, in other words, "caused" his ace. You may also say that Simpson, who is not a golfer but is an exceptional athlete, is a pretty good golfer and is also pretty lucky. If you have never played golf before, you would certainly say that you were lucky; in other words, that some factors outside of your ability and motivation caused you to play so well.

In this example, you attributed the causes of three similar acts to different combinations of personal and environmental factors. You saw Palmer's score as due primarily to personal factors, especially his skill. You attributed Simpson's score to a combination of personal and environmental factors, perhaps ability and good conditions. You credited your own score to environmental factors—luck, or perhaps conditions that made the hole particularly easy on that day.

Whenever we are confronted with such events, we attempt to determine the relative causal contributions of personal and environmental factors. As the golfing example implies, personal forces involve the *ability* of the actor and a *motivational* property, referred to as *trying*. If you are engaged in a contest with a particularly skillful opponent and the score is very close, you may determine that your opponent's ability is high but her motivation is low; she could beat you badly if she tried. The most obvious and direct way to determine whether a person *can* do something is to observe actual behavior; a person can do something if he or she actually does it. But actions may be misleading. If you got a hole-in-one playing golf your first time out, most observers would not conclude that your ability and motivation produced it. Instead, they would probably attribute it to luck or some other external factor.

In evaluating whether a person can do something, we also assess the difficulty of the task. If the task is easy and a person doesn't do it, then we are apt to attribute the failure to lack of motivation; he or she didn't want to do it. If the task is difficult and the person doesn't do it, then we are apt to attribute the failure to the environment, or to the difficulty of the task, rather than to motivation or ability. If the task is difficult and a person does it, we are likely to seek further evidence before deciding that the causes of success were personal or environmental. Does the person succeed consistently? If the person succeeds only once in a great while in performing a difficult task, observers are likely to attribute success to the environment, to luck. This can been seen in an observation made by William Foote Whyte (1943) in his study of a street-corner gang. Whyte reports that a favored activity of the Norton Street gang was bowling. Members of the gang judged a bowler not by his strikes, but by his ability to get spares. The strike, a highly inconsistent occurrence, was considered a matter of chance.

It is important to remember that attribution theory is concerned less with the actual causes of a person's behavior than with observers' inferences about those causes. The fact that we believe Palmer's hole-in-one is due to skill is psychologically important whether or not it is accurate. We are dealing with *perceived* causes of behavior, not with *actual* causes.

Jones and Davis' Theory of Correspondence   The theory developed by E. E. Jones and Davis (1965) was intended to account "for a perceiver's inferences about what an actor was trying to achieve by a particular action" (p. 222). Jones and Davis emphasize those inferences that relate to some personal disposition or characteristic of the actor.

An observer is provided with some behavior and the effects of that behavior, as well as some information about the situation in which the behavior takes place. On the basis of these types of information, the observer will attempt to infer the underlying causes of the behavior. Jones and Davis are concerned with whether the behavior is perceived as intentional, and whether the cause of the behavior is seen to lie in the person or in the environment.

When an observer infers that a behavior was caused by some personal disposition of the actor, that inference is *correspondent* to the extent that it adequately explains the behavior in question. In general, correspondence will be high when the actor's behavior has a low probability of occurrence in the situation and the actor has a high degree of choice in whether or not to perform the act. We may think of correspondence as accuracy of inference. A few examples will help to clarify these concepts.

How much information can we gain from the behavior of a person in a particular situation? Observers make an appraisal of the situation and decide how likely certain behaviors are to occur. A student might engage in a number of different behaviors during a lecture. Each of these behaviors has a somewhat different likelihood of occurrence. From most to least probable, they are: facing the front of the room while taking notes; facing the front of the room while talking to a student in the next seat; facing the front of the room while reading a newspaper; facing the front of the room while sleeping; facing the rear of the room.

According to Jones and Davis, the least likely behaviors provide the observer with the most information about the personal dispositions of the actor. Students whose behavior is most probable—those who face the front of the room and take notes during a lecture—may do so for any number of reasons, some personal and some environmental. They may want to learn, may wish to do well on the next exam, may be worried about losing their scholarships, may be embarrassed if the lecturer notices they are not paying attention, or they may be conforming to a social norm. The first two reasons are personal; they refer to the students' intentions and motives. The last three reasons are external; they refer to environmental pressures that force the students to behave in a certain fashion.

In general, behavior that conforms to expectations provides the observer with little information about the personal motives or intentions of the actor, since there are usually external pressures to conform to such expectations (E. E. Jones, Davis, & Gergen, 1961; see also Calder, 1974). On the other hand, when behavior is strong enough to overcome expectations, observers are apt to ascribe some personal cause to the actor. A student who faces the rear of the room during a lecture must overcome external pressures to face the front. Therefore, observers are likely to infer that such behavior is caused by some desire, motive, or intention on the part of that student.

There are two consequences of such distinctive behaviors. First, observers tend to infer that the behaviors are caused by personal characteristics of the actor rather than by environmental characteristics. Second, observers are more *confident* in their attributions of the causes of unexpected behavior than they are of in-role, conforming behavior (cf. Berscheid, Graziano, Monson, & Dermer, 1976).

The perceived freedom of the actor to engage in particular behaviors also influences attributions about the causes of those behaviors. If a person is coerced or pressured into performing an act, inferences about the actor's intentions and motives will be ambiguous. But if someone freely chooses to do something, then observers are likely to infer that the behavior reflects some desire, motivation, or intention of the actor (see Bem, 1967; I. D. Steiner, 1970).

One implication of Jones and Davis' analysis of causal attribution is that two people may engage in the same behavior, but attributions about the causes of their behavior may differ, depending on observers' analyses of the situation. In studies by Thibaut and Riecken (1955), for example, subjects were introduced to two students, one with high status (a graduate student) and one with low status (an undergraduate student). In one of the studies, the subjects constructed a crossword puzzle with either a high- or low-status student. The subjects soon found they needed the help of the student. The experimenter encouraged the subjects to ask for help by writing a request to the student. After several such requests, the student complied with the subjects' requests for assistance. Later the subjects were asked whether they thought the student helped them because "he is a nice guy or because you put pressure on him?"

The results indicate that the student of high status was perceived as helping because he was a nice guy; that is, attribution about the cause of his behavior was internal. The low-status helper was seen as helping because he was persuaded by the subject's notes; that is, external pressure caused him to help. Thus, the same behavior can be interpreted as either internally or externally caused depending on the analysis of the situation.

Similar research by Jones and his colleagues on the use of compliments also demonstrates that compliments from high-status persons are perceived as sincere, while those from low-status persons are seen as insincere flattery and ingratiation strategies (E. E. Jones, 1964; E. E. Jones, Gergen, & Jones, 1963; Taylor & Jaggi, 1974).

In general, these studies demonstrate that when there is a sufficient external cause for a behavior, observers tend to see that external cause as the explanation for the behavior. When no external cause is available to account for a behavior, observers tend to attribute the cause to some characteristic of the actor.

Further development of attribution theory by Harold Kelley viewed the process in a wide variety of contexts and enabled social psychologists to explore attributional processes as a basic form of social perception.

Kelley's Theory of Attribution   Like scientists, lay people in general tend to draw conclusions about the causes of events and behavior by using inductive logic. In particular, Kelley (1967, 1973) notes similarities between the scientist's use of statistical techniques, namely, the analysis of variance (see Chapter 2), and the comparisons that people make in general. The analysis of variance requires the statistician to compare events across time, people, and different circumstances. Likewise, causal inferences are based on variability in behavior over time, situations, and people. These three variables are the basic constructs in Kelley's attribution theory.

There are, as Kelley notes, two situations in which attributions are made. In the first, the observer has information over time, from multiple observations. For example, we may observe a particular

In football as in science, a single observation tells us very little about a behavior. Did the referee make a bad call? Is the coach mad because his team is losing? Or are both men putting on a good show for the fans? We can't tell from this one photographic observation.

person in a variety of situations, and on the basis of all this information, draw inferences about the causes of that person's behavior. In the second case, we observe a single individual in a single situation at only one moment. Here, we attempt to assess the situation, determine how other people might behave in that situation, and then draw conclusions about the causes of the actor's behavior.

In the case of multiple observations, or "covariation," the observer can make a confident attribution to the environment if (1) the actor's response is distinctively associated with the object or stimulus; (2) the response is similar to responses made by other persons to the same object; and (3) the response is consistent over time. These three variables are referred to as (1) *distinctiveness*, (2) *consensus*, and (3) *consistency*.

To use a much-borrowed example from Leslie McArthur (1972), if John laughs at a comedian, and almost everyone who hears this comedian laughs at him (high consensus), while John does not laugh at most other comedians (high distinctiveness), and, in the past, John has always laughed at the same comedian (high consistency), then observers will attribute the cause of John's laughter to the environment, that is, to the comedian. When distinctiveness, consensus, and consistency are high, attributions should be made to the environment. When consensus and distinctiveness are low, attributions should be made to the person. For example, if John laughs at Don Rickles, and hardly anyone else laughs at Rickles (low consensus), and if John also laughs at most other comedians (low distinctiveness), but in the past has not laughed at Rickles (high consistency), then John's laughter will be attributed to some characteristic of John. In general, McArthur's research supports Kelley's model, although she found that attributions toward dispositions of the actor were influenced more by distinctiveness information than by consensus or consistency (see also Nisbett & Borgida, 1975; Ruble & Feldman, 1976; Suls & Miller, 1976.)

In the case of a single observation, which Kelley (1973) refers to as configuration, attributions are made on the basis of an assessment of a single situation. Kelley proposes that "the role of a given cause in producing a given effect is discounted if other plausible causes are also present." This is referred to as the *discounting principle*. If both internal and external causes for a given action are plausible, the internal cause is apt to be discounted, or given less weight. This is evident in the Thibaut and Riecken (1955) study discussed earlier. The discounting principle can also be seen in the case of a person attempting to determine the causes of his or her own behavior, as well as in causal attribution for the behavior of others. Daryl Bem (1967), who has taken a radical behaviorist position, argues that self-perceptions are based on much the same kinds of information as the perceptions of others. If a person does something and then is asked, "Why did you do that?" there is a tendency to examine the environment for plausible causes of the behavior. If such external causes are present, the person attributes the behavior to the environment. If external causes are absent, the person attributes the behavior to some internal disposition.

E. E. Jones and Nisbett (1971) proposed that there is a tendency to attribute the causes of an actor's behavior to some disposition of the actor, that is, to see another's behavior as a reflection of personality and temperament. There is an opposite tendency when it comes to attributing the causes of our own behavior. In self-attribution, we tend to see the causes of our own behavior as a result of environmental influences. Thus, if you observe Fred in an argument with Tom, you are likely to perceive Fred as argumentative and aggressive. If you were involved in an argument with Tom, you would most likely attribute your behavior to the circumstances, seeing Tom as an instigator or defending your behavior as "the only thing to do in that situation." (See also Monson & Snyder, 1977.)

There are a number of reasons for this difference in other- and self-perception. As an actor, your focus tends to be on the immediate situation. As an observer of another, your focus is primarily on the other's behavior. These results have been replicated in a number of studies (e.g., Nisbett, Caputo, Legant, & Maracek, 1973; Storms, 1973), and are widely accepted as general attributional tendencies. They are not all-pervasive, however, because a reversal of these typical findings may be seen in a number of examples. People who have become famous overnight are frequent guests on television talk shows. As I write these pages, Farrah Fawcett-Majors is the most prominent example (though as you read them, you may wonder who she is). Such guests are perceived to have had lucky breaks, to have been in the right place at the right time. Their success, in other words, is perceived to be the result of external factors. When asked about their instant stardom, however, they frequently describe their success as the result of long, hard training, self-sacrifice, and business acumen. They see as the causes of their own success internal, personal dispositions. This reversal is probably due to the quality of the behavior. When behavior is negative or unfavorable, we tend to hold others responsible; when it is positive or favorable, we tend to see ourselves as the causal agents (e.g., Arkin, Gleason, & Johnston, 1975; Monson & Snyder, 1977; Weiner, 1974; Weiner, Frieze, Kukla, Reed, Rest, & Rosenbaum, 1971).

Social deviance is one of the areas in which this tendency to attribute the causes of others' behavior to personal traits and our own behavior to situational traits is clear. Beginning with the work of Thomas Szasz (1961), the question of whether people can suffer from "psychopathology" has been raised. Are people whose behavior

This girl is probably wondering what her mother will say about the accidental demise of tonight's dessert. Would the boy be more upset if his sister had dropped Mother's best vase?

is distinctive, low in consistency, and low in consensus correctly diagnosed as "abnormal personalities"? Or is the tendency to label as "mentally ill" someone whose behavior seems bizarre merely a result of attributional tendencies? While this issue will be dealt with in detail in Chapter 13, it can be stated here that diagnosing mental (or physical) illnesses is a problem in attribution. Psychologists, psychiatrists, and physicians may see some people's behavior as the result of their personalities; if their behavior is bizarre, then their personalities are also perceived as bizarre. However, when such people are asked to analyze their own behavior, they rarely see it as the product of an abnormal personality (Menapace & Doby, 1976).

Attribution of Responsibility Most of the theories of attribution considered thus far have been concerned with determining which of an actor's behaviors, and which of the effects of those behaviors, are intentional and which are caused by characteristics of the environment. Research on attribution of responsibility deals explicitly with unintentional consequences of actions.

Psychologists' interest in attribution of responsibility can be traced to Jean Piaget's work on moral judgment in children (1932/1950). Piaget described a sequential series of moral stages through

Table 4.2.
Mean Responsibility Assigned for the Accident

	Car Damage		Car Damage + Injury to Bystander	
	Mild Consequences	Severe Consequences	Mild Consequences	Severe Consequences
Amount of responsibility assigned to Lennie	2.5	3.0	2.6	3.2

Note: The higher the mean, the more responsibility assigned to Lennie. From Walster (1966, p. 77).

which children progress. At the earliest stages, only the consequences of an action influence moral judgments, while at later stages of moral judgment, the intentions of the actor are taken into consideration. For example, if Ann accidentally breaks an expensive object and Betty intentionally breaks an inexpensive object, children at the earlier stages of moral development will judge Ann to be more responsible than Betty. Children at higher levels of moral judgment will judge Betty to be more responsible, because it was her intention to break something (see also Sampson, 1978).

If intentions are held constant, then there is a tendency to make attributions of responsibility on the basis of consequences. In an early social psychological study on attribution of responsibility, Elaine Walster (1966) presented college students with descriptions of various car accidents. In all cases, she emphasized that the events were not intended by the actors. In half the cases, the actor's car was seriously damaged, while in the other half, it was only slightly damaged. Crossed with this variable was either slight or serious injury to an innocent bystander. In all cases, the students were told that the actor, Lennie, had parked his car on a hill and set the hand brake. They were told that the brake cable had probably snapped and that the car had rolled downhill, with consequent slight or severe damage to Lennie's car or to a bystander. Subjects, after hearing one of the four versions of the story, were asked to make judgments about Lennie's responsibility for the accident. The results support Walster's hypothesis that more responsibility would be assigned to Lennie when the damage was severe than when it was slight. There was a tendency to attribute greater responsibility when another party was involved, as the data in Table 4.2 indicate.

The results of the Walster study have been qualified by more recent research. In particular, attribution of responsibility to the actor has been found to be greatest when there is some personal relationship between subject and victim (Shaver, 1970), when the victim is seen as respectable (C. Jones & Aronson, 1973), when subjects do not expect to find themselves in circumstances similar to the actor in the near future (Chaikin & Darley, 1973), and when subjects are in a group and the accident is presented as having had negative consequences (Mynatt & Sherman, 1975).

All these studies found that there is a tendency to attribute responsibility, or blame, for the serious consequences of an accident. Various other considerations determine how much the victim is held responsible and how much responsibility is attributable to the environment (usually to luck or chance). In reality, most accidents are caused by a series of events occurring over time, not just a single event.

The studies mentioned thus far all concern configurational situations, observations made at a single time. There may be covariational situations in which an observer has information from more than one temporal point. Such was the situation investigated by Brickman, Ryan, and Wortman (1975). They presented college students with information about an accident and varied the immediate cause (by presenting the accident as caused by internal or external attributes) and the prior cause of the accident. The immediate cause of the accident was either internal (the driver was not looking at the road) or external (the steering failed). The prior cause was either internal (the driver had experienced steering problems before but had not had the car checked) or external (a mechanic improperly repaired the car) or unclear.

The results of the experiment indicate that prior causes can cancel the effects of immediate causes; that greater importance is attached to internal causes than to external causes, regardless of whether they are immediate or prior; and that there are differences in the impact of immediate and prior causes when they are both internal and both external. The driver was held most responsible for the accident when there were both internal immediate and internal prior causes. The driver was held least responsible when there were both external immediate and external prior causes. There was a tendency for subjects to assign responsibility when one or both causes were internal to the driver. This has been reported in other studies as well (e.g., Lerner, 1970; Walster, 1966) and may represent a defensive bias against viewing accidents as caused by external factors because this would imply that they could happen to anyone, including oneself. Brickman and colleagues also report that "immediate causes were rated as more important in internal chains, while prior causes were rated as more important in external chains" (p. 1066).

Summary

Social perception is a broad and pervasive topic. Because social psychologists are nearly always interested in situations in which two or more people interact, it is important to understand some of the ways in which people perceive one another, the kinds of judgments they make about others, and the processes that influence their impressions and perceptions of social events.

Whether we are discussing impression formation, attribution of causality, or object perception, one principle underlies these processes: the need to make psychological sense of our experience. We tend to see other people as whole entities, consistent in a number of ways. We tend to see their behavior as caused by personal and environmental features; and we assign responsibility to them for the outcomes of their behavior partly on the basis of its importance and meaning to us as observers.

Nearly all the theory and research discussed in this chapter has a cognitive/rationalist perspective. While there are noncognitive approaches to social perception, they have not been very influential in contemporary social psychology.

The motivations to form impressions, to perceive people as whole entities, to evaluate the causal bases for events, all stem from the cognitive assumption that people have a need to make sense of their experience. Social psychologists studying person perception and attribution are less concerned with how these judgments arise and with how they influence behavior. As the sociologist W. I. Thomas proposed, "If men define situations as real, they are real in their consequences." Social psychologists studying social perception have tried to assess such consequences.

Perception is not a passive process. It is influenced by expectations, past experiences, language, and culture. Objects that we are used to seeing, those that we are set to see, and those for which we have readily available linguistic categories are most readily perceived. Our perceptions, then, are determined in part by our cognitions, which set limits on what we are most likely to perceive.

Implicit theory of personality refers to the notion that we believe certain personality traits are closely related to other traits. When we learn that a person possesses one of these traits, we assume the other traits are also present.

Implicit theories of personality arise from past experience; they are, in other words, learned ways of perceiving others. Psychologically, implicit theories may be seen as devices to simplify perception. As Gestalt theorists have argued, perception tends to be as simple and unified as conditions permit. Just as people tend to perceive incomplete figures as closed, they also tend to see other people as having rounded, complete, and integrated personalities.

While people in different cultures seem to have different notions of personality structure, there are common elements in various cultures' implicit theories of personality. In particular, distinctive information about others is more often used as the basis for impressions of them than information common to many or all people.

Implicit theories provide us with expectations about the behavior of others. Expectations in general are powerful determinants of perception and may lead to self-fulfilling prophecies. What we believe to be the case may actually occur as the result of our behavior. For example, teachers who believe that certain of their students are gifted will behave so as to encourage these students to outperform their classmates.

Heider, Jones, and Davis, and Kelley have proposed that attribution of causality is a basic component of human social behavior. They assume there is a human need to make causal assessments of events in the environment. Social psychologists have gone beyond a concern with the actual causes of physical and social events and have focused on the perceived causes of events. These perceived causes of behavior and events are studied under the heading of attribution.

Suggested Readings

* Hastorf, A. H., Schneider, D., & Ellsworth, P. *Person perception,* 2nd. ed. Reading, Mass.: Addison-Wesley, 1979.
* La France, M., & Mayo, C. *Moving bodies: Nonverbal communication in social relationships.* Monterey, Calif.: Brooks/Cole, 1978.
Shaver, K. G. *An introduction to attribution processes.* Cambridge, Mass.: Winthrop, 1975.

* Available in paperback edition.

5
ATTITUDE CHANGE, PROPAGANDA, AND COMMUNICATION

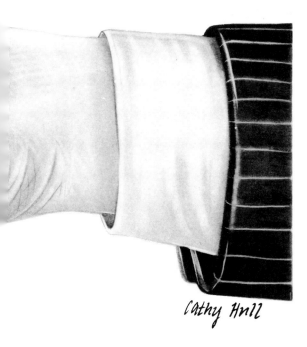

Cathy Hull

Only humans have a sense of history. We know that a civil war was fought in the United States in the last century, though none of us witnessed it. We know of such historical events because we've read about them, seen photographs of them, and heard verbal reports from those who were there. It is only through communication and physical artifacts that we are aware of our ancestral past. Communication often makes life difficult for us; but without communication, a sense of who we are, where we came from, and where we're going would be impossible.

Language is sometimes regarded as the major distinction between *Homo sapiens* and other species. Our culture is passed on from one generation to the next, largely through written and oral communication. Without communication, each generation would have to learn nearly everything anew and cumulative progress from one generation to another would disappear.

Social psychologists interested in communication have generally explored the development and nature of language; persuasive communications and their effects on attitudes and behavior; the mass media of communication; and the communication of meaning through nonverbal gestures and expressions. We reviewed some of the work on language development and nonverbal communication in Chapter 4. In this chapter, we examine the effects of persuasive communications and mass media.

THE NATURE OF COMMUNICATION

Communication is the process whereby meaning or information is conveyed from one person to another. In any act of communication there is always a *source* of a *message* delivered through some *channel* to some *recipient* or *audience* with some *effects*. The process of communication, then, involves who says what to whom through which medium and with what consequences (Lasswell & Casey, 1946). The effects may include purely cognitive responses, such as attention, comprehension, and retention, as well as behavioral responses, such as yielding to the message and acting on its behalf (McGuire, 1969). Social psychologists have generally focused on yielding to a communication, that is, on accepting the conclusions or implications of a message and acting or altering behavior as a consequence of having received a message.

Communication is a social process in which both parties, the communicator and the recipient, are actively involved. Not only is communication a social process, it is in many respects the most fundamental social act. Nearly every other social behavior, including attribution, altruism, conformity, aggression, and attraction, depends on the communication of intentions, needs, wants, and infor-

Although mass communication is usually one-way and impersonal, the general public can respond through person-on-the-street interviews and letters to the editor. We also choose our favorite newspaper or TV channel.

mation from one person to another. Communication actively involves both parties whether or not they are in a face-to-face setting. In face-to-face, or personal, situations, the parties engaged in communication typically alternate positions of communicator and recipient (Gallois & Markel, 1975). First, one person speaks to the second, who in turn then speaks to the first, and so on. In impersonal situations, such as mass-media-like newspapers and television, there is generally a fixed direction of communication, with the media serving as sources of messages and the recipients as the audience. Of course, most newspapers and some television programs allow for comments from the audience in the form of letters to the editor or the expression of opposition viewpoints, but even without these responses, the audience is still active in that it is selectively attending to and interpreting the communications presented.

It is possible to analyze communication processes from the viewpoint of communicator–recipient relationships; that is, who says what to whom (Watson et al., 1948). We know that some people are more likely to communicate certain things to certain other people (S. Rosen & Tesser, 1970). Social psychologists have studied the network of communications in small groups of people in order to map the frequency with which any given individual communicates with any other. They have also imposed certain communication rules on groups in order to determine the effects of communication structure on other characteristics of the group (see Chapter 9). We know, too, that certain kinds of communication are most apt to follow the general social structure, with superiors directing orders and even jokes at subordinates (Brown & Gilman, 1960; Castell & Goldstein, 1977; Coser, 1960). There is considerable interest, too, in studying particular types of communications, such as gossip and rumors (Rosnow & Fine, 1976), requests for assistance (Langer & Abelson, 1972), and social aspects of language (Ervin-Tripp, 1969).

Mass communication has been studied extensively by social psychologists, particularly the effects of portrayals of violence on television (see Chapter 8). Some interesting work has also been done on other social effects of the mass media, including radio, television, and newspapers (e.g., Himmelweit, Oppenheim, & Vince, 1958; Payne & Payne, 1970; G. A. Steiner, 1963; W. Weiss, 1969), and the messages presented in the mass media have been studied to determine their social or political implications (e.g., Bagdikian, 1962; Holsti, 1969; Suedfeld, 1978). In addition to studying the communicator, channel, and message, social psychologists have investigated the characteristics of the recipients in order to determine which types of individual are most apt to respond to a communication under certain circumstances (e.g., Janis, Hovland, Field, Linton, Graham, Cohen, Rife, Abelson, Lesser, & King, 1959; M. B. Smith, Bruner, & White, 1956). Before analyzing these aspects of the communication process, we will review the theories of attitude change and social influence, which will serve as background to a more detailed analysis of the communication process.

Communications are designed to influence their recipients in some ways. Sometimes the influence process is largely cognitive; for example, in education, where knowledge is presumably communicated to students. At other times the purpose of communication is to change the attitudes or behaviors of the audience. We may speak of these latter types of communications as *persuasive communications*, or propaganda, and of their effects as a type of *social influence*. Because communication is always a social process, its effects on attitudes and behaviors are the products of social influence.

SOME THEORIES OF ATTITUDE CHANGE

Because of the profound influence of two very different social psychologists, one a field/cognitive theorist and one a learning theorist, there are essentially two primary types of attitude change theory today. One sizable group of theories, known as *cognitive consistency* theories, stems from the work of Kurt Lewin. There is also a variety of behaviorist/learning theories of attitude change, and most of these can be traced to the influence of Carl I. Hovland. There are, of course, many variations on these two general themes (McGuire, 1969; Oskamp, 1977; Ostrom, 1968).

While there are many different theories of attitude change and social influence, they frequently make the same predictions about the occurrence or extent of change, and often are applicable only to limited aspects of the communication setting (e.g., Fazio, Zanna, & Cooper, 1977; A. G. Greenwald, 1975b). Some theories seem to be more appropriate for explaining public events, while others are best able to account for private beliefs. Some theories are better at explaining the effects of different communicators on persuasion, while others focus primarily on the message and its construction. Still other theories, for example, psychoanalytic theory, focus largely on the needs served by a change in attitudes (e.g., D. Katz, 1960). The great diversity of theory, in other words, does not mean that one theory is right and all others wrong. As we shall see, most theories have received at least modest empirical support and are worth retaining until we have a more comprehensive theory with which to replace them (see Fishbein & Ajzen, 1975). It is best to think of these theoretical approaches as complementary rather than as mutually exclusive.

COGNITIVE CONSISTENCY THEORIES

The underlying basis for cognitive consistency theories is the Gestalt notion that people have a need to organize, simplify, and integrate their perceptions and cognitions. When people are shown incomplete figures, for example, they tend to round them off, to form "good *Gestalten*" from them. This is assumed to be as true of cognitions as of perceptions. Our beliefs and thoughts about the external world are assumed to be organized into meaningful, unified, and "symmetrical" structures. Lewin contributed the idea that such perceptions or cognitions exist in a dynamic field and can exert pressure on one another toward change. Hence, if one or more cognitions does not seem to fit with others, an uncomfortable state of psychological tension is produced in the person, who then becomes motivated to reduce this discomfort by resolving the inconsistency in some way.

Take as an example a person who holds fundamentalist religious beliefs; let's call him Graham Roberts. To Mr. Roberts, God is even-handed and just and rules the universe according to a beneficent grand scheme (see Lerner, 1970). Suppose that on the way to a fund-raising affair for orphans, a good friend of Graham's is seriously injured in an automobile accident. This cognition—the knowledge that a "good person" was injured while attempting to perform a charitable act—does not square with Graham's other cognitions about the just and orderly nature of the universe. The fact that all these cognitions do not fit together neatly and consistently produces a state of psychological discomfort in Graham, and this discomfort becomes a motivational force to resolve the inconsistency.

Graham may do one of the following to reduce his feelings of discomfort: (1) change his view of the benign and just nature of God; (2) change his view of his friend, who may not have been as altruistic as Graham at first believed; (3) conclude that some events in the universe are random or meaningless and are not part of God's grand scheme; (4) decide that his friend's accident is totally irrelevant to the nature of God and the universe; (5) believe that God is still just and the universe still operates on a divine scheme, but that such events happen because of the sinful nature of man; (6) view the accident as trivial. Any of these changes in cognition will help reduce the inconsistency produced by the friend's accident. Many cognitive consistency theories treat the causes and resolutions of such inconsistencies. We will review a few of the more important theories here.

Heider's Balance Model   The balance model of Fritz Heider (1958) was discussed in Chapter 1, and variants of the theory, in particular that proposed by Newcomb (1953), are discussed in Chapter 6. Balance theory is somewhat limited for understanding attitude change and communication. It is applicable only to situations in which two people have attitudes toward some object. For example, if Paul and Olivia each have some attitude toward X-rated movies, balance theory can determine whether that interpersonal system is balanced. If Paul and Olivia share the same attitude toward X-rated movies, the system is balanced. If they do not share the same attitude, the system is unbalanced and a motivational force to restore balance is established. When unbalanced states exist, the theory predicts that one of the attitudes in the system will change or that some cognitive distortion or misperception will occur. Clearly, a useful theory of attitude change based on cognitive consistency has to be more general than balance theory. Despite several attempts to increase the generality of Heider's ideas, most notably by Cartwright and Harary (1956) and Abelson and Rosenberg (1958), it was not until Leon Festinger proposed the cognitive dissonance theory (1957) that we had a general consistency model of attitude change.

Festinger's Theory of Cognitive Dissonance   Cognitive dissonance theory is perhaps the most interesting theory in all of social psychology. Not only is it the most highly researched theory in the field, it is also one of the most controversial. Since its appearance in 1957, dissonance theory has been attacked—and defended—on grounds of internal logic, implications for research, and the methodology by which research has been conducted (e.g., Chapanis & Chapanis, 1964; Nuttin, 1975; M. J. Rosenberg, 1965; Silverman, 1964; Tedeschi, Schlenker, & Bonoma, 1971; Wicklund & Brehm, 1976b).

Festinger's theory can be seen both as an extension of Heider's balance model and as a continuation of Festinger's earlier work on social comparison and social support (Festinger, 1954; Festinger, Riecken, & Schachter, 1956). Unlike previous cognitive consistency theories, however, dissonance theory is broadly applicable to a variety of social and personal situations. Like unbalanced states, cognitive dissonance is a motivational state that arises whenever two or more cognitions are not logically consistent with one another. For example, the cognition that God is just and the knowledge that a friend is injured in an accident are not logically consistent and will produce a state of dissonance. Unlike Heider's original notion of imbalance, dissonance may vary in degree or intensity. The magnitude of dissonance depends on the importance and number of cognitions that are inconsistent. The greater the importance of the involved cognitions and the more cognitions that are logically inconsistent, the greater the degree of dissonance. The magnitude of dissonance may be expressed as the number of dissonant over the number of consonant cognitions.

$$\text{Magnitude of dissonance} = \frac{\text{number of dissonant cognitions}}{\text{number of consonant cognitions}}$$

Festinger proposed three ways by which dissonance can be reduced. Suppose that someone who smokes cigarettes believes that smoking is bad for her health. This inconsistency produces dissonance, which can be reduced by (1) changing a behavior (stop smoking); (2) changing an environmental cognition (distort the extent of the health hazard, for example, by saying that smoking isn't all that dangerous); or (3) adding other cognitions to reduce the extent of dissonance (e.g., "Smoking may be dangerous, but it relaxes me").

In general, research on dissonance theory has been conducted along three main lines of inquiry: selective exposure to information, insufficient justification or forced compliance, and postdecision processes.

According to dissonance theory, people are motivated both to avoid situations that produce dissonance and to seek situations that are consonant with existing cognitions, attitudes, and beliefs. If you have just purchased a new car, for example, the theory predicts that you will continue to read advertisements for your make of car because the ads tend to justify your choice by telling you how good your car is. You will avoid advertisements for other makes of automobile because these are dissonant with your decision. This is referred to as *selective exposure to information.*

In an early study on this type of selective exposure, it was found that people tend to seek consonant information, but do not tend to avoid dissonance-increasing information (D. Ehrlich, Guttman,

Schönbach, & Mills, 1957). Other research has also failed to find support for the dissonance theory prediction that people always avoid inconsistent or dissonant information (e.g., Freedman, 1965). Rhine (1967) has pointed out that it is hard to tell whether people are seeking or avoiding information if they are given a choice between only two types of information. For example, suppose you are asked to choose between a pamphlet entitled "How to Quit Smoking" and one called "How to Enjoy Your Cigarette More." It would be impossible for a researcher to determine whether you chose the one you did because you were seeking information, or did not choose the other one because you wanted to avoid certain information. It has been suggested that people may intentionally expose themselves to dissonant information in order to refute it. A smoker might choose the dissonant pamphlet on quitting smoking in order to argue that the techniques in the booklet wouldn't work for him. When dissonant information is easy to refute, then people will attend to it (Kleinhesselink & Edwards, 1975). The evidence with regard to seeking consonant information is fairly consistent and supports the theory.

How often have you done something you really didn't want to do, only to find that it wasn't quite as bad as you thought it would be? According to dissonance theory, when we do something with *insufficient justification*, this produces a state of dissonance that can be reduced either by exaggerating the external justification or by changing our attitude toward the behavior performed. For example, imagine that someone asks you to argue for a position in which you don't believe, say, for a hike in tuition at your college. To induce you to take this dissonant position, he is willing to pay you $1. Being an impoverished student, you accept. You argue for a tuition hike, after which you are asked how you really feel about raising tuition. What do you say? According to dissonance theory, it would be dissonant to argue for a tuition hike when you are personally opposed to one. So these two cognitions are dissonant. But consonant with your decision to argue for a tuition hike was your thirst for money; the $1 mitigates the extent of dissonance somewhat. Surely you would have more dissonance than someone in the same position who received $20 for making the same argument, and less dissonance than someone who argued for a tuition hike for no incentive at all.

In early studies on just this type of situation (A. R. Cohen, 1962; Festinger & Carlsmith, 1959), it was found that those who received the least external incentives for taking dissonant stands changed their attitudes the most in the direction of their public positions. Those who argued for a tuition hike for very little external justification came to believe that tuition should be raised to a higher level than those who received a great deal of justification, such as $20, for taking a similar stance.

In the initial study in this area, Festinger and Carlsmith (1959) had male college students spend an hour working on a boring task (turning pegs and packing spools). At the end of the hour, they were told that the experiment was over but that the experimenter would like to hire them to introduce the next subject to the experiment. It was explained that the research assistant who generally did this had failed to show up. The subject was to tell the next subject in the waiting room that the experiment was enjoyable and fun. Some of the subjects were offered $1 (low reward) and some $20 (high reward) to act as assistant. After each subject/assistant told the waiting subject about the experiment, he was interviewed about his reactions to the experiment. He was asked, among other things, to indicate how enjoyable the experimental tasks were and whether he was suspicious about the experiment. Of over 50 subjects in the two reward groups, more than 20 percent were eliminated because of suspicions about the procedure or because of their refusal to lie to the waiting subject. For the remaining subjects, the results show that the enjoyment of the task was greatest for the low-reward subjects.

These studies did not sit well with many psychologists, particularly those of a learning theory orientation, who viewed monetary incentives as reinforcements. The greater the magnitude of positive reinforcement for engaging in a behavior, the more that behavior should be learned. So, a subject who argues that a boring task was fun and receives $20 for doing so should learn that attitude better than someone who receives only $1 for making the same argument. Learning theorists conducted their own set of studies on this problem with quite different results. Several studies varied the reward for complying with the experimenter's request to write counterattitudinal essays, which were said to be required for a worthwhile (high-reward) or not worthwhile (low-reward) sponsor (Elms & Janis, 1965; Janis & Gilmore, 1965). The results of these studies tend to support a learning theory interpretation: greater rewards produced more attitude change in the direction of the written essay.

When two major theories make opposite predictions and each of them has some empirical support, it is probable that each is correct only under certain circumstances. It took quite a while for these differences between dissonance and learning theories to be resolved to any degree. But after a decade of research it seems that a set of conditions may be specified to indicate when minimum justification will lead to greater attitude change (the dissonance theory position) and when maximum incentives will lead to maximum change (the learning theory position). The dissonance theory predictions hold only when subjects in the research feel that they are performing the dissonant behavior out of free choice. If they feel forced to perform the behavior, then the learning theory effects will occur (Brehm &

Cohen, 1962; Calder, Ross, & Insko, 1973; Collins & Hoyt, 1972; D. Linder, Cooper, & Jones, 1967). Also, if the dissonant behavior is performed publicly (for example, telling a lie to another person), the dissonance theory predictions hold, while if it is privately performed (for example, writing an anonymous essay), the learning theory position is upheld (Carlsmith, Collins, & Helmreich, 1966; Frey & Irle, 1972).

Whenever a person must make a decision between two or more alternatives, dissonance occurs as a result of the decision. This is called *postdecision dissonance.* Suppose Les Brayns is going to buy a new car and has narrowed the choice down to a Ford or a Chevy. He likes the handling ease and better gas mileage of the Ford and the looks and pep of the Chevy. After much deliberation, Les decides to buy the Chevy and gives the dealer a deposit on the car. At the point Les makes up his mind, dissonance is created. He has chosen a Chevy, which contains some features he does not like, and has rejected a Ford, which contains some features he does like. Both sets of cognitions produce dissonance. The dissonance can be reduced in several ways: by exaggerating the positive features of the chosen alternative, for example, by stressing the clean lines of the Chevy; by minimizing the negative features of the chosen alternative, for example, by saying that the gas mileage isn't as important as the pickup. Dissonance can also be reduced by exaggerating the negative features of the rejected alternative (by saying the Ford is really ugly) and by minimizing its positive features (by saying that it handled all right, but not nearly as well as a Jaguar).

According to dissonance theory, dissonance is created every time we enter into a decision freely and whenever we commit ourselves to one alternative. There is considerable support for these postdecision processes in the research literature, including studies conducted in natural settings. For example, Knox and Inkster (1968) found that, after—rather than just before—placing their bets, bettors at a racetrack are more confident that their horse will win. It is dissonant to place money on a horse we do not feel stands a good chance of winning. Once the decision has been made, however, dissonance is created and can be reduced by increasing our confidence in the correctness of the decision.

A RADICAL BEHAVIORIST
APPROACH TO ATTITUDES: BEM'S
SELF-PERCEPTION THEORY

Cognitive theories of attitude, and cognitive dissonance theory in particular, have been criticized from their inception by behaviorists (e.g., A. G. Greenwald, Brock, & Ostrom, 1968; Nuttin, 1975; Tedeschi, Schlenker, & Bonoma, 1971; Totman, 1973). The behaviorist criticisms revolve about three issues. Cognitive theories are not

According to Knox and Inkster, bettors, after they place their bets, become more confident that their horses will win. Perhaps these men are playing long shots.

parsimonious; that is, they are not as simple and succinct as behaviorists think they should be. Furthermore, concepts such as balance and dissonance are inferred states, in no way observable, and behaviorists abhor such unmeasurable abstractions. Finally, the research methods of the cognitivists can easily be criticized, particularly on the point that large numbers of subjects in dissonance experiments have had to be excluded from the data analysis because of their suspicions about the research or because the independent variable manipulations failed to produce dissonance in them.

Many of the critics of dissonance theory refused to take the results of dissonance research at face value. They believe the results are due to measurement errors, experimenter artifacts, apprehension on the part of the research subjects, and confinement to very limited settings. The learning theorists, in their debate over the effects of small and large incentives on counterattitudinal behavior, are within this group. On the other hand, the criticisms offered by Daryl J. Bem (1965, 1967, 1972) not only accept the results of dissonance studies as reliable, but provide an alternative method for producing them as well. For example, Bem does not doubt that Festinger and Carlsmith found greater liking for a boring task among subjects receiving $1 for telling another person it was enjoyable than among subjects who received $20 for telling the same lie. What he does doubt is that this finding was the result of any psychological process remotely resembling cognitive dissonance.

Borrowing from B. F. Skinner's *Verbal behavior* (1957), Bem argues that attitudes are not psychological entities but self-descriptive statements. If a person is asked her attitude toward chocolate ice cream and says, "I like chocolate ice cream very much," she is merely describing in a summary way her past behavior; in the past she has enjoyed chocolate ice cream and may even have gone out of her way to obtain some. When subjects in experiments are asked to describe their attitudes toward some topic or behavior, they attempt to summarize their own recent behavior. If their behavior with regard to an object can be explained on the basis of environmental forces (called *mands* by Skinner and Bem), their private attitude is uncertain; the behavior was under the control of these external forces and so might not be a reflection of their attitude. But if there are no external forces acting on the person, then his past behavior probably reflects his own attitude toward the object.

Let us take as an example a man who has just signed a murder confession. If asked to state his true belief about having committed homicide, he will look to the environment to determine whether his behavior was under the control of external influences. If he sees a bunch of men standing around with rubber hoses and firearms, he is apt to conclude that he was coerced into signing the confession. His behavior—signing the confession—can be explained by external or environmental causes, and so does not necessarily reflect his "true" attitude. On the other hand, if the man signs the confession when he is alone in his room, he is apt to conclude that his behavior was not caused by external forces and therefore represents his own personal belief.

Bem argues that in cognitive dissonance experiments, subjects make a similar environmental analysis in order to determine how closely their behavior reflects their attitudes. When strong environmental forces can be invoked to account for the behavior, subjects are more likely to infer that their behavior was determined by these forces. When no such external explanations are present, the subjects perceive the behavior as reflecting their own attitudes. Thus, in the Festinger and Carlsmith experiment, when asked what their attitude toward the boring task was, subjects receiving $20 made an environmental appraisal and found quite sufficient reason, namely, $20, for stating to another person that the task was fun. This not inconsequential amount of money was a sufficient external cause for telling a lie. So, when asked what they really thought about the task, the subjects said they thought it was boring because it *was* boring.

Subjects paid $1 were in a different situation. Imagine, for the sake of argument, that they received no money, instead of $1. When asked their attitude toward the task, they would find nothing in the environment to explain why they said the task was fun. Finding no environmental reasons for saying it was fun, they would conclude that their statement that it was fun reflected their true feelings. Why say something was fun unless it was? In the original experiment, however, some subjects received $1, so when they made an appraisal of the environment they found that $1 was an external force pressuring them to say the task was enjoyable. But surely such a small sum was not as potent a force as $20. The subjects concluded that although part of their reason for saying the task was fun was the external force of $1, this force was insufficient to cause them to make the statement and therefore those subjects concluded that the task couldn't have been all that boring.

Bem does not invoke the concept of cognitive dissonance in this analysis. He simply assumes that whenever people are asked what their attitudes are, they determine whether there are external forces that can account for their behavior. If there are few or no such environmental forces, people assume that their behavior reflects their attitudes.

This self-perception theory was highly damaging to dissonance theory, for it provided not only an alternative theoretical interpretation of dissonance phenomena that was much simpler in structure and logic, but also a methodology capable of producing cognitive dissonance-like results without engendering any cognitive conflict in subjects. Bem (1965, 1968, 1972) calls this method *interpersonal replications*.

In his interpersonal replication of the Festinger and Carlsmith (1959) experiment, Bem (1967) had college undergraduates listen to a tape recording that described a college sophomore who had participated in an experiment. They heard that he had performed two motor tasks. Control subjects were asked at this point to evaluate the sophomore's attitude toward these tasks. Two other groups of subjects heard that the sophomore had accepted an offer of either $1 or $20 to go into a waiting room and tell the next subject that the tasks had been enjoyable. The subjects in Bem's experiment then estimated the sophomore's attitude toward the tasks. In this interpersonal replication, Bem tried to present to his subjects the situa-

Table 5.1.

Attitudes and Estimates of Attitudes toward the Tasks for Each Condition

| | Experimental Condition | | |
Study	Control	$1 Compensation	$20 Compensation
Festinger–Carlsmith	−0.45	+1.35	−0.05
Bem Interpersonal Replication	−1.56	+0.52	−1.96

The key question was enjoyableness of the task, rated on a scale of −5 (extremely dull) to +5 (extremely enjoyable). Adapted from Bem (1968, p. 204).

tion actually experienced by a subject in the original experiment. Table 5.1 shows the mean ratings of the tasks for both the original Festinger and Carlsmith study and the Bem study. In this and other interpersonal replications, none of the subjects actually engaged in any dissonant behavior and so could not have experienced dissonance themselves. Yet they were able to predict the results of dissonance experiments quite accurately.

Is there any way to distinguish between cognitive dissonance theory and self-perception theory so that we may choose the better of the two? It has been proposed that the two theories are perhaps only different ways of saying the same thing and that they cannot be experimentally distinguished (A. G. Greenwald, 1975b). But more recent research has shown that dissonance theory can predict results in particular domains where self-perception theory cannot. Dissonance theory has been proposed as a sufficient explanation for behavior that is quite discrepant with initial attitudes, such as telling a lie, while self-perception theory has been offered as the best explanation for behavior that is not so discrepant with initial attitudes (Fazio et al., 1977). And debate goes on.

SOCIAL JUDGMENT THEORY

From the beginning, psychologists have studied perception and the judgment of physical objects, such as the intensity of a light or the loudness of a sound. This research is called *psychophysics* because it explores psychological sensations that result from changes in the physical properties of stimuli. Suppose that rather than judging the extremity of a light or sound, we judge a communication? Here we may apply the techniques of psychophysics to a topic of interest to social psychologists. Attitudes, in this view, are judgments, and attitude change is a perceptual–judgmental process based on our perception of a communicator and a communication. This view is best expressed in the work of Muzafer Sherif (C. W. Sherif, Sherif, & Nebergall, 1965; M. Sherif & Cantril, 1947; M. Sherif & Hovland, 1961), and others (e.g., Helson, 1964).

According to Sherif and his colleagues, we judge a communication (or any other stimulus) not solely in terms of its physical or objective qualities, but also in terms of our subjective scale of reference. For every individual there is a range of acceptable attitudinal positions and a series of unacceptable positions on any given topic. Suppose that Phil Anthropy believes that we should donate 50 percent of our income to charity. Phil is apt to agree that it would be good if people donated as little as 40 percent, and would certainly be pleased if someone donated as much as 70 percent. The positions between 40 and 70 percent represent what Sherif refers to as Phil's *latitude of acceptance*. But Phil would find it unacceptable if we wanted to

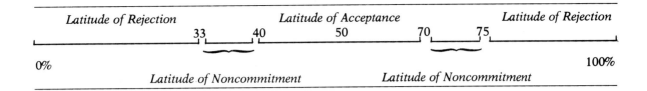

Figure 5.1.
Percent of income to be donated to charity: the latitudes of acceptance, rejection, and noncommitment for Phil Anthropy.

donate less than a third of our income to charity, and might also believe that donating more than three-fourths to charity would not leave enough for us to live on. So, between 0 and 33 percent and between 75 percent and 100 percent would be unacceptable to Phil. These unacceptable areas are referred to as the *latitudes of rejection.* The positions intermediate between the latitude of acceptance and the latitude of rejection are referred to as the *latitudes of noncommitment* (C. W. Sherif et al., 1965). (See Figure 5.1.)

When communications advocate positions that fall within the individual's latitude of acceptance, they are perceived to be closer to the individual's own attitudinal position than they actually are. These communications are *assimilated* toward the person's own position. Communications expressing a position within the person's latitude of rejection are seen as more discrepant from the person's own position than they actually are; they are *contrasted* with the person's position. For example, suppose that Phil meets two people, Ms. Anthropy, who believes that charity undermines people's initiative, and Benny Factor, who thinks we should offer most of what we have to others. Phil is apt to contrast Ms. Anthropy's position and see it as extreme and quite at variance with his own. Depending on how he interprets "most," Phil is likely to assimilate Benny Factor's position and see it as fairly close to his own position.

With regard to attitude change, M. Sherif and Hovland (1961) propose that if we encounter a message advocating a position that lies within our latitude of acceptance, the communication is apt to change our attitude in the direction of the communication. If the position advocated in the message falls within our latitude of rejection, the communication is likely to be contrasted, that is, seen as more extreme than it actually is, and is apt to have little or no influence on our attitudes.

Social judgment theory has been used in some attitude change research, but is more capable of explaining distortions in the judgment of communications and communicators (e.g., Asch, 1948; C. W. Sherif, Kelly, Rodgers, Sarup, & Tittler, 1973) than in explaining the effects of communications on attitude change. Social judgment theory has been useful in studying the effects of discrepancy between a communication's position and the audience's initial position. As we shall see in the section on "The Nature of the Persuasive Communication," social judgment theory has been used to account for the finding that messages advocating increasing amounts of change are more effective in producing change, but only up to a point. Social judgment theory tells us that that point is somewhere between the latitude of acceptance and the latitude of rejection.

ATTITUDE CHANGE AND THE COMMUNICATION PROCESS

We have seen that few, if any, theories of attitude change are broad enough to encompass the entire spectrum of communication effects. Therefore, in order to present important concepts and research on communication and social influence, we will examine each aspect of the communication process separately.

SOURCE CHARACTERISTICS AND PERSUASION

Because much of the early work on persuasion was conducted by learning theorists, a great deal of attention was focused on source and message characteristics, since these comprise the "stimuli" to which attitude change is the "response" (Hovland, Janis, & Kelley, 1953; Hovland, Lumsdaine, & Sheffield, 1949). A traditional learning theory approach to persuasion implies that the recipient must perceive the stimulus, that is, pay attention to the communication, understand it, and adopt the attitude suggested in the communication. This will be done, according to the learning theorists, if the new attitude is seen by the recipient as more rewarding than the recipient's initial attitude.

Among the rewards for paying attention to and accepting the conclusions of a message are the personal benefits that may accrue from going along with the message and doing the same thing as someone whom you respect. For example, if you use Snuggle-up toothpaste, the love of your life will suddenly notice how attractive you are and love, beauty, and health—not to mention clean teeth— will be yours. If you make your coffee in a Mr. Coffee, you can take comfort in the fact that Joe DiMaggio's coffee tastes just like yours. According to learning theory, we tend to attend to and be influenced by a message whose source is seen as highly credible.

Source credibility initially referred to the expertise and trustworthiness of the source of a message (Hovland & Weiss, 1951). The more expert, reliable, and trustworthy the source, the higher its credibility. In recent years, investigators have added several more dimensions to the concept of source credibility. In general, sources perceived as physically attractive (Mills & Aronson, 1965), sources seen as having had relevant experiences similar to those of the recipient (Berscheid, 1966; Brock, 1965), and sources who argue against their own best interests in an apparent show of sincerity (Walster, Aronson, & Abrahams, 1966) are perceived by the audience as more credible. Hence they have more influence than other sources presenting identical communications.

Source Credibility and the "Sleeper Effect" In one of the classic studies on source effects in persuasion, Hovland and Weiss (1951) presented identical communications to two groups, but for one group the communicator was portrayed as "trustworthy," and for the other the communicator was "untrustworthy." For example, one of the communications dealt with whether an atomic-powered submarine was practical. The high-credibility source was the well-known physicist J. Robert Oppenheimer, and the low-credibility source was *Pravda*. In this case, 36 percent of the subjects changed their opinions in the direction of the communication when the source was highly credible, compared to 0 percent when the source was low in credibility.

Hovland and Weiss measured their respondents' opinions immediately after they read the communications, and again four weeks later. There were no differences between the two groups in recall of information from the communication, but there was a difference in change of opinions during the four-week period. The group that had been exposed to the high-credibility communicator showed a decrease in the extent of their agreement with him, while the group exposed to the low-credibility source showed increased agreement with the source. Apparently, the effects of source credibility diminish over time. The authors called this the *sleeper effect*. While the high-credibility source was immediately effective in changing opinions, after four weeks this effectiveness diminished. While the low-credibility source was not very effective immediately, after a period of four weeks there was greater agreement with this position.

A theoretical explanation for the sleeper effect was presented by Kelman and Hovland (1953), who suggested that people are more likely to remember the contents of a message than its source. How often, for example, have you heard someone say, "I read this interesting article about a new diet, but I can't remember where I read it"? Dissociation of source from message presumably leads to the sleeper effect. In their research, Kelman and Hovland, just prior to giving out the delayed opinion questionnaire, reinstated the source by reminding some of the subjects who had communicated the message three weeks earlier. With the source reinstated, there was no evidence of a sleeper effect.

In more recent attempts to produce a sleeper effect, Gillig and Greenwald (1974) failed to find evidence for the full effect in seven experiments. While a highly credible source's message did become less influential over time, there was no evidence of increasing influence of a low-credibility source's message. In reviewing the literature, Gillig and Greenwald suggest that the sleeper effect is not very potent. The statistical significance of the effect is generally weak, and only if we control for the audience's tendencies to counterargue during the reception of a message do we obtain any evidence for the effect (Gruder, Cook, Hennigan, Flay, Alessis, & Halamaj, 1978; Cook et al., 1979).

What can we conclude about the sleeper effect? First, the findings of Gillig and Greenwald do not negate the effects of source credibility on persuasion. High-credibility sources are, in general, more effective than low-credibility sources, both immediately after reception of a message and at any time thereafter (see Zimbardo et al., 1977). Second, Kelman and Hovland's suggestion that a person tends to dissociate the message from the source over time may also be true; in fact, there seems to be evidence that this separation of message from source is fairly common. What the Gillig and Greenwald results suggest is that the sleeper effect is not nearly so robust or so prevalent as previously thought.

It will come as no surprise to you to learn that cognitive dissonance theory often predicts that a low-credibility source will produce more attitude change than a high-credibility source. This, of course, assumes that we are willing to pay attention to such a communicator and comply with the communicator's recommendations. In studies in which subjects were induced to listen to a message whose position they disagreed with, or to engage in behavior they found distasteful, dissonance theory predictions of more effectiveness for low-credibility communicators were often obtained (e.g., Powell, 1965; Smith, 1961). Low-credibility communicators are apt to be more effective than high-credibility communicators only under a set of fairly limited conditions, namely, when the audience commits itself to attending to and adopting the message.

THE NATURE OF THE PERSUASIVE COMMUNICATION

One issue of great interest to social psychologists involves both the communicator and the position advocated by the message. If a citizens' lobby is trying to convince a conservative politician to reduce the military budget, how extreme should the lobbyists' position be? Should they ask for a reduction of 1 percent, 10 percent, or 50 percent? While the lobbyists might regard a budget cut of 1 percent as trivial, the politician might regard it as threatening the security of the United States.

As we saw in our discussion of social judgment theory, our own

A skilled communicator knows how to present a convincing message that will be accepted by the majority. Since politicians have been successfully practicing this technique for centuries, perhaps this woman should contact her representative.

position on an issue influences our perceptions of others' positions. If someone takes a stand at variance with the audience's position, there is a great risk that the audience will misperceive the communicator's position. Should our lobbyists ask for a small, medium, or large cut in the defense budget? Some research suggests that the more change we advocate, the more we are apt to receive (Hovland & Pritzker, 1957). Other studies find that this is true only up to a point, that seeking too much change can have a *boomerang effect* and actually produce no change or change in the opposite direction (Hovland, Harvey, & Sherif, 1957).

As it happens, the effects of discrepancy between the audience's position on attitude change and that of the communicator depend on several additional factors. If the communicator has high credibility, then asking for more change, that is, taking a more extreme position, will result in greater attitude change. If the communicator has low credibility, an extreme position will result in less change than a more moderate position (Aronson, Turner, & Carlsmith, 1963; Bochner & Insko, 1966). Also, if the audience is not highly involved in the issue, there will be greater change with a more discrepant message. If the audience is highly involved in the issue, that is, if it is a controversial issue, a very discrepant message will produce less change than a moderately discrepant message (Freedman, 1964). Finally, asking for increasing amounts of change within the audience's latitude of acceptance will result in increasing attitude change. But if the communicator is advocating positions in the audience's latitude of rejection, asking for more change will actually produce less (Whittaker, 1967).

Emotional versus Rational Appeals Early work on persuasion by Hovland and his associates focused on propaganda during World War II (Hovland et al., 1949). In this research, different communications were written in order to determine their effects on the attitudes and morale of American soldiers. Hovland and his associates introduced several variables: i.e., the explicitness of the conclusions in different messages; whether the communications presented only one side of an issue or acknowledged the opposing sides; or whether communications appealed to reason or emotion. All these variables were found to interact with characteristics of the audience. Better educated audiences were most influenced by rational, two-sided arguments that allowed them to draw their own conclusions. Less educated audiences were most influenced by one-sided messages with explicit conclusions. (For reviews of this literature, see Karlins & Abelson, 1970; Oskamp, 1977; Rosnow & Robinson, 1967; Zimbardo et al., 1978.) Perhaps the broadest message characteristic studied by the Hovland group was the effect of emotional content on persuasion, particularly the effect of fear-arousing communications.

One of the earliest field experiments in social psychology was conducted by George Hartmann (1936), who ran as a candidate of the Socialist party in Allentown, Pennsylvania. The voting districts were divided into three groups. In one district, leaflets with emotional appeals in support of the Socialist ticket were distributed (for example, "Our future as American citizens ... looks dark. ... We have learned what awful wars have taken place under both Republicans and Democrats. ... We beg you in the name of ... early memories and spring-time hopes to support the Socialist ticket."). In a second district, the leaflets distributed contained rational arguments in favor of the Socialist party. For example, the following items were included in the form of a test: "No gifted boy or girl should be denied the advantages of higher education ... AGREE—DISAGREE." "The only way most people will ever be able to live in modern sanitary homes is for the government to build them on a nonprofit basis ... AGREE—DISAGREE." In a control district, no leaflets were distributed. On the basis of votes received in these three districts, Hartmann reports that the emotional appeal was most influential. In the control area, 2.44 percent of the votes cast were for the Socialist candidate; in the wards receiving the rational appeal, the figure was 1.76 percent; and in the emotional wards, it was 4.00 percent.

There is evidence, however, that emotional appeals are not always effective in influencing attitudes (though it should be noted that the Hartmann study used behavior, not attitude, as the dependent variable). A study by Janis and Feshbach (1953) reported that recommendations on dental hygiene were less likely to be followed when the message aroused high fear, for example, by referring to cancer, than when it aroused minimal fear. Since this early study, social psychologists have had to modify their positions on fear and persuasion several times (Duke, 1967).

Communications that arouse fear can be effective when the communicator has high credibility (Hewgill & Miller, 1965), and high fear is more persuasive than low fear when it is accompanied by specific recommendations about how to reduce that fear (Leventhal, 1970; Leventhal & Singer, 1966). The relationship between fear and persuasion is so complex because two different types of effects seem to be involved: what McGuire (1969) calls reception and yielding. The greater the amount of fear that is aroused, the greater the likelihood that the recipient will be tuned in to his or her own emotions, and thus less likely to pay attention to the communication. So, high fear is probably negatively correlated with the reception of a communication. But in those who do receive the message, high fear will produce insecurity and a motivation to try to reduce the fear, probably by complying with (or yielding to) the recommendations of the message. So, fear is positively correlated with yielding.

Appeals may be made not only to our emotions, but also to our values—decency, truth, and other virtues—and it is at these appeals that Madison Avenue seems to excel.

Some Techniques of Propaganda We can define *propaganda* as any attempt to influence another person's attitudes, values, or behavior. In this broad view, perhaps a majority of communications are propagandistic. Education, which is designed to change the content and process of our thoughts, is propagandistic, though we tend to view this sort of influence as benefiting the recipient. The popular view of propaganda is attempted influence that is not beneficial to the recipient. This more limited view carries the connotation that propagandistic communications are distortions of the truth. Political speeches, self-aggrandizing statements, and commercial advertising all employ various propaganda strategies. In order to give you some of the flavor of propagandistic communications, we will briefly examine some recent television commercials.

The effects of mass media are discussed elsewhere in this chapter and in Chapter 8; we will deal here only with the content and intended effects of television commercials. To what extent do these attempts at persuasion influence viewer behavior and attitudes? The evidence is not abundant on this issue, but it suggests that television has relatively little direct influence on consumer attitudes and behavior—this despite the fact that advertisers spend more than $3 billion dollars a year on television commercials!

Mass-media advertising seems to interact with other variables. One variable is viewer familiarity with the product or service advertised. If we are unaware that the General Greed Corporation makes a product to put grease stains in blue jeans, then a TV commercial about Greaso will have informational value. Of course, if we already know that Greaso is on the market, the commercial will have little or no informational value. Assuming we know that

Greaso exists, the effect of the commercial depends on two factors: whether we believe that Greaso works as described, and whether, assuming we believe it works, we have any need or desire for more grease stains on our jeans. Awareness of the product may be correlated with sales to the extent that the product fulfills a need. A commercial about a new product may be related to sales, then (see, for example, Coleman, Katz, & Menzel, 1957). For audiences already aware of a product, commercials are apt to be less effective (Haskins, 1966). This, perhaps, is the reason so many old products are relabeled "new" or "improved." These adjectives suggest that the commercial is about a different product, and so they might increase consumer awareness and lead to increased sales.

Many of the persuasive appeals used in commercial advertising and propaganda employ fallacies of logic. For example, a TV commercial for a brand of aspirin shows a distinguished man in a trench coat standing before the Washington monument, looking for all the world like a reporter. As though he were reporting a major news story from Washington, he says that in a government-sponsored study, aspirin substitutes were *not* proved more effective than aspirin. This ambiguous report can mean one of several things: Aspirin and aspirin substitutes are equally effective; neither aspirin nor aspirin substitutes are at all effective; or there is a slight difference in effectiveness, but the difference fails to reach the level of statistical significance (though that level is not specified). The implications of the purported study are ambiguous because the viewer is not provided with enough information to draw a conclusion.

Another commercial, for a medium-priced automobile, says it has more trunk space than a Lincoln Continental, more leg room than a Cadillac, and more head room than a Mercedes. What is not said is that this may mean the car has less trunk space than a Cadillac or Mercedes, less leg room than a Lincoln or Mercedes, and less head room than a Lincoln or a Cadillac.

A fallacy is an argument that seems to be sound without in fact being so. Common types of fallacies are circular arguments, or "begging the question," in which something is said to be true because it is true. For example, "Schooldaze helps you relax because Schooldaze is a tranquilizer." The most common logical fallacy in commercials seems to be the fallacy of argumentative leap, or *non sequitur*. Here, a conclusion consistent with the premises is presented even though the premises do not prove the conclusion, as in this commercial for Geritol: "Women need 50 percent more iron than men. That's why I take Geritol every day." There seems to be some relationship between the first, factual statement and the conclusion, but, in fact, there is no necessary connection between them.

Appeals to credible sources are common in commercials, even though the expertise of the source may lie in quite a different area.

Sometimes it pays to advertise that you are not being paid to advertise.

Joe DiMaggio advertises coffeemakers and savings banks, and athletes, actors, and comedians endorse clothes, automobiles, and insurance companies. There is one singer (who is not even credible as a musician, as far as I'm concerned) who endorses pasta, cars, restaurants, and tennis racquets.

One attempt at influence employs the most rational of appeals: the appeal to "scientific evidence." Because science has positive connotations for many people, advertising claims backed by "science" seem irrefutable. Because most items advertised in television commercials are not significantly different from competitors' products (soap, toothpaste, deodorant, detergent, junk food, pop records, department stores, cars, refrigerators, banks), there is unlikely to be hard evidence for the superiority of one brand over another. By using various logical errors of omission, differences may appear to exist.

"Crest has been shown to be an effective decay-preventive dentifrice that can be of significant value when used in a conscientiously applied program of oral hygiene and regular professional care," says my tube of toothpaste. Perhaps, but this might also be true of Colgate, other fluoride toothpastes, baking soda, and salt water.

Scientific-looking paraphernalia are often used in TV commercials to enhance the credibility of a source by increasing his or her expertise. White lab coats and stethoscopes are common in commercials for over-the-counter drugs. There was even a commercial (for coffee) that employed Robert Young, for years "Dr. Marcus Welby" on television, who began by saying, "I'm not a real doctor, but ...," and continued as though he were a real doctor.

Graphs are employed in many commercials because they lend an air of scientific respectability to a statement. Often the ordinate of these graphs is not labeled, so that what looks like Figure 5.2 on the TV screen may look like Figure 5.3 when the ordinate is labeled.

These and similar techniques are used not only by advertisers but also by political propagandists and demagogues (E. H. Schein, 1956). All involve attempts to influence our view of reality by withholding or distorting information. These techniques are sometimes effective, if not in influencing behavior directly, then in leading some people to draw erroneous conclusions. In order to be successful, however, persuasive appeals do not have to influence large numbers of people. A successful advertising campaign may increase a product's share of the market by only 1 percent, but this may have a great dollar value to the manufacturer (Bauer, 1964).

It is not only by presenting a distorted view of reality that propagandists influence others; presenting a partial view of reality often is just as effective. Just as many TV commercials use comparative words like "better" without telling us what the product is being compared to, communicators often omit or select information in order to present a particular view of reality. In a study of political bias in *Time, U.S. News & World Report,* and *Newsweek,* Bagdikian (1962) found that the magazines' political positions were reinforced by selective reporting. For example, more space was devoted to Eisenhower than to Stevenson in the 1956 presidential election, flattering photographs of Eisenhower were printed while unflattering photographs of Stevenson appeared, and so on. In this way, while covering the campaign, the magazines were able to make editorial

Figure 5.2.
Unlabeled ordinate.

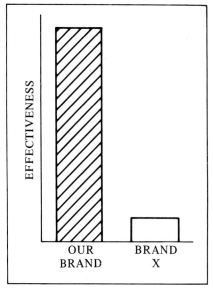

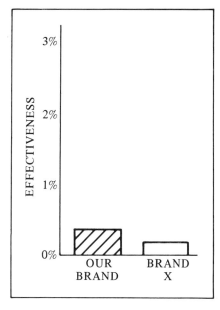

Figure 5.3.
Labeled ordinate.

statements under the guise of objective reporting. Often effective propaganda depends as much on what is not said as on what is.

THE MEDIUM AND THE MESSAGE

Communication must occur through some channel or medium. Communication media vary along several dimensions. Personal media are those in which a communicator is physically present before the audience; impersonal media are those in which the communicator is not present, as in the mass media. The message may be transmitted verbally, visually, through other sense organs, or by any combination of sensory modalities. The messages to which we most often attend are verbal messages, either spoken or written, and visual messages, such as gestures and photographic images on a screen or in print.

When a message is transmitted over a particular channel, there is apt to be some distortion or interference, some "noise" that reduces the pure reception of the message. Channels vary in their signal-to-noise ratios. For example, if we wish to transmit a precise visual image to a mass audience, we might accomplish this by showing the image on television or film. Assuming all other factors are equal, the film will contain less irrelevant, distracting elements than television. This is because the emulsion on a film allows for a more refined and precise representation of an object than the fairly coarse "grain" of a television screen, with its several hundred rows of illuminated dots. One of the topics studied by social psychologists is the effect of irrelevant noise or distraction on the reception and effects of a communication.

Signal-to-Noise Ratio: Distraction and Attitude Change   The first studies on the effects of distraction on persuasion were conducted by Festinger and Maccoby (1964). Fraternity men at three different colleges viewed a film in which a speaker argued against fraternities. Half the subjects viewed a film in which the anti-fraternity speech was accompanied by scenes of campus buildings and views of the speaker. The other half heard the same soundtrack, but instead viewed a highly distracting and amusing film on modern art. Attitudes toward fraternities and the speaker were then measured.

In a study at the University of Minnesota, the authors found no differences in attitudes as a result of the two different films. They attribute this lack of difference to the fact that fraternities at the university were weak in the first place and were under constant attack. The study was then replicated at San Jose State College, where fraternities were strong and were not under attack. Here, and also in a replication at the University of Southern California, they found that those exposed to the distracting visual track were more influenced by the speaker than those not distracted. The students were also more likely to think of the speaker as well qualified and fair when they viewed the distracting version of the film.

Festinger and Maccoby interpret these findings in terms of the notion of counterarguing. They assume that people exposed to communications that are contrary to their own attitudes have a tendency to refute arguments made in the communications (Brock, 1967; Thistlethwaite & Kamenetzky, 1955). But when they are distracted while attending to the message, they must exert more effort to understand the communication and so tend to counterargue less. Thus, distraction is assumed to reduce counterarguing, and a reduction in counterarguing is associated with increased acceptance of the communication.

Since these early studies, the distraction-persuasion effect has been found by others, but only under limited conditions. As so often happens in scientific research, early findings are qualified by later research. In the case of distraction, its effects depend on the focus of the subjects' attention. If the audience is set to focus on the message rather than on the distracting activity, distraction leads to increased attitude change (Insko, Turnbull, & Yandell, 1974; Zimbardo, Snyder, Thomas, Gold, & Gurwitz, 1970). If the audience attends primarily to the distracting activity, there is less attitude change and also less recall of the message's contents. Distraction may even decrease attitude change if it is particularly difficult to refute the persuasive communication (Petty, Wells, & Brock, 1976).

Generally, when we think of the effects of the various media, we are concerned with their *relative* effectiveness. Is a communicator better off presenting a message in person, by film, television, in print, or in some combination of these? There is, of course, no final answer to this question; the answer depends on the nature of the intended audience, the intentions of the communicator, and the structure of the message.

In some attitude change experiments, a persuasive message was presented in writing, on audiotape, or on videotape or film (Chaiken & Eagly, 1976; Hovland et al., 1949; Lana, 1963; McGinnies, 1965). In general, the more information transmitted to the audience, the greater the attitude change. Naturally, this depends on how difficult the message is to comprehend, and on whether the visual presentation (film or videotape) includes nonverbal gestures and expressions that may convey additional information.

The Multimedia Flow of Communication   In an age of instantaneous broadcasts and satellite communications, we do not often think of face-to-face communication as particularly powerful or prevalent. Still, it seems clear that personal communications are more frequent, more potent, and more influential than mass-media communications. This notion is referred to as the *two-step flow of communications* and was proposed by Lazarsfeld, Berelson, and Gaudet in 1948. When they studied voting patterns and preferences for candidates during a presidential election, they found that personal contact was the decisive factor in political preference, particularly among those who were initially undecided and those who switched their preference. They proposed that some people, whom they termed *opinion leaders*, pay particular attention to the mass media—that is, they read newspaper and magazine advertisements, listen to the news on radio and television—and that these opinion leaders then influence others with whom they come into contact. The two-step flow theory proposes that most people are influenced by the mass media only indirectly, through opinion leaders, and thus that personal communication has the greatest and most immediate impact on attitudes and behavior.

More than political preference is influenced by personal contact. A study by Coleman et al. (1957) examined the use of a new drug by physicians in four small midwestern American towns. The question studied by these researchers was: What are the social processes that intervene between the initial trials of the drug by a few local innovators and its final use by virtually the whole medical community? The drug, given the fictitious name Gammanym by the researchers, was widely used within 15 months of its introduction. Some physicians used it almost immediately after it was introduced, while others took a considerable amount of time before deciding to use Gammanym.

Opinion leaders are usually more effective influencers than the mass media. This young woman may not yet have persuaded all of her listeners, but she certainly has their rapt attention.

Nearly every physician in the four communities studied was interviewed. The extent to which the doctors read medical journals, did research and published, and were integrated into the local medical community was assessed. The doctors were also asked to list their three closest medical friends, those physicians to whom they turned for advice and so on. These sociometric choices were closely related to the time of adoption of Gammanym. The results indicated that the more frequently a doctor was named by colleagues as a friend or discussion partner, the more likely it was that that doctor was an innovator with respect to the new drug. These sociometric choices were more closely related to drug adoption than any personal characteristics, such as age and medical school, or any other sources of influence, such as medical journals. Those who were not often chosen as close friends or influential colleagues tended to be hesitant about prescribing the drug, and, in fact, did not prescribe it until it had been used by the innovators for some time. Additional studies, including some on changes in fashion, buying habits, and general attitudes, have confirmed the importance of face-to-face communications in social influence (E. Katz, 1957; Merton, 1949).

Although face-to-face communications seem to play a primary role in adopting new fashions and techniques, it would be unwise to underestimate the importance of the mass media. Recently, the unidirectional notion of the two-step flow—from mass media to opinion leaders to the general public—has been questioned (Oskamp, 1977; Weiss, 1969). For one thing, it has been found that the so-called opinion leaders are leaders only on limited topics and so are difficult to identify, and for another, that the opinion leaders who can be identified do not seem to try very hard to influence the opinions of others (Kingdon, 1970). In reality, information about a topic of importance is generally acquired through a combination of personal and mass-media channels. For example, the shooting of President Kennedy in 1963 was known by nearly 70 percent of the American public within 30 minutes, and this diffusion occurred largely by word of mouth. But people then turned to radio and television for confirmation of the event and additional information.

THE AUDIENCE AND PERSUASION

As mentioned previously, the audience is never completely inactive in the communication process. Recipients of a message must attend to the message, understand it, integrate it with other information they may have, evaluate it, and decide what, if anything, to do on the basis of this new information. Much research by social and personality psychologists has been concerned with whether particular types of audiences are more easily influenced by propaganda than others (e.g., Hovland & Janis, 1959). Are youngsters more readily influenced by TV commercials than their parents? Females more than males? The uneducated more than the educated? These are some of the stereotypic views of persuasibility, but, as we shall see, there is little truth in such generalizations.

In general, we may agree with McGuire (1969), who, in a review of individual differences and persuasibility, concluded, "The results regarding the the relationship between any given individual-difference variable and susceptibility to social influence tend to be extremely complex and seemingly contradictory" (p. 243). McGuire points out that any variable, such as the recipient's age, level of self-esteem, or gender, may be positively, negatively, or curvilinearly related to persuasibility. The exact nature of the relationship depends on how the trait is measured, whether it is experimentally manipulated, the audience's normal level of the trait, and the type of persuasion being measured. Some traits, such as age, self-esteem, and sex, seem to have a small but consistent relationship with certain types of social influence, but not enough to make prediction from the trait to persuasion reliable. While few audience traits are consistently and strongly related to persuasion, some audience characteristics and behaviors are related to resistance to persuasion.

Resistance to Persuasion   It is interesting, though not too surprising, that social psychologists studied persuasion processes for some time before becoming interested in how people might immunize themselves to propaganda. It is obvious to anyone who views American commercial television that most people are remarkably resistant to persuasive attempts. Watching television for even one evening a week exposes the viewer to thousands of commercial advertisements in a year. The fact that people are influenced by so few of these commercials is at least as remarkable as the fact that they are sometimes influenced by some of them.

In the 1960s, a series of studies and theoretical positions began to deal exclusively with the problem of resistance to social influence. Some of these simply proposed that the absence of variables related to persuasion would lead to nonpersuasion. So, if people were generally more influenced by a high-credibility communicator, they would be less influenced by a communicator low in credibility. If it was assumed that people argued along with a persuasive communication, then it was proposed that they would be less influenced if they were made to counterargue. But just as the absence of aspirin is not the cause of a headache, it is not necessarily true that the absence of factors related to persuasion is the cause of resistance to persuasion. Two theories in particular concern the resistance to persuasion: reactance theory and inoculation theory.

Reactance theory was proposed by J. W. Brehm in 1966 and has been elaborated upon by Brehm and his colleagues since then (Wicklund, 1974). The theory assumes that people have a need to choose their own behaviors freely and that any threat to this freedom creates *reactance,* a motivational state that is directed toward the reestablishment of the lost or threatened freedom. When a communicator tries to force a position on a person, reactance is created and the individual should move away from the position the communicator is trying to force upon him. If something is censored, an increased desire for the censored material should follow. There is some empirical support for the reactance notion, but it is difficult in the typical persuasion situation to weigh the importance of reactance against the rewards accompanying compliance, the need for cognitive consistency, and the perceptual distortion of the communicator and his or her position. There is, no doubt, a tendency to resist overt influence attempts; nevertheless, some effects of persuasive communications on attitudes and behavior are often seen. Perhaps these effects would be greater if there were no reactance. At the moment, we have no satisfactory method for measuring the degree of reactance in an individual, and this is a serious handicap in testing and evaluating reactance theory. A more satisfactory theory of the resistance to persuasion is McGuire's inoculation theory.

Beginning in 1961, William J. McGuire developed a theory of resistance to persuasion that is referred to as *inoculation theory* (McGuire, 1961, 1964). The theory derives its name from an analogy in biology in which a person's resistance to disease is enhanced by

If you push your point of view too forcefully, you may stir up more resistance than agreement, as these men are demonstrating.

preexposure to a small dose of the attacking bacteria or virus, the dose being strong enough to stimulate the natural defenses, but not so strong as to overcome them. McGuire attributes the original notion for persuasive inoculations to Janis, Lumsdaine, and Gladstone (1951), though it was most fully developed by McGuire.

McGuire argues that some beliefs, such as those concerned with certain health issues, exist in a "germ-free environment" where they are unlikely ever to be attacked. Hence, the individual has little defense against an attack. For example, it is almost universally accepted that brushing one's teeth is a good thing to do after each meal. Most people have never heard this belief attacked; it is, in McGuire's phrase, a *cultural truism*. But because such a belief has never been attacked, the person has no experience in defending it, and hence the belief is particularly vulnerable to attack. Inoculation theory suggests that in order to defend such a belief against a possible persuasive attack, the individual must build up some immunity either by learning to refute attacks or by learning to defend the belief with supportive arguments.

Inoculation theory proposes that there are two possible types of defense for a belief: refutational defenses and supportive defenses. Refutational defenses entail the development of arguments that refute attacks upon the belief. Supportive defenses consist of arguments in favor of the belief. Of course, these types of defense may be passively or actively learned. Passive defenses are supportive of refutational defenses received from another party; active defenses are those made up by individuals. The theory predicts that refutational defenses provide greater resistance to subsequent attacking propaganda than supportive defenses. Experiments generally support this view. Students provided with refutations of attacking arguments are more resistant to later persuasive attempts than those given only bolstering or supportive information. McGuire has argued that passive defenses, and particularly passive refutational defenses, are more effective than active defenses in conferring immunity to subsequent persuasion, because people are not motivated to defend cultural truisms and have had little practice in defending them. When left to their own defenses, people find them weak. Hence, they are more resistant to persuasion when they are provided with refutational defenses by the experimenter.

Can McGuire's inoculation theory lead to the development of immunity to persuasive arguments for attitudes and beliefs that are not cultural truisms? Surprisingly little research has been conducted on this issue and so we don't know much about the extent to which the theory can be generalized to other types of belief.

Summary

Our culture is transmitted by means of communication, which is the process of passing on information from one person to another. The process always involves a source, a message, a channel, a recipient or audience, and an effect. Because two or more people are always involved, communication is an inherently social process. This chapter focuses on communications that are designed to influence people, particularly persuasive communications—those designed to influence attitudes and behaviors.

Several basic theories of attitude change are reviewed. Two important cognitive consistency theories are presented: Heider's balance theory and Festinger's theory of cognitive dissonance. Dissonance theory is a generalized version of balance theory and has been the subject of much research and controversy in social psychology. Dissonance theory research can be divided into three types: selective exposure, insufficient justification, and postdecision processes. The studies on insufficient justification in particular led learning theorists to propose alternative explanations for the dissonance findings. One explanation, based on Skinner's radical behaviorism, was proposed by Bem and is referred to as self-perception theory. According to this view, we do not need to use concepts such as "cognitive dissonance" to explain why insufficient justifications may produce attitude change. While the debate continues over which of these two approaches, dissonance or self-perception, better explains certain behaviors, some social psychologists have concluded that it is impossible to decide the issue.

Theories based on psychophysics and traditional learning theories are briefly discussed. Because no single theory encompasses the entire communication process, each basic component of communication is discussed separately.

Source credibility consists of those characteristics of a communicator that make the message more believable to an audience. In general, sources are seen as more credible when they are expert, trustworthy, attractive, and have had experiences similar to the audience's. Early research by Hovland and his associates reported that the effects of source credibility tended to dissipate with time. This is known as the "sleeper effect." Recent research has been unable to replicate these early findings and the sleeper effect is now regarded as a somewhat special case of persuasion, occurring only under certain conditions.

Social psychologists have studied characteristics of the message that enhance persuasion. In particular, they have been interested in the effects of fear-producing messages on attitudes and behavior. When messages arouse a great deal of fear, reception of the message may be interfered with and thus less change may occur. Assuming that the message is received, however, fear seems to be positively related to change. Propagandists of all sorts attempt to structure their messages so that they have maximum impact on an audience. Some of the techniques of advertisers are reviewed in order to indicate how messages may be structured to produce change.

All communications must be presented through some medium or channel. The amount of noise and distraction in a channel may influence yielding. Face-to-face communications are often more influential than those presented in the mass media, and several studies demonstrating this point are reviewed. There are people, referred to as opinion leaders, who pay particular attention to the mass media, and these opinion leaders may influence many others in face-to-face contact. Thus, the mass media have an indirect effect on a great many people, although they directly influence a relatively small group. This is referred to as the two-step flow of communications.

Characteristics of the audience, particularly intelligence, activities engaged in while listening to a message, and personality traits, may all influence the effects of a communication. But none of these effects is simple and direct. Likewise, audience characteristics may be related to resistance to persuasion, either through counterarguing and reactance, or through active refutation of communications, as predicted by inoculation theory.

Suggested Readings

Himmelfarb, S., & Eagly, A. H. *Readings in attitude change.* New York: Wiley, 1974.

Oskamp, S. *Attitudes and opinions.* Englewood Cliffs, N.J.: Prentice-Hall, 1977.

*Zimbardo, P., Ebbesen, E. B., & Maslach, C. *Influencing attitudes and changing behavior* (4th ed.). Reading, Mass.: Addison-Wesley, 1978.

*Available in paperback edition.

6
INTERPERSONAL ATTRACTION: STRANGERS, FRIENDS, AND LOVERS

Love, what is it? Answer. 'Tis very much like light, a thing that everybody knows, and yet none can tell what to make of it. 'Tis not money, fortune, jointure, raving, stabbing, hanging, romancing, flouncing, swearing, ramping, desiring, fighting, dicing, though all those have been, are, and still will be mistaken and miscalled for it. . . . 'Tis extremely like a sigh, and could we find a painter who could draw one, you'd easily mistake it for the other. [The Ladies Dictionary, *1694 (quoted by M. M. Hunt, 1959)]*

I had my first date with her about three months after we both started to work in the firm. One day we worked together on an assignment and we made a date for that Saturday night to go to a movie. At that time it was nothing but another date. I liked her general appearance and personality. . . . I would say that I was definitely interested our first night out. I know that on my first date I wanted more dates. . . . I would say that within the first two months we were going together I felt I was in love with her, and that I'd like to marry her. Our understanding was brought on very gradually, however. It was never actually stated, but I gave her my frat ring about nine months after we started dating and that was it. I don't know which of us fell in love first. I think it came on both of us in the same way. I think it just started out as plain dating, and gradually developed into love from there on. (College student describing falling in love for the first time, in Burgess and Wallin, 1953)

All societies recognize that there are occasional violent attachments between persons of opposite sex, but our present American culture is practically the only one which has attempted to capitalize these and make them the basis for marriage. . . . Their rarity in most societies suggests that they are psychological abnormalities to which our own culture has attached an extraordinary value just as other cultures have attached extreme values to other abnormalities. The hero of the modern American movie is always a romantic lover just as the hero of the old Arab epic is always an epileptic. (Ralph Linton, 1936)

What causes us to become attracted to other people? Is there something about *them* that causes us to like them, or something about *us* that impels us to like them? Perhaps it is a combination of traits in both the lover and the loved. Or perhaps, as the anthropologist Ralph Linton suggests, love is a psychological abnormality, reinforced by cultural norms and institutions. These are some of the issues that social psychologists have explored under the general heading of Interpersonal Attraction. Though romantic love is the prime concern of this chapter, we will approach it gradually, examining first the nature of attraction in general, and only later romantic and sexual attraction. Along the way we will discuss friendship and liking, make several side trips to affiliation and other emotions, and attempt to demystify some of love's mysteries.

I should caution you not to expect too much from psychologists as your guides on this journey. There will be plenty of mysteries left when this excursion has ended. As the eminent psychologist Harry Harlow once remarked, "So far as love is concerned, psychologists have failed in their mission. The little we know about love does not transcend simple observation, and the little we write about it has been written better by poets and novelists" (1958, p. 673). I have no quarrel with Harlow's statement about the quality of the writing, but I believe that psychologists know more about love and attraction than we once did, and that not all of what we have learned is common sense.

The study of liking and loving is not merely an academic exercise. Only a few years ago there was one divorce for every three marriages in the United States; as I write this, the figure is closer to one divorce for every two marriages. If psychologists do not know very much about love, it is clear that the rest of the population doesn't either.

LEVELS OF ATTRACTION

Just as the college student quoted by Burgess and Wallin perceives love as a process occurring over time, our approach in this chapter will be to view love as a state reached only after earlier stages of attraction have been transcended. In general, the view taken here is adapted from the work of George Levinger (Huston & Levinger, 1978; Levinger, 1974; Levinger & Snoek, 1972; see also the interview with George Levinger, this chapter).

Attraction between two people, P and O, can range from no awareness of each other to a deep, mutual response (see Figure 6.1). Between these two extremes lie states of awareness of the other, surface contact with minimal attraction, and varying degrees of mutual concern. Research on all these levels has been carried out in social psychology. The different levels will be discussed here in order of increasing interaction and mutuality. At the lower levels, simple awareness of the other and minimal contact, we will be dealing with the relationship between people who are acquaintances, and later, friends, but not romantic partners. At the more intense levels of interaction, we will focus on companionate and romantic love. Not surprisingly, more research has been devoted to the less complex topic of attraction than to the more complex concepts of love and romantic attraction.

A considerable amount of theorizing and research has explored the characteristics of the judge and the judged that make for attraction. Much of this work provides college students with some information about a real or hypothetical stranger and asks the

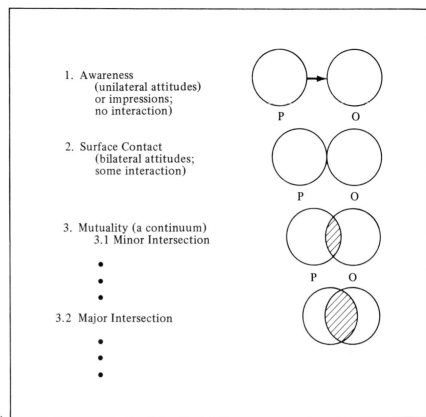

1. Awareness
   (unilateral attitudes)
   or impressions;
   no interaction)

2. Surface Contact
   (bilateral attitudes;
   some interaction)

3. Mutuality (a continuum)
   3.1 Minor Intersection

        •

        •

        •

    3.2 Major Intersection

        •

        •

        •

Figure 6.1.
Levels of relatedness.

students to judge the degree to which they think they would like the stranger, either as a friend, a work partner, or a date. The next level of attraction studied in research has the subjects interact with a stranger for fairly brief periods of time, after which they are asked to state their degree of liking for the other. At the next level, studies have been conducted over long periods of time with people who have lived together or worked together extensively. Finally, there are studies and theories that deal with close relationships and engaged or married couples.

ATTRACTION TOWARD STRANGERS AND BRIEF ACQUAINTANCES

Just as research on person perception and impression formation began with studies of hypothetical people, described to research participants only by a series of adjectives or other minimal information, so too has research on interpersonal attraction emphasized attitudes toward hypothetical strangers. The study of liking for real

George Levinger was born in Berlin, Germany, and educated in the United States. He received his A.B. degree from Columbia University, his M.A. from Berkeley, and his Ph.D. from the University of Michigan. He has taught at Bryn Mawr College, Western Reserve University, and the University of Massachusetts at Amherst, where he is professor of psychology. He has been a visiting scholar at Yale University, Universität Konstanz in Germany, and the Institute for Social Research in Oslo, Norway. He has written extensively on interpersonal attraction, close relationships, marriage, and divorce, and has co-edited two books, *Close relationships* (1977) and *Divorce and separation* (1979).

JHG: A few years ago you published an important theoretical paper which you titled "A New Look at Interpersonal Attraction." What was *new* in your approach?

GL: In one sense, perhaps, nothing. After all, the notion of two persons' lives becoming increasingly interwoven is age old. The very word "breakup" of a relationship implies that two partners have constructed something worthy and unique, whose destruction is painful. And my metaphor of two circles going from 0 to 100 percent overlap is not entirely surprising [see Figure 6.1]. What *was* new, though, was our attempt to connect this metaphor systematically to ongoing social psychological research that had largely ignored relational aspects of social attraction.

JHG: Perhaps you can tell a bit more about where social psychological work in the area of attraction was going.

GL: The term "interpersonal attraction" first received prominence in an APA Presidential Address by Theodore Newcomb [1956] in a report on his longitudinal study of how liking develops among college dorm mates. Newcomb's work on attraction was conducted mainly in field settings—as earlier work on networks of choices and rejections

(Continued on next page)

or hypothetical strangers is closely allied to the topics of person perception and impression formation discussed in Chapter 4. In that research, the dependent variables are usually designed to measure how a stranger is perceived and what traits he or she is believed to possess. In attraction research, the dependent variable is usually liking for the stranger or willingness to interact with the stranger in the future. Because liking is in part determined by how the other is perceived, you should not be surprised to learn that some of the theories designed to explain person perception can be brought to bear on attraction.

SIMILARITY AND ATTRACTION

Probably no social psychological notion is older or more clearly established than the relationship between similarity and attraction.

AN INTERVIEW WITH
GEORGE LEVINGER

(Continued)

had been conducted in classrooms or camps [Moreno, 1934], or a large study of attraction and communication in a housing project [Festinger et al., 1950].

Since the natural phenomena associated with attraction appeared elusive, later social psychologists tried to put them under the microscope. That meant studying attraction under carefully controlled experimental conditions. It meant creating attraction where it had not hitherto existed—by bringing a laboratory subject into contact with a stimulus person whose attributes could be systematically manipulated and the effects examined. To vary these attributes, the stimulus person had to be a stranger—even a "hypothetical stranger" in the well-known investigations of Byrne [1971]. Those experimental studies yielded considerable knowledge about determinants of *initial* social contacts, but such knowledge was inadequate for predicting the development and maintenance of subsequent interaction. And it is deeper interaction that interested

me—and still does.

JHG: How did you happen to come by these interests? Did you intend at the outset to study close relationships?

GL: By the back door, perhaps. I didn't start out to spend my life studying pair relationships, but I have focused much of my work on them since around 1962. My graduate training at Michigan was in group dynamics. After I left Michigan, I became interested in applying group concepts to family interaction, and we did several observational studies of family groups from both school and psychiatric clinic populations. But that work was plagued with complications. Because the two parents were generally the central figures, I eventually decided to limit my research to the parents' marital relationship—as the core of "family strength and problem-solving." That decision led me to focus on pair interaction—first between spouses, and later between dating partners and other sorts of

Aristotle was perhaps the first to describe such a relationship:

And they are friends who have come to regard the same things as good and the same things as evil, they who are friends of the same people, and they who are the enemies of the same people. . . . We like those who resemble us, and are engaged in the same pursuits. . . . We like those who desire the same things as we, if the case is such that we and they share the things together. (1932, pp. 103–105)

The similarity–attraction relationship was also noted by Spinoza, nearly 2000 years later:

If we conceive that anyone loves, desires, or hates anything which we ourselves love, desire, or hate, we shall thereupon regard the thing in question with more steadfast love, etc. On the contrary, if we think that anyone shrinks from something that we love, we shall undergo vacilla-

close friends.

JHG: Does the study of such close relationships require any special research tools?

GL: One of our consistent findings was that in order to understand or predict the development of relationships, ordinary measures of attitude or personality similarity were of little value. In close pairs, the characteristics of the relationship itself were found to be far more important than the separate personalities of the individual members (Levinger et al., 1970).

We thus began to look at the inside of relationships. My co-workers and I have been trying to describe what happens when two people are intimate, how relationships change as they progress in closeness, how the behavior of friendly acquaintances differs from that of extremely close friends. One recent study found that people's expectations about what goes on in a relationship are fairly widely shared, but that today's expectations are systematically different from those of fifty years

ago (Rands & Levinger, 1979).

JHG: Do you have any personal biases that you think might affect your research, or any special feelings about close relationships as a result of having studied them for so long?

GL: In each of us there seems to be something of both the ant and the grasshopper. The ant aims for security, the grasshopper for fun and excitement. The ant struggles ploddingly, sacrificing today for tomorrow; the grasshopper flits around, ignoring tomorrow for the pleasures of today. A recurring human question is how to balance our life so as to have the best of both today and tomorrow. My own belief is that we are often capable of heightening the novelty of our existing relationships in ways that combine present enjoyment with future stability. But there seem to be no simple formulas about where, when, and how to do so. Research on attraction and relationships will not find any easy answers, but perhaps it will help us be more realistic in our questions and our expectations.

tion of soul. . . . It follows that everyone endeavors, as far as possible, to cause others to love what he himself loves, and to hate what he himself hates. (1951, p. 151)

A number of social psychological theories, representing a wide variety of viewpoints, have also described this relationship between similarity and attraction. While there is widespread agreement on the existence of such a relationship, there is considerable disagreement as to the reasons for it. Therefore, we will present some of the evidence for the relationship and then give some theoretical interpretations of the relationship.

Empirical Evidence for the Similarity–Attraction Relationship   Scores of studies have been designed to determine the extent to which a person likes another who is described as having similar attitudes, values, beliefs, social status, or physical appearance. Much of this work has been conducted by Donn Byrne and his students (see Byrne, 1969, 1971, for reviews). In Byrne's research, subjects, usually college students, complete a questionnaire asking them about their attitudes, beliefs, or other personal characteristics. They are then given an identical questionnaire, ostensibly completed by another person. Actually, this is a bogus questionnaire completed by the experimenter and made to appear either similar or dissimilar to the subject's questionnaire. After reading the "other's" questionnaire, the subjects complete the Interpersonal Judgment Scale, developed by Byrne to measure attraction. The subjects are asked, among other things, how much they would like the other person and how much they would like working with the other person in another experiment. The sum of the responses to these two items is interpreted by Byrne as a measure of liking.

In early studies (e.g., Byrne, Bond, & Diamond, 1969; Byrne, Clore, & Worchel, 1966), Byrne and his colleagues reported that the more similar a hypothetical stranger was to the subject, the more favorably the stranger was rated on the Interpersonal Judgment Scale. In later research (Byrne & Lamberth, 1971; Byrne & Nelson, 1965), Byrne emphasized that the *proportion*, rather than the number of similar attitudes held by the stranger, is the better predictor of attraction. Thus, if one subject completes an attitude questionnaire consisting of eight items, while another subject completes a 16-item questionnaire, a stranger who agrees with only four of the items will be liked better by the first subject ($^4/_8$ = 50 percent similarity) than by the second subject ($^4/_{16}$ = 25 percent similarity).

An impressive number of studies have found a positive relationship between the similarity of one person to another and that person's liking for the other. While most of the research conducted by Byrne and associates concerns attraction toward a hypothetical stranger, there is also some evidence that similarity may play a central role in situations in which the two parties interact (e.g., Berscheid, Dion, Walster, & Walster, 1971; Byrne, Ervin, & Lamberth, 1970; Griffitt & Veitch, 1974; Insko, Thompson, Stroebe, Shand, Pinner, & Layton, 1973; Nahemow & Lawton, 1975; Newcomb, 1961).

A field study by Theodore Newcomb (1961) examined the development of attraction among college students residing together in a small house. Newcomb invited 17 college men to live rent-free in the house provided they were willing to participate in a research project. The 17 students were initially strangers, and Newcomb measured at periodic intervals their growing friendships with one another. The study was conducted a second time, using a different group of 17 students. In both cases, the *perceived* attitude similarity of other housemates was a strong correlate of attraction toward them. Subjects liked housemates they perceived as very similar to themselves

Do smilarity and attraction go together? Many studies have shown that people who share similar attitudes and interests are attracted to one another. The noted child psychologists Sheldon and Eleanor Glueck seem to support this hypothesis with enthusiasm.

more than they liked residents they perceived as less similar. Newcomb reports that while actual similarity between two people was also related to attraction, perceived similarity was more closely related to liking (Newcomb, 1978).

In general, research has supported Newcomb's finding that people's perception of the similarity between themselves and others is a more potent determinant of attraction than actual similarity. Byrne and Blaylock (1963) studied the actual and assumed similarity of husbands and wives. Thirty-six married couples completed questionnaires about their political opinions. The participants completed their own questionnaire and one for their spouse. This enabled the researchers to determine actual similarity by comparing the husband's and wife's responses, and assumed similarity by comparing responses made for a spouse with those the spouse actually made.

Byrne and Blaylock did find that husbands and wives had similar attitudes, but the assumed similarity was even greater than the actual similarity. Of course, it is impossible to tell from this study whether actual similarity existed before marriage or whether it developed during the course of the marriage. Nor, as the authors point out, do the results enable us to determine whether assumed similarity increased over time relative to actual similarity. They do suggest, however, that the assumption that others are more similar to ourselves than they actually are plays an important role in maintaining a relationship. Whether we perceive others to be more similar to ourselves than they actually are depends to some extent on how we perceive the relative similarity of still other people. For example, if you believe that other couples are not at all similar to each other, then you will tend to assume that you and your mate are more similar than you actually are (Hensley & Duval, 1976).

There is some cross-cultural evidence that similarity is positively related to attraction. Byrne, Gouaux, Griffitt, Lamberth, Murakawa, Prasad, Prasad, and Ramirez (1971) presented students in Hawaii, India, Japan, Mexico, and the continental United States with attitude questionnaires ostensibly completed by another student. The proportion of attitudes similar to the subjects' was determined and their evaluations of the stranger (on the Interpersonal Judgment Scale) were obtained. The results, summarized in Table 6.1, indicate that as the proportion of responses similar to the subjects' increased, attraction increased. These results were obtained in each of the five samples. Note that in this study the attraction under consideration is toward a hypothetical stranger, not toward someone with whom the subjects have interacted.

Theoretical Explanations for Similarity and Attraction

Reinforcement theory.   Byrne does not believe that it is similarity per se that leads to attraction. Rather, his explanation of the similarity–attraction relationship is based on a learning theory analysis of similarity. He takes the position that people like others who reward them and dislike those who punish them. He notes that "the expression of similar attitudes by a stranger serves as a positive reinforcement" (1971, p. 338). What is being reinforced by a similar

Table 6.1.
Mean Attraction toward Strangers in Five Samples

| | Proportion of Similar Responses | | | |
	.00–.40	.47–.60	.67–1.00	Total
Hawaii	7.03	8.27	8.46	7.92
India	7.19	8.34	9.40	8.31
Japan	6.27	6.94	7.53	6.91
Mexico	7.31	8.55	9.11	8.32
U.S.	6.00	7.33	7.38	6.90
Total	6.76	7.89	8.37	

Adapted from Byrne, Gouaux, Griffitt, Lamberth, Murakawa, Prasad, Prasad, and Ramirez (1971).

attitude is some validation of a person's own attitudes. If other people share your attitudes, they are essentially affirming that your attitudes are "correct."

The reinforcement theory interpretation of similarity and attraction has been criticized on a number of grounds (see Byrne, Clore, Griffitt, Lamberth, & Mitchell, 1973; Kaplan & Anderson, 1973). Fishbein and Ajzen (1975) argue that, as with most reinforcement notions, no precise definition is provided for the concepts of positive and negative reinforcement. "Specifically, similarity is said to lead to attraction because of its reinforcement value, and we know that it has reinforcement value when it produces attraction. . . . [L]earning theory specifies that the amount of attraction should be a function of the *number* of reinforced trials. Byrne's (1971) conclusion that attraction is only a function of proportion and not of number of similar opinions is in direct opposition to most reinforcement theories"(Fishbein & Ajzen, pp. 268–269).

It is not only on theoretical grounds that the reinforcement interpretation of similarity–attraction research has been criticized. There are a number of studies (which will be reviewed shortly) that either do not find a positive relationship between similarity and liking or find the relationship only under certain, limited conditions.

Cognitive balance. Heider's influential book, *The psychology of interpersonal relations* (1958), contains an exposition of sentiments toward other people and toward objects. Consistent with his Gestalt/cognitive orientation, Heider proposes that our sentiments toward others depend upon the extent to which they share our views of the world:

By a balanced state is meant a harmonious state, one in which the entities comprising the situation and the feelings about them fit together without stress. That naïve psychology has little difficulty detecting situations of imbalance can be seen in the following examples:
p *hates* **o** *because he is so similar to* **o.**
He always imitates people he dislikes.
He always hates people with whom he has to work.
He hates **q** *because* **q** *is similar to his friend* **o.**
He avoids people he likes. . . .
In some way we sense that the factors in the situation "do not add up"; they seem to pull in different directions. They leave us with a feeling of disturbance that becomes relieved only when change within the situation takes place in such a way that a state of balance is achieved. (p. 180)

Heider's balance model assumes that there will be a tendency toward balance, harmony, or "mental homeostasis" in our sentiments toward others. Such a state of balance occurs when one person and another hold similar attitudes toward the same object (see top of Figure 6.2), and when the person likes the other. The clear prediction from this theory is that we tend to like others whose attitudes agree with our own. When there is disagreement, the person will tend not to like the other (see bottom of Figure 6.2).

Newcomb's model for interpersonal settings is similar to Heider's balance model. Newcomb (1953, 1956, 1978) proposed a cognitive model concerned with interpersonal relations between two individuals. There is a tendency, he suggested, for interpersonal relations to be in *symmetry*, just as Heider suggested that an individual's cognitions tend to be balanced. When asymmetry exists, as when there is disagreement between two individuals in their attitudes, communications will be exchanged between them in an effort to restore symmetry. So Newcomb proposes that there is a tendency for attitudinal differences to be reduced by interpersonal communication, just as Heider proposed that the perception of a disagreement will lead to cognitive changes within a single person.

Murstein (1971) has specified nearly a dozen difficulties with Heider's balance theory. Most of them deal with the lack of quantification of variables. For example, Heider sees a system involving two individuals and their attitudes toward some object as either balanced or imbalanced; there are no degrees of balance in his scheme. (This problem has been addressed, however, by others, most particularly Newcomb, 1971, and Cartwright and Harary, 1956.) Likewise, liking is either present or absent, according to Heider, although clearly, liking can vary in degree. And Heider gives an attitude toward an object the same weight as an attitude toward a person. Murstein notes that Heider's implication that balance is good or desirable "does not completely jibe with human experience" (p. 24). Tension, ambivalence, and imbalance may all be desirable for some people, at least to a certain extent. Heider also is vague in stating how imbalance is resolved. Murstein concludes that Heider's balance theory has proved to be an important source of research hypotheses, but that it is too simple to provide an adequate explanation of the complexities of interpersonal attraction.

Expected liking. An interpretation of the similarity–attraction research that has some features in common with both the reinforcement interpretation and the balance model is based on the notion of expected liking. People may like others with similar attitudes, beliefs, or traits because they expect that those people will like them in return. In other words, we do not expect to be rejected by someone who is similar to us. In an early test of this hypothesis, Walster and Walster (1963) led some students to believe that they would be disliked by others, while a different group of students was led to believe that others would like them. The students were then asked to pick from a list of similar or dissimilar others those with whom

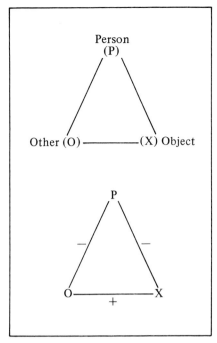

Figure 6.2.
Balance theory and attraction.

they most desired to associate. If the subjects were assured of being liked, they were more willing to interact with dissimilar others. Those who were assured of being disliked most often chose similar others. Additional support for this proposition has been obtained by Walster (1965) and Berscheid et al. (1971). It is entirely possible, then, that we like similar others because we believe they will not reject us and because we fear that dissimilar others will not like us. (See "Making a Date If You Are Shy," pp. 198–199.)

Methodological explanations. It is also possible that the empirical relationship between similarity and liking is due in part to the particular ways in which similarity has been measured or manipulated. Imagine that a person, Jim, is described to you as "intelligent, friendly, a good basketball player, moderately good looking." If you think of yourself as bright, friendly, of average looks, and if you are an avid basketball player, then you will probably tend to like Jim. This would demonstrate a positive relationship between similarity and attraction. But you may like Jim because you think the traits of intelligence and friendliness and the ability to play basketball are in some sense "good." In other words, Jim's particular attitudes, characteristics, or abilities may appear to be positive to you, and you will like Jim not because he is similar to you but because he possesses traits that you view positively. There is some evidence that the manipulation of similarity in much of the attraction research results in a simultaneous, and quite inadvertent, manipulation of

**MAKING A DATE IF
YOU ARE SHY**

Dating is a social contact that is often anxiety-provoking for shy people, because of its promise of intimacy and the more than usual emotional intensity it demands. Shy daters feel great vulnerability to imagined threats of rejection. For many, this anxiety outweighs the anticipated rewards and they "just don't date." Perhaps for this reason, more and more dating is becoming a group activity: "A bunch of us are going bowling. Why don't you come along?"

Make your date by telephone. That way you can at least avoid worrying about body language. Plan ahead; have two specific activities in mind.

When you reach the person, clearly identify yourself by name and explain where you met, if necessary: "This is John Simmons. I met you at the Clarks' open house last week." Then:

☐ Be sure you are recognized in turn; if not, establish who you are.

☐ Pay the person a compliment related to your last meeting, one that indicates your regard for his/her ideas, values, position on an issue, sense of humor—that is, some nonsuperficial attribute.

☐ Be assertive in coming to the point of requesting a date: "I was wondering if you'd like to come to a movie with me this Friday." Be specific in your request, state the activity in mind and the time it will take place.

☐ If "yes," decide together on the particular movie and times (have alternatives ready

---

the positive or negative qualities of the stranger's attitudes or traits.

Stalling (1970) had students rate over 120 personality traits (such as "aggressive," "honest") as "pleasant" or "unpleasant" and as "like me" or "unlike me." There was a tendency for subjects to rate traits they saw as positive also as traits most "like me." The correlation between these two ratings was $+.88$. Similarity may lead to attraction, then, because similar traits are also seen as the most pleasant.

A study by Ajzen (1974) manipulated both the similarity of a stranger's traits to the subject's, and whether the attributes of the stranger were positive or negative. He reports that evaluation of the stranger was positive when the stranger was portrayed as having positive personality traits, and was most negative when the stranger was portrayed as having negative personality traits. Whether the stranger was similar or dissimilar to the subjects made relatively little difference in the subjects' ratings.

Does Similarity Always Lead to Attraction? Despite the considerable evidence that similarity leads to attraction, we can still raise questions about the relative importance of similarity in relation to other causes of attraction. Does similarity, assumed similarity, or the implied positiveness of similar traits always lead to attraction? Does similarity lead to attraction only for some people? Only in certain to allow the other person some freedom of choice). End the conversation smoothly, but quickly, and, of course, politely.

☐ If "no," assess whether the activity or the time is not appropriate, and suggest alternatives for each. Or, suggest a more informal get-together if your unexpected request proves too anxiety-provoking for the shy person on the other end of the line: "How about getting together then for a cup of coffee (or a drink) after work sometime?" If the answer is still "no go," the interest is not there at this time and you should politely end the conversation.

Refusal to go on a date does not mean *you* are being rejected.

Health, work, previous commitments, excessive shyness, etc., can all account for a turndown.

Suppose *you* are asked for a date and are not interested in getting to know the person. Never say "yes" out of sympathy or guilt. Do not hesitate to say, "No, thank you. I appreciate your asking, but I'd rather not." Do so without hurting the requester (he or she may also be shy and have spent hours practicing this exercise). You have the right to say "no" to anyone, to be pleased that you are desirable to someone, without offering an explanation of your refusal.

Reprinted from *Shyness: What it is, what to do about it* by Philip Zimbardo, Copyright © 1977, by permission of Addison: Wesley Publishing Co. Reading, Mass., pp. 184–185.

situations? Perhaps similarity is more important in our culture than it is in some others. There is some research on these issues.

If attraction toward real or hypothetical strangers is the dependent measure in studies of similarity and attraction, the relationship tends to be strong, even though it is not easily interpreted. Studies that fail to confirm the predicted effects of similarity on attraction have usually been conducted with people already involved in some relationship, mainly with dating couples. Levinger (1972), Hoffman and Maier (1966), Walster, Aronson, Abrahams, and Rottmann (1966), and Brislin and Lewis (1968) all failed to find evidence of the relationship between similarity and liking. All these studies used as subjects couples who had had at least one date together.

There are, of course, studies with real couples and friends that do find effects for similarity. Griffitt and Veitch (1974) found that attitudinal similarity was positively related to friendship among men living for ten days in a simulated fallout shelter. Newcomb's (1961) study of men living in a co-op house found a comparable relationship. And in a study on dating, Byrne et al. (1970) found that attitudinal similarity as well as the physical attractiveness of the person's date were positively related to attraction and a desire to continue dating the person.

Thus, while there is considerable evidence that liking for another person is positively related to attitudinal and other forms of similarity, the relationship appears strongest where prior interaction with the other person has not yet occurred or has been minimal. Although there is evidence from studies of interacting people to support the similarity–attraction hypothesis, what disconfirming evidence exists has almost always been obtained with interacting individuals. In other words, similarity can better predict attraction toward strangers than it can attraction toward others with whom we have already had some contact. This does not imply that similarity plays no role in real-life attraction, only that the role is limited and may be offset by other variables.

We need to know the conditions under which similarity is relatively unimportant and those variables that take precedence over similarity in particular circumstances. Some work along these lines has been conducted. There are about a dozen studies that demonstrate that, under particular circumstances, people are more attracted to dissimilar than to similar others. When others are known to have some valuable personal resource such as information or expertise, they may be liked because of this resource even if they are dissimilar (Rosenblood & Goldstein, 1969; Walster & Walster, 1963). If others are similar when dissimilarity is sought, similarity will not lead to maximum attraction. For example, a teacher should be dissimilar to her students in her knowledge of subject matter—the teacher should know the material better than her students. If she were similar to her students on this dimension, she would be liked less than if she were dissimilar (Grush, Clore, & Costin, 1975). Likewise, when another who is stigmatized in some sense is similar to a person, the person will like the other less than if the other were dissimilar. For example, a person who is emotionally disturbed will be liked less if he holds similar attitudes to a person, while a normal person will be liked more if he holds similar attitudes (Bleda, 1974).

In most real encounters with others, we know more about them than the similarity of their attitudes, values, and beliefs to our own. In such cases, the similarity of attitudes and traits is interpreted in terms of the totality of things we know about them. Stimuli, including attitudinal similarities, are interpreted in their total context. Sometimes similarity is seen as important, rewarding, and desirable, and sometimes it is not. Recent research has helped us to set limits on the effects of similarity on interpersonal attraction. But there are other than purely empirical reasons for questioning the generality of the similarity–attraction hypothesis. For one, it does not always seem to jibe with experience. This was particularly so for the French social psychologist Serge Moscovici.

I encountered . . . difficulties with some of the maxims implicit in a good deal of current [American] research: "We like those who support us"; "The leader is a person who understands the needs of the members of his group"; "We help those who help us"; "Understanding the point of view of another person promotes cooperation." This "social psychology of the nice person" was to me then—as it still is today— offensive in many ways; it had little relevance to what I knew or had experienced. Its implicit moral stance reminded me of another maxim . . . : "It is better to be healthy and rich than to be ill and poor." I knew from my social experience that we seek out those who differ from us and that we can identify with them; that we can love someone who is contemptuous of us; that leaders may impose themselves on others through violence or through following unremittingly their own ideals—and that often, in doing this, they are not only admired but also loved; and that, after all, is it not an opponent who often comes to know us best? (1972, pp. 18–19)

There is not only research but also considerable theoretical support for Moscovici's contention that people do indeed frequently find themselves attracted to others *because of* their very differences. That, after all, is why many people travel to exotic places for vacations; study cultural anthropology; go out of their way to meet people who have had experiences different from their own. Several psychological theories deal with the importance of novelty and unfamiliarity in social life (see Chapter 3). Berlyne (1960), for example, proposed that individuals are motivated by a need to explore and understand their environments. The presence of a novel, unfamiliar, or unique individual should lead to attraction toward that person, provided there is no evidence that the person is in any way threatening (see Rothbart, 1976; R. W. White, 1959). Curiosity about others may well lead to a desire to associate with those whose experiences are different from our own. Perhaps such dissimilarity and subsequent attraction may be explained on the basis of the need to test the validity of our own perceptions and attitudes so that those with differing views may be refuted, or so that we may practice defending our viewpoints. Then, too, different views may be seen as complementary to our own or as broadening our horizons.

PROPINQUITY

It is not surprising that people are most attracted to those who live or work nearby. As we shall see shortly, this may be in part because we interact most often with neighbors and co-workers. It is an old and common concept in attraction literature that people form attachments most readily and most often to others not physically distant from themselves.

J. H. S. Bossard, the sociologist, reported in 1945 that couples who filed for marriage licenses in Philadelphia tended to live in the same neighborhood. Festinger, Schachter, and Back (1950) found that people living in a campus housing project at MIT tended to form friendships with those who lived closest to them. Nahemow and Lawton (1975) report that proximity was related to friendship in a housing project. In the Nahemow and Lawton study, it was also reported that people tended to make friends with others who were similar in age, race, and sex, regardless of how distant they lived within the project. But if a person lived in close proximity to someone of a different age, sex, or race, friendship still developed, partly because of the frequency and ease of interaction.

While liking and friendship formation are positively associated with propinquity and similarity, there is evidence that aggression and hostility are likewise related to similarity and proximity (e.g., Goldstein, 1975; Wolfgang, 1958). For example, the most common relationship between victim and offender in cases of criminal homicide is that of husband and wife. Crime victims tend to be similar to offenders in terms of sex, social class, race, age, and other demographic characteristics. So it may be that similarity and proximity are positively associated with strong emotions and related behaviors, and not exclusively with liking and attraction (see Chapters 7 and 8).

EXPECTED INTERACTION AND MERE EXPOSURE

Much of the research on attraction has dealt with liking for hypothetical strangers. Such research has been criticized as unrealistic because we may not often make evaluative judgments of strangers, or if we do, they may not be inflexible but may change as we learn new things about their personalities and behaviors. And it has been demonstrated that even the *expected* interaction with another influences our feelings toward the person.

Darley and Berscheid (1967) report that college students who believe they will soon interact with another student in a discussion increase their liking for the other student more than they do for a student who they believe will not take part in the discussion. More recent research by Tyler and Sears (1977) has shown that an increase in liking for a person with whom we expect to interact occurs only when we know little about the other person or when we initially dislike the other, but does not occur when we already have positive attitudes toward the person.

Not only can our attitudes toward another person change on the basis of expected interaction, but they also tend to become more favorable the more we are exposed to the person. This was first proposed by Robert Zajonc (1968) as the *mere exposure hypothesis*. It was proposed, and the hypothesis was supported by considerable evidence, that the more familiar we are with someone or something, the more favorable our attitudes will be toward that person or

object. In the area of interpersonal attraction, this has generally led to research in which participants interact with one another for varying lengths of time. The results show that, in general, the more someone is exposed to another person, the greater the liking for that person (Kail, 1977; Moreland & Zajonc, 1977; Saegert, Swap, & Zajonc, 1973; Stang, 1974).

People tend to make friends with those who are similar to them in age, race, and sex—but living next door leads to a lot of friendships, too.

PHYSICAL ATTRACTIVENESS: SEX APPEAL

It is said that love and justice are blind, but it seems that at least one of them is only nearsighted. If love were blind, physical appearance would not have much of an effect on interpersonal attraction. As we will see, many studies do find a relationship between appearance and at least initial levels of attraction. Of course, many of the studies to be reviewed here were conducted with college students as subjects, and they may demonstrate that appearance is important for casual dating or in the initial stages of a relationship, but not for more deeply felt attachments. There is a considerable amount of research, and very little theory, on physical attractiveness (Walster & Walster, 1978). This is because physical appearance is relatively easy to quantify and is one of the most visible characteristics that enter into dating. It is, in other words, easier to study physical appearance than, say, the role of psychological needs in dating.

Much of the research literature on physical attractiveness has been reviewed by G. Wilson and Nias (1976), and because space will not permit a detailed review of that research here, I recommend it to any interested readers. For present purposes, only a few questions about physical attractiveness will be addressed: Is there cross-cultural agreement on physical attractiveness? What is the role of physical appearance in dating? How do people's physical appearances affect how others perceive them?

G. Wilson and Nias reviewed several studies on judgments of physical attractiveness and concluded that there is widespread agreement among both males and females on the physical attractiveness of women, but not of men. Iliffe (1960), for example, had a dozen photographs of women's faces ranked for prettiness by more than 4000 readers of an English daily newspaper. Regardless of the respondent's age, social class, or sex, there was considerable agreement on which women were the most attractive. G. Wilson and Nias did note, though, that as additional information about others became available, such as information about their interests or personalities, the extent of agreement on ratings of physical appearance decreased. Knowledge of the personal attributes of others influences our judgments of their attractiveness, just as their attractiveness influences our judgments of their personal traits.

It is widely known that different cultures hold different standards of beauty. But "there is fairly universal agreement that the physical appearance of women is more central to their overall attractiveness than it is for men" (Wilson & Nias, 1976, p. 30). What leads men to classify some women as beautiful in Western society? It is generally believed that the woman's figure is an important determinant of judgments of beauty. Ignoring the contribution of facial characteristics to judgments of physical beauty, Wiggins, Wiggins, and Conger (1968) varied the size and shape of a woman's breasts, buttocks, and legs in silhouettes of nude females. In their scientific assault on judgments of feminine beauty, they presented nearly 100 undergraduate men with pairs of nude female silhouettes in which breasts, buttocks, and legs were varied in size. The males rated the most attractive silhouette in each pair. Later, they also completed questionnaires about their personal backgrounds and took several personality tests. Preference for a particular type of figure was then correlated with this demographic and personality information. Some of the findings indicate that a preference for a large figure (large breasts, large buttocks, and large legs) was associated with a high need for achievement. One of the most preferred figures was average in size, and men preferring this "standard figure" tended to be disorganized in their personal habits. Those preferring a small figure tended to be persevering in their work and reported coming from an upper-class background. Several correlates pertained only to a particular body part. For example, men who preferred the large-breasted figures dated often, had strong masculine interests, and read sports magazines and *Playboy* magazine frequently. Those preferring small breasts showed "a lack of orality" as evidenced by their low alcohol consumption, and tended to come from non-working-class families. As a group, they tended to be engineering rather than business majors. Large buttocks were preferred by business majors and they displayed signs of orderliness, passivity, dependence, and guilt, which the authors note is similar to the "anal character" described by Freud. Large legs were preferred by those who abstain from alcohol; they tended to be nonaggressive and self-abasing. A preference for small legs was associated with social participation and needs for nurturance, affiliation, and exhibitionism.

We should not be tempted to overgeneralize from the study by Wiggins et al., which was based on a limited sample of undergraduate midwestern university men. While these researchers noted some relationships between psychoanalytic stages of development and body preference, other studies have failed to find any such relationship. Scodel (1957), for example, failed to find that men with "oral personalities" preferred large-breasted women.

If a study can examine male preferences for female body types, why not a study of female preferences for male body types? This glaring omission from the psychological literature was supplied by Beck, Ward-Hull, and McLear (1976). Their study was similar in design to the study by Wiggins and colleagues, except that they employed 115 women undergraduates who rated pairs of male silhouettes. The silhouettes varied in chest, buttocks, and leg size. As a group, the women most preferred a male of moderate proportions with small buttocks. There was only a slight preference for males with somewhat larger than average chests.

SOME IMPLICATIONS OF BEAUTY

Impressions of people depend, sometimes to a great extent, on their physical appearance. In our culture, there are both positive and negative stereotypes of physically attractive people. While there is some research on the implications of having a physical disability (e.g., Goffman, 1963), there is considerably more on the kinds of attributions made to attractive people. In a typical experiment in this area, Landy and Sigall (1974) presented male college students with an essay supposedly written by a female student. Some students were led to believe that the writer was physically attractive, some that she was unattractive, and some were given no information about her appearance. Half of each group received a good essay and

Standards of beauty tend to differ from one group to the next. Some people would find this man's physique exciting, some would say it's interesting, and some would wonder why he went to all the trouble.

half a poor essay. The students then rated the quality of the essay. The results indicated, first, that the good essay was judged better than the poor one. But the quality of the essay was rated higher when the writer was portrayed as attractive than when she was said to be unattractive. K. Dion, Berscheid, and Walster (1972) had college students rate sets of photographs of both males and females on a number of dimensions. One photo in each set was attractive, one was average in appearance, and one was unattractive. Their results indicate that, regardless of the sex of the subject or of the person depicted in the photographs, attractive people were judged to be happier, to have a greater likelihood of marriage, to have higher status, and to be socially more successful than unattractive persons. Positive implications of physical attractiveness have been obtained in a number of other studies.

Judgments of attractive people are generally more favorable than those of unattractive people. Attractive people are also more effective in influencing others' opinions (Horai, Naccari, & Fatoullah, 1974) and are usually treated more courteously (Sroufe, Chaikin, Cook, & Freeman, 1977).

Because attractive individuals seem to be treated so well and are assumed to be happier than average or unattractive people, it makes sense to examine the quality of their lives to determine whether such judgments are warranted. Mathes and Kahn (1975) found that looks have no relationship to feelings of happiness for men, but are slightly related to happiness for women. Attractive women report that they feel happier, are better adjusted, and have higher feelings of self-esteem than less attractive women.

That beauty is used as a social asset can be seen in an analysis of personal advertisements for dates. A. A. Harrison and Saeed (1977) found that women tended to offer attractiveness in exchange for financial security (for example, "Attractive woman, 35, seeks professional gentleman, 35–50").

Attractiveness has meaning for males and females alike, and that meaning is generally, though not exclusively (e.g., Dermer & Thiel, 1975), favorable. Attractiveness tends to fade with age, however, and perhaps personal happiness or attributions of positive traits tend to diminish with the dissipation of beauty. That, at least, is one implication of a study by Berscheid and Walster (1974). They measured adjustment in middle-aged people and compared this with their attractiveness when they were young by having photographs from their college yearbooks rated by judges. They found that women who were highly attractive when young tended to be less happy and less well adjusted when they were about 50 years of age. This was not the case for men, for whom attractiveness bore no relationship to adjustment in middle age.

MATCHING OF PHYSICAL ATTRACTIVENESS

Because so many theories emphasize the role of similarity in attraction, it is not unreasonable to try to determine whether there is greater attraction between two people whose physical attractiveness is similar than between people who vary greatly in terms of beauty. It is generally assumed that people prefer dates who are roughly similar in physical attractiveness, or who are just slightly better looking than themselves.

In the first large-scale test of this "matching hypothesis," Walster et al. (1966) arranged a computer dance at the University of Wisconsin. Students who signed up for the dance completed personal questionnaires and believed that they would be assigned compatible dates by the computer. When they handed in their questionnaires, they were unknowingly judged for physical attractiveness by two assistants, and were later randomly assigned a date. Toward the end of the dance, each person was interviewed to determine how attracted he or she was to the assigned date. Initially, the researchers expected to find that people would most like a date similar to themselves in personality, background, and physical attractiveness. What they found was that the only important determinant of attraction was the date's physical appearance. People liked their dates most when the dates were attractive. Similar results were obtained at a different university by Brislin and Lewis (1968). Byrne et al. (1970) also found a preference for physically attractive dates, but obtained evidence that attitudinal similarity was also related to the subjects' desire to date the person again.

In the studies on computer dances, the students involved all met and talked with their dates before rating them for attractiveness. According to Berscheid et al. (1971), a person is most likely to prefer a date of comparable physical attractiveness when no interaction has yet taken place. In the computer dance studies, students spent some time with their dates and reported being most attracted to good-looking partners. In actuality, people may fear rejection by attractive others, especially if they are not themselves physically attractive, and so they are unlikely to attempt to date such people in the first place. In their studies, Berscheid et al. had students choose a date from a series of photographs. In this case, rejection by the other was possible because the two had not yet met and "hit it off." As a result, students selected dates who were comparable to themselves in physical attractiveness. Observational studies of dating couples (Silverman, 1971) find that the partners tend to be similar to each other in their level of physical attractiveness. Presumably, then, most people (or perhaps only college students, because they are the participants in nearly all this research) would rather date someone who is physically attractive, but may not attempt to date such a person for fear of rejection. They are most apt to date someone whose physical appearance is comparable to their own.

We have reviewed some of the correlates of physical beauty, examined several aspects of interpersonal attraction, and explored some variables that make for a desire to date others. But we have yet to explore in any detail the social psychological nature of more mature and enduring relationships, a topic to which we now turn.

ROMANTIC ATTRACTION AND LOVE

To poets, love is a mystery; to social psychologists, it is a dependent variable. In order to examine romantic love in a social psychological framework, we must arrive at some measure of love, provide operational definitions of love, and correlate people's feelings of love with some overt behaviors. Examining a deeply held feeling like love from a scientific perspective tends to take some of the mystery and allure from it. There are more than a few people who feel that there are some things about which it is better to know nothing, and love is one of those. But problems in romantic relationships threaten the social fabric as much as drug abuse and crime. Over one-third of America's children live with only one of their natural parents. The rate of unsuccessful marriages has continued to climb throughout the last three decades. Perhaps it would be better to know something about romantic love after all. Not that social psychologists will be able to provide us with all the information we need to have, but they may at least offer us their views of romantic love as a starting

With divorce rates climbing, perhaps social psychologists should spend more time studying romantic love. This couple may not have all the answers, but they certainly are enjoying the research.

point. Social psychological analyses of love will at least have the advantage of being testable, and of being falsifiable if they are incorrect.

As was suggested earlier, there are both theoretical (e.g., Levinger & Snoek, 1972) and empirical (Rubin, 1970) reasons for treating attraction toward strangers and brief acquaintances differently from romantic attachments. In romantic attraction, variables that are unimportant in simpler, more superficial kinds of relationships become important. A distinction between liking and loving has been made by Zick Rubin (1970). Loving entails caring for and feeling an attachment to another, and also involves a component of intimacy. Liking refers only to a favorable evaluation of another person. Rubin developed a scale to measure liking and a scale to measure loving. He thought the two scales would only moderately correlate with each other. For example, items on the loving scale include:

I would do almost anything for _____ .
It would be hard for me to get along without _____.

I heard a man and woman recently who had fallen in love. "Hopelessly in love" was the woman's antique phrase for it. I hadn't realized people still did that sort of thing jointly. Nowadays the fashion is to fall in love with yourself, and falling in love with a second party seems to be generally regarded as bad form.

It may be, of course, that many people are still doing it, but simply not admitting it publicly, perhaps on the assumption that it is a shameful act, as adultery used to be. Nowadays people discuss their adultery with strangers at parties and on airplanes, and not long ago I saw a married couple chatting about theirs on television, the way people used to discuss their car-repair problems.

A possible explanation, I suppose, is that in an age when the fashion is to be in love with yourself, confessing to being in love with somebody else is an admission of unfaithfulness to one's beloved. The truth is probably more complicated.

Consider, for example, the situation of Ed and Jane, a hypothetical modern couple who see each other across a crowded room, feel inexplicable sensations not reducible to computer printouts

and make human contact. After conventional preliminary events, they will naturally want to express what exists between them.

Jane may announce that they "relate" beautifully. Ed may boast about how gratifyingly they "communicate." The beauty of their "relating" and the gratifications of their "communicating" may induce them to "establish a relationship."

Why it is always a "relationship" they establish, and never a "communicationship," I don't know, but "relationship" is the universally approved term. On days when things go badly, they do not have a lovers' quarrel. Instead, Jane says that Ed is not "relating" and Ed says that Jane is not "communicating."

On days when things go well they boast about how "fulfilling" their "relationship" is. Ed and Jane do not dream of living happily ever after. They are more like the Bell Telephone system. They aspire to heavy communicating in a fulfilling relationship.

In fact, they are probably afraid of falling in love; and if, in spite of everything, they nevertheless do fall in love, they are too embarrassed to tell anybody. Why? One reason is that it is such an out-of-date thing

I would forgive _____ for practically anything.
Among the items on the liking scale are the following:
    I think that _____ is unusually well adjusted.
    I think that _____ and I are quite similar to one another.
    _____ is the sort of person whom I myself would like to be.
Among university students who had been dating the same person for some time, the correlations between the liking and the loving scales were +.56 for males and +.36 for females. As Rubin's research suggests, it is possible to construct instruments capable of measuring these two different emotional states.

to do. Falling in love is not scientific. It cannot be described in the brain-numbing jargon of sociology. It can only be described in the words of song writers. People in Cole Porter's antique old songs were always falling in love, and worse, talking about romance. Romance! Astaire and Rogers in a penthouse, and other such musty stuff. We have moved on to Mick Jagger, to John Lennon, who urged everybody to do it in the road instead of in the penthouse.

Falling in love is archaic, like cookouts and tail fins on your Plymouth. Communicating, relating, experiencing fulfilling relationships—these are what up-to-date boys and girls engage in.

When disaster strikes, it is not "the end of a love affair" to make them blue, but "the destruction of our relationship" to make them yearn for new "therapeutic experience."

This grotesque terminology in which Americans now discuss what used to be called affairs of the heart is curious not only for its comic pseudoscientific sound, but also for the coolness with which it treats a passion formerly associated with heat. It takes a very cool pair of cats to talk about the grandest of passions as though it were only an exercise in sociology. Imagine Dante filling pages about the satisfactory nature of communicating with Beatrice, or Juliet raving on through five acts about her fulfilling relationship with Romeo.

The way people talk, of course, reflects the way they think, and this avoidance of the language of love probably reflects a wish to avoid the consuming single-minded commitment to love to which the old words led, often no doubt to the dismay of people who uttered them. Why in our time we should tread so gingerly to avoid commitment to love to the second party is the subject for a monograph. Perhaps it comes from a fear of living too fully, perhaps from the current cultural fashion of conditioning us to believe that whatever interferes with self-love will lead to psychic headache.

Whatever the explanation, it is a bleak era for love, which makes it a time of dull joys, small-bore agonies and thin passions. "I could not love thee, dear, so much, lov'd I not honor more," the poet once could write. Today he could only say, "I could not have so fulfilling a relationship with thee, dear, had I not an even more highly intensified mental set as regards the absurd and widely discredited concept known as honor."

Russell Baker, *New York Times*, 19 March 1978, p. 17.

Because our notions of love come largely from our own Western, and fairly homogeneous, culture, it is worthwhile to examine the universality of romantic love. As I have tried to demonstrate throughout this book, we often gain insights into social processes by exploring them in widely divergent cultural contexts. This cross-cultural undertaking helps us to place social behavior in perspective so that we may try to distinguish better between biological universals and cultural variations.

As Rubin (1973) notes, our conception of romantic love stems from twelfth-century Europe and is in this sense relatively modern.

It has also been noted that there are both historical and cultural variations in the conception of love and in its perceived importance. Paul Rosenblatt (1966, 1974) has reviewed the anthropological research on romantic love and conducted original cross-cultural research on the concept. While the institution of marriage seems to be universal among human cultures, Rosenblatt finds that the importance of romantic love as the basis for marriage is not. He makes a distinction between those cultures that arrange marriages and those in which a person has some choice in spouse. Where there is choice, the concept of romantic love serves as a justification for choosing a particular person as a partner. In general, where free choice of spouse is typical in a culture, where there is little economic dependency between spouses, and where the choice of a particular spouse must be justified, then the importance of love is at its peak. In such cultures, there is an emphasis not only on romantic love but on other "impractical" grounds for marriage, such as beauty, "which suggests that beauty is important only where people must choose spouses on their own and perhaps where decisions are difficult and not easily justified on more practical grounds" (1974, p. 88).

Rosenblatt did not explore the question of whether romantic love is universal, but we may conclude that there are at least some cultures that do not stress it or consider it important. Cultures may either encourage the development of romantic love or discourage it, by providing or preventing opportunities for members of the opposite sex to interact, to be alone, and to spend much time together. In our own culture, of course, romantic love is encouraged. Informal social institutions such as singles bars, personal columns in newspapers, and coed dorms exist for the purpose of fostering heterosexual interaction, free choice of spouse is the norm, and economic pressures do not serve as the foundation of marriage. In cultures where romantic love is a basis for marriage, attempts to interfere with love by placing obstacles between people tend to fail. Driscoll, Davis, and Lipetz (1972) have dubbed this the "Romeo and Juliet" effect. When parents try to disrupt their children's romantic involvements, they are apt to drive the couple closer together.

SIMILARITY AGAIN, AND NEED COMPLEMENTARITY

Until the 1950s, it was thought that similarity of attitudes, values, needs, beliefs, physical appearance, and political and social characteristics formed the basis of lasting relationships. We have already seen the role played by similarity and assumed similarity both in initial attraction and in longer relationships. But we have seen, too, that similarity is not pervasive enough to explain romantic love. And, like the proverbial sadist who becomes devoted to a masochist, there are numerous clinical examples of complementary traits as the

First, the spouses in a workable marriage respect each other. Each spouse finds some important quality or ability to respect in the other—being a good parent, making a lot of money, writing beautiful music, or whatever. The greater the number of areas of respect, the more satisfactory the marriage.

Second, the spouses are tolerant of each other. They see themselves as fallible, vulnerable human beings and can therefore accept each other's shortcomings.

Third, the key ingredient in a successful marriage is the effort of the spouses to make the most of its assets and minimize its liabilities. . . . [I]f the spouses have enough cultural values in common (and usually they would not have married if they did not *think* they did) workability depends on *learning to communicate* in order to negotiate *quid pro quo*'s. This allows them to agree on common goals and progress toward these goals. Further, workability requires the recognition that a marital relationship is not static. Relationship is a process involving constant change; and constant change requires the spouses to *keep*

working on their relationship until the day they die.

Somehow, a myth has arisen in this country which teaches that the first few years of marriage form the period during which all problems "get ironed out." The implication seems to be that thereafter the spouses sit passively while the marital wagon rolls along through life. This conception of the relationship is nonsense. . . . Divorce figures indicate how fallacious this myth really is. Interviews with hundreds of couples clearly show that those who resign themselves to a static relationship are inviting divorce, desertion, or disaster. Disaster comes in many forms in marriage, from psychosomatic and mental illness all the way to the grim life of the Gruesome Twosome.

Perhaps in the rapidly changing world of the twentieth century the traditional family and marriage structure may become anachronistic. But at present the family unit and monogamous marriage still are the keystones of our culture, and we believe they are worth a lot of effort.

THE MAJOR ELEMENTS OF A SATISFACTORY MARRIAGE

From Lederer and Jackson
(1968, pp. 198–199).

basis for enduring relationships. The sociologist R. F. Winch (1958) proposed a theory of mate selection that encompasses both similarity and complementarity.

Winch argued that in order for two people to meet, and in order for them to decide that a relationship may be continued, they must have similarity of interests. If you are outgoing and dominant, you are apt to go to a singles bar where it is unlikely you will meet a shy, passive teetotaler. Instead, you will most likely run into people who are similar to you in some basic respects. While similarity enhances your chances, it is hardly sufficient as a basis for a relationship, according to Winch. The mutual satisfaction of personal needs is the key to enduring attraction. Winch refers to this as *need complementarity.*

Two types of need complementarity are described by Winch. Type I exists when one partner is high on a particular need, such as dominance, and the other partner is low on that need. Type II complementarity exists when one partner is high on one need and the other partner is high on a different but complementary need, such as a male who has a high need for hostility and a female who has a high need for abasement or abuse. After studying 25 married couples, Winch concluded that complementarity may be observed in terms of achievement and passivity, nurturance and dependence, and dominance and deference. When complementarity exists on these three pairs of complementary needs, marital satisfaction will be at its highest.

Winch also proposed that there are four ideal types of marriage, characterized by a different pair of complementary needs. (Note that *ideal type* is used here to refer to a hypothetical rather than an actual state. It is not used in the sense of desirable.) These four types of marriage are Mothers and Sons, Ibsenian, Masters and Servant Girls, and Thurberian. In a Mother and Son marriage, the wife is nurturant and the husband seeks succor and is passive. In the Ibsenian type, based on Ibsen's play *A Doll's House,* the husband is the protector and caretaker of his wife, who plays the role of doll-child. Master and Servant Girl marriages consist of a husband who is head of the household and a wife who is a capable servant. As Swenson (1973) notes, on an overt, public level, the man is dominating, self-assured, and somewhat cold, while the wife is compliant, nurturant, and outgoing. On a deeper level, however, the wife is a nurturing, accepting, and emotionally strong supporter of her husband. In a Thurberian marriage, named for the writings and drawings of James Thurber, the wife is dominant while the husband is passive. The husband's passivity also includes passive hostility, which will be expressed only under great provocation. Winch suggests two dimensions that underlie these four types of marriage: dominant–submissive and nurturant–receptive. These dimensions and types of complementary relationships are shown in Table 6.2.

What is the evidence for the role of need complementarity in romantic attraction? As reviewed by Swenson (1973), when appropriate measures to determine needs are used, and when the researcher examines complementarity in marriage rather than in short-term dating, some support exists for Winch's hypotheses (e.g., Bermann & Miller, 1967; Kerckhoff & Davis, 1962). Nevertheless, some doubt has been cast on Winch's hypotheses both by contradictory research (e.g., Levinger, Senn, & Jorgensen, 1970) and on theoretical grounds (e.g., Barry, 1970; Tharp, 1963).

In a longitudinal study of college couples contemplating marriage,

Kerckhoff and Davis (1962) measured the partners' degree of value similarity and need complementarity. At the end of the school year, they checked on the progress of these relationships. Initial value similarity led to a closer relationship mainly among short-term couples, while high need complementarity led to progress mainly for couples who had gone together for a long time. Kerckhoff and Davis propose that similarity serves as a "filtering factor" early in a relationship, after which need complementarity becomes the predominant concern. This two-stage theory, not very different from the one proposed earlier by Winch, failed to receive support in a study by Levinger et al. (1970).

It is possible, of course, that complementarity is not a static thing. For example, both Punch and Judy may have a high need for dominance. Punch may satisfy his need by being dominant in certain situations or at certain times—perhaps he makes all the decisions about financial matters or chooses what they will do on weekends— while Judy may be dominant in social matters, or at particular other times. This represents Winch's Type I complementarity, which cannot easily be observed at a single time but requires long-term observation of a couple. Then, too, couples may be complementary on dimensions or needs not readily measured, so that it is difficult to determine empirically that complementarity is present. Despite its elusiveness in research, need complementarity has had a lasting influence on the literature of attraction and mate selection because there is a strong belief that *something* beyond simple similarity in attitudes and values is crucial to the growth and prosperity of relationships. In the absence of other testable theories, need complementarity seems a needed and desirable concept.

PASSIONATE LOVE

There are few scientific theories of love, and we have already examined some of the reasons this is so. But there is one social

Table 6.2.
Dimensions and Types of Complementary Marriages

Dominant–Submissive	Nurturant–Receptive	
	Husband nurturant, wife receptive	*Wife nurturant, husband receptive*
Husband dominant, Wife submissive	Ibsenian	Master–Servant Girl
Wife dominant, Husband submissive	Thurberian	Mother–Son

From Winch (1958, p. 214).

How do young couples maintain and strengthen their love? Dynamic theorists tend to agree that lovers may lean on each other too much, unless they develop both mutual and individual interests outside the relationship.

psychological theory of "passionate love" that deserves special attention. It has as its starting point the observation that love, like anxiety and fear, is an intense emotional state.

"You're Not Sick, You're Just in Love" This line from an old song typifies one theoretical interpretation of love as an intense emotion, what we might call "passionate love" (Berscheid & Walster, 1974). While there are very few points of agreement on what love is, almost everyone agrees that it is an emotional experience. So we may learn something of the nature of love by examining emotions in general.

In 1964, the social psychologist Stanley Schachter proposed a theory of emotion based on both physiological and cognitive factors. Assuming that people have a need to evaluate themselves and their emotional states, Schachter (1964) proposed that when people experience noticeable changes in internal body states, they will be motivated to explain or label those bodily states. In research by Schachter and Singer (1962), the physiological states of some subjects were altered by injecting them with adrenalin. The subjects were led to believe that they were testing a vitamin, Suproxin, that influenced vision. Some of the research participants were misinformed or completely uninformed about the effects of the drug. They therefore underwent changes in physiological arousal for which they had no explanation. Another group was correctly informed of the effects of the drug. It was thought that the subjects who had either been misinformed or given no explanation about the drug's effects would feel a need to understand the arousal they experienced. Schachter and Singer theorized that these people would look to their social environments to help them interpret their arousal. If they were placed in a "euphoric" environment where others were enjoying themselves, they should describe themselves as "happy," and if they were placed in an "angry" environment where others were acting aggressively, they should interpret their arousal as anger. These were, in fact, the results obtained by Schachter and Singer. One implication of this theory of emotion is that when people are physiologically aroused and have no ready explanation for the arousal, they tend to describe their emotional states on the basis of their perception of the environment.

If a man experiences arousal and then finds himself in a romantic setting with an attractive woman, he is apt to interpret this arousal as "love," particularly if he does not have any other ready explanation for his state of arousal (e.g., Dutton & Aron, 1974). This theory suggests that love not only is dependent upon our internal states, but takes its cue from situational circumstances as well. This theoretical description of love may help to explain how different cultures are able to influence the amount or extent of "love" experienced by its members. If a culture has no need of the concept of love, that is, if marriages are arranged or if they are based on economic dependency, love can be discouraged by providing people with labels to use when they undergo physiological arousal in the presence of members of the opposite sex. In our culture, an intense arousal boost may be interpreted as love if the conditions are right—if an appropriate person is present and the scene is conducive to romance. In other cultures, however, the same arousal and setting may be labeled "fear," "anxiety," or "anger," depending on the cultural definition of such terms. If this theory is correct, there may be universal physiological responses to particular situations but cultures influence how these responses are labeled.

LOVE AS PROCESS

The application of Schachter's theory of emotion to love has considerable generality. But it does not tell us as much as we would like to know about how the labeling process is learned, how people came to fall out of love, and what couples in love do to maintain and strengthen their relationship. These questions, particularly as they pertain to changes in emotions over time, seem to require something beyond a labeling theory. Because they deal with the issue of time, they require a dynamic theory of love, that is, a theory that recognizes love as a process of change and growth (see "The Major Elements of a Satisfactory Marriage," p. 213.)

Dynamic conceptions of love abound in the psychological and sociological literature (e.g., Fromm, 1956; May, 1969; Kipnis, Castell, Gergen, & Mauch, 1976; Peele & Brodsky, 1976; Tesser & Paulhus, 1976). The notion that a loving couple involves three entities—partner A, partner B, and the AB interactional unit—is implicit in all of them. As social scientists we are better equipped to study the two partners, their attitudes, expectations, and behaviors, than to study their dynamic interaction. Hence, research on the interactions of successful couples is rare.

Most dynamic theorists agree that the behavior of each partner is determined by a consideration for the other. In the words of Harry Stack Sullivan (1953), "When the satisfaction or the security of another person becomes as significant to one as is one's own satisfaction or security, then the state of love exists" (pp. 42–43). Erich Fromm stresses that love is a continuous process in which each partner helps the other to grow rather than a means of satisfying our own needs or a trade-off between our assets and those of our partner. In an exchange orientation, seeking lovers is like "buying real estate [where] the hidden potentialities which can be developed play a considerable role in this bargain." Mature love requires the lover to think, "I want the loved person to grow and unfold for his own sake, and in his own ways, and not for the purpose of serving me" (1956, pp. 81–82).

Love, which at first may provide euphoria, may devolve into something negative, defensive, or unpleasant. A fascinating book by Peele (1976) compares this regression of love with addiction to drugs.

As with heroin and its irrecoverable euphoria, or cigarettes smoked in routine excess, something initially sought for pleasure is held more tightly after it ceases to provide enjoyment. Now it is being maintained for negative rather than positive reasons. The love partner must be there in order to satisfy a deep, aching need, or else the addict begins to feel withdrawal pain. His emotional security is so dependent on this other individual around whom he has organized his life, that to be deprived of the lover would be an utter shock to the system of his existence. If the world he has built with the lover is destroyed, he desperately tries to find some other partner so as to reestablish his artificial equilibrium. For as with heroin and other addictions, it is traumatic for addict lovers to reenter the broader world with which they have lost touch. (pp. 87–88)

When lovers cut themselves off from the outer world, it is easy for them to become dependent on each other in much the same way that drug addicts become dependent on narcotics. To avoid this dependency, it is necessary to maintain integration of the couple as a unit with the external world; each alone and both together should, according to Peele, maintain interests and contacts outside the dyadic relationship.

We would expect, on the basis of the arguments of Peele, Fromm, and others, that certain people are more likely to "fall in love" than others, namely, those who are not well integrated into a social community, those with few outside interests, and those who feel they have little control over their own destinies. Some evidence for this hypothesis exists. K. L. Dion and Dion (1973) report that students who are high on feelings of external control of reinforcement (as measured by Rotter's I–E Scale) report falling in love more than those who feel they influence their own outcomes, the high internals. The first group, known as the externals, view romantic attraction as more mysterious and emotional than the second group, the internals, do, which suggests that those who feel they have little control over their lives are more likely to "fall" in love.

That love *can* easily serve selfish needs is unquestionable. That it *must* serve self-interest, as the need complementarity and exchange theorists argue, is debatable. Without doubt, the solidity of a relationship is often increased when personal needs are satisfied and when external pressures serve to drive a couple closer together (e.g., Driscoll et al., 1972). Unlike material resources, however, love is not diminished by expenditure. Instead, the expenditure of love—giving our partner priority over ourselves—paradoxically increases our fund of love (cf. Foa & Foa, 1974). In this respect, exchange models of love must incorporate not only the needs and reinforcements traditionally exchanged in interpersonal relationships, but also the paradoxical resource of love, which does not dissipate as it is expressed. Social psychological researchers have not yet developed techniques for dealing with these dynamic properties of interpersonal relationships, though important steps in this direction have been taken by family therapists (e.g., Framo, 1972; Minuchin, 1974; Raush, Barry, Hertel, & Swain, 1974; Levinger & Huston, 1978).

Summary

Attraction between two people may range from nonawareness to love, and while most of the social psychological research focuses on attraction toward strangers and new acquaintances, there is some recent work on the correlates and causes of romantic love. There is considerable evidence that attraction between people is heightened by similarity of personality, beliefs, and even physical characteristics. Just why this relationship between similarity and attraction exists is still unclear. A number of theories have been proposed to account for it, including reinforcement, cognitive balance, expected liking, and a variety of methodological explanations. There is some evidence that similarity is not always the only, or even the most important, determinant of attraction. It seems that the more two people interact, the less likely it is that similarity plays a prominent role in their relationship.

Among other determinants of attraction toward strangers and mere acquaintances is propinquity. The proximity between two people is related to their mutual liking. Thus, you are more likely to have a friend who lives in your dorm than one who lives across campus. One reason for this relationship between physical distance and liking may be that you interact more often with people who live nearby, and this interaction may be responsible for liking. Evidence suggests that merely seeing people, as well as interacting with them, increases attraction for them.

Because physical appearance is a more easily quantified feature of a person than the intricacies of personality and mood, there is a substantial amount of research—though very little theory—on its role in heterosexual attraction. Several studies of college students in the 1960s indicate that people most often like dates who are physically attractive, regardless of their own level of attractiveness. This is true mainly of people who are fixed up with a blind date. When people have to select their own dates, they tend to choose people whose physical attractiveness is close to their own. Several studies also suggest that, at least among Western college students, there is a tendency to attribute positive characteristics to more physically attractive people. People who are themselves attractive in appearance, particularly women, report feeling happier than less attractive individuals. However, when they are older—in their 50s—formerly attractive women report feelings less positive than their less attractive counterparts. As feminine beauty fades, so do the positive feelings that accompanied it. The effects of physical appearance on men's self-concepts are less pronounced.

It has been proposed in the theory of need complementarity that similarity may lead to initial attraction, but that complementary personality characteristics are most important for stable, mature relationships. There is only slight evidence to support this notion.

One theory of passionate love is based on Schachter's theory of emotion. According to this theory, love, like any other emotion, involves two components: a physiological component (in this case, heightened arousal) and a cognitive component (in this case, the self-attribution of love). Love, then, becomes a label we attribute to ourselves under conditions of increased physiological arousal. In this view, love is a *state* of an individual. An alternative view is that love is a *process* occurring between individuals. The process view has been expressed by a number of theorists. According to some, the process of love involves mutual growth and development. According to others, love may be seen as a physiological addiction, the withdrawal from a relationship leading to similar physical symptoms as withdrawal from narcotic drugs. According to process models, which are methodologically difficult to study, the proper focus of love is on the interactions between individuals rather than on either party separately.

Suggested Readings

*Berscheid, E., & Walster, E. *Interpersonal attraction* (2nd ed.). Reading, Mass.: Addison-Wesley, 1978.

*Fromm, E. *The art of loving*. New York: Harper, 1956.

Huston, T. (Ed.). *Foundations of interpersonal attraction*. New York: Academic Press, 1974.

*Peele, S. (with A. Brodsky). *Love and addiction*. New York: New American Library, 1976.

*Rubin, Z. *Liking and loving*. New York: Holt, 1973.

*Walster, E., & Walster, G. W. *A new look at love*. Reading, Mass.: Addison-Wesley, 1978.

Wilson, G., & Nias, D. *Love's mysteries: The psychology of sexual attraction*. London: Open Books, 1976.

Pertinent Journals

Journal of Marriage and the Family

Journal of Personality and Social Psychology

Personality and Social Psychology Bulletin

Social Psychology

*Available in paperback edition.

7
ALTRUISM AND
HELPING BEHAVIOR

Cathy Hill

The United States is the most charitable nation on earth. Each year Americans donate several billion dollars to over 5000 different organizations. Private foundations, such as the Carnegie Corporation, Ford Foundation, Guggenheim Memorial Foundation, Kresge Foundation, Lilly Endowment, Mott Foundation, and Rockefeller Foundation, dispense hundreds of millions of dollars for education, research, and social welfare. From the United Way to sidewalk Santas, Americans freely give a greater portion of their incomes to philanthropic endeavors than the peoples of any other country. It is not only through financial contributions that Americans lend assistance to their fellow citizens. There are over 3000 volunteer services in America, from the Red Cross and volunteer fire departments to the candy stripers at local hospitals.

Dec. 21, 1976. San Francisco. For the second time in a week, noontime crowds around Union Square gathered to watch as a man threatened to jump from the roof of a fashionable hotel. As the man stood precariously on the ledge of a twelfth-story window, chants of "Jump! Jump!" emerged from the crowd. Jeers and cries of "Chicken!" could be heard throughout the square.

We find in these two statements what has been referred to as the *altruistic paradox:* we are both kind and cruel toward our fellow creatures (R. Cohen, 1972). Evidence can be garnered to support the contention that we are kind *or* cruel, as many earlier philosophers have suggested. Jean-Jacques Rousseau, Karl Marx, and others have argued that mankind is innately good and that evil is the product of an evil society. Machiavelli, Thomas Hobbes, and Freud have presented a contrary argument: that mankind is inherently evil and society exists to control our evil tendencies. In this chapter and the next, we will examine both arguments, focusing first on kindness and, in Chapter 8, on aggression. We will conclude that mankind is both potentially kind and potentially cruel, and societies likewise. To reach these conclusions, however, we must first examine more closely some of the issues surrounding cruelty and kindness.

For every act of cruelty we find in the daily papers, we can find a charitable act equal in intensity. In this chapter, we will focus on altruism and helping of various types, and also on the failure to act with charity. First, however, it is best to dispense with the formalities of definition so that the meaning of each of these terms will be clear.

SOME DEFINITIONS

Social psychological study of acts of charity most often falls under the headings "prosocial behavior," "altruism," or "helping behavior." Wispé (1972) has defined each of these concepts and several related ones. *Altruism* is concern for the well-being of others without

When you can't turn the handle by yourself, it's nice to have a big sister who will take the time to help you.

concern for one's self-interest. Of course, it can be argued that behavior never occurs unless it is in our interest to perform it. One person may risk her life to save another and thereby be seen as behaving altruistically. However, it is possible that she hoped to obtain a reward or publicity by her actions, and thus had her own interest at heart. While this has become a delicate topic of discussion among social psychologists, we can say that altruism involves considerably more self-sacrifice than apparent self-gain.

Helping is giving aid or assistance to another with a definite goal in mind. It involves giving time and effort, but probably does not entail danger to the helper. *Donating* refers to the act of making a gift or contribution, usually to a charity. *Bystander intervention* is a direct, personal effort on behalf of another person, often involving an element of personal danger, to protect the interests of or to prevent harm from coming to another. *Prosocial behavior,* which will be used here as a broad term that encompasses all the others, is any act that is designed to benefit another person or group of persons whether or not the act involves possible benefits to the actor. The act may be direct or indirect, and may involve time, effort, or money.

THE KITTY GENOVESE CASE

At 3:00 A.M. on a March night in 1964, no less than 38 neighbors in the Kew Gardens Apartments in New York City watched an assault on a young woman, Catherine "Kitty" Genovese. Her assailant, Winston Moseley, spent over thirty minutes murdering his victim. "Oh my God! He stabbed me. Please help me!" she screamed. But no one did. No one even lifted the phone to call the police.

Newspapers across the country editorialized on the reasons for such "apathy" among Ms. Genovese's fellow citizens. Psychiatrists and sociologists pontificated on the implications of the neighbors' passivity. "A fascination with death," said one psychiatrist; "alienation from the urban society," argued a sociologist. The explanations came fast and furious and they all had a common element: none of them could be supported by scientific evidence.

With so much furor raised by the murder and so little scientific information on what actually crossed the minds of those 38 witnesses, it was not surprising that two social psychologists in New York City began a series of studies on what they referred to as "bystander intervention."

BYSTANDER INTERVENTION: THEORY AND RESEARCH

Bibb Latané, then of New York University, and John Darley, then of Columbia University, collaborated on a research program designed to shed light on the processes surrounding people's responses to emergencies. The Kitty Genovese case, and scores like it, served as the backdrop for their research.

Latané and Darley (1970) began by conducting studies on responses to simple nonemergency requests for help, and culminated in a series of laboratory and field experiments in which certain presumably crucial features of the actual Genovese case were present. Their research is an exemplary model of the close interplay between theory development and research, and of the complementary nature of laboratory and field research.

One of the most common popular explanations for the Genovese case was that urban Americans are unconcerned about their fellow citizens, that they are aloof and apathetic. To study this explanation, research assistants set out upon the streets of New York and made simple requests of passersby: for time, directions, change for a quarter, subway fare, or a dime to make a phone call. In all these instances, a majority of those New Yorkers approached responded favorably. Clearly, New Yorkers are not apathetic and unconcerned about their compatriots. Of course, they were more likely to give money when the requester provided a reasonable explanation as to why he or she needed it. If the requester simply said, "Excuse me, I wonder if you could give me a dime? I've spent all my money," only 38 percent provided the requested dime. But if the requester asked for a dime and added, "My wallet has been stolen," the percent of helpers jumped to 72. Help was given most often when the request seemed justified (see also Langer & Abelson, 1972). Females were provided with the requested help more often than males. Females helped female requesters more often than they helped male requesters. But such requests for help seem a long way from the late-night screams of Kitty Genovese. There is no element of danger in requests for change or for a dime; the potential risks involved in giving a dime on the street in broad daylight seem trivial compared to giving help to the victim of an assault. Latané and Darley, of course, were aware of these differences and hence began a series of studies that more closely resembled real-life emergencies.

Undergraduate students at Columbia University were asked by phone whether they would serve in a survey conducted by the Consumer Testing Bureau for two dollars. Each student who accepted the offer was asked to bring a friend who would also be interested in participating. When the subject arrived for his appointment, he was met by an attractive young woman who said that she was a market research representative. She showed him to the testing room, which was partitioned by a folding divider. On one side of the room the student could see a desk, chairs, and a large ramshackle bookcase. The students were asked to fill out a preliminary questionnaire, and while they worked on this, the representative opened the folding divider and said that she would be in her office next door. While they worked on their questionnaires, the students heard the woman moving around in the office, shuffling papers, and opening and closing drawers. After four minutes, they heard her climb up on a chair to get a book from the top shelf. Then they heard a loud crash and a woman's scream as the chair fell over. "Oh, my God, my foot . . . I . . . I . . . can't move . . . it. Oh, my ankle, I . . . can't . . . get . . . this thing off . . . me."

This whole sequence was recorded on tape, but the students next door had no way of knowing that. The main dependent variable was the type of response made to the emergency and the length of time before that response was made. There were four experimental groups of subjects: (1) students alone in the testing room during the emergency; (2) students in the testing room with one other person, who was passive during the emergency; (3) two strangers in the testing room during the emergency; and (4) two friends in the testing room during the emergency.

Seventy percent of all subjects who heard the fall while alone offered to help the victim. When there was a passive person also in the room, who did nothing to intervene, only 7 percent of the subjects offered help. When two strangers heard the fall, in only 40 percent of the groups did any one subject offer help. In 70 percent of the pairs of friends, at least one of them intervened. In postexperimental interviews it was found that pairs of subjects, whether friends or strangers, were less likely to interpret the fall as serious and more likely to decide that no help was needed than subjects who were alone.

Latané and Darley point out that such laboratory experiments, while often instructive, have an unreal quality about them; they are quite removed from our daily experiences. Accordingly, they conducted research in natural settings. In one of these studies, a liquor store was robbed nearly 100 times in a two-week period. The robbers were husky young men dressed in tee-shirts and chinos. Singly or in a pair, they would enter the store and ask the cashier, who was in cahoots with them, for Löwenbrau. The cashier said he would have to look in the back room. While he was gone, the robbers would pick up a case of beer near the front of the store, put the beer in a car, and drive off. On 48 occasions, one robber carried off the theft; on 48 occasions, two robbers were present.

The robberies were staged when there was either one or two people in the store. When the cashier returned from the rear of the store, he went to the checkout counter and resumed waiting on customers. After a minute, if no one had spontaneously mentioned the theft, he inquired, "Hey, what happened to those men who were in here?"

Customers were slightly more likely to report the theft when there were two robbers (69 percent) than when there was only one (52 percent). The sex of the bystander made no difference: females were as likely to report the theft as males. As in the previous studies, the number of bystanders did make a difference: 65 percent of the single customers reported the theft, but only 56 percent of the two-person groups included at least one reporter.

DIFFUSION OF RESPONSIBILITY

How are these studies to be interpreted? Latané and Darley consistently found that individual bystanders were more likely to interpret an event as requiring assistance and more likely to offer assistance than were groups of bystanders. Their interpretation of this reliable finding was stated in terms of a diffusion of responsibility.

If only one bystander is present at an emergency, he bears all the responsibility for dealing with it; he feels all the guilt for not acting and bears all the blame that comes from not intervening. If others are present, the onus of responsibility is shared and the blame does not rest with any one person.

There is nothing in the concept of diffusion of responsibility that

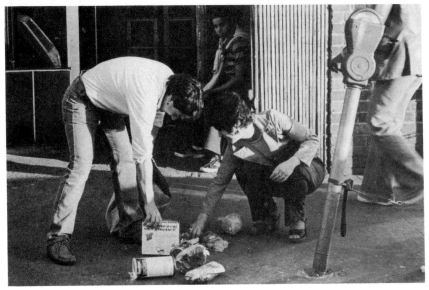

Would this woman have stopped to help if she had been with her husband? Would she stop to help another woman? Research on bystander intervention has shown that the sex of the helper matters less than the number of people witnessing the incident.

remotely resembles the explanations proposed in the newspapers following the murder of Kitty Genovese. The explanations most commonly given at the time depended on personal traits of the bystanders: they were apathetic, they had a fascination for violence, they were alienated from society. Do personality traits play no role in bystander intervention? To examine the role of personality more closely, Latané and Darley administered a number of personality tests to male and female New York University students who participated in a laboratory experiment, presumably involving a discussion of personal problems associated with college life. Subjects completed a scale that measured their feelings of social responsibility, the Marlowe–Crowne Need for Approval Scale, the California F Scale (a measure of authoritarianism), a scale of alienation from social norms and institutions, and the Machiavellianism scale. They also completed a questionnaire that asked for such personal information as church attendance, age, father's education, number of siblings, and size of home town.

The experimental situation involved a discussion with one or more other students that took place over an intercom system. Subjects were placed in separate rooms and could communicate via the intercom. When one person's microphone was on, all others were automatically turned off. Each mike was on for a period of two minutes at a time. In the discussion, one person mentioned that he had difficulty adjusting to New York and to his studies. "Very hesitantly, and with obvious embarrassment, he mentioned that he was prone to seizures, particularly when studying hard or taking exams...." After each subject talked for two minutes, the presumed epileptic (who was in reality working with the experimenters) began to speak. "Somebody er-er-er-give me a little-er-give me a little help here because-er-I-er-I'm-er-er-h-h-having a-a-a real problem-er-right now and I-er-if somebody could help me out it would-it would-er-er s-s-sure be-sure be good ... I could really-er-use some help so if somebody would-er-give me a little h-help-uh-er-er-er-er could some-body-er-er-help-er-uh-uh-uh (choking sounds).... I'm gonna die-er-er-I'm ... gonna die-er-help-er-er-seizure-er (chokes, then quiet)."

Latané and Darley varied the number of other subjects that each subject believed to be present and timed the responses. In the first round of the group discussion, each subject was led to believe that the discussion group consisted of either two, three, or six people.

As in the previous studies, more people responded to the epileptic seizure, and more quickly, when there were fewer people present. When only the subject and the victim were present (two-person group), 85 percent of the subjects responded to the seizure directly, and 100 percent responded within a few minutes. The average time to respond was 52 seconds. When a three-person group was present (subject, victim, and one other subject), 62 percent responded quickly, 85 percent eventually responded, and the average time was 93 seconds. When there were five subjects and a victim, less than a third responded quickly, 62 percent eventually responded, and it took an average of 166 seconds for a response to occur.

What of the personalities of the subjects? Table 7.1 shows the correlations between various personality and demographic measures and the speed of responding to the seizure. Obviously, in this

Table 7.1.
Correlates of Speed of Reporting the Seizure

Personality Item	r
F Scale (authoritarianism)	+.20
Anomia (alienation)	−.10
Machiavellianism	+.08
Need for Social Approval	+.04
Social Responsibility	−.02
Size of community in which subject grew up	−.26
Father's occupation	−.24
Length of stay in New York City	−.18
Number of siblings	+.18
Church attendance	−.17
Age	+.14
Father's education	−.12
Birth order	.00

Adapted from Latané & Darley (1970, pp. 115, 117).

experiment personality traits of the bystanders were unrelated to speed of helping. Alienation, authoritarianism, social responsibility, religiosity, birth order—none of these had any appreciable effect on responding to the epileptic.

At least in this study, the best prediction of response to emergency is based solely on the number of other witnesses present: the fewer the witnesses, the quicker and more likely the response. This, of course, does not mean that personality, either alone or in conjunction with other factors, is unrelated to all kinds of prosocial acts. We will return to the relationship between personality and helping.

In addition to presenting their theory of diffusion of responsibility, Latané and Darley discuss a general theory of helping in emergencies. In order for a bystander to provide help to a victim, the following sequence of events must occur. First, the bystander must *notice* that something is happening. Second, the person aware of an event must *interpret* it as an emergency. Third, the bystander must decide that it is his personal *responsibility* to act. Fourth, the person must consider what *form of assistance* can be given. And finally, the person must decide how to *implement* this assistance. Latané and Darley's research focused primarily on the third stage of this five-stage process. We will subsequently review research that sheds some light on the other stages.

Latané and Darley's research and theory on bystander intervention stimulated other social psychologists to conduct studies of prosocial behavior. Their explanations of bystander intervention, rather than being the last word on the matter, proved to be the first. It was clear to many that while diffusion of responsibility could explain and predict intervention or the failure to intervene, the theory was limited to a relatively small number of situations: those in which several people were present or assumed to be present and in which an event had already been noticed and interpreted as an emergency. Clearly a solitary individual is more likely to help at one time than another. Diffusion of responsibility cannot account for this difference. Shouldn't a single observer of an emergency always help if there are no others present with whom responsibility can be shared? Obviously, additional factors must be involved in explaining why a single bystander helps more in certain situations than in others. Then, too, there are alternative ways of interpreting the results obtained by Latané and Darley (see Clark & Word, 1974; Pomazal & Jaccard, 1976). One such interpretation rests upon social learning theory and involves the processes of modeling and imitation.

Modeling, Imitation, and Helping   While it is generally true that the presence of several bystanders who witness an emergency may result in a diffusion of felt responsibility, other processes may also occur in conjunction with or in lieu of responsibility diffusion. One such process is modeling. Each bystander may serve as a behavioral model for the others, and each person may look to the others for cues as to what should be done. Imagine several people who suddenly encounter a man and woman fighting on the street. The woman is screaming and crying out for help. When you arrive on the scene, four or five people are already present, standing around the embattled couple. What do you do? According to Latané and Darley, you size up the situation and decide whether help is needed. If you decide that the woman needs help, you then decide whether you should help or whether, perhaps, one of the other onlookers should help. As there are several other people present, you are likely to decide that they should help rather than you. So you continue to watch the attack.

A modeling and imitation explanation is somewhat different. When you arrive on the scene and decide that the woman is in need of assistance, you look to the other bystanders to determine just what it is you should do. You notice that none of them is actively doing anything; they are all merely watching the brawl. Because none of them provides you with any cues as to what behavior may be appropriate, you stand with them and watch. Here it is not your lack of a feeling of responsibility that inhibits your tendency to help, but your lack of knowledge of what actions should be taken. In terms of Latané and Darley's model, this is Stage 4.

Suddenly one of the onlookers breaks from the crowd and runs toward the battling couple. Someone else quickly follows, and both are approaching the attacker. You decide that it is time for you to do something and you, too, rush toward the pair with the intention of separating the combatants. In such a situation, you are likely to have taken your cue from the first bystander who intervened. He has served as a model whose behavior you imitated.

In such situations, particularly when the appropriate response is ambiguous (should you intervene directly? call the police? yell for help? yell at the attacker?) or when the situation is ambiguous (is it a lovers' quarrel? who started it? what's it about? are they drunk?), each onlooker serves as a model for all other onlookers. If no one does anything, then all the others imitate that nonintervention response. As soon as one person decides to take some action, that person becomes a model for the others to imitate, by his actions defining the situation as one requiring intervention and modeling behavior appropriate to that situation.

Do models really influence helping? A series of studies by James Bryan and Mary Ann Test suggests that they do. In a shopping center just before Christmas, Bryan and Test (1967) had an adult male serve as a model by approaching a Salvation Army kettle and clearly depositing money in it. All those in visual range of the kettle could

People are twice as likely to help a stranded motorist change a tire if they have just seen someone else help to change a flat. Do you think this helping model of an engine repairman would be equally effective?

see the model donating to charity. In control conditions, no model was present to donate. Donations within two minutes of the model's donation were more frequent than those during the control periods, indicating that charity is enhanced by the observation of a charitable model (Blake, Rosenbaum, & Duryea, 1955; Macaulay, 1970).

While donating money to the Salvation Army at Christmastime is hardly akin to intervention in emergencies, Bryan and Test present evidence that modeling also influences riskier and more demanding kinds of prosocial behavior. Motorists driving along a highway encountered a car on the shoulder of the road with a flat tire and a woman standing helplessly next to it. Would passing motorists stop and offer assistance? Not many of them did offer to change the tire for her, but twice as many were apt to do so if they had previously passed a helping model. The helping model in this case was a man who had pulled over to help another woman change a flat tire about a mile before. So even in situations in which some risk and inconvenience are present, observing a prosocial model increases the likelihood of helping.

According to a modeling and imitation explanation of the Genovese case, people awakened in the night by her screams were undoubtedly aware that others must also have been awakened. Thus they knew that several others must be witness to the attack. Not knowing quite what to do, each observer awaited a cue from one or more of the others. When no one acted to stop the attack, each observer, still waiting for someone to provide an appropriate response, failed to act too. With everyone waiting for someone else to act first, no one acted until it was too late.

The explanations that we have examined so far have at least one thing in common: a bystander's decision to intervene or not to intervene depends upon the social situation. Neither the diffusion of responsibility explanation nor the modeling and imitation explanation involves characteristics of the emergency, nor do they involve very complex psychological processes of the observers as central elements. Surely not all potential helping situations are alike: some are more physically demanding or dangerous than others, some require a greater sacrifice of time or money than others, some involve greater ambiguity than others, and some situations may not be defined as emergencies at all by some bystanders.

A COST–REWARD ANALYSIS

It is possible to examine both diffusion of responsibility and modeling in terms of a cost–reward model and to place somewhat greater emphasis on cognitive processes and characteristics of the situation. This has been done by Walster and Piliavin (1972) and by J. A. Piliavin and Piliavin (1975). In a cost–reward interpretation, a bystander experiences some emotional or physiological arousal upon witnessing an emergency. This arousal is uncomfortable and the bystander is motivated to reduce the arousal. This can sometimes be done by helping, sometimes by not helping, and sometimes by redefining the situation so that arousal is reduced (for example, by saying "This isn't an emergency at all, so I no longer have to think about it."). In any case, the bystander attempts to reduce arousal by choosing the response that most completely reduces the uncomfortable arousal with the lowest physical or psychological costs and the highest potential rewards.

Arousal is apt to be greatest when the emergency is severe, when there is little physical distance between the bystander and the victim, and when the victim is perceived by the bystander to be similar to the bystander or when there is some emotional relationship between bystander and victim (Katz, Cohen, & Glass, 1975; West, Whitney, & Schnedler, 1975). With high arousal, the tendency to act quickly to reduce arousal is great, but so are the costs of intervening if the situation is an extreme emergency. In order to reduce this uncomfortable arousal state, low-cost means may be used—means that do not involve much physical danger or self-sacrifice. Low-cost means are often psychological. Aroused bystanders may alter their perceptions of the emergency in order to reduce arousal. They may either redefine the situation as a nonemergency, thereby reducing arousal, or convince themselves that the victim is not being severely injured. There is some research support for these processes (Brock & Buss, 1962; Glass, 1964; Goldstein, Davis, & Herman, 1975; Sykes & Matza, 1957).

Employing a cost–reward, or equity (Adams, 1965), model enables us to think of diffusion of responsibility and modeling as two processes that influence a bystander's perceived costs. Thus, they can both be considered specific cases of a more general process. The knowledge that others are also witness to an emergency implies that a single individual can share the blame for not helping; thus, a diffusion of responsibility may be seen as a diffusion of cost (blame). Likewise, when a bystander observes a model helping someone, if nothing bad then happens to the model as a result of his helping, that can reduce our perceived costs for helping. Initially a bystander may not intervene because he or she is uncertain of what the consequences will be: Is this really an emergency? Will I be sued if I mess up? Is it dangerous? If a helping model experiences no ill effects, then the costs of helping may be seen as reduced: there is less danger in helping than perhaps the bystander initially thought.

While this is a fairly convenient way to think of helping, it is difficult to *predict* a response to an emergency strictly in these terms. It requires some knowledge of how each bystander perceives the situation and his or her own abilities to help. Clearly, we rarely have such information about most bystanders. So while we can state that a bystander will intervene to reduce arousal by choosing the least costly and most rewarding response, we rarely know enough to predict just what that response will be. Nevertheless, this approach does have some value. It makes us sensitive to the fact that bystanders differ in both abilities and past experience, and that each may define the emergency situation somewhat differently. It also points out the importance of *psychological responses* to emergencies, as opposed to purely behavioral intervention responses. Not intervening directly does not mean that observers of an emergency are apathetic, or that they are not struggling to cope with the emergency in some emotional way. The cost–reward model suggests that purely psychological responses may be one method of reducing the uncomfortable feeling that results from witnessing an emergency. One important psychological process that may be capable of reducing this discomfort involves justifying in some way the plight of the victim. This type of process is presented by Lerner in his notion of the "just-world phenomenon."

THE JUST-WORLD PHENOMENON

In the 1960s, when the furor over the Genovese case was at its height, Melvin Lerner, a social psychologist teaching at a southern medical school, noticed that many of the medical students who were required to work in a hospital clinic resented the fact that they had to treat indigent patients. Why should medical students resent such patients?

After all, isn't that what they go to medical school to learn? Lerner (1970) began to investigate the reasons for this curious phenomenon. He found that many of the med students believed that the poor people who visited the hospital clinic were ill through negligence and ignorance, that they had somehow brought disease upon themselves.

Is this sort of phenomenon, which has also been called "blaming the victim," restricted to young medical students, or is it to be found elsewhere? Lerner found evidence of it in a wide variety of people and situations.

Nearly all religions teach that God is just; that God does not capriciously or randomly make things happen, but always has a greater purpose. Therefore, while God may work in "mysterious ways," there is always some notion of justice behind his actions. It follows, then, that when something bad happens to a person, it is not without reason. The Protestant Ethic, which has been the dom-

According to the just-world phenomenon, this man sleeps in doorways because of something he did in the past. Perhaps he will do something in the future that will improve his situation.

inant philosophical tenet of nineteenth- and twentieth-century America, clearly conveys the notion that hard work and sacrifice are rewarded. Nearly all religions teach us that leading a virtuous life has its rewards; if not in this life, then in the next. When something bad does happen to someone who works hard and leads a virtuous life, he is apt to ask, "Why me, God? What have I done to deserve this?", underscoring the fundamental belief that things don't happen without a reason.

Even the nonreligious are imbued with some sense of this notion. Einstein, in explaining why he looked for simple mathematical equations to account for complex physical phenomena, said, "God does not play dice with the universe." Most people hold this belief, regardless of their conception of God. The world would be a much more difficult place if we believed it to be random, without order or potential meaning. So, when important or dramatic events occur, we assume that there is a rational explanation for them; things don't happen for no reason at all.

It follows from this belief that the world is just and orderly that we can find the order and meaning that lie behind events. When bad things happen to us or to others, we ask why they happen. The same is true for good things. If something good happens to us, we usually attribute it to our hard work and sacrifice. If something good happens to someone else, we assume either that that person deserved it or that it wasn't such a good thing after all (Brickman, Coates, & Janoff-Bulman, 1978). If we are highly motivated to explain why something happened, we can, of course, always come up with some sort of explanation.

These ideas have some surprising implications, which can account for a great variety of seemingly nonrational behaviors. Stereotypes of minority groups, for example, generally portray them as "dirty," "lazy," "ignorant," and "oversexed." This is not a recent or a local phenomenon. Minority groups have been so typified for centuries, everywhere from Great Britain to Latin America to the Soviet Union. Minority groups most often occupy the lowest social positions: they live in substandard housing, receive inadequate medical care, find it more difficult to obtain work, and generally have to attend inferior schools. If a member of the prevailing majority is asked why minorities are not well educated, she or he is apt to tell you that it is because "they are too ignorant to learn." Why are they unemployed? "Because they are too lazy to work." Why do they live in poor housing? "Because they are unclean." And—to return to our medical students, who are almost always majority group members—they are sick "because they are careless and ignorant." It is important to remember that these beliefs are not simple prejudice; they are the logical derivatives of the potent belief that the world is just. It is not entirely a matter of ignorance on the part of the majority groups, but stems from one of their most fundamental beliefs: that the universe is meaningful, orderly, and just. In such a world, apparent injustices must be justified.

Lerner and his associates conducted a number of experiments to test the effects of this fundamental belief in a just world. According to this explanation, people may fail to intervene in an emergency because they assume that if something bad is happening to someone, the victim deserves his fate. In a just world, bad things do not happen to good people. Ergo, if something bad happens to someone, it must be because that person is bad. If we know that the victim deserves his fate, it is much less disturbing.

In his typical experiment, Lerner exposes an innocent victim to harm. If observers feel powerless to curtail that harm effectively, they tend to dislike the victim; they make it seem as though the victim deserved to be harmed. In one study, Lerner and Simmons (1966) had a group of college women observe an experiment on human learning, in which a woman received shocks for errors made on a task. The observers watched this learning experiment on closed-circuit television. They were then asked to describe the personality of the victim by completing a questionnaire.

In one of the experimental conditions, observers were told that they could choose whether the learning experiment would progress using negative reinforcement (shocks), positive reinforcement (payment of 25 cents), or no reinforcement. In the second experimental group, observers were told that they were watching a tape that had been made earlier. The third group was told that the events they were watching on the TV screen were taking place live. One experimental group, called the "martyr" condition, was led to believe that the victim reluctantly agreed to undergo the shock so that the observers could witness the learning experiment. It was in this condition that Lerner and Simmons expected the strongest devaluation and dislike of the victim. The victim in the martyr condition was behaving altruistically.

The results of the study are presented in Table 7.2, where it can be seen that observers found the martyr less attractive than the other victims. It was also found that, of the 25 observers who voted on whether the victim should later be given positive, negative, or no reinforcement, 23 subjects voted for positive reinforcement and the remaining 2 for no reinforcement. Thus, the results indicate that when there is an opportunity to alter the victim's fate, people choose to end her suffering. But when no opportunity exists for reducing the suffering, there is a tendency to dislike the victim—to blame her for her victimization. It has also been found that observers who feel some emotional involvement with the victim do not devalue her (Aderman, Brehm, & Katz, 1974).

If a victim is seen as inherently responsible for being victimized—

Table 7.2.
Ratings of the Victim

	Choice for Future Reward	Past Event	Live Event	Martyr
Attractiveness of Victim	−5.07	−11.10	−12.85	−34.00

NOTE: The more negative the rating, the less attractive the victim was perceived to be. Adapted from Lerner and Simmons (1966).

that is, if the victim brought about his or her situation—there is less need to devalue the victim. When, on the other hand, we have no good explanation for why a person was victimized, the tendency to devalue the victim is stronger (Godfrey & Lowe, 1975).

C. Jones and Aronson (1973) described a rape case to college students. They varied only the description of the victim: she was sometimes said to be married, sometimes to be a virgin, and sometimes to be a divorcee. As they argue, "in this culture, married women and virgins are generally seen as having more social respectability than a divorcee; therefore, we hypothesized that if the victim were married or a virgin, subjects would attribute greater responsibility to her than if she were a divorcee." The reasoning behind this hypothesis stems from Lerner's just-world phenomenon. If the reader does not know the circumstances surrounding the rape, then the discomfort or arousal engendered by the description of the rape has to be reduced. If the world is just, married women and virgins are not raped. Hence, in order to maintain the belief that the world is just, readers tend to attribute blame to the least deserving victims: married women and virgins. The results bear out this line of reasoning. When asked, "How much do you consider the crime to be the victim's fault?" readers attributed the most fault to the married victim and the least fault to the divorced victim.

That these results are not restricted to college students or to laboratory situations can be seen in the way in which rape victims have been treated historically by the courts and law enforcement agencies (see Kahn, Gilbert, Latta, Deutsch, Hagen, Hill, McGaughey, Ryen, & Wilson, 1977; Krulewitz & Payne, 1978). Judges and defense attorneys have frequently argued that women would not be raped if they really didn't want to be, or if they didn't wear provocative clothing. This unfortunate situation now seems to be changing, and there is a greater willingness to prosecute rapists and to recognize that rape victims do not intentionally become victims.

The just-world phenomenon is a dramatic and powerful explanation. It has proved awkward to test in many situations, but there is some convincing supportive evidence (Lerner, 1970; Lerner & Matthews, 1967; Rubin & Peplau, 1973). Of course, not everyone blames a victim for being victimized. It is possible, though psychologically more difficult, to believe in a just world and still recognize that injustices occur and can be redressed. It is even possible to believe that the world is not orderly and meaningful, a belief that is central to existentialist philosophy. But even here, we seek to create order and meaning by our actions. So while the universe is seen to have no *inherent* meaning, it is possible to forge a meaning for ourselves. Providing selfless assistance to others may be one strategy for finding meaning, as some of the cases below attest.

CHRISTIANS WHO SAVED JEWS FROM THE NAZIS: SITUATIONAL AND PERSONALITY FACTORS IN HELPING

A study engendered by the trial of Adolf Eichmann, conceived by a rabbi, publicized by a novelist, and sponsored by a museum was conducted by Perry London and his colleagues. This study aimed to "find out if there are stable traits of character connected with extremely altruistic acts such as those in which the Christians in Nazi-occupied Europe risked their lives trying to save Jews" (London, 1970, p. 241). While the study never reached fruition, it nonetheless provides some rich and interesting data about the motives and situations that lie behind certain types of altruistic behavior.

London and his colleagues in the United States and Israel were able to interview 27 Christians who had rescued Jews during World War II and 42 people who had been rescued by Christians. Although this work was only a pilot study, lack of funds prevented the larger project from being carried out.

We often think of altruism in terms of relatively simple motives and acts, defining an altruist as one who confers a benefit on someone else without profit to himself, or without intention of profiting from his act, or with positive motives to be helpful. The behavior of rescuers cannot easily be classified by any simplistic definition, however. Some were paid a great deal of money for their efforts, usually in connection with essential parts of their operations, such as buying forged papers, food, or arms, or bribing officials. Some spent fortunes and were left destitute as a result. Some who had almost nothing to begin with shared it with good grace—or without. (London, 1970, p. 244)

There were almost no common themes in the rescuers' motives for helping Jews. Some of them had long been affiliated with Jews, others were anti-Semitic. Some began their operations out of beneficence, others just seemed to fall into the role of rescuer.

The Christian owners of this clock shop in Haarlem, Holland, gave temporary shelter to many Jewish refugees who were escaping from Nazi-occupied territory during World War II.

The importance of *situational factors,* as opposed to a pure, internal motivation to be altruistic, can be seen in the case of a wealthy German businessman.

"I was believing in 1942 that the war will be another year. It cannot be any longer. It's impossible. I was then a rich man. I had about 300,000 or 400,000 marks, and I started with one person, then six people, from there to 50, then 100.... People came to me—maybe they like my looks—I don't know what it was—asking me very bluntly and very frankly, 'Will you save me?'"

It began for him when his secretary came to him, said that the Germans were going to kill her Jewish husband and asked for help. He thought at first that she was crazy, and told her, "Germans don't do things like that!" But she was convinced that they were going to kill all the Jews in town so, although he felt it was not true, he agreed to let her husband stay in his office over the weekend. Through this act of compassion he found himself in the business of rescue. Once he found that the Jews' fears were justified, he was pulled in deeper and deeper. He had access to resources that few others had, he had compassion for his hapless clients, and he had the personal resources of wit, tenacity, and courage to remain with it for years. (London, 1970, p. 245)

London points out that many rescuers began their operations, not with forethought, but out of circumstances. Persistence in rescue work for long periods of time, however, required a certain cluster of personality traits: (1) a spirit of adventurousness; (2) a strong identification with a model of moral conduct, usually a parent; and (3) a sense of being socially marginal, of not quite fitting into the mainstream of society.

One rescuer was a Seventh-Day Adventist minister from the Netherlands, a country in which almost everyone is Catholic or Calvinist. Thus, his religion made him a marginal man in Dutch society. The minister, who described himself as mildly anti-Semitic, said that he rescued Jews simply because it was a Christian's duty to do so.

There is also some evidence for the just-world phenomenon in these case studies. A woman's father, who was a miner, became involved in rescue work when he foresaw the massacre of the Jews. After his death, his daughter and wife carried on his work.

The daughter, whom we interviewed, had been in bad health, but with the great responsibilities she assumed—including an increasing risk to her life—her health improved. She even replaced her father in the mines. When we talked to her, she told us that she believed the holocaust happened because the Jews did not keep the laws of the Bible, and that the destruction visited upon them would soon engulf other people. She had a fanatical belief in a God of rewards and punishments, and felt that her reward for helping the Jews was improved health. Later she suffered a mental breakdown, during which she quoted passages from the Old Testament to prove that man suffers for his own misdeeds. (London, 1970, p. 249)

While it would be unwarranted to draw conclusions from such a small number of interviews, there are two themes that run through them. The first is that circumstances seem to play an important role in altruism, and the second is that some aspects of personality may, in conjunction with certain situations, lead to altruistic behavior.

PERSONALITY FACTORS IN HELPING

Latané and Darley failed to find evidence that personality or demographic characteristics of bystanders played any significant role in their study of responses to an epileptic seizure. Their study, however, was limited to a relatively few dimensions of personality and to only one particular type of emergency. It is possible that other personality traits are important determinants of helping and that certain personality characteristics are important for some, but not all, types of emergencies.

Gergen, Gergen, and Meter (1972), Bryan (1975), Krebs (1970), Staub (1978), and Staub and Feinberg (1979) have reviewed the personality literature with respect to altruism. Although no personality trait is highly related to all types of helping, certain traits appear with considerable frequency. People, both adults and children, who have a strong need for social approval tend to help less often than those with weaker approval needs (Darley & Latané, 1968; Rutherford & Mussen, 1968; Staub & Sherk, 1970). This may be because potential helpers are uncertain as to how their intervention will be received by others. While Americans learn that there is a norm to help others, they also learn the counteracting norm to mind their own business. When confronted with an emergency, these conflicting norms fail to make clear just which response—intervention or nonintervention—is the more socially acceptable. So those people who value highly the approval of others tend not to intervene, perhaps because of their lack of certainty about what other people's responses will be.

The bystander's feeling of self-esteem has been found to influence helping, and to contribute to the amount of distress experienced upon witnessing an emergency (Glass, 1964; Walster & Piliavin, 1972). Those with high self-esteem are more likely to experience distress in an emergency and are therefore more likely to act so as to reduce this distress.

Personality characteristics may consist not only of enduring traits of a person but also of temporary states. A series of studies by Alice Isen and her colleagues has shown that a temporary improvement in mood increases a person's tendency to help (Cialdini & Kenrick, 1976; Isen, 1970; Isen, Clark, & Schwartz, 1976; Isen & Levin, 1972).

Findings with respect to the age, race and sex of bystanders have not been at all consistent (e.g., L. Berkowitz & Friedman, 1967; I. Katz et al., 1975; Krebs, 1970; I. M. Piliavin, Rodin, & Piliavin, 1969; J. A. Piliavin & Piliavin, 1972; Staub, 1970; West et al., 1975; Wispé & Freshley, 1971).

On the whole, Gergen et al. (1972) note more inconsistencies than consistencies between measures of personality and helping. They attribute these inconsistencies to the fact that researchers have not taken into account the differences between kinds of helping. It is not illogical to argue that different personality traits are related to different kinds of helping. Gergen et al. had 72 Swarthmore College students complete a battery of personality tests, which consisted of ten different measures of personality traits. They asked them to volunteer for five different types of help: counseling male high school students; counseling female high school students; aiding a faculty research project on thinking; aiding research on altered states of consciousness; and assisting in collating and assembling materials for further use by the class. While there are clearly different kinds of helping involved in these five situations, they only scratch the surface of the many possible situations in which help may be needed. The results of the study indicate that different personality traits were correlated with different types of help. No one personality trait was significantly related to all five types of help. The results are presented in Table 7.3.

Obviously, from this research, we must conclude that helping, altruism, and prosocial behavior are broad terms that include different types of situations and that it would be unwise to expect a single type of personality to correlate highly with all types of helping. What we need is some way to distinguish among important classes of helping situations.

SITUATIONAL FACTORS IN HELPING

The studies reviewed in this chapter have included the following different kinds of helping situations: a woman falls from a chair and hurts her leg; students request money from strangers; people witness a theft; people witness an epileptic seizure; bystanders observe someone receiving shocks as part of an experiment; students are asked to volunteer for a variety of tasks. Do all these situations have something in common, aside from a superficial need for one person to act on behalf of another? According to Gergen et al., they do not. While few clues are available, we can offer at least a tentative list of dimensions on which helping situations differ.

Familiarity–Novelty   Some types of helping events are common or predictable in nature. Each year we expect to see sidewalk Santas collecting money for charity; it is not unusual for solicitors to go door to door collecting money, goods, and clothing for charity; the United Way annually asks for donations. These events are all common and predictable. People learn at a very early age what response is expected of them and how to act in such situations. These events are clearly different from the unanticipated emergencies that people may occasionally encounter: a highway accident, an attack on the street or in the subway, a robbery. These events are neither predictable nor frequent enough for people to become familiar with them. There are uncertainties and ambiguities present in such novel situations and the appropriate response is often unclear.

Table 7.3.
Correlations Relating Ten Trait Dispositions to Five Types of Prosocial Behavior

Trait Dispositions	Counsel High School Males		Counsel High School Females		Thinking Experiment		Altered States Experiment		Collating Class Materials	
	M	F	M	F	M	F	M	F	M	F
Abasement	−.30*	−.39*	−.31*	−.19	−.33*	−.08				
Autonomy			−.30*	−.04			+.19	+.36*	+.29*	+.36*
Change				−.08			+.40*	+.32*		
Deference			−.14	+.32*					+.03	−.33*
Nurturance	+.41*	+.09	+.35*	+.34*						
Order				+.40*					−.28*	−.03
Self-consistency	+.07	−.33*			−.06	+.29*	−.40*	+.22		
Self-esteem							+.16	+.50*	+.01	+.42*
Sensation-seeking	+.01	+.29*			−.28*	+.22	+.45*	+.56*	−.03	+.29*
Succorance	+.38*	−.01					−.05	−.31*		

NOTE: Correlations that are not significant at the .05 level are not entered unless there is a significant correlation for the opposite sex. Correlations followed by * are significant at the .05 level. Adapted from Gergen, Gergen, and Meter (1972, p. 115).

Anonymity–Visibility   Situations also differ in the degree of visibility of the helper. We can donate anonymously to charities and we can call the police anonymously to report a crime. On the other hand, some helping situations make the bystanders highly visible. If we encounter a crime on the street and intervene, both the victim and the offender are apt to get a good look at us. While there is some evidence, which we will review more thoroughly in Chapter 8, that anonymous individuals are more likely to engage in antisocial acts, there is also some evidence that they may engage in more prosocial acts as well (Goldstein, 1975; Newman, 1972; Zimbardo, 1969). Clearly, if there is potential danger or the possibility of retaliation or of involvement in lengthy legal proceedings, visibility serves as a hindrance to helping. But in some cases visibility may increase helping. If people clearly see that their legal or moral duty lies in helping and that not helping may bring penalties, they are likely to help if they can be identified readily. This may be the reason that help is more likely to be given in small towns than in cities (Korte & Kerr, 1975; Latané & Darley, 1970; Milgram, 1970) and in subdued rather than "busy" environments (Korte, Ypma, & Toppen, 1975).

Safety–Danger   Perhaps the overriding dimension on which helping situations differ is the potential for personal danger. In most novel emergencies, such as street crimes or fights, intervention may involve a real and immediate risk. A bystander is less likely to help when potential danger is great even though nonintervention may be psychologically disturbing. It is in these situations that such psychological responses as devaluing the victim and minimizing the perception of the victim's pain are apt to be invoked. J. A. Piliavin and Piliavin (1972) report a study in which a person fell down in a moving subway car. In half the cases, a bloodlike fluid trickled from his mouth; in the remaining half, there was no blood. While it is clear that the presence of blood signals a greater need for assistance than the absence of blood, intervention was less frequent, and took longer in coming, when the victim was bleeding. Apparently, there is no direct relationship between the extent of the emergency and the tendency to respond. The researchers interpret the less frequent and slower response to the bleeding victim as due to the bystander's increased cost of helping—a bystander must "get his hands dirty" to help a bloody victim. It is also possible that the presence of blood signals a more serious emergency or one in which there is more potential danger, and blame, for the helper.

Doubtless there are other dimensions on which helping situations may differ. What is required at this stage is to determine whether such distinctions enhance the ability to predict helping and the role of personality traits in helping, and to determine whether these dimensions have any theoretical importance.

SOCIAL NORMS AND HELPING

In our culture, two especially salient norms seem to pertain to helping: the social responsibility norm and the norm of reciprocity (Gouldner, 1960). We learn that we should act responsibly toward another person who is dependent on us, and also that if someone does us a favor, we are obliged to reciprocate in kind or degree.

As Latané and Darley (1970; also, Darley & Latané, 1970) have pointed out, it is difficult to use a normative approach to explain bystander intervention because in any given situation, inconsistent or contradictory norms are apt to be operating. We learn to feel responsible for our fellow citizens, but we also learn to mind our own business. We learn to "do unto others as you would have them do unto you," but also "not to take candy from a stranger" and "stand on your own two feet," which generally mean don't accept help from others. Of course, norms can always be invoked after an event has occurred to explain that event. If people did not intervene, we could say that they were following the norm of minding their own business; if they did intervene, we could say that they were following a social responsibility norm. If norms are to be scientifically useful, we must be able to predict what people will do in a specific situation. Pepitone (1976) has argued that social norms are made salient or active by particular situations, and we require further knowledge of just which situations activate which norms.

In a study designed to examine the role of norms in helping behavior, Darley and Batson (1973) led some seminary students to believe that they were to give a talk on the parable of the Good Samaritan; others were led to expect they would give a talk on jobs for seminary students. The researchers also varied the amount of time the students had to walk across campus to another building: some were told to get there in a hurry, others to go there directly, and others that they would have several minutes. While in transit, the students encountered a "victim," a confederate of the experimenters, who was slumped in a doorway, groaning. Would those for whom the Good Samaritan parable had been made salient help more than the others? While Darley and Batson initially concluded that their results did not support the helping norm hypothesis, a reanalysis of their data by A. G. Greenwald (1975a) indicates that there is modest support for the notion that students who expected to deliver a talk on the Good Samaritan helped more (53 percent helped), regardless of whether they were in a hurry, than those who expected to talk on a topic unrelated to help-giving (29 percent).

Different cultures may be expected to have different norms concerning helping. Many European countries have laws, which may be seen as a form of norm, that penalize a bystander who does not intervene in an emergency. In the United States, there seem to be more laws that mitigate against helping: for example, a helper who incompletely or incorrectly helps is often liable for damages (see J. Kaplan, 1972; Kaufmann, 1970b). We have seen that Americans are economically more helpful toward their compatriots than people of other countries, but what of direct, personal helping?

CROSS-CULTURAL STUDIES OF HELPING

There are relatively few studies on responses to requests for aid in countries outside North America. In one of the earliest such studies, Feldman (1968) compared the cooperative behaviors of Parisians, Athenians, and Bostonians in a series of field experiments. Simple requests for aid (such as giving directions, mailing a letter) were made by an experimenter who posed either as a native or as a foreign tourist. Feldman found that the citizens of Boston were the most likely to give directions to, and mail a stamped letter for, compatriots. Foreigners were less likely to be granted favors in Boston and Paris than were native Americans or Frenchmen. Athenians treated foreigners better than they treated their compatriots.

Restricting themselves to compatriots, L'Armand and Pepitone (1975) found that American students tend to behave more altruistically toward their peers when they can help at no cost to themselves. Indian students, on the other hand, tended to be less generous toward their peers than toward themselves. L'Armand and Pepitone interpret their results in terms of social norms operating in India and the United States. The behavior of the Indian students was seen as stemming from a view of the world as one involving competition for scarce resources.

With so few cross-cultural studies on helping, it is not possible to conclude that there are important national differences in the tendency to help others. What differences have been found can usually be interpreted either in terms of different social norms about helping others or in terms of the perceived costs of helping to a bystander (see L. Berkowitz & Walker, 1967; Goldstein, Rosnow, Raday, Silverman, & Gaskell, 1975; Schwartz & Gottlieb, 1977).

CROSS-CULTURAL STUDIES ON RECEIVING AID

Kenneth Gergen and his colleagues have conducted a number of cross-cultural studies on responses to receiving, rather than to giving, aid (Gergen, Ellsworth, Maslach, & Seipel, 1975; Gergen, Morse, & Kristeller, 1973). In their research, students in Japan, the United States, Sweden, South Africa, Scotland, Korea, and Taiwan were asked how they would feel about someone who offered to help them. Among other independent variables, they studied the effects of the amount of resources available to the donor, whether the donor required repayment of the aid or not, and whether there were restrictions on how the aid was to be used. Two major dependent variables in this research were attraction to and liking for the donor and whether repayment would be made. In both studies, Gergen and his associates found no major differences between countries in evaluation of the donor or in tendency to repay the donor. The donor was liked most when recipients were obliged to repay the aid. As the obligations attached to the aid increased, the recipients became more resistant to receiving it and more negative in their feelings toward the donor. Greater attraction was found for poor as opposed to wealthy donors. The desire to return money given in aid was greater for poor than for wealthy donors, regardless of whether repayment was originally demanded.

While Gergen's research is designed to be an analogue of international governmental aid, it raises a number of questions for theory and research on interpersonal aid. There have been few studies on how people respond to receiving aid in an emergency. There have been considerably more studies on feelings and characteristics of blood donors and bone marrow donors (e.g., Fellner & Marshall, 1970) than on the responses of recipients. If we acquire a feeling of

Cross-cultural studies on helping are scarce and inconclusive. This young American is not having any trouble getting directions from these Frenchmen, however.

indebtedness as a result of receiving aid, how do we deal with that indebtedness? Do we become more, or less, altruistic? These are among the unanswered questions.

Summary

The murder of Kitty Genovese stimulated social psychological interest in bystander intervention. Beginning with the work of Latané and Darley and continuing actively today, social psychology has produced a variety of theories of prosocial behavior. At best, some of these theories can account for responses to certain types of helping situations, but no single theory that is capable of accurately predicting responses to a wide variety of prosocial settings has yet been proposed.

Latané and Darley presented two theoretical explanations. The first, the notion of diffusion of responsibility, accounts for their finding that individual bystanders are more likely to intervene in an emergency than are groups of bystanders. The second, a general model of helping, involves five sequential stages. In order to provide assistance in an emergency, the bystander must (1) notice that something is happening, (2) interpret it as an emergency, (3) decide that he or she has some responsibility for helping, (4) decide what response is most appropriate, and (5) implement that response.

At any step along the way, the behavior of others may serve to define the situation or appropriate response. The behavior of others thus serves as a model for a bystander to imitate. Observation of a model lending aid to someone may increase the probability that an event will be noticed, that it will be interpreted as an emergency, and that it is the bystander's responsibility to act, and may also help to define what actions are appropriate and how to implement them. These two explanations, then, are not mutually exclusive, but complementary.

One explanation of responses to emergencies focuses on the costs and rewards that a bystander may expect from intervening. According to this explanation, witnessing someone in distress is itself distressing, leading to an emotional arousal that is uncomfortable. Individuals thus aroused are motivated to reduce this uncomfortable state of arousal. This can be done by intervening, by changing one's perception of the emergency, or by leaving the scene. The particular response chosen will be the least costly (in terms of effort, consequences, time, and money) and the most rewarding. One psychological response we may have to an emergency is devaluation of the victim. This notion has been explored by Lerner in his work on the just-world phenomenon.

An analysis of altruism during the Second World War suggests that situational characteristics are particularly important determinants of helping behavior. Christians who saved Jews from the Nazis had little in common. Persistence in rescue operations was partly determined by a cluster of personality traits: a spirit of adventurousness, identification with a moral model, usually a parent, and a feeling of moderate isolation from society.

In general, research on the personalities of altruistic individuals has not produced strong or highly consistent findings. Some research suggests that personality interacts with the particular kind of helping requested. What is clearly required is some way of classifying different types of helping situation.

Some social psychologists have argued that helping is determined in part by social norms, and that differences between helping found in different cultures can be traced to differences in norms for and against helping in those cultures. On the whole, cross-cultural differences in helping and responses to being helped do not seem to be major.

Suggested Readings

Des Pres, T. *The survivor: An anatomy of life in the death camps.* London and New York: Oxford University Press, 1976. Amidst the death and horror of concentration camps, Des Pres focuses on "the small strands of life and decency which constitute . . . a fabric of discernible goodness."

Paley, G. "Samuel." In *Enormous changes at the last minute.* New York: Farrar, Straus & Giroux, 1974. Good intentions of a helper go astray in this short story.

Latané, B., & Darley, J. M. *The unresponsive bystander: Why doesn't he help?* New York: Appleton, 1970.

Piliavin, J. A., & Piliavin, I. M. *The responsive bystander: Why does he help?* New York: MSS Modular Publications, 1975.

Staub, E. *Positive social behavior and morality* (Vol. 1). New York: Academic Press, 1978.

Staub, E. *Positive social behavior and morality* (Vol. 2). New York: Academic Press, 1979.

Cathy Hull

8
THE SOCIAL PSYCHOLOGY OF AGGRESSION

THE NATURE OF HUMAN AGGRESSION

Most of us are familiar with acts of aggression, either through personal experience or through the mass media. A report in *The New York Times* in 1973 indicated that 34 percent of adult women in one congressional district of New York City were victims of serious crimes in 1972. Even if we have not been so victimized, we may have engaged in hitting our siblings, spouses, or children, or have seen combat on the battlefield. We may have been involved in less direct, though no less damaging, acts of aggression, such as refusing food to someone hungry or failing to stop a fight in progress.

A DEFINITION OF AGGRESSION

Ever since psychologists became interested in studying human violence, they have had difficulty in defining aggression. We will define human aggression as *behavior whose intent is the physical or psychological injury of another person*. While this is less than an ideal definition, it is closest to the definitions commonly used in research. Among its difficulties are the exclusion of nonhuman targets of aggression and the fact that it is not at all easy to determine an aggressor's intentions. Nevertheless, we would probably want to exclude injury to organisms such as viruses and insects from our consideration, as well as accidental injuries. Note that the definition includes not only physical injury to others but psychological injury as well. If we were primarily concerned with animal aggression, we would not be interested in psychological injury. But because humans have the capacity to manipulate symbols and to attribute meaning

Biff! A Bobo doll reels from a punch that may actually be intended for a frustrating parent, teacher, or psychologist. Or perhaps this boy is imitating some two-fisted TV hero who solves his problems by hitting bad people. Children must learn which forms of aggression are socially acceptable.

to a wide variety of objects and actions, we will discuss psychological as well as physical injury. While this chapter will be concerned primarily with physical harm, various sorts of psychological harm are discussed elsewhere in this book: failure to help others in need is discussed in Chapter 7, and prejudice and intergroup conflict are discussed in Chapter 10.

Our definition of aggression is a broad one and not all social psychologists would be inclined to accept it (Kaufmann, 1970a; Tedeschi, Smith, & Brown, 1974). Distinctions are frequently made between different types of aggression. L. Berkowitz (1962), for example, discusses *instrumental aggression*, aggressive behaviors that are designed to provide some gain for the aggressor. Buss (1971) and Moyer (1968) distinguish several different categories of aggression. We will discuss these distinctions as the need arises.

MEASUREMENT OF AGGRESSION

In social psychological research, aggression is most often studied in laboratory experiments, where the administration of shock is used as a measure of aggression (Buss, 1961). In the typical study, one subject and one accomplice of the experimenter are together in the laboratory. The subject believes the accomplice to be another subject. After one or more independent variables are manipulated by the experimenter, the real subject is led to believe that he or she is going to teach the other person a task, such as a list of words. Each time the person makes a mistake, the subject is to administer an electric shock, which can vary in intensity from mild to severe. The intensity of the shock and its duration are used as the measures of the subject's aggression level. In actuality, no shocks are delivered to the accomplice, although the subject doesn't find this out until the end of the experiment.

This "teacher–learner" paradigm has been criticized as not being a direct, or even a very reliable, measure of a person's aggressiveness (Baron & Eggleston, 1972; Goldstein, 1976a). However, it is the most common measure found in the experimental social psychological literature of aggression.

Bandura (1973), as well as others, has observed the aggressive behavior of children. Rather than have them participate in the complex teacher–learner situation, researchers permit children to play with toys, some of which give an idea of their aggressiveness. Punching a doll or a punching bag may be indicative of a child's level of hostility, and such measures are often used in studying children's aggression (Baron, 1977).

In order to approach a social psychological understanding of aggression, we must first address some fundamental issues. Foremost among these is the heritability of aggression.

IS AGGRESSION AN INSTINCT?

Throughout modern history the answer to the question of whether aggression is innate or learned has swung first toward one pole, then the other. This has resulted in a great many inconsistencies and uncertainties in Western judicial and legal systems. Current thinking leans toward the instinctual pole because of three major influences: the highly readable accounts of aggression by Konrad Lorenz (1966), Desmond Morris (1967), Robert Ardrey (1966), and Edward O. Wilson (1975); the dramatic research on electrical and chemical stimulation of the brain (Delgado, 1967, 1969); and the popularity and pervasiveness of Freudian theory (Freud, 1930/1962).

One Giant Leap toward Mankind The ethological arguments proposed by Lorenz, Morris, and others can be summarized by saying that there is ample evidence that our animal ancestors were instinctively violent beings, and because we have evolved from them, we too must be the bearers of destructive impulses in our genetic composition. Lorenz states, "There cannot be any doubt, in the opinion of any biologically minded scientist, that intraspecific aggression is, in man, just as much of a spontaneous instinctive drive as in most other higher vertebrates" (1964, p. 49).

There are two difficulties with this argument. First, the evidence that animals, at least higher primates, are instinctively aggressive is not at all convincing (Alland, 1972; Montagu, 1968, 1976; Schneirla, 1968; Scott, 1975). Second, even if the evidence reviewed by the ethologists were sufficient to warrant the conclusion that infrahuman species were innately violent, we would still have to ask whether that proves anything about proneness to aggression in *Homo sapiens*. The answer, of course, is that it does not. The *likelihood* that humans are instinctively aggressive would be increased if all animals were shown to be aggressive. However, we would still have to entertain the possibility that humans, having evolved as an independent species, were not instinctively aggressive.

There is little doubt that humans *can* behave like phylogenetically inferior species. There is no reason whatever why an organism with such a complex nervous system cannot mimic the behavior of animals with less complex nervous systems. But to argue that because humans *can* behave like lower organisms, this is the way they *must* behave is fallacious. If we take learning experiments on animals, particularly those operant conditioning studies in which an organism is rewarded for performing a certain response, there is no neurological or psychological reason why a human being cannot also learn responses in this way. To argue that this is *the* way that humans learn simply because it is *one* way in which they may learn is begging the question. Human beings can and do learn behaviors through operant conditioning (see Chapter 1). However, the preclusion of other uniquely human ways of learning is a serious shortcoming of much contemporary experimental psychology. Likewise, to argue that humans learn aggression in the same ways that animals learn aggression (if, in fact, it is learned in animals) is to ignore the rather likely possibility that there are species-specific aggressions in human beings or that there are specifically human routes to learning and behaving.

Monkeying around in Primate Brains   Research on brain physiology and chemistry, particularly that on electrical and chemical stimulation of the brain, has demonstrated that it is possible in many instances to make normally docile animals—and humans—violent (e.g., Delgado, 1969). The best-known work in this field has been done by José Delgado. After implanting sensitive radio receivers in the hypothalami of cats, monkeys, and other species, Delgado has been able to control the aggressive behavior of his research subjects by activating the hypothalamis electronically.

What implications does this dramatic research hold for an understanding of aggression in humans? Aside from the moral issues involved (such as the possibility that electrodes could be implanted in human brains during routine operations without the recipients' knowledge or consent), the brain stimulation studies are in fact less consistent than is often believed (K. B. Clark, 1971; Moyer, 1971, 1976). In many of the brain stimulation studies on aggression, some animals will not engage in aggression unless certain environmental conditions are present, such as an "appropriate" target for attack (Flynn, 1967; Plotnik, 1974). Thus, brain stimulation does not guarantee that aggressive behavior will ensue, a finding that calls into question the notion that aggression is purely a matter of brain chemistry or physiology. Even if the brain research were entirely reliable, evoking aggression whenever the hypothalamus was stimulated, it still would not prove that human aggression was caused by spontaneous stimulation of the hypothalamus. The electrochemical stimulation research tells us nothing about the intact brain, about brains that do not have electrodes embedded in them. In the normal, intact brain, what simulates the hypothalamus? It is likely that stimuli residing outside the person, in his or her environment, stimulate the production of certain hormones that act upon the hypothalamus. So we will have to look outside the corporal package, to the social and physical environment, in order to understand human aggression fully.

Psychoanalytic Views of Aggression: Freudian Slips   Although Freud initially proposed that there was only one instinctive force motivating human behavior, the life instinct or Eros (1930/1962), his inability to explain the horrors of a world war with this positive instinct led him to modify his theory and add a second instinctive force, Thanatos, or the death instinct (1955). Freud suggested that societies must learn to control the expression of both the life and death instincts. This need for social control results in social mores, rules, and laws that regulate aggressive and sexual conduct.

Contemporary psychoanalytic theorists, building more or less on Freud's work, have retained the notion that aggression is an instinctive drive (Zinberg & Fellman, 1967). Common in current psychoanalytic thinking is the notion that aggression must be discharged periodically, lest it build up to such a point that its expression becomes inevitable, spontaneous, and uncontrollable. Some psychoanalysts go so far as to suggest that war itself serves to discharge the aggression instinct not only for the combatants, but for the civilian population as well. As one psychoanalyst put it, "Crime is the price paid for the domestication of a naturally wild animal, man" (Glover, 1960, p. 7). Of importance here is the notion that aggression is instinctive; that if it is not regularly discharged it will build up to a dangerously high level which leads to excessive and spontaneous aggression; that it is possible to discharge aggression vicariously by observing violence in others, a process referred to as *catharsis* (though this term is now used in a way that would be foreign to Freud).

One additional aspect of psychoanalytic theory deserves mention, and that is the possibility that a person can invoke one or more *ego defense mechanisms* to prevent the expression of aggressive drives. (This is also said of sexual instincts where sexual energy can be denied expression and used in other endeavors, a process known as *sublimation.*) Aggressive energy can be channeled into nonaggressive behaviors, according to Freudian theories. Thus, it is postulated that all people have aggression instincts, but not everyone will behave aggressively, owing to the use of various ego defense mechanisms. This kind of ambiguity makes Freudian theory difficult to test, and it is largely because nearly any research finding can be interpreted as support for the theory that it is still considered viable by so many people. With regard to those parts of the theory that are testable, there is less than overwhelming empirical support that aggression regularly and inevitably increases with the passage of time, and that aggression can be discharged vicariously.

AGGRESSION AS SOCIAL
BEHAVIOR

Aggression is neither automatic, compulsive, nor stereotypic. Over 40 years ago, an introductory psychology text noted that

... *conflict between individuals does not invariably or universally result in the same behavior. Instead of fighting with his fists, the*

Conflict is expressed differently from one culture to the next. Perhaps these two should learn from the Eskimos and sing their aggressions away.

Kwakiutl Indian fights with property in the institution of the "potlatch," in which the more property he can give away or destroy, the more superior he is to his opponent. Eskimos settle their conflicts in a public contest in which each sings abusive songs about the other. When two Indians of Santa Marta quarrel, instead of striking each other they strike a tree or rock with sticks, and the first one breaking his stick is considered the braver and hence the victor. In other societies aggression is expressed in still other ways; even within the same society there may be a wide range of different socially approved expressions of aggression. (Boring, Langfeld, & Weld, 1939, p. 163)

The great differences between cultures in the amount and nature of aggression is evidence that aggression is something more than a unitary instinct. The fact is that aggression is a relatively infrequent form of human interaction; it is more common than most of us would like, but most people learn to control their aggression most of the time. We cannot explain the cultural and personal variations in aggressive behavior except by reference to social factors (Baron, 1977; Goldstein, 1975; Goode, 1969; Montagu, 1976).

THEORIES OF AGGRESSION

Psychologists often use examples from physics to demonstrate the ways in which newly developed theories replace older, less useful theories. This is because physics has such a long and illustrious theoretical history. But in psychology, too, theories are revised and modified on the basis of new observations that don't quite fit existing theories. In the study of human aggression there has been almost continuous updating and revising of theory. Perhaps the best example of this is the frustration–aggression theory (Berkowitz, 1978; Dollard, Doob, Miller, Mowrer, & Sears, 1939).

The frustration–aggression theory is a good example of theory development in psychology and a demonstration of how behaviorist and cognitive ideas may be entwined within a single model. The original formulation of the theory was mostly behaviorist in its assumptions. Some of the more recent versions of the theory incorporate a number of cognitive elements.

FRUSTRATION–AGGRESSION THEORY, THEN AND NOW

The Original Theory   One of the first psychological theories of aggression, besides psychoanalytic theory, was proposed in 1939 by a group of Yale psychologists. The theory of John Dollard, Leonard Doob, Neal Miller, O. Hobart Mowrer, and Robert Sears is referred to as the frustration–aggression hypothesis and it received widespread attention upon its publication. The theory is elegant in its simplicity. It consists primarily of two basic postulates: that aggression is caused by frustration and that all frustration causes aggression. As stated in its original version: "The occurrence of aggression always presupposes the existence of frustration and, contrariwise, that the existence of frustration always leads to some form of aggression" (Dollard et al., 1939).

The theorists were careful to provide concise definitions of both frustration and aggression. Frustration was defined as any "interference with the occurrence of an instigated goal-response at its proper time in [a] behavior sequence." This means that interrupting some ongoing activity is frustrating. Aggression was defined as "a response having for its goal the injury of a living organism." In other words, aggression is the attempt to injure someone.

Of course, we could quibble over these definitions if we were so inclined. For example, yelling at your begonia plant is aggressive according to the definition given in the theory, as it may be construed as an attempt to injure a living organism. Brushing one's teeth is also aggressive because its goal is the destruction of bacteria. But most people make allowances for such actions and say that a behavior is aggressive if it is intended to injure another person, or perhaps higher species of animal.

While the theory contains some ambiguities in its definition of aggression, it is quite clear in stating that frustration and only frustration causes aggression. Of course, if we take the theory literally (and there is no reason why we shouldn't), it is utter nonsense. If frustration is *any* interference with ongoing behavior, then people are frustrated dozens of times each day. Having to open a door that is closed, having to wait for a traffic light to change, waiting in a line, being refused a date—all these are frustrations, according to the theory. And, according to the theory, aggressive behavior should follow each of these frustrations. Most people in most of these situations, however, are not noticeably more aggressive for having been frustrated. In fact, it is quite remarkable how many people are able to tolerate these frustrations, and scores like them, with serenity. It is simply untrue that all frustrations lead to aggression.

The second postulate of the theory, that aggression is always preceded by frustration, is equally false. A good deal of aggression occurs in the absence of any noticeable frustration. Soldiers fighting in a war, children imitating aggressive scenes depicted on television,

This girl seems frustrated by the bewildering choice of cereals—but instead of becoming aggressive, she may just decide that she prefers muffins for breakfast.

bullies picking fights with weaker people—all these are examples of aggression that occur in the absence of frustration. So it is neither true that frustration always causes aggression nor that aggression is always preceded by frustration.

A Modification of the Frustration–Aggression Hypothesis These deficiencies in the theory were noted almost immediately (Barker, Dembo, & Lewin, 1940; Maslow, 1941), and, to their credit, the theorists conceded that many of the criticisms were legitimate. At least two early revisions of the theory were made. In 1941, Robert Sears published a paper on nonaggressive reactions to frustration. Also in 1941, N. E. Miller, in collaboration with Sears, Mowrer, Doob, and Dollard, published a paper in which the frustration–aggression theory was stated in less rigid terms.

Miller acknowledged that the phrasing of the original theory was, to use his word, "unfortunate." In particular, he singled out the statement that "the occurrence of aggression always presupposes the existence of frustration and . . . the existence of frustration always leads to . . . aggression." He said in his 1941 paper that frustration can have effects other than aggression. While frustration always leads to a *tendency* to aggress, the organism may have learned other ways of responding to frustration. Miller modified the theory to read: "Frustration produces instigations to a number of different types of response, one of which is some form of aggression." In other words, frustration does not always lead to aggression, but may result in other, nonaggressive behaviors as well. Miller suggested further that aggression may also be caused by factors other than frustration.

With this modification, the frustration–aggression theory went from being too restrictive to being too ambiguous. Which frustrations lead to aggression? When will aggression occur in the absence of frustration? These questions were not answered in Miller's paper. The original theory did not allow for any nonaggressive responses to frustration, or for any other causes of aggression besides frustration. In its revised version, the theory does not tell us when aggression will result from frustration and when it will not.

Despite the difficulties with both versions of the frustration–aggression theory, it generated a considerable amount of research (L. Berkowitz, 1969). Aside from the psychoanalytic theory of aggression proposed earlier in the century by Freud, there were not many other psychological explanations of aggression until the 1960s. So researchers were pretty much forced to base their investigations of aggression on the frustration–aggression theory.

One of the enticing features of these two versions of the frustration–aggression theory is that they do provide researchers with some non-Freudian explanation of aggression. Here, at least, is a theory with no psychoanalytic mumbo jumbo. No need to bother about such phantoms as ids, egos, superegos, and ego-defense mechanisms. Thwart an instigated goal response and you get "a response having for its goal the injury of a living organism."

The lack of specificity in the Miller modification poses a serious problem, particularly to researchers who wish to base predictions on the theory. Someone may wish to test the theory by frustrating one group of people and not frustrating a second, control group, and observing the extent of aggressive behavior in both groups. If frustrated people are more aggressive than nonfrustrated people, we can conclude that the experiment supports the theory. Suppose, though, that frustrated people are not more aggressive than nonfrustrated people. Can we then conclude that the theory is wrong? Because Miller stated that frustration may lead to responses other than aggression, we cannot know whether this is one of those nonaggressive instances. This places the researcher in an untenable position: If frustration leads to aggression in the study, he may conclude that the theory is correct. But if it does not lead to aggression, he may also conclude that the theory is correct, because Miller said that frustration may lead to nonaggressive responses as well as aggressive ones. Hence, there is no good way to test the theory unless it can specify precisely when frustration will lead to aggression and when it will lead to other responses.

A Further Refinement: The Berkowitz Model In his early effort to apply the frustration–aggression theory to prejudice, particularly to anti-Semitism, Leonard Berkowitz (1959) confronted the problem of the theory's ambiguity. In order to increase the usefulness of the theory, a modification that would state just when frustration causes aggression was required. Berkowitz borrowed a concept from the biologist Nikolaas Tinbergen (1951) and added it to the theory.

Tinbergen was a student of animal behavior who objected to the way biologists used the concept of instinct. Most biologists tended to think of instincts as automatic behaviors that would be expressed at certain critical times. For example, we tend to think of eating and drinking as instinctive. This implies that they are not learned behaviors, but innate biological drives. When we are hungry, though, when the eating instinct should be at its peak, we don't stick just any available object into our mouths. We wait until there is some specific object, namely, food, which is best able to satisfy our hunger. We don't eat pencils, or books, or rocks when we are hungry. And we Westerners don't eat ants, beetles, or insects, even though these may be capable of reducing our hunger. Instead, we select from a large number of possible objects those that we feel are most appropriate. This implies that instincts are not merely internal biological mechanisms but require some *appropriate* external object or situation in order to be expressed.

Tinbergen's best known research on this conception of instinct was done with male stickleback fish (1951). Male sticklebacks are capable of performing an elaborate mating ritual during which they fight off rival male sticklebacks. This ritual is not learned, because males isolated from birth can also perform the ritual. Yet, male sticklebacks don't perform the ritual every day or every month. They perform it only at particular times, and those times are when they see another stickleback with a red belly. The sight of such a stimulus is the triggering mechanism, or external *cue*, that releases this unlearned ritual in the male. Tinbergen proposes that we replace the older notion of instinct as a purely automatic internal behavior with the concept of a *fixed action pattern*. A fixed action pattern is also an unlearned behavior, but it is not purely internal because it requires for its expression some appropriate releasing cue that will set off the behavior. Rather than being purely internal, a fixed action pattern is both internal and external. It consists of some internal potential, but this potential behavior will not be expressed unless external conditions are appropriate.

Berkowitz, using reasoning similar to Tinbergen's, added the notion of external cues to the frustration–aggression theory. While there is an innate aggressive response to frustration and anger, he proposes (1962), it will be expressed only under conditions that are "appropriate." Aggression, like the mating ritual of the male stickleback, requires some external releasing cues in order for it to be expressed. Berkowitz's refinement of the frustration–aggression theory states that frustration or anger causes aggression when appropriate cues are present. If these cues are not present, then the response to frustration will be some nonaggressive behavior.

What are the releasing cues for aggression? Berkowitz has discussed three types of cue: targets, objects, and situations. We can learn, through a number of processes, that there are certain people who are appropriate targets of aggression. In the United States, many people learn to express their anger toward particular groups of people, such as blacks, Jews, or women. Some people may learn that specific individuals are appropriate targets of aggression, such as one's landlord or boss. According to the modified frustration–aggression theory of Berkowitz, an individual who is frustrated or angered will be more likely to express aggression if one of these "appropriate" targets is present than if no such target is present (Berkowitz & Geen, 1967).

Likewise, people often associate particular objects with the expression of aggression, and these too may act as releaser stimuli for the aggression aroused by frustration or by anger. Guns, for example, are closely associated with violence, and so an individual who is frustrated will be more likely to aggress if a weapon is present than if no weapon is present (L. Berkowitz & LePage, 1967). Situations, too, can be associated with violence. People are more likely to express their aggression in bars and in alleyways than in churches or restaurants (Goldstein, 1975).

Over the last twenty years, Berkowitz and his colleagues have conducted scores of studies on this version of the frustration–aggression theory. In recent years, Berkowitz has added another modification to the initial theory, and that is the idea that other strong emotional states, such as anger, may have effects similar to frustration. Two of these studies will be presented here to illustrate several aspects of the theory.

In 1966, Berkowitz and Geen published a study entitled "Film Violence and the Cue Properties of Available Targets." In their research, Berkowitz and Geen angered some subjects and did not anger others. This was accomplished by having another presumed subject (actually a confederate of the experimenters') evaluate the subject's solution to a problem. The confederate indicated either that he liked the subject's solution by administering only one shock to him, or that he did not like the subject's solution by administering seven shocks to him. For half the subjects, the accomplice's name was given as "Kirk Anderson," while for the remaining half, his name was said to be "Bob Anderson." Half the subjects in each of these conditions then viewed a 7-minute film clip of a fight scene from the film *Champion*, starring Kirk Douglas. The remaining half of the subjects saw a seven-minute film of an exciting track race.

The study thus consisted of three independent variables: (1) anger versus no anger; (2) the accomplice's name, Kirk or Bob; and (3) the type of film viewed, either a fight scene with Kirk Douglas or a race. The dependent variable was the subject's subsequent evaluation of a solution to a problem by the accomplice. After viewing the film, the subject was told that he was to evaluate the confederate's solution to a problem by administering shock to signal how good or bad he thought it was. It was assumed that the more unsatisfactory the subject found the confederate's solution, the more shocks he would administer, and that he would dislike the solution in proportion to how aggressive he felt.

The hypotheses of the experiment were that angered subjects would administer more shocks than nonangered subjects; and that more shocks would be administered after viewing the fight film than after viewing the track film, particularly when there was some connection between the film and the situation—that is, when the confederate's name served as an aggressive cue, when his name was "Kirk." The results, presented in Table 8.1, lend support to these hypotheses. The greatest number of shocks was administered by angered subjects who viewed the aggressive film and who could associate the name of the confederate (Kirk) with aggression. In this study, we have an experimentally created aggressive cue. Someone's name, Kirk, has been presented in conjunction with aggressive behavior, and when subjects were angered and could associate the target with aggression, they gave a considerable amount of shock to him. In this study, we also have a classically conditioned cue: the accomplice's name was given aggressive cue properties by associating it with the aggressor in a film.

In the same way that someone's name might serve as an aggressive cue, so might objects be associated with aggression. In a controversial experiment by Berkowitz and LePage (1967), the aggressive cue studied was the presence of a weapon. According to the authors:

For many men (and probably women as well) in our society, these objects (weapons) are closely associated with aggression. Assuming that the weapons do not produce inhibitions that are stronger than the evoked aggressive reactions (as would be the case . . . if the weapons were labeled as morally bad), the presence of the aggressive objects should generally lead to more intense attacks upon an available target than would occur in the presence of a neutral object.

One hundred undergraduate males from the University of Wisconsin served as subjects in the experiment. They were randomly assigned to one of seven groups. As in the Berkowitz and Geen study, half the subjects were angered by a confederate, who administered seven shocks to each of them in evaluation of a problem solution. The nonangered subjects were given only one shock.

It was then the subject's turn to evaluate the confederate. For one group, there was only a shock key on the subject's desk. For two other groups, there was a 12-gauge shotgun and a .38-caliber revolver lying on the table near the shock key. Some of these subjects were informed that the weapons belonged to the confederate ("associated weapons" condition); others were told that they were being used in other research ("unassociated weapons" condition). A fourth group of subjects found badminton racquets and shuttlecocks on the table rather than weapons. The subjects evaluated the confederate's problem solution by administering from one to ten shocks. Then a brief questionnaire was completed. The results of the study are presented in Table 8.2.

Table 8.1.
Mean Number of Shocks Administered in Berkowitz
and Geen Study (1966)

Accomplice's name	Aggressive Film		Track Film	
	Angered	Nonangered	Angered	Nonangered
Kirk	6.09	1.73	4.18	1.54
Bob	4.55	1.45	4.00	1.64

Table 8.2.
Mean Number of Shocks Administered in
Berkowitz and LePage Study (1967)

Condition	Nonangered	Angered
Associated weapons	2.60	6.07
Unassociated weapons	2.20	5.67
No object	3.07	4.67
Badminton racquets	—	4.60

As in previous research, angered subjects (those receiving seven shocks) were most aggressive when aggressive cues (weapons) were present. It made no significant difference whether those weapons were associated with the confederate or not—the number of shocks is approximately the same (6.07 versus 5.67). Both these studies, and numerous others conducted by Berkowitz and his associates (e.g., Berkowitz, 1974; Swart & Berkowitz, 1976), demonstrate the usefulness of this revision of the frustration–aggression hypothesis (see Berkowitz, 1978).

Of all the studies conducted by the Berkowitz group, none has proved more controversial than the Berkowitz and LePage study. As Berkowitz has said of that study (1970), it demonstrates not only that a finger may pull the trigger of a weapon, but also that "the trigger pulls the finger." In other words, the mere possession or presence of a weapon may facilitate violence.

Quite a number of social psychologists have attempted to replicate the results of the Berkowitz and LePage study. Their concern was as much practical as theoretical. Not all the critics raised questions about the usefulness of the modified frustration–aggression theory. Rather, some questioned whether there might not be other explanations for the results of that particular experiment, and whether the results might not have been due to various types of methodological bias. Arnold Buss and his colleagues (Buss, Booker, & Buss, 1972) attempted to replicate the "weapons effect" in nearly half a dozen studies, and in each case they were unable to obtain the finding that weapons facilitated aggression. Other researchers were able to replicate the results (e.g., Frodi, 1975), but often because of particular idiosyncrasies in the Berkowitz and LePage procedures (Page & Scheidt, 1971). So the existence of a "weapons effect" is still open to question (L. Berkowitz, 1971; Ellis, Weinir, & Miller, 1971). What can be said of the Berkowitz and LePage study is that it provided support for the modified frustration–aggression theory, although there are alternative explanations for the findings.

Frustration as Arousal: The Zillmann Modification   Emotions of any sort, frustration and anger among them, may be seen to consist of at least two separate components: a physiological component and a cognitive component (Schachter & Singer, 1962). Frustration may share a particular set of physiological characteristics with other emotions, such as anger, fear, or anxiety. An increase in autonomic nervous system arousal, including increased heart rate, blood pressure, respiratory rate, and electrodermal activity, is one of the physiological aspects of frustration. Anger, fear, and anxiety may also produce autonomic nervous system arousal. A cognitive label that an individual attaches to that state of heightened arousal may be what distinguishes frustration from other emotions. In a sense, we can think of frustration as a label which people assign to certain internal feelings in particular situations. Whenever we refer to an emotion, we are actually referring to two things at once: the physiological state accompanying the emotion and the cognitive label attached to that physiological state. The frustration–aggression theory states that a particular emotion, frustration, leads to a particular behavior, aggression. We can ask whether the crucial element of the hypothesis is the physiological arousal or the cognitive label, or, perhaps, the two together. It may be that only one of the two components of frustration causes aggression, in which case we would have to modify the original formulation in one of two ways. Either it should read "Physiological arousal causes aggressive behavior," or "The cognitive label of frustration causes aggressive behavior." Of course, the original theory may be correct in that both components of frustration together cause aggression.

Dolf Zillman (1971) reasoned that the crucial element of frustration may be physiological arousal in and of itself. He therefore proposed that people who are aroused physiologically, as by a stimulating drug or some external event which is stimulating, should be more aggressive than people who are not physiologically aroused.

In order to test this hypothesis, Zillmann showed groups of college males one of three different films. One film was a relatively boring story that contained no aggressive scenes and no sexual scenes that might arouse the students. A second group of students viewed a film that had been determined to be moderately arousing and highly aggressive in content. A third group saw a highly arousing film with scenes of explicit sexual activity. At various points in the experiment, Zillmann measured the extent of students' arousal by taking blood pressure readings. After viewing the films, students were led to believe that they were teaching a list of words to someone else and that they were to express their approval or disapproval of the other's responses by administering shock. The shock administered could vary in intensity from mild to quite severe. Zillmann used this as his dependent measure of aggression, assuming that the more extreme the shock administered by a subject, the more aggressive he was.

As hypothesized, Zillmann found that aggression could be predicted from a knowledge of the extent of the subjects' arousal. Those students who were most aroused (those viewing the sexually explicit film) gave the most shock. Those who were least aroused (those viewing the boring film) gave the least aggressive responses.

Other studies by different investigators have provided additional support for the notion that arousal causes aggression (Goldstein, Rosnow, Raday, Silverman, & Gaskell, 1975). Geen and O'Neal (1969) found that subjects who are angered and then exposed to high levels of noise are more aggressive than those not exposed to arousing noise. Additional work by Zillmann and his colleagues studying arousal caused by a variety of means, including physical exercise, has added further supporting evidence (Zillmann, 1979; Zillmann & Bryant, 1974; Zillmann, Katcher, & Milavsky, 1972). Aggressiveness is seen by Zillmann as an attribution of anger to oneself due to arousal. Because arousal may subside slowly after, say, physical exercise, the person, when in an appropriate situation, may believe that he is angry and attribute his residual arousal to anger.

These various versions of the frustration–aggression theory take us a long way toward understanding the many forms of human aggression. The theory has been applied to a wide variety of violent situations, including domestic riots and international conflicts. Nevertheless, the theory has some decided defects. It is incapable of explaining numerous kinds of violence, of explaining violence among people who are not angry, frustrated, or otherwise aroused, of explaining the effects of early experience on later aggression. These issues are addressed more fully in Albert Bandura's social learning theory, a behaviorist theory that relies heavily on cognitive content.

SOCIAL LEARNING THEORY

Strict behaviorists generally explain behavior in terms of rewards and punishments. If they were to explain why people are sometimes aggressive, they would say that some people have been rewarded for being aggressive in certain situations in the past, or that they have been punished for being nonaggressive in the past. Bandura (1965b, 1973) has long criticized this simple notion of learning. In fact, he says that people can learn to behave in certain ways even without being rewarded or punished at all. To demonstrate this, he had groups of young children watch a videotape on a television monitor (Bandura, 1965a). One group of children saw an adult woman engage in a series of aggressive acts, punching and kicking an inflatable "Bobo" doll, after which she was rewarded by another adult who offered her soft drinks and candy. A second group saw the same behavior on the TV monitor, but this time the model was punished. She was told that her behavior was bad and that she would not receive soft drinks and candy. A third group of children saw the same tape, but afterward the model was neither rewarded nor punished.

The children were then allowed to play in a large room that contained a number of toys, including a Bobo doll. Each child's behavior was observed and later scored for the extent of aggression shown. What Bandura found in this free-play period was precisely what we would expect from a traditional behaviorist position: the children who observed the model rewarded were considerably more aggressive than those who saw her punished. The children who saw her punished were least aggressive. (See Table 8.3.)

At this point, most behaviorists would have called an end to the study and concluded that the results show that rewards strengthen behavior and punishments inhibit behavior. But Bandura added a second set of dependent variables to the study. He asked each child to imitate the behavior observed on the TV screen. Here he found that all three groups of children were equally capable of imitating the aggressive behavior of the model. Regardless of the distribution of rewards and punishments, children learned the behavior they saw merely by observation.

Bandura concluded from this study that learning can occur in the absence of rewards and punishments. Otherwise, how could we explain the finding that all three groups of children learned the behavior they observed? He also concluded that in a free-choice setting, rewards led to the spontaneous performance of the observed behavior whereas punishments led to a suppression of the observed behavior. Thus, learning occurs merely through observation; it is spontaneous performance that is influenced by reinforcement.

In explaining aggression, Bandura (1973) proposes that children learn aggressive behaviors merely by being exposed to them. Seeing aggression performed on television or by parents is sufficient to cause the child to learn aggressive behaviors. Whether or not the child actually performs the learned behavior will depend on whether the child has been, or has seen others, rewarded or punished for that aggression in the past. Even if the child has been punished for aggressing, the aggressive behaviors will still have been acquired and are therefore potentially capable of being expressed.

Bandura (1965b; Bandura, Ross, & Ross, 1963) has proposed a number of mechanisms to explain why and how observation leads to learning. In general, it is proposed that when observers pay attention to something going on around them, they form mental pictures or *cognitive representations* of what they observe, and they remember these mental pictures. Hence, what is learned through observation is not the behavior of someone else, but a cognitive representation of that behavior. The theory is thus a cognitive learning theory; Bandura refers to it as a cognitive-mediated learning theory.

Table 8.3.
Relative Amount of Aggression in Bandura
Study (1965a)

| | Children Saw the Model: | | |
	Rewarded	Punished	Neither
Spontaneous performance	High	Low	Moderate
Learning	High	High	High

Social learning theory has numerous implications for the understanding of aggression. Not only is it concerned with the acquisition and performance of aggressive behavior, but it has implications for the reduction of violence, for aggression in mass media, sports, and humor, and even for the criminal justice system. One of the interesting aspects of the theory is that it often leads to predictions quite at variance with those based on psychoanalytic theory. Some of these issues are discussed briefly below in order to acquaint you with the breadth of the theory.

Violence in the Mass Media   Within the past two decades, there has been more research conducted on the effects of violence in the mass media than on any other aspect of human aggression. In 1972, the U.S. Surgeon General published a report on television and social behavior that has been summarized by Robert Liebert:

The data suggest consistently that children are exposed to a heavy dose of violence on television. It is also clear that they can and do retain some of the aggressive behaviors which they see, and are often able to reproduce them. Differences in recall as a function of age are in the expected direction (better recall with increasing age). Differences in recall as a function of content are less clearly understood, but violent content appears to be learned and remembered at least as well as nonviolent fare. . . . Punishment to an aggressive model leads children to avoid reproduction of the exemplary behavior, but does not prevent learning or subsequent performance under more favorable circumstances. . . . It is important to note that the correlational results, while generally consistent, point to a moderate (rather than a strong) relationship between watching television violence and subsequent aggressive attitudes and behavior. (1972)

Many of the studies summarized by the Surgeon General's report have been criticized on a number of methodological grounds (Singer, 1971; W. Weiss, 1969). For example, most of the studies were conducted in the laboratory under quite unnatural conditions that people would rarely encounter in their daily lives. Second, much of the research was conducted only in the United States, and the extent to which the results can be generalized to other peoples is unclear. In order to examine some of these issues, Goldstein et al. (1975) conducted a study on the effects of filmed violence in the United States, England, Canada, and Italy, using a full-length film in nonlaboratory settings. The effects of films that were aggressive (e.g., *Clockwork Orange, Straw Dogs*), sexually arousing but not aggressive (X-rated films in each country), and neither aggressive nor sexual (such as *Fiddler on the Roof* and *Born Free*) were studied by obtaining a measure of aggressiveness from male theatergoers either before or after they had seen one of these films. The results of the study, presented in Figure 8.1, indicate that people in all four countries who viewed aggressive films were more hostile afterward than before. There was no such increase for those who had seen neutral films. Observers of sexual films showed a level of aggressiveness somewhere between these two. As part of the study, we were interested in learning whether the effects of films were specific to aggressive behavior, or whether viewing violent films increased the probability of other responses as well. Therefore, some of the subjects were asked to make donations to charity. There were no differences in the amount of money donated as a function of the type of film seen. In other words, the results showed that an increase in aggression occurred for those watching aggressive films, but that there was no effect on the unrelated response of charitableness. The results of the study are most clearly consistent with social learning theory, although there is some evidence that arousal, too, may have played some role, because those who viewed sexually arousing films were more aggressive afterward than those who viewed nonarousing films.

The results of research on mass media effects generally indicate that viewing violence leads to an increase in aggressive behavior. Social learning theory suggests that the mechanism through which this increase occurs is a tendency to imitate the aggressive behavior that models display, provided that the behavior is unpunished. Watching aggressive models may also lead to a reduction in inhibitions against aggressing (Bandura, Underwood, & Fromson, 1975; Wheeler & Caggiula, 1966); when models seem to get away with aggression on screen, this increases the viewer's perception that he or she is likely to aggress with impunity as well.

The effects of the mass media are considered more fully in Chapter 5, but it is worth noting here that people exposed to heavy doses of violence on television differ in a number of ways from those who watch less television (Gerbner & Gross, 1976). Heavy TV viewers are more inclined to view the world through the filter of television drama. Judging solely from programs telecast in the United States, one would think that the world consists almost entirely of white, middle-class, unmarried adults who are constantly being kidnapped, robbed, or bribed. When asked to estimate the amount of crime in

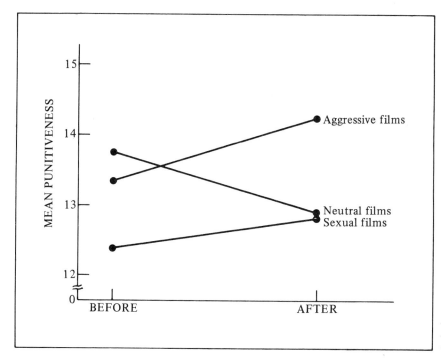

Figure 8.1.
Effects of film content on aggression. Data adapted from Goldstein, Rosnow, Raday, Silverman, and Gaskell (1975).

the United States, the proportion of married to unmarried adults, the proportion of blacks to whites, heavy television viewers tended to give answers based on their unrealistic view of the world as seen on TV. Light viewers were more accurate in their assessments. Not only may the mass media influence aggressive behavior, but they may also influence people's views of aggression and their views of the world in general.

Is There No Such Thing as Aggression Catharsis? While the vast majority of studies on the effects of witnessing violence report that it leads to an increase in aggressiveness, it would be misleading to ignore the fact that there are some studies that do find either direct catharsis or vicarious catharsis (e.g., Bramel, Taub, & Blum, 1968; Calabrese & Goldstein, in press; Doob & Wood, 1972; Feshbach, 1961; Feshbach & Singer, 1971; Fromkin, Goldstein, & Brock, 1977; Konečni, 1975; Quanty, 1976). Taking these studies as a group, it is difficult to determine precisely the conditions under which a reduction in aggressiveness will follow direct aggression or the witnessing of aggression. Konečni (1975), Baron (1977), and Quanty (1976) have attempted to specify the conditions under which catharsis will occur and those under which the more common, imitative effects will occur. Tentatively, we may suggest that a person is most likely to undergo a direct catharsis when he or she is first angered, waits for some time or performs some irrelevant task, and then aggresses

INTERVIEW WITH SEYMOUR FESHBACH

Seymour Feshbach is professor of psychology at the University of California, Los Angeles. He received his Ph.D. from Yale University, and has taught at the University of Pennsylvania and the University of Colorado. He is the author, with Robert D. Singer, of *Television and aggression*, and has contributed chapters on aggression and fantasy to numerous volumes.

JHG: How did you first become interested in the study of aggression?

SF: When I was at Yale, the area in which I was particularly interested was substitute behavior, the drive-reducing properties of substitute activity. For example, for my dissertation I started out working with the basketball team, trying to make predictions about what would happen to players who tried out but didn't make the team. What substitute activities would they be likely to pursue and what would be the fate of the original resolve? I found that it was not practical to work with the basketball team. But I was still interested in the problem of substitution and I wanted to work with important motivations. I couldn't work with achievement motivation, so I worked with aggressive motivation.

JHG: You've been persistent enough to examine the same kinds of problems, those related to catharsis, fantasy, and aggression, for twenty years now. It is unusual in contemporary psychology to find a common thread in someone's work.

SF: There are two common threads. One is that aggression is a motivational system. Once you say you are dealing with a motivational system, then you raise questions about that system, namely, what stimulates it, what satisfies it, and what reduces it? Looking at aggression as a kind of process forces you to come to grips with the question of what satisfies the motive. The second common thread, which led me to the TV and fantasy research, was how do you regulate this motive? That's why I began to look at substitute behaviors. Now I'm looking at the effects of inhibiting aggression on other behavioral systems, such as sexual responsiveness.

JHG: Would you describe some of the issues in this area?

directly against the individual responsible for the anger. A set of conditions for vicarious catharsis involves being angered or frustrated, waiting a fairly long time (perhaps an hour), and then viewing a third party retaliate against the individual responsible for the frustration. This retaliation will result in a lessening of aggressiveness only if it is seen to be proportionate to the person's frustration or anger level. Too much or too little retaliation will not result in catharsis (Fromkin et al., 1977).

These are fairly restricting conditions and no single experiment has been conducted in which all of them have been studied simultaneously. It is both practically and theoretically important to know

SF: We wanted to look at the regulation of aggression and how it affected another behavioral system. For a variety of reasons, we think there is a connection between sex and aggression. We decided first to arouse sexual feelings and then measure aggression because we didn't have very good dependent measures of sexual arousal. We implemented a series of experiments in which we generally found that sexual arousal produced an increase in aggressive behavior; but also we sometimes found an inverse relationship. Other investigators generally interpret the sexual facilitation of aggression within the framework of an arousal effect. I don't think that's an adequate explanation. Sex and aggression are not *arbitrarily* related. There's a reason why, in our society, people censor violence and censor sex. In general, in animals, there are close hormonal and physiological connections. I would say at the human level there is a connection, but it is not an inevitable one. It comes from socialization. Both sex and aggression get socialized in our society with strong taboo connotations. So it is this common taboo quality that joins them together. The way I would interpret the research we've done so far is that a sexually-arousing stimulus is presented and an increase in aggression is obtained. It's not because the stimulus aroused the person, it's because of weakened inhibitions, so that now it becomes "appropriate" to engage in another inhibited response.

JHG: So presumably the inverse should also be true: If you arouse aggression, you should find an increase in sexual behavior.

SF: That's right, and we do find that facilitation of aggression leads to heightened sexual responsiveness. And inhibition of aggression, we found, results in reduced sexual responsivity to erotic stimuli. Similarly, when sex is accompanied by embarrassment, guilt, and conflict, you get strong arousal but a decrement in aggressive behavior. I don't mean to say that ultimately—or for many people—they can't discriminate between sex and aggression. But given current society, given the socialization conditions, and so on, if you lift one taboo, it may affect the other. This is why I think there is a modest *(Continued on next page)*

precisely under what conditions catharsis occurs and for what reasons. As of this writing, our ability to specify these circumstances and reasons is minimal. It is probably safest to conclude that catharsis is a relatively rare response to witnessed violence, and that when it does occur, social psychologists are at a loss to explain why. (See the interview with Seymour Feshbach.)

DEINDIVIDUATION

One of the most obvious facts with which theories of aggression and criminality must contend is that there is a great deal of variation in degree of justification for the conservative position that if you get a society full of erotica, you get an increase in antisocial behavior. I think you might get it—not in Denmark, where sex and aggression may have been separated—but in our own society, a temporary increase in antisocial behavior with a reduction of erotica taboos.

JHG: There is a lot of controversy about the effects of televised violence. In a recent paper you showed that children who believed that a violent TV episode was real became more aggressive, while those who believed it was fantasy became less aggressive.

SF: We tend to talk about stimuli "out there" as if they're all functionally equivalent. The context is really important. There are two ways in which I would look at the fantasy notion, that is, catharsis. By and large, if you're to approximate anything like what Aristotle talked about regarding the effects of drama, the message cannot be the violence, that is, the violence has to be embedded in another context. When the stimulus, say a TV drama, focuses so heavily on the violence that it begins to approximate a how-to-do-it, it

becomes an instructional film, and the message is one of instructing the viewer in techniques of violence.

JHG: You're saying that the standard kind of violence experiment is an oversimplification of what happens in reality. You're making distinctions among both the stimuli and the various kinds of cognitive processes in the observer. The picture you paint of the effects of televised violence is more complicated than that usually presented.

SF: When you read the first few chapters of *Television and aggression*, you can see that we had a lot of complicated hypotheses. Unfortunately, the results were simple in a sense, but the hypotheses were complicated.

To get back to your point, I think there is a fantasy mode that is very difficult to describe in precise terms. What does it mean to act as though something were real when you know that it is not real? All of this is very amorphous and difficult to define sharply, but it does make a difference in behavior. I've seen this with kids watching television. If you say that this is really

any individual's behavior. Even a highly aggressive person is aggressive only a small proportion of the time. What accounts for these individual variations? Answers to this question have been suggested by a number of personality theorists, who tend to see occasional violence either as a manifestation of a buildup in aggressive tension or as the product of assorted personality traits (e.g., Megargee, 1972).

Philip Zimbardo has proposed a theory that involves changes in self-awareness as a function of the environment (1969). His theory revolves around the concept of *individuation*, which was originally used by Carl Jung and also by some early Gestalt psychologists. The Jungian notion of individuation is that an individual behaves as a happening, or is something that actually happened, their reaction is totally different: They cannot easily identify, they cannot participate in vicarious fantasy. It is dealt with in a different way than if it were an imaginative experience.

JHG: Are others misinterpreting and oversimplifying your research findings, or are they simply unable to come up with theoretical models complex enough to incorporate both kinds of findings—a stimulating effect of viewing violence and a cathartic effect?

SF: I think both are true and I think both are fair statements. In *Television and aggression*, people ignore the fact that half the subjects were unaffected by their TV diet, the upper middle-class subjects. I think that is an important parameter. When you attempt to replicate the study using less educated subjects, then you don't get a decrement in aggression.

JHG: You're saying that you found an interaction effect (between watching TV violence and social class), but that others treat it as though you found a main effect (for TV violence)?

SF: That's right. And further, there were some interesting personality differences. Social psychologists have sort of taken over the research on television and aggression, and since they are not terribly oriented to personality dimensions, a whole set of interesting variables gets lost.

JHG: How do you respond when your research is misinterpreted or passed off as a "minority report," since you tend to find that viewing TV violence can lead to a reduction in aggressiveness while the majority of studies conclude that it can only stimulate aggression?

SF: You begin to be criticized on grounds that are irrelevant, and you begin to be put in a defensive posture and start taking positions because you want to be criticized on the right grounds. In general, we go over with a much finer eye one set of findings than another. . . . There are some studies in the Surgeon General's *Report on television and social behavior* that are methodologically unsound and these deficiencies are completely ignored.

distinct personality who is aware of his or her own individuality. Zimbardo uses the concept in a similar way to mean self-consciousness. *Deindividuation*, of course, refers to the lack of feelings of distinctiveness or self-consciousness.

Depending upon the social and physical setting, people feel varying degrees of individuation. Individuation is high when we are in familiar settings, surrounded by others who know us. Deindividuation is high in situations in which we can act with relative anonymity. In large cities, for example, people feel highly deindividuated, whereas in small towns they feel individuated because they are visible to and known by many townsfolk.

People are more likely to act aggressively or criminally in deindividuated states for two reasons: first, because they feel that the likelihood of being identified is less; second, because there is a generally reduced ability or tendency to be socially concerned. In an experiment designed to test these ideas, Zimbardo manipulated deindividuation by treating some of his female subjects anonymously; they were not called by name, the experiment took place in a dark room, and each subject wore a standard lab coat with a hood over her head. The individuated subjects were treated personally, called by name, and did not wear uniforms or hoods. If deindividuated subjects are less socially concerned, as well as less self-conscious, then they should not discriminate as much between one person and another. In the experiment, the subjects administered shocks to another person. Aggression was measured by the intensity of shock administered. Sometimes the victim receiving shocks was portrayed as nice and other times as obnoxious. As hypothesized, the deindividuated group was more aggressive than the individuated group. Deindividuated subjects tended to give both the nice and the obnoxious victims the same amount of shock; individuated subjects gave more shock to the obnoxious victim than to the nice victim.

A cross-cultural test of this theory was conducted by Robert Watson, Jr. (1973), using the Human Relations Area Files (HRAF) as a source of data (see Chapter 2). On the basis of Zimbardo's theory, Watson hypothesized that individuals who wear disguising battle dress commit more atrocities in times of war than those who are not so disguised. Changes in appearance may be accomplished by body or face painting, wearing special garments or masks, or hair cutting. In cultures where such changes in appearance exist, combatants should feel relatively deindividuated—that is, they should not feel identifiable, distinctive, or highly aware of their uniqueness. Watson obtained information from the HRAF on 23 cultures for which data were available both on physical appearance in battle and on the extremity of violence in warfare. Extremity of aggression was measured by the extent to which torturing and mutilating of enemies were carried out and the extent to which prisoners were executed. As predicted, excessive aggression was employed significantly more often in cultures where changes in physical appearance preceded battle than in those cultures where no change in appearance was made.

Aside from changes to one's person (e.g., Diener, 1977, 1979; Diener, Fraser, Beaman, & Kelem, 1976), changes in the physical and social environment may also influence deindividuation (e.g., Newman, 1972). A person would feel more deindividuated in dimly lit places where he or she cannot be readily identified. A person would also feel more deindividuated when some authority figure, such as a parent or policeman, is absent. It is not surprising,

It's easy to get lost in a crowd. We become anonymous and can do things we wouldn't dream of doing with our friends in a place where we might be recognized.

therefore, that increases in police foot patrols and increases in street lighting have a depressive effect on crime (Goldstein, 1975).

Deindividuation may also, apparently, be self-induced. A state somewhat akin to deindividuation may be induced by repeating a two- or three-syllable word over and over rapidly until it loses its denotative meaning and becomes a nonsense word. In the same way, once we engage in some aggressive act, say 10 or 20 times, it ceases for the moment to be "aggressive." We may lose awareness of what we are doing, and the act is repeated in a fairly automatic, un-self-conscious way. Zimbardo (1969) and Goldstein (1975) have proposed that child abuse may be explained in this way.

Deindividuation, Escalation, and Child Abuse Child abuse is the excessive use of physical punishment against children. Rates of abuse per 100,000 children under 18 years of age range from a high of about 31 in Texas to nearly zero in Rhode Island and South Dakota (Gil, 1970). In a nationwide survey, Gil found that the median child abuse rate for the United States as a whole was approximately 4.4 children per 100,000. It is likely, however, that many, if not most, child abuse cases go unreported or undetected by official agencies.

In his nationwide survey, Gil found that over 58 percent of his respondents agreed with the statement that "almost anybody could at some time injure a child in his care." Over 22 percent agreed that they themselves "could at some time injure a child." Those who engage in child abuse may not be very different psychologically from normal, nonabusing parents. In a study of 60 abusing parents, Steele and Pollock (1968) noted, "If all the people we studied were gathered together, they would not seem much different than a group picked by stopping the first dozen people one would meet on a downtown street" (p. 106).

A number of explanations have been proposed to account for child abuse. The majority of these are psychoanalytic in origin and emphasis. For example, M. G. Morris, Gould, and Matthews (1964) have stated that an abusing parent may view his victim not only as a child but also as his own parent who has failed, hurt, and frustrated him. A related explanation is that the parent has a great deal of self-hatred, which is "taken out" on the child. As experimental data on child abuse are virtually nonexistent and official statistics are probably unreliable, there is no sufficiently testable theory for the battered child syndrome (Kempe, Silverman, Steele, Droegemueller, & Silver, 1962). Zimbardo's theory, however, may prove capable of explaining a wide variety of aggressive behaviors, child abuse included.

In a typical situation resulting in abuse, a parent physically disciplines a child for some real or imagined misdeed and the punishment seems to get out of hand. Let us assume that a mother is awakened by her young son's crying. She attempts to quiet him, perhaps by preparing a bottle or by cradling him in her arms. If the

This father and son may be having a misunderstanding, but in a few hours they will probably be eating hot dogs at a baseball game. For some parents, however, a simple attempt at discipline can turn into child abuse.

child persists in crying, the woman may yell at her son out of anger or frustration, because she has exhausted her usual means of comforting her child. This, of course, will make his crying even worse. In desperation, she may strike the child. He cries louder; she strikes him harder. At some point, the woman may no longer be rationally attempting to determine strategies that will quiet her son. She may be involved in an increasingly violent episode in which the aggressive behavior that she has initiated becomes automatic; in other words, she is no longer aware that she is a mother attempting to stop her son from crying. She is barely aware of the total situation at all. Instead, she may reach some critical point beyond which her actions are all that she is aware of, and she is aware of them, not as acts of aggression, but as a series of physical movements. Her behavior, like a repeated word, has lost its meaning to her.

This kind of situation, which begins as a simple attempt at discipline and eventuates in the abuse of a child, is not at all uncommon. Of course, most parents cease their punishment before it reaches this critical level, before they forget what they are doing, why, and to whom. But many parents seem to get "carried away." That is not only their own description of their behavior, but it is apparently an objective description of what happens during many cases of abuse. They lose objective awareness of the situation (Duval & Wicklund, 1972) and their punishment becomes, in a very real sense, automatic—it is no longer under their cognitive control.

Not all cases of child abuse fit this description. In a sizable minority of cases—perhaps 20 percent—the parents intentionally set out to torture their children. In the vast majority of cases, however, there is no premeditated intention to injure a child (see Kalmar, 1977).

Most of the studies of abusive parents have attempted to find the types of personality disorders that lead to abuse (Spinetta & Rigler, 1977). There has been no consistency in the findings of these many studies. Perhaps the most common finding is that children who were abused grow up to abuse their own children, a finding that is readily explainable in terms of social learning theory. Evidence of psychopathology has not been found consistently among abusive parents. It is perhaps because the processes of deindividuation and escalation of aggression are themselves not pathological processes that such parents are so often found to be psychologically normal.

If this tentative explanation of child abuse is at all accurate, it should be possible to find comparable processes in nonabusive people. To this end, a series of experiments was conducted by Goldstein, Davis, and Herman (1975) and Goldstein, Davis, Kernis, and Cohn (in press) in which college students were given the task of teaching a particular verbal response to another person, a "learner." Each time the learner made a mistake, the subject/teacher could administer one of ten levels of negative reinforcement. What the researchers expected to find was that normal college students would be increasingly aggressive as the task progressed. They found that, regardless of whether the learner made many or few mistakes, whether the learner improved as the study progressed, whether the subjects had met, or expected to meet the learner, there was a tendency to escalate the intensity of aggression over time. These studies demonstrate that aggression, once under way, is difficult to curtail. While deindividuation was not directly measured in these studies, the mechanism hypothesized to be responsible for escalation of aggression was the loss of self-consciousness and the increasing involvement in the task itself (cf. Konečni & Ebbesen, 1976).

Aggression may increase over time for reasons other than deindividuation. It may increase because of obedience to a malevolent authority, a topic to which we now turn.

OBEDIENCE TO AUTHORITY

Perhaps the most publicized social psychological research of this century has been that conducted on obedience to authority by Stanley Milgram (1974). The research has been the subject of a play (Abse, 1974), a television drama, at least two educational films, and numerous articles in mass-circulation magazines. It has also served as the focal point of a debate on the ethics of psychological research (Baumrind, 1964). The research that brought about all this furor was fairly simple in design.

A subject enters an experimental laboratory, is introduced to another subject (actually a confederate of the experimenter's), and is told that his job is to teach the other person a verbal task. For example, the subject reads pairs of words to the learner, such as "blue box; nice day; wild duck," and in the testing sequence reads the word "blue" along with four other words, "sky, ink, box, lamp." The learner is to choose which of these four terms was originally paired with the first word. Each time the learner fails to get the correct answer, the subject is to shock him. There were 30 levers on the shock machine, labeled from 15 to 450 volts. Every four switches there was a verbal designation, going from left to right: *Slight Shock, Moderate Shock,* and so on, up to *Extreme Intensity Shock,* and *Danger: Severe Shock.* These designations were followed by one that simply read *XXX.*

Each time the learner made an error, the subject was to administer a shock of greater intensity than the previous shock. The learner made a prearranged number of errors on the task, and the conflict confronting the subject was whether to continue to administer increasingly painful shocks, as the experimenter requested, or to disobey the experimenter and refuse to shock the learner.

Before conducting his experiments, Milgram asked a group of psychiatrists, a class of Yale University students, and a sample of middle-class adults what they thought they might do if they were involved in such an experiment. Not one of the more than 100 people asked thought that they would continue to shock the learner to the end of the shock scale. What actually happened, however, is another matter. Despite the repeated protests of the learner, which began with several grunts at 75 volts and shouts of "I can't stand the pain" at 270 volts, 65 percent of the subjects in the first experiment administered shocks to the end of the scale. Even when the experiment was removed from the prestigious laboratories of Yale and conducted in a rented office building in working-class Bridgeport, Connecticut, the subjects still continued to administer what they thought was 450 volts nearly half the time.

Of course, many of the subjects raised protests during the course of the study; the experimenter said that the subject must continue to administer shocks. One subject, a 50-year-old man, after administering 180 volts, addressed the experimenter:

SUBJECT: I can't stand it. I'm not going to kill that man in there. You hear him hollering?

EXPERIMENTER: As I told you before, the shocks may be painful, but—

SUBJECT: But he's hollering. He can't stand it. What's going to happen to him?

EXPERIMENTER: The experiment requires that you continue, Teacher.

SUBJECT: Aaah, but, unh, I'm not going to get that man sick in there . . . know what I mean?

EXPERIMENTER: Whether the learner likes it or not, we must go on, through all the word pairs.

SUBJECT: I refuse to take the responsibility. He's in there hollering!

EXPERIMENTER: It's absolutely essential that you continue, Teacher.

SUBJECT: There's too many left here; I mean, Geez, if he gets them wrong, there's too many of them left. I mean who's going to take the responsibility if anything happens to that gentleman?

EXPERIMENTER: I'm responsible for anything that happens to him. Continue, please.

SUBJECT: All right. The next one's "Slow—walk, truck, dance, music." Answer, please. (A buzzer indicates the learner has signaled his answer.) Wrong. A hundred and ninety-five volts. (Milgram, 1974, pp. 73–74)

Over a dozen variations on the basic obedience procedure were conducted to determine under which conditions obedience would diminish. Among the findings were that the closer the subject was to the victim (learner), the less likely the subject was to administer strong shocks. Obedience was reduced to 30 percent when the subject was required to place the victim's hand on the shock plate. Likewise, if two experimenters disagreed in the presence of the subject over the subject's obligation to continue to administer shock, obedience completely disappeared: none of the 20 subjects receiving contradictory orders shocked the victim to the end of the shock scale.

There are some obvious parallels between this series of obedience experiments and such important historical events as the Nuremberg Trials and the My Lai massacre. Adolf Eichmann's defense at the Nazi war crime trials was that he was merely following orders. Of course, there are considerable differences between Milgram's experimental situation and events that occur during wartime. But the results of the obedience research indicate that normal and often well-intentioned people are capable of engaging in behaviors that may be lethal when they believe that others are responsible for the results of their actions. The evidence that most of the SS officers responsible for running concentration camps were pathological maniacs is hardly convincing (see, for example, Harrower, 1976); instead, they, like the subjects in Milgram's studies, may have assumed that responsibility for their actions rested upon someone else's shoulders.

What of those subjects who refused to obey? Did they differ in temperament or morality from those who obeyed? There is no evidence that they did (Elms & Milgram, 1966; Kilham & Mann, 1974; Mantell, 1971). Here is a portion of the transcript in which one subject, a 32-year-old industrial engineer who emigrated from Holland after the Second World War, refuses to continue the experiment:

At 250 volts, he pushes the chair away from the shock generator and
    turns to the experimenter.
SUBJECT: Oh, I can't continue this way; it's a voluntary program, if
    the man doesn't want to go on with it.
EXPERIMENTER: Please continue.
SUBJECT: No, I can't continue. I'm sorry.
EXPERIMENTER: The experiment requires that you go on.
SUBJECT: The man, he seems to be getting hurt.
EXPERIMENTER: There is no permanent tissue damage.
SUBJECT: Yes, but I know what shocks do to you. I'm an electrical
    engineer, and I have had shocks . . . and you get real shook up by
    them— especially if you know the next one is coming. I'm sorry.
EXPERIMENTER: It is absolutely essential that you continue.
SUBJECT: Well, I won't—not with the man screaming to get out.
EXPERIMENTER: You have no other choice.
SUBJECT: I *do* have a choice. Why don't I have a choice? I came here
    on my own free will. I thought I could help in a research project.
    But if I have to hurt somebody to do that, or if I was in his place,
    too, I wouldn't stay there. I can't continue. I'm very sorry. I think
    I've gone too far already, probably.

SOCIAL PSYCHOLOGICAL PERSPECTIVES ON WAR

A theory of aggression, if it is sound enough, ought to be capable of explaining (and some would argue, predicting) wars between nations. A good theory should, in addition, have implications for the reduction of violence. The theories and research reviewed to this point have generally been limited to aggression between two people. We may ask whether frustration–aggression theory, psychoanalytic theory, or social learning theory has anything to tell us about international aggression. A brief review of these theories with reference to war is presented below.

Before we begin this brief excursion into the social psychology of war and peace, something should be said about this approach to the topic. I do not by any means believe that the complete and ultimate explanation of war is to be found in social psychological analysis. In fact, as we will see, social psychologists have had relatively little to say on the matter. This is partly because war is difficult to study by the conventional methods of social psychological research. War requires a psychological explanation to some extent, however, because it is the result of human judgments, values, and behaviors. A few years ago I was told of a symposium on war held at a large university. The panel consisted of a distinguished economist, a political scientist, a psychologist, and a sociologist, each of whom gave a brief talk on the major causes of war. The economist saw wars as largely caused by social factors such as poverty and alienation. The psychologist thought that wars were fought primarily over economic issues. The political scientist believed that the personalities of national leaders caused wars; that is, that they were psychologically caused. And the sociologist thought that wars were caused by particular political ideologies. Each expert believed that the best explanation for war was to be found in someone else's bailiwick, perhaps because none of them was very confident his own discipline presented a satisfactory explanation. Certainly the social psychological theories reviewed in the following pages are incomplete explanations of international conflict; they ignore other equally important issues. Economic, political, and historical factors are obviously necessary for a complete theory of war, and I am ill equipped to discuss such issues. But a theory that overlooked social psychological factors would be equally incomplete.

FRUSTRATION AS A CAUSE OF WAR

In examining the frustration–aggression theory within the context of nations rather than individuals, it is necessary to distinguish between two types of political violence: revolutionary violence within a single country and international warfare between two or more countries. Frustration–aggression theories have more often been applied to the former than the latter.

In perhaps the best studies of frustration and revolutionary violence, Ivo Feierabend, a political scientist, and Rosalind Feierabend, a social psychologist, examined various sources of frustration and their effects on violence within political units (1966, 1972). They used archival methods (see Chapter 2) for their research.

For 84 nations they obtained information on variables such as the percentage of population that was literate, the number of radios, newspapers, and telephones per 1000 people, the number of physicians in the nation, the per capita income and gross national product, and the percentage of population living in urban and rural areas. They also obtained information about the degree of aggression within the country. They determined both the amount of aggression directed by individuals and groups within the political system against other groups or officeholders, and the amount of aggression directed by those officeholders against others in the country. Table 8.4 shows the relative amount of political violence (called "instability" by Feierabend & Feierabend) for these countries. Political violence included strikes, riots, terrorist acts, mass political arrests, *coups d'état*, and political executions.

Frustration in this research was defined as unsatisfied needs, expectations, or aspirations of many people. This is, in fact, a definition of *relative deprivation* or *relative frustration* (Merton & Kitt, 1952); it considers a situation as frustrating only when individuals are deprived of something they want or expect to have. Thus, of two nations with the same number of telephones per 1000 population, only one of them may have high frustration because the people expect or want telephones, while the other may be low in frustration because the people neither expect nor want phones. Feierabend and Feierabend reasoned that in countries with a largely urban population and a high degree of literacy, people would be aware of, and would consequently expect, more phones, newspapers, medical care, money, and food. In one study, Feierabend and Feierabend (1972) found that in those countries where frustration was greatest, political violence was high (see Table 8.5).

Does this way of conceptualizing frustration also account for international aggression? The Feierabends, with Frank Scanland (1972), examined international hostility, including formal protests, accusations, expulsion of diplomats, troop movements, the severing of diplomatic relations, military actions, and declarations of war. For the period 1955–1960, the relative amount of international hostility for 75 nations is given in Table 8.6. For the 53 nations for which data are available, it was found that internal frustrations

Table 8.4.
Frequency Distribution of Countries in Terms of Their Degree of Relative Political Stability, 1955–1961 (Stability Score Shown for Each Country)*

0	1	2	3	4	5	6
				France 499		
				U. of S. Africa 495		
				Haiti 478		
				Poland 465		
				Spain 463		
				Dom. Rep. 463		
				Iran 459		
				Ceylon 454		
				Japan 453		
				Thailand 451		
				Mexico 451		
				Ghana 451		
				Jordan 448		
				Sudan 445		
				Morocco 443		
				Egypt 438		
				Pakistan 437		
				Italy 433		
				Belgium 432		
				Paraguay 431		
			Tunisia 328	USSR 430		
			Gr. Britain 325	Nicaragua 430	India 599	
			Portugal 323	Chile 427	Argentina 599	
			Uruguay 318	Burma 427	Korea 596	
			Israel 317	Yugoslavia 422	Venezuela 584	
			Canada 317	Panama 422	Turkey 583	
			US 316	Ecuador 422	Lebanon 581	
	Norway 104		Taiwan 314	China 422	Iraq 579	
	Netherlands 104		Libya 309	El Salvador 421	Bolivia 556	
	Cambodia 104	W. Germany 307	Austria 309	Liberia 415	Syria 554	
	Sweden 103	Czech. 212	E. Germany 307	Malaya 413	Peru 552	Indonesia 699
	Saudi Ar. 103	Finland 211	Ethiopia 307	Albania 412	Guatemala 546	Cuba 699
	Iceland 103	Romania 206	Denmark 306	Greece 409	Brazil 541	Colombia 681
	Philippines 101	Ireland 202	Australia 306	Bulgaria 407	Honduras 535	Laos 652
N. Zea. 000	Luxembourg 101	Costa Rica 202	Switzer. 303	Afghanistan 404	Cyprus 526	Hungary 652
0	*1*	*2*	*3*	*4*	*5*	*6*

STABILITY INSTABILITY

From Feierabend and Feierabend (1972).

were positively related to external aggression (the correlation being +.33). Not surprisingly, those countries that exhibited the greatest amount of internal violence also were the most externally aggressive ($r = +.52$).

To the extent that the Feierabends' concept of frustration is similar to that of Dollard and his colleagues (1939), we can conclude that both revolutionary violence within a country and warfare between countries are positively related to frustration. This analysis based on frustration–aggression theory accounts for neither all warfare nor all internal violence. Nor does it provide a very detailed

Table 8.5.

Relationship between Level of Frustration and Degree of Internal Violence

Degree of Internal Violence	High Frustration			Low Frustration		
HIGH	Bolivia Brazil Bulgaria Ceylon Chile Colombia Cuba Cyprus Dom. Republic Ecuador Egypt El Salvador Greece Guatemala Haiti India Indonesia	Iran Iraq Italy Japan Korea Mexico Nicaragua Pakistan Panama Paraguay Peru Spain Syria Thailand Turkey Venezuela Yugoslavia	(34)	Argentina Belgium France Lebanon Morocco Union of South Africa	(6)	
LOW	Philippines Tunisia	(2)		Australia Austria Canada Costa Rica Czechoslovakia Denmark Finland West Germany Great Britain Iceland Ireland Israel Netherlands	New Zealand Norway Portugal Sweden Switzerland United States Uruguay	(20)

From Feierabend and Feierabend (1972). Data are for the period from 1948 to 1962.

Table 8.6.
External Aggression Profile, 1955–1960

Country	Score	Country	Score	Country	Score
USSR	4516	Yugoslavia	4036	Netherlands	3035
USA	4505	Haiti	4035	Afghanistan	3033
UAR	4353	Iran	4035	Thailand	3021
Israel	4245	Cambodia	4030	Canada	3020
China	4204	Honduras	4030	Brazil	3016
India	4185	Chile	4025	Bolivia	3015
France	4180	N. Korea	4022	El Salvador	3014
Jordan	4174	Paraguay	4022	Belgium	3012
UK	4156	U. of S. Africa	4022	Nepal	3011
Indonesia	4099	Costa Rica	4021	Philippines	3011
Cuba	4096	Albania	4019	Japan	2064
Pakistan	4087	Burma	4017	Czechoslovakia	2029
S. Korea	4079	Australia	4015	Sweden	2023
Lebanon	4076	Colombia	4014	Switzerland	2018
Iraq	4068	Ecuador	4014	Panama	2016
Argentina	4067	Peru	4013	Romania	2016
Hungary	4065	Uruguay	4011	Norway	2012
Formosa	4063	Spain	4011	Denmark	2011
Turkey	4054	Ethiopia	4009	Bulgaria	2009
E. Germany	4051	Irish Republic	3137	Portugal	1006
Nicaragua	4050	Poland	3073	New Zealand	1003
Guatemala	4049	Italy	3043	O. Mongolia	1002
Venezuela	4045	Saudi Arabia	3042	Liberia	1002
W. Germany	4043	Dom. Republic	3041	Ceylon	1002
Mexico	4040	Greece	3039	Finland	0000

From Feierabend and Feierabend (1972). Based on data collected by Rudolph J. Rummel and Raymond Tanter. The higher the score, the more aggressive the country.

description of the particular mechanisms that operate to determine revolutions or wars. For example, it does not tell us whether political instability (a high degree of internal violence) follows or precedes international violence. It is conceivable that international acts of aggression are strategically employed to undermine internal revolutions by providing the population with a common focus in the form of a foreign enemy. Nor does the theory tell us which countries will be aggressed against. On the whole, however, the evidence indicates that the level of frustration of a nation's population is positively associated with both domestic and international aggression.

PSYCHOANALYTIC THEORY

The psychoanalytic theory of war is loosely organized and largely untested. Freud discussed the causes of war briefly in a number of places, most notably in *Civilization and its discontents* (1930/1962), and engaged in an exchange of views with Albert Einstein (1934) published as *Why war?* But there are a number of Freudian-derived theories and analyses of war.

Most psychoanalytic analyses of war involve the following elements: unconscious motives, ego defense mechanisms, and innate aggression. Perhaps the major contribution of psychoanalytic theory to our understanding of human behavior is its emphasis on unconscious determinants of behavior. While there is much disagreement over how much behavior is unconsciously motivated, there is little doubt that *some* behaviors are caused by nonconscious motives. Ego defense mechanisms function on an unconscious level. The familiar devices of rationalization, projection, displacement, denial, and identification act beneath the level of consciousness to protect the ego from threatening thoughts or feelings. Taking these two ideas together—unconscious motivation and ego defense mechanisms—it is fairly easy to understand how wars may be rationalized (Klineberg, 1964).

Wars are rarely begun in a psychologically offensive manner. Nations do not perceive themselves as acting aggressively in war, but rather as acting defensively. People see their country as acting rationally and with good intentions when it enters into warfare. This is true for all parties to the conflict. Each party sees its opponents as acting irrationally and unjustly. This state of affairs may come about through the ego defense mechanisms of rationalization, projection, displacement, denial, and identification. Rationalization of aggression leads people to emphasize the evil qualities of the opponent. The anthropologist E. A. Hooton has stated it this way:

Man incessantly seeks to compromise with his conscience, or with his innate humanitarianism, by rationalizing his predatory behavior. He must convince himself that the act of grabbing is somehow noble and beautiful, that he can rape in righteousness and murder in magnanimity. He insists upon playing the game, not only with an ace up his sleeve, but with the smug conviction that God has put it there. (1937, p. 151)

Unconscious aggressive motives may also be projected onto one's enemies. Instead of saying that it is I who hates you, I say that it is you who hates, and I therefore am justified in taking preventive action against your hatred.

Displacement plays a role in the psychoanalytic theory of war by transferring aggressive impulses toward parents to another object, such as some generally accepted enemy. Maurice Farber (1955) has written that "an unconscious hatred of the father carried over from unresolved Oedipal conflict may be displaced onto strong authority figures and manifested specifically by a resentment against the United States on the part of a citizen of a weak country."

Denial may be involved in ignoring events or ideas that may be threatening to the ego. Thus, people often believe that nuclear weapons will not be used because their effects will be catastrophic. Identification is involved in the development of a strong sense of nationalism, in which threats to the mother country or the fatherland will not be tolerated.

Some psychoanalytic writers have suggested that international conflicts may reflect the need periodically to discharge a buildup of aggressive energy. But as we have already seen, such a notion of energy storage and discharge is probably misconceived (see Archer & Gartner, 1976; Mannheim, 1941).

It is very difficult to obtain empirical data to test these notions. It is clear that people tend to see their nation's behavior as justified in times of war, and that they see the enemy as aggressive and unjust. But this does not mean that these effects occur *because of* rationalization and projection. They can be explained by notions of cognitive consistency (e.g., Abelson, Aronson, McGuire, Newcomb, Rosenberg, & Tannenbaum, 1968). For example, it would be psychologically uncomfortable to live in a nation that had just sent troops to a foreign country for no apparent reason. Because private citizens cannot reduce this discomfort by recalling their nation's troops, they try to reduce it by providing some justification for the troops' deployment. We do not need the invocation of unconscious motives or processes in order to explain why people tend to justify events that have already occurred.

CONFLICT RESOLUTION

A theory of conflict resolution designed specifically to provide a technique for reducing conflict already under way has been proposed by Charles Osgood. He calls his theory GRIT, which stands for Graduated and Reciprocated Initiatives in Tension-reduction.

As described by Osgood (1962), "GRIT is the application of *interpersonal* communication and learning principles to *international* relations—where the communication is more by deeds than by words. . . . "

In Osgood's analysis of the "cold war" between East and West, each side alternately increases international tension and the threat of war by building and stockpiling more and more lethal weapons. Such escalation is designed to reduce tension by making the nation's people feel less threatened and more secure. The psychological effects, however, seem to be the reverse—increasing distrust for the opposing side and the probability of war. Osgood proposed a system

Table 8.7.
Events in the Kennedy Experiment

US	Joint	USSR
1. June 10, 1963: Kennedy announces decision to stop nuclear testing in atmosphere.		
		2. June 11: USSR removes its objection to sending UN observers to Yemen.
		3. June 15: Khrushchev halts production of strategic bombers; radio jammers turned off, permitting Voice of America broadcasts to reach Moscow.
4. June 22: United States removes its objection to restoration of full UN status to Hungary.		
		5. June 20: Soviets agree to a direct America–Russia communications link.
	6. July 1963: Multilateral negotiations on nuclear testing treaty. Signed in Aug.	

in which the arms race would be run in reverse, with each side alternately taking tension-reducing steps.

In order to begin this gradual tension reduction, one country must initiate a unilateral and unambiguous policy of de-escalation: for example, deactivating a foreign military base or scrapping a weapons development program. Osgood is not proposing total unilateral disarmament; this would probably increase domestic tension and the feeling of threat or vulnerability. He proposes only a single initial act of tension reduction. Such an act by one side would increase trust and decrease tension in the other side. This effect should then stimulate a reciprocal tension-reducing act by the side that would approximate the first act in magnitude. Each side would, in turn, begin a reciprocal de-escalation.

Osgood proposes the following guidelines for implementing GRIT:

US	Joint	USSR
		7. Sept. 19: Foreign Minister Gromyko calls for nonaggression pact between East and West.
8. Sept. 20: Kennedy addresses UN and suggests joint US–USSR exploration of space. 9. Oct. 9: Kennedy approves sale of $250 million of wheat to Soviet Union.		
	10. Oct. 19: UN General Assembly with joint US–USSR backing passes resolution prohibiting orbiting of nuclear weapons. 11. Oct. 1963: Exchange of released spies.	
12. Late Oct.–Nov.: Slowdown in US initiatives.		12. Late Oct.–Nov.: Slowdown in Soviet reciprocations.

1. Unilateral initiatives should be publicly announced before their execution.
2. Explicit invitations to reciprocate should be announced publicly.
3. Initiatives should be continued over a considerable period of time, and they should be subject to verification by the other side.
4. Beginning initiatives should not reduce a nation's capacity to retaliate against an enemy. Initiatives should be graduated, with smaller concessions coming first.
5. The initiatives should be seen by the enemy as voluntary.

In 1963, during the Kennedy administration, a series of events occurred that, in retrospect, may be interpreted as a test of the GRIT model. To what extent President Kennedy had this model, or one like it, in mind remains unclear. But the events, as chronicled by the sociologist Amitai Etzioni (1967), suggest that tension-reducing initiatives are in fact reciprocated. The sequence of events, as shown in Table 8.7, indicates that the first tension-reducing step was initiated by President Kennedy in a speech at American University on June 10, 1963. During that speech, which was delivered soon after the Cuban missile crisis, Kennedy took a conciliatory tone. He said that "constructive changes" in the Soviet Union might "bring within reach solutions which now seem beyond us." He also announced his decision to stop the testing of nuclear weapons in the atmosphere.

The following day, June 11, 1963, the Soviet Union removed its objection to a UN proposal to send observers to war-torn Yemen. The United States had originally backed this proposal.

There then followed no less than ten tension-reducing steps by both sides. From June to mid-October, each side responded to conciliatory gestures by the other. By late October, there was a marked slowdown in American initiatives. Etzioni notes several reasons for this: the administration felt that the psychological mood of optimism and rising expectations about Soviet–American relations were running too high; allies, particularly West Germany, objected bitterly; and in the pre-election year, the administration did not want to seem overly accommodating toward the Russians. This analysis of complex historical events after the fact is less than the ideal test of the theory. However, some laboratory simulations also provide support for the model (e.g., Pilisuk & Skolnik, 1968).

Summary

Human aggression is behavior whose intent is the injury of another person. Three common arguments for the belief that aggression is an instinct in humans—from biology, physiology, and psychoanalytic theory—lead us to conclude that aggression in humans is most likely a learned set of behaviors. In laboratory research on aggression, electric shock is often used as the dependent measure, and it is less than ideal as a measure of human aggression. Studies of children's aggression tend to observe aggression during play.

Frustration–aggression theory has been modified several times since its inception in 1939, first by some of its original authors, later by Berkowitz, and then by Zillmann's notions of arousal and attribution. Berkowitz believes that frustration as well as anger may lead to aggression only when appropriate environmental cues are present. Such cues are learned in humans and may include appropriate targets, places, and means of aggressing. The notion of an aggressive cue is analogous to the concept of a releaser cue in biology.

Bandura's social learning theory notes that aggressive behavior may be learned merely through observation, and that rewards and punishments are not necessary for learning to occur. Among the implications of social learning theory is that violence in the mass media stimulates violence in real life. This hypothesis runs counter to the psychoanalytic notion of catharsis, whereby viewing violence will reduce a person's level of aggression. A review of the literature on catharsis suggests that it is a real, though fairly rare and complex, response to witnessed violence. Zimbardo's notion of deindividuation also has many implications for aggressive behavior. Among these are the notion that child abuse and other forms of escalation of aggression are not pathological responses but common outcomes of cognitive changes that accompany repetitive acts of violence.

Milgram has studied destructive obedience to authority. He finds that there is a high level of conformity to an experimenter's commands to administer shock to another person.

Social psychologists have long had an interest in studying international conflict. Psychoanalytic and frustration–aggression theories, in particular, have been used to account for the prevalence of war. Osgood's model of international tension reduction, GRIT, suggests that there should be a reciprocal and graduated series of gestures toward peace between two opponents, so that each side remains secure as the de-escalation process unfolds.

Suggested Readings

Baron, R. A. *Human aggression.* New York: Plenum, 1977.

*Feierabend, I. K., Feierabend, R. L., & Gurr, T. R. (Eds.). *Anger, violence, and politics.* Englewood Cliffs, N.J.: Prentice-Hall, 1972.

Gaskell, G. D., & Pearton, R. Violence and sport. In J. H. Goldstein (Ed.), *Sports, games, and play.* Hillsdale, N.J.: Erlbaum, 1979.

Geen, R. G., and O'Neal, E. C. *Perspectives on aggression.* New York: Academic Press, 1976.

*Goldstein, J. H. *Aggression and crimes of violence.* London and New York: Oxford University Press, 1975.

Kelman, H. C. (Ed.). *International behavior: A social psychological analysis.* New York: Holt, 1965.

*Milgram, S. *Obedience to authority.* New York: Harper, 1974.

*Montagu, A. *The nature of human aggression.* London and New York: Oxford University Press, 1976.

Moyer, K. E. *Psychobiology of aggression.* New York: Harper, 1976.

Pertinent Journals

Aggressive Behavior

Journal of Conflict Resolution

*Available in paperback edition.

9
THE NATURE OF GROUPS

Who are you? Most people answer this question in terms of group memberships. "I am a Catholic. I'm Italian. I'm in Tau Kappa Epsilon. I'm an American . . . a violinist . . . a Democrat . . . a sophomore . . . a male . . . a Teamster." No two individuals are exactly alike, and one important way in which we differ from one another is in the constellation of groups to which we belong. There are lots of Italian-American, Catholic, Democratic males, but not many Italian-American, Catholic, Democratic, male, sophomore TKE's who play violin and are members of the Teamsters' Union. All these attributes are derived from group memberships, even though they serve to describe a particular individual. Individual identities exist largely at the intersection of group memberships (Simmel, 1955). Our uniqueness is both caused by and definable by our particular combination of group loyalties.

THE SOCIAL PSYCHOLOGICAL STUDY OF GROUPS

Floyd H. Allport, in his 1924 textbook, remarked that groups exist only in men's minds. "You can't stumble over a group," he said. But as you will see in this chapter, social psychologists do have a way of stumbling over groups. Social psychologists have not adequately come to grips with the reality of group phenomena. Groups are not real in the same sense that individuals are real, but groups do indeed exist as psychological entities that exert forces, pressures, and counterpressures on individuals. They exist in the same way that democracy exists, as an abstraction that may profoundly alter peoples' lives.

There are fads and fashions in social psychology just as there are in most other human endeavors (Sorokin, 1956). The study of groups was fashionable at one time, most notably in the 1940s, when the world was engaged in a bitter war. Following World War II, interest in group phenomena was replaced by a concern with the individual, and that individualistic orientation persisted to the mid-1970s. But according to one analyst (I.D. Steiner, 1974), that is changing. There was a resurgence of interest in group phenomena in the late 1970s which may become dominant by the mid-1980s. According to Steiner:

When society is serene, and only a few wrong-headed deviants disturb our tranquility, we focus our attention on individuals or on large organizations. But when many small segments of society are vying with one another, our attention is drawn to units of an intermediate size. We go where the action is: the prison courtyard, the commune, the assembly line, the committee room, or wherever people assemble and discuss, plot, act, or commiserate. And we find ourselves studying such nebulous things as leadership, cohesion, social facilitation, role systems, and all the rest. (p. 105)

In these days of minority movements to assert autonomy and legal egalitarianism, of burgeoning religious cults, of medical and dietary fads, it is not surprising that a return to the study of group phenomena is predicted for social psychology.

For purposes of this chapter, we will define a *group* as two or more people who come into contact for a specific purpose and who consider this contact meaningful. This implies that the members of a group are aware of one another, that they share a common goal, sentiment, or purpose, and that they interact in some fashion. The degree to which this awareness, purpose, and interaction occur varies from one type of group to another.

DO GROUPS REALLY EXIST?

It has been argued for generations whether groups consist merely of individuals who are in the same place at the same time or transcend individuals and have a reality of their own (see, for example, F.H. Allport, 1924; Billig, 1976; Freud, 1921/1960; LeBon, 1896; Shaw, 1976). This is a complex issue and by no means an easy one to resolve empirically, for it often appears that groups are capable of actions that their individual members cannot perform. Groups were often seen as more than the sum of their individual members, and this supra-individual characteristic was called the *group mind*. Psychologists and sociologists no longer adhere to any such notion. They recognize that concepts like "group mind" entail logical fallacies, in this case, the *fallacy of reification*, treating an abstract idea as though it had an actual existence.

A related issue is whether the behavior of a group can be predicted from a knowledge of the characteristics of its individual members. Many modern behaviorists support this notion, while other psychologists, particularly those with a cognitive orientation, argue that this is impossible. As Shaw (1976) notes, both viewpoints have some merit: There is no group behavior apart from the behavior of individual members, but individuals in a group react to the other individuals who comprise the group. As he concludes, "The group is not more than the sum of its parts, but rather it is *different* from the sum of its parts. An individual behaves differently in the group situation because he is experiencing a different set of stimuli" (p. 336).

DO SOCIAL PSYCHOLOGISTS
ACTUALLY STUDY GROUPS?

Groups have been defined as two or more people who have something meaningful in common. We all have things in common with everyone else—a liver, a need for sleep, feelings—but these do not mean that we are all members of the same group. In order for a group to exist, there must be awareness that there is a common element and that this commonality pertains to the group's existence. A group is distinguished from an *aggregate*, a mere gathering of people who do not have common bonds except perhaps accidental or trivial ones. Aggregates do not take one another into consideration. Lines at a movie theater or football game, for example, constitute aggregates. Groups, on the other hand, are characterized by purpose and organization: groups have goals and they almost invariably involve interaction among some or all of their members; they also have some discernible structure or organization, such as a leader. This is no less true of social groups, such as baseball teams or sororities, than it is of more highly structured groups, such as congressional subcommittees or student governments.

Nearly all the research on groups in social psychology involves aggregates rather than actual groups. This is particularly true of laboratory research, in which several students are placed in the same room and given some task to perform. Do the students working on this task constitute a group? Do they interact, or expect to interact in the future? Is there any organization or structure to their interaction? Do they take one another into account when speaking or acting? In most cases, the answer is no. We can, of course, learn some valuable lessons from studying aggregates in the laboratory, but we may learn less about groups than is often supposed. Because there are relatively few social psychological studies of groups per se, particular attention will be devoted here and in Chapter 10 to studies of intact groups, such as families, co-workers, sports teams, and hospital staffs.

TYPES OF GROUPS

A married couple, a men's club, a sorority, a ski club, Republicans, relatives, psychology professors, Pittsburgh Steelers, Texans, and Trekkies: These are all groups, but they are quite different from one another. Because groups are so numerous and so prevalent in our lives, researchers and theorists have found it convenient to divide them into various categories. The most important distinctions will be presented here, though others have also been made. The variables on which groups differ are size, intimacy, function, and membership requirements.

SOCIAL COMPARISON THEORY

Critics of social psychology often note the lack of well-developed, testable theories. One example of sound theory in social psychology is Leon Festinger's social comparison theory (1954; Latané, 1966; Suls & Miller, 1977). The theory deals with the reasons people join groups and why they join the particular groups they do. Festinger proposes a series of hypotheses in social comparison theory, several of which are presented below.

There exists in humans a drive to evaluate their opinions and abilities. That is, we all have a need to know how good or bad our opinions and abilities are relative to those of other people.

To the extent that objective, nonsocial means are not available, people evaluate their opinions and abilities by comparison with the opinions and abilities of others. For many of the opinions and abilities most important to us, such as how friendly we are, how popular, how intelligent, there is no objective means of evaluation. The theory hypothesizes that we compare ourselves with others whom we assume will be somewhat similar to ourselves in opinion or ability. That is, we engage in a process of *social comparison.* For example, if you want to know how intelligent you are, you first attempt to find some objective means of assessing your intelligence. If none is available, you compare yourself to others, particularly to those you believe are roughly similar in intelligence: you do not compare yourself to grade school children or your physics professor, but most likely to other college students.

Subjective evaluations of opinions or of abilities are stable when comparison is available with others who are judged to be close to one's opinions or abilities. A person will be less attracted to situations where others are very divergent from him than to situations where others are close to him.

The existence of a discrepancy in a group with respect to opinions or abilities will lead to action on the part of members of that group to reduce the discrepancy. In other words, a person who holds a deviant opinion will feel pressure from others in the group to change that opinion to conform more closely to other members.

There is a unidirectional drive upward in the case of abilities, which is largely absent in opinions. In our culture, at least, people prefer to perform better on most tasks, while there is no "better" with regard to opinions.

When a discrepancy exists with respect to opinions or abilities, there will be a tendency to change one's own position so as to move closer to others in the group. Pressure to change, then, comes not only from others in the group, but also from oneself.

When a discrepancy exists, there will be tendencies to change others in the group to bring them closer to oneself. Festinger is proposing

Festinger believes that people join groups primarily for self-evaluation. If one member of this chess club is not as skilled as the others, he will probably feel pressures to improve or to leave the club.

here that deviance in a group tends to lead to pressures to conform to the group norm.

When a discrepancy exists, there will be tendencies to cease comparing oneself with those in the group who are very different from oneself. Here is a proposal that may account for the dissolution of groups, or the resignation of certain members from groups. When a member holds an opinion or ability that is very discrepant from that of other members, there is a tendency, if pressure to reduce the discrepancy fails, for that member no longer to compare himself to other members of the group.

The stronger the attraction to the group, the stronger will be the pressure toward uniformity concerning abilities and opinions within that group. Thus, attractive groups exert greater pressure on individual members to conform.

People join groups primarily for self-evaluation, and groups tend to be relatively homogeneous on at least one opinion or ability. For example, if you are interested in knowing how well you play chess, you may join a chess club if you believe that you play about as well as the members of the club. While members may differ considerably in age, politics, and ethnicity, they will tend to be fairly homogeneous in their chess skills. Still, there are bound to be differences among members. Those who are most divergent from the majority will feel pressure to change. If you are not a very good player, you will feel both internal pressure and pressure from other group members to improve. If you are unable to reduce this discrepancy, you will cease comparing yourself to the others and will probably drop out of the club. There is a great deal of research to support most of the hypotheses and derivations from the theory (see Suls & Miller, 1977), and some of it will be reviewed in the following section.

INFORMATION AND FEEDBACK AS
SOURCES OF GROUP
ATTRACTIVENESS

Social comparison theory proposes that people affiliate with groups because groups provide self-evaluative feedback; groups enable members to assess the value or correctness of their opinions and abilities. Little is said in Festinger's theory about emotional evaluation, about a need to assess the correctness of our emotional reactions to events. Research by Stanley Schachter (1959) deals primarily with the information provided by others on emotional states and affiliation.

The Schachter Affiliation Studies Schachter published in 1959 a number of studies on the role of emotion in affiliation based on Festinger's social comparison theory. The prototypical experiment involved college women who were told that the experiment in which they were about to participate involved either severe or mild electric shocks. The women were then given an opportunity to wait alone or with others while the equipment was being set up. Choosing to wait with others was used as a measure of affiliation.

Those expecting severe shocks ("high anxious" subjects) preferred to wait with others, while those expecting only mild shocks ("low anxious" subjects) preferred to wait alone or didn't care whether they waited alone or not. Results from one of these experiments is presented in Table 9.1.

In a series of such experiments, Schachter found that the tendency to want to affiliate with others is greatest for those experiencing "high anxiety." Affiliation preferences are not indiscriminate; subjects preferred to wait with others who were undergoing the same emotional experience rather than with others who were not experi-

Table 9.1.
Relationship of Anxiety to the Affiliative
Tendency

	Number Choosing to Wait		
Subjects	Together	Didn't Care	Alone
High Anxiety	20	9	3
Low Anxiety	10	18	2

Adapted from Schachter (1959, p. 18).

encing anxiety at the time. Schachter also found that the tendency to affiliate with others was influenced by birth order. Firstborns and only children were more likely to want to wait with others than subjects who had older siblings. In one experiment, hunger also influenced affiliative preferences. Hunger was manipulated by depriving subjects of food for varying lengths of time. Those experiencing the greatest hunger chose to wait with others more often than those experiencing moderate or low hunger.

Two plausible explanations for these results were proposed by Schachter. First, affiliating with others helps to reduce anxiety, and second, others help us evaluate our own emotional states. While there is evidence to support both these contentions, it is the need for self-evaluation that seems most consistent with the data. As Schachter summarizes, "ambiguous situations or feelings lead to a desire to be with others as a means of socially evaluating and determining the 'appropriate' and proper reaction" (p. 132).

There have been numerous replications of Schachter's main findings. Several studies, however, have called for some modifications or limits on his generalizations. First, a distinction must be made between "anxiety" and "fear." It was unfortunate that Schachter used the term "anxiety" to refer to the threat of electric shock, and he himself seemed to recognize the ambiguity of this term. Anxiety is an emotional state that has no specific objective cause (English & English, 1958). Fear, on the other hand, is an equally unpleasant state that does have an objective cause. We can fear something, such as electric shock; we are anxious for some nonconscious reason. While Freud distinguished several types of anxiety, it is generally agreed that nearly all of them have unconscious determinants.

In order to distinguish between the affiliative effects of anxiety and fear, Sarnoff and Zimbardo (1961) manipulated both emotional states in an experiment similar in format to Schachter's studies. To produce anxiety, Yale undergraduates were led to expect that they would have to suck on nipples, baby bottles, and pacifiers. Fear was manipulated by threat of shock. Subjects were then given a choice of waiting with others or alone while the experimenters set up the laboratory. The results show that 95 percent of high-fear subjects chose to wait with others, while less than half of the high-anxiety subjects chose to wait with others. These findings suggest that it is fear, rather than anxiety, that increases the tendency to affiliate. These results have been replicated by Firestone, Kaplan, and Russell (1973) and Teichman (1973).

Schachter's findings with respect to birth order and affiliation have not always been successfully replicated. Occasionally, no relationship between birth order and affiliation is found (e.g., Teichman, 1973), and sometimes birth order effects are obtained only with females (e.g., M. F. Hoyt & Raven, 1973). Recent research on the social and psychological effects of birth order (Davis, Cahan, & Bashi, 1977; Zajonc & Markus, 1975) suggests that position in the family is a complex factor, having multiple effects and interacting with other social variables. Birth order is certainly not the simple, unidimensional concept that earlier psychologists believed it to be (cf. Adler, 1931).

Of the dozens of studies on fear and affiliation published since Schachter's initial studies (1959), only one examined what those who chose to wait with others actually discussed among themselves. In a study by W.N. Morris, Worchel, Bois, Pearson, Rountree, Samaha, Wachtler, and Wright (1976), fear (threat of shock), anxiety (the experimental task involved explicit sexual material), and ambiguity (the task was unclear) were manipulated. When waiting with others, which all subjects were required to do in this study, only those in the fear condition discussed the experiment per se in an attempt to clarify the situation. As Schachter proposed, fear leads to a desire to be with others because they serve as comparison persons who are able to help the individual evaluate his or her own emotional reactions to the situation.

The work on emotional arousal and affiliation may be taken as support for social comparison theory, provided we expand the theory to say that individuals have a need to evaluate their opinions, abilities, and emotional states.

AFFILIATION AND SOCIAL EXCHANGE

Whereas Festinger and Schachter approach group affiliation from a cognitive point of view, arguing that individuals obtain information from group members about their own abilities, opinions, and emotions, there are reinforcement and exchange theories that argue that other types of reward, in addition to information and feedback, are influential in affiliation. Two related theories in this framework are Thibaut and Kelley's (1959,1978) social exchange theory, and Foa and Foa's (1974) resource exchange theory.

According to both theories, individuals are attracted to groups to the extent that they receive from them social, psychological, and material satisfactions that exceed their inputs or costs. We may receive prestige, status, satisfying social experiences, affection, and a variety of goods and services, from a group. Of course, while all these may be derived from group membership, it is primarily the nonmaterial resources of status, affection, and information that most commonly are exchanged in interpersonal encounters. Costs or inputs for participating in a group include not only a sacrifice of our time, but also the obligation to provide some of these same resources for others—giving prestige and status to other group members, for example. Thibaut and Kelley note that we assess the relative rewards and costs of participating in a group and evaluate the net profit (outcomes minus inputs) in terms of a personal *comparison level*, some general expectation of how rewarding a relationship should be. Beyond this, we may also recognize other groups or relationships in which we may participate. For example, if Joseph Kollidge is a member of Gro Ur Own fraternity, he cannot simultaneously be a member of other fraternities. But he may compare his satisfaction at being in GUO to his expected satisfaction if he were in another fraternity. He will leave GUO when he believes that he will be more satisfied in another fraternity. Hence, while his rewards may exceed his costs in GUO, he may think that the profit will be even greater in Buy Ur Own. This comparison with alternative affiliations is called the *comparison level for alternatives*.

Foa and Foa have proposed a similar theory, though theirs is a bit less explicit in its reinforcement notions. Participation in a group entails the exchange of resources that are most abundant to the individual for less abundant resources. Thus, we may join a group in which we provide expert information about a topic of concern in exchange for status and respect from others.

COHESIVENESS

Cohesiveness refers to the overall attractiveness of a group to its members. There are two broad sources of cohesion: internal and external (Festinger et al., 1950). There are characteristics of the group per se that members find attractive. These include the similarity of group members (Terborg, Castore, & DeNinno, 1976), the opportunity to interact personally with others (Marshall & Heslin, 1975), the occasionally drive-reducing and relaxing effects of others (Kissel, 1965), and the opportunity for social comparison. Then, too, we may gain relative anonymity in a group, a state referred to as *deindividuation* (Cannavale, Scarr, & Pepitone, 1970; Festinger, Pepitone, & Newcomb, 1952; Zimbardo, 1969; see the discussion of deindividuation in Chapter 8). There are also outside pressures that tend to keep groups together. Sometimes these external sources of cohesion are informal social pressures, such as prejudice and discrimination, and sometimes they are practical, often economic, in nature. In most large American cities, for example, there are neighborhoods consisting mainly of blacks, Hispanics, Irish, Italians, Jews, Orientals, Poles, and so on. These neighborhoods exist because of both internal and external factors. There are various sources of social and personal satisfaction in living among one's kinsmen: it is possible to speak one's native language, to obtain ethnic foods, to engage in social and recreational activities most consistent with one's interests. One needn't worry about prejudice from outsiders in

People tend to be more relaxed when they interact with group members who share similar interests, like these members of a Weight Watchers club.

an ethnically homogeneous community. External pressures are also responsible for these "nations within a nation." Economic, educational, occupational, and social institutions exert various kinds of pressure on individuals to remain in these segregated neighborhoods. It is the combination of support and satisfaction from members of one's own group and threats and pressures from outsiders that leads to maximum cohesion. A classic study on group cohesion was conducted by Festinger, Riecken, and Schachter (1956).

When Prophecy Fails In the early 1950s, publicity was given to a group that had predicted the destruction of the earth by flood. Mrs. Keech, the leader of the group, was in contact with inhabitants of the planet Clarion. She received messages from Clarion that she and her followers would be saved. Members of her cult gathered around her in anticipation of the arrival of a spacecraft from Clarion. Among her followers were three social psychologists (Festinger et al., 1956), who were interested in studying the members' response to the failure of her prophecy. What would members do if, at the appointed hour, the earth was not destroyed and no spaceship appeared? There were three possibilities: (1) the group could disband, denouncing Mrs. Keech as a false prophet; (2) cohesiveness might remain the same, and Mrs. Keech could decide that she had somehow got her messages confused; (3) the group could become even more cohesive. Unless I am mistaken, the earth was not destroyed in the 1950s and Mrs. Keech's predictions were shown to be in error. Which of the three possible responses did the group have? It was the final one. Not only did the members of the group fail to admit that they were in error, but they took credit for saving the earth from imminent destruction. Rather than disbanding, the group began to recruit new members. Cohesiveness increased because of both internal and external pressures. Members had sacrificed a great deal in preparing to leave the earth, and so cognitive dissonance may have played an important role in their unwillingness to admit their error (see Chapter 5). External forces, too, acted to increase cohesion: Members of the group had been singled out by the mass media and would have been branded as lunatics by the public had they retracted their pronouncements. If unfulfilled prophecies are to lead to greater cohesiveness among group members, it seems essential that the members lend strong support to one another (Hardyck & Braden, 1962).

The effects of false prophecies may be culturally determined, at least in part. In 1974, the leader of a new religious sect in Osaka, Japan, predicted that an earthquake would occur on June 18 at 8 A.M. Members of his sect distributed 100,000 leaflets concerning the forthcoming disaster. The earthquake failed to occur. Unlike the leader of the American group, however, the religious leader in Japan attempted suicide and later disbanded the sect (Sanada & Norbeck, 1975). It seems, then, that we must consider not only group members, but the larger social and cultural context in which groups, and prophecies, function as well.

Cognitive Dissonance and Group Cohesiveness One of the early studies designed to test Festinger's (1957) theory of cognitive dissonance, which we discussed in Chapter 5, is pertinent to our discussion of affiliation and cohesiveness. Aronson and Mills (1959) deduced from the theory the hypothesis that we come to value a group to the extent that we make sacrifices and exert effort on its behalf. That is essentially the interpretation placed on the early studies of failed prophecies discussed above. It would be dissonance-producing to work hard for something, such as membership in a group, and then find the group unattractive. In their research, Aronson and Mills studied college women who had volunteered to participate in a series of group discussions about sex. A prescreening session was held to ensure that each of the women could frankly and openly discuss such a topic. Three different "initiations" into the group were held. One-third of the women underwent no initiation or screening, serving as a control group. One-third of them underwent a mild initiation, in which they had to read sex-related words aloud.

A third group of women, the severe initiation group, had to read obscene words and erotic passages to a male experimenter. After this initiation, the women listened to one of the group discussions, and what they heard was a dull discussion of the sexual behavior of animals. After having been allowed to join the group, and then learning that it was boring, how would the three groups of women come to view the group? The results indicate that the women who had undergone the embarrassing severe initiation thought the group was more attractive and interesting than those who underwent a mild initiation or no initiation. Thus, attraction to a group may be related to the extent that we suffer or sacrifice for it (Gerard & Mathewson, 1966).

GROUP STRUCTURE

Groups are rarely static entities; they are constantly changing, exerting various pressures and counterpressures on members, changing their feelings, thoughts, and behaviors. In this section, we consider three aspects of group structure: the measurement of member relations in a group, leadership, and communication among group members.

MEASUREMENT OF GROUP STRUCTURE

Most social psychological research employs fairly arbitrary and makeshift techniques of measurement. However, several measurement devices were developed exclusively for work with small groups, and their use is fairly common. Perhaps the best known techniques are Moreno's sociometric methods.

Sociometry   J. L. Moreno (1934, 1947) believed that social systems, including small groups, are based largely on preference or "attraction–repulsion" systems, that is, on members' likes and dislikes for other members. He further argued that objective statistical methods are inadequate to describe these mutual feelings. It is more accurate to allow each group member to indicate his or her own feelings toward others in the group than for a researcher to describe members' sentiments. In a sociometric study of group structure, each member is asked to indicate the two or three other members most liked, or those he or she would most like to work with on some task. These choices are then arranged in a *sociometric matrix* (see Table 9.2), and later converted to a graphic display called a *sociogram* (see Figure 9.1).

Sociometric methods are widely used to study influence and friendship structures in a group. A member who is attractive to many other members is a "sociometric star" (person B in Figure 9.1), while one who is rarely chosen is an "isolate" (C, E, and F in Figure 9.1). Friendship cliques, subgroups whose members are mutually attracted, may be observed using these methods (A, B, and D in Figure 9.1) (see Kerckhoff, Back, & Miller, 1965).

Some individuals may have more than one power base, and the kind of influence they use will depend on their perceptions of the other group members (Goldman & Fraas, 1965), the kind of task confronting the group (Gibb, 1969), and their own personalities (Goodstadt & Hjelle, 1973; Kipnis, 1976).

Bales' Interaction Process Analysis   In order to measure ongoing interaction in a small group, R. F. Bales (1950, 1955, 1970) developed a procedure that enables trained observers to categorize any act that takes place during a group meeting. In most of his research, Bales arranged for several people to discuss complex human relations problems. Through a one-way screen, observers recorded every act that occurred between group members—an *act* being defined as a single statement, question, or gesture. Acts are divided into two broad classes: task relations and social–emotional relations (see Table 9.3).

In Bales' research, subjects are given information about a problem, and they discuss the problem for about 40 minutes, meeting as a group on four separate occasions. He found that there are between 15 and 20 acts per minute in a typical group session. About half of these acts are pertinent to the problem under discussion, and half of them consist of positive and negative reactions and questions. If a group session is analyzed over time, some noticeable changes are

Table 9.2.
Sociometric Matrix

Member Choosing	Member Chosen					
	A	B	C	D	E	F
A		x		x		
B	x			x		
C		x		x		
D	x	x				
E		x	x			
F	x	x				
Total	*3*	*5*	*1*	*3*	*0*	*0*

In a group of six people, each person is asked to choose the two members he or she likes best. The choices are then cast into a matrix.

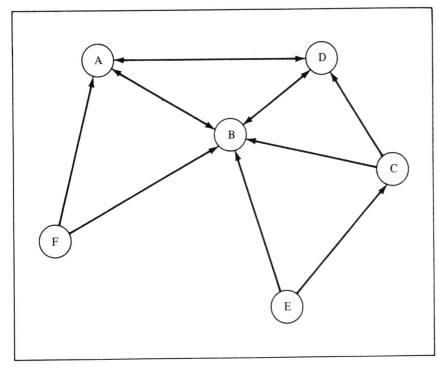

Figure 9.1.
Sociogram using choices in Table 9.2.

found. During the first third of the session, the most frequent act tends to be giving information. Opinions tend to be given most often during the middle portion of a session, and suggestions are offered most frequently in the last third of the session.

Bales reports that acts tend to alternate between socio–emotional and task- or problem-solving attempts. When too much emphasis is given to the problem, socio–emotional relations may become strained; emphasis is then placed on socio–emotional relations, and the problem is returned to later.

Following each session, group members were asked to complete a questionnaire on which they ranked other members in terms of the quality of their ideas, their likableness, and so on. The person considered to have the best ideas is usually the one who does the most talking and who offers more than the average number of suggestions and opinions. As we will see in our discussion of leadership, the member who contributes the best or most influential ideas is not usually the one who is most liked by others. The originator of ideas must be forceful enough to overcome resistance by other group members, and so is not usually the most popular. The reverse also seems to be true: Group members who do not push too hard for the acceptance of their ideas are likely to be popular.

Table 9.3.
Observation Categories for Group Interaction

SOCIAL–EMOTIONAL RELATIONS

Positive
Reactions

1. Shows solidarity, raises others' status, gives help and reward
2. Shows tension release; jokes, laughs, and shows satisfaction
3. Agrees, showing passive acceptance; understands, concurs, and complies

TASK RELATIONS

Attempted
Answers

4. Gives suggestion and direction, implying autonomy for others
5. Gives opinion, evaluation, and analysis; expresses feelings and wishes
6. Gives orientation and information; repeats, clarifies, and confirms

a b c d e f

Questions

7. Asks for orientation, information, repetition, and confirmation
8. Asks for opinion, evaluation, analysis, and expression of feeling
9. Asks for suggestion, direction, and possible ways of action

SOCIAL–EMOTIONAL RELATIONS

Negative
Reactions

10. Disagrees, showing passive rejection and formality; withholds help
11. Shows tension and asks for help; withdraws from field
12. Shows antagonism, deflating others' status and defending or asserting self

a. Problems of orientation   d. Problems of decision
b. Problems of evaluation   e. Problems of tension management
c. Problems of control   f. Problems of integration

From Bales (1950).

LEADERSHIP

Despite such common phrases as "he's a natural leader," or "she has leadership qualities," leadership is not a characteristic that resides within a single person. Instead, it defines a particular type of relationship between two or more people. We can define leadership as "the presence of a particular influence relationship between two or more persons. Social influence, however, is not equivalent to leadership. . . . Rather, leader influence suggests a positive contribution toward the attainment of group goals" (Hollander & Julian,

1969). In order for a person to be a leader, there must be one or more followers. It would be ridiculous for me to claim to be the leader of an organization whose membership included only myself. A leader needs followers, perhaps even more than followers need a leader.

If leadership is the ability of one person to influence others, those others generally agree to be influenced because they see it as being in their best interests. As our definition suggests, the leader facilitates the attainment of group goals. One person can sometimes force others to do something, but this is not what we mean by leadership (Gibb, 1969). Leadership is more than a personality trait of an individual. It is influenced by the structure and composition of the group, and the tasks involved, as well as the qualities of the person wielding influence. Since leadership is generally defined as power or control over others, we will first examine various bases of social power.

The Bases of Social Power   In a classic analysis of social power, French and Raven (1959) proposed that one person can influence another if at least one of the following sources of power is present:

1. Legitimate power: The followers believe that the leader, by virtue of his or her position, has a legitimate right to exert influence over them.
2. Coercive power: The leader can punish followers, for example, by firing them.
3. Reward power: The leader possesses some resource that followers value, such as promotions and raises.
4. Referent power: The leader is attractive to followers, who identify with him or her, and so voluntarily follow.
5. Expert power: The leader possesses some special skill or knowledge that the followers need.

Some individuals may have more than one power base, and the kind of influence they use will depend on their perceptions of the other group members (Goldman & Fraas, 1965), the kind of task confronting the group (Gibb, 1969), and their own personalities (Goodstadt & Hjelle, 1973; Kipnis, 1976).

The Great Man Theory of Leadership: "Leaders Are Born"   A great deal of modern history has been written as if historical events were directly shaped by the personalities of leaders. Hitler, Gandhi, Churchill, and Nixon have all shaped the course of world events on the basis of their personal strengths and weaknesses. A popular pastime of contemporary historians is writing psychohistorical analyses of world leaders. Whether such analyses of politicians are at all capable of explaining complex international events is highly questionable. Instead, we must look to the historical, social, economic, and political circumstances surrounding a leader. Here are two characterizations of very different types of leaders. Would Gandhi have become a leader in the Germany of the 1930s, or Hitler in India?

[Gandhi] is a small frail man, with a thin face and rather large protruding eyes, his head covered with a white cap, his body clothed in coarse white cloth, barefooted. He lives on rice and fruit, and drinks only water. He sleeps on the floor—sleeps very little, and works incessantly. His body does not seem to count at all. There is nothing striking about him—except his whole expression of "infinite patience and infinite love. . . ." He feels at ease only in a minority, and is happiest when, in meditative solitude, he can listen to the "still small voice" within. This is the man who has stirred three hundred million people to revolt, who has shaken the foundations of the British Empire, and who has introduced into human politics the strongest religious impetus of the last two hundred years. (Eriksen, 1961, quoting R. Rolland)

Leaders, as we have emphasized, need followers, and they must be ready to follow. Having examined Hitler's rise to power, Cantril (1941/1963) made the following observations of Hitler and the German social climate:

By 1920, the institutional structure which had held sway in Germany for several generations had broken down. Neither the state nor the church could claim the allegiance of the individual. No new institutions with promises of stability, no new social values with clearly defined goals had arisen to replace what had gone. . . . The individual felt himself a more or less isolated unit in a loosely united, multidirectional society. . . . When institutions and social values are disturbed and when people are disturbed they are anxious to regain mental stability. The easiest and most usual way of accomplishing this is to look for a leader, identify oneself with him, transfer one's troubles to him, and believe that he can always cope with things, that he always has another trick up his sleeve, that he can safely protect one against external dangers. . . . It is no wonder, then, that the message of Hitler, his own obvious belief in the righteousness of his program, his sincerity, and his faith in himself made an indelible impression on those who heard him. In a period of doubt and uncertainty, here was a speaker who did not argue the pros and cons of policies but who was fanatically self confident; who did not quietly suggest that he and his program were possible solutions, but who actually shouted certainty at the top of his lungs. (pp. 233–236)

There are personality characteristics that make some people more predisposed to leadership than others. Yet, the situation must be

Although some people are predisposed to leadership, they still need followers. Winston Churchill was greatly admired during the two world wars, but his popularity waned in peacetime.

appropriate, and followers must be ready to accept a leader who possesses those particular traits.

Leaders vary in their *style* of leadership. Some are more democratic than others. In a well-known early study of leadership style, Lewin, Lippitt, and White (1939) placed children in groups with either an authoritarian leader who controlled and directed their activities, a democratic leader who allowed the children to play a role in deciding what they would do, or a laissez-faire leader who simply let the children do as they wished. They reported that the authoritarian leader produced aggressiveness among members, while the democratic leader produced more efficient and more satisfied groups. These results have not always been replicated in other cultures (e.g., Meade, 1967). In general, research on personality characteristics of leadership have not yielded very reliable or consistent findings (Borgatta, Couch, & Bales, 1954; Stogdill, 1948). As Stogdill (1969) has concluded in his review of this literature:

A person does not become a leader by virtue of the possession of some combination of traits, but the pattern of personal characteristics of the leader must bear some relevant relationship to the characteristics, activities, and goals of the followers. Thus, leadership must be conceived in terms of the interaction of variables which are in constant flux and change. (p. 125)

An Interaction Model of Leadership: The Contingency Model If the personality traits of leaders are generally unrelated to leadership, then we must consider the group situation in addition to personalities. The contingency model of Fred Fiedler (1964, 1967, 1971) examines the interaction between leadership and situational characteristics.

The contingency model consists of three dimensions: task structure, the leader's position power, and leader–member relations. Individuals are asked to think of all those with whom they have ever worked, and to describe the one person with whom they could work least well. The traits listed in the description yield the individual's *least-preferred co-worker* (LPC) score. A high LPC score indicates a person who is oriented toward interpersonal relationships, while a low LPC score indicates a person who is motivated primarily toward working on the task. The LPC score is the measure of leader–member relations. We can ask whether the leader is liked by his followers, whether he has the power to reward and punish followers, and whether he has some expert power as well. These are used to determine "leader position power." Finally, the kinds of tasks confronting the group are divided into those that are highly structured with clear solutions, and those that are more ambiguous and unstructured. These three dimensions are then used by Fiedler to predict the kind of leader who is most effective in various kinds of situations.

In general, task-motivated leaders (those with low LPC scores) tend to perform better than relationship-motivated leaders in very favorable and in very unfavorable situations. Very favorable situations are those with structured tasks and strong leader position power. Very unfavorable situations are those with unstructured tasks and weak leader position power. High LPC leaders, those motivated toward personal relationships, tend to perform better in situations of intermediate favorableness. The findings from dozens of studies by Fiedler tend to support the contingency model, and suggest that domineering leaders and human-relations-oriented leaders can each be effective provided they are placed in situations that are appropriate to their orientations. Although the model has been criticized on methodological grounds (Graen, Orris, & Alvares, 1971), there is considerable support for it from studies of a wide variety of groups in a wide variety of cultures.

COMMUNICATION

By definition, members of a group communicate with one another in some way. Occasionally, especially in large organizations, formal networks of communication are established that limit access to certain members. For example, an assembly-line worker in a plant may be able to communicate with other assembly-line workers, with the shop steward, and with the foreman, but not with the company vice president or with workers in another part of the plant. Bavelas (1948) and Leavitt (1951) studied various versions of *communication networks* and found that satisfaction correlated positively with independence in a network, that is with the ability to communicate with many others. Task performance is generally better, especially when the task is a simple one, in centralized networks, those in which communications must pass through a central member (Shaw, 1964).

Even in groups less formal than those examined in communication network studies, certain people are more likely to be in contact with particular others, depending on their position in the group. At staff conferences in a psychiatric hospital, for example, humorous remarks, particularly hostile ones, are always directed at a subordinate. The psychiatrists are likely to make fun of a nurse, who in turn is most likely to pick on an orderly, who is most apt to make a joke at the expense of a patient (e.g., Coser, 1960; Goodchilds, 1972). As a general rule, communications of a hostile nature are directed downward in a group's hierarchy, from leaders to subordinates. Other types of communications, however, may be directed upward in the hierarchy, particularly those designed to protect members' status (Cohen, 1958).

Festinger's social comparison theory also deals with communication in groups. According to the theory, attempts should be made by group members to keep deviates from getting too far out of line. If these influence attempts are unsuccessful, the theory predicts that communications to the deviate will eventually stop. In a study designed to test these hypotheses, Schachter (1951) arranged for a paid confederate to participate in a group. In some groups, the confederate voiced the same opinions as other members. In other groups, he began with deviant opinions but gradually moved toward the others' positions. In yet other groups, the confederate remained deviant in his opinions throughout. Some of the groups were made attractive or cohesive to members, while others were not. The groups discussed a case that was either relevant or irrelevant to the group's stated purpose.

Schachter was primarily interested in communications to the deviant. According to Festinger (1950, 1954), groups would be most likely to attempt to bring the deviant into line when they were high in cohesiveness and when they were discussing a relevant problem. The results lend only some support to social comparison theory. The cohesive groups discussing a relevant problem did decrease the number of communications directed toward the deviate during the last part of the group session, but the greatest overall number of communications to the deviate was found for the noncohesive, irrelevant groups. It is unclear why these groups were so concerned with bringing the deviate into line, except perhaps to note that they may have been relatively unconcerned about the task.

As Bales has found in his analysis of small group interaction, communications serve two primary purposes: they help the group accomplish its explicit goals, and they facilitate fluid social–emotional relations among group members. The jokester in a group, who always seems to be interfering with the business at hand, may be equally important to the smooth functioning of the group as the more serious problem-solvers.

GROUP PROCESSES

Groups consist not only of individual members but of the interactions and interrelationships among members, the interdependencies that develop over time, and the influences that each member has upon the others. In this section we will be concerned with processes that occur in groups but cannot be found from an analysis of individuals in isolation. Perhaps the most fundamental question we can ask about groups is how the mere presence of other people influences the behavior of a single individual. This is generally considered under the somewhat misleading heading of "social facilitation."

SOCIAL FACILITATION

In what is often regarded as the earliest experiment in social psychology, Triplett (1897) compared the performance of bicycle racers, and in a later study, that of children winding fishing reels, alone and in the presence of others. He found that cyclists racing only against time did less well than those using a pacer and that those racing in competition did best of all. On the whole, Triplett found that children wound fishing reels better when they were in competition than when they performed the task alone. From this and several other early experiments (e.g., Dashiell, 1930; Travis, 1925), it appeared that the presence of other people facilitated or improved performance. Hence the term "social facilitation."

Social facilitation studies show that the performance of well-learned tasks improves with competition and an audience. So the winner of this close race may find he has done his best time ever.

However, not all studies found an improvement in performance with the presence of others. Pessin (1933) had students learn lists of nonsense syllables either alone or in the presence of an audience. In general, learning a series of nonsense syllables was accomplished faster when students were alone than when they were in front of spectators. Here is a case (and there are numerous others; e.g., F. H. Allport, 1920; Husband, 1931) where the presence of others interfered with performance.

These inconsistent findings occurred not only with human subjects but also with various animal species. Rats and chickens were found to eat more in groups than when alone (Harlow, 1932; C. W. Tolman & Wilson, 1965), and ants excavated more soil in the same time period when other ants were working simultaneously with them than when they worked alone (Chen, 1937). These animal experiments all point to a facilitation of behavior when others of the same species are present. But in some animal experiments, notably those in which the animals were learning a maze or learning to make fine discriminations among variously shaped objects, the animals did better when alone (e.g., Gates & Allee, 1933; Klopfer, 1958).

The research on the effects of working alone versus working with others was thus truly contradictory. This state of confusion reigned for over 60 years. It was not until Robert Zajonc (1965) carefully reviewed all the literature on this subject that a clear theoretical explanation of social facilitation was provided. Zajonc noted that essentially two types of tasks were studied in social facilitation research: tasks that required the performance of well-learned responses, and tasks that required the acquisition of new responses. This is the familiar distinction made by many learning theorists (e.g., Bandura, 1965b) between *learning* and *performance*.

If we divide all the tasks studied in social facilitation research into learning tasks and performance tasks, the results are not contradictory at all. When the task requires the subject to acquire some new response, such as learning nonsense syllables or learning to negotiate a maze, performance is better when the subject is alone than when others are present. When the task requires only the performance of some well-learned or instinctual response, such as riding a bicycle or eating food, performance is better when others are present.

Zajonc was not content merely to make this distinction. He also wanted to explain why learning was impaired and performance enhanced by the presence of others. For this he borrowed the concepts of response hierarchy and general drive from learning theory. For any given task or stimulus there is a range of possible responses an organism can make. If the task is well learned or instinctive, such as eating food or riding a bicycle, the dominant or most probable response in the hierarchy is correct. If the task requires learning, the most probable or dominant response is apt to be incorrect. This can most clearly be seen in a motor task such as typing. When you first learn to type, positioning your fingers on the keyboard is awkward and your first efforts at typing are apt to look like this:

Nwo is het tIme forlal goo dmen to com eto the aid . . .

Once you have mastered the task of typing, the dominant response is likely to be correct. You no longer need to look at the keyboard while typing, you somehow "know" when you're doing it right. So, the dominant response to novel, learning tasks is usually incorrect, while the dominant response to performance tasks, those that are well learned, is correct. We can now state that the presence of others enhances the emission of dominant responses. According to learning theory (e.g., Spence, 1956), one reason that dominant responses are likely to be emitted is because general drive level or activation is high. Zajonc then proposed that the presence of others increases drive or arousal, and this increase in arousal accounts for the emission of dominant responses and for the fact that novel tasks are better learned alone while performance tasks are better performed in the presence of others.

This elegant bit of detective work by Zajonc not only makes sense of scores of contradictory studies, but also serves to highlight the importance of theory as a tool in explaining behavior. Since Zajonc's original formulation, there have been additional studies confirming his hypothesis that the presence of others is a source of arousal (e.g., P. J. Hunt & Hillary, 1973; Martens, 1969; R. F. Weiss & Miller, 1971), and there have been some refinements in the theory as well. Cottrell (1968; Cottrell, Wack, Sekerak, & Rittle, 1968) has argued that the presence of others is not an innate biological source of drive but a learned source of drive in humans. He proposes that the presence of others increases arousal primarily when the audience is evaluating the subject, and there is some research to support this contention (Geen, 1977; Henchy & Glass, 1968; Paulus & Murdock, 1971). This theory has been used to explain the "home-team effect" in sports, that is, why teams have a better won–lost record at home than on the road (J. D. Edwards, 1979).

THE DEVELOPMENT OF GROUP NORMS

The behavior of people in groups is guided not only by the personalities of group members and by sets of formal rules and proscriptions, but also by a set of standards or norms that emerge from the group. The classic study of group norms was conducted by Muzafer Sherif (1936).

Sherif's Research with the Autokinetic Effect If a single star is seen in the sky, it may appear to move. Likewise, a point of light in a dark room appears to have movement. Sherif used this phenomenon, known as the *autokinetic effect*, to study the formation of norms in small groups (1936). Two sets of experimental conditions were used: Individual subjects were exposed to the light alone and asked to judge how far it moved, or they were exposed to the light in groups of two or three and each subject was to judge the degree of movement. Sherif was interested in whether individuals would arrive at a standard distance. For example, on 100 trials, would a single subject judge the movement of the light to be about the same on each trial? In group situations, would subjects agree with one another about the average distance? What would happen when individuals were then placed in groups, and when group members were then tested individually?

Sherif found that individuals tended to see a narrow range of distances in which the light seemed to move. While this range differed from one person to the next, each subject was fairly consistent in estimating the distance of movement. For example, Subject A might estimate the distance as around seven inches on the average. On one trial, he might guess the light moved nine inches, while on another trial he might guess five inches. Subject B, on the other hand, might estimate that the light moved between three inches and nine inches, and all her responses would fall within this range. When these individuals were then placed in a group setting, the judgments of group members tended to converge. Subject A might give his first response in a group setting as eight inches, while Subject B might say three inches. On the second trial, Subject A might say seven

Figure 9.2.
Distance judgments made by subjects alone and in a group experiment using a stationary light (autokinetic phenomenon). Subject A, dotted line; subject B, solid line. Adapted from Sherif, 1936, p. 208.

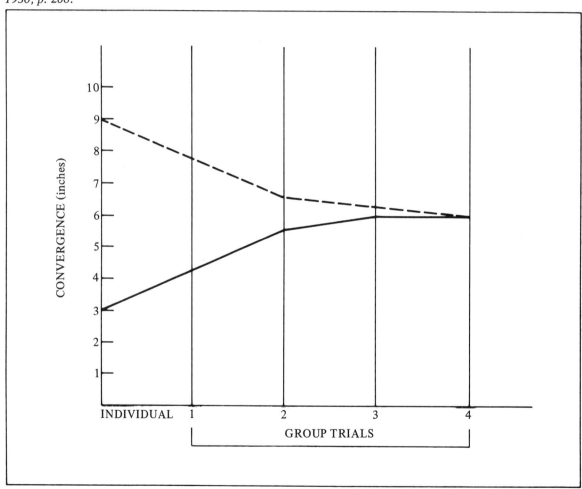

inches and B estimate five inches. On successive trials, A and B converge toward a single judgment, as can be seen in Figure 9.2.

For those who began their judgments in a group setting rather than alone, there was also evidence of convergence. As each person called out the estimate of distance moved, others tended to modify their own estimates; the final result was a fairly narrow range of responses for all group members. Thus, the members of a group came to agree on the distance moved by the stationary light, indicating that they had formed an agreed-upon and shared *social norm*, a standard against which they evaluated their own perceptions. When group members were tested individually, they perceived the light movement in terms of the group norm. The norm established in the group influenced the person's judgments even when the person was isolated from other group members.

The autokinetic situation used by Sherif in these classic studies is a highly ambiguous one. Because there is no reference point in a dark room against which to judge the apparent movement of the light, subjects may have little confidence in their own perceptions and may therefore be easily influenced by others in the group. When subjects are told that the movement of the light is erratic, there is little tendency for judgments to converge (Alexander, Zucker, & Brody, 1970).

One interpretation of these studies (Moscovici, 1974) is that

convergence is not motivated by the characteristics of the physical environment (its ambiguity) nor by the internal needs of each individual; it is motivated by the way in which the consensus is reached. In this influence modality, the search for a common and assured frame of reference is essentially inspired by the tendency to avoid conflict and disagreement with respect to this framework. The objective is to determine what is reasonable rather than what is true. (p. 216)

There is some evidence that group norms are not arbitrary but must be somewhat in accord with members' own perceptions. In one experiment (Jacobs & Campbell, 1961), confederates were used in the autokinetic situation to establish norms that were several times greater than the perceptions of the group members. Whereas group members judged the movement of the light to be about four inches, the confederates' judgments were closer to 15 inches. One by one, the confederates were removed from the group and replaced by naïve subjects. While the confederates' judgments influenced the judgments of naïve subjects for several "generations," there was a tendency for judgments to converge toward four inches, and away from the arbitrarily established 15-inch norm.

MacNeil and Sherif (1976) have argued that the group norm "disintegrated" in the Jacobs and Campbell study because it was so discrepant from the natural judgments of subjects. In their experi-

SCHOOLGIRLS LAUGH
UNCONTROLLABLY AS
"EPIDEMIC" STRIKES
TANZANIA

DAR ES SALAAM, Tanzania (UPI)—
Health officials in southwestern
Tanzania report that 18 high school
girls have been hospitalized after
being struck by "laughing
sickness."

The officials, in the Mbeya region,
said that nine of the girls were in
"unsatisfactory condition,"
laughing uncontrollably.

Doctors in Dar es Salaam said
"laughing sickness" was a kind of
mass hysteria that sometimes
affects adolescent girls in Tanzania.
They said it was serious only in
that it disrupts classes.

From *New York Times,*
7 August 1977.

ment, MacNeil and Sherif had confederates give highly arbitrary
responses, quite different from those of naïve subjects, or only mildly
arbitrary responses, somewhat different from those of the subjects.
They found that the highly arbitrary norm tended to decay as the
confederates were replaced by naïve subjects, but that the moderately arbitrary norm tended to be passed on for many generations of
the group. Since new members quickly acquired the group norm
when it was mildly arbitrary and passed it on to still newer members,
the norm was perpetuated even when there was a complete turnover
in group membership. It has also been shown (Montgomery, Hinkle,
& Enzie, 1976) that the tendency to perpetuate a very discrepant
norm is more likely to occur in groups consisting of highly authoritarian members than in nonauthoritarian groups.

The Sherif studies on the formation of group norms are closely
allied with the topic of conformity and influence processes. Each
member in the group setting in the Sherif studies influenced other
members, with the result that their judgments of light movement
converged. When judgments of some group members are extremely
deviant there is some tendency to resist them, as evidenced in the
Jacobs and Campbell, and MacNeil and Sherif studies. To what
extent do people adopt the perceptions of others?

CONFORMITY

"Conformity"—the word itself has a negative flavor. It smacks of
dependency, loss of individuality, and mindless obedience. Yet society depends on some amount of conformity for its very existence.
In a political sense, the opposite of conformity is anarchy. Behavior
that conforms to norms, rules, and expectations plays a major part
in people's lives, though they are usually unaware of the extent to
which they are dependent on their own and others' conformity. It
would be difficult to plan even the most routine activities if people
failed to live up to our expectations of them. We could not drive a

car from one place to another if motorists refused to conform to local and national driving customs. There is, of course, a certain amount of autonomy and individuality involved in even such mundane activities as driving a car. While most people stick to the legal speed limit, some go a bit slower and some a bit faster than the law allows. But within fairly narrow limits, nearly all drivers conform to the posted limit. It is difficult to say precisely why drivers adhere so closely to such rules, and there are at least three possible explanations. (1) Since there are dangers, both legal and personal, for deviating significantly from the speed limit, drivers may conform because of these external pressures. The sudden reduction in speed of cars is certainly noticeable when there is a police patrol ahead. So it seems clear that external threats and pressures influence the degree of conformity. (2) People may drive at or around the speed limit because that is what other drivers are doing. Their behavior, in other words, is influenced by the behavior of others around them. If other drivers accelerate, they will drive faster, too. (3) People may drive at the speed limit because they have internalized beliefs that such signs are to be followed strictly. Drivers may believe that the posted speed limit is indeed the best, safest, most efficient speed at which to travel. In this case, the presence or absence of a police patrol or the sudden change in driving speed of others around them will have little effect on their own driving speed. These three bases of conformity to a norm or a rule are referred to as *compliance*, *identification*, and *internalization*, respectively (Kelman, 1958).

As we will see, conformity occurs for all these reasons, and even in a single instance of conformity, more than one of these mechanisms may be in operation. To what extent does conformity occur?

The Asch Studies on Conformity   One of the basic tenets of Gestalt psychology and Lewinian field theory is that social entities, such as

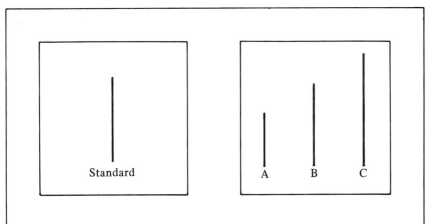

Standard

A   B   C

Figure 9.3.
Experimental task employed in the Asch conformity study. One subject, along with several confederates of the experimenter, was asked to indicate which of three lines was closest in length to a standard line. It was arranged that confederates would give incorrect judgments on some trials before the subject was asked to give his or her own judgment.

groups, exert pressures on individuals' perceptions, emotions, and behaviors. Asch (1951) was concerned with the effects of group pressure on perceptual judgments. In one study, fifty males were to choose which of several lines came closest to a standard line, as in Figure 9.3. The subjects were run in groups of from three to fifteen members. All but one of the subjects were accomplices of the experimenter. The real subject gave his judgment last, after hearing the judgments of the other group members. Asch arranged for his accomplices to give incorrect answers on certain trials.

Asch found that nearly one-third (32 percent) of the subjects, when confronted with an incorrect judgment by all other group members, gave incorrect responses themselves. Of course, this means that two-thirds of the subjects were not influenced by the others' judgments, but Asch focused upon that third who did conform. Regardless of group size, if the judgments of accomplices were unanimous, the extent of conformity from naïve subjects was the same. However, if one accomplice agreed with the real subject, the tendency to conform to the incorrect majority decreased from one-third to 10 percent. In interviews with the subjects following this perceptual judgment task, Asch found that there were three distinct motives for yielding to the pressure exerted by the incorrect majority: (1) wanting to appear the same as the others in the group; (2) a lack of confidence, doubts about their own perceptions, and (3) an unawareness of being incorrect. Some subjects actually perceived the incorrect response of other group members as the correct response— or so they reported. If this is so, conformity may occur without awareness.

While the Asch studies have occasionally been criticized on methodological and other grounds (e.g., C. N. Alexander, & Sagatun, 1973; L. Ross, Bierbauer, & Hoffman, 1976; Schulman, 1967), such criticisms miss their essential point. Groups do exert pressures on members, and these pressures, while they may be responded to in a variety of ways and for different reasons, play a role in the behavior or group members.

Several refinements in the concept of conformity have been offered. Willis and Hollander (1964) distinguished conformity from independence and from anti-conformity. Conformity consists of behavior that is consistent with the expectations of a particular group, as in the Asch studies. Independence is the ability to resist social pressures, even though the person may be aware of them. Anti-conformity is behavior that is influenced by pressure from group members but in a direction opposite to the group. For example, if, when given a choice in the Asch situation of choosing line A or line B, all group members said A, the anti-conforming subject would say B. Anti-conformity may be seen as determined by others' behavior, and may be viewed in terms of Brehm's (1966) notion of reactance (see Chapter 5).

More recent research on conformity has concerned the external validity of the laboratory phenomena demonstrated by Asch (e.g., Stech, McClintock, Fitzpatrick, & Babin, 1976) and the processes that lead to compliance and conformity (Allen & Levine, 1969; Godwin & Restle, 1974; Kiesler & Kiesler, 1969). With regard to qualifications of the Asch findings, people are more likely to conform when the situation is ambiguous, when members are uncertain of the correctness of their own judgments (Mausner, 1954), and when other group members are personally present (Deutsch & Gerard, 1955).

Is conformity an American trait? Cross-cultural research on conformity finds that it occurs, to some extent, in all cultures. Using variations on the Asch situation, Milgram (1961) studied conformity in Norway and France. In five different types of conformity situation, the Norwegians conformed to a slightly greater extent than the French. In one study, involving the judgment of tones rather than lines, 60 percent of the Norwegian subjects, as compared to 58 percent of the French subjects, conformed to the majority. In his research on obedience to authority (see Chapter 8), Milgram (1974) found that one-third to two-fifths of American subjects obeyed the experimenter's request to continue administering shock to another person. In a replication of this study in Germany (Mantell, 1971), the percentage of subjects obeying the experimenter's request was about the same as in the United States.

What of the minority in such conformity experiments? Attention has almost always been focused on the majority's influence on the minority but, historically, all important social and political movements have begun as minority responses. After all, there is no way to explain any sort of social change if the majority always has its way. It was this concern that has motivated a good deal of research on conformity among European social psychologists.

Moscovici, Lage, and Naffrechoux (1969) planted a minority of two confederates in groups of six people. The minority of two always gave incorrect responses on a perception task (judging colors). When the minority gave thoroughly consistent responses (saying "green" when the correct answer was blue), over 8 percent of the true subjects said "green," compared to a control group with no confederates where less than 0.5 percent said "green." However, when the two confederates were not consistent in their position, saying "green" on some trials and "blue" on others, naïve subjects were not swayed by their judgments. Thus, when the minority is not consistent in its judgments, the majority is not at all influenced, but when the minority is consistent and persistent, a significant proportion of the majority is influenced. More recent research (e.g., Allen, 1975) has been concerned with those factors that increase the *non*conformity of individuals. Independence of judgment is found to increase when the individual has support from another group member.

The Bennington College Studies: How the Liberal Arts Make Some Students Liberal We know from the studies of Sherif and Asch that given fairly ambiguous perceptual tasks to perform in laboratory situations, individual group members are influenced by other members of the group. Theodore Newcomb (1952) extended research on group influence beyond the laboratory to a more convincing and complex setting.

Newcomb studied the entire student body of over 600 students at Bennington College between 1935 and 1939. He was particularly interested in "the manner in which the patterning of behavior and attitudes varied with different degrees of assimilation into the [college] community" (p. 215). Students at Bennington College came primarily from conservative and well-to-do homes, and as freshmen they entered college with the conservative attitudes of their parents. Seniors at Bennington, however, tended to be considerably more liberal than underclassmen (over half of them were Democrats, compared to 29 percent of the freshmen). Parents, of course, are often appalled when their children return from liberal arts colleges as liberals. How does this transformation occur?

The Bennington students generally identified strongly with their college; it was, in other words, a *positive reference group* for them. There were rewards for being nonconservative; the students with the most prestige on campus were those who were most liberal. Newcomb selected 24 nonconservative and 19 conservative seniors for intensive study. Seniors who remained conservative throughout their four years at Bennington tended to be those who identified more strongly with "home and family." They were not well integrated into the college community, and tended to return home on weekends. For them, the college community was not a positive reference group. Some of the conservative students were aware of the conflict between the values of the college and those of their parents and home communities, and quite consciously decided to go along with their parents' values. Those who did identify with the Bennington community gradually found that their attitudes converged toward the predominant and rewarded liberal attitudes of their peers (Newcomb, 1952).

TASK PERFORMANCE

Most cultural products, both material and intellectual, are produced by groups. Bombs and the decision to use them, television sets and the programs broadcast, textbooks and the ideas they include, are products of group decisions and group behaviors. How well a group

Building a house is a divisible task. These Peace Corps workers are pooling their resources to complete this building with maximum efficiency and productivity.

performs a particular task or solves a certain problem depends upon three sets of variables: task demands, resources, and group process (Steiner, 1972).

Task demands consist of the requirements of the task and the rules under which the task must be performed. I. D. Steiner (1972) identifies tasks as being either unitary or divisible. *Unitary tasks* are those that cannot be easily or profitably broken into smaller subtasks. For example, if a group has only one problem to solve, little or nothing can be gained by having one person do the thinking and another the writing. For unitary tasks, no division of labor is possible. On many tasks, there are specific subtasks that can profitably be assigned to some group members. These are called *divisible tasks*. If a group has a number of different problems to solve, some problems can be assigned to particular members. Making an automobile is a divisible task in that it permits different people to perform different actions, some working on the engine, others on the electrical system, and so on. Resources include all the relevant knowledge, abilities, skills, and tools possessed by the individuals who make up the group. As Steiner notes, task demands and resources together determine the maximum level of productivity that can be achieved. "If an individual or group possesses all the needed resources, it has the potential to perform the task" (p. 8). If the group has the needed resources but fails to accomplish the task, then its actual productivity is less than its potential productivity. This may occur because of errors, inefficiencies, or misuse of resources during the problem-solving process.

Groups often fail to achieve their maximum productivity. There are various pressures toward uniformity and conformity in groups. Minority views are often discouraged, and it may be the minority view that is the best or correct solution (L. R. Hoffman, 1965). People may agree with other members if they believe that such agreement will make them more popular. The differential rate of participation in group discussions may also interfere with group productivity. L. R. Hoffman and Maier (1964) found that the proposed solution that receives the greatest number of favorable comments during group discussion tends to become the solution adopted by the group, but that most of these comments may come from a single member. The most talkative member is therefore likely to promote his or her solution. As the size of the group increases, fewer members contribute to the discussion, and so relatively few possible solutions are aired.

There is perhaps no better analysis of how these normal group processes interfere with effective problem-solving than Irving Janis' (1972) analysis of decision-making during the Bay of Pigs invasion of Cuba. President Kennedy's advisers included Dean Rusk, Robert McNamara, Douglas Dillon, Robert Kennedy, McGeorge Bundy, Arthur Schlesinger, Jr., and Allen Dulles—"one of the greatest arrays of intellectual talent in the history of American Government" (Janis, 1971, p. 43). They decided to send CIA-trained Cuban exiles to Cuba to overthrow the Castro government. The invasion proved to be a disaster. The exiles were captured or killed, the United States was embarrassed, and Cuba solidified its relationship with Russia. "How could we have been so stupid?" President Kennedy asked. Janis argues that it was not stupidity, but *groupthink* that led to the fiasco. The main principle of groupthink is "The more amiability and esprit de corps there is among the members of a policymaking ingroup, the greater the danger that independent critical thinking will be replaced by groupthink, which is likely to result in irrational and dehumanizing actions directed against outgroups" (p. 44). Among the processes that led to the invasion decision was the illusion that the policy advisers were unanimous in their approval of the plan.

Schlesinger (1965) wrote, "Our meetings were taking place in a curious atmosphere of assumed consensus. Had one senior adviser opposed the adventure, I believe that Kennedy would have canceled it. Not one spoke against it." There were strong pressures toward conformity among the advisers, so that those who had doubts about the policy remained silent.

According to social comparison theory (Festinger, 1954) and other analyses of group structure, there is a tendency for groups to be fairly homogeneous in composition. This can interfere with problem-solving, especially if the problem requires an unusual or highly creative solution. If group members tend to share the same attitudes and thought patterns, then it is unlikely that one of them will be able to arrive at a highly original solution to such a problem. Often more effective problem-solving can be achieved by a heterogeneous group, but this requires being able to overcome the tendency for similar people to join groups.

Janis suggests a number of ways for preventing groupthink and for increasing problem-solving effectiveness. Among these devices are the willingness to tolerate differences of opinion, the bringing in of outside experts, including those who may disagree with the group, and the assignment of a group member to play the role of devil's advocate, challenging each solution proposed by others.

Hackman and Morris (1975) have presented a model of group task performance that includes specific strategies for improving group productivity. They propose that there are three general variables that influence group performance: (1) the effort brought to bear on the task by group members; (2) the strategies used by group members in carrying out the task; and (3) the knowledge and skills (resources) of group members. All these variables may be influenced by what happens during group interaction. Performance strategies may be influenced by group norms; effort can be increased by redesigning the group task; the level and utilization of member knowledge and skill can be improved by altering group composition.

As we have seen, group norms often minimize the tendency of individuals to speak up when they disagree or hold a minority view. Hackman and Morris suggest that these norms, which often exist on a nonconscious level, limit the group's strategies. If feedback about these norms, either by group members themselves or by outsiders, is provided, the norms may be altered or their tendency to limit problem-solving strategies may be minimized.

The effort expended by group members on the solution of the task is influenced largely by group norms (e.g., Homans, 1950) and the quality of experiences members have as they work on the task. If the task is altered, then members' experiences may be altered to increase effort. For example, effort and motivation are heightened when the individual has a variety of specific tasks to perform, when the tasks

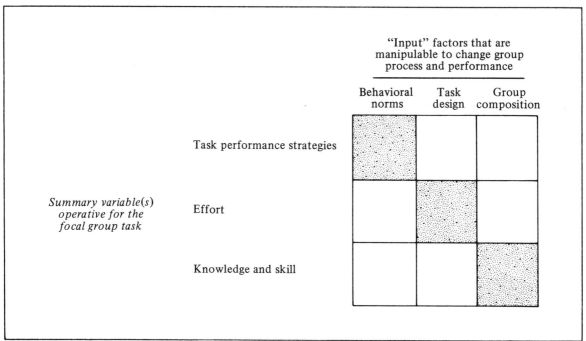

"Input" factors that are manipulable to change group process and performance

	Behavioral norms	Task design	Group composition
Task performance strategies	░░░		
Effect		░░░	
Knowledge and skill			░░░

Summary variable(s) operative for the focal group task

Figure 9.4.
Three summary variables and "input" factors that may be altered to influence them. Shaded cells represent especially promising sites for change aimed at improving group performance effectiveness.

are important ones, and when the individual has some autonomy and job discretion.

The efficient use of member knowledge and skill may be increased by teaching group members how to deal effectively with individual differences within the group and how to create a climate that supports learning and the sharing of learning. These proposed variables for enhancing group effectiveness are summarized in Figure 9.4.

COLLECTIVE BEHAVIOR

We have been concerned with groups of people and with individuals who interact with some purpose and who share some common goals and bonds. As we noted earlier, distinct from a group is an *aggregate*, people who happen to be in the same place at the same time, but with no structure, purpose, or shared sense of identity. Despite this distinction between groups and aggregates, the behavior of masses of people often appears to be meaningful, patterned, and caused (Aveni, 1977). The study of mass or aggregate behavior is generally considered under the topic of *collective behavior*. Collective behavior, which includes crowd behavior, riots, crazes, panics, fads, mass hysteria, protest movements, rebellions, revolutions, and social movements, usually emerges spontaneously, without a prior plan of action. Examples of collective behavior range from the looting that occurred during the New York City blackout of 1977 to Erhard Seminars Training and religious cults.

A thorough treatment of all the forms of collective behavior is well beyond the scope of this textbook, and adequate summaries of the sociological and psychological literature are widely available (Milgram & Toch, 1969; Rosnow & Fine, 1977; Rudé, 1964; Schultz, 1964; Smelser, 1963; Toch, 1965; Turner & Killian, 1957). We shall therefore limit ourselves to a brief discussion of the relationship between small group theory and research and collective phenomena, and to a more detailed examination of a few forms of collective behavior, in particular, panics, riots, and crowds.

Social psychologists study collective behavior for a number of reasons (Milgram & Toch, 1969). The very first social psychology textbooks published in the United States devoted considerable attention to crowds and collective phenomena. Another reason is that the study of collective behavior raises problems of social significance for social psychology; it brings social psychology into the social and political arena. A third reason is that an understanding of social upheavals in the form of riots, panics, and revolutionary social movements illuminates the bases of social stability. It is only when disorders occur that we become aware of the meaning of order. A fourth is that the dynamic relationship between individual and group activity is perhaps best illustrated in the study of collective behavior. This last point is illustrated by Milgram, discussing a civil rights rally he attended:

I had been standing on the perimeter of the crowd, but by 2:50 P.M., without doing anything, I found myself no longer on the fringe. A great mass of people had formed behind me, and I was now in a relatively central part of the crowd. Somewhat the same feeling as waiting at the very end of the line at a movie theatre, and then with great surprise noticing how many people had formed behind me. By doing nothing, my position shifted in a changing structure.

The observation is representative of a general property of crowds. There is a separation of intention and consequence. A man becomes immersed in a situation whose properties are continually changing. He decides to stand on the fringe, yet finds himself at the core; he wishes to remain stationary, but the dense flow of bodies carries him forward. The choices made by a plurality of others in interstimulation create altered conditions for him that are independent of his intentions; in turn, his response to the conditions creates constraints and pressures for others. (Milgram & Toch, 1969, p. 523)

Finally, collective phenomena are ubiquitous in daily social life.

On nearly any day, we can read in the newspaper of strikes, riots, social, religious, and political movements, and the unfortunate consequences of panic during a fire, flood, or earthquake. Like so many seemingly patternless events, these behaviors are no more random than decision-making or attitude change; they are therefore amenable to study by traditional scientific methods.

PANIC

We begin with the study of panic because it was one of the first aspects of collective behavior to be subjected to experimental research. The classic study of panic was conducted by Alexander Mintz (1951). Mintz noted that because it normally takes only a few minutes for patrons to file out of a theater or restaurant, deaths that occur during fires are a result of nonadaptive behavior, such as blocking exits and pushing other people. Generally, these panics have been explained by reference to emotional excitement, contagion, or suggestion (e.g., LeBon, 1896; E. A. Ross, 1908). Mintz proposed that the decisive factor is not emotional excitement but rather the reward structure of the situation. In most panic situations, there is a conflict of interest: If everyone cooperates, all can escape, but if a few individuals do not cooperate, if they push and shove, then anyone who does not push will be burned. Thus, when mutual cooperation breaks down, there is a conflict between self-interest and social interest, a conflict also found in analyses of ecology (e.g., Hardin, 1968; Stern, 1976) and in simulated games such as the Prisoner's Dilemma Game (Dawes, 1975; Kelley & Grzelak, 1972). Mintz conducted experiments in which groups of people had the task of pulling cones out of a glass bottle. Each subject was given a piece of string to which a cone was attached. Cooperation on the part of the subjects was required if the cones were to come out, since the neck of the bottle would permit only one cone at a time to pass. Mintz believed that this task was analogous to going out a theater exit, which only one person could pass through at a time. Subjects could win or lose money depending on how much time elapsed before they pulled out the cone. In some experiments, water began to fill the bottle, and success was defined as retrieving a dry cone. In control conditions, no rewards or fines were levied.

In order to test the emotion explanations of panic, Mintz also instructed some accomplices to scream, behave excitedly, and swear during the task. In all, 42 experiments were conducted. Results indicate that there were no "traffic jams" in the no reward or fine groups. Emotional excitement on the part of some subjects had little effect on group efficiency. But in over half of the reward–fine experiments, traffic jams developed as soon as the bottle neck was temporarily blocked. The introduction of a screen to prevent subjects

Table 9.4.
Mean Percentages of Escapes

	High Threat	Low Threat
High Reward	46.6	43.1
Low Reward	16.3	59.5

From Kruglanski (1969, p. 462).

from seeing one another had no effect on traffic jams; thus, emotional facilitation as an explanation for panics was ruled out. According to Mintz's research, panics occur when people are penalized for failure to escape and when they are rewarded for successful escape.

In order to examine the role of threat or danger in panic more closely, Kelley, Condry, Dahlke, and Hill (1965) varied the penalties for failure to escape. They found that nonadaptive behavior increased as the penalties increased. In two experiments that varied both threats (shock) and monetary rewards and fines, Schultz (1965) and A. L. Klein (1976) found contradictory results. Schultz found, as Mintz had, that only the reward–fine group displayed evidence of panic, while Klein found, as Kelley et al. had, that personal threat increased panic.

Kruglanski (1969) also varied rewards (from 3 cents to $5) and threat (shock versus no shock) and found an interaction between the two. When threat is high for failure to escape, stronger rewards for delaying an individual's escape result in many people's escaping. When there are few rewards for waiting, then high threat leads to the most panic (see Table 9.4).

RIOTS

Like panics, riots are relatively spontaneous, uncoordinated collective phenomena. They seem to be unpredictable and, for the most part, uncontrollable. The storming of the Bastille, the food riots in eighteenth-century Britain, the draft riots in New York during the Civil War, the race riots of the 1940s and 1960s, and riots that have occurred during fires, floods, blackouts, and other unusual events have all been analyzed by observers. Early explanations of riots centered on the immorality of participants, the spread of emotional excitement, and the individual's feelings of anonymity in a crowd. Gustav LeBon (1896) and Freud (1921/1960) proposed that rioters act on instinct and that emotional excitement spreads through a crowd contagiously. The belief that crowds engage in random acts of violence and destruction was widespread. So, too, was the notion that there are no restraints or norms serving to inhibit the behavior of crowds.

Systematic research on crowds and riots, however, quite clearly demonstrates that behavior is not random; that contagion does not spread indiscriminately through participants; and that there are norms and other regulatory mechanisms that limit the extent of violence and damage. Emotionality is passed from one person to another, but the pattern that this contagion takes is orderly and predictable. In a study of hysterical contagion in which workers at a small factory were "bitten" by insects (which, in fact, did not exist), the imaginary bug first infected sociometric isolates, and only later did it spread through close circles of friends (Kerckhoff et al., 1965). Looting that occurs in urban riots is not indiscriminate, but shows a pattern of deliberate retaliation against shops and stores thought to be unfair to customers (Berk & Aldrich, 1972). Likewise, individual acts of vandalism occurring during the Los Angeles riot of 1967 indicate that in only about 20 percent of the instances in which rioting spread to a new geographical area did the contagion involve a contiguous area.

Riots and crowd behavior, then, are complex, dynamic processes. Collective behavior is dynamic; it emerges over time. Twenty people do not suddenly turn into a rioting mob. Certain conditions must exist before a particular precipitating event turns a mass of people into a crowd.

Lieberson and Silverman (1965) correlated the occurrence of riots with a variety of economic, political, and social conditions. In general, in their analysis of over 75 racial disturbances in the United States up to 1916, demographic and housing conditions had no effect on the probability of a riot, but the job situation for blacks and characteristics of local government did have a significant effect. Economic indices have fairly consistently been shown to relate to instances of collective violence. Hovland and Sears (1940) correlated the number of lynchings in the South for the years 1882 to 1930 with the price of cotton and found that as the price of cotton fell, the number of lynchings increased.

Two theories of crowd behavior are of interest, the first because it relies heavily on concepts derived from the study of small groups, and the second because it shows the dynamic and historical nature of crowds. These are Turner and Killian's (1957) emergent norm theory, and Smelser's value-added theory (1963).

We have seen from the studies of Asch (1951) and Sherif (1936) that a group of people who interact for a period of time will eventually evolve a common set of norms. Once these norms are established, they influence most members of the group. Turner and Killian propose that in ambiguous situations, where the outcome is uncertain, communication in the form of mingling with others and passing rumors creates a sense that something must be done. Rumors and other forms of communication take on the function of norms, suggesting what actions might be undertaken. According to this emergent norm theory, people in a crowd act the way they do because they believe it is appropriate or required—in other words, they conform to a norm—and not because of some emotional contagion or pre-existing propensity for riotous behavior. The initial impetus for this process is some ambiguous or unstructured situation. This precipitating event may be a rumor, a violent incident, such as a shooting, or any of a number of unusual occurrences that require interpretation or clarification (such as the lights suddenly going out, which triggered riots in New York City in 1977).

Smelser proposes a series of determinants of collective behavior in which each stage must be reached successively. First there must be *conduciveness to collective behavior* in the social system. There is little rioting, for example, in totalitarian countries because such behavior is not tolerated. The second stage is *perception of strain*, the belief that things are "out of whack," that injustices exist, or that needs are unmet. Then there must be the *spread and growth of a belief* among participants; that is, they must come to see the strain in a similar manner. Once people have a shared view of the problem, they can *mobilize for action*, forming groups or gathering among themselves. Collective behavior itself will most often be triggered by some *specific event*—an arrest or a fight, for example. Finally, there is some *resolution* to the collective action. The police may break up a demonstration, make mass arrests, or the collective group may achieve its purposes. While this theory has been criticized (by Milgram & Toch, 1969) on a number of grounds, it emphasizes the point that seemingly spontaneous crowds and riots do not materialize out of nothing. Certain social, psychological, and environmental conditions must exist before collective behavior arises (see also Mann, 1979).

Summary

Groups are characterized by individuals who are aware of one another and who take one another into account in working toward specific task or socio–emotional goals. Aggregates or collectivities consist of a number of individuals who do not share common mutual feelings or goals, but who nevertheless influence and occasionally interact with one another.

Groups may vary along a number of dimensions, three important ones being the relative size, intimacy, and function of the group. Individuals join groups for a variety of reasons, including the propinquity of groups and the need to evaluate opinions, abilities, and emotions in social comparison when nonsocial means of evaluation are unavailable or nonexistent. There may also be psychological or material rewards attendant on affiliation with a particular group. Some theorists have explained group affiliation in terms of social exchange processes, wherein one offers resources that one has in abundance in exchange for resources that one desires.

Cohesiveness refers to the attraction of group members to the group. The more satisfying the group is to members, the more attractive the group is. Beyond this, cohesiveness varies over time as a function of the external pressures placed on the group as well as the sources of satisfaction obtained within the group. As external pressures mount, there is a tendency for group cohesiveness to increase. Another source of cohesiveness is the result of dissonance reduction; individuals come to like most those groups for which they have unnecessarily suffered.

Groups also have a discernible structure, usually along such dimensions as leader–follower, patterns of communication, and patterns of friendship. Such structures can be measured by sociometric techniques, social distance scales, and interaction process analysis techniques. Leadership involves the influence of one or more persons by another. Viewed in terms of influence, leadership depends greatly on the bases of social power held by the leader. Early theories of leadership tended to focus on the personalities of leaders, while more recent theories take into account not only personal characteristics of the leader, but also the type of task confronting the group and the leader's perception of group members. In this view of leadership, the effectiveness of a leader is a product of the interaction of the leader's traits and situational characteristics.

The mere presence of others increases physiological arousal, and this has important implications for the ability of individuals to learn and perform tasks in group settings. Groups tend to develop standards or norms that guide the behavior of members. Particularly in ambiguous situations, the tendency to form and conform to group norms is strong. Conformity to group norms serves to reduce the uncertainty or ambiguity of external events and it enhances the individual's attractiveness to other group members. Conformity is apt to be greatest when individuals strongly identify with the groups of which they are members. Conformity tends to be less when individuals have an ally in the group and when the group is not particularly attractive to the individual.

The ability of groups to solve problems and perform tasks is a function of three sets of variables: characteristics of the group members, particularly their skill and knowledge; characteristics of the task or problem to be performed; and processes that occur during the actual performance of the task. Many of the processes that naturally occur in groups, such as conformity and adherence to group norms, often tend to undermine effective problem-solving. But it is possible to increase problem-solving efficiency by structuring groups in a certain way or by providing them with training.

The behavior of aggregates was reviewed under the heading of collective behavior. Despite their seeming chaos, panics and riots are often patterned and systematic events. Their development depends upon the immediate situation, the growth and development of shared beliefs and perceptions among individuals, and an agreed-upon course of action.

Suggested Readings

*Davis, J. H. *Group performance* (2nd ed.). Reading, Mass.: Addison-Wesley, 1979.

*Janis, I. L. *Victims of groupthink.* 1972.

Janis, I. L., & Mann, L. *Decision making.* New York: Free Press, 1977.

*Peter, L. J., *The Peter principle.* New York: Bantam, 1970.

Steiner, I. D. *Group process and productivity.* New York: Academic Press, 1972.

Weick, K. E. *The social psychology of organizing* (2nd ed.). Reading, Mass.: Addison-Wesley, 1979.

*Available in paperback edition.

Cathy Hull

10
INTERGROUP RELATIONS: PREJUDICE, CONFLICT, AND COOPERATION

Most Americans endorse the principles of freedom, democracy, religious liberty, equality of opportunity, and enlightened self-interest. This creed conflicts with the knowledge that not every American enjoys such freedoms and opportunities. This conflicting set of facts, particularly with regard to the treatment of black Americans, is called an "American dilemma" by Gunnar Myrdal (1944). But it is not only with respect to race that values and ideals may conflict.

Nearly everyone in this country believes in equal educational and occupational opportunities for others as well as for themselves. Only when these values conflict, such that there are more applicants than openings in a school or for a position, is a person forced to choose between these values. The resolution of this conflict may result in discriminatory behavior and the development or manifestation of prejudice.

Most people who are considered prejudiced by others probably do not consider themselves to be so, and they may endorse such concepts as equality and fair-mindedness almost to the same extent as those who are free of bigotry. The person's behavior is clearly prejudicial only when a concept like equality conflicts with other values, such as economic self-interest. While the "dominative racists" are consistently and overtly bigoted, most forms of prejudice are more subtle, occasional, and as a result, pernicious. Most bigotry is passive; this has been called "aversive" racism when applied to racial intolerance (J. M. Jones, 1972; Kovel, 1970; McConahay & Hough, 1976). In this chapter, we examine intergroup conflict and prejudice, first, with respect to ethnic prejudice and sexism, and second, with respect to other types of group conflict, such as international hostility.

At this point in American history, we tend to think of intergroup relations as primarily concerned with race and sex discrimination. This has not always been the case in the United States, and is certainly not the case in most other nations. At various times in our history, the groups most involved in conflict with one another were union and nonunion laborers, lower and middle social classes, recent and second-generation immigrants, northerners and southerners, urban and rural dwellers. In other countries, intergroup hostility occurs along linguistic lines, such as between Flemish- and French-speaking Belgians or English- and French-speaking Canadians; along geographic lines, as between the northern and southern Italians; or along social class lines, as in Japan (see Klineberg, 1971). All these intergroup conflicts have certain common features, which are the primary focus of this chapter, though we use racial and sexual discrimination as the primary examples. Some attempt is made to discuss conflict in a general way so that we may understand conflicts in other countries and cultures as well as current types of intergroup conflicts in the United States.

A NOTE ON RACE AND SEX DIFFERENCES

Because race and gender will be used frequently as examples, it is important to discuss research and theories that find racial or sex differences in abilities, habits, and personal characteristics. These differences will not generally be mentioned in the remainder of this chapter, and it is worthwhile to discuss the reasons for this omission. I will not, for example, discuss, except in passing, the literature on racial differences in IQ test scores, or differences between males and females in shyness and aggressiveness. The reason for the absence of such discussions is that these kinds of findings are not reduced to a level where they can be intelligently interpreted by the social scientist; they are not reduced to the lowest common denominator. Where, for example, do sex differences in aggression come from? Are they really due to gender? If a nonaggressive female underwent a sex-change operation, would her passivity disappear along with her ovaries? If not, then aggressiveness is not caused by gender but by something else, and it is that "something else" that should probably be studied. Undoubtedly, females in a particular culture share certain experiences that males, for the most part, do not; just as most males experience treatment that females do not. This differential treatment is probably what underlies most sex differences in personality and behavior. Hence, what should be the focus of study is the differential treatment accorded males and females and how this affects such traits as aggressiveness.

Whenever discussing race, sex, social class, religious, linguistic, or national differences, it is important to remember that these categories are merely correlated with the behavior under study and not the causes of that behavior (see Chapter 3). Other factors that are themselves correlated with these categories are probably the root cause of the behavior. So, genetic differences aside, race differences on IQ tests, to whatever extent they may exist, are not caused by race; sex differences in aggression are not caused by gender; religious differences in political ideology are not caused by religion; and national differences in authoritarianism are not caused by nationality (see D. W. Edwards, 1974; Mack, 1974). While it may be a convenient way to summarize complex findings in psychological research, we will not term such differences "race differences," "sex differences," and so on, because that is not precisely what they are.

As social psychologists, we are interested less in describing human behavior (that is presumably what newspaper reporters and historians do) than in understanding it by developing and testing theories. Race, sex, national, religious, and linguistic differences are merely shorthand descriptions of relationships in the world, and as such are of little interest to the social scientist. What is of more interest is

"IT TAKES ONE TO KNOW ONE"—NOTES ON INTERGROUP RESEARCH

Some of the things on which I do research seem to be—and perhaps are—frivolous. When people find out that I study humor, they often ask me, somewhat accusingly, I think, why. The implication is that I ought to study what they consider to be more fundamental social problems. (I do not perceive humor to be a "social problem," though I could make a case that the lack of it is one.) I am generally considered somewhat suspect by colleagues and students who want to study social problems. In recent years, there has been an extraordinary amount of controversy over the issue of racial differences in intelligence (e.g., Eysenck, 1971; Jensen, 1969; Kamin, 1974; Tobach, Gianutsos, Topoff, & Gross, 1974). I believe the central questions in this controversy are insoluble,* and I question the motives of researchers who undertake such research in the first place. Especially when no theory is being tested, the appearance of having an ax to grind is unavoidable.

As a general rule of thumb, I believe that teams of researchers whose preconceptions are apt to differ, or perhaps even to cancel one another out, should work together in research on sensitive issues. Research on American race relations should probably be conducted by black and by white

what causes certain relationships to exist in the first place, and we begin our discussion of intergroup differences with an examination of prejudice. (See " 'It Takes One to Know One'—Notes on Intergroup Research," above.)

THE NATURE OF PREJUDICE

This section carries the same title as a book by Gordon Allport (1954), partly because his treatment is still one of the best in this area. In this section, definitions of prejudice are presented, along with theory and research on prejudice. We will define prejudice, following J. M. Jones (1972, p. 61), as "the prior negative judgment of the members of a race or religion or the occupants of any other significant social role, held in disregard of facts that contradict it."

Prejudice, then, refers to an invalid negative evaluation of a group or of its members on the basis of their membership in the group. Often, social psychologists distinguish among various types of prejudice, such as a negative evaluation of another and negative behavior toward another. This distinction makes sense if we treat prejudice as a private judgment, or as an attitude toward others, in which case we must somehow relate this attitude to overt behavior. Sometimes prejudice and related behaviors are viewed as constituting an

*Since psychologists do not know very well how to measure intelligence and there is a good deal of confusion as to what "race" is, and these two factors are compounded by the need to deal with correlational data, the issue is perhaps an impossible puzzle.

researchers working together, perhaps also with non-American collaborators. In this way, distortions in language, perception, and interpretation of events and data are likely to be minimized if all can agree on a final report. If diverse researchers agree on certain points, this is fairly compelling evidence of their validity; if they disagree, this should serve as a signal that certain events or interpretations are in dispute and therefore may depend on yet further data or on social and political biases.

The issue here is the extent to which a researcher's values may bias and influence the results and interpretation of his or her research. There is no doubt that such distortions can and have occurred (Rosenthal & Jacobson, 1968; Rosenthal & Rosnow, 1969). I have argued (Chapters 1 through 3) that the choice of topic, method, and theoretical approach are also influenced by personal philosophy. If we are ever to approximate objective knowledge in social psychology, it will come about through the cooperation of those with competing ideologies.

attitude. In this view, the negative affect toward another is called prejudice, and it corresponds to the affective component of an attitude. The beliefs about the other, such as that he is aggressive, correspond to the cognitive component and generally consist of stereotypes. The behavioral component consists of discriminatory actions against others. While it will sometimes be useful for us to distinguish between beliefs and behavior in this chapter, we do not treat prejudice and its related aspects as an attitude, but rather as a norm of a group. Prejudices shared by group members about members of another group are likely to influence their perceptions and actions toward the others, while uniquely held views of out-group members are not likely to have much effect on one's actions. Only when prejudices are shared with others do they become important for social psychological purposes.

AN EXAMPLE OF PREJUDICE

Let me begin our discussion of ethnic prejudice with a description of discrimination and its consequences, because there are several lessons in this and similar examples for an understanding of prejudice.

There are various names for the group I will describe, some of them most unflattering. For the moment, let us refer to this group by the Greek letter Eta. The Eta are not a genetically distinct group, and if differences between Eta and the rest of the population exist, those differences were created by generations of segregation and inferior social status. Because the Eta are forced to spend so much of their time with only one another (non-Eta will not associate with them), and because their education is minimal, they have developed distinct speech patterns that immediately identify them as Eta, much as the lower-class Cockney of London developed distinctive habits of speech. The Eta are a fairly sizable minority, numbering in the millions, and are scattered throughout the country, where they live in slums or ghettos. They are regarded as unclean and fit only for the most undesirable occupations. Intermarriage with the Eta is taboo, although there is some occasional "passing." The average IQ of an Eta is about 16 points lower than that of the general population (88 compared to 104). The measures of school achievement show the Eta to be considerably below others, with more absenteeism from school, greater truancy, and a delinquency rate over three times as high as that found among other youth. These differences between Eta and others are generally regarded as signs of "innate racial inferiority," and are used to justify further discrimination.

This sounds all too familiar to Americans. Yet the Eta exist as a group, known less pejoratively as the Burakumin, in Japan (DeVos & Wagatsuma, 1966; Klineberg, 1971). The Burakumin are not distinguishable by the color of their skin or by their physical appearance, but by their speech, their occupation, their place of residency, and their identity papers. The manifestations of prejudice and the consequences of centuries of discrimination are strikingly similar to those found for blacks in the United States. Though the stereotypes of the Burakumin, the beliefs and attitudes of the majority group toward them, are similar to racial prejudice in the United States, this is not a prejudice based on race.

Prejudice and discrimination, regardless of whether they are based on physical, cultural, social, or other traits, serve similar social and psychological functions for the prejudiced group. To understand the origins of prejudice we must study the bigot rather than the targets of bigotry. While blacks live with the burden of white racism every day, they are no more the cause of that racism than canvas is the cause of a Picasso painting. So, we will generally focus our attention on the majority group, what William Graham Sumner (1906) called the "in-group," and only occasionally examine the characteristics of the out-group that make it a useful scapegoat.

CATEGORIZATION AND STEREOTYPING

Because our environment is so complex, it can most efficiently be perceived and dealt with by categorizing similar objects into broad classes and groups. While no two street lights are precisely the same, for example, we place them in the category "street light" and respond to them as though they were all identical: If the light is red, we stop. This is as true of the social environment as of the physical. We tend to categorize people into groups so that we may more easily perceive and respond to them. When we are having a prescription filled at the local pharmacy, it makes little difference to us who the pharmacist is as long as he or she is competent. The fact that one pharmacist likes Baroque music and another doesn't is of little consequence. Individual pharmacists are unique and have distinctive traits, but it is only important for us as customers to perceive them as having one common trait, the ability to fill a prescription. However, if we are introduced to a pharmacist at a party, the ability to fill a prescription may be irrelevant. To assume that all pharmacists are alike in a social encounter is to assume that people who are members of one category on the basis of one trait share other traits that do not define the category. So, if we assume that pharmacists are political conservatives, and therefore this pharmacist must be conservative, we are overgeneralizing, stereotyping, or prejudging.

The process of establishing a social object as a member of a social category involves minimizing its individual differences and maximizing its categorical properties. To categorize a social object implies that the criterial similarities are more important for that object and like objects than any differences among them.... [Y]ou may need very little information to decide that a person is Jewish, but once you assign him to this category you now (ostensibly) know a great deal about him—which is to say that you think you know a great deal about Jewish persons. (Ehrlich, 1973, p. 38)

Categorization is a useful, perhaps inevitable, process. It helps us simplify our interactions with a complex physical and social environment. But categorization is also a potentially dangerous process because it so easily leads to overcategorization, generalization, and prejudgment of others. Of course, it is not only others who are categorized and labeled; we do the same to ourselves. We label ourselves as friendly, intelligent, or musical, and tend to think of ourselves as belonging to homogeneous groups with similar individuals. When we read a flattering article about a fellow musician, we may swell with pride, as though what applies to one member of a category applies to all.

Categorization is an interesting process, for its very existence tends to lead to emotional responses. When young children are arbitrarily divided into two competitive athletic teams, they develop positive sentiments toward their teammates and negative feelings toward competitors (Sherif, Harvey, White, Hood, & Sherif, 1961). Such feelings tend to develop even when there is no competition between groups (Allen & Wilder, 1975; Doise, Csepeli, et al., 1972;

AN INTERVIEW WITH
JAMES M. JONES

James M. Jones is currently the director of the Minority Fellowship Program of the American Psychological Association. He received his B.A. degree from Oberlin College, his master's from Temple University, and his Ph.D. in psychology from Yale. He has taught at Harvard University. Dr. Jones's research has dealt with humor, play, and sports. He is the author of *Prejudice and racism* (1972).

JHG: In your book *Prejudice and racism,* you distinguish among several kinds of racism, including what you call "cultural racism." Would you define this concept?

JMJ: I wanted to write a book in which the full gamut of racial conflicts was reflected. Thus, the first step was to go from an individualistic psychological analysis of *prejudice* to the broader concept of racism. The unique notion that tied individual and institutional racism together was *cultural* racism. The positivist social scientific view is culture bound; its normative bias has meant that cultural forms and functions different from the WASP culture are seen as deficient. There is no principle of psychology based on a *positive* analysis of a cultural group. Cultural –racial groups of color are pejoratively described and understood. This is broadly the observation to which cultural racism refers.

JHG: In *Prejudice and racism,* you mention that much of the social science literature on race is seriously confounded by social class, and that much is not relevant to racism. Would you elaborate on these criticisms?

JMJ: Because of discrimination and oppression, large segments of black and Hispanic groups are in the lower economic echelon. Therefore, people are willing to interpret the entirety of their cultural experience as a class phenomenon. There is obviously some truth to it, and you find that when you control for class, racial differences are severely diminished, if they don't disappear altogether. If you look at variables that emerge from a materialistic conceptual base in the Protestant ethic, it's not surprising that class accounts for a substantial percentage of the variance. If you had a psychology that was based on a spiritual, nonmaterialistic, nonpositivistic posture, I think you would find cultural differences heightened and sharpened and class differences diminished. But our psychology is very scientific and materialistic.

JHG: Can you think of a nonmaterial variable that psychologists might study that would diminish class differences and heighten racial differences?

JMJ: The kind of variable I find compelling from a cultural point of view is a concept like rhythm: how time is sliced up—such things as gait, movement, chronology. Rhythm is, for me, a way of identifying the flow of behavior against a temporal background. If you look at music, there are bars and notes that have certain temporal values. I think behavioral episodes have a similar kind of pattern. If psychologists looked at such variables, I think they would find heightened differences between, for example, colored racial groups and Western or white racial groups.

For a long time the notion that black people "had rhythm" was seen as a pejorative stereotype. I think it's remarkable when a very fundamental basis of a people's culture is denigrated to such a degree that they themselves have attempted to deny it. I think rhythm is important to black culture, but rhythm is a fundamental phenomenon. It's not that one group has it and another doesn't, but that there are differences. A march is a Western phenomenon. I don't think you'd ever see a march coming out of any African country. What you do have is essentially movement that is nonlinear. It's not only nonlinear but polyrhythmic. One talks about "primitive" societies of Africa. They're primitive with respect to certain logical–cognitive domains that have gained ascendancy in the West, but with respect to rhythm, they're very complicated. Western classical music is very primitive rhythmically.

JHG: In 1978, you published an editorial in the *APA Monitor* ("Neither Request nor Demand," Vol. 9 [July], p. 2) in which you noted that psychology as a whole would benefit from increased cultural pluralism and greater numbers of ethnic minorities in the field. In what ways would psychology benefit?

JMJ: As psychologists, we have been unable to admit that the characteristics of other groups are influential in the development of American society. I don't know of any statement that has general currency that argues for the cultural contribution of any group to American culture outside of what

we might think of as the Puritans. Let's take sports as an example. The "revolution" in sports that Jack Scott wrote about is a revolution occasioned by the entrance of blacks into sports. As more blacks went into sports, they brought not only their abilities but also their life styles. If you are socialized into black basketball, you play informally, for fun. It is nevertheless the case that patterns of achievement follow from individual expression and style, conspicuous skill and innovation, and ego combat. You don't have any allegiance to a coach. The coach, it is felt, wants you only to the degree that you can make money or win ball games. You also don't adhere to the myth that sport is a character-building enterprise. Black athletes have not played sports because they built character. They've played because sports were available, because they were fun, because blacks were good at them, and because they were a source of upward economic mobility and ego gratification. They didn't want any of this metaconceptual basis for their performance. Since they didn't conform to the traditional role, there was a persistent set of problems between white authority and black performers in sports. Eventually white athletes began responding in a similar way, and eventually a revolution was under way. Now it's so widespread that there's no particular racial pattern to it. If psychology could accept the input of other groups, it would be more relevant and accurate in what it says about intergroup relations and individual psychic capacities.

JHG: How can one translate what you're saying into training for psychologists? As director of the   *(Continued)*

Minority Fellowship Program, what kinds of changes do you think could be made that take into account the need for cultural pluralism?

JMJ: It's partially a human resources problem. I was not trained in the things I'm talking about. I was trained in cognitive dissonance theory. People study what interests them in their experience. That's all well and good. But given that psychologists have traditionally been white males, it's not surprising that there are lacunae in the knowledge that they have generated. It seems to me that one of the things you have to do is train more people who have different kinds of experiences on the assumption that they will develop research interests and approaches that will reflect that. But that's not enough, because the profession must recognize that these different perspectives are valuable to have in its journals, taught in the universities, and ultimately represented throughout the profession. It's my view that racial and cultural differences are really part of the stuff that psychology is made of. Psychology is sterile without them.

JHG: So, you're saying that racial and cultural issues are implicit in most of psychology in the first place.

JMJ: Absolutely.

JHG: You've done research on humor and sports and written a book on racism. Do you see any common thread running through these varied interests?

JMJ: The thread has emerged over time. The Puritans of New England are the dominant force in the character of America. Their culture was religiously dominated by the materialism of Calvin, a belief in economic determinism, and a belief that humanism was what man could do *here*. This ethos exalted the human spirit when it was strong and materially successful, and dominated the environment, including one's physical being. So, denial and hard work and sacrifice were very much part of that ethic. That ethic is white and is opposed to any kind of gaiety or joy. When you juxtapose that mentality with the mentality of a culture that believes in celebration, festival, religious fealty and respect and reverence for the natural order of things, what can you expect? The Puritans thought that play was only slightly worse than blacks as a thing with which to be associated. There were even laws against play. I think Freud was off target when he talked about the dominance of sex. Look at the wild boy of Aveyron. He didn't have any sexual drive, but he needed to play. Play was really more dominant. The Puritans had to somehow rationalize this act that they didn't condone. I think a lot of the philosophy of the value of athletics is in the context of work, not play. You get the development of authority, discipline, and so on, superimposed on play. And when you get a group of people who enjoy play and you put them into this authority structure, you get another conflict, a culture conflict. Again and again I find myself coming back to that kind of basic conflict between the fundamental, simple tenets of this culture and the way in which I think large segments of the population fail to fit with them.

Gerard & Hoyt, 1974; Tajfel, Billig, Bundy, & Flament, 1971). Thus, the tendency to categorize cognitively or label something results in some emotional attachment to the category.

Despite the inevitability of categorization and the development of in-group–out-group sentiments, aren't some people more prone to overgeneralize about others and to make stereotyped judgments? In other words, aren't there personality correlates of prejudice?

PERSONALITY AND PREJUDICE: THE AUTHORITARIAN PERSONALITY

The "authoritarian personality" is a complex cluster of personality traits that tend to characterize certain highly prejudiced individuals. While Adorno, Frenkel-Brunswik, Levinson, and Sanford (1950) recognized that people prejudiced against one group, such as Jews, were not necessarily prejudiced against other groups, such as blacks or Catholics, they also believed that there was a general tendency for some people to perceive the world in a totalitarian way. On the basis of psychoanalytic theory, they proposed that the highly prejudiced, or authoritarian, individual would be characterized by a rigid adherence to middle-class values, submission to moral authority figures of the in-group, generalized hostility, and an exaggerated concern with sexuality. These traits were hypothesized to result from childhood experiences, particularly harsh and rigid parental standards of child rearing.

Adorno and his colleagues developed a scale, the F-(for Fascism) scale, to measure these general tendencies. People who scored high on the F-scale were found to be highly prejudiced, while those who scored low were considered tolerant and nonauthoritarian. In one study, Hartley (1946) found that those scoring high on the F-scale were not only intolerant of Jews and blacks, as measured by social distance scales, but also tended to be intolerant of three purely fictitious nationalities: the Wallonians, the Pirenians, and the Danerians. Knowing nothing about these groups, highly authoritarian subjects tended to view them with suspicion and animosity. This makes authoritarians highly *xenophobic*, afraid of people who are strange, unknown, or different from themselves.

The authoritarian personality studies have been heavily criticized, with respect to both the methodology of the research (Christie & Jahoda, 1954; Rokeach, 1960) and the underlying emphasis on personality as the cornerstone of prejudice (Billig, 1976; Brown, 1965). Rokeach, in particular, noted that the authoritarian was defined largely in terms of a set of beliefs and traits that were projected onto out-groups. But the *content* of those beliefs might be less important in prejudice than their *structure*. Perhaps, Rokeach

According to the theory of belief congruence, prejudice is based on belief rather than race. When people of different races share similar religious beliefs, they tend to like believers more than atheists, regardless of their race.

argued, prejudiced individuals can be characterized by the way their beliefs are organized rather than by the specific beliefs they hold. Rokeach's analysis of prejudice suggests that the highly prejudiced individual has a *closed mind,* tends to see things in a rigid fashion, and is not open to new ways of looking at things or to new information. Rokeach also argued that the authoritarian personality was conceived of as a right-wing bigot; he proposed that bigots might also exist on the left wing of the political spectrum, and both types might be characterized by a closed-minded approach to thought. To measure this closed-mindedness he developed two scales, the *dogmatism* scale and the *opinionation* scale. As Billig (1976) notes, these two scales, while representing something of an advance over the F-scale, nevertheless do not measure the purely structural aspects of beliefs, but also measure the content of beliefs. For example, one item asks whether people believe that "Communism and Catholicism have nothing in common." This is clearly not a content-free item.

A more damaging criticism of the authoritarian personality studies and the concept of dogmatism is that they seek to explain prejudice primarily on the basis of the bigot's personality, without taking into consideration the cultural and intergroup context in which these beliefs and personality characteristics develop.

There is, as a consequence, the implication that prejudice might possibly be eradicated, if authoritarians could be in some way "cured" of their irrational predilections. This implication, however, conflicts with the view that there are sound historical reasons for the development of prejudiced ideologies in particular places at particular times; similarly it conflicts with the view that outgroup prejudice is more than the product of individuals' psychological disturbances, since it is linked to fundamental social forces. (Billig, 1976, pp. 118–119)

Perhaps beliefs enter into prejudice in a somewhat different way than that proposed by Adorno et al., or in Rokeach's concept of dogmatism. Prejudice may be a consequence not only of our own beliefs or belief structures, but also of the beliefs we assume that others hold. This notion, too, was first proposed by Rokeach, and led to what is known in social psychology as the "race versus belief controversy."

RACE AND BELIEF AS CAUSES OF PREJUDICE

In a paper entitled "Two Kinds of Prejudice or One?" Rokeach, Smith, and Evans (1960) proposed that racial prejudice was not caused primarily by physical differences between whites and blacks but by the *assumption* of differences in beliefs and values. Whites, believing that blacks held different beliefs and values, tended to dislike them on the basis of this assumed discrepancy. There is some evidence (e.g., Byrne & Wong, 1962) that highly prejudiced whites do assume that blacks hold different fundamental beliefs than they.

If Rokeach and his colleagues are correct in their assertion that prejudice is not so much racial as intellectual, then a white should like a person of different race whose beliefs are congruent with his own more than a person whose race is the same but whose beliefs differ. So, if one individual were described as "a Negro who believes in God," and another as "a white who is an atheist," a religious white should prefer the first to the second individual as a friend, at least according to the *belief congruence* notion of Rokeach. And indeed there are several studies that show just such a preference, at least among college students (Anderson & Cote, 1966; Insko & Robinson, 1967; Smith, Williams, & Willis, 1967).

This intriguing notion is capable of explaining a number of instances of prejudice. If we can see that a person differs from us in one respect, such as race, it is not difficult to imagine that the person also differs in other respects, such as beliefs. But there is also a sense of comparing two incomparable characteristics in these studies, like apples and oranges. As noted by Kidder and Stewart (1975), some beliefs are important and others trivial. How much of a belief difference is equivalent to a skin color difference? How do we equate the two to determine which is the more potent determinant of prejudice? Especially since the very concept of race is unclear (Montagu, 1965), there may be no way to know whether race or belief is the *more* important cause of prejudice. Some kinds of evaluations of others may be determined by belief congruence, but others may not be. When dealing with intimate acceptance of others, such as the likelihood of falling in love with them, then race becomes more relevant than belief (Stein, Hardyck, & Smith, 1965; Triandis & Davis, 1965; Triandis & Triandis, 1960).

Table 10.1.
Male and Female Stereotypes in England,
Ireland, and the United States

Males		
Active	Daring	Rational
Adventurous	Dominant	Reckless
Aggressive	Enterprising	Robust
Assertive	Forceful	Rude
Autocratic	Handsome	Severe
Boastful	Humorous	Stern
Coarse	Inventive	Strong
Confident	Lazy	Tough
Courageous	Logical	Unemotional
Cruel	Masculine	Unexcitable

Females		
Affectionate	Fussy	Submissive
Appreciative	Gentle	Sympathetic
Attractive	High-strung	Talkative
Changeable	Mild	Timid
Dreamy	Nagging	Warm
Emotional	Poised	Whiny
Excitable	Sensitive	Worrying
Feminine	Soft-hearted	
Frivolous	Sophisticated	

NOTE: The adjectives used to describe males and females were chosen by both male and female subjects.

Adapted from Williams, Giles, Edwards, Best, & Daws (1977).

Table 10.2.
Stereotypes of Three Generations of College Students

	D. Katz and Braly Study (1933)		Gilbert Study (1951)		Karlins et al. Study (1969)	
Americans						
	Industrious	48	Materialistic	37	Materialistic	67
	Intelligent	47	Intelligent	32	Ambitious	42
	Materialistic	33	Industrious	30	Pleasure-loving	28
	Ambitious	33	Pleasure-loving	27	Industrious	23
	Progressive	27	Individualistic	26	Intelligent	20
	Favorableness	.99		.86		.49
Jews						
	Shrewd	79	Shrewd	47	Ambitious	48
	Mercenary	49	Intelligent	37	Materialistic	46
	Industrious	48	Industrious	29	Intelligent	37
	Grasping	34	Mercenary	28	Industrious	33
	Intelligent	29	Ambitious	28	Shrewd	30
	Favorableness	.24		.45		.66
Negroes						
	Superstitious	84	Superstitious	41	Musical	47
	Lazy	75	Musical	33	Happy-go-lucky	27
	Happy-go-lucky	38	Lazy	31	Lazy	26
	Ignorant	38	Ignorant	24	Pleasure-loving	26
	Musical	26	Pleasure-loving	19	Ostentatious	25
	Favorableness	−.70		−.37		.07

NOTE: Numbers represent percent of students checking the trait. Favorableness is based on a scale from −2 to +2. Adapted from Karlins, Coffman, and Walters (1969).

STEREOTYPES

Although in-group members may sometimes assume erroneously that out-group members hold different beliefs than they, some real differences in beliefs often do exist between groups. In the case of prejudice, however, these differences are exaggerated or given a prominence unwarranted by an objective assessment of the out-group. Some stereotypes are fabricated out of whole cloth by in-group members—such as the notion that Jews are heavily involved in the banking industry—but others are distortions of some attribute possessed by the group. There is sometimes considerable agreement among in-group members about the traits of minorities, and at other times little agreement about their characteristics (except that whatever traits they possess are at the least undesirable) (see Tables 10.1 and 10.2).

Which traits of a group will result in stereotypes? According to Campbell (1967), "The greater the real difference between groups on any particular custom, detail of physical appearance, or item of material culture, the more likely it is that that feature will appear in the stereotyped imagery each group has of the other" (p. 821). Does this mean there is "a grain of truth" in all stereotypes (see Triandis & Vassiliou, 1967)? Of course not. It means only that stereotypes may contain some actual differences in distorted form, though other aspects of a stereotype may be totally fabricated.

The distinctiveness of a trait is apt to influence its prominence in both the perception of others (Bochner & Ohsako, 1977) and in self-perception (McGuire & Padawer-Singer, 1976). If a person is the only male in an otherwise all-female household, then masculinity will become a central aspect of his self-concept, since it is this trait that sets him apart from others. In a study by Bochner and Ohsako, Japanese, Australian, and Hawaiian-Japanese subjects were shown a slide depicting either a Japanese or a Caucasian couple. They were asked to describe ways in which the two people in the slide were similar. The Japanese subjects tended to describe the Caucasian, but not the Japanese, couple in terms of race; the Australians described the Japanese, but not the Caucasian, couple in terms of race; and the Hawaiian-Japanese described both couples in ethnic terms.

Ehrlich (1973) presents nearly 125 words taken from the literature on stereotypes that have been used to portray various minority groups. It is interesting to note that many of these words, and those appearing in Tables 10.1 and 10.2 as well, can be divided into roughly three groups on the basis of the Freudian notion of fixation and projection (see Chapter 3). Several words appear to represent oral traits (e.g., "loud," "boisterous"); several anal traits (such as "dirty," "lazy"); and some sexual traits ("pleasure-loving," "over-sexed"). It may be, as Adorno et al. proposed in their study of the authoritarian personality, that one of the bases for stereotypes is the projection of potentially threatening self-attributes onto others. Although this notion is not easily tested, and although there is not generally much empirical support for a psychoanalytic interpretation of prejudice (e.g., I. E. Alexander & Blackman, 1957), it is an intriguing idea that has yet to be refuted. How else are we to account for the fact that not only American college students, but also Japanese, Greeks, Germans, and others, employ similar traits to characterize out-groups? Within a single culture, we could easily explain similarities in stereotypes on the basis of common exposure to mass media and propaganda. But this could hardly explain why, for example, the Japanese stereotype the Burakumin as dirty and lazy.

Is the tendency to stereotype out-groups universal? Do all groups develop antagonisms toward and stereotypes of other groups? According to a thorough review of the literature in anthropology by LeVine and Campbell (1972), the "ethnocentric syndrome" is not universal. They note cases in which individuals have multiple group membership and belong to both the in- and out-groups. Conjoint membership prevents stereotyping. There are also cases in which out-groups serve as reference groups, in which in-group feelings are aroused only under very special circumstances, and in which various ethnic groups all coexist as positive reference groups. Thus, the tendency to stereotype out-groups does not seem to be universal; however, it does appear to be the norm.

THE SCAPEGOAT HYPOTHESIS: FRUSTRATION AND DISPLACED AGGRESSION

One of the most popular explanations for the development of discrimination against minorities is the scapegoat hypothesis. According to this notion, severe parental discipline for a child's aggression actually increases the child's tendency to aggress. Because the child has learned that he or she will be severely punished for being aggressive toward anyone in the in-group, such as members of the family, the aggression is *displaced* from the original source of frustration onto out-group members (N. E. Miller & Bugelski, 1948). Suppose that Raymond Syst has learned that he will be punished for aggressing against his little sister. When he is frustrated by his sister, for example, by having to share his toys with her, he is tempted to aggress against her, but fears the consequences of such aggression. He may then choose a substitute target, a *scapegoat*. This scapegoat may be anyone whom he can aggress against without eliciting punishment from his parents, and very often this substitute target is a member of a minority group. Thus, Ray's frustration caused by his sister is now displaced onto someone else.

We have already seen (Chapter 8) that a simple causal link between frustration and aggression does not exist. One modification has it that frustration will cause aggression only when a "suitable" target is present. Minority groups often are perceived as "suitable targets" of aggression, and so minorities may serve as scapegoats for the frustrations of the majority. This is certainly a plausible explanation for much anti-Semitism, anti-Catholicism, and racism.

In an early test of the displacement hypothesis, Hovland and Sears (1940) found that the frequency of lynchings in the South between 1882 and 1930 correlated significantly with economic indices such as the value of cotton. When the per acre value of cotton declined, lynchings increased. Thus, according to Hovland and Sears, economic frustrations were displaced onto blacks.

Overall, the evidence with respect to the scapegoat hypothesis is inconclusive. There are studies that suggest frustration arouses a tendency to aggress, but fear of punishment leads to the displacement of that aggression onto an "acceptable" target (L. Berkowitz & Green, 1962; Cowen, Landes, & Schaet, 1959). Some research, however, has failed to find evidence of displaced aggression toward a third party (e.g., Stagner & Congdon, 1955). More crucial than the conflicting evidence is the fact that the scapegoat hypothesis overlooks several important issues and is not so much incorrect as incomplete. For example, why are certain groups chosen as scapegoats rather than others? Could we have predicted conflict between French- and Flemish-speaking Belgians rather than between French- and German-speaking Swiss? And it is not always a minority that is the target of discrimination. Jews, for example, may harbor prejudices toward gentiles, blacks toward whites, and women toward men. Are these examples of scapegoating, too? Some intergroup conflict is realistic and represents, not displacement, but antagonism toward the source of one's frustrations. The scapegoat hypothesis ignores the social aspects of prejudice and conflict. The point is not that a frustrated *individual* displaces aggression onto an individual scapegoat, but that there is large-scale intergroup conflict. Scapegoaters develop a group norm that deems certain out-groups appropriate targets of prejudice, discrimination, and violence. It makes little difference, then, if minority group member A or member B is attacked; the victim is seen as representative or symbolic of the group. So, the scapegoats themselves are not responded to as individuals but as members of a group. This intergroup character of conflict is overlooked by the scapegoat hypothesis.

LEARNING AND PREJUDICE

Social psychology has tended to treat prejudice as an attitude; that is, as something personal and individual, acquired in the same way as other attitudes. While there is some merit to this position, I have chosen to treat prejudice as a social norm, acquired from the members of one's reference groups. In this broader view, it is easier to explain why so many people in a culture share similar prejudices. But while I prefer to think of prejudice as a group phenomenon, it is also true that individuals carry prejudices around with them and that these prejudices, even though widely shared by others in the individual's group, *can* be viewed as attitudes. Within this more limited, attitudinal framework, it is easy to discuss some of the origins of prejudice. As we have seen in the chapter on socialization (Chapter 3), individuals acquire attitudes and other behavioral dispositions from the *pta* (parents, teachers, associates). This learning may occur through a variety of mechanisms, from classical and operant conditioning, to imitation and modeling, effects of past experience, and exploration and mastery of the environment.

In this section, prejudice is treated as a learned response or a

If prejudice is a learned response, so is friendship— and it's hard to maintain negative stereotypes about your friends.

learned attitude. The people responsible for teaching prejudice have had their own attitudes and behaviors shaped by still other individuals and groups. Thus, the socializing agents share their prejudices with other members of their reference groups and pass these prejudices along to others. While children thus acquire prejudices in the same way they acquire other attitudes and dispositions, these particular responses are widely shared by the socializing agents' reference groups.

A simple demonstration of classical conditioning and attitudes was performed by Staats and Staats (1957). College students were exposed to the names of various nationalities on a screen (such as Swedish, Italian, Dutch). Soon after one of these names appeared, a word was read aloud. For two of the nationalities, the words were always positive or always negative (words such as "happy," "sacred," or "ugly," "failure"). For the remaining nationalities, the words were neutral. Each nationality was exposed 18 times, and 18 different words were read for each. Following exposure to these stimuli, the students were asked to indicate how pleasant or unpleasant they found each nationality. When students saw the nationality "Swedish" paired with positive words, they rated "Swedish" more favorably than they rated "Dutch." When "Swedish" was paired with negative words, they rated it less favorably than "Dutch."

While some critics have argued that subjects cannot remain unaware of the purpose of such an experiment, there is evidence that classical conditioning procedures are capable, for whatever reason, of instilling positive or negative attitudes toward previously neutral groups (Zanna, Kiesler, & Pilkonis, 1970).

Operant conditioning procedures, too, may culminate in favorable or unfavorable attitudes toward groups. A person may be rewarded or punished for associating with or expressing an attitude toward a member of a particular group, and so may repeat or fail to repeat similar expressions or behaviors. Social learning theory also is applicable to the development of prejudice. Children who identify with adults are apt to internalize the prejudices of those adults, particularly parents and teachers. Even without reinforcement, children tend to acquire the prejudices of those around them.

There are more subtle ways in which attitudes and prejudices may be conveyed. We may learn implicit views of others by being exposed to them in various situations. For example, without expressly stating that women are incompetent to engage in professional careers, textbooks that never show women in professional roles are implicitly suggesting a certain view of women. There are a great many ways in which such implicit attitudes may be expressed. Ethnic humor is one.

ETHNIC HUMOR—IT ISN'T FUNNY

Let me be the first to introduce you to East Frisian jokes. "Why does it take 22 East Frisians to hammer in a nail?" "One to hold the hammer, one to hold the nail, and 20 to shove the wall toward the nail." Another one? "Have you heard about the East Frisian jigsaw puzzle? One piece." Not very funny, eh? Perhaps if you could substitute one of the following groups for East Frisians you would enjoy the jokes more:

Arabs	Homosexuals	Psychiatrists
Atheists	Irishmen	Puerto Ricans
Basques	Italians	Republicans
Blacks	Jews	Russians
Catholics	Men	Scientists
Communists	Mexicans	Scotsmen
Cubans	New Yorkers	Slavs
Democrats	Nuns	Sophomores
Englishmen	Poles	Turks
Frenchmen	Politicians	WASPs
Gentiles	Priests	Women
Greeks	Professors	

An acquaintance of mine from Alabama served in Poland for seven years with the U.S. State Department. His children, now 10 and 12, went to Polish schools, having learned the language with the ease of the very young. Now back in Virginia, the two children, despite their pure Anglo-Saxon Baptist features, are the constant object of playground abuse. Children shout "goulash!" at them. They are called "Hunky." They are the constant butt of "dumb Polack" jokes. On one occasion when the oldest lad could bear the humiliation no longer, he had an inspiration. He turned on those who were taunting him with a challenge: "Can you speak Polish?" The others fell silent and then he hit them: "How does it feel to be dumber than a Polack?"

Too many Americans make a joke out of Polish jokes. They expect people of Slavic descent (all of whom suffer under these jokes; no one can tell us apart) to take these jokes as funny, to show our own sense of humor, gracefully to laugh at ourselves. If mere graciousness were at stake, we could easily oblige.

The intent of Polish jokes, however, is not humor alone. Should blacks laugh at nigger jokes? There are mean anti-Semitic jokes no Jew or Arab ought to tolerate. Not all humor is humor; different genera require different responses.

THE SHARED BARBS

Ethnic humor is one of the great resources of this nation. There are forms of laughing at oneself and at others, usually based on the daily absurdities of mutual noncomprehension or double meaning. These are truly amusing, probably the most amusing jokes in the American repertoire. In this humor, all ethnic groups are equal; the barbs are shared by everybody at the same time.

But there is a second genus of ethnic joke. It does not gain its force from that double understanding of the same word or doubly misapprehended event that characterizes multi-cultural perception. It is based on demeaning the character of one ethnic group, in line with a stereotype, and its function is to make the majority feel superior to the minority. Told in the presence

(Continued)

THE STING OF POLISH JOKES

by Michael Novak*

*Novak, a philosopher and writer, is the author of The joy of sports.

In the event that you are unfamiliar with East Frisians, they reside in West Germany, and jokes such as the above are widely circulated about them in that country (The New York Times, 1973). What we think of as ethnic humor is not new and is not exclusively American. The type of humor we now associate with the Polish joke can be traced to the "sick jokes" of the 1950s and early 1960s, and the rise of black comedians, such as Dick Gregory, in the 1960s. In fact, it can be traced to the traveling Commedia dell'Arte of the Italian Renaissance, where stereotypes of various professions and nationalities were regularly spoofed.

THE STING OF POLISH JOKES

Michael Novak
(Continued)

of the minority, these jokes further require those who are their butt to acquiesce in their own humiliation, to laugh obediently, to accept their ascribed inferiority. (Nudging elbow: "No offense, friend. Only a joke.") The tactic is structurally the same as those techniques that force inmates to embrace their own degradation. Rage is not permitted. One must stand there helplessly and acquiesce.

Southern and Eastern Europeans in the United States are subject to the last respectable bigotry. (Let me modify that: anti-German jokes, the heritage of two world wars, are still so legitimate that even Lufthansa Airlines and other German firms are forced to play upon them in their advertising.) Such bigotry flourishes for "unofficial" minorities, while "official" minorities are protected.

THE DOUBLE BIND

Recently, in Pennsylvania, I saw a huge, newly painted garbage truck. On its front bumper in large letters was printed: POLISH CAMPER. Suppose the words had been: NIGGER CAMPER or JEWISH CAMPER? Liberal organizations would certainly have protested.

So deep is the Anglo-American tradition of disdain for Eastern Europeans, however, so explicit have been the texts of the past, and so deep is ignorance even among highly educated people of cultures they never studied in school, that many Americans do not realize the systematic structure of the stereotype Eastern Europeans confront.

Nor do they suspect the double bind—outraged justice and deeply internalized self-contempt—that the constant pressure of ugly jokes and stereotypes imposes. Most of those of us who are children of Eastern European Christian immigrants know we are the children of peasants. We do not have in our family experience many models of learning, status and public grace. We have a sufficient sense of our modest origins. The sting of Polish jokes is that they make our deepest self-doubts public. They keep us in our place. They canonize a caste from which many see no escape. Land of opportunity?

Figures as diverse as George Blanda, Sen. Edmund Muskie and Bobby Vinton have voiced their anger at Polish jokes that even they

Responses to ethnic jokes may well reflect the listener's attitude toward the group being derided. If you have no idea who East Frisians are, then there is little or no humor to be found in the above jokes. However, if you are familiar with the group being ridiculed, your response to the jokes will more likely be positive if you dislike the group than if it is one toward which you hold favorable attitudes. This attitudinal component of humor can best be seen in terms of Heider's (1958) balance model. If you dislike Group O and a joke implies something negative about Group O, then you will tend to appreciate the joke (see Goldstein, 1976).

There appears to be an exception to the general balance model are asked to tolerate. Blanda tried to explain why he sympathizes so much with young black kids: "I've heard 'dumb Polack' as often as they've heard the word 'nigger.' . . ."

Paul Wrobel, a brilliant young anthropologist who is now working in Detroit, has shown from many hundreds of hours of inquiry in one Polish-American neighborhood how deeply the public stereotype has been internalized by many Polish-Americans. When a news dispatch carried his findings back to Detroit from the scholarly meeting in Boston where he presented them, the Detroit papers received a most touching deluge of letters from sad and hurt Polish-Americans. Their own self-image was exactly as he described: poignantly aware of being stigmatized as dull, dumb, and stolid, and painfully aware of how unfair that image is, they could hardly bear to have the subject discussed. One cannot read these letters without piercing recognition and dismay.

THE LAST LAUGH

One woman wrote that the news stories based on Wrobel's study "added to the already anti-Polish climate." A man declared that "the damage inflicted upon Polish-American boys was devastating." A mother wrote: "We were blessed with a good sense of humor but we feel [these stories] will stir up a hornet's nest."

Cannot some major center of learning conduct a study of how much damage is done to the psyches of people constantly stereotyped in public? Can't the American Civil Liberties Union and a wide range of anti-defamation societies join in protests to the magazines, television channels and gatherings of (otherwise) sophisticated people who tell ethnic jokes of the inherently demeaning kind? We don't need Supreme Court decisions, perhaps, but we do need a basic sense of public fairness. Eastern Europeans cannot halt Polish jokes alone. The help of all is required.

This is supposed to be a nation of civility toward all, bigotry toward none. It is not. But when the laughter rings, it rings for thee.

interpretation of intergroup humor and that is humor that is directed against one's own group. When we laugh at a derogatory joke about our own presumably positive reference group, the predictions made on the basis of balance theory no longer hold. For example, there are any number of jokes about Jews told most often by Jews. Many of these jokes emphasize or exaggerate the stereotypes of the Jew prevalent among non-Jews at that historical moment. Some jokes dramatize the stereotype of the overbearing Jewish mother.

Mrs. Cohen was bursting with pride. "Did you hear about my son, Louie?" she asked Mrs. Greenblatt.

"No, what's with your son, Louie?"
"He's going to a psychiatrist. Twice a week."
"Is that good?"
*"Is that good? Of course, it's good. Forty dollars an hour he pays.
And all he talks about is me!"*

Other jokes satirize the philosophical outlook on life common among
Talmudic scholars.

Schwartz and Goldberg were in a cafeteria, drinking tea.
*Schwartz studied his cup and said with a sigh, "Ah, my friend, life
is like a cup of tea."*
*Goldberg considered this for a moment and said, "But why is life
like a cup of tea?"*
And Schwartz replied, "How should I know? Am I a philosopher?"

What purposes might be served by directing stereotypic jokes
against one's own group? There are several possibilities. One is to
strengthen in-group ties, to increase feelings of solidarity by saying,
in effect, that this is how others see us. We have already seen that
threats from out-groups strengthen in-group cohesiveness. Ethnic
jokes may remind people that they are threatened by out-groups. A
second purpose of self-directed group humor may be for the jokester
to dissociate him or herself from these stereotypes. For example, if
Jews laugh at an anti-Semitic joke, they may be indicating by their
approval that they are unlike the Jews depicted in that joke. While
they may hold Jews in high esteem generally, they may, at the same
time, dislike the stereotypic Jew portrayed in the joke. So laughter
at derogatory jokes about one's own group may be a means of
indicating that the jokes deal with a particular subgroup and these
members of the group are to be perceived negatively.

Some ethnic humor is less an attack on a group than a means for
people to overcome some real or imagined obstacle. Laughter at
some of these self-disparaging jokes may be a way of affirming
ourselves, of saying that our predicaments are absurd. Through an
ethnic joke, we may step back to look at ourselves from a distance.
This use of humor to objectify and thus make laughable our faults
and predicaments may explain why humor is so often found in the
most unlikely places, in prisons and concentration camps, during
natural disasters, and wherever people undergo stress.

If telling ethnic jokes is an indication of the joker's attitude toward
the ethnic group, and if such humor also tells us something about
the audience's attitude, it does not tell us very much about what it
means to be the target of such humor when told by an out-group
member. As social psychologists, we know surprisingly little of what
it means to be the victim of prejudice. Most of what we do know has
come from novels, biographies, and autobiographies of minority

group members in various cultures. The study of the consequences of discrimination for its victims is gradually being addressed by social scientists (Dion & Earn, 1975; Harrison, 1974).

BEING A VICTIM OF PREJUDICE

There are various accounts of people who suddenly find themselves the targets of prejudice and who, for the first time, must confront bigotry. There is the classic case of John Howard Griffin (1961), who, to experience what it was like to be black in this country, had the color of his skin changed. One of the consequences of prejudice for the victim is the toll it takes on the victim's concept of self. This is seen in studies of racial preference among black children and in some of the notions of women's achievement motivation.

Racial Preference Studies Research initiated by Kenneth B. Clark and Mamie Clark in the 1930s (1939, 1950) showed that, as early as age three or four, black children were conscious of race and tended to hold many of the prejudices of the white majority. In particular, black children showed a preference for playing with white, as opposed to black, dolls.

This phenomenon was frequently explained in psychoanalytic terms as *identification with the aggressor* (Bettelheim, 1943; Maliver, 1965; Milner, 1973). Black children were assumed to identify with whites and to share their views of blacks, in part, because whites forced this view on blacks and, in part, because blacks were socially and economically dependent on whites (Maliver, 1965). A similar phenomenon has been observed among Jews (Bettelheim, 1943; Lewin, 1941; Sarnoff, 1951) and women.

Of course, it is possible to explain this "identification" not in terms of personality dynamics and dependencies, but more simply in terms of the dominant social norms of the culture (cf. R. Epstein & Komorita, 1966). Blacks and whites in the United States have been exposed repeatedly to negative stereotypes of blacks. These stereotypes can be found not only among the majority of the population in everyday social situations, but also in textbooks, the entertainment media, humor, news reports, and so on (Fiske, 1978; FitzGerald, 1979).

As the black power movement gained force in the 1960s, and anti-discrimination legislation was passed and enforced, black children began to prefer black dolls to white dolls (e.g., Crooks, 1970; Y. M. Epstein, Krupat, & Obudho, 1976; J. H. Greenwald & Oppenheim, 1968; Hraba & Grant, 1970; Teplin, 1977; Ward & Braun, 1972).

Sexism and Some of Its Consequences A similar change in self-identity has occurred among women. Prior to the women's movement, women's views of themselves were largely imposed by men. It was actually the norms and values of men that women used to evaluate themselves. In this regard, some women were as prejudiced against women as were men (P. A. Goldberg, 1968). This changed when there was a change in reference group. At first, a few women redefined and refocused several aspects of womanhood. The women's movement said, in effect, that women should develop their own norms and standards and not rely on those of men for self-evaluation. Many women began to look anew at their roles and identities from the point of view of women's experiences rather than men's. A change in reference group led to a number of fundamental changes in attitudes, values, and behavior.

One effect of this change in reference group is that it deprives the former reference group of some of its social power. In traditional majority–minority group settings, the minority uses the majority as a reference group, adopting its values and norms. This type of identification gives the majority group power over the minority. Once the minority begins to define norms and standards for itself, the majority loses some of this identification power. This may be one reason men so often resist the women's movement: It reduces their social power.

It is easy to document the prejudices against women in contemporary Western society: for example, they are paid less than men for identical work and are underrepresented in the most prestigious professions. I recall that Shirley Chisholm, when she represented a district in New York in the U.S. Congress, remarked that she had encountered more obstacles in her career as a woman than as a black. Research by social psychologists also demonstrates the relatively low esteem accorded women when they violate traditional sex roles. When college students were told that more and more women would enter five high-status professions, their ratings of prestige and desirability for those professions decreased (Touhey, 1974). This was true of both female and male students.

The effects of prejudice on the victim can be seen quite clearly in what has been labeled "fear of success" by Matina Horner (1970). When responding to the sentence, "After first-term finals, Ann finds herself at the top of her medical school class," females, as well as males, tend to view Ann as guilt-ridden, socially rejected, and unfeminine (Monahan, Kuhn, & Shaver, 1974). Since males view successful women as being anxious and possessing other negative traits to at least the same extent as other females, these findings probably do not represent a fear of success among women. Rather, they seem to indicate that negative characteristics will be attributed to anyone who violates widely accepted sex-role expectations (see also Weitz, 1977). If women attributed these negative traits to successful women and men did not, we might say that women

*"Women are helpless people
who can't fix machines."
These women decided to
fight the negative stereotype
and get better-paying jobs by
training to become auto
mechanics.*

demonstrated a fear of succeeding. But since men, too, attribute
negative characteristics to successful women, it may be simply that
violating a social norm leads to negative stereotyping. Regardless of
the underlying explanation, both males and females tend to view
women who succeed at traditionally masculine tasks in negative
terms. Women who are successful at masculine tasks are viewed not
only as less happy than other women, but also as less skillful than
successful men (Deaux & Emswiller, 1974). While men who succeed
are generally viewed as skillful, women who succeed are seen as
lucky (see also Feather & Simon, 1975). In all these studies, women
and men share a common framework—that certain tasks are unfeminine, that to succeed in such tasks is to invite psychological and

social turmoil, and so on. Just as there has been a reversal in color preference of dolls by black youngsters, we may soon find that women, when given a choice, do not choose dolls at all.

REDUCING PREJUDICE

CAN SOCIAL PSYCHOLOGY HELP?

Billig (1976) has argued that, regardless of how much we learn about attitudes, personality, small-group processes, and individual psychology, we will never be able to understand and prevent prejudice and discrimination with these tools alone. After finding that many southerners were prejudiced against blacks but did not score high on the F-scale, Prothro (1952, p. 108) remarked, "It would seem from these results that the problem of 'the American dilemma' cannot be solved by approaching it from the level of personality dynamics alone. Situational, historical, and cultural factors appear to be of considerable, perhaps major, import." This conclusion was reached also by Lewin (1948), who argued that prejudice must be seen in a larger social–political–historical–economic context.

If this argument is correct, prejudice and discrimination should change whenever the larger social–political–historical–economic context changes. This does not often appear to happen (Hampel & Krupp, 1977). But, we will probably not be able to alter dramatically the extent or structure of prejudice based only on a knowledge of social psychological principles. There is considerable evidence, for example, that even within the recent history of the United States, patterns of prejudice and discriminatory behavior have changed, and such changes are probably not due to any increase in our knowledge of attitudes, personality, small-group processes, or fundamental psychological phenomena. In many ways, the changes were instigated by changes in the legal system, such as Supreme Court decisions and court-ordered desegregation and sex-discrimination rulings. Since I am a social psychologist, I will focus here on social and psychological aspects of prejudice reduction, while acknowledging the possibility that this larger historical–political–economic context plays an important role in intergroup relations.

THE CONTACT HYPOTHESIS

One of the most persistent social psychological ideas for the reduction of intergroup conflict is contact between the antagonistic groups (G. W. Allport, 1954; Deutsch & Collins, 1951; Lewin, 1948; MacKenzie, 1948; F. T. Smith, 1943; Wilner, Walkley, & Cook, 1952). For example, F. T. Smith (1943) had graduate students spend two successive weekends in Harlem, living and socializing with blacks at their invitation. Compared with students unable to attend the weekends, those who took part in the program showed increased favorability in their attitudes toward blacks.

As Allport (1954, p. 254) notes, this and similar studies do "not prove that every visit to Chinatown, Harlem, or Little Italy will result in lessened prejudice Many people start with stereotypes, and the tourist mode of contact is unlikely to change them." In other words, it is the *nature of the contact* rather than the mere fact of contact that is of crucial importance in changing attitudes. Despite evidence that any contact is better than none in altering prejudices (e.g., Clement, Gardner, & Smythe, 1977), *equal-status contact* in nonthreatening settings is more effective in reducing prejudice than inequitable contact (Amir, 1969; Triandis & Vassiliou, 1967; Tsukashima & Montero, 1976). And *mutual cooperation* among members of conflicting groups is even better.

There may be some tasks that force members from antagonistic groups to work together. These are called *superordinate goals* by Sherif et al. (1961). In their study of boys at a summer camp, Sherif and his colleagues found that the introduction of a series of superordinate goals reduced fighting and hostility between two groups of campers. The groups were required to work together to restore the camp's water supply for their mutual benefit, and to cooperate in order to see a movie. In other studies (e.g., Eaton & Clore, 1975; Worchel, Andreoli, & Folger, 1977), mutual cooperation also reduced intergroup conflict. In a study at a recently desegregated school, liking toward former out-group members increased when black children and white children were given tasks that required mutual cooperation for successful completion (Aronson, Blaney, Sikes, Stephan, & Snapp, 1975). These studies demonstrate that when people are forced by circumstances to cooperate on a task that is mutually beneficial, they tend to form a new in-group and develop positive sentiments toward one another that gradually replace the antagonisms built up by prior in-group –out-group distinctions.

It is not only with regard to children or to interracial situations that the contact hypothesis receives empirical support. Exchange students and foreign business executives also show increased tolerance with increased contact (e.g., Triandis & Vassiliou, 1967).

The contact hypothesis is not based so much on the individual's personality or even on individual attitudes undergoing change. It is based on the development of new group identities and in-group sentiments, and is thus a basically social psychological hypothesis of intergroup conflict reduction.

Nevertheless, some people will, as Allport noted, persist in stereotypically thinking about others and may manage to keep their prejudices pretty much intact despite frequent contact with others.

Is there any hope for such people? Perhaps a technique developed by Triandis and his colleagues (Triandis, 1977) might help to break down stereotypic images. The technique is called the *culture assimilator* and was developed for use by Peace Corps volunteers, students, and business people going to new cultures for the first time.

THE CULTURE ASSIMILATOR

One of the most difficult problems for members of different groups is to "speak the same language," to use the same frame of reference when responding to each other. Misunderstandings and miscommunications commonly occur because each person is dealing with a different set of assumptions, experiences, and expectations.

An illustration of the culture assimilator prepared by Slobodin, Collins, Crayton, Feldman, Jaccard, Rissman, and Weldon (1972) is given below. This version was used to train white supervisors of black hard-core unemployed males.

On page 205–1, the following incident appears:

Several hard-core unemployed Blacks had been hired by Jones Tool & Die Company. Mac Grove was one of the supervisors who was supposed to train the Blacks in the procedures of their new jobs. After he had explained the use of one machine, he asked:

"Are there any questions?"

One of the Black workers replied: "Yes, Mr. Grove . . . " At which time Mac interrupted, saying: "Oh, call me Mac. Everybody does."

Mutual cooperation tends to reduce intergroup conflict. These boys are united in their team efforts to win the tug of war, and nothing else matters right now.

The group moved on to another machine and Mac explained its function. He was surprised when one of the other Black workers again addressed him as Mr. Grove.

On page 205–2, we find the following:

Why did the Black workers call him Mr. Grove?
1. They thought Whites in positions of authority expect to be called Mr. by Blacks.

> *Please go to page 205–3.*

2. They felt that Mr. was more appropriate under the circumstances.

> *Please go to page 205–4.*

3. They didn't feel comfortable about calling a White by his first name.

> *Please go to page 205–5.*

4. They didn't believe that Mac really wanted to be called Mac. . . .

> *Please go to page 205–6.*

The people using the assimilator would turn to the page indicated after they selected the answer they felt most correct and would get the following feedback:

On page 205–3:

You selected 1: They thought Whites in positions of authority expect to be called Mr. by Blacks.
While this might be true, it doesn't explain why they continued to call him Mr. after he told them to call him Mac.

> *Please go back to page 205–1.*

On page 205–4:

You selected 2: They felt that Mr. was more appropriate under the circumstances.
Yes. Our data indicate that hard-core unemployed Blacks feel that formal speech indicates mutual respect and provides status. They also feel that establishing this mutual respect indicates friendship and trust. It is a good thing to keep in mind that hard-core unemployed Blacks may prefer the more formal use of Mr. until they have established a good relationship with another person. They may prefer to be called Mr. themselves, at first. . . .

> *Please go to page 206.*

On page 205–5:

You selected 3: They didn't feel comfortable about calling a White by his first name.
This is not necessarily true. Hard-core Blacks call friends, White or

Black, by their first names. However, they may have felt uncomfortable about calling the foreman Mac until they got to know him better.

Please go back to page 205–1.

On page 205–6:

You selected 4: They didn't believe that Mac really wanted to be called Mac. . . .

This is not the best answer. There is no evidence given in the incident to assume this.

Please go back to page 205–1.

Following the correct completion of each section, the person using the assimilator is provided with a summary of the principles covered in that section.

As Triandis (1977) notes, the culture assimilator can provide various kinds of training that reward correct judgments about another group's or culture's expectations. In general, the culture assimilator enables us to view the world from the point of view of another person. This facilitates understanding of the person's behavior and makes cooperative social interaction more likely (Landis, Day, McGrew, Thomas, & Miller, 1976).

The culture assimilator, or a similar type of cognitive training, might, when used in conjunction with equal-status contact, be a significant method of reducing prejudice and stereotypic thinking. Note that the assimilator is generally used *before* contact actually takes place. This should make whatever contact does occur less likely to be distorted or unpleasant for the participants.

REDUCING OTHER TYPES OF INTERGROUP CONFLICT

Possibly the most concrete contribution of social psychology to human welfare was the important role it played in the 1954 Supreme Court decision on desegregation (see Meltzer, Note 4). Social psychological research, particularly that by Clark and Clark, which showed that black children preferred white to black dolls, was especially influential. While social psychology may have influenced society in this rather indirect way, there are also some specific interventions designed to produce immediate and beneficial results in a political context.

An example of the application of social psychology to the political domain is the *conflict resolution workshop* (Doob, 1970; Doob & Foltz, 1973; Kelman & Cohen, 1976). In such workshops, the conflicting parties are brought together by a third party in an effort to increase

376   INTERGROUP RELATIONS: PREJUDICE, CONFLICT, AND COOPERATION

communication and understanding that will eventually lead to a resolution of the conflict.

A preliminary study of the effectiveness of such a workshop was conducted by Cohen, Kelman, Miller, and Smith (1977). Israeli and Palestinian men were brought together in a two-day workshop to discuss the Middle East conflict. The third party, whose role was to foster communication, employed theoretical ideas taken from the literature on small-group research, social influence, theories of nationalism, and conflict resolution.

Each party to the conflict was first met in preworkshop sessions to develop some cohesion and internal structure that might later facilitate cooperative problem-solving. These sessions provided the third party with important information about the perceptions of the conflicting parties and increased the participants' commitment to the workshop. In the particular workshop studied by S. P. Cohen et al., discussion quickly centered on the willingness of the Israelis to recognize the legitimacy of Palestinian nationalism. The Israelis were quite willing to concede this point, and when asked whether they would sign a statement to that effect, agreed to do so. The remainder of the workshop was devoted to the drawing up of a document to be signed by the Israelis and Palestinians. By the time the precise wording of the document was agreed upon, the time allotted to the workshop had expired.

As the authors note, the document was a relatively minor point to the Israelis, but of major importance to the Palestinians. Because it was unimportant to one party, the authors see its signing as a symbolic act.

Mistrust and hostility may be at such a profound level that symbolic acts have a much greater significance than is usually supposed. Furthermore, each side in a conflict has difficulty assessing the depth of its adversary's emotional commitment to specific symbols and perceptions. Paradoxically, this means that each party may have sources of power and influence over the other side of which it is unaware. It may have resources that the other side desperately wants but which are considered of little or no value to the possessor. . . . One potentially creative contribution of problem-solving workshops is in identifying symbolic gestures that are not very costly to the initiator but are ideologically significant to the recipient." (pp. 181–182)

All participants believed the workshop to be beneficial and felt that further progress would have been made had there been time to continue.

In this study, the participants were not military or political leaders. Such workshops are better conducted with those who have decision-making capabilities. Nevertheless, the change in attitudes and reduction in polarization of positions among the participants may have indirect effects in that the participants may try to influence others in positions of power.

Summary

Prejudice is an invalid negative evaluation of a group or of its members on the basis of their membership in the group. While it is customary to view prejudice as an attitude, with cognitive (stereotypes), affective (prejudicial feelings), and behavioral (discrimination) components, the view taken here is that it is a widely shared group norm. While race and sex prejudice are used as modern examples of prejudice, all prejudices share common elements.

Stereotyped thinking often arises because of the need to categorize objects and people. Being able to place some object or person into a category simplifies our interaction with a complex physical and social environment. When this act of categorization becomes overgeneralized, we may speak of stereotypic thinking. This entails attributing some trait to the members of a category that does not serve to define the category; for example, attributing a political trait to a group of people defined by their religious belief.

Prejudice is a complex phenomenon. As such, explanations for its development and manifestation are varied. Early psychological research, based loosely on psychoanalytic theory, looked for personality types that were particularly prone to stereotyped thinking and discriminatory behavior. Foremost among the personality types associated with prejudice is the "authoritarian personality" studied by Adorno and his colleagues. The authoritarian was assumed to have had harsh standards of behavior while growing up and to have particular beliefs about morality and order in the world. Rather than stress the particular beliefs of prejudiced individuals, Rokeach stressed their style of thinking. He proposed that certain individuals were closed-minded; that their thinking was rigid and that they were not receptive to new information. He developed the dogmatism scale to measure this type of thought structure.

Rokeach also proposed that, in racial prejudice, skin color was less important than the assumption made by whites that blacks held different basic beliefs than they. The research designed to test whether race or belief was the major determinant of racial prejudice led to the conclusion that the two were not really comparable and the question not really answerable. Some beliefs are important and some not; sometimes race is a relevant dimension and sometimes it is not.

Minority groups are often used as scapegoats by the majority. According to the scapegoat hypothesis, the majority takes out its frustrations on the minority. The majority displaces its aggression onto a minority because of fear of reprisals or punishment for direct aggression against the original source of frustration. Like the frustration–aggression hypothesis itself, the scapegoat hypothesis is an oversimplified version of interracial prejudice.

Prejudices may be acquired in the same way that other dispositions are acquired: from parents, teachers, and associates. The processes by which this acquisition takes place include classical and operant conditioning, social learning, and imitation. Learning may also occur in more subtle contexts, such as in books and literature that depict minorities in certain ways, and in ethnic jokes that portray minorities in certain roles.

There is some research on the effects of prejudice on its victims. Until the mid-1960s, black children preferred to play with white dolls, and generally had low levels of self-esteem. That situation seems to have changed recently with a change in reference group for many blacks. Likewise, women show little esteem for successful women. This has been called the "fear of success" among women, but may instead reflect a widely held view of traditional sex roles.

There are a few social psychological theories on reducing intergroup conflict. Included among them are the effects of contact between antagonistic groups and their mutual cooperation on superordinate goals. Some specific tools for reducing miscommunication and misunderstanding between groups are the culture assimilator and the conflict resolution workshop.

Suggested Readings

*Allport, G. W. *The nature of prejudice.* New York: Doubleday, 1954. Still one of the best analyses available.

*Goldschmid, M. L. (Ed.), *Black Americans and white racism.* New York: Holt, 1970. A collection of articles, mostly by psychologists, but also including some sociological studies, an address to the American Psychological Association by Martin Luther King, etc.

*Guthrie, R. V. *Even the rat was white: A historical view of psychology.* New York: Harper, 1976. A history of the study of race in psychology and of black psychologists in the United States.

*Jones, J. M. *Prejudice and racism.* Reading, Mass.: Addison-Wesley, 1972. A good overview of psychological research.

*Weitz, S. *Sex roles.* London and New York: Oxford University Press, 1977. An integrated survey of the literature on biological, psychological, and social bases of sex differences.

*Available in paperback edition.

11
SOCIAL BEHAVIOR IN THE PHYSICAL ENVIRONMENT

THE ENVIRONMENT: OBJECTIVE AND SUBJECTIVE

POPULATION AND BEHAVIOR: SPACING, TERRITORIALITY, AND CROWDING
PERSONAL SPACE/RESPONSES TO VIOLATIONS OF PERSONAL SPACE/ HUMAN TERRITORIALITY/CROWDING AND POPULATION DENSITY

CITY LIFE
THE "CHICAGO SCHOOL" AND THE CITY/SOCIAL PATTERNS OF CITIES/A THEORY OF URBAN BEHAVIOR: STIMULUS OVERLOAD/COGNITIVE MAPS/AESTHETICS AND ENVIRONMENTAL DESIGN

SUMMARY

SUGGESTED READINGS

All behavior takes place in some physical setting, which sets limits on the kinds of behavior that may occur. The physical environment influences behavior both directly and indirectly. It consists of objects and stimuli to which people respond immediately. Sometimes the environment forces people into close proximity, as when they are on a bus or in an airplane or attending a concert. At other times, as in a library or museum, there is ample room to spread out. How does this spatial distribution of people affect their moods, abilities, and behavior toward others?

In general, the environment influences all our senses (with the possible exception of taste), and these, in turn, are apt to influence our behavior and feelings. How do we interact with someone whom we cannot see, as when speaking over the telephone? How does noise influence social and intellectual behavior? What sort of information might we gain from our sense of smell? These are questions that environmental psychologists have dealt with over the past dozen years or so.

Most of this chapter will be concerned with the constructed rather than the natural environment; that is, with cities, buildings, and architectural design rather than the elements, mountains, lakes, and forests. The constructed environment was largely a response to the threats of the natural elements, yet now it has become something of a threat in itself. The constructed environment was built by humans to serve our needs, yet we find that we must adapt our behavior to its demands.

Two variables we long took for granted in psychological studies are time and space. These are among the most fundamental dimensions of theories in the physical sciences, but have, until recently, been almost totally ignored by social psychologists. While there is some recent work dealing with time (e.g., Albert, 1977, 1978; Fraisse, 1974; Ornstein, 1970), it is space that first caught the interest of social psychologists.

Concern by psychologists with the environment has many historical antecedents (Proshansky & O'Hanlon, 1977; Stokols, 1977), but an often overlooked one is the effects of space exploration. Humans were largely unconcerned with the environment until they could step away from it and view it from a distance. There were a number of warnings and cries from the wilderness about the disastrous effects of pollution and overpopulation (e.g., Carson, 1962; P.R. Ehrlich, 1968), and there was also some early work by psychologists on the effects of the physical environment on behavior (e.g., Barker, 1968; Bates, 1953; R. Blake, Wedge, & Mouton, 1956; Festinger, Schachter, & Back, 1950; Shelford, 1935). But it was not until men were propelled into the stratosphere that we could have an "Earth Day," which marked the beginning of widespread concern with the environment. This, plus research on population density and regulation and research on small and large groups, may be seen as the immediate roots of environmental social psychology. The research of biologists on population density and population regulation in animals has been a major influence on modern-day thinking (e.g., Calhoun, 1962; Wynne-Edwards, 1962). There was a tendency, if not in the initial investigators, then at least in the popular press, to generalize these animal studies to human beings. The ensuing controversy over the effects of overcrowding on humans drew psychologists into the battle. None of this would have become the least bit controversial if birth control techniques had not enabled humans to regulate family size effectively and thus to have fairly direct control over changes in population. We rarely argue over issues when no choice is possible.

A second important influence on environmental issues emerged out of studies of small groups (e.g., Mark, 1954; Sommer, 1959, 1967; Steinzor, 1950; Strodtbeck & Hook, 1961) and larger, cultural groups (Hall, 1959, 1966). This research explored questions dealing with the optimal size of groups engaged in different tasks and the distribution of individuals engaged in group tasks, and it was found that these spatial dimensions influenced group functioning. This quickly led to research on group ecology and the spacing of individuals in different situations, and provided a link between the animal research on population density and the social psychological work on spacing and group size among humans (Wohlwill & Carson, 1972).

Theory and research on various aspects of spatial and environmental behavior proliferated in the 1970s to such an extent that there are now several journals devoted exclusively to these issues (see Suggested Readings), as well as a newly formed division of the American Psychological Association on environmental psychology. Since the field is still in the process of formation, I will discuss separately a few of the more fundamental aspects of environmental psychology.

THE ENVIRONMENT: OBJECTIVE AND SUBJECTIVE

If social psychologists study effects of the physical environment, how do they differ from architects or urban planners? The primary difference is that social psychologists are interested less in the objective features of the environment than in the subjective, or perceived, features of the environment that give rise to feelings and actions. Of course, in order to understand people's perceptions better, it is often useful to have an objective description of an environment; but for understanding the immediate causes of people's behavior, this objective information is not necessary. If a person believes that it is hot and crowded in a room where she is standing, she is apt to behave in certain ways, despite the fact that no one else believes the room to be hot or crowded.

For the sake of convenience, the term *environment* will be used to refer to the constructed environment—that is, to buildings, cities, towns. The term *natural environment* will be used when reference is being made to climatic conditions such as humidity and temperature, rivers, mountains, and countryside. Other distinctions are possible and will sometimes be desirable in this chapter, such as that between rural and urban environments and that between public and private types of space (Altman, 1976). These will be introduced as the need arises.

POPULATION AND BEHAVIOR: SPACING, TERRITORIALITY, AND CROWDING

As Freedman (1975) points out, human beings are highly social. They tend to congregate in cities and can usually be found more or less huddled together on fairly small plots of land. Urban centers are nothing new; in the pre-Christian era, cities of many thousands of people existed (see Mumford, 1961). Despite this human tendency to gregariousness, it is clear that we also enjoy a modicum of privacy and solitude (Altman, 1975). While we are social animals, we also have something of the lone wolf in our makeup. It is possible to perceive an equilibrium point between too much and too little social contact. Contact with too few people may be just as unpleasant as contact with too many. One of the ways in which this concern with numerical and spatial regulation of humans has been studied is through observation of interpersonal distance, or personal space.

PERSONAL SPACE

The term *personal space* was popularized by the psychologist Robert Sommer (1959, 1969). In general, it refers to "the area individual humans actively maintain around themselves into which others cannot intrude without arousing discomfort" (Hayduk, 1978, p. 118). Personal space may be thought of as an invisible bubble surrounding a person that encloses space thought of as "private." This invisible bubble changes shape and size depending upon the immediate circumstances. If you are walking down a crowded city street during lunch hour, your personal space contracts and may consist of only a few inches on either side of you. If you are sitting in a school lounge studying, your personal space may consist of a few feet.

The rush of the city may be exciting, but the solitude of the park also has its rewards.

Personal space is one of the specific areas of interest in the general area of *proxemics*. Proxemics is the scientific study of human spatial behaviors, including personal space, nonverbal communication, crowding, and population density (Hall, 1959).

Personal space not only expands or contracts with the circumstances, but also differs from one culture to another (e.g., Hall, 1966; S.E. Jones & Aiello, 1973). There is some (albeit controversial) evidence that certain types of individuals, such as violent prisoners, have larger personal spaces than others (Kinzel, 1971; Lothstein, 1971, in D. E. Linder, 1974). Personal space, unlike the concept of territoriality, moves with a person. It expands and contracts according to circumstance, but is always a space that has the person at its core. Territory is an area of space that a person considers "his" and that is used fairly regularly over a period of time (Edney, 1974). A person can leave his territory, to return to it later, but he cannot leave his personal space, for it is "part" of him.

Intrusion of personal space leads to discomfort and individuals attempt to reduce this discomfort by defending or reestablishing their personal space. Intrusion into personal space does not seem to be a very common occurrence in our culture. Most of us learn quite early to respect the spatial privacy of others (e.g., Eberts & Lepper, 1975; Guardo, 1969; Scherer, 1974). As early as age 10, most American children recognize that they should not encroach upon others' space either in public or in private places. Children are repeatedly told by their parents to leave others alone, even when they clearly are not imposing on others but are merely in close proximity to them.

Some Meanings of Space The anthropologist E. T. Hall (1959, 1966) has suggested that the various spatial distances maintained between individuals can be conveniently divided into four types: intimate, personal, social, and public (see Little, 1965). *Intimate distance* between two individuals ranges from physical contact to about 18 inches. Hall notes that "This is the distance of love-making and wrestling," for in purely spatial terms both are highly intimate behaviors. What makes close distances intimate? While there is some theoretical disagreement about this, part of the answer involves a restricted visual field and the involvement of more sensory receptors at such close distance. We can see and smell only the other person, can hear subtle changes in breathing, and may even be able to perceive changes in the other's body temperature.

A distance from about 1.5 feet to 4 feet (.3 to 1.3 meters) is called *personal distance*. At this distance, the other is at "arm's length," but near enough to provide a sense of closeness. *Social distance*, ranging from 4 to 12 feet (about 1.3 to 3.5 meters), is common among people working cooperatively on a task or engaging in social conversation. Hall refers to a distance of 12 feet (3.5 meters) and beyond as *public distance*. The field of vision includes not only the other person but also people in the general vicinity. Here, a person is literally and psychologically keeping his or her distance.

Cultural Variations in Personal Space Hall is responsible for popularizing the fact that spatial dimensions hold different meanings for people in different cultures. There is a cultural norm of appropriate distance between two individuals engaged in informal conversation, for example. When someone stands too close, or too far away, while we are speaking with them, we feel that something is wrong. Hall discusses speaking distance in the United States, England, and Arabic countries and notes that, compared to Americans, the English tend to feel most comfortable with greater distance between two speakers, while Arabs tend to feel most comfortable with closer distances. This cultural difference is likely to give rise to emotional reactions on the part of an American conversing with an English or an Arab person, and perhaps even to stereotypic judgments of the English as "cold" or "aloof" and of the Arabs as "aggressive" or "inconsiderate."

Hall (1969) gives striking examples of differences in the meaning of space in different cultures:

For the Arab, there is no such thing as an intrusion in public. Public means public. With this insight, a great range of Arab behavior that had been puzzling, annoying, and sometimes even frightening began to make sense. I learned, for example, that if A is standing on a street corner and B wants his spot, B is within his rights if he does what he can to make A uncomfortable enough to move. In Beirut only the hardy sit in the last row in a movie theater, because there are usually standees who want seats and who push and shove and make such a nuisance that most people give up and leave. . . .

. . . In the Western world, the person is synonymous with an individual inside a skin. And in northern Europe generally, the skin and even the clothes may be inviolate. You need permission to touch either if you are a stranger. . . . For the Arab the location of the person in relation to the body is quite different. The person exists somewhere down inside the body. The ego is not completely hidden, however, because it can be reached very easily with an insult. It is protected from touch but not from words. The dissociation of the body and the ego may explain why the public amputation of a thief's hand is tolerated as standard punishment in Saudi Arabia. . . . (pp. 146–147)

There is also systematic evidence on the existence of cultural variations in proxemic behavior. W. R. Berkowitz (1971) observed over 20,000 pedestrians in cities in the United States, Europe, and the Middle East, noting the percentage of people alone or with others, and the percentage of people who had physical contact with their companions. As can be seen in Table 11.1, there is considerable variation in the extent to which companions engage in contact. Berkowitz's results are not entirely consistent with the observations of Hall on speaking distance. A higher percentage of English pedestrians had contact with their companions than Middle Easterners ("Moslem" in the Table). Of course, the two measures — speaking distance and physical contact with companions — are different, and that may account for the discrepancy. Some studies of culture and interpersonal distance fail to find any consistent differences. For example, Forston and Larson (1968) did not find any differences in interpersonal distances between Latin Americans and North Ameri-

Table 11.1.
Percentage of Pedestrians in Groups Who
Were Also in Contact

Country	Percent in Contact
Sweden	18.1
United States	19.4
"Moslem"	15.4
England	24.1
West Germany	26.4
Italy	29.8

From W. R. Berkowitz (1971).

AVOIDING *FAUX PAS* WHEN VISITING A FOREIGN COUNTRY

When you head for an unfamiliar country on short notice, some cramming on its customs could pay more dividends than a crash program in the language.

Unless you have been conjugating the local verbs for years, your business will probably be done in English. But while your foreign hosts won't expect you to spout the local patois, your innocent failures in nonverbal communication could offend them. Or you could misread their actions, with bad results.

Even a friendly grin can go wrong. Americans usually smile when shaking hands, but some German-speaking people find smiles too affectionate for new . . . acquaintances. So, while you're sizing up a German as a cold fish, he or she may be pegging you as the overly familiar type.

Try to break the ice in Germany with the *"Wie geht's?"* ("How goes it?") you got from watching war movies, and you'll be twice wrong. The expression is too informal and the question too personal for first encounters.

In Chinese-speaking areas, though, inquiring after a person's health is a proper first greeting, especially for the elderly.

But compliments are tricky in the Orient. You exchange them more readily there than in the United States, but pay a Chinese-speaking person a compliment and he or she will surely decline it. Disagreeing is merely the way they accept praise. So if an Oriental compliments you, best be modest about it.

You can get into trouble by being too complimentary about objects in a Chinese or Japanese home; your host may feel obliged to give you the item.

The French are also evasive about compliments. They never say *"merci"* in response to praise, and if you respond to a compliment with "thanks," a French-speaking person could even interpret it as ridicule.

cans working together on a task. In cooperative tasks, we might reasonably expect individuals, regardless of culture, to work at what Hall has termed a social distance, and the demands of the immediate situation may override whatever cultural differences may exist between Latin Americans and North Americans. Thus, it seems fair to say that differences in the use of space depend not only on culture and social norms, but also on the immediate demands of the situation and the type of interaction in which people engage.

Theories of Personal Space   It is not always possible to maintain the optimum distance for every occasion. Sometimes circumstances force people into close contact or prevent them from achieving desired levels of intimacy. In these cases, compensating mechanisms may be used so that the desired level of intimacy is achieved.

Formality is a must in France. Frenchmen who have worked side by side in an office for decades stick to formal pronouns when addressing each other, unless they also happen to have been school or military buddies.

And while using first names in business encounters is regarded as an American vice in many countries, nowhere is it found more offensive than in France.

Hand gestures are far from international. Italians wave goodbye with palm up and fingers moving back and forth—a beckoning signal to Americans. But when people wave the fingers with the palm down in China, Japan, and other Oriental areas, it's not goodbye—they mean "come here."

People who speak a romance language use more hand gestures than most Americans, but you can go wrong imitating them. For example, if you form a circle with thumb and forefinger, most Europeans will know you mean "it's the best," or "O.K." But in some Latin American countries the same gesture has a vulgar connotation.

The easiest place to have a gesture misunderstood abroad is in someone's home. Bearing gifts is expected in Japan, but can be considered a bribe in the Soviet Union. Portuguese and Brazilians like to bring foreigners home for dinner, but when it's time for you to go, politeness may compel them to insist that you stay. In some countries punctuality is expected; in others the custom is to arrive late. No matter where you go abroad, you can never assume that your best table manners will carry the day. You need a thorough rundown on local etiquette before your visit.

From *Business Week* (December 12, 1977), pp. 115–116.

Four different theories of space are reviewed by Hayduk (1978), but only two of them have generated enough research to warrant discussion here: equilibrium theory and sensory stimulation theory. *Equilibrium theory* was proposed by Argyle and Dean in 1965. According to them, personal space, or the distance between two individuals, is a component of intimacy. The greater the intimacy between two people, the more likely they are to discuss personal topics, to smile at each other, to have a high degree of eye contact, and to maintain a small amount of distance between themselves. If something interferes with one of these mechanisms for expressing intimacy, there is a tendency to compensate by changing other mechanisms. For example, if a person is prevented from having eye contact with an intimate acquaintance, compensation might take the form of standing closer to that person. Thus, the same level of

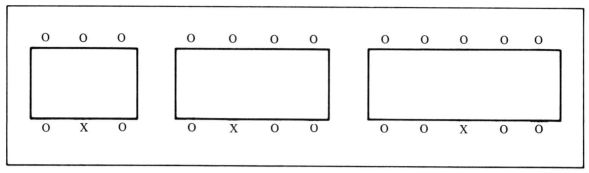

Figure 11.1.
Optimal positions for the defense of personal space.

intimacy is expressed by striking a balance between distance, eye contact, smiling, and discussion topic.

Equilibrium theory has stimulated a considerable amount of research, partially because there is so little testable theory in this area. Much of the research is supportive of the theory (G. N. Goldberg, Kiesler, & Collins, 1969; M. L. Patterson, 1975; M. L. Patterson, Mullens, & Romano, 1971), though it is sometimes difficult to conduct adequate tests of the theory, such as in measuring the degree of eye contact between two individuals (Carr & Dabbs, 1974; Knight, Langmeyer & Lundgren, 1973; Russo, 1975; Stephenson & Rutter, 1970).

With *stimulation theory*, proposed by Desor (1972), we can begin to see the relationship between personal space and other proxemic behaviors such as crowding. A person is crowded when he or she *feels* crowded (Stokols, 1972), and that usually occurs when a person receives excessive stimulation from other people. The differences in personal space found under various circumstances are mechanisms for regulating the amount of stimulation a person receives from others. This, of course, can be closely related to intimacy. The stimulation theory proposes that it is not intimacy per se that is regulated by variations in space but social and sensory stimulation. We would expect these two variables to correlate negatively in the real world; a person who lives in a complex, crowded, intense stimulus environment would probably not feel very intimate toward a given stranger and would avoid eye contact and closeness. In general, stimulation intensity may lead to a feeling of intimacy or of lack of intimacy, and either feeling may, in turn, lead to variations in interpersonal distance. The issue of stimulation and its regulation is discussed in the section entitled "City Life."

RESPONSES TO VIOLATIONS OF
PERSONAL SPACE

By definition, personal space is that distance whose violation by

Table 11.2.

Perceived Crowdedness

Sex of Subject	Spatial Relationship between Subject and Invader		
	Adjacent	1 Seat Away	Across
Male	11.48_b	8.50_b	17.04_a
Female	16.60_a	8.39_b	14.76_a

NOTE: Means with common subscripts are not different from one another at the .05 level. The possible range of scores is from 4 (least crowded) to 28 (most crowded). From Fisher and Byrne (1975).

another causes feelings of discomfort. When discomfort occurs, we naturally expect a person to attempt to reduce it. This can be done by withdrawing, by standing one's ground and attempting to drive off the intruder, or by avoiding situations in which personal space might be violated by others.

These and other reactions have been investigated most extensively by Robert Sommer (1969). In studies conducted at a university library, for example, Sommer found that certain defensive actions may be taken to prevent spatial invasion. When asked where a person would sit at a rectangular table with six, eight, or ten chairs, students predicted that, to discourage others from sitting at the same table, they would sit in the positions marked by an "X" in Figure 11.1. When the students left their chairs temporarily, various kinds of "markers" were used to signal that the chairs were occupied. People draped a sweater over the back of a chair or left an open book or notebook in front of it. When such markers were used in a library, the chairs were never occupied by someone else.

When a public place, such as a library, becomes crowded, we use various defensive behaviors to maintain and protect our personal space. Barriers of books and belongings may be erected between ourselves and others; we may change the angle of our seat to minimize eye contact with others; or we may move to a less crowded part of the room. In such behaviors there appear to be sex differences, at least among American college students. Fisher and Byrne (1975) found that males respond more negatively than females to invasions of personal space from the front, while females respond more negatively to side-by-side invasions of personal space. When asked to rate how crowded they felt when a male invaded their space, females felt most crowded when he was next to them, while males felt most crowded when he was across from them (see Table 11.2).

Of course, how we respond emotionally to such invasions depends on other information we might have about the invader. If we have reason to believe that the invader is friendly, we are less likely to erect defensive barriers and interpret his or her actions as hostile (cf. Storms & Thomas, 1977). Individuals feel uncomfortable not only when their personal space has been invaded by others but also when circumstances force them to invade the personal space of others (Efran & Cheyne, 1974). There is considerable evidence that there are potent norms for the preservation of one's own and others' personal spaces.

HUMAN TERRITORIALITY

Territoriality is a concept closely related to personal space. Unlike personal space, which moves with the person, territory refers to behavior designed to preserve a particular geographical space such as one's home. Many animal species are territorial. They establish home territories, tend to live in them, depend on them for food, shelter, and the rearing of offspring, and defend them against intruders. These territories are often delineated by *territorial markers* to ward off other members of the same species. Rabbits, for example, urinate around the perimeter of their territories to signal to other rabbits that "this land is occupied."

There are some striking parallels between animal territoriality and human behavior. Humans also appear to "mark" their territories. They put fences around their yards, names on their mailboxes, numbers on their doorposts, distinctive decorations on their houses or lawns, and signs on their office doors. When leaving a seat temporarily in an airplane, we can place on it a sign provided by the airline that tells others that seat is ours—in no less than three languages: OCCUPIED, OCCUPÉ, OCUPADO.

These similarities between animal and human behavior should be interpreted only as analogs. Rabbits instinctively urinate around their territories; people do not instinctively put up mailboxes with their names on them, nor, except in rare circumstances, do they urinate around their dwellings. "It is virtually undisputed that humans exhibit territoriality, at the national, family home, or temporary (my-seat-in-the-bus) level, but the question remains how meaningful the similarities are to animal territoriality" (Edney, 1974, p. 961). Unlike animals', the humans' defense and use of territories are quite flexible. Territories seem to serve largely biological purposes for animals, whereas humans use them for social and recreational purposes. Animals use only a single territory for multiple purposes, whereas humans have separate territories, such as home, office, and fishing lodge, for different purposes. And, perhaps most important, humans engage in many behaviors in which they share territories with others, such as dining at a table at a restaurant, and then leaving it to be used by others (Sundstrom & Altman, 1974). Edney (1974) adds still another important difference: Humans appear to be the only species that uses home territories for entertaining others without antagonism.

It is often suggested that there is a relationship between size of territory and status. A person is assumed to have higher status if he or she has a large house with ample grounds. Although this generally is the case, there are some exceptions that suggest we need to consider the location of the property and the resources found on it. For example, someone might give up a large country home for a small town house. Owning 50 acres of farmland is not generally as prestigious as owning a downtown block in a city. Would-be trespassers also seem to recognize differences in territorial status. By varying the size of a group and the status of its members, Knowles (1973) discovered that fewer pedestrians would walk through a stationary high-status group of people than through a low-status group.

We must distinguish between areas that may be marked but not defended and those, such as our homes, that are defended. Becker and Mayo (1971) found that although spaces in a cafeteria may be marked, they are rarely defended against intruders. Over 90 percent of the occupants moved when their tables were spatially invaded. Therefore, such "temporary territories" should not be thought of as leading to territorial behavior, but rather as mechanisms for the regulation of personal space.

CROWDING AND POPULATION
DENSITY

Because a number of animal studies demonstrate that population density may have negative social and physiological effects (e.g., Calhoun, 1962), there is a widespread assumption that crowding has comparable negative effects on humans. But it is far from clear that, for humans, density is destiny.

What is "crowded" or "overpopulated"? Tokyo is more densely populated than New York City; the Netherlands is more densely populated than the United States. Do these facts explain any of the differences in social behavior between these different locations?

Perhaps we should begin this section by clarifying some terms. First, we must distinguish between *population density*, the number of people in a given area (such as 100 people per acre), and *crowding*, the subjective feeling that there are too many people present for comfort or freedom of movement (Schopler & Stockdale, 1977). Second, we must distinguish between *short-term crowding*, such as being in an elevator with many other people for a few minutes, and *long-term crowding*, such as living in Tokyo for 10 or 15 years.

Freedman (1975) has summarized and criticized the literature on crowding in animals. While there is evidence that animals housed for many generations in densely populated conditions display increased aggressiveness or increased passivity, a deterioration in normal social and sexual behavior, and increased infant mortality, these effects are not likely to be caused solely or directly by crowding. Freedman suggests that the presence of additional animals intensifies certain physiological responses and social interaction, and perhaps this intensification accounts for these observed effects in animals. In other words, the evidence that crowding per se has deleterious effects on animal species is, at best, inconclusive.

In much of his own research, Freedman and his colleagues (Freedman, Klevansky, & Ehrlich, 1971; Freedman, Levy, Buchanan, & Price, 1972) have examined behavioral and emotional effects of short-term population density in humans. The findings indicate no main effect for density on tests of creativity, memory, performance of various tasks, or aggressiveness. When one considers the sex of the subjects, however, Freedman, as well as others (e.g., M. Ross, Layton, Erickson, & Schopler, 1973), finds that there is a heightening of affect. Males, for example, who are generally more aggressive than females, become more aggressive under densely populated conditions, while females become less aggressive. In other words, there does not appear to be any unidirectional effect of short-term population density. We must consider additional variables in evaluating the effects of density on behavior and emotion, such as the initial emotional state of the subject.

One such additional consideration is the extent to which people interact with others. When individuals do not interact in a densely populated area, there are few short-term effects due to density. However, when interaction between people in a densely populated area is great, there is a decrement in the performance of cognitive and behavioral tasks (Heller, Groff, & Solomon, 1977). We must also consider the fact that, in natural settings, there is a tendency for density and temperature to vary together; when it is crowded in a small area, it is usually hot. When increased temperature is added to increased population density, there is a general arousal of negative emotions and a decrease in liking for others in the immediate vicinity (Griffitt & Veitch, 1971).

Studies of long-term crowding are difficult to conduct with acceptable degrees of scientific rigor. Comparing mood and behavior in a densely populated area, such as the Watts area of Los Angeles, with a sparsely populated area, such as Marin County, California, can tell us little about the effects of density, since there are so many other differences between these two areas and their inhabitants. It is generally true that indices of behavior such as the Uniform Crime Reports of the FBI show more criminal behavior in densely populated areas, but such studies are, from a scientific point of view, nearly worthless (Goldstein, 1975). The fact is that we know very little

Short-term crowding can be a lot of fun if you enjoy street festivals.

about the consequences of long-term crowding on humans, and what we do know suggests that factors other than population density per se are most strongly associated with illness, psychopathology, aggression, and crime (e.g., Freedman, Heshka, & Levy, 1975; Galle, Gove, & McPherson, 1972; Giel & Ormel, 1977; Levy & Herzog, 1974).

Because of the difficulties encountered in studying consequences of long-term population density on humans, social psychologists have turned to a more readily measurable behavior, the perception of crowding. Because crowding is a subjective feeling in response to population density, factors that influence the intensity of the feeling of crowding have been studied. The issues dealt with are: Under what circumstances will people feel most or least crowded? When density cannot be avoided, what do people do to avoid feeling crowded? Once we begin to explore the perception of crowding, we find that not only is there sound scientific research but also a number of theories designed to explain the sensations of crowding. These theories propose that other people can become impediments to our freedom of space, movement, or privacy. Whenever such interference comes about, we experience crowding.

That crowding is different from mere population density can be seen in several studies of architectural design (Desor, 1972). Keeping room area constant while varying architectural features such as partitions and number of doors, Desor found that individuals would place more people in an uncrowded room when the structure of the

AMERICAN CITIES: SOME GOOD AND SOME BAD

On the basis of over 100 statistical indices, such as economics, crime, housing, weather, pollution, health, and education, the Midwest Research Institute of Kansas City, Missouri, published a relative "quality of life" index for 243 urban areas. The following cities, listed according to population, are judged "good places to live" or "not-so-good places to live."

Good	Not-So-Good
Over 500,000 Population	
Portland, Ore.	Jersey City, N.J.
Sacramento, Cal.	Birmingham, Ala.
Seattle, Wash.	New Orleans, La.
San Jose, Cal.	San Antonio, Tex.
Minneapolis–St. Paul, Minn.	Jacksonville, Fla.
Rochester, N.Y.	Greensboro–Winston-Salem, N.C.
Hartford, Conn.	Norfolk, Va.
Denver, Colo.	Memphis, Tenn.
San Francisco, Cal.	Philadelphia, Pa.
San Diego, Cal.	Tampa–St. Petersburg, Fla.
200,000–500,000 Population	
Eugene, Ore.	Mobile, Ala.
Madison, Wis.	Charleston, S. C.
Appleton, Oshkosh, Wis.	Macon, Ga.
Santa Barbara, Cal.	Montgomery, Ala.
Stamford, Conn.	Columbus, Ga.
Des Moines, Ia.	Fayetteville, N.C.
Lansing, Mich.	Greenville, S. C.
Kalamazoo, Mich.	Columbia, S. C.
Ft. Wayne, Ind.	Huntington, W. Va.
Ann Arbor, Mich.	Augusta, Ga.
Less than 200,000 Population	
La Crosse, Wis.	Laredo, Tex.
Rochester, Minn.	Pine Bluff, Ark.
Lincoln, Nebr.	McAllen, Pharr, Tex.
Topeka, Kan.	Ft. Smith, Ark.
Green Bay, Wis.	Lawton, Okla.
Ogden, Utah	Brownsville, Tex.
Norwalk, Conn.	Albany, Ga.
Sioux Falls, S.D.	Tuscaloosa, Ala.
Fargo, N.D.	Savannah, Ga.
Bristol, Conn.	Gadsden, Ala.

From *Quality of Life in the U.S. Metropolitan Areas, 1970,* 1975.

room minimized social interaction. Thus, in a space that is partitioned, an increase in population density does not necessarily lead to an increase in feelings of overcrowding.

Worchel and Teddlie (1976) have argued that feelings of crowding result from two sequential processes. First is the violation of personal space by others, then the attempt to attribute the cause of this violation. Because there are many people in the person's immediate environment, the tendency is to attribute the discomfort to them. In research designed to test this personal space–attribution model, Worchel and Teddlie distracted some people in densely populated conditions by placing pictures on the walls. In densely populated rooms with these distracting pictures, there was less tendency to attribute personal space violations to others; people did not feel as crowded as when no "distractors" were present (see also Greenberg & Firestone, 1977). It is not only personal space that others may interfere with in densely populated settings, but a whole variety of behaviors. When there are many people in a relatively small area, freedom of movement, ability to attain personal goals, and ease of communicating are all interfered with, and it is this interference that results in the perception of crowding (Schopler and Stockdale, 1977).

Since crowding is an uncomfortable subjective state, individuals will avoid feeling crowded if possible, or will attempt to reduce the feeling when it arises. This may explain, for example, why so many people in elevators watch the floor numbers change as the elevator ascends or descends; by avoiding eye contact with others, they may reduce their feelings of crowding. We can postulate a homeostatic mechanism for dealing with densely populated areas in which individuals will avoid large numbers of people if they live in densely populated areas, and will seek out large numbers of people if they live in sparsely populated areas (Baum, Harpin, & Valins, 1975; Tucker & Friedman, 1972).

In a study by Munroe and Munroe (1972), three East African societies that differed in population density were studied: the Logoli (1440 people per square mile), the Gusii (691 people per square mile), and the Kipsigis (253 people per square mile). Munroe and Munroe proposed that in the most densely populated societies, there would be less touching during casual encounters, such as hand holding with friends, and less value placed on group affiliation. Observations of casual encounters were made and the importance of affiliation was measured by asking people to remember such affiliation words as "friend" or "party." Both hypotheses were supported: The Logoli were least likely to hold hands and were least able to remember affiliation words on a short-term memory task. Therefore, when population density is great, social norms and psychological mechanisms minimize additional contact with others.

CITY LIFE

Cities are an ancient phenomenon. Most of what we know of life in pre-Christian times comes from archeological digs of ancient cities (Mumford, 1961). Scientific study of city life, however, is a modern undertaking, dating only from the Industrial Revolution. The Industrial Revolution of the eighteenth and nineteenth centuries gave rise to factory towns and to industry-related cities, which, in turn, resulted in changing patterns of population. A "working class" and a class of *"nouveau riche"* arose, and novel forms of social, political, and economic life began to emerge.

European sociologists and philosophers scrutinized these changes and contrasted them with pre-industrial life or with life in the

Figure 11.2.
Burgess's conception of the structure of the city.

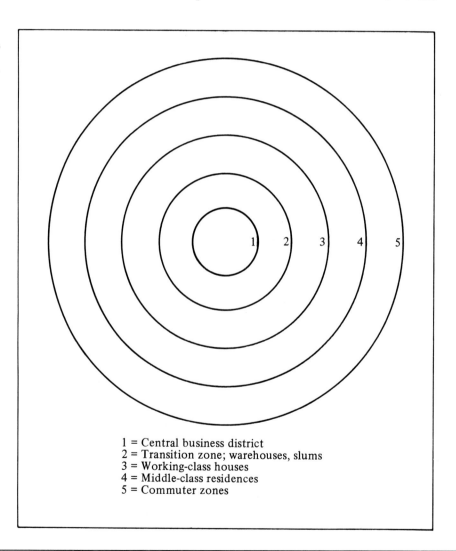

1 = Central business district
2 = Transition zone; warehouses, slums
3 = Working-class houses
4 = Middle-class residences
5 = Commuter zones

countryside. Ferdinand Tönnies (1887/1940), for example, distinguished between the traditional community that existed in France before the Industrial Revolution (*Gemeinschaft*) and the heterogeneous and more fragmented community of the post-industrial world (*Gesellschaft*). There was much armchair theorizing on the nature and effects of the city, but it was not until the present century that the city became a "laboratory" for social research.

THE "CHICAGO SCHOOL" AND THE CITY

If we assume, as nearly all social psychologists do, that human behavior is a function of the environment—both social and physical—it would seem of utmost importance to specify the nature of that environment. This was first done by sociologists at the University of Chicago in the early decades of the twentieth century. Under the leadership of R. E. Park (1915) and E. W. Burgess (1925), a series of studies on the social organization and social character of Chicago was conducted. Using Chicago as their research laboratory, this group produced important studies on immigrants to the city (Cressey, 1932), family disorganization and divorce (Mowrer, 1927), juvenile gangs (Thrasher, 1926), and mental illness (Faris & Dunham, 1939).

The Chicago School was primarily interested in describing the city's physical characteristics and their effects on social structure and organization. Burgess (1925) suggested that the ecology of the city consisted of "natural areas" of growth emanating from a central business district at the core to working-class, middle-class, and finally commuter zones (see Figure 11.2). This conception of the city has been criticized as an oversimplified model, since some cities have developed along the main lines of transportation (H. Hoyt, 1937) or, like New York, have multiple core areas rather than a single business district.

These early views of the city also overlook the fact that cities are characterized more by their social than by their physical nature (Karp, Stone, & Yoels, 1977). It is probably more important for an understanding of behavior to describe a city in terms of patterns of social interaction and friendship then in terms of architecture and zones of residential and business dwellings. This type of description was presented by Duncan and Reiss in 1956, and more recently by other social psychologists (e.g., Milgram, 1967). Furthermore, Burgess's objective map of the city does not necessarily correspond to residents' or visitors' conceptions of the city. People's subjective or cognitive maps of a physical environment often differ from an objective description of the environment (Lynch, 1960).

SOCIAL PATTERNS OF CITIES

The city's reputation has suffered in the writings of sociologists and psychologists. In early studies, cities were contrasted with the more "natural" and sedentary existence of the small, personal communities and were seen as impersonal, unfriendly places where individuals counted for little. Cities are neither worse nor better than small towns and rural areas; they are merely different. And because they are different, the social and psychological needs of their residents must be satisfied in different ways.

Duncan and Reiss (1956) examined intimate friendships in rural and urban areas and reported that city dwellers have many more close friends than rural residents. Milgram (1970) reports that within a ten-minute radius of one's office by foot or car, one can meet more than 20,000 persons in a moderate-sized city like Newark, New Jersey, and nearly a quarter of a million people in midtown Manhattan! It is this possibility for social encounter that appeals to so many city dwellers.

Where else but in a city—in this case, Philadelphia—could you find organizations as specialized and diverse as the Alliance Française, Anti-Vivisection Society, Slavic Cultural Foundation, Chinese Benevolent Association, Council for the Advancement of Science Writing, Cuban Community Center, Filipino American Seaman's Club, Bicycle Coalition, Committee to Reopen the Rosenberg Case, Folk Song Society, Society of Parapsychology, Single Parents Society, Women Strike for Peace, and clubs for playing backgammon, bridge, chess, golf, racquetball, squash, and tennis? If intimate friendships are more difficult to establish in a city than in a smaller community, organizations such as these are established to make such contact possible. That is also why cities have discos, singles bars, and lonely hearts advertisements in the press.

Because cities are larger and more diverse than rural areas, they afford some measure of anonymity. In cities, people who are in some sense deviant are more apt to be tolerated because privacy is respected. Just as intimacy is not a natural product of city living, neither is privacy a natural result of urban life. Again, specialized social institutions and shared social norms are established for the creation and preservation of privacy. Privacy and anonymity are possible in a city because to behave otherwise would be too costly. To treat each person as a unique individual, to express concern for every drunk on the street and everyone who requests money, would occupy the city dweller's every waking hour. Therefore, city dwellers establish mechanisms to enable them to carry on a daily routine uninterrupted by strangers. The purpose of these mechanisms is to minimize the amount of social and sensory stimulation received from the environment. This idea has been discussed earlier with respect to personal space and crowding, and has been developed by Milgram with respect to the city in general.

A THEORY OF URBAN BEHAVIOR: STIMULUS OVERLOAD

Early analyses of urban life emphasized that the hustle and bustle of the city would take its "psychic toll" on the urbanite (Simmel, 1950). Milgram (1970) has proposed that there is a superabundance of visual, auditory, and social stimulation in the typical city and city dwellers must learn to adapt to this stimulus overload. They do so by developing specific norms to minimize their involvement with others. We learn to ignore beggars, to avoid drunks on the street, and not to talk to strangers. These and similar norms are ways to minimize the amount of sensory stimulation. Milgram suggests a number of additional ways that this overload may be handled. For example, a person may spend only the minimum amount of time necessary for any social transaction, such as with a store clerk. An unlisted phone number may be used to prevent others from calling. Business and government organizations have established elaborate bureaucracies to protect executives from the public.

In addition to social mechanisms for adapting to the excessive stimulation of the city, there are psychological mechanisms as well. Glass and Singer (1972a) have studied the mechanisms used to adapt to loud noise. Their primary hypothesis is that such adaptations are accomplished only at some psychological or physical cost. We can filter out certain kinds of noise so that they are no longer distracting. But in order to do this, we must sacrifice some cognitive abilities, such as the ability to solve problems and perform intellectual tasks. This is especially true if the noise is loud and unpredictable or irregular in pattern. Glass and Singer suggest that "exposure to uncontrollable noise produces feelings of helplessness which interfere with later functioning" (p. 462).

Mechanisms for adapting to the complexity of urban living may include simplifying the image of the city to make it more manageable. Such simplification may follow the familiar cognitive mechanisms of leveling, sharpening, and assimilating various features of the environment to form maximally meaningful structures. These views of the city are referred to as *cognitive maps*.

COGNITIVE MAPS

Cognitive maps were first studied by Kevin Lynch (1960), who wished to learn how people subjectively structure their environments. Lynch instructed residents to draw a quick map of their city "as if you were making a rapid description of the city to a stranger,

Although many people remember cities they visit by the social encounters they have, there are also some landmarks that leave memorable impressions.

covering all the main features." While this may not be the ideal set of instructions to use to elicit people's subjective images of their city (see Porteus, 1977, p. 102), it does provide sufficient information to be of some interest to social psychologists.

Lynch proposed that images of the city consist of five types of elements. *Paths* are the channels along which we customarily or occasionally move. In Boston, one of the cities studied by Lynch, Commonwealth Avenue is a commonly mentioned path. *Edges* are boundaries, such as walls, shorelines, railroad cuts, and rivers. In Boston, the Charles River is an edge. *Districts* are distinctive sections of the city. Boston Common and Beacon Hill are often mentioned as two districts. *Nodes* are the strategic spots where a person can enter the city and are the primary focuses of travel. They may be intersections or transportation terminals, such as the Back Bay rail station in Boston. Finally, cognitive maps contain *landmarks*—buildings, signs, stores, or physical terrain used for orientation.

Not all of these elements exist in every individual's cognitive map of his or her city. Imagine that you are giving directions to a stranger to get to where you are now from a distant point in your town. Assume that the stranger has a car. What would you tell him to do? Most people mention paths (streets) and landmarks, using edges and nodes for additional reference. Districts are not apt to be mentioned often in directions from one point to another. Naturally, individual experience influences the image of a city. We would expect those areas in which a person spends most of his or her time to be most differentiated and detailed. Your directions to a stranger would probably contain more and more detail as they describe the approach to your present location. You are more apt to remember the names of streets, the names of stores used as landmarks, and the type of gasoline sold in the station in your own neighborhood. Milgram, Greenwald, Kessler, McKenna, and Waters (1972) propose that the recognizability of a location is a function of its centrality to the flow of people and to its architectural or social distinctiveness. Thus, nearly everyone who knows New York City includes Times Square in his or her cognitive map of the city.

We can use cognitive mapping to study any characteristic of interest. For example, a person may ask a group of New Yorkers where they go to find peace and quiet, or where they do not go for fear of crime. In this way, we find that cognitive maps often differ from geographical maps in that they leave out whole sections of a city that are not known or are considered irrelevant for certain purposes.

AESTHETICS AND ENVIRONMENTAL DESIGN

The study of subjective maps of cities provides us with some understanding of how people orient themselves in various places. Such cognitive maps, however, only occasionally include social encounters. Yet many people's views of cities are based on just such interaction. When travelers are asked what they remember most about foreign cities, they most frequently respond with some personal encounter they've had. My most memorable impressions of London concern encounters with Londoners, and of Paris, with a shopkeeper. Although we orient ourselves by the Post Office Tower and Hyde Park in London, or the Seine and the Eiffel Tower in Paris, they are merely guides for negotiating the physical obstacles of the city. Social interactions are more important than physical landmarks in forming lasting impressions of places.

Of course, the physical presence of a place has some bearing on its emotional tone. A New Yorker feels immediately that London and Paris, because they have few tall buildings, are not nearly so imposing and impersonal as New York City. Parisian streets provide the American visitor with a different sense of space and time. Sidewalks are wide and filled with benches and cafés, encouraging one to stop or to move on at leisure. In contrast, American streets seem hardly to take pedestrians into account; they are clearly designed for automobiles, pedestrians having been relegated to subordinate status. Our impressions of cities are based on their apparent scale. When buildings spread horizontally instead of vertically, when we are encouraged to move through the city in the open air instead of in a steel and glass bubble, our view of the city and our emotional responses to it are apt to be quite different.

These observations are as true of neighborhoods as of entire cities. As we drive through an unfamiliar neighborhood, we can judge whether it would be a pleasant place to live. This judgment is engendered as much by the nature of public and semi-public spaces as by the lavishness of the dwellings. Do the streets and parks seem to be made for walking and sitting? Or are they merely means of channeling people from their residences to the nearest parking lot, public conveyance, or shopping center? Are the spaces, to use the terms of Humphrey Osmond (1957), sociopetal or sociofugal? *Sociopetal spaces* encourage interaction between people, while *sociofugal spaces* discourage interaction. Airport waiting rooms are usually sociofugal spaces, with immovable chairs facing other immovable chairs too far apart for comfortable conversation.

By changing the nature of space, it is possible to change both people's feelings about the environment and their behavior. This was shown most dramatically by Oscar Newman (1972) and the Clason Point Gardens development.

Changing the Physical Environment to Change Behavior Clason Point Gardens is a two-story public housing development in the Bronx, New York, consisting of about 400 duplex apartments located in over 40 row-house buildings. At the time of Newman's study, one third of the tenants were elderly white families, about 10 percent were younger whites, one-fourth were Puerto Rican families, and about one-third were Negro families. Interviews with the tenants revealed that they were extremely fearful of being victimized by criminals, particularly by adolescents from neighboring projects who used the grounds as a congregation area.

Newman reasoned that increased surveillance of the grounds by tenants would help reduce crime. If tenants could be induced to spend more time in the common grounds and take greater pride in their residences, these changes, too, would lead to a reduction in crime. Clason Point Gardens were redesigned so that these desirable effects might occur. Pedestrian paths were widened and paved with decorative effects; small private front lawns with low walls were made for each dwelling; public seating in the center of public paths was added, close enough to buildings to ensure visibility by tenants. Small playgrounds were created for young children, with seating nearby to allow supervision by adults. Increased lighting along the public paths and near recreation areas extended residents' surveillance potential. Buildings were refaced in colors selected by the tenants. The large central area of Clason Point was transformed into special areas for young children.

These changes in the physical design of the project increased the use of public areas and the visibility of open spaces. The number of outsiders and trespassers was reduced by increasing the visibility of these areas, and there was a corresponding decrease in crime. After one year, Newman reports,

felonies were down to one-third of the previous years' level. Measures of tenant satisfaction showed statistically significant improvement in the reduction of fear, in increased surveillance on the part of tenants, and in their evaluation of the quality of their living environment. The newly modified central play area is very intensively used by the community, and this has succeeded in discouraging its use by drunks and addicts. Tenants now maintain some 80 percent of the project grounds, appreciably reducing the workload of the maintenance staff. (1972, p. 174)

Changes in the physical design of structures might influence not only crime, but, as in the case of Clason Point Gardens, tenants' feelings of satisfaction with their environment as well. This is surely a more desirable response to crime than the more common act of sealing oneself off from others. High-rise buildings in the central parts of cities, with their security guards, 24-hour doorman service, and one main entrance, are like fortresses in the midst of decaying neighborhoods. These dwellings contribute to urban decay by reducing tenants' surveillance potential and sense of common property.

Summary

Since all behavior must occur in some sort of environment, it is reasonable to study the effects of that environment on behavior. A basic question of environmental psychology is: Given all the same circumstances except the physical environment, will the same behavior occur?

We know that what people think is often more important than objective conditions. It is people's *perceptions* of their environment that influence their behavior. If someone believes that a room is hot and crowded, then for all practical purposes, it *is*. That is why it is important to distinguish between the objective features of the environment and people's perception of that environment. Social psychologists are more apt to study the latter than the former.

Environmental psychology is a relatively new area of study. A few of the more fundamental topics in the field are personal space, human territoriality, and crowding. *Personal space* is the area surrounding a person the violation of which by another produces discomfort in the person. Personal space varies with situation, and with culture. When personal space is invaded by others, there is some effort to reestablish that space or to withdraw. Two theories of personal space, both dealing with the notion that there is an optimal amount of distance between people, are *equilibrium theory* and *stimulation theory*. Equilibrium theory, first proposed by Argyle and Dean, suggests that personal space varies with the intimacy between individuals. The more intimate, the closer they will tend to stand. Other components of intimacy include eye contact, smiling, and the nature of discussion topics. If one of these means of expressing intimacy is interfered with, there will be a tendency to compensate by making changes in one or more of the other mechanisms. Stimulation theory, proposed by Desor, among others, states that varying personal distance is a means of reducing or increasing social and sensory stimulation.

The areas referred to as territoriality and crowding draw heavily on similarities between animal and human behavior. These striking parallels, however, should not lead to premature conclusions that humans are territorial in the same way that most other primates are, nor should studies of the negative consequences of high population density in animals be generalized to humans. In both cases, there are enough differences between human and animal behavior to warrant caution in generalizing.

A topic only beginning to receive attention from social psychologists concerns the conditions that lead people to conclude that their environments are crowded. Crowding is the perception that a place is overcrowded, and because it is a psychological judgment, it is to be distinguished from population density (the number of people in a given area).

In recent years, interest in the city as a social psychological phenomenon has grown. Cities, because they are so diverse, give rise to coping mechanisms that may not easily be studied in other contexts. This is the *stimulus overload theory*, a more general version of stimulation theory.

Individuals' perceptions of their physical environments can be studied by examining their *cognitive maps* or personal views of the structure of a city. In addition to these mental images of the city, social encounters influence people's impressions of a place. This is more apt to be true of distant than of close places.

If the physical environment influences behavior, changes in that environment should lead to changes in behavior. An example of environmental design change, Clason Point Gardens, indicates how people's feelings and behaviors may change as a result of well-planned environmental change.

Suggested Readings

*Hall, E. T. *The silent language.* Garden City, N.Y.: Doubleday, 1959; *The hidden dimension.* 1966. Two well-written books on the uses and meanings of space, with emphasis on cultural differences.

*LaFrance, M., and Mayo, C. *Moving bodies: Nonverbal communication in social relationships.* Monterey, Calif.: Brooks/Cole, 1978. An overview of theory and research on nonverbal communication.

*Leff, H. L. *Experience, environment, and human potentials.* London and New York: Oxford University Press, 1978. A difficult but highly original work on changing the pattern of human life so that it is "more ecologically sound."

*Lynch, K. *The image of the city.* Cambridge, Mass.: MIT Press, 1960. A book on how people perceive their environments, particularly Boston, Jersey City, and Los Angeles, by a city planner.

*Newman, O. *Defensible space.* New York: Collier-Macmillan, 1972. How the environment may be changed to reduce crime and to increase people's feelings of social responsibility.

*Sommer, R. *Personal space.* Englewood Cliffs, N.J.: Prentice-Hall, 1969. A summary of research on personal space.

Pertinent Journals

Environment and Behavior

Environmental Psychology and Nonverbal Behavior

*Available in paperback edition.

Cathy Hull

12
APPLIED SOCIAL PSYCHOLOGY

PROSPECTS FOR AN
APPLIED SOCIAL
PSYCHOLOGY

Most of the problems confronting society today are human problems—overcrowding, poverty, pollution, maleducation, prejudice, war. A science that studies the interpersonal behavior of humans certainly ought to have something to say about the solutions to human problems (G. A. Miller, 1969). The preceding chapters have discussed child rearing, attribution, persuasion, attraction, pro- and anti-social behavior, problem-solving and conflict, among other topics. The roots of many of our problems lie in just these areas. Yet, as we will see, social psychology has contributed little to the amelioration of these problems. Forty years after the social psychologist Otto Klineberg noted that "It may seem premature to speak of an Applied Social Psychology, or to attempt to relate our findings to the problems of human welfare" (1940, p. 549), we may comfortably echo his remarks.

If social psychology has not contributed in a major or direct fashion to the solution of social problems, it is largely because of philosophical, social, psychological, and political processes. We might even say that one of the social problems confronting modern society is the failure to apply psychological knowledge to the solution of social problems. In this chapter, we will first examine some of the philosophical, social psychological, and other reasons for the relative absence of an applied social psychology. Then we will discuss what applied social psychology might accomplish, using examples of social psychology in action (two words, "in action," not one, "inaction").

SOME PHILOSOPHICAL AND
THEORETICAL PROBLEMS

"Applied Science": A Contradiction in Terms The term *applied social psychology* is in a fundamental sense a paradox. If social psychology is a science, and if science, as defined in Chapter 1, is concerned primarily with theory development, then *applied science* is a contradiction in terms. The goal of application is to effect change; the goal of science is to build theory. Applications are aimed at producing some desired result: a bridge, a change in attitude, the passage of legislation. Attempting to apply social psychological theories or research findings to some real-world behaviors is not a science, because the goals of the two are different. Application involves taking something from one system, the scientific system, and attempting to produce some change in another system, the real world. As with any translation from one system to another, errors of various sorts may occur. Something may be lost in the translation.

The tenuous relationship between science and real-world change is not peculiar to psychology; it exists as well in all areas of technology and engineering. "[E]ngineering is 'the art or science of making practical application of the knowledge of pure sciences.' In other words, although engineers are not scientists, they study the sciences and use them to solve problems of practical interest ..." (Florman, 1976, p. x). Engineering, whether of a physical or a social nature, borrows from science and relies heavily on science; however, the application of information from science to reality is not in itself a scientific enterprise.

Still Not Convinced? A Hypothetical Example Imagine that social psychology has produced a well-supported theory of racial prejudice. As part of a program to reduce prejudice in New York City, a governmental agency decides to apply this theory in randomly selected areas of the city. The appropriate materials are prepared and distributed, and appropriate control areas are established. Now let us suppose that after a period of one year, prejudice and discrimination can be reliably measured in New York. And further, that the results of this measurement indicate that the sections of New York City exposed to the experimental treatment show a significant decline in discrimination and prejudice, while the control areas show no change whatever. We have in this hypothetical case an example of what applied social psychology might look like. But, you may well ask, is it science?

Even if the theory is a very good one and the research is adequately conducted, the theory may still be false, and the results of the experiment may be due to factors other than those proposed by the theory. No theory may be accepted as absolutely true and any theory may be false, if not in the present, then at some time in the future. Because of the tentative and probabilistic nature of all science, theoretical models can never be applied to any situation with absolute certainty. We cannot expect that any attempt to apply social psychology to a real-life problem will *ever* be a foolproof scheme for changing individuals or society.

This is as true for physical technology as for social technology (Varela, 1975). We do not know everything there is to know about metallic alloys, rocket propulsion, astrophysics, weightless states, or interplanetary communication, yet our imperfect knowledge of these, based on scientific theories, enables us to send a man to the moon. Technology involves taking imperfect ideas from the scientific realm and combining them to accomplish a specific task.

In the application of theory to the real world, just as in conducting a laboratory experiment on the theory, there may be errors in (1) sampling; (2) the manipulation of variables; (3) the control of extraneous, irrelevant variables; and (4) measurement of effects.

1. Sampling errors. Social psychological research is usually conducted with college students as subjects. The results of such research may not be obtained with other populations. In other words, the external validity of much psychological research may be low. It would not be surprising, therefore, to find that many of our research results or theories are applicable only to a limited segment of the total population. Hence, the application of social psychology to large populations may fail to produce the desired or expected results because it may simply be irrelevant to the particular people involved.

2. Manipulating variables. Even if theories are widely applicable to various populations, the social technologist must still manipulate variables in the real world. Many of the variables found to be important in laboratory research, such as cognitive dissonance, are difficult to produce in natural settings and for large numbers of people. Then, too, there is the problem of ensuring that the desired variables have indeed been manipulated successfully in the natural setting. Again, errors in translation, manipulation, and control may prevent the successful application of social psychological knowledge to the real world.

3. Control of extraneous variables. If we wish to apply social psychological knowledge to the real world, it may be important to limit or control, or at least to measure, other variables that may interfere with the effect of the independent variable. In many situations, this is simply not possible. There is often little or no control over the myriad of things that transpire in people's lives. It is widely known in psychological research (e.g., Berelson & Steiner, 1964) that the very people we wish to influence are often those least likely to pay attention. For example, information campaigns to influence voters' opinions about a candidate, or campaigns to influence people's attitudes toward preventive health care, are most likely to be attended to by people already convinced of the candidate's desirability or already most concerned with maintaining good health.

4. Measurement of effects. While it may not be mandatory that the social psychologist measure the success of an intervention, this is often desirable. When the technologist sets out to solve a specific problem, as many civil engineers do when building a bridge, for example, it is evident whether or not he has been successful. There is no need to build a control bridge alongside the new bridge to determine whether people can get from San Francisco to Oakland. But for the accomplishment of a nonmaterial goal such as changing people's attitudes, it is necessary to establish adequate measurement procedures to determine whether we have, in fact, succeeded. Social psychologists are only beginning to address themselves to this problem. Using procedures that come under the heading *evaluation research* (Campbell, 1969, 1970), they are developing measurement methods that help determine the effects of social and political

These delegates have worked hard for the candidate of their choice. If their candidate is elected, will the delegates know, when the re-election campaign is underway, which strategies actually helped to win the election?

programs. But, as with any sort of psychological measurement, such methods contain numerous possibilities for error and bias.

Pragmatics For some programs, or for some social technologists, it is sufficient to produce a specific effect in a particular group of people, regardless of the reasons for that success. A political candidate, for example, might apply a variety of social psychological strategies culled from the literature on person perception and attitudes in her efforts to win an election. She is concerned, perhaps, only with getting elected, not with which of the applied principles were responsible for her winning the election. In such applications of psychological information, it may be only the end result which is important. But there is something to be said for the evaluation of effects even in this case. Four years hence, when our candidate comes up for reelection, it would be helpful if she could tell her staff just which of the many principles she applied successfully in the past were responsible for her being elected. This would provide specific guidelines for her reelection campaign, and might be of value to other candidates running for office. While it might appear practical in many situations to produce a change, it may be more practical still to determine the reasons for success (or failure), for then change can be produced more easily in the future or in other, related settings.

THERE IS NOTHING SO GOOD AS
A PRACTICAL THEORY: THE NEED
FOR A THEORY OF APPLICATION

How should the interested social technologist go about applying social psychological information to real-world settings? Hornstein (1975) has proposed a number of ways in which a social psychologist might use his or her expertise in effecting social change. The social psychologist might act as an expert on relevant matters, work in collaboration with a client such as a politician or an activist group, or serve as an advocate. The various forms of intervention might include conducting research on social problems, trying to orient people by providing them with scientific information pertinent to a social problem, and serving as a model of change, as a Rogerian therapist does. But while a social psychologist may play any, or all, of these roles, there is little to guide him or her in the direct application of theory and research to the solution of a social problem.

In an important and influential book on applied social psychology, Varela (1971) provides a number of basic philosophical principles that should underlie applications, but does not tell us how to translate ideas from the scientific realm to the real world. The application of social psychological knowledge to real-world problems has been pretty much a hit-or-miss proposition. In the hands of a sensitive and skillful practitioner like Varela, there have been more hits than misses. But how does the average practitioner learn how to apply social psychology to social problems successfully? According to Morton Deutsch (1975):

We must develop a theory about the utilization of social psychology and institutionalize a set of ethical guidelines to enhance the likelihood that social psychology will be used for rather than against the well-being of mankind. . . . Any theory of utilization will inevitably raise many fundamental ethical issues about the interrelations between the social psychologist, his client system, and other relevant third parties. These ethical issues center about the question of under what conditions does one party have the right to influence another? (pp. 9–10)

Deutsch raises two important issues here. The first is the need for a theory of application, that is, for a set of interrelated propositions about the utilization of psychological knowledge. The second concerns the moral and legal aspects of influencing other individuals.

Until a theory of application, or at least a set of principles for application, of scientific knowledge to social problems is formulated, we will have to be content with trial-and-error solutions based, whenever possible, on the most reliable findings and best-supported theories in the field. This leaves much room for error and, as a result, we should not be surprised to find that when such social engineering has been undertaken, it has not always proved successful.

WHAT IS A SOCIAL PROBLEM?

Before we can apply social psychology to social problems, we must define the nature of those problems. It is common to think of social problems in large-scale terms; for example, racism, war, urban terrorism, pollution, the invasion of privacy, and other impediments to individual liberty and satisfaction. The mere identification of a social problem tells us nothing about how to solve it. However, the way in which a problem is defined will tell us where we might look for a solution (Caplan & Nelson, 1973; J. G. Manis, 1976). There are two aspects to this issue.

The first is that there is no universal agreement on what problems need solving or the order of importance of different problems. It is commonplace to argue that anything detrimental to human well-being is a social problem (J. G. Manis, 1976), but what is detrimental to one person may be enjoyable or profitable to another.

This can be seen clearly in what Garrett Hardin (1968) has called *The tragedy of the commons*. In Colonial New England villages, a common grazing area was provided for cattle. Anyone could graze his cows freely in the Commons. Since use of the Commons was free, every owner could make more money by increasing the number of cattle that he grazed there. But, as the number of cattle increased, the grass became scarcer, until finally it was destroyed and everyone wound up with a loss. Each individual acting to his own advantage in the short term led to collective ruin in the long run. Was the Commons area a "social problem" or not? The answer would depend on whom you asked and at what point in the process. (A number of similar problems are discussed by Platt (1973) under the heading of *social traps*.)

What we choose to label a social problem, then, depends largely upon our values and politics. And, of course, there is greater agreement that certain things are problems—such as poverty and war—than other things. In the following sections of this chapter, I will discuss a number of human behaviors that I believe are social problems that require solution. Since there is no scientific way to determine whether something is a problem, these choices reflect my own biases and are restricted by the work that other social psychologists have done.

The second aspect of the issue of defining a social problem is that the definition and conceptualization of a problem influence where we look for solutions. The definition of a problem is based not only on our own values but also on assumptions about the causes of the problem. We might define juvenile delinquency as a social problem, but how we conceive of the causes of delinquency will influence the types of strategies we implement to reduce delinquency.

If the causes of delinquency ... are defined in person-centered *terms (e.g., inability to delay gratification, or incomplete sexual identity), then it would be logical to initiate* person-change *treatment techniques and intervention strategies to deal with the problem. . . . If, on the other hand, explanations are* situation centered, *for example, if delinquency were interpreted as the substitution of extralegal paths for already preempted, conventionally approved pathways for achieving socially valued goals, then efforts toward corrective treatment would logically have a* system-change *orientation. Efforts would be launched to create suitable opportunities for success and achievement along conventional lines. . . . (Caplan & Nelson, 1973, p. 200)*

Caplan and Nelson are saying that our presuppositions about the nature and causes of a problem will influence our proposed solutions. Once a problem is defined in a particular way and a proposed

Many prisons are called correctional institutions, implying that the prisoners criminal tendencies will be reduced by some kind of personality-altering treatment. But few prisons have such treatment programs.

solution is attempted, there is a tendency among psychologists to maintain their definition of the problem even if the solution is a failure. In other words, psychologists are subject to the same human foibles and distortions of reality as everyone else: once they have formed some conception of reality, they find it difficult to abandon it in favor of a new conception. It is for this reason that social technologists must ensure open lines of communication between themselves and the public they are trying to serve.

All this implies that what we know, or think we know, about some problem can blind us to what we don't know. Defining a problem in a certain way, viewing it through a particular theory, may prevent us from seeing alternative definitions and solutions. For years the problem of starvation in third world countries was defined as one of inadequate agricultural technology. Concern was focused on improving crop yield and on more efficient agricultural methods. These emphases made it easy to overlook the related issue of population growth in third world countries and ignored the question of which crops should be grown. Likewise, our tendency to define many social problems, such as unemployment, inadequate education, poverty, poor medical care, crime, and delinquency, in terms of personal characteristics limits our ability to see other, impersonal causes, such as the social and physical environment and political and economic conditions.

ETHICAL AND LEGAL CONSIDERATIONS IN SOCIAL TECHNOLOGY

In addition to the philosophical, theoretical, and methodological problems involved in applying social psychological knowledge to real-world settings, the social engineer must confront difficulties of a legal and ethical nature. To what extent does a person or group of people have the legal or moral right or obligation to effect changes in others? If social problems are broadly conceived as obstacles to individual freedom, then the social engineer who implements a program of change may also contribute to the realm of problems. These issues have been explored by a number of social scientists (e.g., Abelson & Zimbardo, 1970; Argyris, 1975; Deutsch, 1975; Wilson & Donnerstein, 1976).

The social technologist must devote attention to legal matters, but laws are inconsistent from one jurisdiction to another and seem to depend heavily on the specific nature of the application. Invasion of privacy, the legality of obtaining information surreptitiously, and the restriction of freedom of choice are topics that have been dealt with in U.S. courts.

Of perhaps greater importance are the ethical and moral issues of application. Do we have the right to interfere with what, for lack of a better term, might be called the "natural order" of things? This is a consideration that no social technologist can afford to ignore. I must confess that I find some of the applications reviewed in the remainder of this chapter ethically questionable—that is, I would not consider undertaking them myself. Some of them might now be held illegal in certain courts of law. Nevertheless, these studies are presented without comment on their legality or ethicality to provide you with as wide a sample as possible of applied research.

Jacobo Varela who has applied social science findings to human problems, deals with the matter of ethics in this way:

It has also been mentioned that many people seem shocked at the use of what might be considered deception in some of the techniques. That is precisely the position of Alceste, the principal character in Molière's Le Misanthrope. *He insists that one must be absolutely sincere and say nothing but what is absolutely true and comes from the heart. He detests mankind for its deceit. Philinte, his friend, of a more practical nature, says,*

> *There are many places where to be perfectly frank*
> *Would be ridiculous and little allowed.*
> *And often, hoping not to displease your austere honor,*
> *It's wise to hide what one has in one's heart.*

Amelioration of social ills is possible when we tell little white lies. If everyone said immediately what he thinks of everyone else (T-group training notwithstanding), life would be horrible. Part of living in civilization is saying, "I'm pleased to meet you," or "Glad to see you." We do this all the time because we have become quite accustomed to it. Yet, when there are new forms of saying things we are not *accustomed to, we may react as Alceste does. However, it is quite probable that if we could only induce this type of character to be more civilized, his bitterness would cease. (1971, pp. 285–286)*

Varela is arguing that, in some situations, the means justify the ends they serve. But in his actual role of social engineer, Varela is careful to respect the integrity of his "subjects," and to employ deception as infrequently as possible (see Chapter 2). And there are some social psychologists who argue that it is immoral *not to* use the knowledge we have of social problems to try to reduce human misery (Baumrin, 1970).

One of the most perceptive analyses of applied social psychology has been made by Chris Argyris (1975). He argues that since so much scientific social psychology is based on the manipulation and control of variables in laboratory experiments, it is only logical that when psychologists attempt to solve social problems they do so by trying to manipulate and control variables in the natural world. An alternative strategy, both for conducting research and for producing social change, is to enlist the cooperation of people in the enterprise of collecting data or producing change. In this "Model Two" strategy, people are not seen as "subjects" but as co-workers in an enterprise that can serve the mutual interests of psychologist and co-worker.

VARIETIES OF APPLIED SOCIAL PSYCHOLOGY

APPLICABLE VERSUS APPLIED SOCIAL PSYCHOLOGY

Much of the material you have studied in this course has potential application to real-world problems and events. Latané and Darley's (1970) work on bystander intervention, research on television and aggression, problem-solving and influence in groups, attitude change, socialization, and crowding can all be extended to situations of actual behavior. These will be considered "applicable social psychology," for, by extension, the theories and research can be applied to some real-life context. Though a great deal of social psychology is applicable—that is, it *could be* used in dealing with real-life problems—relatively little social psychology has, in fact, been applied.

For several years now social psychologists have been concerned with the social and political relevance of their field (e.g., Helmreich, 1975; M. B. Smith, 1973; Streufert, 1973; Meltzer, Note 4). In the early 1970s, a number of books appeared bearing titles like "The Relevance of Social Psychology," and it was considered somehow relevant to conduct a cognitive dissonance attitude change experiment where the persuasive message was about the Vietnam War rather than about buying toothpaste. While it is true that this concern with relevance influenced the field, it was only a superficial influence. This section is concerned not with social psychology that *may be* applicable to some human needs, but with actual applications of social psychology to alleviate human misery.

In some logical fashion, we could argue either that all science has some as yet unforeseen relevance to the real world, or that certain aspects of science are fairly close to real-world concerns. This is a facile argument since there is no hard evidence available to support or refute it. It is easy to point to engineering, where the most esoteric and abstract theories in physics and chemistry have been used for technological purposes, such as in the space program. But we cannot, with a few exceptions, point to technological progress based on social psychology that has met with even a modicum of success. It is the purpose of this section to examine technological programs based on social psychological information.

SCIENCE AND IMMEDIATE SOCIAL GOALS

A decade ago, science and technology were perceived as the means for achieving the principal national goals of the time, including better health, more affluence, improved defense, and adventurous space exploration. Since it was highly relevant, research was accorded prestige, funds, and considerable freedom. Society now is most concerned with a new set of problems, and science and technology no longer seem so central. Correspondingly, their prestige, funds, and freedom have been eroded. Of the three, the loss of freedom is the most damaging. When a scientist cannot work at what to him is most interesting and important, he is not effective. Loss of freedom has come in two ways. Some scientists have placed expediency above freedom and have chosen work for which they have little talent. More serious has been increasing pressure by the public and politicians through the control of federal funds to force scientists to work on "relevant" projects.

The public and the politicians in general are not sufficiently well informed to make good judgments as to the potential of science and technology in meeting societal needs. They seize on slogans as a substitute for thought. Because of some dramatic feats, there is excessive confidence in the power of technology. The typical response to the successful Apollo mission was, "If we can go to the moon, we can do anything." Subsequently, as the public contemplated such matters as the environment, it became impatient for instant change. Any performance short of the miraculous seemed to indicate lack of good will or an inappropriate set of priorities.

The public needs to understand that science and technology cannot be applied successfully to the fulfillment of every wish. In part this is because the "state of the art" is not sufficiently advanced. This is true of sociology and social problems. It also is true of medicine, where our desires for magical cures will always exceed

I do not mean to suggest that the basic research and theory building of scientific social psychology is irrelevant to human needs. It is relevant in a number of ways. First, it may provide us with new and better ways of understanding ourselves and others. Certainly Freud's theories of human nature have influenced untold millions of people in their views of their own and others' behavior. Second, we can appreciate basic science in much the same way we appreciate other abstract and creative endeavors. For example, I am not a physicist, but I find the comprehensible parts of Einstein's theory of general relativity as intellectually satisfying as a good novel or symphony. Third, it is impossible to know just which of the many theories and findings of social psychology will have important applications in the future. There is always a time lag between scientific discovery and technological application. In Varela's (1971) version of social technology, theories from the 1950s and 1960s were what the wisest men can deliver. Even in the physical sciences, which give man enormous power for accomplishments, there are limitations. One that has not been emphasized sufficiently is the long period of time needed to harness effectively the technology to meet a social goal. This matter was discussed recently by Harvey Brooks, dean of the School of Applied Physics at Harvard University. He pointed out that there is ample evidence to show that it takes about 10 years to arrive at a technological goal having significant impact on society. He has listed a number of the major goals of 10 years ago in education and in lunar exploration, all of which were achieved. However, even before the goals were reached, the public was turning its attention toward new goals. As Brooks puts it, technology is being asked to shoot at moving targets. When such targets come and go within a period of a few months, there is an impossible mismatch with the long time span required for research to be converted into practical application.

Commenting on the need to achieve a reasonable balance between demands for relevance and the need to maintain a viable scientific enterprise, the National Goals Research Staff (1970) has said, "To the extent that society insists that basic scientists do work that is more relevant to present social needs . . . scientists will be less able to work where nature appears willing to answer their questions. They may be required to work on relevant questions that perhaps cannot be answered at all at present, or can be answered only with uneconomic use of resources. Thus, excessive efforts to make science more productive in terms of immediate social goals may actually make it far less productive in the long run."

An editorial by P. H. Abelson, *Science*, August 21, 1970, *169*.

used successfully in social problem-solving in the 1970s. Who can say just which of the theories of the 1970s will have important applications in the 1990s? Finally, I believe one measure of a society is the freedom it allows people in their pursuit of knowledge, and social psychologists, like everyone else, should be permitted to study whatever they wish. In this kind of freewheeling science, findings discovered serendipitously may turn out to be important.

To some degree, it is possible to be a scientific researcher and at the same time be concerned with the potential applicability of one's findings. This is what Kurt Lewin (1947) referred to as *action research*. Lewin's concept of action research centered on studying things by changing them and observing the effects of change. "This seems very close to common sense. It is the way to solve any practical problem or learn any skill. Yet for Lewin this kind of involvement with practical problems was a never-failing source of theoretical ideas and knowledge of fundamental social psychological relationships" (Sanford, 1970, p. 4). We can study small-scale social changes, generate theories from them, and proceed to larger scales of change. In this way, the theory-building and theory-testing activities of the scientist are integrated with social technology.

VARELA'S SOCIAL TECHNOLOGY

Jacobo Varela is a social technologist in Montevideo, Uruguay. He was educated at Princeton, where he received a degree in engineering. He is therefore acutely aware of the techniques used by engineers in drawing information from the basic sciences for the purposes of problem-solving. Varela found that many of the problems with which he had to deal as an engineer for a large South American company were social rather than physical. So he began to use the techniques of engineering, with the literature in social psychology as his basic science, to solve these social problems (see Varela, 1975). Social engineering requires a broad knowledge of the social science literature, some expertise in evaluating problems, and experience in using the scientific literature for the solution of those problems.

In any kind of engineering, it is important to prepare the blueprint for the problem-solving program before implementing the program. The engineer should know just what he or she is trying to accomplish and how to go about it. In the example below, Varela even set a deadline for the complete solution. The problem to be solved involved a medium-sized South American company with about 600 employees. There was a clear organizational structure, with the board of directors at the top, general managers for each division, and design, production, and service departments within each division.

Varela was called in to solve an acute crisis. A technician, following the suggestions of two members of the board, had designed an important component for a new product. One of the board members claimed that there was a flaw in the design of the new component because the technician had failed to follow his advice. The entire board saw this as insubordination and ordered a change in the design. The technicians saw this order as punishment and virtually ceased work; they talked of the possibility of a strike.

When Varela came on the scene, the first thing he did was to analyze both the structure of the company and the personalities of the individuals involved. In particular, he was interested in the abilities, political leanings, and personality traits of the board members, manager, and technicians. The members of the board, with one exception, were politically conservative, while many of the managers and technicians had a history of liberal politics.

Before Varela's arrival, the board members had issued a series of

Small, informal meetings can help to resolve differences and correct misunderstandings. Varela used this technique as part of his social technology.

arbitrary directives to increase efficiency. They attributed the company's lack of efficiency to deliberate activity by infiltrated left-wing agitators. Most of the board's directives were in the form of direct orders about how to perform tasks in various departments and severe penalties for breaking rules or not following the board's orders.

The Technical Department's reaction to these orders was to exercise as much independence as possible on technical matters. Varela's interpretation of this reaction was in terms of psychological reactance (J. W. Brehm, 1966). The liberal technicians blamed the situation on a "fascist" plot by the board to try to get rid of those who did not share their conservative political views. As Varela notes, "The exaggerations and distortions in perception are clearly seen on both sides" (p. 198).

The strategy for resolving this conflict involved a series of meetings, held twice weekly during working hours, with members of the board, the manager, and the heads and assistant heads of all departments. "At these meetings several social-science principles were expounded and freely discussed in relation to their current problems. The main principles discussed were: positive reinforcement, approach–avoidance conflict, cognitive dissonance, win–lose conflict, individual differences in ability, and social pressure" (p. 199).

The assessment of the participants' personalities included designating those who were most involved and those who were involved only to a lesser extent. The design of the solution was to persuade the involved parties to change their attitudes on several issues. The board needed to recognize the necessity of delegating authority; the technicians had to recognize that they enjoyed a certain freedom in their designs, within the general objectives of the organization. "Since it was felt that these aims would be impossible to obtain in one step, due to the high degree of polarization and intensity of feeling on both sides, it was decided to first adopt more limited objectives . . . to have the technicians admit that the initial design could be improved upon. The improvement need not necessarily be in the direction indicated by the opposing party" (1971, p. 204).

Beginning with those least involved in the crisis, Varela drew up a list of statements with which particular individuals would most likely agree or disagree. During his conversations with these individuals, he tried to obtain agreement with the statements that were in line with the desired solution. Beginning with Prentice, a relatively noninvolved worker, Varela engaged in the following conversation:

V: In your experience, when designs are prepared, do you believe that they are final or is there always a chance for making some improvement?

P: Well, in general there is a limit of how far you can go on improving things. . . . The improvement obtained may not warrant the effort expended.

V: Do you think the projects made here in general always reach that stage?

P: By no means . . . I'd say that a good portion of the work is well below an acceptable standard.

V: You feel that if there were not so many distracting circumstances due to all these conflicts the work could come out better and that everyone would be less disturbed?

P: I've no doubt about it. . . .

V: Have you seen Witkin's design?

P: Yes. . . .

V: Do you feel that it is the best possible?

P: (Immediately on guard) I don't know. . . . But the Board should certainly not try to get in on details.

V: . . . Forgetting the Board's suggestion, do you think it would be absolutely impossible to improve on Witkin's design in any way?

P: . . . Well, probably [it could be improved on]. . . . If he didn't have to work under this kind of pressure, he probably could improve on it.

V: Do you think Heder [a more involved technician] thinks as you do?

P: I don't know. We might ask him. But I'll tell you. He sure is standing by his boys.

V: Why don't we call him in and ask him? Remember—we don't want to ask him if he's willing to accept the Board's ruling, but whether he thinks that under calmer circumstances Witkin or maybe somebody else couldn't improve on some aspect or other of the design.

P: There's no harm in trying. I don't think he'll have objections to going along with that. [Note that by a method of successive approximations agreement has been obtained from Prentice that it may be possible to make improvements on the design. Prentice will now reduce the dissonance this admission causes by trying to persuade Heder that Witkin could, under more favorable circumstances, turn out a better design. He will seek social support from Heder. . . .]

This conversation was repeated with Heder and others. Varela notes that as the persuader in these situations, his role was limited to asking questions and getting commitments to a new point of view. Once the technicians had agreed that it was possible to improve on Witkin's design, Varela set to work on the board of directors. One of the board members, Baker, had been involved in radical politics as a youth, and Varela began by talking with him.

V: I see you are having trouble with the technicians. I'm sorry to see that.

B: Yes, but we must be firm. We can't let these upstarts have their way every time.

V: You believe then that firm, iron discipline is what the young technicians need. [This statement was reactance-provoking. In his younger years, Baker had been quite liberal and had prided himself upon fighting against iron discipline.]

B: I wouldn't go as far as to say that iron discipline is what we need. That would be going too far, but we are facing a rebellion, and a minimum of respect for authority is what I ask for.

V: I see. You mean that the sign of a good, loyal technician is one who does exactly as he is told and no more. [This is, again, reactance-provoking . . .]

B: No. A good, loyal technician is one who is able to carry out orders but who also uses his imagination in order to create something. Otherwise, we wouldn't need technicians.

V: In your past career, did you ever face someone who insisted on telling you exactly what to do at every step?

B: I should say so! . . . [Here Baker launched into a long story about the time he worked under an authoritarian who wouldn't allow him any leeway. . . . By getting him to admit the validity of a reasoning that was once favorable to him, he must now maintain cognitive consistency by changing his present attitude.]

v: Do you think that the fact you were closer to the work situation put you in a better condition to think up new ideas than your boss? In other words, was he as close to the work as you were?

b: Of course not. . . . He couldn't possibly know all the details I knew, yet somehow he insisted on giving an opinion on the slightest detail. . . . [Again, Baker is committing himself to a principle on an unrelated issue, which nevertheless applies to the case at hand. He must therefore change his belief in the present crisis in order to reduce the dissonance that this causes. . . .]

v: Do you think then that in general people who are close to the work can apply information about details better than, say, a General Manager?

b: Of course. As people rise in organizations, they have to keep a more general view of the whole domain . . . ; and they can't keep up to date on every detail.

v: Even if he had the capacity to keep up to date on every detail, do you think that is the role of the person higher up?

b: By no means. He can't abandon detail altogether, but there is a great danger that if he gets into too much detail, he will lose sight of the general picture.

At this point, Varela has gotten a member of the board to commit himself to the general principle of delegation of authority.

v: Would you feel then that you personally would be seen in a better light by everyone by giving detailed instructions or rather by giving broad directives?

b: I think it is much more effective to give broad directives, provided the personnel are able and willing to carry them out.

v: Do you think the technicians of this corporation are able to carry the broad directives out?

b: Yes, they are able. They don't seem to be willing.

v: But is the matter under discussion a matter of broad policies or of detail?

b: Well, actually it's a matter of detail.

v: Is it in some way similar to the experiences you had?

b: Well, I suppose it is, except that now they aren't even willing to talk.

v: But assuming the hypothetical case of their being willing to talk and to recognize the Board's authority, would you admit to them that it's the Board's duty to give broad directives only?

b: Yes, but I don't think that's possible.

v: And if I were to tell you that I have spoken to Witkin and the other technicians and that they are not only willing but eager to talk . . . ?

B: I don't believe it! . . .

V: Under the circumstances then, in view of their willingness to talk and reach some sort of agreement, would you admit to them that the Board's job is to give broad directives?

B: Yes, I personally would, but I don't know what [the others] would say. . . .

One by one, the other board members were persuaded to agree that they should give only broad directives to the technicians and leave the details to them.

As Varela notes, this conflict was resolved by correcting misunderstandings, using cognitive dissonance and reactance, providing positive reinforcement for certain positions and statements, and eventually bringing the two sides together. True conflict resolution is not a compromise, but a process in which the two parties reach an agreement on the fundamental issues that led to the conflict (1971, p. 192). The process of conflict resolution that Varela engaged in was not one of arbitration. An arbitrator usually decides that one party is right and the other wrong, with the result that the latter usually feels cheated. In this example of problem-solving Varela enabled each side to agree on the fundamental position of delegation of authority.

I have spent so much time on Varela's version of social technology because it represents a departure from the usual conception of applied social psychology. First, rather than attacking large-scale social problems, Varela deals with a specific, concrete interpersonal or intergroup conflict. He deals with problems one by one, the way any engineer must. Each bridge must be constructed to achieve a particular aim and must take into account the specific conditions peculiar to that span. Likewise, Varela states the need to evaluate the situation and the participants in as much detail as possible. Rather than attacking a problem in the abstract, Varela deals with specific individuals who manifest the problem. Second, it may seem to you that a different social technologist might perceive the problem differently and propose different solutions. No doubt that is true. But it is also true of other engineering problems. A different civil engineer might build an altogether different bridge. But each of them would manage to solve the problem, though in different ways. Third, the social technologist does not expend effort trying to determine who is to blame for the problem. That, he says, is irrelevant to the solution.

When an attempt is made to solve a problem, there is no point whatever in trying to fix the blame on someone. As in most cases of conflict, there is not just one cause but an extremely complex situation in which each party sees his position as just, while maintaining that the position of the other party is untenable. In a situation like this, trying to fix blame or to find out who is right is about the most useless and often most damaging thing one could do. (1971, p. 201)

While Varela does not explicitly state how the various theories and findings in social psychology may solve social problems, he does provide a general framework that the social technologist should use. This framework is a set of guiding principles for the social engineer.

1. There are great individual differences among human beings.
2. Positive incitement is a better modifier of behavior than punishment or threat.
3. Social problems are solved by correcting causes, not symptoms.
4. Human conflict is no more inevitable than disease and can be solved, or even better, prevented.
5. Irrational feelings must be reduced before people can reason.
6. Human motivation is complex; no one does or fails to do something for only one reason.
7. Problems are solved more effectively in groups than individually.
8. Perceptions are more relevant to social problems than "true facts."
9. Time and effort are not available in infinite amounts for problem-solving.
10. Responsibility for individual improvement of subordinates, students, and others should shift largely from them to higher authorities.
11. Supervisors and teachers should receive intensive training in social science technology.

I am not aware of any systematic programs of applied social psychology on the scale of Varela's. He has worked on a large number of social problems, in such areas as health, group cooperation, and job stability. There are a number of other instances in which social psychological principles have been applied to various problems, and several of these will be reviewed below to familiarize you with the variety of applied social psychology programs that have been implemented to date.

MEDICINE AND SOCIAL PSYCHOLOGY

At least since the days of Breuer and Freud (1895/1955), it has been recognized that nonphysical factors often play a role in physical well-being. Stress, anxiety, interpersonal conflicts, the "will to live," and other personal and social states all influence one's bodily condition. In recent years especially, social psychologists have investigated the social correlates of smoking (Erickson & Cramer, 1976; Janis & Hoffman, 1970; Schachter, 1977; Suedfeld, 1973), heart disease (Glass, 1977), recovery from medical procedures such as surgery (Johnson & Leventhal, 1974; J. M. Levy & McGee, 1975; Sime, 1976), obesity (Rodin & Slochower, 1976), and alcohol and drug abuse (Jessor, Jessor, & Finney, 1973; Schlegel, Crawford & Sanborn, 1977), as well as social factors associated with what is usually referred to as mental illness (S. S. Brehm, 1976; Glass & Singer, 1972b; Klein, Fencil-Morse, & Seligman, 1976; Thorell, 1976; Vinokur & Selzer, 1975).

Little of this research has been applied in the sense that specific science-based intervention strategies were developed in order to produce a change in health or health-related behaviors. Among the applied work in the area of health is that of Suedfeld (1973) on the reduction of cigarette smoking.

Suedfeld modified earlier procedures on persuasion in isolated situations to reduce the consumption of cigarettes. When college students were placed in sensory-deprivation chambers, where there was little light and sound, and then exposed to a persuasive taped message arguing against cigarette smoking, it was found that there was a significant change both in attitudes about smoking and in actual smoking behavior. Three months after this treatment, the sensory-deprivation subjects smoked 38 percent fewer cigarettes than they had before treatment; a control group, exposed to the same persuasive message but not in sensory-deprivation chambers, showed a reduction in smoking of only 23 percent.

While it is not my intention to discuss smoking here, it should be noted that several social psychological theories are pertinent to the reduction and control of tobacco use. Erickson and Cramer (1976) attempted to determine which of three social psychological theories—reference group theory, cognitive dissonance theory, or psychoanalytic theory—best accounted for the modification of smoking.

Table 12.1.
Smoking Habits of Friends and Family of Ex-Smokers and Smokers

	Close Friends Smoking			Family Members Smoking
	Most Do	Mixture	Most Don't	
Ex-smokers				
When smoking	39	8	3	39
Now	10	7	33	15
Smokers	21	14	15	31

From Erickson and Cramer (1976).

In general, support was strongest for reference group theory. People who had once smoked cigarettes but no longer did showed a change in the smoking habits of their friends. Whereas when they smoked, most of their friends also smoked, once they had given up cigarettes, they tended to have more nonsmokers among their friends (see Table 12.1). It seems that friends and family may provide social support for the decision to stop smoking.

Giving Plants to Grandmother: Personal Change among the Institutionalized Elderly For a variety of reasons that social psychological theories can explain, older people, especially those who are isolated in institutions for the aged, often feel that their control over their own lives is minimal. In particular, a nursing home can be seen as a "decision-free" environment where all important decisions are made for the residents by the staff. Having few decisions to make, residents lose their sense of responsibility and control. Langer and Rodin (1976) attempted to reverse the chain of events that help lead to feelings of powerlessness by telling some residents that "many of you don't realize the influence you have over your own lives here." These residents were told that they had responsibility for the arrangement of their rooms, for deciding how to spend their time, for where they would meet visitors, and so on. A comparison group was told primarily about the variety of activities in the home and the dedication of the staff to making life comfortable and pleasant for them; they were not told about their own responsibilities. All residents were given a plant as a present. The experimental (responsibility-induced) group was told they had to make two decisions: first, whether or not they wanted a plant at all, and second, which plant they wanted. The plants were theirs to keep and take care of as they liked. The members of the comparison group were also given plants, but were told that while the plants were theirs, the nurses would water and care for them.

What effects did emphasizing personal responsibility have on people? The responsibility-induced group reported being happier and more active three weeks after this intervention. They were rated as more alert by the interviewers, and, according to the nurses, spent more time visiting other patients, talking to the staff, and entertaining their visitors. They also tended to assume responsibility and control over other areas of their lives.

Similar results were obtained in a field experiment by Schulz (1976), who had college students visit institutionalized elderly people. The residents of the retirement home were given various degrees of control over the number and timing of visits. When the visits were predictable, particularly when the residents had control over their timing, there was a marked improvement in the health, behavior, and attitudes of the residents.

ONE BUSINESS OF SOCIAL TECHNOLOGY IS BUSINESS: MOTIVATING ECONOMIC ACHIEVEMENT

Partly because business organizations and factories are relatively small, controlled social systems, they have been studied and experimented on for some time (e.g., Coch & French, 1948/1952; French, Israel, & As, 1960; Lawler, Hackman, & Kaufman, 1973; Zander & Armstrong, 1972). Much of this work was initiated by Lewin in the belief that changing one part of a social system would lead to changes in other parts. A good deal of the current work by psychologists on economics and productivity does not derive at all from social psychological research or theory, however. The primary concerns are with the effects of changes in the work week on productivity and morale (e.g., Goodale & Aagaard, 1975; Ivancevich, 1974; V. E. Schein, Maurer, & Novak, 1977) and with redesigning jobs and changing the decision-making structure of an organization (Lawler et al., 1973). One important exception is the work of McClelland and

Elderly people tend to be healthier and happier if they have some responsibilities and can control their own lives. It's also nice to be needed and appreciated.

Winter (1969), who attempted to influence economic productivity in underdeveloped areas by changing people's motivations and aspirations. Their research and application are, to a large extent, based on social psychological theory.

The social psychologist David C. McClelland has for many years been interested in motivation, particularly in what he has called *achievement motivation.* Rather than viewing a motive such as the need for achievement or the need for social approval as a static and unalterable component of human nature, McClelland and his colleagues believe that motivational states can be altered at any point in a person's life.

In his work on the need for achievement, McClelland and others have found that individuals who have a high need for achievement tend to be more enterprising and to set moderately difficult goals for themselves, are interested in success for its own sake rather than for money or power, are more interested in concrete feedback on how well they perform a task, and have a greater future time perspective than those with lower achievement needs. McClelland and Winter (1969) wanted to put the theory to the test by trying to influence the achievement motivation levels of businessmen in economically underdeveloped countries. They reasoned that an increase in the levels of achievement need among some businessmen would lead to more enterprising behavior, which in turn would lead to the opening of more businesses and the hiring of more workers, all to the economic benefit of the community.

McClelland and Winter chose to give a course in increasing the need for achievement in a city in Andhra Pradesh, India. The course would be given to some businessmen, while others in the town would constitute a control group. Businessmen in a comparable town in the same state would serve as a second control group. Data from the experimental town of Kakinada and the control town of Rajahmundry were collected over a period of five years, beginning two years before the training commenced.

The need-for-achievement course consisted of about ten days of training in four specific types of behavior.

1. Achievement syndrome. The participants were trained to recognize and produce fantasies and stories that were related to a high need for achievement. It is through an analysis of such stories that a person's level of achievement need is measured. So, in short, participants learned how to score high on the need for achievement tests.

2. Self-study. The participants were given various homework assignments in which they had to relate the material from the classroom to their own personal and business lives. As McClelland and Winter note, "The scientific implication of the research findings is inescapable. If they want to do a better entrepreneurial job, then the

Table 12.2.
Some Economic Effects of Training in Need Achievement

	Before Course 1962–1964	After Course 1964–1966
Percentage Working Longer Hours		
Trained (N = 61)	7	20
Controls (N = 44)	11	7
Percentage Starting New Businesses		
Trained (N = 51)	6	27
Kakinada, controls (N = 22)	5	5
Rajahmundry, controls (N = 35)	9	14
Percentage in Charge of Firm Employing More People		
Trained (N = 33)	32	58
Kakinada, controls (N = 14)	23	21
Rajahmundry, controls (N = 24)	35	42

Adapted from McClelland and Winter (1969).

scientific evidence shows that the means to that end is to learn to think, talk, and act like a person with high need Achievement" (p. 59).

3. Goal setting. Participants learned to set goals for themselves that reflected a high need for achievement; that is, goals that were moderately difficult to attain. The goal setting included training in various types of games such as ringtoss, in which an individual could make the task easy by standing close to the pegs, or difficult by standing a great distance away. Participants in the course learned to set moderately difficult goals in this and other tasks.

4. Interpersonal supports. The course participants quickly formed a close-knit group in which they reinforced and supported one another.

While the training was fairly intense over the ten-day period of the course, it was enjoyable and not terribly difficult for the participants.

What effects did the training have? There were two types of dependent measure in this study: individual measures of the participants' behavior and economic measures of the impact of the course on the town of Kakinada. As the authors summarize, "Analysis of several measures of individual behavior and economic effects demonstrated that the participants in achievement motivation courses showed significant improvement in many aspects of entrepreneurial performance, both as compared with themselves before the course and as compared with three matched groups of controls. Course participants show more active business behavior . . ." (p. 230). In particular, participants in the training course worked longer hours, made more investments in new and fixed capital, employed more workers, and had increased gross income in their firms. About 135 new jobs were created in Kakinada. Some of the economic effects are shown in Table 12.2.

In a note appended to the 1971 edition of their report on the project, the authors noted that, in general, the effects of this fairly brief training in need for achievement persisted for several years, and thus had a lasting impact on the economic well-being of the town of Kakinada. They also noted that training in achievement motivation is not a panacea for economic ills. The training was more effective for participants who were initially most dissatisfied with themselves and who believed that they might be able to solve some of their own economic problems. The course provided them with some of the skills and attitudes necessary to solve these problems. Training in achievement motivation would not be as effective in places where there was little opportunity or incentive for entrepreneurial behavior.

SOCIAL PSYCHOLOGY IN THE
POLITICAL ARENA

Social psychological theory and research in politics revolve around three basic issues: voting, the effects and formulation of public policy, and national and international conflict. Although considerable research, much of it applicable, has been carried out on each of these issues, little has been done to change the voting habits of constituents, to influence public policy, or to reduce social conflict.

For example, there are numerous studies on the social and psychological processes involved in the decision to vote and the choice of candidate (e.g., Granberg & Brent, 1974; Knoke, 1972; Kraut & Lewin, 1975; G. S. Rotter & Rotter, 1966; Shikiar, Wiggins, & Fishbein, 1976). Much research has been done on how public policy is formulated (Hughes, Rao, & Alker, 1976; McCann, 1972; H. L. Ross, Campbell, & Glass, 1970; Steinman, Smith, Jurdem, & Hammond, 1977) and how it is received by the general public (Cooper, Boltwood, & Wherry, 1974; Goodwin & Tu, 1975; Wortman, Hendricks, & Hillis, 1976). And there has been a great deal of theoretical analysis and simulation research on intergroup and international conflict (Deutsch, 1973; Kelman, 1965; R. K. White, 1977; see also Chapter 8).

It has been said that the most concrete contribution of social psychology to human welfare was the important role it played in the 1954 Supreme Court decision on desegregation (see Meltzer, Note 4). Social psychological research, particularly that by Kenneth B. Clark and Mamie P. Clark (1947), which showed that black children preferred white to black dolls, was especially influential. (In more recent years, that finding has not been replicated; see

For nearly two decades social scientists have been talking about the desirability of having a voice in the highest policy-making councils of the nation. Some have favored placing in the White House a Council of Social Advisers, which would function like the Council of Economic Advisers. Others would rather add social scientists to that council.

More recently, high-level representation has been in disfavor among social scientists because they believe that such "high visibility" would make them into whipping boys of Congress. This is feared because social science tends to deal with value-laden issues and to have a relatively weak basis for many of its positions. . . .

Putting aside the question of how social science's voice is to be heard in national policy-making, it seems that despite its fledgling status, social science has significant contributions to make.

First, its representatives would provide an institutionalized source of basic social facts policy-makers are quick to ignore—for example, that many welfare clients are not able-bodied males, but old or disabled Americans, or mothers of several young children. . . .

There are literally thousands of such social facts, many summarized in Berelson and Steiner's *Human behavior* (1964) and Rothman's *Planning and organizing for social change.* Unfortunately books do not speak, and institutionalized occasions are needed to call attention to their content and to spell out their implications.

In addition to facts, social science perspectives ought to be represented in councils, which often contain only persons whose background is politics, law, or natural science. Thus, politicians typically tend to believe in the potency of the "Madison Avenue" approach. However, social scientists will point out that the view of human nature as subject to manipulation through advertising is probably erroneous. Ads may work well for products people already have a preference for, and are effective in switching people around among nearly identical products, but to overcome addictions or prejudices ads tend to be ineffectual. This has been established by studies on attitudes toward everything from campaigns against smoking to drives against prejudice. Can one, for example, expect an addict to heed such an emotionally shallow and brief input as a 60-second ad, compared to all the social, psychological, and physiological forces that bind him? Or, to put it more technically, can formal communication fight values and peer relations, community and social structure, personality, and biology?

True, social scientists will often not agree on what advice to give, but advisers from other specialties also disagree. And out of the heat of give-and-take a light does arise. Policy-makers should certainly not base their decisions solely on social science, but they might well be better off if they formed them after the social scientists' voices have been heard.

An editorial by Amitai Etzioni, *Science,* December 10, 1976, *194.*

SOCIAL SCIENCE IN THE WHITE HOUSE

Greenwald and Oppenheim, 1968; Hraba and Grant, 1970; see also Chapter 10.) While social psychology may influence society in this rather indirect way, there are some specific interventions designed to produce immediate and beneficial results. An example of the application of social psychology to the political domain is in what has been called the conflict resolution workshop discussed in Chapter 10.

JUVENILE DELINQUENCY AND SOCIAL PSYCHOLOGY

Ostrom, Steele, Rosenblood, and Mirels (1971) borrowed several concepts from social psychology to modify the behavior of juvenile delinquents, following principles of engineering much like those used by Varela. Their primary concern was to influence the values and attitudes of the delinquents and to alter their anti-social behavior. They note that "By the time a youth is labeled a 'juvenile delinquent' by society, he is likely to have developed a resistance to the conventional means society uses to transmit values and encourage law-abiding behavior" (p. 119). It therefore becomes necessary to overcome the youth's resistance to communication and influence, and this they attempted to accomplish by using notions from the literature in social psychology.

The subjects in their intervention study were delinquents who had been placed on probation by a juvenile court in Ohio. The intervention itself took place in a setting that would not have negative connotations to the delinquents, the Ohio State University laboratories. The delinquents were given maximum freedom to participate in the project and were told that they would be released from visits with parole officers if they agreed to serve as "consultants in a project designed to understand 'why kids get into trouble.'" Attendance at the experimental sessions was purely voluntary since "making participation a compulsory requirement can destroy the effectiveness of influence attempts." At two-hour sessions held weekly for two months, topics relating to delinquency were discussed and the participants engaged in a number of role-playing procedures in which they took the part of parents, policemen, victims, law breakers, judges, teachers, gang leaders, and innocent bystanders. To increase commitment during these role-playing sessions, videotape recordings were made, reviewed, and discussed by the boys. They were rewarded with a letter of praise for behavior that was self-initiated and internally motivated. A control group of delinquents did not participate in these sessions.

The effect of this broad theory-based intervention was determined both by paper-and-pencil tests given to the subjects and by examination of their school and court records. Nearly twice as many members of the control group committed one or more delinquent acts during the ten months following the intervention. During the four months after intervention, 50 percent of the control group, but only 8 percent of the treatment group, had at least one arrest. The difference between the experimental and control groups diminished with the passage of time, which suggests either that intervention should persist for longer than two months or that there should be periodic reinstatement of the treatment. The boys in the experimental group, however, did show a lasting increase in self-supportive attitudes that did not diminish over time.

Various kinds of intervention strategies have been used with juvenile delinquents and their families. The theoretical bases for these interventions generally come from a single source, such as learning theory (e.g., Switzer, Deal, & Bailey, 1977), role theory (Chandler, 1973), or behavior therapy (J. F. Alexander & Parsons, 1973; Hawkins, Peterson, Schweid, & Bijou, 1966). Only rarely is a genuine engineering approach taken in which strategies are based on a wide range of theories and research findings (e.g., Patterson, Cobb, & Ray, 1973).

PREVENTIVE SOCIAL PSYCHOLOGY

Many social problems are difficult—and may ultimately prove to be impossible—to solve. Like most other problems, social problems are considerably easier to prevent than to solve.

Most phenomena associated with societies and people grow exponentially if not restrained. That is why crises appear to come on so suddenly, why problems seem unimportant one season and out of hand the next. It is probable that we can still control most of the serious problems we face, the population explosion and all its by-products, such as misery, crowding, famine, lack of education, poverty, or the spread of nuclear arsenals, or the pollution of the air and the seas.... [E]nvironmental and social diseases are much easier to prevent or arrest than reverse. Prevention requires legislation and restraint, while undoing environmental damage which requires vast physical projects and undoing the human damage of a social error, such as allowing children to grow up in poverty or without adequate proteins in their diets, may prove to be impossible. (Wiesner, 1970, p. 89)

When social scientists discuss the possible relevance of their discipline to social problems, they almost always refer to the uses of science for the solution of existing, usually large-scale, problems. But perhaps social science should learn a lesson from medicine and devote a considerable portion of its efforts to heading off problems before they arise. It has been possible to eradicate virtually dozens of once-lethal diseases, not by the development of treatments to cure them, but by the development of vaccines to prevent their occurrence and spread. Likewise, social scientists might develop strategies to prevent social problems.

Preventive social psychology might consist of several activities: basic research on the antecedents of problems; methods to alter the social environment to minimize the likelihood of the occurrence of social problems; a focus on positive social behaviors; continuous liaison with legislative bodies to keep them abreast of these activities; and continuous communication between social psychologists and the public, both to keep people informed of situations that foster problems and to gather information about their perceived needs and desires. This last component of preventive social psychology is particularly important, for not only does much research in science depend upon public funds and require public support, but as psychologists, we know that people's perceptions of the causes of problems are perhaps as important as the actual causes. If, for example, people believe that they can reduce crime by arming themselves and forming vigilante groups, then that is what many people will do whether it actually reduces crime or not. The theories that people assume are true are likely to be acted upon. It is social psychologists' responsibility not only to keep the public informed, but also to treat people's beliefs as possible sources of social problems and to use these beliefs in the solutions of problems.

There are numerous opportunities for the misuse of preventive social science. Project Camelot perhaps epitomizes the misuse of applied social science.

MISAPPLIED SOCIAL SCIENCE: PROJECT CAMELOT

Camelot was the name given to a project for measuring and forecasting the causes of revolutions and insurgencies primarily in underdeveloped areas of the world. It was also concerned with finding ways to eliminate the causes of revolutions. The project was sponsored by the U.S. Army at a cost of about $5 million.

In a recruiting letter sent to scholars all over the world in 1964, Camelot was presented as a study to "make it possible to predict and influence politically significant aspects of social change in the developing nations of the world" (quoted in Horowitz & Katz, 1975, p. 102). Scholars were informed that the research was designed to identify the potential for internal war within societies and to identify "with increased degrees of confidence, those actions which a government might take to relieve conditions which are assessed as giving rise to a potential for internal war." While Camelot was intended to be conducted in Latin America, Asia, Africa, and Europe, the initial research was begun in Chile.

When word of the project was leaked, Camelot was canceled, with all parties greatly embarrassed: the scientists for failing to take control of the project and for doing military research under the guise of science; the military for enlisting social scientists to formulate counterinsurgency plans; and the Congress for allowing the Department of Defense, rather than the State Department, to conduct international research. The scientists working on Project Camelot failed to take into account the beliefs and attitudes of the Chilean people, and the United States as a whole was embarrassed by the ill-fated project. One lesson of Project Camelot was stated in another context by Aronson and Sherwood (1972, quoted in Zuniga, 1975): "The researchers learned that skill in their craft requires more than technical knowledge. In fact the ability to be diplomatic is perhaps as important as any. We learned that success requires close cooperation among the researchers, the program designers, and the practitioners." (And, one might add, the subjects of the research as well.)

If there is ever to be a preventive social technology, it must consider what is being prevented, at what expense, and for what purpose. Too much of what is taken for granted in science, and too much of what is portrayed as "objective," is in fact politically charged. As we saw in Chapter 10, research on prejudice almost always studies prejudice as an attitude of the prejudiced person. Relatively little is known about the psychological impact of prejudice on its victims. While prejudice itself may not be a political topic, the choice of subjects to study, theories to test, and methods to use involves political considerations. For this reason, it is probably advisable to have as great a diversity of opinion represented on policy research committees as possible. This will help reduce the implicit political and moral bias of so much applied research.

Summary

In this chapter, I have tried to show both the pitfalls and the promise of applying social psychology to social and personal problems. Some people fear that psychology is too powerful a tool to be left in the hands of a scientific or political elite. They argue for the widest dissemination of psychological research and theory. But I don't think that psychological knowledge is so potent or precise as to be a dangerous weapon of control. Actions undertaken in the name of "science" or "research" can, of course, be misused, as Project Camelot clearly shows. Applied social psychology does not have to involve manipulation of other people, but may instead enlist the cooperation of others and provide them with information that may enable them to take control of some aspects of their lives (Argyris, 1975).

The application of any scientific knowledge to the real world involves some degree of risk. Because all science is speculative, there is no certainty that an application to the real world will be successful. Even if a social problem can be solved by applying psychological knowledge, there are still moral, economic, social, and political factors to be considered before intervening in the lives of other people.

The task of solving social problems with psychological knowledge would be greatly facilitated if we had a theory that specified how we could translate information from the scientific system to the real world. That is much less a problem in the physical sciences, where both theories and problems may be expressed in mathematical terms. Since most theories in psychology are entirely verbal, the precise meaning of concepts and relationships is often ambiguous. A theory of application would enable us to determine the extent of this ambiguity and to weigh alternative strategies for solutions.

Despite the many difficulties of applying social psychology, a number of successful applications have been made. Two in particular have been the focus of this chapter: one deals with small-scale problems that require changing individuals' attitudes in an industrial setting (Varela, 1971), and the other deals with large-scale economic changes in an underdeveloped community (McClelland & Winter, 1969). Other varieties of application have been briefly reviewed to show the potential range of problems to which social psychology might be directed.

A distinction was made between applicable social psychology and applied social psychology. Only actual applications were discussed in this chapter, and those applications dealt primarily with human problems. The following chapter is concerned with social psychological studies that may be applicable to a variety of phenomena, such as music, art, humor, sports, and recreation. These topics concern not social problems but areas which may enrich our lives, and it is here that a preventive social technology might be developed that would forestall social problems before they arise.

Suggested Readings

Brehm, S. S. *The application of social psychology to clinical practice.* Washington, D.C.: Hemisphere, 1976.

Deutsch, M., & Hornstein, H. A. (Eds.). *Applying social psychology.* Hillsdale, N.J.: Lawrence Erlbaum Associates, 1975.

*J. H. Hamsher & H. Sigall. *Psychology and social issues.* New York: Macmillan, 1973.

Korten, F. F., Cook, S. W., & Lacey, J. I. (Eds.). *Psychology and the problems of society.* Washington, D.C.: American Psychological Association, 1970.

Marrow, A. J. *The practical theorist: The life and work of Kurt Lewin.* New York: Basic Books, 1969.

Mitcham, C., & Mackay, R. (Eds.). *Philosophy and technology*. New York: Free Press, 1972.

Varela, J. A. *Psychological solutions to social problems*. New York: Academic Press, 1971.

The following journals are most apt to contain articles on social technology and applied psychology: **Pertinent Journals**

Evaluation and Program Planning (Contains articles on evaluation research and policy formulation.)

Journal of Applied Behavior Analysis (A journal concerned with the application of Skinner's operant conditioning principles to problems in schools and hospitals, to psychotherapy, medicine, and so on.)

Journal of Applied Behavioral Science (Concerned largely with T groups, but also has articles dealing with organization development.)

Journal of Applied Psychology (Publishes articles based on a variety of approaches dealing largely with industry, business, and advertising.)

Journal of Applied Social Psychology (Contains research papers that are primarily applications of basic social psychological principles; both applicable and applied research.)

Journal of Social Issues (Publication of the Society for the Psychological Study of Social Issues. Each quarterly issue is devoted to a specific topic, such as population planning, conflict, desegregation, and so on.)

Social Problems (A sociologically oriented journal containing articles on crime, racism, poverty, education, and politics.)

13

THE SOCIAL PSYCHOLOGY OF . . .

Cathy Hull

Social psychology can be broadly defined so that most behaviors involving one or more persons may be considered part of the field. All but the natural sciences may fit within this broad definition. Consistent with this view is the study of the effects of human creations, such as art or architecture, on the behavior of others. Therefore, a social psychologist might choose to study certain aspects of the arts and aesthetics, formal social institutions such as the law, historical events, and so on. Of course, as a *scientific* social psychologist, one's purpose would still be to employ accepted scientific methods with the aim of testing and developing theoretical explanations for certain events.

It is possible to take nearly any theory in social psychology and use it as a tool for explaining almost any behavior. Cognitive dissonance theory, for example, has been tested in such a variety of contexts that it is possible to discuss political campaigns, voting, sexism, child rearing, sports, gambling, education, and attraction with the aid of this one theory alone (Wicklund & Brehm, 1976a). It was this broad applicability of theory that led Kurt Lewin to remark that there is nothing so practical as a good theory. Because theories are written in the abstract, they may be generalized to an almost unlimited number of particulars. (This is a distinction discussed in more detail in Chapter 12 as "applicable" versus "applied" social psychology.)

In this chapter a number of topics are discussed whose study is not incidental to theory development. A number of topics are of growing interest to social psychologists. For a sampling of these, some current theory and research are reviewed. Some of these topics, such as humor, aesthetics, and abnormal behavior, are of particular interest to me and are included here because I would like to share my enthusiasm for them with the reader. Other areas, such as the legal system, science, and the social psychology of social psychology, are becoming increasingly prominent in the field and may become central to it in the years ahead.

This assortment of topics is also designed to allow you to use your newly acquired social psychological perspective for the study and analysis of any given behavior. For example, one of the sections deals with the social psychological analysis of sports and games. Before reading that section, try to think as a social psychologist would about what features of sports might be amenable to social psychological analysis. Watch a team sport, such as a football or basketball game, and, while watching, ask yourself which of the many things going on would be of most importance to a social psychologist. Once you have become familiar with the tools and theories of social psychology, you should be able to see any social situation from this particular vantage point. One purpose of this chapter, then, is to prepare you for examining everyday situations in social psychological terms.

. . . ABNORMAL BEHAVIOR

Among the most important lessons you can learn as a student of social psychology is that behavior at any moment is a function not only of a person's internal state, but also of a person's social, physical, and psychological environment. In a sense, this is true for group as well as individual behavior. It is not true in the *strictest* sense because if we are talking about a group of people, it is unwise to speak of the group as a unit possessing cognitive traits. Although these traits might be shared by all the individuals composing the group, the group itself does not have a "mind." Nevertheless, when many individuals begin to display certain behaviors at roughly the same time in the same place, it is wise to look for the causes not only in those individuals, but also in their social environment. For this reason, sociologists, and, more recently, social psychologists, have taken an interest in collective behavior and personality disorders (see Chapter 9), for these mass phenomena might best be explained by reference to the individuals in their social environments. Mental illness will be used as an illustration of the social psychological approach to mass behavior.

In order to examine the behavior of many individuals as a function of the social context, we must take a more or less historical view of the behavior in question. For example, does it occur more frequently at different historical periods, or in different places, or among different groups of people? We know that what is termed "mental illness" has not always been considered either an illness or mental (G. Rosen, 1968; Szasz, 1961). We know, too, that its prevalence in different places and among different groups of people varies considerably (Gruenberg, 1954). For example, the lower one's social class, the more likely it is one will be diagnosed as severely mentally ill (Hollingshead & Redlich, 1958).

A historical analysis of the frequency and distribution of mental illness quite clearly shows that it varies with time, place, and circumstance. The most interesting analyses have been made by sociologists, historians, and social philosophers, who have demonstrated that before science became the leading social institution, and medicine one of the leading sciences, there were quite different explanations for abnormal behavior (Foucault, 1965; G. Rosen, 1968). Before science dominated Western thought, the church was the institution with the greatest esteem and political power. Behavior was judged in large measure by how closely it conformed to accepted church doctrine. Nonconforming behavior, especially of the old, the poor, and women, was thought to be indicative of possession by the devil, and in Europe and North America, suspected witches were persecuted until the beginning of the nineteenth century.

As the church's influence faded and science ascended in the

public's esteem, talk of witchcraft and the devil became an occasion for ridicule and suspicion. What scientifically minded person believed in invisible demons in the enlightened Age of Reason? Yet, deviant behavior persisted, especially among those who had the least means to conform to social customs, the poor and the disenfranchised. Rather than being discussed as the devil's work, deviant behavior was discussed in more rational terms, as the work of still invisible but now tangible demons—"illness," "disease." Poor old women were no longer thought to be witches, but wretches caught in the throes of a mental disease, and were treated as other sick people (Spanos, 1978). This medical view of deviance is the most prevalent today in Western society. The language with which we discuss nonphysical abnormalities is almost entirely medical: mental illness, psychiatric hospital, diagnosis, treatment, therapy, symptom. As Szasz (1961) notes, if an illness is real, it is not mental; if it is mental, it is not an illness. Over the past few hundred years, people formerly given the power to define and deal with deviance from a religious base have given way to those who treat deviance from a medical–scientific base. In both instances, a metaphor for explaining and dealing with deviance has given way to a widespread belief in the reality of the metaphor. Because people behave as though they are sick does not mean they are sick.

It is not clear whether this replacement of witchcraft with the medical view was a step forward. It is still the case that the dominant social institution, science, is left with the power to decide which people are mentally ill and what should be done about them. Thomas Szasz (1970) has argued that the psychiatric establishment is not firmly based on scientific principles and most often serves its own political and economic ends. It is well known in the West that the Soviet Union, for example, commonly places political dissidents in psychiatric institutions to remove them from society at large (Medvedev & Medvedev, 1972). In the United States, people who engage in certain deviant acts are thought to be mentally disturbed and are allowed to plead such in a court of law.

LABELING THEORY AND DEVIANCE

There are several variations on the general notion of labeling as a primary determinant of "psychopathology." Two related versions are Thomas Scheff's (1966) labeling theory and the views of Philip Zimbardo (Note 5).

According to this general approach, most behavior conforms pretty closely to accepted social norms, rules, and customs. On those rare occasions when a person's behavior does not conform to generally accepted standards, either we have some ready explanation for the individual's failure to adhere to custom, or we are motivated

Although no one seems to agree with this fan, we would hardly label his behavior as deviant. We might wonder why he's sitting with supporters of the opposing team, however.

to seek an explanation for the failure to conform. For instance, take the behavior of driving a car in an 80 kilometer per hour zone. Nearly everyone will drive within a fairly narrow range of the posted speed limit, between 70 and 90 kilometers per hour. This slight deviance from the norm is well within tolerable limits to most people and we would think little about anyone driving at these speeds. But suppose someone deviates considerably from this normal range by going either 20 kilometers per hour or 140 kilometers per hour. Given the severity of the deviance, we would probably be motivated to find an explanation for the person's failure to conform. We might satisfy ourselves upon passing the slow vehicle to learn that the car suffers a mechanical problem, thus explaining the driver's deviance. Or we might assume that the person driving at 140 kilometers per hour is late for an important appointment. In either case, we would be apt to attribute the cause of the deviance to some factor external to the individual, or perhaps to some combination of internal and external factors, such as the desire to reach a certain destination quickly and the crowded traffic conditions. Only rarely would we be likely to attribute the driver's behavior to "mental illness." That is because driving speed is one of those behaviors of rule breaking that is socially tolerated and for which we often have adequate explanations.

Let us take another example of deviance, in which the rules are not so well established and explanations are not generally available—paying attention to others when they speak to us. Imagine that you and a friend are having a conversation. Your friend is telling you about some problem of hers and she suddenly realizes that you have been staring off into space, having heard nothing of what she said. She is apt to ask why you weren't paying attention to her. There are a few acceptable answers: you were thinking of something important or interesting; you were distracted by some external event you heard or saw; you were thinking about something she said earlier; you were thinking about a problem of your own. In our culture, these are all acceptable reasons for not listening to someone, but they are acceptable only occasionally. If you never listen when people speak to you, these will no longer be accepted as reasonable excuses for not paying attention. In this case, which Scheff refers to as *residual rule breaking*, because there is no general explanation for why someone does not pay attention, being deviant makes one susceptible to an internal explanation for nonconformity. If you are a chronic residual rule breaker, if you never pay attention when spoken to, your friend may assume there is something wrong with you. When there are no ready explanations for residual rule breaking, the person becomes vulnerable to the attribution of mental illness.

Mental illness is a broadly shared social stereotype, learned from the media and used to characterize chronic residual rule breakers. In most instances, the person so labeled must be more or less willing to accept this stereotype and to play the role of a mentally ill person. Once a person is categorized as mentally ill, it becomes exceedingly difficult to shed the stereotype. This is nowhere better illustrated than in a study by David Rosenhan (1973).

Rosenhan had eight "sane" people gain admission to nearly a dozen psychiatric facilities. (At least they were as sane as three psychologists, a psychology graduate student, a pediatrician, a psychiatrist, a painter, and a housewife generally tend to be.) After making an appointment at the hospital, the "pseudo-patients" complained of hearing voices that said "empty," "hollow," and "thud."

Beyond stating these symptoms and using a fictitious name, employer, and vocation, the eight pesudo-patients presented factual information about themselves and their circumstances. All of them were admitted, most with a diagnosis of schizophrenia. Once admission was gained, they ceased simulating any symptoms of abnormality. Their goal was now to convince the staff that they were sane and should be released.

The length of hospitalization ranged from 7 to 52 days, with an average of 19 days. During their stay, the pseudo-patients were largely ignored by the staff, and were in other ways depersonalized. For example, Rosenhan reports that in the presence of an entire ward of men, a nurse unbuttoned her uniform to adjust her bra, as though the patients were not even there. During their hospitalization, the eight pseudo-patients were given close to 2100 pills of various sorts, nearly all of which were, like much medication given to actual patients, pocketed or deposited in the toilet.

It appears from this study that once they are assumed to be mentally ill, people find it difficult to demonstrate their sanity. Even when the pseudo-patients were discharged, it was most often not as "sane" but as having schizophrenia "in remission." This label means that the staff still considered the pseudo-patients to be suffering from mental illness, though the overt symptoms were no longer apparent.

Of course, Rosenhan does not deny that people often engage in deviant behavior or that they may suffer from depression and anxiety. He does conclude that our ability to diagnose sanity and insanity are, at best, unreliable.

Quite a different picture of a psychiatric facility emerges from a paper by Killian and Bloomberg (1975). One of the authors, a prominent social psychologist, was admitted to a "therapeutic community" and reported his impressions of the therapeutic process. He was well aware of the stigma associated with mental illness.

In spite of years of study of social psychology, all my professional sophistication vanished now. "Insane" was only the worst of the frightening words that flashed through my disordered mind. "Institutionalized," "psychiatric ward," "mentally ill," "deviant," are only a few of the others that I can remember. Not only did I know that, in terms of what we sociologists call "labeling theory," my friends would hereafter perceive me differently; I was already experiencing the pain of a new self-definition. Just the day before I had gotten my driver's license renewed. One of the questions on the application had been, "Have you even been hospitalized for mental illness?" Never again would I be able to answer "No" to this question. The realization was devastating. (pp. 42-43)

Killian began his stay by identifying more with the staff than with the patients. He was, after all, nearer to the staff in age, education, and interests. But he quickly learned that the staff would not tolerate this and that he would have to assume the role of patient. He came to believe that it was in his best interests to identify with the patients rather than with the staff, and by surrendering himself to the therapeutic process, he was able to make sufficient progress to be released in less than three weeks.

I include this example both because I do not wish to reduce all psychological problems to a purely deviance/labeling/attribution

Aesthetic values often stir passionate arguments. This art form may not appeal to you, but your neighbors may go out of their way just to have another look.

level, and because, as Killian's narrative shows, even one well versed in the labeling perspective may be willing either to accept the label of mental illness or on some level play the role of a psychiatric patient. This is not to deny that "problems in living" are often traumatic and that professional help may facilitate their resolution. This general section on abnormal behavior is simply designed to shed some light on the social and historical context of psychopathology and to present you with one way in which social psychologists have approached the problem.

. . . AESTHETICS

Individual tastes seem to predominate in the arts, perhaps more than anywhere else. Even close friends, who may agree on most matters, may disagree on the quality of a painting, song, book, film, or play. While the aesthetic sensibility is complex and variable, it is not unique to each individual. If each person had a private set of criteria for judging an object of art, such mass events as concerts, long-running plays, waiting lines at art museums, bestsellers, and box-office hits would not exist. There seem to be fairly large subgroups of people, each with different aesthetic values.

Psychologists have taken considerable pains to explain appreciation of the arts. Most of these attempts at explanation have emphasized personality characteristics of the audience and their relationship to various aspects of the art object. There is considerable research and theory on the need for stimulation in individuals and the fulfillment of this need by relatively complex and novel patterns in art, music, drama, humor, and literature (e.g., Berlyne, 1971, 1972, 1974). Individuals are said to appreciate those works that most closely satisfy their particular need for stimulation.

Freud and later psychoanalysts (Arieti, 1978; Freud, 1964; Kris, 1962) were much interested in individual differences in aesthetic taste. Both the creation of works of art and the appreciation of such works were thought to derive from the unconscious expression of id impulses. Individual differences in appreciation were explained on the basis of differential, unconscious drive strength, different childhood experiences in dealing with impulses, and the use of various ego defense mechanisms. According to most psychoanalytic views of aesthetics, appreciation for particular artistic creations must be understood on the unconscious rather than the conscious level. We often hear someone say, "I know what I like," even though the person may not be certain just why he or she likes something. This is because we like aesthetic objects for reasons that are bound up with unconscious wishes, and, by definition, we are unaware of the reasons for aesthetic taste.

The Gestalt psychologists have had perhaps the longest historical interest in aesthetics among all psychologists. The very first Gestalt experiment was on music, demonstrating that the transposition of a melody from one key to another did not alter its recognition by listeners. According to the Gestalt approach to aesthetics, art, music, and so on cannot be studied by examining their isolated elements. One cannot use a "synthetic" method, where stimuli are studied in isolation, but must use an "analytic" method in which "real" works of art are used as stimuli (Sargent-Pollock & Konečni, 1977). This is because the Gestalt psychologists believe the whole object consists not of isolated elements, such as complexity, shape, color, and tone, but of a unique arrangement and organization of these elements. In their terms, "the whole is greater than the sum of its parts."

Much of the early theoretical work on aesthetics by psychologists tended to ignore the social aspects of art appreciation. Just as there are trends in fashion, politics, and other realms of behavior, there are also historical trends in art, music, and literature. These changes over time are best explained through the mechanisms of social interaction, the development and transmission of social norms, and the processes of social influence. We know people respond more positively to art and music that they believe others like or that were created by well-known artists (Chapman & Williams, 1976; Weick, Gilfillan, & Keith, 1973). We know, too, that change in artistic style and content are correlated with changes in society as a whole. What has not been stressed strongly enough is that artists are apt to be influenced as much by their contacts with fellow artists as by "society" at large, and there is little research on just how this small-group process of social influence takes place.

An interesting approach to aesthetics has recently been taken by Louis Moffett (1975a, 1975b), and it is perhaps the most social psychological of all views of aesthetics. Moffett treats art objects as social stimuli, much like people, to which observers respond. He notes that people often treat inanimate objects and animals as people, attributing human qualities to pets, automobiles, and mechanical objects. If art objects are treated as persons, then a host of social psychological theories becomes applicable to understanding aesthetics. Festinger's (1954) social comparison theory, for example, suggests that people, especially under conditions of moderate fear, might be more apt to expose themselves to works of art. There is some research to support this view (Roubertoux, 1970). Art preferences can be seen in terms of the cognitive consistency notion, in which people like those objects that seem to express a sentiment or attitude with which they agree. Likewise, the literature on interpersonal attraction may be relevant and would enable us to predict that people are most drawn to objects of art that seem to express traits similar to their own. These suggestions, of course, require much elaboration, and research is needed before the value of this metaphor can be determined.

. . . HUMOR

Within the past decade or so, psychologists have devoted considerable attention to behaviors previously thought of as frivolous. Beginning perhaps with Harlow's early studies of love (1958) through the research of Berlyne on curiosity and exploratory behavior (1960), and to the emphasis given to positive forms of behavior and well-being by humanistic psychologists (Schutz, 1967), there has been something of a reorientation among many contemporary psychologists. The imbalances of past research, which told us more about aggression than altruism, anxiety than serenity, depression than joy, are slowly being corrected. Part of this redress involves the study of humor and laughter. While humor has been sporadically studied by psychologists for decades (Keith-Spiegel, 1972), it now seems firmly entrenched as a legitimate area of contemporary research.

Most research on humor involves an attempt either to examine the personality correlates of a "sense of humor" or to explore the cognitive and developmental processes involved in the appreciation of humor (McGhee, 1979). There is relatively little research on the social psychology of humor; that is, who tells what kinds of jokes to whom and in what social settings. Anthropologists, beginning with Radcliffe-Brown (1940), have long noted the existence of *joking relationships*, the lighthearted banter that takes place between individuals who occupy certain social roles, such as a man and his mother-in-law. But these relationships rarely involve the spontaneous telling of a joke or a humorous remark.

Among the first social psychological studies of humor are two observational studies conducted in psychiatric hospitals. Goodrich, Henry, and Goodrich (1954) recorded laughter at 23 weekly staff conferences, and Coser (1960) recorded joking incidents at staff meetings in a mental hospital. The results of both studies indicate that joking is a frequent event at formal meetings and that jokesters and the targets of their wit reflect the social structure. At over 20 staff meetings, Goodrich et al. found an average of 7.7 funny remarks at each; that is about one every ten minutes. Over one-third of these consisted of derogatory remarks directed at colleagues. Sarcastic sorts of humor also characterized the staff meetings observed by Coser. She reported that senior members of the staff directed their sarcasm at junior staff members, while junior personnel directed their humor at patients or peers, but not at senior staff. Those occupying prestigious positions are rarely the butt of jokes made by underlings—at least in face-to-face situations. In these two studies, there were just two instances in which junior staff directed hostile humor at senior staff members, and in both instances, the senior staff members had just left the room!

A study by Smith and Goodchilds (1959) examined spontaneous humor during a five-day management development course in a large eastern corporation. Among their findings, Smith and Goodchilds note that more men than women made jokes, and that of all those who did make jokes, only men made sarcastic or hostile jokes. In general, the witty group members also were more active in group discussions and were more favorably rated by themselves and by their peers than were nonwits (see Goodchilds, 1972).

Pollio and Edgerly (1976) review early studies that employed "humor diaries" in which people were asked to make note of all the jokes they heard during a certain period of time. This technique was used in a 1926 study by Kambouropoulou with Vassar students, in a 1937 study by Young with college students, and in a more recent study by Pollio and Edgerly (1976). In all three studies, covering a span of nearly 50 years, students reported that the most frequent type of humorous remark was a wisecrack, put-down, or some form of hostile humor. Also, in all three studies, students reported that they laughed between 15 and 20 times a day. In the Young and the Pollio and Edgerly studies, students indicated that they laughed at formal jokes (as opposed to mistakes, pratfalls, blunders) in only about 20 percent of all laugh-provoking occasions. In other words, jokes per se are relatively infrequent sources of humor in natural settings (see Goldstein, 1979b).

When students keep track of all the formal jokes they hear, it is found that they are exposed to an average of only six per week, and that most of these are sexual jokes or hostile jokes, mainly about minority groups (Middleton & Moland, 1959). Again, it is reported that men tell such jokes more often than women.

These and similar studies suggest that joking is in some ways a "masculine" activity, a finding that is perhaps not inconsistent with the notion that joking also reflects the social structure. The fact that in the late 1970s there was an increase in women comedians indicates that the status differential between the sexes may be changing.

Goldstein and Kernis (Note 6) analyzed letters written to the advice column *Dear Abby* in order to see which letters would be given purely serious replies and which would receive humorous replies. Joking replies were more often given to older females than to older males, though this situation was reversed for younger writers.

Male and female college students in Belgium, Hong Kong, and the United States were asked to indicate the last time they laughed, what it was that made them laugh, who was present, and so on. In this study (Castell & Goldstein, 1977), we again found that males

People laugh more often at funny situations than at formal jokes. This photograph would probably produce a chuckle more readily than would a lengthy in-law joke, especially if you forgot the punch line.

were more likely than females to joke. Females in all three countries were more likely to be the butt of jokes, and when females made some sort of verbal mistake, they were more apt to elicit laughter from males than were males who made a similar mistake. Much laughter depends on the social setting. In mixed company, both males and females laugh at the mistakes of females, but rarely do they laugh at males. Females would tell jokes to other females in all three countries, and often these jokes contained aggressive or sexual themes. When males were present, however, we found not one instance in which females told a sexual or aggressive joke. Males, on the other hand, often told sexual and hostile jokes in the presence of other males and equally often in the presence of females. In short, female joking seems to be dependent on the social setting, while male joking is consistent across different social settings.

Sex differences are difficult to explain, and more so when they are consistent across cultures. Sex differences in humor may reflect important personality differences (Leventhal & Cupchik, 1976), or may merely reflect the status difference between the sexes in different cultures (Goldstein, 1977).

Psychologists are also concerned with the psychological mechanisms that underlie laughing at certain kinds of jokes. For example, why do some people find ethnic humor so funny, while others find it distasteful? There have been essentially two answers proposed for this sort of humor preference. LaFave and his colleagues (LaFave, 1972, 1977; LaFave, Haddad, & Maesen, 1976) have suggested that

Social psychologists cannot agree on whether violence in sports transfers to other situations. Both James and Freud suggest, however, that the tendency toward violence may be lessened after watching a rugby match.

appreciation of certain kinds of jokes depends on the reference groups to which a person belongs. If, for example, you identify positively with minority groups, then jokes that make fun of those groups will not be humorous to you. If you feel negatively about a group, then disparaging jokes will be humorous. One needn't think of the butt of a joke as a member of a reference group; it is sufficient merely to hold some predisposing attitude toward the target of a joke (Goldstein, 1976b; Zillmann & Cantor, 1976). This view is generally consistent with the idea mentioned earlier that joking tends to move downward in the social hierarchy.

A second explanation concerns the effects of jokes on a person's physiological or cognitive state of arousal. According to this view, people appreciate specific jokes because they provide pleasurable levels of complexity, arousal, or challenge. Once we are able to master the meaning of a joke, our pleasure is expressed suddenly in laughter (Berlyne, 1972; Cantor, Bryant, & Zillmann, 1974; Chapman, 1976; Goldstein, Suls, & Anthony, 1972; Schachter & Wheeler, 1962; Suls, 1972, 1976).

. . . SPORTS

The playing of games and sports is a complex social phenomenon that can be analyzed on several levels, from the formal structure of play (Garvey, 1977) and its relationship to other types of social behavior (Lieberman, 1977; Sherrod & Singer, 1979; Zillmann, Bryant, & Sapolsky, 1979) to sports as organized industry and mass entertainment (Goldstein & Bredemeier, 1977; Michener, 1976). While there is growing interest among social psychologists in sports and play generally (Goldstein, 1979a), most of their attention has been focused on two aspects of sports: the relationship between sports, especially those referred to as body-contact sports, and aggression; and the social psychology of the sports fan.

SPORTS AND AGGRESSION

For decades people have written about sports and other forms of vigorous physical activity, including manual labor, as physically, morally, and psychologically healthy. While there is little dispute with the claim that exercise in many forms is physically beneficial, the belief that it builds character and serves positive social functions is open to question. Two modern sources of the belief that sports are psychologically and morally uplifting are a paper by William James (1911) on the "moral equivalent of war" and Freud's psychoanalytic notion of catharsis (Freud, 1930/1962; Storr, 1968). James and Freud both suggest that people's tendencies toward violence and disharmony may be diminished by participating in, or witnessing, sports contests. The philosophy underlying the modern Olympic Games is consistent with this view.

What little research exists on sports and violence belies this notion, and there is considerable anecdotal evidence to suggest that a relatively strong relationship exists between violence on the playing field and violence in the streets. Lever (1969) has even traced the roots of a war between El Salvador and Honduras to a soccer match. Riots at soccer matches are not at all uncommon, especially during World Cup play, and thousands of players, officials, and fans have lost their lives at such games (Gaskell & Pearton, 1979; Mann, 1979). Violence is becoming more prevalent among spectators and players alike at boxing matches, hockey and football games, and to some extent at baseball games. But it is quite rare to find violence at tennis, gymnastics, track, or horse racing events. One obvious difference between these two groups of sports is that the first group includes the more violent sports.

It seems plausible to ask whether the physical contact of soccer, football, hockey, and boxing contributes to the violent outbursts of players and fans. As we have seen in Chapter 8, social learning theory suggests that observers tend to learn and to imitate the unpunished violence they witness in others. It would therefore be surprising to find that watching aggressive sports diminished, rather than increased, observers' own levels of aggression. After all, there is no sound reason for suspecting that the effects of violence in sports would be different from the effects of other forms of violence.

These two positions, one suggesting that observing aggression in sports leads to a general lowering of aggression and the other suggesting that it leads to a heightening of aggression, are not the only possible views of violence and sports. On the basis of the general notion of frustration and aggression (Chapter 8), we might expect an increase in aggression only among those observers who in some way are frustrated. Frustration might come about if a person wanted Team A to win and Team B actually won. For the spectators whose preferred team loses a game, we might predict an increase in aggressiveness, while those whose preferred team wins might show no increase, or perhaps even a decrease, in aggression.

We might translate losing a game not only as frustration but also as "punishment." If a preferred team loses a game, it is in a sense punished for its aggressive play, while the winning team is rewarded. Thus, social learning theory might lead us to expect that those whose preferred team wins a game will actually become more aggressive than those whose preferred team loses.

These various explanations for the relationship between aggressive sports and hostility were examined in a study by Goldstein and Arms (1971) at the 1969 Army–Navy football game. Male spectators were interviewed either before or after the game and their general level of hostility was measured. For control purposes, the same interview was given to male spectators at an Army–Temple gym meet in order to determine whether watching a nonaggressive sport had any appreciable effect on observers' aggressiveness. The primary results of the study are presented in Table 13.1. A significant increase in hostility was found for spectators at the football game, while no significant increase was found for those watching the gym meet. All groups of spectators at the Army–Navy game had higher hostility scores after the game whether their team won or lost. It will be noted that the increase for the pro-Army spectators was greater than that for the Navy fans. In other words, the larger increase in hostility was for those who favored the winning team. This finding lends some support to the social learning interpretation of aggression and sports. Comparable results, though not always with comparable explanations, have been obtained by others (Berkowitz & Alioto, 1973; Lefkowitz, Walder, Eron, & Huesmann, 1973; Russell & Drewry, 1976; Russell & Arms, in press).

There are at least two general types of violence at sports events: collective or group violence, in which fans of opposing teams engage in brawls with one another; and individual acts of violence, in which two fans, perhaps even of the same side, fight. The first type is much less spontaneous than the second and can be seen to serve largely a ritual function in which serious injury of the opponent is less important than showing support for the team and demonstrating bravery (Gaskell & Pearton, 1979). There is probably a more direct relationship between violence in a sport and individual acts of aggression among spectators than between violence in a sport and collective violence, such as that engaged in by "soccer hooligans" in Britain, who destroy property and engage in ritual battle before important matches.

THE SPORTS FAN

What is there about certain sports—football, soccer, and boxing foremost among them—that attracts 70 million people to a single televised game, or 100 million to a heavyweight bout? The word "fan" derives from a Latin word meaning possessed by the gods or mad, and implies a certain irrationality. Research on the sports fan's behavior suggests that he or she may be no less rational than anyone else.

Research by Sloan (1979) and Zillmann et al. (1979) suggests that sports fans are motivated by a need to enhance self-esteem and validate their own attitudes. Over the last century, critics of sports have tended to view the sports fan as having a need to escape from the chores of everyday life, a need for stimulation, or an excess amount of physical or aggressive energy. More recent views of the sports fan by social psychologists suggest that the fan's loyalty to a player or team fulfills important social needs. Sloan (1979; Cialdini, Borden, Thorne, Walker, Freeman, & Sloan, 1976) has proposed an

Table 13.1.
Mean Hostility Scores

	Football Game			Gym Meet
	Preferred Team			
	Army (winning team)	Navy (losing team)	No preference	
Pregame	n = 38 10.42	n = 47 11.72	n = 12 11.67	n = 49 12.00
Postgame	n = 18 13.33	n = 30 13.17	n = 5 15.00	n = 32 13.40

The higher the score, the greater the hostility. From Goldstein and Arms (1971).

Table 13.2.
Viewers' Appreciation of Tennis as a Function of Perceived Dispositions of the Players Manipulated through Commentary

Dependent Measure	Reported Relationship between Players		
	No Particular Relationship Specified	Personal Friendship, Mutual Admiration	Bitter Rivalry, Mutual Hatred
Appreciation of play:			
Enjoyable	17[a]	18[a]	34[b]
Exciting	11[a]	10[a]	19[b]
Involving	13[a]	14[a]	25[b]
Interesting	13[a]	18[a]	30[b]
Perception of players:			
Hostile	8[a]	1[a]	40[b]
Tense	9[a]	6[a]	22[b]
Competitive	17[a]	14[a]	39[b]

NOTE: Comparisons are within measures only. Means having different superscipts are significantly different at the .05 level.
Adapted from Zillmann, Bryant and Sapolsky (1979).

achievement-seeking motive for the behavior of fans. According to this notion, the fan perceives himself to be a member of the reference group centered around a team, and when the team wins a game, identification is increased and the fan experiences a momentary increase in achievement or self-esteem. After a win, the fan is more likely to refer to the team as "we" than as "they," and, at colleges, is more apt to wear apparel, such as a school sweatshirt, identifying him as a member of the winning school. When students have had a recent experience that called their abilities into question, such as failing an exam, the tendency to identify with a team's victory by referring to it as "we" is enhanced. Thus, the identification with a team by sports fans is not an irrational act but an act designed to increase the fans' sense of achievement and worth.

But it is not only the outcome of a game or match that spectators find enjoyable; it is the sports contest itself that provides excitement and interest. Zillmann et al. (1979) review several theories on the appreciation of sports by observers. Most of these focus on the aesthetic appreciation of skill and grace that are part of nearly all sports. They note that spectators do *not* generally appreciate athletic skill or beauty for its own sake, but that appreciation depends on the context in which it occurs. A long pass in a practice football game will not elicit the excitement among fans that it would in a playoff game. A well-executed play by a favorite team will be seen as more skillful and important than the identical play executed by the opposing team. Zillmann et al. have stated that we appreciate sports to the extent that we have positive attitudes toward the player and/or team that is successful. In order to test these ideas, they videotaped a tennis match and imposed three different soundtracks on it. One voice-over was an objective description of the match. A second added the information that the opposing players were the best of friends. The third soundtrack noted that the players were bitter rivals who hated each other. College subjects saw one of the three tapes and rated the enjoyment and excitement of the match. The results are shown in Table 13.2. The tennis match was seen as most enjoyable, exciting, involving, and interesting when observers believed that it involved bitter rivals.

These studies suggest that sports fans appreciate sports not solely for their aesthetic appeal, but also because they involve basic human emotions that permit identification with a player or team. Through identification, a spectator might come to have increased feelings of solidarity with other fans and greater feelings of self-worth.

. . . THE LAW

Nearly every major topic in social psychology has some bearing on the legal process, and may be particularly relevant to proceedings in a court of law. Persuasion and attitude change, impression formation and attribution, group dynamics, conflict resolution, and the effects of the physical environment all play a role in the criminal trial. Social psychological research in the legal process has focused on the jury trial, despite the fact that most civil and criminal cases are decided without the presence of a jury, both because jury trials are more dramatic and because they afford the researcher a better opportunity to apply social psychological theories to this real-life behavior.

Because of the secrecy surrounding the operation of jury deliberations, much of the psychological research has relied on simulations of jury trials (Bermant, Nemeth, & Vidmar, 1976). Since it is fairly convenient to focus on the various aspects of jury trials, research has examined the selection of jurors, events that transpire in the courtroom, and the process of deliberation and arrival at a verdict.

JURY SELECTION

Much of the research into jury selection has relied on survey data in an effort to correlate age, sex, social class, and other demographic information with jury verdicts. Several highly publicized trials have involved the use of ideal juror profiles, developed by social scientists, in order to help defense attorneys select "favorable" jurors. The Harrisburg conspiracy and Angela Davis trials are among these. Profiles of jurors who might be expected to favor the defense are developed by social scientists, and the defense lawyers then use these profiles while questioning prospective jurors during the *voir dire* (juror selection process). The employment of such juror profiles raises a number of sensitive issues, including those of professional ethics, jury tampering, and violation of confidentiality (Bermant et al., 1976).

There is some evidence that jurors who are high on the personality variable of authoritarianism judge defendants more harshly under some circumstances, and that they reach a decision about the guilt or innocence of the defendant early in the course of a trial and are highly resistant to changing that initial opinion (R. W. Davis, 1979). Much of this research, of course, comes from studies of college students who role-play as jurors while deliberating an actual case presented to them either on videotape or in written form. Therefore, there is some question as to whether the findings from these simulated studies are applicable to actual jury trials (Gerbasi, 1977; Saks, 1977).

THE COURTROOM

During the opening remarks of the attorneys and the presentation of evidence, jurors form impressions of the individuals involved in the case and interpret evidence in various ways. Jurors may complicate their tasks by attending to nonevidential aspects of the trial as well. For example, jurors may attend to the attorneys' physical appearance and demeanor; the defendant's sex, marital status, and physical attractiveness; and the amount of suffering of the defendant and victim (e.g., W. N. Brooks & Doob, 1975; Stephan, 1975). Data on sex differences in jurors' verdicts is contradictory and appears to depend on the type of case and whether the crime is seen as a stereotypically male one or not. There is also some recent research on the effects of pretrial publicity on the jurors' behavior (R. W. Davis, 1979). In general, being exposed to even prejudicial publicity about a trial prior to deliberation does not seem to have much effect on jurors.

DELIBERATIONS

Because jury deliberations are conducted in privacy, little is known about them (Kalven & Zeisel, 1966). Using simulated jury deliberations, psychological research has found that the person elected foreperson generally sits at the head of the jury table, is well educated, male, and tends to be high on authoritarianism (Simon, 1967; Strodtbeck, James, & Hawkins, 1957).

The number of options available to a jury (such as a simple guilty–not guilty choice of verdict, or a more complex set of choices including guilty of first degree murder, second degree murder, manslaughter, or not guilty) may influence deliberations and the verdict. The typical two-choice option of guilty or not guilty may seem to jurors overly restrictive and therefore result in more acquittals. When choices also include middle-ground options, such as second-degree murder and manslaughter, there are fewer acquittals (Vidmar, 1972).

Recent Supreme Court rulings permit juries of six people (as well as the more common 12-person jury) and allow for less than unanimous verdicts. Experimental research on the effects of jury size has produced mixed results (J. H. Davis, Kerr, Atkin, Holt, & Meek, 1975; Saks, 1977), although with strong evidence of the defendant's guilt, smaller juries are more likely than 12-person juries to convict the defendant (Valenti & Downing, 1975).

At this point, research into the legal process is only in its infancy. What has rarely occurred until now is genuine cooperation between social psychologists and those more directly involved in the legal system, namely lawyers and judges.

. . . SCIENCE

Very often, scientists and lay persons alike see science as an independent intellectual discipline. Individual scientists are free to do research and write technical papers pretty much as they please. Colleges and universities provide the setting and the sense of individual freedom needed to "do" science. Knowledge and discipline are all one needs to become an outstanding scientist, according to this stereotype. Scientists who are bright enough and diligent enough will see their achievements recognized within the field, as in a Nobel Prize, or perhaps outside it, as in a mention in *The New York Times*.

This picture of the free-spirited scientist, which closely fits the idealized view of the American frontiersman as a rugged individualist, is highly misleading. While scientists are often more or less free to study what they wish, their interests may be strongly influenced by social psychological factors (and by political and economic forces, though these will not be discussed here; for a discussion of economics and science, see Price, 1965, and Ben-David, 1971). What scientists study, the methods and theories they use in their studies, and how they choose to present their results are all decisions influenced by nonscientific variables. For example, Nobel Prize-winning scientists tend to have a number of demographic similarities, such as having studied at one of only a handful of universities, having studied under previous Nobel laureates, and being comparable in age (Zuckerman, 1967). Beyond that, there are often personal encounters in the early intellectual lives of prominent scientists that profoundly influenced the direction of their interests. Many report having attended a single lecture or read a single book by an important figure that led them to the decision to devote their intellectual life to a particular field. Here is what some prominent psychologists have said about their initial interest in psychology.

The two men whose books influenced me most as an undergraduate were the biological ultramechanist Jacques Loeb and the proponent of emergent evolution C. Lloyd Morgan. I finally decided, especially after reading Howard C. Warren's Human Psychology, *that psychology rather than anatomy or physiology was the best place for me. . . ."* (Leonard Carmichael, 1967, p. 32)

I started graduate work at Harvard with the intention of working toward a Ph.D. degree in philosophy, but the arrival of E. G. Boring from Clark University at the beginning of my second year was responsible for my change to psychology. With Boring, whose courses I audited because I was ostensibly a philosophy major, a new, fresh wind seemed to blow across the psychological horizon. After the second or third lecture, I remember looking across the room at Beebe-Center who, when he caught my glance, gave a solemn nod of approval as if to say, "This is what we have been looking for." And indeed it was. (Harry Helson, 1967, pp. 199–200)

In my sophomore year I took elementary psychology, and a mixture of solid facts and high, wide, and handsome speculations suited me to a tee. With Thorndike's theory of bonds and William James's theory of habits leading me on into more complex conceptualizations in the Titchener-dominated experimental psychology which was the core of my "psychology major," I was being drawn into psychology in part because I loved all that stuff about the mind, and was good at it as far as academic standards go. . . . At the same time, I was sure I wanted to go into psychical research, and as it became clear to me that I needed a Ph.D. in psychology to achieve that goal, I became henceforth a double personality, one personality adapting to the environment known as scientific or laboratory psychology, the other personality being concerned with a vast array of interesting phenomena which looked like telepathy, clairvoyance, precognition, and all the rest of what William James was talking about under the head of psychical research. . . . (Gardner Murphy, 1974, p. 325)

During my sophomore year . . . I happened to take Introductory Psychology and then an advanced course with the late Prof. Theodore Karwoski. . . . I found what I had been, unknowingly, looking for all the time—the right combination of demand for rigor and room for creativity—and I forgot about writing The Great American Novel. (Charles Osgood, 1974, p. 347–348)

The sociology and psychology of science can be approached in several different ways (Crane, 1972). The relationships between science and other social institutions can be explored (e.g., Merton,

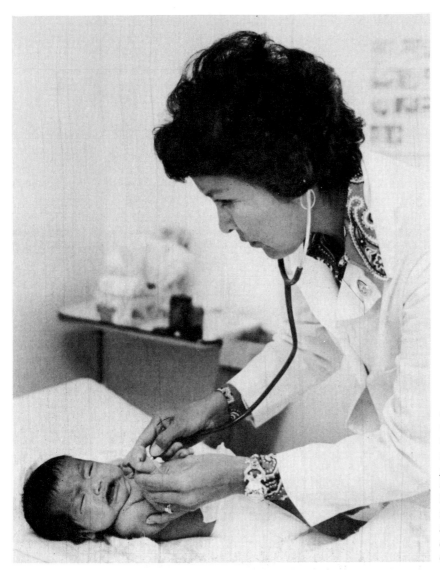

Research scientists are constantly developing new medicines, which are useless unless both doctors and patients learn about the benefits and risks involved. This tiny patient seems to be resisting the advances of science, but his parents have already given their informed consent.

1957). Science can be viewed as a social system, consisting of individuals, rules, norms, groups, and social exchanges (Hagström, 1965). The psychologist can look for individual differences, early childhood experiences, and personality traits of scientists (Coan, 1973; Klausner, 1968; Roe, 1953; Terman, 1955). We might look for historical changes in the nature of science (Kuhn, 1962). Or, we might look at the social and psychological fads and fashions in a science (Ray, 1977).

These different approaches raise a number of interesting questions about science. For example, how is knowledge produced and diffused? How does it spread within a scientific community and from the scientific community to the public at large? What conditions must be set to increase knowledge in a particular area? How can the individual scientist best make a contribution to a given field? Why are some scientists adherents of a particular theory while others hold to different theories? We know from recent experience that these are practical as well as intellectual issues. The American space program is an example of a successful attempt to direct the future course of science. Questions about recombinant DNA research and the use of human subjects in biomedical and psychological research may also be seen as part of the social psychology of science.

This area of study is only beginning to emerge in psychology. For many years, sociologists have had an interest in science, including the social sciences, as a social institution. They tend to view science as embedded in the larger social system, influenced by and influencing political, social, and economic institutions. A social psychology of science sees science not only as an "institution," but also as a social network consisting of individuals and groups of individuals who have needs, desires, goals, and personality traits, and who attempt to influence one another in a variety of ways. This social psychological view of science is only beginning to develop and it has focused on the subject matter closest to home, social psychology itself. We therefore will conclude this book with a social psychological discussion of social psychology.

. . . SOCIAL PSYCHOLOGY

Social psychology recently has been going through "a crisis" (Strickland, Aboud, & Gergen, 1976). Actually, it is more like several crises, some of them independent of the others. All of them can be seen, however, as growing pains or side effects of historical development. Thus, rather than signaling a fatal illness, these crises may herald a new maturity and self-awareness.

Social psychologists have never been as sensitive to the philosophical or historical bases of their field as, say, physicists or sociologists. They have tended to take the view of science employed by nineteenth- and early-twentieth-century physicists. In this mechanistic and fairly simple model, the universe operates according to basic, discoverable principles, with the scientist seen as an impartial observer, attempting to discover "nature's secrets." Such a view is unfounded and leaves its proponents open to attack on several grounds. If we adopt an unquestioned set of beliefs, they become, in McGuire's (1964) terms (see Chapter 5), "cultural truisms" vulnerable to attack because little or no effort was made to defend these beliefs in the past. This seems to have been the case with experimental social psychologists in the 1960s and early 1970s. When criticism did come, it caused more turmoil than it might have, had social psychologists been better versed in the history and philosophy of their discipline.

By this point in the book, you have a good idea of what social psychologists do and how many of them think. Before reading of the criticisms that have been leveled at the field by some social psychologists, ask yourself what the major weaknesses of social psychology are. What are the limitations on social psychological knowledge? Can these be overcome with better methods or theories? With greater dedication by psychologists? By studying different subject matter? Or are the weaknesses inherent in the current subject matter of the field and therefore insurmountable?

The first of the recent papers to raise basic questions about what social psychologists were doing was by Kenneth Ring (1967). Ring accused many social psychologists of engaging in "fun and gamesmanship" in the research laboratory.

One sometimes gets the impression that an ever-growing coterie of social psychologists is playing (largely for one another's benefit) a game of "can you top this?" Whoever can conduct the most contrived, flamboyant, and mirth-producing experiments receives the highest score on the kudometer. There is, in short, a distinctly exhibitionistic flavor to much current experimentation. . . . (p. 117)

Ring cautioned against laboratory experiments that were too complex or that involved too much deception or were too far removed either from theory or from human concerns.

William McGuire (1967) responded to Ring's criticisms by noting that a growing number of social psychologists were conducting field studies that were indeed relevant to both theory and human needs, and that, after all, one of the advantages of a scientific career was that those who undertook it were relatively free to study what and how they wanted.

The next, and perhaps the most important, step in this progression was a paper published in 1973 by Kenneth Gergen (1973b). Social psychologists often had doubts about whether a science of human behavior could employ the same models and methods as the physical sciences. Gergen argued forcefully that it could not. "It is the purpose of this paper to argue that social psychology is primarily an historical inquiry. Unlike the natural sciences, it deals with facts that are largely nonrepeatable and which fluctuate markedly over time. Principles of human interaction cannot readily be developed over time because the facts on which they are based do not generally remain stable."

AN INTERVIEW WITH KENNETH GERGEN

Ken Gergen received his B.A. from Yale University and his Ph.D. from Duke University. He is professor and chairman of the Department of Psychology at Swarthmore College. He has been on the faculties of Harvard University, the University of Colorado, and the University of North Carolina, and he has been visiting professor at Kyoto University in Japan, Copenhagen University in Denmark, the National Institute of Psychology in Rome, and the Sorbonne in Paris. He is the author of numerous papers on social psychology, and of *The Self in Social Interaction* (with C. Gordon), *The Study of Policy Formation* (with R. A. Bauer), *Personality and Social Behavior* (with D. Marlowe), and *The concept of self*, among other books.

JHG: What was the initial impetus for your "Social Psychology as History" paper?

KG: Actually, the seeds of that paper were planted as early as 1960, when I was in graduate school. The experimentation in which I was involved then was on the psychology of self-esteem. There is a long-standing assumption in the discipline concerning self-esteem that holds that people develop a basic or fundamental conception of who they are (including their own value or worth). So you have people who are basically high in self-esteem as opposed to low, and individual differences in basic self-esteem should, from the traditional standpoint, predict various kinds of behaviors. For a variety of reasons, it seemed worth examining this set of suppositions rather closely. At least in my own life, they did not appear to be the case. If anything, it seemed that my self-esteem changed a great deal from one situation to another, and from one relationship to another. And I couldn't grasp anything that seemed to be very fundamental or lasting across situations. That unleashed a set of studies that tried to show how self-conception changed over time across situations, often very rapidly.

At that point, I also began to develop questions about a whole set of other concepts that we have in social psychology, concepts that essentially try to build durability into the organism. We have been a field that looks for the durable, the fundamental. Take the concept of attitude; an attitude is defined as a reliable disposition to respond to certain objects in favorable or unfavorable ways. Both prejudice and attraction have also been considered attitudes, and thus of enduring and stable consequence.

This was no mere critique of methods or theories but a blow to the very heart of scientific social psychology. Gergen argued that a science of social behavior was not even theoretically possible. Some reliable experimental findings in the past were no longer found to be reliable. Circumstances changed, and so did the behavior and factors that caused them. Social psychologists, Gergen argues, are engaged in describing contemporary affairs, using largely experimental procedures. Some of the things we study are more long-lasting than

Processes of conformity, group decision making, and causal perception have also been considered stable parts of the human makeup. But are they?

At this early point, I was also very interested in Goffman's (1959) work on self-presentation and in E. E. Jones' (1964) research on ingratiation (i.e., what kinds of tactics people use to make others like them). Now, if you flesh out the assumptions underlying this work, you begin to see that the work implies something about human functioning that is quite different from the stable cause-and-effect models so traditional in the field. It implies a model of choice whereby an individual from moment to moment can change tactics for a variety of reasons. It suggests that much of what we take to be built-in, reflex-like, unchangeable, could be viewed as tactical within interpersonal settings. Such tactics could change as they become more or less rewarding.

JHG: You seem to be painting a picture of someone choosing strategies to accomplish goals on an entirely conscious level. What of people, for example, whose behavior is not adaptive?

KG: I don't mean to imply by the notion of strategy that people always choose their actions consciously. However, by making another conscious of a set of behaviors, you can often change these behaviors. For example, it's much like a baseball player's learning to bat. He doesn't know exactly how he's putting together the swing, the follow-through, and so on. He doesn't know how it's all being coordinated; he's just doing it. He's trying always to operate adaptively, that is, to get more hits. You wouldn't call his behavior unconscious in a Freudian sense; that is, unavailable to consciousness; but the batter is certainly not aware of everything he's doing. However, at any point, a coach could say, "Look, your stance is too wide. You're holding the bat too far back." By drawing the batter's attention to these factors, making them conscious, the coach may enable the batter to change his actions—to adopt a new strategy of hitting.

If you begin to consider the various patterns of behavior we have traditionally considered durable in social psychology—that is, patterns of conformity, of attitude change, of social perception, and so on—as being convenient strategies, heuristics, or adaptive patterns that the person need not adopt, but does because they seem appropriate or useful at

(Continued)

others, but we should not assume that any of our findings are trans-historical.

A response to Gergen was made by Schlenker (1974). He noted that there is considerable evidence that much social behavior is consistent over long periods of time. "If social processes were as transient as Gergen believes, it would be difficult to explain why the writings of Aristotle, Plato, Marcus Aurelius, Kant, Locke, Rousseau, Hobbes, and other philosophers and social commentators of more or a given time and place, then you must begin to question the entire notion of fundamental patterns.

JHG: You're saying something different than that personality is situationally determined. You're saying that even if you have a good accounting of situations, you still can't predict the kind of self-presentation or strategies that a person will use.

KG: You could determine for any given individual a set of patterns that he or she finds relatively reasonable and useful over time and circumstance, which we would call that person's "personality." However, what is there about behavior that can't be jettisoned at any point? What kind of pattern have we ever studied in social psychology about which you couldn't say, "I don't want to do that today; I think I won't"? In contrast, you can't make such decisions about, say, your digestive tract or your nervous system, in general. You can't say, "Well, I don't think I'm going to see color today." You are going to see color regardless of your choice, the pattern is durable and not generally subject to historical circumstance.

JHG: Do you see your arguments

about social behavior undermining the claims of sociobiologists that much of social behavior is genetically determined?

KG: Yes, this does argue strongly against a sociobiology notion. It is dead set against much of what sociobiology would argue. I don't see that a very strong argument can be made that most of our behavior is such that we couldn't do otherwise if we wanted to. This is to say that there isn't much about our activities that is guaranteed by our genetic constitution.

JHG: In saying that people can change—that attitudes or self-presentation are not as consistent as is sometimes thought—how would you account for the fact that there seems to be relatively little change over time in what we might call "human nature"? If one reads Plato and Aristotle, Spinoza, Hobbes, and so on—you can take your pick of political points of view, man as animal or as civilized organism—one finds relative continuity over a period of thousands of years.

KG: There are several problems with that argument. One is that many ideas are generated in any culture,

less 'ancient' origin still affect contemporary conceptualizations of man" (p. 5). Schlenker also argues that theories must be stated in terms abstract enough so that concrete data, even if they are contradicted by other data, can be successfully accommodated. In other words, interaction effects do occur in nature and a good theory will enable such interactions to be predicted and explained.

It was no accident that several criticisms by highly respected social psychologists appeared at about the same time. In 1973, and if you look back in history, chances are you can find something in any given era or in any given culture that resembles something you agree with today. For any idea you could probably find somebody in the past who said something that seems similar.

JHG: The impression I have from your most recent papers is that you envision two future schools of social psychology: theoretical and applied research. What would the researchers research?

KG: Empirical research would have several functions. One of them would be a sort of pragmatic prediction, much like econometric forecasting in economics. You could also use research as a means of transforming society. It seems to me that Milgram's obedience research, for example—which has very little value theoretically—has had a catalytic effect that causes one to rethink what people are capable of, and what we have to safeguard against. The research upsets our settled assumptions about social life. And that is a fairly useful kind of enterprise.

JHG: Suppose there were two theories that differed in explaining the same phenomenon. In a dialectical sense, you might end up with a third theory, whereas in the traditional positivist sense, you end up with one discredited. In talking about research and the role of theory, you suggest that it's not a matter of right and wrong; such an issue can't even be decided.

KG: That's correct. Ultimately, if you have two different theories, even if one of them predicts correctly, you wouldn't know if that theory had anything to do with the correct prediction. It's similar to the traditional tests of one form of therapy against others. If your therapy works, you don't really know if the theory has been vindicated because there are a thousand different things that can account for the empirical differences: the patients you have studied, the training of the therapists, the patients they selected, and so on. So many things could explain the results that they don't really validate the theory.

JHG: So a "crucial experiment" is not only impossible, it isn't even desirable.

KG: Correct. To search for a critical experiment is largely a waste of *(Continued)*

William McGuire published his own critique of the field. Whereas in 1967, McGuire had urged social psychologists to study socially relevant behavior in natural settings, he now noted that that solution was no solution at all. A great many psychologists were clever enough to arrange laboratory situations or to find natural settings in which their hypotheses could be supported. They were, in McGuire's phrase, "finders." What seemed missing in 1973 was social psychologists with the ability to think creatively about social behavior, to time. You can always explain any research results or reinterpret them in a variety of ways.

JHG: You've spoken of the "orienting capacity" and "generative function" of theories. Would you elaborate on this idea?

KG: If it is true that one cannot validate general theories (given the problems of changing patterns of behavior, ambiguous meaning of concepts, preselection of data), then it must also be the case with implicit theories we hold in everyday life. They must not be empirically valid either. If that is true, then it seems to me that any set of implicit or shared understandings about the social world is potentially dangerous. It directs attention in certain ways, it acts like blinders, and it restricts our options. Thus one can make a case for theory that has as its primary function cutting away the basis for commonsense assumptions and building alternative potentials. To reexamine the principles that we live by, and try to provide other kinds of alternatives, are highly useful functions of theorizing.

JHG: Where do you think—or where would you like to see—social psychology go in the next decade or so?

KG: There is a set of what we might call dissident groups in social psychology, all of which criticize traditional positivist social psychology. For example, in Germany you have a group who call themselves "critical psychologists." In Great Britain, the ethogenics group has become extremely influential. In the United States, there are the ethnomethodologists, the life-span developmental psychologists, and the dialectic movement, all of which are set against the traditional assumptions of the field. I don't believe any of these groups is strong enough to turn the tide independently. I don't think that any one of them will become *the* wave of the future. My own feeling is, however, that as they become knitted one with another, which I think is happening, we will see the development of an opposing paradigm. It is possible that within 50 years, social psychology will be a very different discipline.

develop hypotheses that added something to our way of thinking about behavior. We need more social philosophers and hypothesis generators.

There followed a depressing number of papers answering one or more of the criticisms, looking far and wide for additional problems with social psychology, and proposing a variety of solutions, from leaving the field altogether to developing new statistical techniques. What was often overlooked was that all these criticisms and responses were themselves social psychological phenomena understandable in social psychological terms. Such an analysis was most cogently made by Alan Elms (1975).

Elms analyzed the "crisis of confidence in social psychology" in terms of social comparison theory, aspiration level, and so on. The public at large, and social psychologists in particular, had high expectations about the possible contribution of social psychology to human problems. Our experience with problems of poverty and the Vietnam war made it clear that we could do less to solve these dilemmas than we, the public, or federal funding agencies thought. Our research techniques had been shown to contain various sources of bias (Rosenthal, 1966; Rosenthal & Rosnow, 1969). Psychology had been declared a "pre-science" by a noted philosopher of science (T. S. Kuhn, 1962), despite the fact that the physicists still served as a comparison group. These seemed to be the general reasons behind the criticisms. Elms made a number of proposals for dealing with these problems, including to "work harder at developing a sound moral and philosophical stance, to lower one's aspiration level, and to be less insistent on immediate payoffs" (p. 975). In other words, social psychology will have to weather the storm.

The storm of criticism, mainly from within the field, but also to some extent from outside it, is not to be deplored. No field can continue to develop without serious, difficult challenges. As a social psychologist, I am less certain of what social psychology will be like in the twenty-first century than I was only a few years ago. That makes it a more exciting prospect.

Summary

Any scientific field, including social psychology, consists of a body of theory and research that is general in scope and, therefore, broadly applicable. Current theories and research methods in social psychology have been used to increase our understanding of a variety of complex behaviors, several of which are reviewed in this chapter.

While what is referred to as "mental illness" or "abnormal behavior" (the choice of terms depends to a great extent on one's theoretical perspective) can be found in all segments of the population, there is great variation between social classes. The lower the social class, the greater the likelihood of severe "psychopathology." One social psychological approach to this phenomenon asks, not whether there are mentally ill people and how their illness may have arisen, but who is capable of deciding whether an individual is mentally ill and what is to be done about it. The labeling theory of mental illness can be seen as an extension of attribution theory in which people are motivated to explain someone's behavior and, on the basis of certain social norms and customs, apply the label "mental illness" to certain people at certain times. This approach does not assume that there is any such thing as mental illness; only that certain individuals in our society—judges, psychiatrists, psychologists—are in a position to apply the label to others. The consequences of being labeled mentally ill are examined briefly. One advantage of this perspective on psychopathology is that it enables us to look at abnormal behavior from afar, incorporating in our view not only the behavior of the person labeled mentally ill but also the behavior of the person doing the labeling. The judgment that someone is mentally ill involves at least two people: an actor and a labeler. The social psychological perspective forces us to consider the behavior of each separately and in interaction.

Likewise, in examining aesthetics, particularly responses to works of art and music, the social perspective forces us to look at the interaction between the individual perceiving the art and the features of the art "stimulus." Psychoanalytic theories of aesthetic appreciation involve the unconscious expression of id impulses, namely, aggressive and sexual drives. Gestalt psychologists suggest that certain features of the work of art must fit together into a meaningful whole in order to elicit favorable responses. One social psychological approach to art appreciation is to view the object as a "person" and to apply the theories and methods of impression formation research (reviewed in Chapter 4).

As with art, there are psychoanalytic, Gestalt, and social psychological perspectives on the appreciation of humor. As a rule, joking tends to reflect the relative social status of the individuals involved, with higher-status people making fun of lower-status people by telling aggressive jokes about them or by telling jokes about taboo topics. Appreciation of certain types of jokes, such as ethnic jokes, can also reflect an individual's attitudes toward the butt of the humor.

There is a growing interest in the psychology of sports and play. The research reviewed in this chapter focused on aggression in sports and on the social psychology of the sports fan. While violence among sports spectators may serve a partly ritual function, there is also considerable evidence that sports and violence are closely related. As a rule, the more violent the sport, the more violent the spectators' reactions. Thus, there have been numerous riots at soccer, football, and hockey games. The notion that viewing violence in sports (or on television; see Chapter 8 for a discussion of this issue) is a healthy outlet for pent-up hostility is unfounded. What little research exists on this issue indicates that viewers of aggression are more, rather than less, aggressive afterward, especially if they perceive the action of the game as violent in itself.

Identification with a team or with an individual player serves several functions. For one thing, it provides fans with an opportunity to bask in the reflected glory of their team's success. Identification also enables fans to experience intense, often pleasant, emotions, to share their feelings with other fans, and to enhance their self-esteem.

Social psychology has been applied to the analysis of jury trials both by psychologists and by lawyers and judges. In several well-known cases, social psychologists assisted in the jury selection process. Research on the jury process has shown that jurors often respond to irrelevant and extraneous features of a trial. Research has focused on three aspects of the jury process: jury selection, arguments and evidence presented during the trial, and the deliberation process. One of the problems with jury research is that it almost invariably involves the use of simulated rather than actual juries, and so its external validity is unknown.

If science is viewed as a behavioral process, then it, too, is amenable to social psychological analysis. We might ask why people become scientists, how they choose particular problems for study, and why they adopt particular methods or theoretical points of view. Although this topic has only recently aroused the curiosity of social psychologists, it is clear that many of these decisions are based, not on objective evidence, but on social influence, communication networks, personality, and social norms and values.

Finally, social psychologists can stand back from their everyday work and look at their own field as a dynamic social entity. Why do social psychologists study what they do, and why do their interests shift from time to time? How does our view of social psychology as a science limit what—and how—we can know about social behavior? These issues have led to a turning point in the field and to considerable debate about the future course of social psychology. The more sensitive we are to what we, as social psychologists, do and why we do it, the more likely it is that we will make contributions to both the knowledge of social behavior and the solutions to social problems.

Suggested Readings

Abnormal Behavior:

*Goffman, E. *Asylums: Essays on the social situation of mental patients and other inmates.* Garden City, N.Y.: Anchor Doubleday, 1961.

Hall, C. S., & Lindzey, G. *Theories of personality* (3rd ed.). New York: Wiley, 1978.

*Price, R. H. *Abnormal behavior: Perspectives in conflict.* New York: Holt, 1972.

*Rosen, G. *Madness in society.* New York: Harper, 1968.

Smith, R. J. *The psychopath in society.* New York: Academic Press, 1978.

*Sontag, S. *Illness as metaphor.* New York: Farrar, Straus & Giroux, 1978.

Aesthetics:

Berlyne, D. E. *Studies in the new experimental aesthetics.* Washington, D.C.: Hemisphere,1974.

*Seashore, C. E. *The psychology of music.* New York: Dover, 1935.

Humor:

Chapman, A. J., & Foot, H. C. *It's a funny thing, humour.* Oxford: Pergamon, 1977.

*Koestler, A. *The act of creation.* New York: Dell, 1964.

*McGhee, P. E. *Humor: Origins and development.* San Francisco: Freeman, 1979.

Sports:

*Coakley, J. J. *Sport in society: Issues and controversies.* St. Louis: Mosby, 1978.

Goldstein, J. H. (Ed.). *Sports, games, and play.* Hillsdale, N.J.: Lawrence Erlbaum Associates, 1979.

*Novak, M. *The joy of sports.* New York: Basic Books, 1976.

Law:

Bermant, G., Nemeth, C., & Vidmar, N. *Psychology and the law.* Lexington, Mass.: Heath, 1976.

*Thibaut, J., & Walker, L. *Procedural justice.* Hillsdale, N.J.: Erlbaum, 1975.

Science:

Goldstein, M., & Goldstein, I. F. *How we know: An exploration of the scientific process.* New York: Plenum, 1978.

Merton, R. K. *The sociology of science.* Chicago: University of Chicago Press, 1973.

Zuckerman, H. The Sociology of the Nobel Prizes. *Scientific American,* 1967, *217,* 25–33.

Social Psychology:

*Armistead, N. (Ed.). *Reconstructing social psychology.* Baltimore: Penguin, 1974.

Israel, J., & Tajfel, H. *The context of social psychology.* New York: Academic Press, 1972.

Strickland, L. H., Aboud, F. E., & Gergen, K. J. *Social psychology in transition.* New York: Plenum, 1976.

Pertinent Journals

Abnormal Behavior:
Journal of Abnormal Psychology
Journal of Consulting and Clinical Psychology
Social Psychiatry

Aesthetics:
Journal of Creative Behavior
Journal of Experimental Aesthetics

Humor:
Humor Research Newsletter

Sports:
International Journal of Sport Psychology
Journal of Leisure Research
Journal of Sport History
Research Quarterly

Law:
Journal of Criminal Law and Criminology
Law and Human Behavior
Law and Society Review

Science:
Science
Science and Society
Social Studies of Science

Social Psychology:
Journal of the History of the Behavioral Sciences
Personality and Social Psychology Bulletin

*Available in paperback edition.

Abelson, R. P., Aronson, E., McGuire, W. J., Newcomb, T. M., Rosenberg, M. J., & Tannenbaum, P. H. *Theories of cognitive consistency: A sourcebook.* Chicago: Rand McNally, 1968.

Abelson, R. P., & Rosenberg, M. J. Symbolic psycho-logic: A model of attitudinal cognition. *Behavioral Science*, 1958, *3*, 1–13.

Abelson, R. P., & Zimbardo, P. G. *Canvassing for peace.* Ann Arbor, Mich.: Society for the Psychological Study of Social Issues, 1970.

Abse, D. *The dogs of Pavlov.* London: Valentine, Mitchell, 1974.

Adams, J. S. Toward an understanding of inequity. *Journal of Abnormal and Social Psychology*, 1963, *67*, 422–436.

Adams, J. S. Inequity in social exchange. In L. Berkowitz (Ed.), *Advances in experimental social psychology* (Vol. 2). New York: Academic Press, 1965.

Aderman, D., Brehm, S. S., & Katz, L. B. Empathic observation of an innocent victim: The just world revisited. *Journal of Personality and Social Psychology*, 1974, *29*, 342–347.

Adler, A. *What life should mean to you.* Boston: Little, Brown, 1931.

Adorno, T. W., Frenkel-Brunswik, E., Levinson, D., & Sanford, R. N. *The authoritarian personality.* New York: Harper, 1950.

Ajzen, I. Effects of information on interpersonal attraction: Similarity versus affective value. *Journal of Personality and Social Psychology*, 1974, *29*, 374–380.

Albert, S. Temporal comparison theory. *Psychological Review*, 1977, *89*, 485–503.

Albert, S. Time, memory, and affect: Experimental studies of the selective past. In J. T. Fraser & N. Lawrence (Eds.), *The study of time.* New York: Springer, 1978.

Alexander, C. N., & Sagatun, I. An attributional analysis of experimental norms. *Sociometry*, 1973, *36*, 127–142.

Alexander, C. N., & Weil, H. Players, persons, and purposes: Situational meaning and the prisoner's dilemma game. *Sociometry*, 1969, *32*, 121–144.

Alexander, C. N., Zucker, L. G., & Brody, C. L. Experimental expectations and autokinetic experiences: Consistency theories and judgmental convergence. *Sociometry*, 1970, *33*, 108–122.

Alexander, I. E., & Blackman, S. Castration, circumcision, and anti-Semitism. *Journal of Abnormal and Social Psychology*, 1957, *55*, 143–144.

Alexander, J. F., & Parsons, B. V. Short-term behavioral intervention with delinquent families: Impact on family process and recidivism. *Journal of Abnormal Psychology*, 1973, *81*, 219–225.

Alland, A., Jr. *The human imperative.* New York: Columbia University Press, 1972.

Allen, V. L. Social support for nonconformity. In L. Berkowitz (Ed.), *Advances in experimental social psychology* (Vol. 8). New York: Academic Press, 1975.

Allen, V. L., & Levine, J. M. Consensus and conformity. *Journal of Experimental Social Psychology*, 1969, *5*, 389–399.

Allen, V. L., & Wilder, D. A. Categorization, belief similarity, and intergroup discrimination. *Journal of Personality and Social Psychology*, 1975, *32*, 971–977.

Allport, F. H. The influence of the group upon association and thought. *Journal of Experimental Psychology*, 1920, *3*, 159–182.

Allport, F. H. *Social psychology.* Boston: Houghton Mifflin, 1924.

Allport, G. W. *The nature of prejudice.* Boston: Addison-Wesley, 1954.

Allport, G. W. The historical background of modern social psychology. In G. Lindzey & E. Aronson (Eds.), *Handbook of social psychology.* Reading, Mass.: Addison-Wesley, 1968.

Altman, I. *The environment and social behavior.* Monterey, Calif.: Brooks/Cole, 1975.

Altman, I. Environmental psychology and social psychology. *Personality and Social Psychology Bulletin*, 1976, *2*, 96–113.

American Psychological Association. *Ethical principles in the conduct of research with human participants.* Washington, D.C.: APA, 1973.

Amir, Y. Contact hypothesis in ethnic relations. *Psychological Bulletin*, 1969, *71*, 319–342.

Anderson, N. H. Averaging versus adding as a stimulus-combination rule in impression formation. *Journal of Experimental Psychology*, 1965, *70*, 394–400.

Anderson, N. H. Integration theory and attitude change. *Psychological Review*, 1971, *78*, 171–206.

Anderson, C. C., & Côté, A. D. J. Belief dissonance as a source of dissatisfaction between ethnic groups. *Journal of Personality and Social Psychology*, 1966, *4*, 447–453.

Anderson, R., Manoogian, S. T., & Reznick, J. S. The undermining and enhancing of intrinsic motivation in preschool children. *Journal of Personality and Social Psychology*, 1976, *34*, 915–922.

Archer, D., & Gartner, R. Violent acts and violent times: A comparative approach to postwar homicide rates. *American Sociological Review*, 1976, *41*, 937–963.

Ardrey, R. *The territorial imperative.* New York: Atheneum, 1966.

Argyle, M., & Dean, J. Eye-contact, distance and affiliation. *Sociometry*, 1965, *28*, 289–304.

Argyris, C. Dangers in applying results from experimental social psychology. *American Psychologist*, 1975, *30*, 469–485.

Arieti, S. *Creativity.* New York: Basic Books, 1978.

Aristotle. *The rhetoric.* New York: Appleton, 1932.

Arkin, R. M., Gleason, J. M., & Johnston, S. Effect of perceived choice, expected outcome, and observed outcome of an action on the causal attributions of actors. *Journal of Experimental Social Psychology*, 1975, *11*, 427–438.

Armistead, N. (Ed.). *Reconstructing social psychology.* Baltimore: Penguin, 1974.

Arms, R. L., Russell, G. W., & Sandilands, M. L. Effects of viewing aggressive sports on the hostility of spectators. *Social Psychology*, in press.

Aronfreed, J. *Conduct and conscience: The socialization of internalized control over behavior.* New York: Academic Press, 1968.

Aronson, E., Blaney, N., Sikes, J., Stephan, C., & Snapp, M. Busing and racial tension: The jigsaw route to learning and liking. *Psychology Today*, 1975, *8*, 43–50.

Aronson, E., & Mills, J. The effect of severity of initiation on liking for a group. *Journal of Abnormal and Social Psychology*, 1959, *59*, 177–181.

Aronson, E., Turner, J., & Carlsmith, J. M. Communicator credibility and communication discrepancy as determinants of opinion change. *Journal of Abnormal and Social Psychology*, 1963, *67*, 31–36.

Asch, S. E. Forming impressions of personality. *Journal of Abnormal and Social Psychology*, 1946, *41*, 258–290.

Asch, S. E. The doctrine of suggestion, prestige, and imitation in social psychology. *Psychological Review*, 1948, *55*, 250–276.

Asch, S. E. Effects of group pressure upon the modification and distortion of judgments. In H. Guetzkow (Ed.), *Groups, leadership, and men*. Pittsburgh: Carnegie Press, 1951.

Asch, S. E. *Social psychology*. Englewood Cliffs, N.J.: Prentice-Hall, 1952.

Aveni, A. F. The not-so-lonely crowd: Friendship groups in collective behavior. *Sociometry*, 1977, *40*, 96–99.

Backman, C. W., Secord, P. F., & Pierce, J. R. Resistance to change in the self-concept as a function of consensus among significant others. *Sociometry*, 1963, *26*, 102–111.

Bagby, J. W. Dominance in binocular rivalry in Mexico and the United States. *Journal of Abnormal and Social Psychology*, 1957, *54*, 331–334.

Bagdikian, B. H. Bias in the weekly newsmagazines. In R. M. Christenson & R. O. McWilliams (Eds.), *Voice of the people*. New York: McGraw-Hill, 1962.

Bakan, D. *Freud and the Jewish mystical tradition*. New York: Schocken, 1965.

Baker, R. Meaningful relationships. *New York Times* March 19, 1978, p. 17.

Bales, R. F. *Interaction process analysis*. Cambridge, Mass.: Addison-Wesley, 1950.

Bales, R. F. How people interact in conferences. *Scientific American*, 1955, *192*(3), 31–35.

Bales, R. F. *Personality and interpersonal behavior*. New York: Holt, 1970.

Bandura, A. Influence of models' reinforcement contingencies on the acquisition of imitative responses. *Journal of Personality and Social Psychology*, 1965, *1*, 589–595. (a)

Bandura, A. Vicarious processes: A case of no-trial learning. In L. Berkowitz (Ed.), *Advances in experimental social psychology* (Vol. 2). New York: Academic Press, 1965. (b)

Bandura, A. *Aggression: A social learning analysis*. Englewood Cliffs, N.J.: Prentice-Hall, 1973.

Bandura, A., Ross, D., & Ross, S. A comparative test of the status envy, social power, and secondary reinforcement theories of identificatory learning. *Journal of Abnormal and Social Psychology*, 1963, *67*, 527–534.

Bandura, A., Underwood, B., & Fromson, M. E. Disinhibition of aggression through diffusion of responsibility and dehumanization. *Journal of Research in Personality*, 1975, *9*, 253–269.

Barker, R. G. *Ecological psychology*. Stanford, Calif.: Stanford University Press, 1968.

Barker, R. G., Dembo, T., & Lewin, K. *Frustration and regression: An experiment with young children*. Iowa City: University of Iowa Studies in Child Welfare, 1940.

Barnes, K. E. Preschool play norms: A replication. *Developmental Psychology*, 1971, *5*, 99–103.

Baron, R. A. *Human aggression*. New York: Plenum, 1977.

Baron, R. A., & Ball, R. L. The aggression-inhibiting influence of nonhostile humor. *Journal of Experimental Social Psychology*, 1974, *10*, 23–33.

Baron, R. A., & Eggleston, R. J. Performance on the "aggression machine": Motivation to help or harm? *Psychonomic Science*, 1972, *26*, 321–322.

Barry, H., III, Bacon, M. K., & Child, I. L. A cross-cultural survey of some sex differences in socialization. *Journal of Abnormal and Social Psychology*, 1957, *55*, 327–332.

Barry, W. A. Marriage research and conflict: An integrative review. *Psychological Bulletin*, 1970, *73*, 41–54.

Barthell, C. N., & Holmes, D. S. High school yearbooks: A nonreactive measure of social isolation in graduates who later became schizophrenic. *Journal of Abnormal Psychology*, 1968, *73*, 313–316.

Bassili, J. N. Temporal and spatial contingencies in the perception of social events. *Journal of Personality and Social Psychology*, 1976, *33*, 680–685.

Bates, M. Human ecology. In A. L. Kroeber (Ed.), *Anthropology today*. Chicago: University of Chicago Press, 1953.

Bauer, R. A. The obstinate audience: The influence process from the point of view of social communication. *American Psychologist*, 1964, *19*, 319–328.

Baum, A., Harpin, R. E., & Valins, S. The role of group phenomena in the experience of crowding. *Environment and Behavior*, 1975, *7*, 185–198.

Baumrin, B. H. The immorality of irrelevance: The social role of science. In F. F. Korten, S. W. Cook, & J. I. Lacey (Eds.), *Psychology and the problems of society*. Washington, D.C.: American Psychological Assoc., 1970.

Baumrind, D. Some thoughts on ethics of research: After reading Milgram's "Behavioral study of obedience." *American Psychologist*, 1964, *19*, 421–423.

Bavelas, A. A mathematical model for group structures. *Applied Anthropology*, 1948, *7*, 16–30.

Beck, S. B., Ward-Hull, C. I., & McLear, P. M. Variables related to women's somatic preferences of the male and female body. *Journal of Personality and Social Psychology*, 1976, *34*, 1200–1210.

Becker, F. D., & Mayo, C. Delineating personal distance and territoriality. *Environment and Behavior*, 1971, *3*, 375–381.

Becker, H. S. *The outsiders*. Glencoe, Ill.: Free Press, 1963.

Bell, R. Q., & Harper, L. V. *Child effects on adults*. Hillsdale, N.J.: Erlbaum, 1977.

Bem, D. J. An experimental analysis of self-persuasion. *Journal of Experimental Social Psychology*, 1965, *1*, 199–218.

Bem, D. J. Self-perception: An alternative interpretation of cognitive dissonance phenomena. *Psychological Review*, 1967, *74*, 183–200.

Bem, D. J. Attitudes as self-descriptions: Another look at the attitude-behavior link. In A. G. Greenwald, T. C. Brock, & T. M. Ostrom (Eds.), *Psychological foundations of attitudes*. New York: Academic Press, 1968.

Bem, D. J. Self-perception theory. In L. Berkowitz (Ed.), *Advances in experimental social psychology* (Vol. 6). New York: Academic Press, 1972.

Ben-David, J. *The scientist's role in society*. Englewood Cliffs, N.J.: Prentice-Hall, 1971.

Bender, I. E., & Hastorf, A. H. On measuring generalized empathic ability (social sensitivity). *Journal of Abnormal and Social Psychology*, 1953, *48*, 503–506.

Berelson, B., & Steiner, G. A. *Human behavior: An inventory of scientific findings*. New York: Harcourt, 1964.

Berk, R. A., & Aldrich, H. E. Patterns of vandalism during civil disorders as an indicator of selection of targets. *American Sociological Review*, 1972, *37*, 533–547.

Berkowitz, L. Anti-semitism and the displacement of aggression. *Journal of Abnormal and Social Psychology*, 1959, *59*, 182–187.

Berkowitz, L. *Aggression: A social psychological analysis*. New York: McGraw-Hill, 1962.

Berkowitz, L. *Roots of aggression: A re-examination of the frustration-aggression hypothesis*. New York: Atherton, 1969.

Berkowitz, L. Impulse, aggression and the gun. *Psychology Today*, September 1970.

Berkowitz, L. The "weapons effect," demand characteristics and the myth of the compliant subject. *Journal of Personality and Social Psychology*, 1971, *20*, 332–338.

Berkowitz, L. Some determinants of impulsive aggression: Role of mediated associations with reinforcements for aggression. *Psychological Review*, 1974, *81*, 165–176.

Berkowitz, L. Whatever happened to the frustration-aggression hypothesis? *American Behavioral Scientist*, 1978, *21*, 691–708.

Berkowitz, L., & Alioto, J. T. The meaning of an observed event as a determinant of its aggressive content. *Journal of Personality and Social Psychology*, 1973, *28*, 206–217.

Berkowitz, L., & Friedman, P. Some social class differences in helping behavior. *Journal of Personality and Social Psychology*, 1967, *5*, 217–225.

Berkowitz, L., & Geen, R. G. Film violence and the cue properties of available targets. *Journal of Personality and Social Psychology*, 1966, *3*, 525–530.

Berkowitz, L., & Geen, R. G. Stimulus qualities of the target of aggression: A further study. *Journal of Personality and Social Psychology*, 1967, *5*, 364–368.

Berkowitz, L., & Green, J. A. The stimulus qualities of the scapegoat. *Journal of Abnormal and Social Psychology*, 1962, *64*, 293–301.

Berkowitz, L., & LePage, A. Weapons as aggression-eliciting stimuli. *Journal of Personality and Social Psychology*, 1967, *7*, 202–207.

Berkowitz, L., & Walker, N. Laws and moral judgments. *Sociometry*, 1967, *30*, 410–422.

Berkowitz, W. R. A cross national comparison of some social patterns of urban pedestrians. *Journal of Cross-Cultural Psychology*, 1971, *2*, 129–144.

Berlyne, D. E. *Conflict, arousal and curiosity*. New York: McGraw-Hill, 1960.

Berlyne, D. E. *Aesthetics and psychobiology*. New York: Appleton, 1971.

Berlyne, D. E. Humor and its kin. In J. H. Goldstein & P. E. McGhee (Eds.), *The psychology of humor*.

New York: Academic Press, 1972.

Berlyne, D. E. *Studies in the new experimental aesthetics.* Washington, D.C.: Hemisphere (Wiley), 1974.

Bermann, E., & Miller, D. R. The matching of mates. In R. Jessor & S. Feshbach (Eds.), *Cognition, personality and clinical psychology.* San Francisco: Jossey-Bass, 1967.

Bermant, G., Nemeth, C., & Vidmar, N. *Psychology and the law.* Lexington, Mass.: Heath, 1976.

Bernstein, L. *The unanswered question.* Cambridge, Mass.: Harvard University Press, 1976.

Berscheid, E. Opinion change and communicator - communicatee similarity and dissimilarity. *Journal of Personality and Social Psychology,* 1966, *4,* 670–680.

Berscheid, E., Dion, K., Walster, E., & Walster, G. W. Physical attractiveness and dating choice: A test of the matching hypothesis. *Journal of Experimental Social Psychology,* 1971, *7,* 173–189.

Berscheid, E., Graziano, W., Monson, T., & Dermer, M. Outcome dependency: Attention, attribution, and attraction. *Journal of Personality and Social Psychology,* 1976, *34,* 978–989.

Berscheid, E., & Walster, E. A little bit about love. In T. L. Huston (Ed.), *Foundations of interpersonal attraction.* New York: Academic Press, 1974.

Best, D. L., Williams, J. E., Cloud, J. M., Davis, S. W., Robertson, L. S., Edwards, J. R., Giles, H., & Fowles, J. Development of sex-trait stereotypes among young children in the United States, England, and Ireland. *Child Development,* 1977, *48,* 1375–1384.

Bethlehem, D. W. Cooperation, competition and altruism among school-children in Zambia. *International Journal of Psychology,* 1973, *8,* 125–135.

Bettelheim, B. Individual and mass behavior in extreme situations. *Journal of Abnormal and Social Psychology,* 1943, *38,* 417–452.

Bieri, J. *Clinical and social judgment.* New York: Wiley, 1966.

Billig, M. *Social psychology and intergroup relations.* New York: Academic Press, 1976.

Blake, R. R., Wedge, R. B., & Mouton, J. Housing architecture and social interaction. *Sociometry,* 1956, *19,* 133–139.

Blake, R. R., Rosenbaum, M., & Duryea, R. Gift-giving as a function of group standards. *Human Relations,* 1955, *8,* 61–73.

Bleda, P. R. Toward a clarification of the role of cognitive and affective processes in the similarity-attraction relationship. *Journal of Personality and Social Psychology,* 1974, *29,* 368–373.

Blumenthal, M. D., Kahn, R. L., Andrews, F. M., & Head, K. B. *Justifying violence: Attitudes of American men.* Ann Arbor, Mich.: Institute for Social Research, 1972.

Bochner, S., & Insko, C. A. Communicator discrepancy, source credibility, and opinion change. *Journal of Personality and Social Psychology,* 1966, *4,* 614–621.

Bochner, S., & Ohsako, T. Ethnic role salience in racially homogeneous and heterogeneous societies. *Journal of Cross-Cultural Psychology,* 1977, *8,* 477–480.

Bogardus, E. S. Measuring social distance. *Journal of Applied Psychology,* 1925, *9,* 299–308.

Borgatta, E. F., Couch, A. S., & Bales, R. F. Some findings relevant to the great man theory of leadership. *American Sociological Review*, 1954, *19*, 755–759.

Boring, E. G. *Psychology for the fighting man*. Washington, D.C.: U.S. Army, 1944.

Boring, E. G., Langfeld, H. S., & Weld, H. P. *Introduction to psychology*. New York: Wiley, 1939.

Bossard, J. H. S. Residential propinquity as a factor in marriage selection. *American Journal of Sociology*, 1931, *38*, 219–224.

Bossard, J. H. S. Law of family interaction. *American Journal of Sociology*, 1945, *50*, 292–294.

Braginsky, B., & Braginsky, D. *Mainstream psychology*. New York: Holt, 1974.

Bramel, D., Taub, B., & Blum, B. An observer's reaction to the suffering of his enemy. *Journal of Personality and Social Psychology*, 1968, *8*, 384–392.

Brehm, J. W. *A theory of psychological reactance*. New York: Academic Press, 1966.

Brehm, J. W., & Cohen, A. R. *Explorations in cognitive dissonance*. New York: Wiley, 1962.

Brehm, S. S. *The application of social psychology to clinical practice*. Washington, D.C.: Hemisphere, 1976.

Breuer, J., & Freud, S. *Studies on hysteria*. London: Hogarth, 1955. (Originally published, 1895).

Brickman, P., Coates, D., & Janoff-Bulman, R. Lottery winners and accident victims: Is happiness relative? *Journal of Personality and Social Psychology*, 1978, *36*, 917–927.

Brickman, P., Ryan, K., & Wortman, C. B. Causal chains: Attribution of responsibility as a function of immediate and prior causes. *Journal of Personality and Social Psychology*, 1975, *32*, 1060–1067.

Brislin, R. W., & Lewis, S. A. Dating and physical attractiveness: A replication. *Psychological Reports*, 1968, *22*, 976.

Brislin, R. W., Lonner, W. J., & Thorndike, R. M. *Cross-cultural research methods*. New York: Wiley, 1973.

Brock, T. C. Communicator-recipient similarity and decision change. *Journal of Personality and Social Psychology*, 1965, *1*, 650–654.

Brock, T. C. Communication discrepancy and intent to persuade as determinants of counterargument production. *Journal of Experimental Social Psychology*, 1967, *3*, 296–309.

Brock, T. C., & Buss, A. H. Dissonance, aggression, and evaluation of pain. *Journal of Abnormal and Social Psychology*, 1962, *65*, 197–202.

Brooks, R. S. Reference group influence on political party preference. In J. G. Manis & B. N. Meltzer (Eds.), *Symbolic interaction*. Boston: Allyn & Bacon, 1967.

Brooks, W. N., & Doob, A. N. Justice and the jury. *Journal of Social Issues*, 1975, *31*, 171–182.

Brown, R. W. *Social psychology*. Boston: Little, Brown, 1965.

Brown, R. W., & Gilman, A. The pronouns of power and solidarity. In T. Sebeok (Ed.), *Style in language*. Cambridge, Mass.: MIT Press, 1960.

Brown, R. W., & Lenneberg, E. H. A study in language and cognition. *Journal of Abnormal and Social Psychology*, 1954, *49*, 454–462.

Bruner, J. S., & Goodman, C. C. Value and need as organizing factors in perception. *Journal of Abnormal and Social Psychology*, 1947, *42*, 33–44.

Bruner, J. S., Goodnow, J., & Austin, G. A. *A study of thinking.* New York: Wiley, 1956.

Bruner, J. S., & Perlmutter, H. V. Compatriot and foreigner: A study of impression formation in three countries. *Journal of Abnormal and Social Psychology*, 1957, *55*, 253–260.

Bryan, J. H. "You will be advised to watch what we do, instead of what we say." In D. DePalma & J. Folley (Eds.), *Moral development.* Hillsdale, N.J.: Lawrence Erlbaum Associates, 1975.

Bryan, J. H., & Test, M. A. Models and helping: Naturalistic studies in aiding behavior. *Journal of Personality and Social Psychology*, 1967, *6*, 400–407.

Burgess, E. W. The growth of the city. In R. E. Park, E. Burgess, & R. McKenzie (Eds.), *The city.* Chicago: University of Chicago Press, 1925.

Burgess, E. W., & Wallin, P. *Engagement and marriage.* Philadelphia: Lippincott, 1953.

Business Week "Personal Business." B. Hitchings, ed. 12 Dec 1977, pp 115–116.

Buss, A. H. *The psychology of aggression.* New York: Wiley, 1961.

Buss, A. H. Aggression pays. In J. L. Singer (Ed.), *The control of aggression and violence.* New York: Academic Press, 1971.

Buss, A. H., Booker, A., & Buss, E. Firing a weapon and aggression. *Journal of Personality and Social Psychology*, 1972, *22*, 296–302.

Buss, A. H., & Durkee, A. An inventory for assessing different kinds of hostility. *Journal of Consulting Psychology*, 1957, *21*, 343–348.

Byrne, D. Attitudes and attraction. In L. Berkowitz (Ed.), *Advances in experimental social psychology* (Vol. 4). New York: Academic Press, 1969.

Byrne, D. *The attraction paradigm.* New York: Academic Press, 1971.

Byrne, D., & Blaylock, B. Similarity and assumed similarity of attitudes between husbands and wives. *Journal of Abnormal and Social Psychology*, 1963, *67*, 636–640.

Byrne, D., Bond, M. H., & Diamond, M. J. Response to political candidates as a function of attitude similarity-dissimilarity. *Human Relations*, 1969, *22*, 251–262.

Byrne, D., Clore, G. L., Griffitt, W., Lamberth, J., & Mitchell, H. E. When research paradigms converge: Confrontation or integration? *Journal of Personality and Social Psychology*, 1973, *28*, 313–320.

Byrne, D., Clore, G. L., & Worchel, P. Effect of economic similarity-dissimilarity on interpersonal attraction. *Journal of Personality and Social Psychology*, 1966, *4*, 220–224.

Byrne, D., Ervin, C. R., & Lamberth, J. Continuity between the experimental study of attraction and real-life computer dating. *Journal of Personality and Social Psychology*, 1970, *16*, 157–165.

Byrne, D., Gouaux, C., Griffitt, W., Lamberth, J., Murakawa, N., Prasad, M. B., Prasad, A., & Ramirez, M., III. The ubiquitous relationship: Attitude similarity and attraction. A cross-cultural study. *Human Relations*, 1971, *24*, 201–207.

Byrne, D., & Lamberth, J. Cognitive

and reinforcement theories as complementary approaches to the study of attraction. In B. I. Murstein (Ed.), *Theories of attraction and love.* New York: Springer, 1971.

Byrne, D., & Nelson, D. Attraction as a linear function of proportion of positive reinforcements. *Journal of Personality and Social Psychology,* 1965, *1,* 659–663.

Byrne, D., & Wong, T. J. Racial prejudice, interpersonal attraction, and assumed dissimilarity of attitudes. *Journal of Abnormal and Social Psychology,* 1962, *65,* 246–253.

Cairns, R. B. Attachment and dependency: A psychobiological and social-learning synthesis. In J. L. Gewirtz (Ed.), *Attachment and dependency.* Washington, D.C.: Winston, 1972.

Calabrese, F., & Goldstein, J. H. *Type of aggression as a mediator of catharsis.* In press.

Calder, B. J. An analysis of the Jones, Davis, and Gergen attribution paradigm. *Representative Research in Social Psychology,* 1974, *5,* 55–59.

Calder, B. J., & Ross, M. *Attitudes and behavior.* Morristown, N.J.: General Learning Press, 1973.

Calder, B. J., Ross, M., & Insko, C. A. Attitude change and attitude attribution: Effects of incentive, choice, and consequences. *Journal of Personality and Social Psychology,* 1973, *25,* 84–99.

Calhoun, J. B. Population density and social pathology. *Scientific American,* 1962, *206,* 139–148.

Campbell, D. T. Ethnocentric and other altruistic motives. In D. Levine (Ed.), *Nebraska Symposium on Motivation* (Vol. 13). Lincoln: University of Nebraska Press, 1965.

Campbell, D. T. Stereotypes and perception of group differences. *American Psychologist,* 1967, *22,* 812–829.

Campbell, D. T. Reforms as experiments. *American Psychologist,* 1969, *24,* 409–429.

Campbell, D. T. Considering the case against experimental evaluations of social innovations. *Administrative Science Quarterly,* 1970, *15,* 110–113.

Campbell, D. T. Measuring the effects of social innovations by means of time series. In J. M. Tanur, F. Mosteller, W. H. Kruskal, R. F. Link, R. S. Pieters, & G. R. Rising (Eds.), *Statistics: A guide to the unknown.* San Francisco: Holden-Day, 1972. (a)

Campbell, D. T. On the genetics of altruism and the counter-hedonic components in human culture. *Journal of Social Issues,* 1972, *28,* 21–37. (b)

Campbell, D. T., & Stanley, J. C. *Experimental and quasi-experimental designs for research.* Chicago: Rand McNally, 1966.

Cannavale, F., Scarr, H., & Pepitone, A. Deindividuation in the small group: Further evidence. *Journal of Personality and Social Psychology,* 1970, *16,* 141–147.

Cannon, W. B. *The wisdom of the body* (2nd ed.). New York: Norton, 1932.

Cantor, J. R., Bryant, J., & Zillmann, D. Enhancement of humor appreciation by transferred excitation. *Journal of Personality and Social Psychology,* 1974, *30,* 812–821.

Cantril, H. *The psychology of social movements.* New York: Wiley, 1941.

Caplan, N., & Nelson, S. D. On being useful: The nature and consequences of psychological research on social problems. *American Psychologist*, 1973, *28*, 199–211.

Carlsmith, J. M., Collins, B. E., & Helmreich, R. L. Studies of forced compliance: The effect of pressure for compliance on attitude change produced by face-to-face role playing and anonymous essay writing. *Journal of Personality and Social Psychology*, 1966, *4*, 1–13.

Carmichael, L. Autobiography. In E. G. Boring & G. Lindzey (Eds.), *A history of psychology in autobiography* (Vol. 5). New York: Appleton, 1967.

Carr, S. J., & Dabbs, J. M., Jr. The effects of lighting, distance and intimacy of topic on verbal and visual behavior. *Sociometry*, 1974, *37*, 592–600.

Carson, R. *Silent spring*. Boston: Houghton Mifflin, 1962.

Cartwright, D., & Harary, F. Structural balance: A generalization of Heider's theory. *Psychological Review*, 1956, *63*, 277–293.

Cashdan, S. *Abnormal psychology*. Englewood Cliffs, N.J.: Prentice-Hall, 1972.

Castell, P. J., & Goldstein, J. H. Social occasions for joking: A cross-cultural study. In A. J. Chapman & H. C. Foot (Eds.), *It's a funny thing, humour*. Oxford: Pergamon, 1977.

Chaiken, S., & Eagly, A. H. Communication modality as a determinant of message persuasiveness and message comprehensibility. *Journal of Personality and Social Psychology*, 1976, *34*, 605–614.

Chaikin, A. L., & Darley, J. M. Victim or perpetrator: Defensive attribution of responsibility and the need for order and justice. *Journal of Personality and Social Psychology*, 1973, *25*, 268–275.

Chandler, M. J. Egocentrism and antisocial behavior: The assessment and training of social perspective-taking skills. *Developmental Psychology*, 1973, *9*, 326–332.

Chapanis, N. P., & Chapanis, A. Cognitive dissonance: Five years later. *Psychological Bulletin*, 1964, *61*, 1–22.

Chapman, A. J. Social aspects of humorous laughter. In A. J. Chapman & H. C. Foot (eds.), *Humour and laughter*. New York: Wiley, 1976.

Chapman, A. J., & Williams, A. R. Prestige effects and aesthetic experiences: Adolescents' reactions to music. *British Journal of Social and Clinical Psychology*, 1976, *15*, 61–72.

Chase, S. Foreword. In J. B. Carroll (Ed.), *Language, thought and reality: Selected writings of Benjamin Lee Whorf*. Cambridge, Mass.: MIT Press, 1956.

Chein, I. The environment as a determinant of behavior. *Journal of Social Psychology*, 1954, *39*, 115–127.

Chen, S. C. The leaders and followers among the ants in nest building. *Physiological Zoology*, 1937, *10*, 437–455.

Chesler, P. *Women and madness*. New York: Doubleday, 1972.

Chomsky, N. *Syntactic structure*. Den Hague: Mouton, 1957.

Christie, R., & Jahoda, M. *Studies in the scope and method of the authoritarian personality*. New York: Free Press, 1954.

Cialdini, R. B., Borden, R. J., Thorne, A., Walker, M. R., Freeman, S., & Sloan, L. R. Basking in reflected glory: Three (football) field studies. *Journal of Personality and Social Psychology*, 1976, *34*, 366–375.

Cialdini, R. B., & Kenrick, D. T. Altruism as hedonism: A social development perspective on the relationship of negative mood state and helping. *Journal of Personality and Social Psychology*, 1976, *34*, 907–914.

Clairborn, W. L. Expectancy effects in the classroom: A failure to replicate. *Journal of Educational Psychology*, 1969, *60*, 377–383.

Clark, K. B. The pathos of power. *American Psychologist*, 1971, *26*, 1047–1057.

Clark, K. B., & Clark, M. P. The development of consciousness of self and the emergence of racial identification in Negro preschool children. *Journal of Social Psychology*, 1939, *10*, 591–599.

Clark, K. B., & Clark, M. P. Racial identification and preference in Negro children. In T. M. Newcomb & E. L. Hartley (Eds.), *Readings in social psychology*. New York: Holt, 1947.

Clark, K. B., & Clark, M. P. Emotional factors in racial identification and preference in Negro children. *Journal of Negro Education*, 1950, *19*, 341–350.

Clark, R. D., III, & Word, L. E. Where is the apathetic bystander? Situational characteristics of the emergency. *Journal of Personality and Social Psychology*, 1974, *29*, 279–287.

Clement, R., Gardner, R. C., & Smythe, P. C. Inter-ethnic contact: Attitudinal consequences. *Canadian Journal of Behavioural Science*, 1977, *9*, 205–215.

Coan, R. W. Toward a psychological interpretation of psychology. *Journal of the History of the Behavioral Sciences*, 1973, *9*, 313–327.

Coch, L., & French, J. R. P. Overcoming resistance to change. In G. E. Swanson, T. M. Newcomb, & E. L. Hartley (Eds.), *Readings in social psychology*. New York: Holt, 1952. (Originally published in *Human Relations*, 1948, *1*, 512–532.)

Cohen, A. R. Upward communication in experimentally created hierarchies. *Human Relations*, 1958, *11*, 41–53.

Cohen, A. R. An experiment of small rewards for discrepant compliance and attitude change. In J. Brehm & A. Cohen (Eds.), *Explorations in cognitive dissonance*. New York: Wiley, 1962.

Cohen, R. Altruism: Human, cultural, or what? *Journal of Social Issues*, 1972, *28*, 39–57.

Cohen, S. *Social and personality development in childhood*. New York: Macmillan, 1976.

Cohen, S. P., Kelman, H. C., Miller, F. D., & Smith, B. L. Evolving intergroup techniques for conflict resolution: An Israeli-Palestinian pilot workshop. *Journal of Social Issues*, 1977, *33*(1), 165–189.

Cole, M., & Scribner, S. *Culture and thought*. New York: Wiley, 1974.

Coleman, J., Katz, E., & Menzel, H. The diffusion of an innovation among physicians. *Sociometry*, 1957, *20*, 253–270.

Collins, B. E., & Hoyt, M. F. Personal responsibility for consequences: An integration and extension of the forced compliance literature. *Journal of Experimental Social Psychology*, 1972, *8*, 558–593.

Condry, J. Enemies of exploration: Self-initiated versus other-initiated learning. *Journal of Personality and Social Psychology*, 1977, *35*, 459–477.

Cook, H., & Stingle, S. Cooperative

behavior in children. *Psychological Bulletin*, 1974, *81*, 918–933.

Cook, S. W. Ethical issues in the conduct of research in social relations. In C. Selltiz, L. S. Wrightsman, & S. W. Cook (Eds.), *Research methods in social relations* (3rd ed.). New York: Holt, 1976.

Cook, T. D. & Campbell, D. T. *Quasi-experimentation*. Chicago: Rand McNally, 1979.

Cook, T. D., & Diamond, S. S. *Field experimentation in basic and applied social science*. New York: Free Press, 1976.

Cooley, C. H. *Human nature and the social order*. New York: Scribner's, 1902.

Cooley, C. H. *Social organization*. New York: Scribner's, 1909.

Cooper, M. R., Boltwood, C. E., & Wherry, R. J., Sr. A factor analysis of air passenger reactions to skyjacking and airport security measures as related to personal characteristics and alternatives to flying. *Journal of Applied Psychology*, 1974, *59*, 365–370.

Coser, R. L. Laughter among colleagues. *Psychiatry*, 1960, *23*, 81–95.

Cottrell, N. B. Performance in the presence of other human beings: Mere presence, audience and affiliation effects. In E. C. Simmel, R. A. Hoppe, & G. A. Milton (Eds.), *Social facilitation and imitative behavior*. Boston: Allyn & Bacon, 1968.

Cottrell, N. B., Wack, D. L., Sekerak, G. J., & Rittle, R. H. Social facilitation of dominant responses by the presence of an audience and the mere presence of others. *Journal of Personality and Social Psychology*, 1968, *9*, 245–250.

Cowen, E. L., Landes, L., & Schaet, D. E. The effects of mild frustration on the expression of prejudiced attitudes. *Journal of Abnormal and Social Psychology*, 1959, *58*, 33–38.

Crane, D. *Invisible colleges: Diffusion of knowledge in scientific communities*. Chicago: University of Chicago Press, 1972.

Cressey, P. G. *The taxi dance hall*. Chicago: University of Chicago Press, 1932.

Cronbach, L. J. Processes affecting scores on "understanding of others" and "assumed similarity." *Psychological Bulletin*, 1955, *52*, 177–193.

Crooks, R. C. The effects of an interracial preschool program upon racial preference, knowledge of racial differences, and racial identification. *Journal of Social Issues*, 1970, *26*, 137–144.

Darley, J. M., & Batson, C. D. "From Jerusalem to Jericho:" A study of situational and dispositional variables in helping behavior. *Journal of Personality and Social Psychology*, 1973, *27*, 100–108.

Darley, J. M., & Berscheid, E. Increased liking as a result of the anticipation of personal contact. *Human Relations*, 1967, *20*, 29–40.

Darley, J. M., & Latané, B. Bystander intervention in emergencies: Diffusion of responsibility. *Journal of Personality and Social Psychology*, 1968, *8*, 377–383.

Darley, J. M., & Latané, B. Norms and normative behavior: Field studies of social interdependence. In J. Macaulay & L. Berkowitz (Eds.), *Altruism and helping behavior*. New York: Academic Press, 1970.

Darwin, C. *The descent of man*. New York: Appleton, 1871.

Darwin, C. *The expression of the emotions in man and animals.* London: Murray, 1872.

Dashiell, J. F. An experimental analysis of some group effects. *Journal of Abnormal and Social Psychology,* 1930, *25,* 190–199.

Davis, D., Cahan, S., & Bashi, J. Birth order and intellectual development: The confluence model in the light of cross-cultural evidence. *Science,* 1977, *196,* 1470–1471.

Davis, J. H., Kerr, N. L., Atkin, R. S., Holt, R., & Meek, D. The decision process of 6- and 12-person mock juries assigned unanimous and two-thirds majority rules. *Journal of Personality and Social Psychology,* 1975, *32,* 1–14.

Davis, R. W. The influence of pretrial publicity and trial timing on the deliberation process and verdicts of simulated jurors. Doctoral dissertation, Temple University, 1979.

Dawes, R. M. Formal models of dilemmas in social decision making. In M. F. Kaplan & S. Schwartz (Eds.), *Human judgment and decision processes: Formal and mathematical approaches.* New York: Academic Press, 1975.

Deaux, K., & Emswiller, T. Explanations of successful performance on sex-linked tasks: What is skill for the male is luck for the female. *Journal of Personality and Social Psychology,* 1974, *29,* 80–85.

Deci, E. *Intrinsic motivation.* New York: Plenum, 1975.

Delgado, J. M. R. Aggression and defense under cerebral radio control. In C. D. Clemente & D. B. Lindsley (Eds.), *Aggression and defense: Neural mechanisms and social patterns.* Los Angeles: University of California Press, 1967.

Delgado, J. M. R. *Physical control of the mind.* New York: Harper, 1969.

Denzin, N. K. Play, games, and interaction: The contexts of childhood socialization. *Sociological Quarterly,* 1975, *16,* 458–478.

Dermer, M., & Thiel, D. L. When beauty may fail. *Journal of Personality and Social Psychology,* 1975, *31,* 1168–1176.

Desor, J. A. Toward a psychological theory of crowding. *Journal of Personality and Social Psychology,* 1972, *21,* 79–83.

Deutsch, M. *The resolution of conflict.* New Haven, Conn.: Yale University Press, 1973.

Deutsch, M. Introduction. In M. Deutsch & H. A. Hornstein (Eds.), *Applying social psychology.* Hillsdale, N.J.: Lawrence Erlbaum Associates, 1975.

Deutsch, M., & Collins, M. E. *Interracial housing: A psychological evaluation of a social experiment.* Minneapolis: University of Minnesota Press, 1951.

Deutsch, M., & Gerard, H. B. A study of normative and informational social influence upon individual judgment. *Journal of Abnormal and Social Psychology,* 1955, *51,* 629–636.

Deutsch, M., & Krauss, R. M. *Theories in social psychology.* New York: Basic Books, 1965.

DeVos, G., & Wagatsuma, H. *Japan's invisible race.* Berkeley: University of California Press, 1966.

Diamond, R., & Carey, S. Developmental changes in the representation of faces. *Journal of Experimental Child Psychology,* 1977, *23,* 1–22.

Diener, E. Deindividuation: Causes and consequences. *Social Behavior and Personality,* 1977, *5,* 143–155.

Diener, E. Deindividuation, self-awareness, and disinhibition. *Journal of Personality and Social Psychology*, 1979, *37*, 1160–1171.

Diener, E., Fraser, S. C., Beaman, A. L., & Kelem, R. T. Effects of deindividuation variables on stealing among Halloween trick-or-treaters. *Journal of Personality and Social Psychology*, 1976, *33*, 178–183.

Dillehay, R. C. On the irrelevance of the classical negative evidence concerning the effect of attitudes on behavior. *American Psychologist*, 1973, *28*, 887–891.

Dion, K. K., Berscheid, E., & Walster, E. What is beautiful is good. *Journal of Personality and Social Psychology*, 1972, *24*, 285–290.

Dion, K. L., Baron, R. S., & Miller, N. Why do groups make riskier decisions than individuals? In L. Berkowitz (Ed.), *Advances in experimental social psychology* (Vol. 5). New York: Academic Press, 1970.

Dion, K. L., & Dion, K. K. Correlates of romantic love. *Journal of Consulting and Clinical Psychology*, 1973, *41*, 51–56.

Dion, K. L., & Earn, B. M. The phenomenology of being a target of prejudice. *Journal of Personality and Social Psychology*, 1975, *32*, 944–950.

Doise, W., Csepeli, G., Dann, H. D., Gouge, C., Larsen, K., & Ostell, A. An experimental investigation into the formation of intergroup representations. *European Journal of Social Psychology*, 1972, *2*, 202–204.

Dollard, J., Doob, L. W., Miller, N. E., Mowrer, O. H., & Sears, R. R. *Frustration and aggression.* New Haven, Conn.: Yale University Press, 1939.

Doob, A. N., & Gross, A. E. Status of frustrator as an inhibitor of horn-honking responses. *Journal of Social Psychology*, 1968, *48*, 213–218.

Doob, A. N., & Wood, L. E. Catharsis and aggression: Effects of annoyance and retalitation on aggressive behavior. *Journal of Personality and Social Psychology*, 1972, *22*, 156–162.

Doob, L. W. *Resolving conflict in Africa: The Fermeda workshop.* New Haven, Conn.: Yale University Press, 1970.

Doob, L. W., & Foltz, W. J. The Belfast workshop: An application of group techniques to a destructive conflict. *Journal of Conflict Resolution*, 1973, *17*, 489–512.

Driscoll, R., Davis, K. E., & Lipetz, M. E. Parental interference and romantic love: The Romeo and Juliet effect. *Journal of Personality and Social Psychology*, 1972, *24*, 1–10.

Duke, J. D. Critique of the Janis and Feshbach study. *Journal of Social Psychology*, 1967, *73*, 71–80.

Duncan, O. D., & Reiss, A. *Social characteristics of urban and rural communities.* New York: Wiley, 1956.

Dutton, D. G., & Aron, A. P. Some evidence for heightened sexual attraction under conditions of high anxiety. *Journal of Personality and Social Psychology*, 1974, *30*, 510–517.

Duval, S., & Wicklund, R. A. *A theory of objective self-awareness.* New York: Academic Press, 1972.

Dweck, C. S., & Reppucci, N. D. Learned helplessness and reinforcement responsibility in children. *Journal of Personality and Social Psychology*, 1973, *25*, 109–116.

Dworkin, R. H., Burke, B. W., Maher, B. A., & Gottesman, I. I. A longitudinal study of the genetics of personality. *Journal of Personality and Social Psychology*, 1976, *34*, 510–518.

Eaton, W. O., & Clore, G. L. Interracial imitation at a summer camp. *Journal of Personality and Social Psychology*, 1975, *32*, 1099–1105.

Eberts, E. H., & Lepper, M. R. Individual consistency in the proxemic behavior of preschool children. *Journal of Personality and Social Psychology*, 1975, *32*, 841–849.

Edney, J. J. Human territoriality. *Psychological Bulletin*, 1974, *81*, 959–975.

Edwards, D. W. Blacks versus whites: When is race a revelant variable? *Journal of Personality and Social Psychology*, 1974, *29*, 39–49.

Edwards, J. D., The home field advantage. In J. H. Goldstein (Ed.), *Sports, games, and play*. Hillsdale, N.J.: Lawrence Erlbaum Associates, 1979.

Efran, M. G., & Cheyne, J. A. Affective concomitants of the invasion of shared space: Behavioral, physiological, and verbal indicators. *Journal of Personality and Social Psychology*, 1974, *29*, 219–226.

Ehrlich, D., Guttman, I., Schönbach, P., & Mills, J. Postdecision exposure to relevant information. *Journal of Abnormal and Social Psychology*, 1957, *54*, 98–102.

Ehrlich, H. J. *The social psychology of prejudice*. New York: Wiley, 1973.

Ehrlich, P. R. *The population bomb*. New York: Ballantine. 1968.

Eisenberger, R. Is there a deprivation-satiation function for social approval? *Psychological Bulletin*, 1970, *74*, 225–275.

Ekman, P., & Friesen, W. V. Detecting deception from the body or face. *Journal of Personality and Social Psychology*, 1974, *29*, 288–298.

Ekman, P., Sorenson, E. R., & Friesen, W. V. Pan-cultural elements in facial displays of emotion. *Science*, 1969, *164*, 86–88.

Elashoff, J. D., & Snow, R. E. *A case study in statistical inference: Reconsideration of the Rosenthal-Jacobson data on teacher expectancy*. Stanford, Calif.: Stanford University School of Education, 1970. (Cited in Seaver, 1973.)

Ellis, D. P., Weinir, P., & Miller, L. Does the trigger pull the finger? An experimental test of weapons as aggression-eliciting stimuli. *Sociometry*, 1971, *34*, 453–465.

Elms, A. C. The crisis of confidence in social psychology. *American Psychologist*, 1975, *30*, 967–976.

Elms, A. C., & Janis, I. Counter-norm attitudes induced by consonant versus dissonant conditions of role playing. *Journal of Experimental Research in Personality*, 1965, *1*, 50–60.

Elms, A. C., & Milgram, S. Personality characteristics associated with obedience and defiance toward authoritative command. *Journal of Experimental Research in Personality*, 1966, *2*, 282–289.

Emmerich, W. Evaluating alternative models of development: An illustrative study of preschool personal-social behaviors. *Child Development*, 1977, *48*, 1401–1410.

English, H. B., & English, A. C. *A comprehensive dictionary of psychological and psychoanalytical terms*. New York: McKay, 1958.

Epstein, R., & Komorita, S. S. Prejudice among Negro children as related to parental ethnocentrism and punitiveness. *Journal of Per-*

sonality and Social Psychology, 1966, 4, 643–647.

Epstein, Y. M., Krupat, E., & Obudho, C. Clean is beautiful: Identification and preference as a function of race and cleanliness. Journal of Social Issues, 1976, 32, 109–118.

Erickson, L. G. W., & Cramer, J. A. Smoking behavior development and modification: An empirical application of three social psychological theories. Journal of Applied Social Psychology, 1976, 6, 369–386.

Eriksen, E. H. Gandhi's truth. New York: Norton, 1961.

Ervin-Tripp, S. M. Sociolinguistics. In L. Berkowitz (Ed.), Advances in experimental social psychology (Vol. 4). New York: Academic Press, 1969.

Estes, S. G. Judging personality from expressive behavior. Journal of Abnormal and Social Psychology, 1938, 33, 217–236.

Etzioni, A. The Kennedy experiment. Western Political Quarterly, 1967, 20, 361–380.

Eysenck, H. J. The I.Q. argument: Race, intelligence & education. New York: Library Press, 1971.

Farber, M. L. Psychoanalytic hypotheses in the study of war. Journal of Social Issues, 1955, 11, 29–35.

Faris, R. E. L., & Dunham, H. W. Mental disorders in urban areas. Chicago: University of Chicago Press, 1939.

Faucheux, C. Cross-cultural research in experimental social psychology. European Journal of Social Psychology, 1976, 6, 269–322.

Fazio, R. H., Zanna, M. P., & Cooper, J. Dissonance and self-perception: An integrative view of each the-

ory's proper domain of application. Journal of Experimental Social Psychology, 1977, 13, 464–479.

Feather, N. T., & Simon, J. G. Reactions to male and female success and failure in sex-linked occupations: Impressions of personality, causal attributions, and perceived likelihood of different consequences. Journal of Personality and Social Psychology, 1975, 31, 20–31.

Feierabend, I. K., & Feierabend, R. L. Aggressive behavior within polities, 1948–1962: A cross-national study. Journal of Conflict Resolution, 1966, 10, 249–271.

Feierabend, I. K., & Feierabend, R. L. Systemic conditions of political aggression: An application of frustration-aggression theory. In I. K. Feierabend, R. L. Feierabend, & T. R. Gurr (Eds.), Anger, violence, and politics: Theory and research. Englewood Cliffs, N.J.: Prentice-Hall, 1972.

Feierabend, I. K., Feierabend, R. L., & Scanland, F., III. The relation between sources of systemic frustration, international conflict, and political instability. Study 5. In I. K. Feierabend, R. L. Feierabend, & T. R. Gurr (Eds.), Anger, violence, and politics: Theory and research. Englewood Cliffs, N.J.: Prentice-Hall, 1972.

Feldman, R. E. Response to compatriot and foreigner who seek assistance. Journal of Personality and Social Psychology, 1968, 10, 202–214.

Feleky, A. M. The expression of the emotions. Psychological Review, 1914, 21, 33–41.

Fellner, C. H., & Marshall, J. R. Kidney donors. In J. Macaulay & L. Berkowitz (Eds.), Altruism and helping behavior. New York: Academic Press, 1970.

Ferster, C. B., & Skinner, B. F. *Schedules of reinforcement.* New York: Appleton-Century-Crofts, 1957.

Feshbach, S. The stimulating versus cathartic effects of a vicarious aggressive activity. *Journal of Abnormal and Social Psychology,* 1961, *63,* 381–385.

Feshbach, S., & Singer, R. D. *Television and aggression.* San Francisco: Jossey-Bass, 1971.

Festinger, L. Informal social communication. *Psychological Review,* 1950, *57,* 271–292.

Festinger, L. Theory of social comparison processes. *Human Relations,* 1954, *7,* 117–140.

Festinger, L. *A theory of cognitive dissonance.* Stanford, Calif.: Stanford University Press, 1957.

Festinger, L., & Carlsmith, J. M. Cognitive consequences of forced compliance. *Journal of Abnormal and Social Psychology,* 1959, *58,* 203–210.

Festinger, L., & Maccoby, N. On resistance to persuasive communications. *Journal of Abnormal and Social Psychology,* 1964, *68,* 359–366.

Festinger, L., Pepitone, A., & Newcomb, T. M. Some consequences of de-individuation in a group. *Journal of Abnormal and Social Psychology,* 1952, *47,* 382–389.

Festinger, L., Riecken, H., & Schachter, S. *When prophecy fails.* Minneapolis: University of Minnesota Press, 1956.

Festinger, L., Schachter, S., & Back, K. *Social pressures in informal groups: A study of human factors in housing.* New York: Harper, 1950.

Fiedler, F. E. A contingency model of leadership effectiveness. In L. Berkowitz (Ed.), *Advances in experimental social psychology* (Vol. 1). New York: Academic Press, 1964.

Fiedler, F. E. *A theory of leadership effectiveness.* New York: McGraw-Hill, 1967.

Fiedler, F. E. *Leadership.* New York: General Learning Press, 1971.

Fiedler, W. R., Cohen, R. D., & Finney, S. An attempt to replicate the teacher expectancy effect. *Psychological Reports,* 1971, *29,* 1223–1228.

Fine, G. A. Humor in situ. In A. J. Chapman & H. C. Foot (Eds.), *It's a funny thing, humour.* Oxford: Pergamon, 1977.

Firestone, I. J., Kaplan, K. J., & Russell, J. C. Anxiety, fear, and affiliation with similar-state versus dissimilar-state others: Misery sometimes loves nonmiserable company. *Journal of Personality and Social Psychology,* 1973, *26,* 409–414.

Fishbein, M. An investigation of the relationship between beliefs about an object and the attitude toward the object. *Human Relations,* 1963, *16,* 233–240.

Fishbein, M., & Ajzen, I. *Belief, attitude, intention, and behavior.* Reading, Mass.: Addison-Wesley, 1975.

Fisher, J. D., & Byrne, D. Too close for comfort: Sex differences in response to invasions of personal space. *Journal of Personality and Social Psychology,* 1975, *32,* 15–21.

Fiske, E. B. Children's books depicting blacks, while rising, are still only 1 in 7. *The New York Times,* Jan. 8, 1978, p. 41.

FitzGerald, F. *America revised.* Boston: Atlantic–Little, Brown, 1979.

Flaste, R. What's in a name? *The New York Times,* February 4, 1977, p. A12.

Florman, S. C. *The existential pleas-*

ures of engineering. New York: St. Martin's, 1976.

Flynn, J. P. The neural basis of aggression in cats. In D. C. Glass (Ed.), *Neurophysiology and emotion.* New York: Rockefeller University Press, 1967.

Foa, U. G. Interpersonal and economic resources. *Science,* 1971, *171,* 345–351.

Foa, U. G., & Foa, E. B. *Societal structures of the mind.* Springfield, Ill.: Thomas, 1974.

Foa, U. G., Megonigal, S., & Greipp, J. R. Some evidence against the possibility of utopian societies. *Journal of Personality and Social Psychology,* 1976, *34,* 1043–1048.

Foa, U. G., Triandis, H. C., & Katz, E. W. Cross-cultural invariance in the differentiation and organization of family roles. *Journal of Personality and Social Psychology,* 1966, *4,* 316–327.

Foa, U. G., & Turner, J. L. Psychology in the year 2000: Going structural? *American Psychologist,* 1970, *25,* 244–247.

Forston, R. F., & Larson, C. U. The dynamics of space: An experimental study in proxemic behavior among Latin Americans and North Americans. *Journal of Communication,* 1968, *18,* 109–116.

Foucault, M. *Madness and civilization.* New York: Pantheon, 1965.

Fraisse, P. *The psychology of time.* (J. Leith, trans.) Westport, Conn.: Greenwood, 1975.

Framo, J., ed. *Family interaction: A dialogue between family researchers and family therapists.* New York: Springer, 1972.

Freedman, J. L. Involvement, discrepancy, and change. *Journal of Abnormal and Social Psychology,* 1964, *69,* 290–295.

Freedman, J. L. Preference for dissonant information. *Journal of Personality and Social Psychology,* 1965, *1,* 287–289.

Freedman, J. L. *Crowding and behavior.* San Francisco: Freeman, 1975.

Freedman, J. L., Heshka, S., & Levy, A. Population density and pathology: Is there a relationship? *Journal of Experimental Social Psychology,* 1975, *11,* 539–552.

Freedman, J. L., Klevansky, S., & Ehrlich, P. R. The effect of crowding on human task performance. *Journal of Applied Social Psychology,* 1971, *1,* 7–25.

Freedman, J. L., Levy, A., Buchanan, R. W., & Price, J. Crowding and human aggressiveness. *Journal of Experimental Social Psychology,* 1972, *8,* 528–548.

French, J. R. P., Israel, J., & As, D. An experiment in participation in a Norwegian factory. *Human Relations,* 1960, *13,* 3–19.

French, J. R. P., & Raven, B. The bases of social power. In D. Cartwright (Ed.), *Studies in social power.* Ann Arbor: University of Michigan Press, 1959.

Freud, A., & Dann, S. An experiment in group unbringing. *Psychoanalytic study of the child,* 1951, *6,* 127–168.

Freud, S. *Group psychology and the analysis of the ego.* London: Hogarth, 1945. (Originally published, 1921.)

Freud, S. *Totem and taboo.* New York: Norton, 1952. (Originally published, 1913.)

Freud, S. *Civilization and its discontents* (J. Strachey, trans.). New York: Norton, 1962. (Originally published, 1930.)

Freud, S. *Dora: An analysis of a case*

of hysteria. New York: Macmillan, 1963. (a)

Freud, S. *Three case histories.* New York: Macmillan, 1963. (b)

Freud, S. *Leonardo da Vinci and a memory of his childhood* (A. Tyson, trans.). New York: Norton, 1964.

Freud, S. *Beyond the pleasure principle.* New York: Bantam, 1970. (Originally published, 1920.)

Freud, S., & Einstein, A. *Why war?* London: Hogarth, 1934.

Frey, D., & Irle, M. Some conditions to produce a dissonance and an incentive effect in a "forced-compliance" situation. *European Journal of Social Psychology,* 1972, *2,* 45–54.

Frijda, N. H. Recognition of emotion. In L. Berkowitz (Ed.), *Advances in experimental social psychology* (Vol. 4). New York: Academic Press, 1969.

Frodi, A. The effects of exposure to weapons on aggressive behavior from a cross-cultural perspective. *International Journal of Psychology,* 1975, *10,* 283–292.

Fromkin, H. L., Goldstein, J. H., & Brock, T. C. The role of "irrelevant" derogation in hostility catharsis: A field experiment. *Journal of Experimental Social Psychology,* 1977, *13,* 239–252.

Fromm, E. *The art of loving.* New York: Harper, 1956.

Galle, O. R., Gove, W. R., & McPherson, J. M. Population density and pathology: What are the relations for man? *Science,* 1972, *176,* 23–30.

Gallois, C., & Markel, N. N. Turn taking: Social personality and conversational style. *Journal of Personality and Social Psychology,* 1975, *31,* 1134–1140.

Gamson, W. A., & Scotch, N. Scape- goating in baseball. *American Journal of Sociology,* 1964, *70,* 69–72.

Gardner, H. *The quest for mind: Piaget, Lévi-Strauss, and the structuralist movement.* New York: Knopf, 1973.

Garfield, E. The 100 articles most cited by social scientists, 1969–1977. *Current Contents,* 1978, *10*(32), 5–14.

Garfinkel, H. *Studies in ethnomethodology.* Englewood Cliffs, N.J.: Prentice-Hall, 1967.

Garvey, C. *Play.* Cambridge, Mass.: Harvard University Press, 1977.

Gaskell, G. D., & Pearton, R. Aggression and sport. In J. H. Goldstein (Ed.), *Sports, games, and play.* Hillsdale, N.J.: Lawrence Erlbaum Associates, 1979.

Gates, M. J., & Allee, W. C. Conditioned behavior of isolated and grouped cockroaches on a simple maze. *Journal of Comparative Psychology,* 1933, *15,* 331–358.

Geen, R. G. Effects of anticipation of positive and negative outcomes on audience anxiety. *Journal of Consulting and Clinical Psychology,* 1977, *45,* 715–716.

Geen, R. G., & O'Neal, E. C. Activation of cue-elicited aggression by general arousal. *Journal of Personality and Social Psychology,* 1969, *11,* 289–292.

Gerard, H. B., & Hoyt, M. F. Distinctiveness of social categorization and attitude toward ingroup members. *Social Psychology,* 1974, *29,* 836–842.

Gerard, H. B., & Mathewson, G. C. The effect of severity of initiation on liking for a group: A replication. *Journal of Experimental Social Psychology,* 1966, *2,* 278–287.

Gerbasi, K. C. Justice needs a new

blindfold: A review of mock jury research. *Psychological Bulletin*, 1977, *84*, 323–345.

Gerbner, G., & Gross, L. The world of the television viewer. *Psychology Today*, 1976 (April), 41–45, 89.

Gergen, K. J. The codification of research ethics: Views of a doubting Thomas. *American Psychologist*, 1973, *28*, 907–912. (a)

Gergen, K. J. Social psychology as history. *Journal of Personality and Social Psychology*, 1973, *26*, 309–320. (b)

Gergen, K. J., Ellsworth, P., Maslach, C., & Seipel, M. Obligation, donor resources, and reactions to aid in three cultures. *Journal of Personality and Social Psychology*, 1975, *31*, 390–400.

Gergen, K. J., Gergen, M. M., & Meter, K. Individual orientations to prosocial behavior. *Journal of Social Issues*, 1972, *28*, 105–130.

Gergen, K. J., Morse, S. J., & Kristeller, J. L. The manner of giving: Cross-national continuities in reactions to aid. *Psychologia*, 1973, *16*, 121–131.

Gewirtz, J. L., & Baer, D. M. Deprivation and satiation of social reinforcers as drive conditions. *Journal of Abnormal and Social Psychology*, 1958, *57*, 165–172.

Gibb, C. A. Introduction. In C. A. Gibb (Ed.), *Leadership*. Baltimore: Penguin, 1969.

Giel, R., & Ormel, J. Crowding and subjective health in the Netherlands. *Social Psychiatry*, 1977, *12*, 37–42.

Gil, D. *Violence against children*. Cambridge, Mass.: Harvard University Press, 1970.

Gilbert, G. M. Stereotype persistence and change among college students. *Journal of Abnormal and Social Psychology*, 1951, *46*, 245–254.

Gillig, P. M., & Greenwald, A. G. Is it time to lay the sleeper effect to rest? *Journal of Personality and Social Psychology*, 1974, *29*, 132–139.

Glass, D. C. Changes in liking as a means of reducing cognitive discrepancies between self-esteem and aggression. *Journal of Personality*, 1964, *32*, 531–549.

Glass, D. C. *Behavior patterns, stress, and coronary disease*. Hillsdale, N.J.: Lawrence Erlbaum Associates, 1977.

Glass, D. C., & Singer, J. E. Behavioral aftereffects of unpredictable and uncontrollable aversive events. *American Scientist*, 1972(a), *60*, 457–465.

Glass, D. C., & Singer, J. E. *Urban stress*. New York: Academic Press, 1972(b).

Glover, E. *The roots of crime*. New York: International Universities Press, 1960.

Godfrey, B. W., & Lowe, C. A. Devaluation of innocent victims: An attribution analysis within the just world paradigm. *Journal of Personality and Social Psychology*, 1975, *31*, 944–951.

Godwin, W. F., & Restle, F. The road to agreement: Subgroup pressures in small group consensus processes. *Journal of Personality and Social Psychology*, 1974, *30*, 500–509.

Goffman, E. *The presentation of self in everyday life*. Garden City, N.Y.: Doubleday, 1959.

Goffman, E. *Asylums: Essays on the social situation of mental patients and other inmates*. New York: Aldine, 1961.

Goffman, E. *Stigma*. Englewood Cliffs, N.J.: Prentice-Hall, 1963.

Goffman, E. *Frame analysis*. New York: Colophon, 1974.

Goldberg, G. N., Kiesler, C. A., & Collins, B. E. Visual behavior and face-to-face distance during interaction. *Sociometry*, 1969, *32*, 43–53.

Goldberg, P. A. Are women prejudiced against women? *Trans-Action*, 1968, *5*, 28–30.

Goldman, M., & Fraas, L. A. The effects of leader selection on group performance. *Sociometry*, 1965, *28*, 82–88.

Goldstein, J. H. *Aggression and crimes of violence*. London and New York: Oxford University Press, 1975.

Goldstein, J. H. Conducting field research on aggression: Notes on "Effects of observing athletic contests on hostility." In M. P. Golden (Ed.), *The research experience*. Itasca, Ill.: F. E. Peacock, 1976. (a)

Goldstein, J. H. Theoretical notes on humor. *Journal of Communication*, 1976, *26*, 102–112. (b)

Goldstein, J. H. Cross-cultural research: Humour here and there. In A. J. Chapman & H. C. Foot (Eds.), *It's a funny thing, humour*. Oxford: Pergamon, 1977.

Goldstein, J. H. In vivo veritas: Has humor research studied humor? *Humor Research Newsletter*, 1978, *2*, 3–4.

Goldstein, J. H. (Ed.), *Sports, games, and play*. Hillsdale, N.J.: Lawrence Erlbaum Associates, 1979. (a)

Goldstein, J. H. Outcomes in professional team sports: Chance, skill and situational factors. In J. H. Goldstein (Ed.), *Sports, games, and play*. Hillsdale, N.J.: Lawrence Erlbaum Associates, 1979. (b)

Goldstein, J. H., & Arms, R. L. Effects of observing athletic contests on hostility. *Sociometry*, 1971, *34*, 83–90.

Goldstein, J. H., & Bredemeier, B. J. Sport and socialization: Some basic issues. *Journal of Communication*, 1977, *27*, 154–159.

Goldstein, J. H., Davis, R. W., & Herman, D. Escalation of aggression: Experimental studies. *Journal of Personality and Social Psychology*, 1975, *31*, 162–170.

Goldstein, J. H., Davis, R. W., Kernis, M., & Cohn, E. S. Retarding the escalation of aggression. In press.

Goldstein, J. H., Rosnow, R. L., Goodstadt, B., & Suls, J. M. The "good subject" in verbal operant conditioning research. *Journal of Experimental Research in Personality*, 1972, *6*, 29–33.

Goldstein, J. H., Rosnow, R. L., Raday, T., Silverman, I., & Gaskell, G. D. Punitiveness in response to films varying in content: A cross-national field study of aggression. *European Journal of Social Psychology*, 1975, *5*, 149–165.

Goldstein, J. H., Suls, J. M., & Anthony, S. Enjoyment of specific types of humor content: Motivation or salience? In J. H. Goldstein & P. E. McGhee (Eds.), *The psychology of humor*. New York: Academic Press, 1972.

Good, I. J. *The scientist speculates*. New York: Capricorn, 1965.

Goodale, J. G., & Aagaard, A. K. Factors relating to varying reactions to the four-day workweek. *Journal of Applied Psychology*, 1975, *60*, 33–37.

Goodchilds, J. D. On being witty: Causes, correlates, and consequences. In J. H. Goldstein & P. E. McGhee (Eds.), *The psychology of humor*. New York: Academic Press, 1972.

Goode, W. Violence among intimates. In D. J. Mulvihill & M. M. Tumin (Eds.), *Crimes of violence.* Washington, D.C.: U.S. Government Printing Office, 1969.

Goodmonson, C., & Glaudin, V. The relationship of commitment-free behavior and commitment behavior: A study of attitude toward organ transplantation. *Journal of Social Issues,* 1971, *27,* 171–183.

Goodrich, A. J., Henry, J., & Goodrich, D. W. Laughter in psychiatric staff conferences: A sociopsychiatric analysis. *American Journal of Orthopsychiatry,* 1954, *24,* 175–184.

Goodstadt, B. E., & Hjelle, L. A. Power to the powerless: Locus of control and the use of power. *Journal of Personality and Social Psychology,* 1973, *27,* 190–196.

Goodwin, L., & Tu, J. The social psychological basis for public acceptance of the social security system: The role for social research in public policy formation. *American Psychologist,* 1975, *30,* 875–883.

Gordon, C., & Gergen, K. J. *The self in social interaction.* New York: Wiley, 1968.

Gottschaldt, K., & Frauhauf-Ziegler, C. On the development of cooperative behavior in young children. *Zeitschrift für Psychologie,* 1958, *162,* 254–278. (Cited in Cook & Stingle, 1974.)

Gouldner, A. The norm of reciprocity: A preliminary statement. *American Sociological Review,* 1960, *25,* 161–178.

Graen, G., Orris, J., & Alvares, K. The contingency model of leadership effectiveness: Some experimental results. *Journal of Applied Psychology,* 1971, *55,* 196–201.

Grahamjun, C. D. *Metal Progress,* 1957, *71,* 75–76.

Granberg, D., & Brent, E. E., Jr. Dove-hawk placements in the 1968 election: Application of social judgment and balance theories. *Journal of Personality and Social Psychology,* 1974, *29,* 687–695.

Greenberg, C. I., & Firestone, I. J. Compensatory responses to crowding: Effects of personal space intrusion and privacy reduction. *Journal of Personality and Social Psychology,* 1977, *35,* 637–644.

Greenwald, A. G. Does the Good Samaritan parable increase helping? A comment on Darley & Batson's no-effect conclusion. *Journal of Personality and Social Psychology,* 1975, *32,* 578–583. (a)

Greenwald, A. G. On the inconclusiveness of "crucial" cognitive tests of dissonance vs. self-perception theories. *Journal of Experimental Social Psychology,* 1975, *11,* 490–499. (b)

Greenwald, A. G. Consequences of prejudice against the null hypothesis. *Psychological Bulletin,* 1975, *82,* 1–20. (c)

Greenwald, A. G., Brock, T. C., & Ostrom, T. M. (Eds.). *Psychological foundations of attitudes.* New York: Academic Press, 1968.

Greenwald, A. G., & Ronis, D. L. Twenty years of cognitive dissonance: Case study of the evolution of a theory. *Psychological Review,* 1978, *85,* 53–57.

Greenwald, H. J., & Oppenheim, D. B. Reported magnitude of self-misidentification among Negro children: Artifact? *Journal of Personality and Social Psychology,* 1968, *8,* 49–52.

Griffin, J. H. *Black like me.* New York: New American Library, 1961.

Griffitt, W., & Veitch, R. Hot and crowded: Influences of population density and temperature on interpersonal affective behavior. *Journal of Personality and Social Psychology*, 1971, *17*, 92–98.

Griffitt, W., & Veitch, R. Preacquaintance attitude similarity and attraction revisited: Ten days in a fall-out shelter. *Sociometry*, 1974, *37*, 163–173.

Gruder, C. L., Cook, T. D., Hennigan, K. M., Flay, B. R., Alessis, C., & Halamaj, J. Empirical tests of the absolute sleeper effect predicted from the discounting cue hypothesis. *Journal of Personality and Social Psychology*, 1978, *36*, 1061–1074.

Gruenberg, E. M. Epidemiology of mental disease. *Scientific American*, 1954, *190*(3), 38–42.

Gruner, C. R. *Understanding laughter.* Chicago: Nelson-Hall, 1979.

Grusec, J. E., & Brinker, D. B., Jr. Reinforcement for imitation as a social learning determinant with implications for sex-role development. *Journal of Personality and Social Psychology*, 1972, *21*, 149–158.

Grush, J. E., Clore, G. L., & Costin, F. Dissimilarity and attraction: When difference makes a difference. *Journal of Personality and Social Psychology*, 1975, *32*, 783–789.

Grusky, O. Managerial succession and organizational effectiveness. *American Journal of Sociology*, 1963, *69*, 21–31.

Guardo, C. J. Personal space in children. *Child Development*, 1969, *40*, 143–151.

Gurwitz, S. B., & Dodge, K. A. Adults' evaluations of a child as a function of sex of adult and sex of child. *Journal of Personality and Social Psychology*, 1975, *32*, 822–828.

Guthrie, G. M., & Bennett, A. B., Jr. Cultural differences in implicit personality theory. *International Journal of Psychology*, 1971, *6*, 305–312.

Hackman, J. R., & Morris, C. G. Group tasks, group interaction process, and group performance effectiveness: A review and proposed integration. In L. Berkowitz (Ed.), *Advances in experimental social psychology* (Vol. 8). New York: Academic Press, 1975.

Hagström, W. *The scientific community.* New York: Basic Books, 1965.

Hall, E. T. *The silent language.* Garden City, N.Y.: Anchor Doubleday, 1959.

Hall, E. T. *The hidden dimension.* Garden City, N.Y.: Doubleday, 1966.

Hampel, R., & Krupp, B. The cultural and the political framework of prejudice in South Africa and Great Britain. *Journal of Social Psychology*, 1977, *103*, 193–202.

Hamsher, J. H., Geller, J. D., & Rotter, J. B. Interpersonal trust, internal-external control and the Warren Commission report. *Journal of Personality and Social Psychology*, 1968, *9*, 210–215.

Hardin, G. The tragedy of the commons. *Science*, 1968, *162*, 1243–1248.

Harding, J., Proshansky, H., Kutner, B., & Schein, I. Prejudice and ethnic relations. In G. Lindzey & E. Aronson (Eds.), *Handbook of Social Psychology* (Vol. 5). Reading, Mass.: Addison-Wesley, 1969.

Hardyck, J. A., & Braden, M. Prophecy fails again: A report of a failure to replicate. *Journal of Abnormal and Social Psychology*, 1962, *65*, 136–141.

Hare, A. P. *Handbook of small group*

research (2nd ed.). New York: Free Press, 1976.

Harlow, H. F. Social facilitation of feeding in the albino rat. *Journal of Genetic Psychology*, 1932, *43*, 211–221.

Harlow, H. F. The nature of love. *American Psychologist*, 1958, *13*, 673–685.

Harrison, A. A., & Saeed, L. Let's make a deal: An analysis of revelations and stipulations in lonely hearts advertisements. *Journal of Personality and Social Psychology*, 1977, *35*, 257–264.

Harrison, G. A bias in the social psychology of prejudice. In N. Armistead (Ed.), *Reconstructing social psychology*. Baltimore: Penguin, 1974.

Harrower, M. Were Hitler's henchmen mad? *Psychology Today*, 1976, *10*, July, 76–82.

Hartley, E. L. *Problems in prejudice*. New York: King's Crown Press, 1946.

Hartmann, G. W. A field experiment on the comparative effectiveness of "emotional" and "rational" political leaflets in determining election results. *Journal of Abnormal and Social Psychology*, 1936, *31*, 99–114.

Haskins, J. Factual recall as a measure of advertising effectiveness. *Journal of Advertising Research*, 1966, *6*, 2–8.

Hastorf, A. H., & Bender, I. E. A caution respecting the measurement of empathic ability. *Journal of Abnormal and Social Psychology*, 1952, *47*, 574–576.

Hastorf, A. H., & Cantril, H. They saw a game: A case study. *Journal of Abnormal and Social Psychology*, 1954, *49*, 129–134.

Hastorf, A. H., Schneider, D. J., & Polefka, J. *Person perception*. Reading, Mass.: Addison-Wesley, 1970.

Hawkins, R. P., Peterson, R. F., Schweid, E., & Bijou, S. W. Behavior therapy in the home: Amelioration of problem parent-child relations with the parent in a therapeutic role. *Journal of Experimental Child Psychology*, 1966, *4*, 99–107.

Hay, D. F. Following their companions as a form of exploration for human infants. *Child Development*, 1977, *48*, 1624–1632.

Hayduk, L. A. Personal space: An evaluative and orienting overview. *Psychological Bulletin*, 1978, *85*, 117–134.

Heider, F. *The psychology of interpersonal relations*. New York: Wiley, 1958.

Heider, F. Gestalt theory: Early history and reminiscences. In M. Henle, J. Jaynes, & J. J. Sullivan (Eds.), *Historical conceptions of psychology*. New York: Springer, 1973.

Heider, F., & Simmel, M. An experimental study of apparent behavior. *American Journal of Psychology*, 1944, *57*, 243–259.

Heller, J. F., Groff, B. D., & Solomon, S. H. Toward an understanding of crowding: The role of physical interaction. *Journal of Personality and Social Psychology*, 1977, *35*, 183–190.

Helmreich, R. Applied social psychology: The unfulfilled promise. *Personality and Social Psychology Bulletin*, 1975, *1*, 548–560.

Helson, H. *Adaptation-level theory*. New York: Harper, 1964.

Helson, H. Autobiography. In E. G. Boring & G. Lindzey (Eds.), *A history of psychology in autobiography* (Vol. 5). New York: Appleton, 1967.

Henchy, T., & Glass, D. C. Evaluation apprehension and the social facilitation of dominant and subordinate responses. *Journal of Personality and Social Psychology*, 1968, *10*, 446–454.

Hensley, V., & Duval, S. Some perceptual determinants of perceived similarity, liking, and correctness. *Journal of Personality and Social Psychology*, 1976, *34*, 159–168.

Hess, R. D. Political attitudes in children. *Psychology Today*, January 1969, pp. 24–28.

Hewgill, M., & Miller, G. Source credibility and response to fear-arousing communications. *Speech Monographs*, 1965, *32*, 95–101.

Himmelweit, H. T., Oppenheim, A. N., & Vince, P. *Television and the child*. London and New York: Oxford University Press, 1958.

Hitchcock, J. L., Munroe, R. L., & Munroe, R. H. Coins and countries: The value-size hypothesis. *Journal of Social Psychology*, 1976, *100*, 307–308.

Hoffman, L. R. Group problem solving. In L. Berkowitz (Ed.), *Advances in experimental social psychology* (Vol. 2). New York: Academic Press, 1965.

Hoffman, L. R., & Maier, N. R. F. Valence in the adoption of solutions by problem-solving groups: Concept, method, and results. *Journal of Abnormal and Social Psychology*, 1964, *69*, 264–271.

Hoffman, L. R., & Maier, N. R. F. An experimental reexamination of the similarity-attraction hypothesis. *Journal of Personality and Social Psychology*, 1966, *3*, 145–152.

Hoffman, M. L. Altruistic behavior and the parent-child relationship. *Journal of Personality and Social Psychology*, 1975, *31*, 937–943.

Hollander, E. P., & Julian, J. W. Leadership. In E. F. Borgatta (Ed.), *Social psychology: Readings and perspectives*. Chicago: Rand McNally, 1969.

Hollingshead, A. B., & Redlich, F. C. *Social class and mental illness*. New York: Wiley, 1958.

Holsti, O. Content analysis. In G. Lindzey & E. Aronson (Eds.), *Handbook of social psychology* (2nd ed.). Reading, Mass.: Addison-Wesley, 1969.

Homans, G. C. *The human group*. New York: Harcourt, Brace, 1950.

Homans, G. C. *Social behavior: Its elementary forms*. New York: Harcourt, Brace, & World, 1961.

Hooten, E. A. *Apes, men, and morons*. New York: Putnam, 1937.

Horai, J., Naccari, N., & Fatoullah, E. The effects of expertise and physical attractiveness upon opinion agreement and liking. *Sociometry*, 1974, *37*, 601–606.

Horner, M. S. Femininity and successful achievement: A basic inconsistency. In J. Bardwick, E. M. Douvan, M. S. Horner, & D. Guttmann (Eds.), *Feminine personality and conflict*. Belmont, Calif.: Brooks/Cole, 1970.

Hornstein, H. A. Social psychology as social intervention. In M. Deutsch & H. A. Hornstein (Eds.), *Applying social psychology*. Hillsdale, N.J.: Lawrence Erlbaum Associates, 1975.

Horowitz, I. L. *Rise and fall of project Camelot: Studies in the relationship between social science and practical politics*. Cambridge, Mass.: MIT Press, 1967.

Horowitz, I. L., & Katz, J. E. *Social science and public policy in the United States*. New York: Praeger, 1975.

Hovland, C. I. Reconciling conflicting results derived from experimental and survey studies of attitude change. *American Psychologist*, 1959, *14*, 8–17.

Hovland, C. I., Harvey, O. J., & Sherif, M. Assimilation and contrast effects in communication and attitude change. *Journal of Abnormal and Social Psychology*, 1957, *55*, 242–252.

Hovland, C. I., & Janis, I. L., (Eds.) *Personality and persuasibility*. New Haven, Conn.: Yale University Press, 1959.

Hovland, C. I., Janis, I. L., & Kelley, H. H. *Communication and persuasion*. New Haven, Conn.: Yale University Press, 1953.

Hovland, C. I., Lumsdaine, A. A., & Sheffield, F. D. *Experiments on mass communication*. Princeton, N.J.: Princeton University Press, 1949.

Hovland, C. I., & Pritzker, H. Extent of opinion change as a function of amount of change advocated. *Journal of Abnormal and Social Psychology*, 1957, *54*, 257–261.

Hovland, C. I., & Sears, R. R. Minor studies of aggression. VI. Correlations of lynchings with economic indices. *Journal of Psychology*, 1940, *9*, 301–310.

Hovland, C. I., & Weiss, W. The influence of source credibility on communication effectiveness. *Public Opinion Quarterly*, 1951, *15*, 635–650.

Hoyt, H. City growth and mortgage risk. *Insured Mortgage Portfolio*. Washington, D.C.: U. S. Federal Housing Administration, 1937. (Cited in Karp, Stone, & Yoels, 1977).

Hoyt, M. F., & Raven, B. H. Birth order and the 1971 Los Angeles earthquake. *Journal of Personality and Social Psychology*, 1973, *28*, 123–128.

Hraba, J., & Grant, G. Black is beautiful: A reexamination of racial preference and identification. *Journal of Personality and Social Psychology*, 1970, *16*, 398–402.

Hughes, G. D., Rao, V. R., & Alker, H. A. The influence of values, information, and decision orders on a public policy decision. *Journal of Applied Social Psychology*, 1976, *6*, 145–148.

Hull, C. L. *Principles of behavior*. New York: Appleton, 1943.

Hull, C. L. Clark L. Hull. In E. G. Boring (Ed.), *A history of psychology in autobiography* (Vol. 4). Worcester, Mass.: Clark University Press, 1952.

Hunt, M. M. *The natural history of love*. New York: Minerva Press, 1959.

Hunt, P. J., & Hillary, J. M. Social facilitation in a coaction setting: An examination of the effects over learning trials. *Journal of Experimental Social Psychology*, 1973, *9*, 563–571.

Husband, R. W. Analysis of methods in human maze learning. *Journal of Genetic Psychology*, 1931, *39*, 258–277.

Huston, T. L. (Ed.). *Foundations of interpersonal attraction*. New York: Academic Press, 1974.

Huston, T. L., & Levinger, G. Interpersonal attraction and relationships. *Annual Review of Psychology*, 1978, *29*, 115–156.

Hyman, H. H. *Political socialization: A study in the psychology of political behavior*. New York: Free Press, 1959.

Iliffe, A. H. A study of preferences in

feminine beauty. *British Journal of Psychology*, 1960, *51*, 267–273.

Insko, C. A. *Theories of attitude change.* New York: Appleton, 1967.

Insko, C. A., & Cialdini, R. B. *Interpersonal influence in a controlled setting: Verbal reinforcement of attitude.* Morristown, N.J.: General Learning Press, 1971.

Insko, C. A., & Robinson, J. E. Belief similarity versus race as determinants of reactions to Negroes by Southern white adolescents: A further test of Rokeach's theory. *Journal of Personality and Social Psychology*, 1967, *7*, 216–221.

Insko, C. A., Thompson, V. D., Stroebe, W., Shaud, K. F., Pinner, B. E., & Layton, B. D. Implied evaluation and similarity-attraction effect. *Journal of Personality and Social Psychology*, 1973, *25*, 297–308.

Insko, C. A., Turnbull, W., & Yandell, B. Facilitative and inhibiting effects of distraction on attitude change. *Sociometry*, 1974, *37*, 508–528.

Isen, A. M. Success, failure, attention and reaction to others: The warm glow of success. *Journal of Personality and Social Psychology*, 1970, *15*, 294–301.

Isen, A. M., Clark, M., & Schwartz, M. The duration of the effect of good mood on helping: "Footprints in the sands of time." *Journal of Personality and Social Psychology*, 1976, *33*, 385–393.

Isen, A. M., Horn, N., & Rosenhan, D. L. Effects of success and failure on children's generosity *Journal of Personality and Social Psychology*, 1973, *27*, 239–247.

Isen, A. M., & Levin, P. F. Effect of feeling good on helping: Cookies and kindness. *Journal of Personal-*

ity and Social Psychology, 1972, *21*, 354–358.

Israel, J., & Tajfel, H. (Eds.). *The context of social psychology.* New York: Academic Press, 1972.

Ivancevich, J. M. Effects of the shorter workweek on selected satisfaction and performance measures. *Journal of Applied Psychology*, 1974, *59*, 717–721.

Jacobs, R. C., & Campbell, D. T. The perpetuation of an arbitrary tradition through several generations of a laboratory microculture. *Journal of Abnormal and Social Psychology*, 1961, *62*, 649–658.

Jahoda, G., & Harrison, S. Belfast children: Some effects of a conflict environment. *Irish Journal of Psychology*, 1975, *1*, 1–19.

James, W. The moral equivalent of war. In W. James, *Memories and Studies.* New York: Longmans, Green, 1911.

James, W. *Principles of psychology.* New York: Dover, 1950. (Originally published, 1890.)

Janis, I. L. Groupthink. *Psychology Today*, 1971, *5*(6), 43–50, 78–84.

Janis, I. L. *Victims of groupthink: A psychological study of foreign-policy decisions and fiascoes.* Boston: Houghton Mifflin, 1972.

Janis, I. L., & Feshbach, S. Effects of fear-arousing communications. *Journal of Abnormal and Social Psychology*, 1953, *48*, 78–92.

Janis, I. L., & Gilmore, J. The influence of incentive conditions on the success of role playing in modifying attitudes. *Journal of Personality and Social Psychology*, 1965, *1*, 17–27.

Janis, I. L., & Hoffman, D. Facilitating effects of daily contact between partners who make a decision to cut down on smoking. *Journal of*

Personality and Social Psychology, 1970, *17*, 25–35.

Janis, I. L., Hovland, C., Field, P., Linton, H., Graham, E., Cohen, A., Rife, D., Abelson, R., Lesser, G., & King, B. *Personality and persuasibility.* New Haven, Conn.: Yale University Press, 1959.

Janis, I. L., Lumsdaine, A. A., & Gladstone, A. I. Effects of pre-preparatory communication on reactions to subsequent news events. *Public Opinion Quarterly*, 1951, *15*, 487–518.

Jensén, A. R. How much can we boost IQ and scholastic achievement? *Harvard Educational Review*, 1969, *39*, 1–123.

Jessor, R., Jessor, S. L., & Finney, J. A social psychology of marijuana use: Longitudinal studies of high school and college youth. *Journal of Personality and Social Psychology*, 1973, *26*, 1–15.

Johnson, J. E., & Leventhal, H. Effects of accurate expectations and behavioral instructions on reactions during a noxious medical examination. *Journal of Personality and Social Psychology*, 1974, *29*, 710–718.

Jones, C., & Aronson, E. Attribution of fault to a rape victim as a function of respectability of the victim. *Journal of Personality and Social Psychology*, 1973, *26*, 415–419.

Jones, E. E. *Ingratiation.* New York: Appleton, 1964.

Jones, E. E., & Davis, K. E. From acts to dispositions: The attribution process in person perception. In L. Berkowitz (Ed.), *Advances in experimental social psychology* (Vol. 2). New York: Academic Press, 1965.

Jones, E. E., Davis, K. E., & Gergen, K. J. Role playing variations and their informational value for person perception. *Journal of Abnormal and Social Psychology*, 1961, *63*, 302–310.

Jones, E. E., Gergen, K. J., & Jones, R. G. Tactics of ingratiation among leaders and subordinates in a status hierarchy. *Psychological Monographs*, 1963, *77* (Whole No. 566).

Jones, E. E., & Nisbett, R. E. *The actor and the observer: Divergent perceptions of the causes of behavior.* Morristown, N.J.: General Learning Press, 1971.

Jones, J. M. *Prejudice and racism.* Reading, Mass.: Addison-Wesley, 1972.

Jones, S. E., & Aiello, J. R. Proxemic behavior of black and white first-, third-, and fifth-grade children. *Journal of Personality and Social Psychology*, 1973, *25*, 21–27.

Junod, H. A. *The life of a South African tribe.* New York: Macmillan, 1927.

Kagan, J., & Klein, R. E. Cross-cultural perspectives on early development. *American Psychologist*, 1973, *28*, 947–961.

Kahn, A., Gilbert, L. A., Latta, R. M., Deutsch, C., Hagen, R., Hill, M., McGaughey, T., Ryen, A. H., & Wilson, D. W. Attribution of fault to a rape victim as a function of respectability of the victim: A failure to replicate or extend. *Representative Research in Social Psychology*, 1977, *8*, 291–305.

Kail, R. V., Jr. Familiarity and attraction to pictures of children's faces. *Developmental Psychology*, 1977, *13*, 289–290.

Kalmar, R. *Child abuse: Perspectives on diagnosis, treatment and prevention.* Dubuque, Iowa: Kendall/Hunt, 1977.

Kalven, H., Jr., & Zeisel, H. *The American jury*. Boston: Little, Brown, 1966.

Kambouropoulou, P. Individual differences in the sense of humor. *American Journal of Psychology*, 1926, *37*, 268–278.

Kamin, L. J. *The science and politics of IQ*. Hillsdale, N.J.: Lawrence Erlbaum Associates, 1974.

Kaplan, J. A legal look at prosocial behavior: What can happen for failing to help or trying to help someone. *Journal of Social Issues*, 1972, *28*, 219–226.

Kaplan, M. F., & Anderson, N. H. Information integration theory and reinforcement theory as approaches to interpersonal attraction. *Journal of Personality and Social Psychology*, 1973, *28*, 301–312.

Karlins, M., & Abelson, H. I. *Persuasion: How opinions and attitudes are changed* (2nd ed.). New York: Springer, 1970.

Karlins, M., Coffman, T. L., & Walters, G. On the fading of social stereotypes: Studies in three generations of college students. *Journal of Personality and Social Psychology*, 1969, *13*, 1–16.

Karp, D. A., Stone, G. P., & Yoels, W. C. *Being urban: A social psychological view of city life*. Lexington, Mass.: Heath, 1977.

Katz, D. The functional approach to the study of attitudes. *Public Opinion Quarterly*, 1960, *24*, 163–204.

Katz, D., & Braly, K. W. Racial prejudice and racial stereotypes. *Journal of Abnormal and Social Psychology*, 1933, *30*, 175–193.

Katz, E. The two-step flow of communication: An up-to-date report on an hypothesis. *Public Opinion Quarterly*, 1957, *21*, 61–78.

Katz, E., & Lazarsfeld, P. F. *Personal influence: The part played by people in the flow of mass communications*. New York: Free Press, 1955.

Katz, I., Cohen, S., & Glass, D. Some determinants of cross-racial helping behavior. *Journal of Personality and Social Psychology*, 1975, *32*, 964–970.

Kaufmann, H. *Aggression and altruism*. New York: Holt, 1970. (a)

Kaufmann, H. Legality and harmfulness of a bystander's failure to intervene as determinants of moral judgment. In J. Macaulay & L. Berkowitz (Eds.), *Altruism and helping behavior*. New York: Academic Press, 1970. (b)

Keith-Spiegel, P. Early conceptions of humor: Varieties and issues. In J. H. Goldstein & P. E. McGhee (Eds.), *The psychology of humor*. New York: Academic Press, 1972.

Kelley, H. H. The warm-cold variable in first impressions of persons. *Journal of Personality*, 1950, *18*, 431–439.

Kelley, H. H. Two functions of reference groups. In G. E. Swanson, T. M. Newcomb, & E. L. Hartley (Eds.), *Readings in social psychology*. New York: Holt, 1952.

Kelley, H. H. Attribution theory in social psychology. In D. Levine (Ed.), *Nebraska Symposium on Motivation*, Vol. 15. Lincoln: University of Nebraska Press, 1967.

Kelley, H. H. The processes of causal attribution. *American Psychologist*, 1973, *28*, 107–128.

Kelley, H. H., Condry, J. C., Dahlke, A. E., & Hill, A. H. Collective behavior in a simulated panic situation. *Journal of Experimental Social Psychology*, 1965, *1*, 20–54.

Kelley, H. H., & Grzelak, J. Conflict between individual and common interest in an N-person relationship. *Journal of Personality and Social Psychology*, 1972, *21*, 190–197.

Kelley, H. H., Shure, G., Deutsch, M., Faucheux, C., Lanzetta, J., Moscovici, S., Nuttin, J. M., Rabbie, J., & Thibaut, J. W. A comparative experimental study of negotiation behavior. *Journal of Personality and Social Psychology*, 1970, *16*, 411–438.

Kelman, H. C. Compliance, identification, and internalization: Three processes of attitude change. *Journal of Conflict Resolution*, 1958, *2*, 51–60.

Kelman, H. C. *International behavior.* New York: Holt, 1965.

Kelman, H. C., & Cohen, S. P. The problem-solving workshop: A social-psychological contribution to the resolution of international conflicts. *Journal of Peace Research*, 1976, *13*, 79–90.

Kelman, H. C., & Hovland, C. I. "Reinstatement" of the communicator in delayed measurement of opinion change. *Journal of Abnormal and Social Psychology*, 1953, *48*, 327–335.

Kempe, C. H., Silverman, F. N., Steele, B. F., Droegemueller, W., & Silver, H. K. The battered child syndrome. *Journal of the American Medical Association*, 1962, *181*, 17–24.

Kerckhoff, A. C., Back, K. W., & Miller, N. Sociometric patterns in hysterical contagion. *Sociometry*, 1965, *28*, 2–15.

Kerckhoff, A. C., & Davis, K. E. Value consensus and need complementarity in mate selection. *American Sociological Review*, 1962, *27*, 295–303.

Kershaw, D. N. A negative-income-tax experiment. *Scientific American*, 1972, *227*, 19–25.

Kidder, L. H., & Stewart, V. M. *The psychology of intergroup relations: Conflict and consciousness.* New York: McGraw-Hill, 1975.

Kiesler, C. A., Collins, B. E., & Miller, N. *Attitude change: A critical analysis of theoretical approaches.* New York: Wiley, 1969.

Kiesler, C. A., & Kiesler, S. B. *Conformity.* Reading, Mass.: Addison-Wesley, 1969.

Kilham, W., & Mann, L. Level of destructive obedience as a function of transmitter and executant roles in the Milgram obedience paradigm. *Journal of Personality and Social Psychology*, 1974, *29*, 696–702.

Killian, L. M., & Bloomberg, S. Rebirth in a therapeutic community: A case study. *Psychiatry*, 1975, *38*, 39–54.

Kingdon, J. W. Opinion leaders in the electorate. *Public Opinion Quarterly*, 1970, *34*, 256–261.

Kinzel, A. F. Body-buffer zones in violent prisoners. *New Society*, January 28, 1971, pp. 149–150.

Kipnis, D. Does power corrupt? *Journal of Personality and Social Psychology*, 1972, *24*, 33–41.

Kipnis, D. *The powerholders.* Chicago: University of Chicago Press, 1976.

Kipnis, D., Castell, P. J., Gergen, M., & Mauch, D. Metamorphic effects of power. *Journal of Applied Psychology*, 1976, *61*, 127–135.

Kipnis, D. M. Changes in self concepts in relation to perceptions of others. *Journal of Personality*, 1961, *29*, 449–465.

Kissel, S. Stress-reducing properties of social stimuli. *Journal of Personality and Social Psychology*, 1965, *2*, 378–384.

Klausner, S. Z. Choice of metaphor in behavioral research. *Methodology and Science*, April, 1968, pp. 1–23.

Klein, A. L. Changes in leadership appraisal as a function of the stress of a simulated panic situation. *Journal of Personality and Social Psychology*, 1976, *34*, 1143–1154.

Klein, D. C., Fencil-Morse, E., & Seligman, M. E. P. Learned helplessness, depression, and the attribution of failure. *Journal of Personality and Social Psychology*, 1976, *33*, 508–516.

Kleinhesselink, R. R., & Edwards, R. E. Seeking and avoiding belief-discrepant information as a function of its perceived refutability. *Journal of Personality and Social Psychology*, 1975, *31*, 787–790.

Klineberg, O. *Social psychology*. New York: Holt, 1940.

Klineberg, O. *The human dimension in international relations*. New York: Holt, 1964.

Klineberg, O. Black and white in international perspective. *American Psychologist*, 1971, *26*, 119–128.

Klopfer, P. H. Influence of social interaction on learning rates in birds. *Science*, 1958, *128*, 903–904.

Knight, D. J., Langmeyer, D., & Lundgren, D. C. Eye-contact, distance and affiliation: The role of observer bias. *Sociometry*, 1973, *36*, 390–401.

Knoke, D. A causal model for the political party preferences of American men. *American Sociological Review*, 1972, *37*, 679–688.

Knowles, E. S. Boundaries around group interaction: The effect of group size and member status on boundary permeability. *Journal of*

Personality and Social Psychology, 1973, *26*, 327–332.

Knox, R. E., & Inkster, J. A. Postdecision dissonance at post time. *Journal of Personality and Social Psychology*, 1968, *8*, 319–323.

Koch, S. The image of man implicit in encounter group therapy. *Journal of Humanistic Psychology*, 1971, *11*, 109–128.

Kohlberg, L. Moral development and identification. In H. W. Stevenson (Ed.), *Child psychology: Sixty-second yearbook of the National Society for the Study of Education*. Chicago: University of Chicago Press, 1963.

Konečni, V. J. Annoyance, type and duration of postannoyance activity, and aggression: The "cathartic" effect. *Journal of Experimental Psychology, (General)*, 1975, *104*, 76–102.

Konečni, V. J., & Ebbesen, E. B. Disinhibition versus the cathartic effect: Artifact and substance. *Journal of Personality and Social Psychology*, 1976, *34*, 352–465.

Korte, C., & Kerr, N. Response to altruistic opportunities under urban and rural conditions. *Journal of Social Psychology*, 1975, *95*, 183–184.

Korte, C., Ypma, I., & Toppen, A. Helpfulness in Dutch society as a function of urbanization and environmental input level. *Journal of Personality and Social Psychology*, 1975, *32*, 996–1003.

Kovel, J. *White racism: A psychological history*. New York: Pantheon, 1970.

Kraut, R. E., & Lewis, S. H. Alternative models of family influence on student ideology. *Journal of Personality and Social Psychology*, 1975, *31*, 791–800.

Kraut, R. E., & Price, J. D. Machiavellianism in parents and their children. *Journal of Personality and Social Psychology*, 1976, *33*, 782–786.

Krebs, D. L. Altruism—An examination of the concept and a review of the literature. *Psychological Bulletin*, 1970, *73*, 258–302.

Krebs, D. L. Infrahuman altruism. *Psychological Bulletin*, 1971, *76*, 411–414.

Kris, E. *Psychoanalytic explorations in art*. New York: International Universities Press, 1962.

Kruglanski, A. W. Incentives in interdependent escape as affecting the degree of group incoordination. *Journal of Experimental Social Psychology*, 1969, *5*, 454–466.

Kruglanski, A. W. Much ado about artifact. In L. Berkowitz (Ed.), *Advances in experimental social psychology* (Vol. 9). New York: Academic Press, 1975.

Krulewitz, J. E., & Payne, E. J. Attributions about rape: Effects of rapist force, observer sex, and sex role attitudes. *Journal of Applied Social Psychology*, 1978, *8*, 291–305.

Kuhn, M. H., & McPartland, T. S. An empirical investigation of self-attitudes. *American Sociological Review*, 1954, *19*, 68–76.

Kuhn, T. S. *The structure of scientific revolutions*. Chicago: University of Chicago Press, 1962.

Kurtines, W., & Greif, E. B. The development of moral thought: Review and evaluation of Kohlberg's approach. *Psychological Bulletin*, 1974, *81*, 453–470.

Kutner, B., Wilkins, C., & Yarrow, P. R. Verbal attitudes and overt behavior involving racial prejudice. *Journal of Abnormal and Social Psychology*, 1952, *47*, 649–652.

LaFave, L. Humor judgments as a function of reference groups and identification classes. In J. H. Goldstein & P. E. McGhee (Eds.), *The psychology of humor*. New York: Academic Press, 1972.

LaFave, L. Ethnic humour: From paradoxes towards principles. In A. J. Chapman & H. C. Foot (Eds.), *It's a funny thing, humour*. Oxford: Pergamon, 1977.

LaFave, L., Haddad, J., & Maesen, W. A. Superiority, enhanced self-esteem, and perceived incongruity theory. In A. J. Chapman & H. C. Foot (Eds.), *Humour and laughter*. New York: Wiley, 1976.

Lana, R. E. Interest, media, and order effects in persuasive communications. *Journal of Psychology*, 1963, *56*, 9–13.

Lana, R. E. *Assumptions of social psychology*. New York: Appleton, 1969.

Landis, D., Day, H. R., McGrew, P. L., Thomas, J. A., & Miller, A. B. Can a black "culture assimilator" increase racial understanding? *Journal of Social Issues*, 1976, *32*, 169–183.

Landy, D., & Sigall, H. Beauty is talent: Task evaluation as a function of the performer's physical attractiveness. *Journal of Personality and Social Psychology*, 1974, *29*, 299–304.

Langer, E. J., & Abelson, R. P. The semantics of asking a favor: How to succeed in getting help without really dying. *Journal of Personality and Social Psychology*, 1972, *24*, 26–32.

Langer, E. J., & Rodin, J. The effects of choice and enhanced personal responsibility for the aged: A field experiment in an institutional setting. *Journal of Personality and Social Psychology*, 1976, *34*, 191–198.

Langlois, J. H., & Stephan, C. The effects of physical attractiveness and ethnicity on children's behavioral attributions and peer preferences. *Child Development*, 1977, *48*, 1694–1698.

LaPiere, R. T. Attitudes vs. actions. *Social Forces*, 1934, *13*, 230–237.

L'Armand, K., & Pepitone, A. Helping to reward another person: A cross-cultural analysis. *Journal of Personality and Social Psychology*, 1975, *1*, 189–198.

Lasswell, H. D., & Casey, R. D. *Propaganda, communication, and public opinion*. Princeton, N.J.: Princeton University Press, 1946.

Latané, B (Ed.). Studies in social comparison. *Journal of Experimental Social Psychology*, 1966 (1).

Latané, B., & Darley, B. *The unresponsive bystander: Why doesn't he help?* New York: Appleton, 1970.

Lauer, R. H., & Handel, W. H. *Social psychology: The theory and application of symbolic interactionism.* Boston: Houghton Mifflin, 1977.

Lawler, E. E., III, Hackman, J. R., & Kaufman, S. Effects of job redesign: A field experiment. *Journal of Applied Social Psychology*, 1973, *3*, 49–62.

Lazarsfeld, P. F., Berelson, B., & Gaudet, H. *The people's choice.* New York: Columbia University Press, 1948.

Leavitt, H. J. Some effects of certain communication patterns on group performance. *Journal of Abnormal and Social Psychology*, 1951, *46*, 38–50.

LeBon, G. *The crowd.* London: Benn, 1896.

Lederer, W. J., & Jackson, D. D. *The mirages of marriage.* New York: Norton, 1968.

Lee, S. G. Social influences in Zulu dreaming. *Journal of Social Psychology*, 1958, *47*, 265–283.

Leeper, R. W. The role of motivation in learning: A study of the phenomenon of differential motivation control of the utilization of habits. *Journal of Genetic Psychology*, 1935, *46*, 3–40.

Lefkowitz, M. M., Walder, L. O., Eron, L. D., & Huesmann, L. R. Preference for televised contact sports as related to sex differences in aggression. *Developmental Psychology*, 1973, *9*, 417–420.

Lepper, M. R., Greene, D., & Nisbett, R. E. Undermining children's intrinsic interest with extrinsic reward: A test of the "overjustification" hypothesis. *Journal of Personality and Social Psychology*, 1973, *28*, 129–137.

Lerner, M. J. The desire for justice and reactions to victims. In J. Macaulay & L. Berkowitz (Eds.), *Altruism and helping behavior.* New York: Academic Press, 1970.

Lerner, M. J., & Matthews, G. Reactions to suffering of others under conditions of indirect responsibility. *Journal of Personality and Social Psychology*, 1967, *5*, 319–325.

Lerner, M. J., & Simmons, C. H. Observer's reaction to the "innocent victim:" Compassion or rejection? *Journal of Personality and Social Psychology*, 1966, *4*, 203–210.

Leventhal, H. Findings and theory in the study of fear communications. In L. Berkowitz (Ed.), *Advances in experimental social psychology* (Vol. 5). New York: Academic Press, 1970.

Leventhal, H., & Cupchik, G. C. A process model of humor judgment. *Journal of Communication*, 1976, *26*, 190–204.

Leventhal, H., & Singer, R. P. Affect arousal and positioning of recommendations in persuasive communications. *Journal of Personality and Social Psychology*, 1966, *4*, 137–146.

Lever, J. Soccer: Opium of the Brazilian people. *Trans-action*, 1969, *7*(2), 36–43.

Levine, R., Chein, I., & Murphy, G. The relation of intensity of a need to the amount of perceptual distortion: A preliminary report. *Journal of Psychology*, 1942, *13*, 283–293.

LeVine, R. A., & Campbell, D. T. *Ethnocentrism: Theories of conflict, ethnic attitudes and group behavior.* New York: Wiley, 1972.

Levinger, G. Little sand box and big quarry: Comment on Byrne's paradigmatic spade for research on interpersonal attraction. *Representative Research in Social Psychology*, 1972, *3*, 3–19.

Levinger, G. A three-level approach to attraction: Toward an understanding of pair relatedness. In T. L. Huston (Ed.), *Foundations of interpersonal attraction.* New York: Academic Press, 1974.

Levinger, G., & Raush, H. L. *Close relationships.* Amherst: University of Massachusetts Press, 1977.

Levinger, G., Senn, D. J., & Jorgensen, B. W. Progress toward permanence in courtship: A test of the Kerckhoff-Davis hypothesis. *Sociometry*, 1970, *33*, 427–443.

Levinger, G., & Snoek, J. D. *Attraction in relationship: A new look at interpersonal attraction.* New York: General Learning Press, 1972.

Levy, J. M. & McGee, R. K. Childbirth as crisis: A test of Janis's theory of communication and stress resolution. *Journal of Personality and Social Psychology,* 1975, *31*, 171–179.

Levy, L., & Herzog, N. Effects of population density and crowding on health and social adaption in the Netherlands. *Journal of Health and Social Behavior*, 1974, *15*, 228–237.

Lewin, K. *Principles of topological psychology.* New York: McGraw-Hill, 1936.

Lewin, K. Group decision and social change. In T. M. Newcomb & E. L. Hartley (Eds.) *Readings in social psychology.* New York: Holt, 1947.

Lewin, K. Self-hatred among Jews. *Contemporary Jewish Record*, 1941, *4*, 219–232. (Cited in Maliver, 1965.)

Lewin, K. *Resolving social conflicts.* New York: Harper, 1948.

Lewin, K. Lippitt, R., & White, R. K. Patterns of aggressive behavior in experimentally created "social climates." *Journal of Social Psychology*, 1939, *10*, 271–299.

Lieberman, J. N. *Playfulness: Its relationship to imagination and creativity.* New York: Academic Press, 1977.

Lieberson, S., & Silverman, A. R. The precipitants and underlying conditions of race riots. *American Sociological Review*, 1965, *30*, 887–898.

Liebert, R. M. Television and social learning: Some relationships between viewing violence and behaving aggressively. In J. P. Murray, E. A. Rubinstein, & G. A. Comstock (Eds.), *Television and social behavior.* Washington, D. C.: U. S. Government Printing Office, 1972.

Linder, D. E. *Personal space.* Morristown, N. J.: General Learning Press, 1974.

Linder, D. E., Cooper, J., & Jones, E. E. Decision freedom as a determinant of the role of incentive magnitude in attitude change. *Journal of Personality and Social Psychology*, 1967, *6*, 245–254.

Linton, R. *The study of man*. New York: Appleton, 1936.

Little, K. B. Personal space. *Journal of Experimental Social Psychology*, 1965, *1*, 237–247.

London, P. The rescuers: Motivational hypotheses about Christians who saved Jews from the Nazis. In J. Macaulay & L. Berkowitz (Eds.), *Altruism and helping behavior*. New York: Academic Press, 1970.

Lorenz, K. Ritualized fighting. In J. Carthy & E. Ebling (Eds.), *Natural history of aggression*. New York: Academic Press, 1964.

Lorenz, K. *On Aggression*. New York: Harcourt, 1966.

Lothstein, L. M. *Personal space in assault-prone male adolescent prisoners*. Doctoral dissertation, Duke University, 1971. (Cited in Linder, 1974.)

Lyman, S. M., & Scott, M. B. Territoriality: A neglected sociological dimension. *Social Problems*, 1967, *15*, 236–249.

Lynch, K. *The image of the city*. Cambridge, Mass.: MIT Press, 1960.

Macaulay, J. R. A shill for charity. In J. Macaulay & L. Berkowitz (Eds.), *Altruism and helping behavior*. New York: Academic Press, 1970.

Maccoby, E. E., & Jacklin, C. *The psychology of sex differences*. Stanford, Calif.: Stanford University Press, 1974.

Mack, D. E. The power relationship in black families and white families. *Journal of Personality and Social Psychology*, 1974, *30*, 409–413.

MacKenzie, B. K. The importance of contact in determining attitudes toward Negroes. *Journal of Abnormal and Social Psychology*, 1948, *43*, 417–441.

MacNeil, M. K., & Sherif, M. Norm change over subject generations as a function of arbitrariness of prescribed norms. *Journal of Personality and Social Psychology*, 1976, *34*, 762–773.

Main, E. C., & Walker, T. G. Choice shifts and extreme behavior: Judicial review in the federal courts. *Journal of Social Psychology*, 1973, *91*, 215–221.

Malinowski, B. *Sex and repression in savage society*. New York: Harcourt, Brace, 1937.

Maliver, B. L. Anti-Negro bias among Negro college students. *Journal of Personality and Social Psychology*, 1965, *2*, 770–775.

Manis, J. G. *Analyzing social problems*. New York: Praeger, 1976.

Manis, J. G., & Meltzer, B. N. *Symbolic interaction*. Boston: Allyn & Bacon, 1967.

Manis, M. Social interaction and the self-concept. *Journal of Abnormal and Social Psychology*, 1955, *51*, 362–370.

Manis, M. Social psychology and history: A symposium. *Personality and Social Psychology Bulletin*, 1976, *2*, 371–465.

Mann, L. On being a sore loser: How fans react to their team's failure. *Australian Journal of Psychology*, 1974, *26*, 37–47.

Mann, L. Sports crowds viewed from the perspective of collective behavior. In J. H. Goldstein (Ed.), *Sports, games, and play*. Hillsdale, N. J.: Lawrence Erlbaum Associates, 1979.

Mannheim, H. *War and crime*. London: Watts, 1941.

Mantell, D. M. The potential for violence in Germany. *Journal of Social Issues*, 1971, *27*(4), 101–112.

Mark, R. W. Ecological patterns in an industrial shop. *Social Forces*, 1954, *32*, 351–356.

Marrow, A. J. *The practical theorist.* New York: Basic Books, 1969.

Marshall, J. E., & Heslin, R. Boys and girls together: Sexual composition and the effect of density and group size on cohesiveness. *Journal of Personality and Social Psychology*, 1975, *31*, 952–961.

Martens, R. Palmar sweating and the presence of an audience. *Journal of Experimental Social Psychology*, 1969, *5*, 371–374.

Maslach, C. Negative emotional biasing of unexplained arousal. *Journal of Personality and Social Psychology*, 1979, *37*, 953–969.

Maslow, A. H. Deprivation, threat, and frustration. *Psychological Review*, 1941, *48*, 364–366.

Matheny, A. P., Jr., & Dolan, A. B. Persons, situations, and time: A genetic view of behavioral change in children. *Journal of Personality and Social Psychology*, 1975, *32*, 1106–1110.

Mathes, E. W., & Kahn, A. Physical attractiveness, happiness, neuroticism, and self-esteem. *Journal of Psychology*, 1975, *90*, 27–30.

Mausner, B. The effect of prior reinforcement on the interaction of observer pairs. *Journal of Abnormal and Social Psychology*, 1954, *49*, 65–68.

May, R. *Love and will.* New York: Norton, 1969.

McArthur, L. A. The how and what of why: Some determinants and consequences of causal attribution. *Journal of Personality and Social Psychology*, 1972, *22*, 171–193.

McCann, J. C. Differential mortality and the formation of political elites: The case of the U. S. House of Representatives. *American Sociological Review*, 1972, *37*, 689–700.

McClimont, W. *Shipbuilding and Shipping Record*, 1958, *91*, 301.

McClelland, D. C. *Motivational trends in society.* New York: General Learning Press, 1971.

McClelland, D. C., & Winter, D. *Motivating economic achievement.* New York: Free Press, 1969 & 1971.

McConahay, J. B., & Hough, J. C., Jr. Symbolic racism. *Journal of Social Issues*, 1976, *32*, 23–45.

McGhee, P. E. Humor: Its origins and development. San Francisco: Freeman, 1979.

McGinnies, E. A cross-cultural comparison of printed communication versus spoken communication in persuasion. *Journal of Psychology*, 1965, *60*, 1–8.

McGinnies, E., & Ward, C. D. Persuasibility as a function of source credibility and locus of control: Five cross-cultural experiments. *Journal of Personality*, 1974, *42*, 360–371.

McGuire, W. J. Resistance to persuasion confirmed by active and passive prior refutation of the same and alternative counter-arguments. *Journal of Abnormal and Social Psychology*, 1961, *63*, 326–332.

McGuire, W. J. Inducing resistance to persuasion: Some contemporary approaches. In L. Berkowitz (Ed.), *Advances in experimental social psychology* (Vol. 1). New York: Academic Press, 1964.

McGuire, W. J. Some impending reorientations in social psychology. *Journal of Experimental Social Psychology*, 1967, *3*, 124–139.

McGuire, W. J. The nature of attitudes and attitude change. In G.

Lindzey & E. Aronson (Eds.), *Handbook of social psychology* (2nd ed.), Reading, Mass.: Addison-Wesley, 1969.

McGuire, W. J. The yin and yang of progress in social psychology: Seven koan. *Journal of Personality and Social Psychology*, 1973, *26*, 446–456.

McGuire, W. J. *Personality and Social Psychology Bulletin*, 1976, *2*.

McGuire, W. J., & Padawer-Singer, A. Trait salience in the spontaneous self-concept. *Journal of Personality and Social Psychology*, 1976, *33*, 743–754.

Mead, G. H. *Mind, self and society.* Chicago: University of Chicago Press, 1934.

Mead, G. H. *George Herbert Mead on social psychology.* Chicago: University of Chicago Press, 1964.

Meade, R. D. An experimental study of leadership in India. *Journal of Social Psychology*, 1967, *72*, 35–43.

Meade, R. D., & Barnard, W. A. Conformity and anticonformity among Americans and Chinese. *Journal of Social Psychology*, 1973, *89*, 15–24.

Medvedev, Z., & Medvedev, R. A. *A question of madness.* New York: Random House, 1972.

Megargee, E. I. *The psychology of violence and aggression.* Morristown, N.J.: General Learning Press, 1972.

Meltzer, B. N. Mead's social psychology. In J. G. Manis & B. N. Meltzer (Eds.), *Symbolic interaction.* Boston: Allyn & Bacon, 1967.

Menapace, R. H., & Doby, C. Causal attributions for success and failure for psychiatric rehabilitees and college students. *Journal of Personality and Social Psychology*, 1976, *34*, 447–454.

Merton, R. K. The self-fulfilling prophecy. *Antioch Review*, 1948, *8*, 193–210.

Merton, R. K. Patterns of influence: A study of interpersonal influence and communications behavior in a local community. In P. F. Lazarsfeld & F. N. Stanton (Eds.), *Communications research, 1948–1949.* New York: Harper, 1949.

Merton, R. K. *Social theory and social structure.* Glencoe, Ill.: Free Press, 1957.

Merton, R. K., & Kitt, A. S. Contributions to the theory of reference group behavior. In R. K. Merton & P. F. Lazarsfeld (Eds.), *Studies in the scope and method of "The American Soldier."* New York: Free Press, 1950.

Michener, J. A. *Sports in America.* New York: Random House, 1976.

Middleton, R., & Moland, J. Humor in Negro and white subcultures: A study of jokes among university students. *American Sociological Review*, 1959, *24*, 61–69.

Milgram, S. Nationality and conformity. *Scientific American*, 1961, *205*, (6), 45–51.

Milgram, S. Behavioral study of obedience. *Journal of Abnormal and Social Psychology*, 1963, *67*, 371–378.

Milgram, S. The small-world problem. *Psychology Today*, May 1967, *1*, 60–67.

Milgram, S. The experience of living in cities. *Science*, 1970, *167*, 1461–1468.

Milgram, S. *Obedience to authority.* New York: Harper, 1974.

Milgram, S., Greenwald, J., Kessler, S., McKenna, W., & Waters, J. A psychological map of New York City. *American Scientist*, 1972, *60*, 194–200.

Milgram, S., & Toch, H. Collective behavior: Crowds and social movements. In G. Lindzey & E. Aronson (Eds.), *Handbook of social psychology* (Vol. 4). Reading, Mass.: Addison-Wesley, 1969.

Mill, J. S. *System of logic* (J. M. Robson, Ed.), Toronto: University of Toronto Press, 1973. (Originally published, 1842.)

Miller, G. A. Psychology as a means of promoting human welfare. *American Psychologist*, 1969, *24*, 1063–1075.

Miller, N. E. The frustration-aggression hypothesis. *Psychological Review*, 1941, *48*, 337–342.

Miller, N. E., & Bugelski, R. Minor studies in aggression: The influence of frustrations imposed by the in-group on attitudes toward out-groups. *Journal of Psychology*, 1948, *25*, 437–442.

Mills, J., & Aronson, E. Opinion change as a function of the communicator's attractiveness and desire to influence. *Journal of Personality and Social Psychology*, 1965, *1*, 173–177.

Milner, D. Racial identification and preference in 'black' British children. *European Journal of Social Psychology*, 1973, *3*, 281–295.

Mintz, A. Non-adaptive group behavior. *Journal of Abnormal and Social Psychology*, 1951, *46*, 150–159.

Minuchin, S. *Families and family therapy*. Cambridge, Mass.: Harvard University Press, 1974.

Moffett, L. A. Sculpture preferences, craftsmanship, and aesthetic sensitivity. *Journal of Social Psychology*, 1975, *95*, 285–286. (a)

Moffett, L. A. Art objects as people. *Journal for the Theory of Social Behaviour*, 1975, *5*, 215–223. (b)

Monahan, L., Kuhn, D., & Shaver, P. Intrapsychic versus cultural explanations of the "fear of success"

motive. *Journal of Personality and Social Psychology*, 1974, *29*, 60–64.

Monson, T. C., & Snyder, M. Actors, observers, and the attribution process: Toward a reconceptualization. *Journal of Experimental Social Psychology*, 1977, *13*, 89–111.

Montagu, M. F. A. *Man's most dangerous myth: The fallacy of race*. New York: World, 1965.

Montagu, M. F. A. *Man and aggression*. London and New York: Oxford University Press, 1968.

Montagu, M. F. A. *The nature of human aggression*. London and New York: Oxford University Press, 1976.

Montgomery, R. L., Hinkle, S. W., & Enzie, R. F. Arbitrary norms and social change in high- and low-authoritarian societies. *Journal of Personality and Social Psychology*, 1976, *33*, 698–708.

Moreland, R. L., & Zajonc, R. B. Is stimulus recognition a necessary condition for the occurrence of exposure effects? *Journal of Personality and Social Psychology*, 1977, *35*, 191–199.

Moreno, J. L. *Who shall survive?* (No. 58). Washington, D.C.: Nervous & Mental Disease Monograph Series, 1934.

Moreno, J. L. Contributions of sociometry to research methodology in sociology. *American Sociological Review*, 1947, *12*, 287–292.

Morris, D. *The naked ape*. New York: McGraw-Hill, 1967.

Morris, M. G., Gould, R. W., & Matthews, P. J. Toward prevention of child abuse. *Children*, 1964, *11*, 55–60.

Morris, W. N., Worchel, S., Bois, J. L., Pearson, J. A., Rountree, C. A., Samaha, G. M., Wachtler, J., & Wright, S. L. Collective coping with stress: Group reactions to fear, anxiety and ambiguity. *Journal of Personality and Social Psychology*, 1976, *33*, 674–679.

Moscovici, S. Society and theory in social psychology. In J. Israel & H. Tajfel (Eds.), *The context of social psychology: A critical assessment.* New York: Academic Press, 1972.

Moscovici, S. Social influence. I. Conformity and social control. In C. Nemeth (Ed.), *Social psychology.* Chicago: Rand McNally, 1974.

Moscovici, S., Lage, E., & Naffrechoux, M. Influence of a consistent minority on the responses of a majority in a color perception task. *Sociometry*, 1969, *32*, 365–380.

Mosteller, F. A resistant analysis of the professional football schedule. In J. H. Goldstein (Ed.), *Sports, games, and play.* Hillsdale, N. J.: Lawrence Erlbaum Associates, 1979.

Mowrer, E. Family Disorganization. Chicago: University of Chicago Press, 1927.

Mowrer, O. H. *The crisis in psychiatry and religion.* Princeton, N.J.: Van Nostrand-Reinhold, 1961.

Moyer, K. E. Kinds of aggression and their physiological bases. *Communications in Behavioral Biology*, 1968, *2A*, 65–87.

Moyer, K. E. *The physiology of hostility.* Chicago: Markham, 1971.

Moyer, K. E. *The psychobiology of aggression.* New York: Harper, 1976.

Mueller, C., & Donnerstein, E. The effects of humor-induced arousal upon aggressive behavior. *Journal of Research in Personality*, 1977, *11*, 73–82.

Mumford, L. *The city in history.* New York: Harcourt, 1961.

Munroe, R. L., & Munroe, R. H. Population density and affective relationships in three East African societies. *Journal of Social Psychology*, 1972, *88*, 15–20.

Murdoch, G. P., Ford, C. S., Hudson, A. E., Kennedy, R., Simmons, L. W., & Whiting, J. W. M. *Behavior science outlines* (3rd ed., Vol. 1). New Haven, Conn.: Human Relations Area Files, 1950.

Murphy, G. There is more beyond. In T. S. Krawiec (Ed.), *The psychologists* (Vol. 2). London and New York: Oxford University Press, 1974.

Murstein, B. I. Critique of models of dyadic attraction. In B. I. Murstein (Ed.), *Theories of attraction and love.* New York: Springer, 1971.

Mynatt, C., & Sherman, S. J. Responsibility attribution in groups and individuals: A direct test of the diffusion of responsibility hypothesis. *Journal of Personality and Social Psychology*, 1975, *32*, 1111–1118.

Myrdal, G. *An American dilemma.* New York: Harper, 1944.

Nahemow, L., & Lawton, M. P. Similarity and propinquity in friendship formation. *Journal of Personality and Social Psychology*, 1975, *32*, 205–213.

Nelson, L., & Madsen, M. Cooperation and competition in 4 year olds as a function of reward contingency and subcultures. *Developmental Psychology*, 1969, *1*, 340–344.

Nemeth, C. Interactions between jurors as a function of majority vs. unanimity decision rules. *Journal of Applied Social Psychology*, 1977, *7*, 38–56.

Newcomb, T. M. Attitude development as a function of reference groups: The Bennington study. In G. Swanson, T. Newcomb & E. Hartley (Eds.), *Readings in social psychology*. New York: Holt, 1952.

Newcomb, T. M. An approach to the study of communicative acts. *Psychological Review*, 1953, *60*, 393–404.

Newcomb, T. M. The prediction of interpersonal attraction. *American Psychologist*, 1956, *11*, 575–586.

Newcomb, T. M. *The acquaintance process*. New York: Holt, 1961.

Newcomb, T. M. Dyadic balance as a source of clues about interpersonal attraction. In B. I. Murstein (Ed.), *Theories of attraction and love*. New York: Springer, 1971.

Newcomb, T. M. The acquaintance process: Looking mainly backward. *Journal of Personality and Social Psychology*, 1978, *36*, 1075–1083.

Newman, O. *Defensible space*. New York: Collier-Macmillan, 1972.

New York Times, August 8, 1973.

Nisbett, R. E., & Borgida, E. Attribution and the psychology of prediction. *Journal of Personality and Social Psychology*, 1975, *32*, 932–943.

Nisbett, R. E., Caputo, C., Legant, P., & Maracek, J. Behavior as seen by the actor and as seen by the observer. *Journal of Personality and Social Psychology*, 1973, *27*, 154–164.

Norman, W. T. Toward an adequate taxonomy of personality attributes: Replicated factor structure in peer nomination personality ratings. *Journal of Abnormal and Social Psychology*, 1963, *66*, 574–583.

Novak, M. The sting of Polish jokes. *Newsweek*, April 12, 1976, p. 13.

Nuttin, J. M., Jr. *The illusion of attitude change*. New York: Academic Press, 1975.

O'Neal, E. C. Influence of future choice importance and arousal upon the halo effect. *Journal of Personality and Social Psychology*, 1971, *19*, 334–340.

O'Neal, E. C., & Mills, J. The influence of anticipated choice on the halo effect. *Journal of Experimental Social Psychology*, 1969, *5*, 347–351.

Ornstein, R. *On the experience of time*. Baltimore: Penguin, 1970.

Osgood, C. E. *An alternative to war or surrender*. Urbana: University of Illinois Press, 1962.

Osgood, C. E. Exploration in semantic space: A personal diary. In T. S. Krawiec (Ed.), *The psychologists* (Vol. 2). London and New York: Oxford University Press, 1974.

Osgood, C. E., Suci, G., & Tannenbaum, P. H. *The measurement of meaning*. Urbana: University of Illinois Press, 1957.

Oskamp, S. *Attitudes and opinions*. Englewood Cliffs, N. J.: Prentice-Hall, 1977.

Osmond, H. Function as the basis of psychiatric ward design. *Mental Hospitals*, 1957, *8*, 23–30.

Ostrom, T. M. The emergence of attitude theory: 1930–1950. In A. G. Greenwald, T. C. Brock, & T. M. Ostrom (Eds.), *Psychological foundations of attitudes*. New York: Academic Press, 1968.

Ostrom, T. M., Steele, C. M., Rosenblood, L. K., & Mirels, H. L. Modification of delinquent behavior. *Journal of Applied Social Psychology*, 1971, *1*, 118–136.

Page, M. M., & Scheidt, R. J. The elusive weapons effect: Demand awareness, evaluation apprehension, and slightly sophisticated subjects. *Journal of Personality and Social Psychology*, 1971, *20*, 304–318.

Park, R. E. *Human communities*. New York: Free Press, 1915.

Parsons, A. Is the Oedipus complex

universal? The Jones–Malinowski debate revisited and a South Italian "nuclear complex." In W. Muensterberger & S. Axelrod (Eds.), *The psychoanalytic study of society* (Vol. 3). New York: International Universities Press, 1964.

Parsons, T., & Bales, R. F. *Family, socialization and interaction process.* Glencoe, Ill.: Free Press, 1955.

Passini, F. T., & Norman, W. T. A universal conception of personality structure? *Journal of Personality and Social Psychology*, 1966, *4*, 44–49.

Patterson, G. R., Cobb, J. A., & Ray, R. S. A social engineering technology for retraining the families of aggressive boys. In H. Adams & I. Unikel (Eds.), *Issues and trends in behavior therapy.* Springfield, Ill.: Thomas, 1973.

Patterson, M. L. Eye contact and distance: A re-examination of measurement problems. *Personality and Social Psychology Bulletin*, 1975, *1*, 600–603.

Patterson, M. L., Mullens, S., & Romano, J. Compensatory reactions to spatial intrusion. *Sociometry*, 1971, *34*, 114–121.

Paulus, P. B., & Murdock, P. Anticipated evaluation and audience presence in the enhancement of dominant responses. *Journal of Experimental Social Psychology*, 1971, *7*, 280–291.

Payne, D. E., & Payne, K. P. Newspapers and crime in Detroit. *Journalism Quarterly*, 1970, *47*, 233–238.

Peele, S., with Brodsky, A. *Love and addiction.* New York: New American Library, 1976.

Peevers, B. H., & Secord, P. F. Developmental changes in attribution of descriptive concepts to persons. *Journal of Personality and Social Psychology*, 1973, *27*, 120–128.

Pepitone, A. Toward a normative and comparative biocultural social psychology. *Journal of Personality and Social Psychology*, 1976, *34*, 641–653.

Pessin, J. The comparative effects of social and mechanical stimulation on memorizing. *American Journal of Psychology*, 1933, *45*, 263–270.

Petty, R. E., Wells, G. L., & Brock, T. C. Distraction can enhance or reduce yielding to propaganda: Thought disruption versus effort justification. *Journal of Personality and Social Psychology*, 1976, *34*, 874–884.

Piaget, J. *The moral judgment of the child.* London: Routledge, 1950. (Originally published, 1932.)

Piaget, J. *The construction of reality in the child.* New York: Basic Books, 1954.

Piliavin, I. M., Rodin, J., & Piliavin, J. A. Good Samaritanism: An underground phenomenon? *Journal of Personality and Social Psychology*, 1969, *13*, 289–299.

Piliavin, J. A., & Piliavin, I. M. The effect of blood on reactions to a victim. *Journal of Personality and Social Psychology*, 1972, *23*, 353–361.

Piliavin, J. A., & Piliavin, I. M. *The good samaritan: Why does he help?* New York: MSS Modular Publications, 1975.

Pilisuk, M., & Skolnik, P. Inducing trust: A test of the Osgood proposal. *Journal of Personality and Social Psychology*, 1968, *8*, 121–133.

Platt, J. R. Strong inference. *Science*, 1964, *146*, 347–353.

Platt, J. R. Social traps. *American Psychologist*, 1973, *28*, 641–651.

Plotnik, R. Brain stimulation and aggression: Monkeys, apes, and humans. In R. L. Holloway (Ed.), *Primate aggression, territoriality, and xenophobia*. New York: Academic Press, 1974.

Pollio, H. R., & Edgerly, J. Comedians and comic style. In A. J. Chapman & H. C. Foot (Eds.), *Humour and laughter*. New York: Wiley, 1976.

Pomazal, R. J., & Jaccard, J. J. An informational approach to altruistic behavior. *Journal of Personality and Social Psychology*, 1976, *33*, 317–326.

Popper, K. *The logic of scientific discovery*. New York: Basic Books, 1959.

Porteus, J. D. *Environment and behavior: Planning and everyday urban life*. Reading, Mass.: Addison-Wesley, 1977.

Powell, F. A. The effects of anxiety-arousing messages when related to personal, familial, and impersonal referents. *Speech Monographs*, 1965, *32*, 102–106.

Price, D. K. *The scientific estate*. Cambridge, Mass.: Harvard University Press, 1965.

Proshansky, H. M., & O'Hanlon, T. Environmental psychology: Origins and development. In D. Stokols (Ed.), *Perspectives on environment and behavior*. New York: Plenum, 1977.

Prothro, E. T. Ethnocentrism and anti-Negro attitudes in the deep south. *Journal of Abnormal and Social Psychology*, 1952, *47*, 105–108.

Quanty, M. B. Aggression catharsis: Experimental investigations and implications. In R. G. Geen & E. C. O'Neal (Eds.), *Perspectives on aggression*. New York: Academic Press, 1976.

Radcliffe-Brown, A. R. On joking relationships. *Africa*, 1940, *13*, 195–210.

Rands, M., & Levinger, G. Implicit theories of relationship: An intergenerational study. *Journal of Personality and Social Psychology*, 1979, *37*, 645–661.

Rapp, A. *The origins of wit and humor*. New York: Dutton, 1951.

Raush, H. L., Barry, W. A., Hertel, R. K., & Swain, M. A. *Communication conflict and marriage*. San Francisco: Jossey-Bass, 1974.

Ray, R. D. Psychology experiments as interbehavioral systems: A case study from the Soviet Union. *Psychological Record*, 1977, *2*, 279–306.

Resnik, J. H., & Schwartz, T. Ethical standards as an independent variable in psychological research. *American Psychologist*, 1973, *28*, 134–139.

Rhine, R. J. Some problems in dissonance theory research on information selectivity. *Psychological Bulletin*, 1967, *68*, 21–28.

Riecken, H. W., & Boruch, R. F. (Eds.), *Social experimentation: A method for planning and evaluating social intervention*. New York: Academic Press, 1974.

Ring, K. Experimental social psychology: Some sober questions about some frivolous values. *Journal of Experimental Social Psychology*, 1967, *3*, 113–123.

Rodin, J., & Slochower, J. Externality in the nonobese: Effects of environmental responsiveness on weight. *Journal of Personality and Social Psychology*, 1976, *33*, 338–344.

Roe, A. *The making of a scientist*. New York: Dodd, Mead, 1953.

Roethlisberger, F. J., & Dickson, W. J. *Management and the worker*. Cambridge, Mass.: Harvard University Press, 1939.

Rogers, C. R. *Client-centered therapy*. Boston: Houghton Mifflin, 1951.

Rokeach, M. (Ed.). *The open and closed mind*. New York: Basic Books, 1960.

Rokeach, M., Smith, P. W., & Evans, R. I. Two kinds of prejudice or one? In M. Rokeach (Ed.), *The open and closed mind*. New York: Basic Books, 1960.

Rosen, G. *Madness in society*. New York: Harper, 1968.

Rosen, S., & Tesser, A. On reluctance to communicate undesirable information: The MUM effect. *Sociometry*, 1970, *33*, 253–263.

Rosenberg, M. J. When dissonance fails: On eliminating evaluation apprehension from attitude measurement. *Journal of Personality and Social Psychology*, 1965, *1*, 28–42.

Rosenberg, S., Nelson, C., & Vivekananthan, P. S. A multidimensional approach to the structure of personality impressions. *Journal of Personality and Social Psychology*, 1968, *9*, 283–294.

Rosenblatt, P. C. Origins and effects of group ethnocentrism and nationalism. *Journal of Conflict Resolution*, 1964, *8*, 131–146.

Rosenblatt, P. C. A cross-cultural study of child rearing and romantic love. *Journal of Personality and Social Psychology*, 1966, *4*, 336–338.

Rosenblatt, P. C. Cross-cultural perspective on attraction. In T. L. Huston (Ed.), *Foundations of interpersonal attraction*. New York: Academic Press, 1974.

Rosenblood, L. K., & Goldstein, J. H. Similarity, intelligence, and affiliation. *Proceedings of the 77th Annual Convention of the American Psychological Association*, 1969, *4*, 341–342.

Rosenhan, D. L. On being sane in insane places. *Science*, 1973, *179*, 250–258.

Rosenthal, R. *Experimenter effects in behavioral research*. New York: Appleton, 1966.

Rosenthal, R., & Jacobson, L. *Pygmalion in the classroom*. New York: Holt, 1968.

Rosenthal, R., & Rosnow, R. L. (Eds.). *Artifact in behavioral research*. New York: Academic Press, 1969.

Rosenzweig, S. The picture-association method and its application in a study of reactions to frustration. *Journal of Personality*, 1946, *14*, 3–23.

Rosnow, R. L., & Fine, G. A. *Rumor and gossip: The social psychology of hearsay*. New York: American Elsevier, 1976.

Rosnow, R. L., & Robinson, E. J. *Experiments in persuasion*. New York: Academic Press, 1967.

Rosnow, R. L., & Rosenthal, R. The volunteer subject revisited. *Australian Journal of Psychology*, 1976, *28*, 97–108.

Ross, E. A. *Social psychology*. New York: Macmillan, 1908.

Ross, H. L., Campbell, D. T., & Glass, G. V. Determining the social effects of a legal reform: The British "breath-alyser" crackdown of 1967. *American Behavioral Scientist*, 1970, *13*, 493–509.

Ross, L., Bierbrauer, G., & Hoffman, S. The role of attribution processes in conformity and dissent: Revisiting the Asch situation. *American Psychologist*, 1976, *31*, 148–157.

Ross, M., Layton, B., Erickson, B., & Schopler, J. Affect, facial regard, and reactions to crowding. *Journal of Personality and Social Psychology*, 1973, *28*, 69–76.

Roszak, T. *The making of a counterculture*. New York: Doubleday, 1969.

Rothbart, M. K. Incongruity, problem-solving and laughter. In A. J. Chapman & H. C. Foot (Eds.), *Humour and laughter*. New York: Wiley, 1976.

Rothbart, M. K., & Maccoby, E. E. Parents' differential reactions to sons and daughters. *Journal of Personality and Social Psychology*, 1966, *4*, 237–243.

Rotter, G. S., & Rotter, N. G. The influence of anchors in the choice of political candidates. *Journal of Social Psychology*, 1966, *70*, 275–280.

Rotter, J. B. *Social learning and clinical psychology*. Englewood Cliffs, N. J.: Prentice-Hall, 1954.

Rotter, J. B. Generalized expectancies for internal versus external control of reinforcement. *Psychological Monographs*, 1966, *80*(1, Whole No. 609).

Rotter, J. B., Chance, J. E., & Phares, E. J. *Applications of a social learning theory of personality*. New York: Holt, 1972.

Rotter, J. B., & Hochreich, D. *Personality*. Chicago: Scott, Foresman, 1975.

Rubin, Z. Measurement of romantic love. *Journal of Personality and Social Psychology*, 1970, *16*, 265–273.

Rubin, Z. *Liking and loving*. New York: Holt, 1973.

Rubin, Z., & Peplau, A. Belief in a just world and reactions to another's lot: A study of participants in the national draft lottery. *Journal of Social Issues*, 1973, *29*(4), 73–93.

Ruble, D. N., & Feldman, N. S. Order of consensus, distinctiveness, and consistency information and causal attributions. *Journal of Personality and Social Psychology*, 1976, *34*, 930–937.

Rubovits, P. C., & Maehr, M. L. Pygmalion analyzed: Toward an explanation of the Rosenthal-Jacobson findings. *Journal of Personality and Social Psychology*, 1971, *19*, 197–203.

Rudé, G. *The crowd in history*. New York: Wiley, 1964.

Rushton, J. P. Generosity in children: Immediate and long-term effects of modeling, preaching, and moral judgment. *Journal of Personality and Social Psychology*, 1975, *31*, 459–466.

Russell, G. W., & Drewry, B. R. Crowd size and competitive aspects of aggression in ice hockey: An archival study. *Human Relations*, 1976, *29*, 723–735.

Russo, N. F. Eye contact, interpersonal distance, and the equilibrium theory. *Journal of Personality and Social Psychology*, 1975, *31*, 497–502.

Rutherford, E., & Mussen, P. Generosity in nursery school boys. *Child Development*, 1968, *39*, 755–765.

Saegert, S., Swap, W., & Zajonc, R. B. Exposure, context, and interpersonal attraction. *Journal of Personality and Social Psychology*, 1973, *25*, 234–242.

Saks, M. J. *Jury verdicts: The role of group size and social decision rule*. Lexington, Mass.: Lexington Books, 1977.

Sampson, E. E. Scientific paradigms and social values: Wanted—a scientific revolution. *Journal of Personality and Social Psychology*, 1978, *36*, 1332–1343.

Sanada, T., & Norbeck, E. Prophecy continues to fail: A Japanese sect. *Journal of Cross-Cultural Psychology*, 1975, *6*, 331–345.

Sanford, N. Whatever happened to action research? *Journal of Social Issues*, 1970, *26*(4), 3–23.

Sargent-Pollock, D. N., & Konečni,

V. J. Evaluative and skin-conductance responses to Renaissance and 20th-century paintings. *Behavior Research Methods and Instrumentation*, 1977, *9*, 291–296.

Sarnoff, I. Identification with the aggressor: Some personality correlates of anti-Semitism among Jews. *Journal of Personality*, 1951, *20*, 199–218.

Sarnoff, I., & Zimbardo, P. G. Anxiety, fear, and social affiliation. *Journal of Abnormal and Social Psychology*, 1961, *62*, 356–363.

Schacter, S. Deviation, rejection, and communication. *Journal of Abnormal and Social Psychology*, 1951, *46*, 190–207.

Schachter, S. *The psychology of affiliation*. Stanford, Calif.: Stanford University Press, 1959.

Schachter, S. The interaction of cognitive and physiological determinants of emotional state. In L. Berkowitz (Ed.), *Advances in experimental social psychology* (Vol. 1). New York: Academic Press, 1964.

Schachter, S. Studies of the interaction of psychological and pharmacological determinants of smoking, *Journal of Experimental Psychology (General)*, 1977, *106*, 3–40.

Schachter, S., & Singer, J. E. Cognitive, social and physiological determinants of emotional state. *Psychological Review*, 1962, *69*, 379–399.

Schachter, S., & Wheeler, L. Epinephrine, chlorpromazine and amusement. *Journal of Abnormal and Social Psychology*, 1962, *65*, 121–128.

Schaie, K. W., & Parham, I. A. Social responsibility in adulthood: Ontogenetic and sociocultural change. *Journal of Personality and Social Psychology*, 1974, *30*, 483–492.

Scheff, T. J. *Being mentally ill: A sociological theory*. Chicago: Aldine, 1966.

Schein, E. H. The Chinese indoctrination program for prisoners of war. *Psychiatry*, 1956, *19*, 149–172.

Schein, V. E., Maurer, E. H., & Novak, J. F. Impact of flexible working hours on productivity. *Journal of Applied Psychology*, 1977, *62*, 463–465.

Scherer, S. E. Proxemic behavior of primary school children as a function of their socioeconomic class and subculture. *Journal of Personality and Social Psychology*, 1974, *29*, 800–805.

Schlegel, R. P., Crawford, C. A., & Sanborn, M. D. Correspondence and mediational properties of the Fishbein model: An application to adolescent alcohol use. *Journal of Experimental Social Psychology*, 1977, *13*, 421–430.

Schleifer, M., & Douglas, V. I. Effects of training on the moral judgment of young children. *Journal of Personality and Social Psychology*, 1973, *28*, 62–68.

Schlenker, B. R. Social psychology and science. *Journal of Personality and Social Psychology*, 1974, *29*, 1–15.

Schlenker, B. R. In L. Berkowitz (Ed.) On the ethogenic approach: Etiquette and revolution. *Advances in experimental social psychology* (Vol. 10). New York: Academic Press, 1977.

Schlesinger, A., Jr. *A thousand days*. Boston: Houghton Mifflin, 1965.

Schlosberg, H. The description of facial expressions in terms of two dimensions. *Journal of Experimental Psychology*, 1952, *44*, 229–237.

Schneider, D. J. Implicit personality theory: A review. *Psychological Bulletin*, 1973, *79*, 294–309.

Schneirla, T. C. Instinct and aggression. In M. F. A. Montagu (Ed.), *Man and aggression*. London and New York: Oxford University Press, 1968.

Schopler, J., & Stockdale, J. E. An interference analysis of crowding. *Environmental Psychology and Nonverbal Behavior*, 1977, *1*, 81–88.

Schulman, G. I. Asch conformity studies: Conformity to the experimenter and/or to the group? *Sociometry*, 1967, *30*, 26–40.

Schultz, D. P. (Ed.), *Panic behavior*. New York: Random House, 1964.

Schultz, D. P. Group behavior in a simulated escape situation. *Journal of Psychology*, 1965, *61*, 69–72.

Schulz, R. Effects of control and predictability on the physical and psychological well-being of the institutionalized aged. *Journal of Personality and Social Psychology*, 1976, *33*, 563–573.

Schutz, W. *Joy*. New York: Grove, 1967.

Schwartz, S. H., & Gottlieb, A. Bystander reactions to a violent theft: Crime in Jerusalem. *Journal of Personality and Social Psychology*, 1977, *34*, 1183–1210.

Scodel, A. Heterosexual somatic preference and fantasy dependency. *Journal of Consulting Psychology*, 1957, *21*, 371–374.

Scott, J. P. *Aggression* (2nd ed.). Chicago: University of Chicago Press, 1975.

Sears, R. R. Non-aggressive reactions to frustration. *Psychological Review*, 1941, *48*, 343–346.

Seaver, W. B. Effects of naturally induced teacher expectancies. *Journal of Personality and Social Psychology*, 1973, *28*, 333–342.

Segall, M. H., Campbell, D. T., &

Herskovits, M. J. *The influence of culture on perception*. Indianapolis: Bobbs-Merrill, 1966.

Seligman, M. E. P. *Helplessness*. San Francisco: Freeman, 1975.

Shaver, K. G. Defensive attribution: Effects of severity and relevance on the responsibility assigned for an accident. *Journal of Personality and Social Psychology*, 1970, *14*, 101–113.

Shaw, M. E. Communication networks. In L. Berkowitz (Ed.), *Advances in experimental social psychology* (Vol. 1). New York: Academic Press, 1964.

Shaw, M. E. An overview of small group behavior. In J. W. Thibaut, J. T. Spence, & R. C. Carson (Eds.), *Contemporary topics in social psychology*. Morristown, N. J.: General Learning Press, 1976.

Shaw, M. E., Briscoe, M., & Garcia-Esteve, J. A cross-cultural study of attribution of responsibility. *International Journal of Psychology*, 1968, *3*, 51–60.

Shaw, M. E., & Costanzo, P. R. *Theories of social psychology*. New York: McGraw-Hill, 1970.

Shelford, V. E. The physical environment. In C. Murchison (Ed.), *A handbook of social psychology*. Worcester, Mass.: Clark University Press, 1935.

Sherif, C. W., Kelly, M., Rodgers, H. L., Sarup, G., & Tittler, B. I. Personal involvement, social judgment, and action. *Journal of Personality and Social Psychology*, 1973, *27*, 311–327.

Sherif, C. W., Sherif, M., & Nebergall, R. E. *Attitude and attitude change: The social judgment-involvement approach*. Philadelphia: Saunders, 1965.

Sherif, M. *The psychology of social*

norms. New York: Harper, 1936.

Sherif, M. Superordinate goals in the reduction of intergroup conflict. *American Journal of Sociology,* 1958, *63,* 349–356.

Sherif, M., & Cantril, H. *The psychology of ego-involvements.* New York: Wiley, 1947.

Sherif, M., Harvey, O. J., White, B. J., Hood, W. R., & Sherif, C. W. *Intergroup conflict and cooperation: The Robber's Cave experiment.* Norman: University of Oklahoma Press, 1961.

Sherif, M., & Hovland, C. I. *Social judgment.* New Haven, Conn.: Yale University Press, 1961.

Sherrod, L., & Singer, J. L. The development of imaginative play in children. In J. H. Goldstein (Ed.), *Sports, games, and play.* Hillsdale, N. J.: Erlbaum, 1979.

Shikiar, R., Wiggins, N. H., & Fishbein, M. The prediction of political evaluation and voting preference: A multidimensional analysis. *Journal of Research in Personality,* 1976, *10,* 424–436.

Silverman, I. In defense of dissonance theory: Reply to Chapanis and Chapanis. *Psychological Bulletin,* 1964, *62,* 205–209.

Silverman, I. Physical attractiveness and courtship. *Sexual Behavior,* 1971, *7,* 22–25.

Sime, A. M. Relationship of preoperative fear, type of coping, and information received about surgery to recovery from surgery. *Journal of Personality and Social Psychology,* 1976, *34,* 716–724.

Simmel, G. The metropolis and mental life. In K. Wolff (Ed.), *The sociology of Georg Simmel.* New York: Free Press, 1950.

Simmel, G. *Conflict and the web of group affiliations.* Glencoe, Ill.: Free Press, 1955.

Simon, R. J. *The jury and the defense of insanity.* Boston: Little, Brown, 1967.

Singer, J. L. The influence of violence portrayed in television or motion pictures upon overt aggressive behavior. In J. L. Singer (Ed.), *The control of aggression and violence.* New York: Academic Press, 1971.

Skinner, B. F. *Verbal behavior.* New York: Appleton, 1957.

Skinner, B. F. *Beyond freedom and dignity.* New York: Knopf, 1971.

Skinner, B. F. *About behaviorism.* New York: Random House, 1974.

Skinner, B. F. Why I am not a cognitive psychologist. *Behaviorism,* 1977, *5,* 1–10.

Sloan, L. R. The function and impact of sports for fans. In J. H. Goldstein (Ed.), *Sports, games, and play.* Hillsdale, N. J.: Lawrence Erlbaum Associates, 1979.

Slobin, D. I. *Psycholinguistics.* Glencoe: Scott, Foresman, 1971.

Slobodin, L. F., Collins, M. I., Crayton, J. L., Feldman, J. M., Jaccard, J. J., Rissman, K., & Weldon, D. E. *Culture assimilator for interaction with the economically disadvantaged.* Urbana: University of Illinois, 1972. (Cited in Triandis, 1977.)

Smelser, N. J. *Theory of collective behavior.* New York: Free Press, 1963.

Smith, C. R., Williams, L., & Willis, R. H. Race, sex, and belief as determinants of friendship acceptance. *Journal of Personality and Social Psychology,* 1967, *5,* 127–137.

Smith, E. E. The power of dissonance techniques to change attitudes. *Public Opinion Quarterly,* 1961, *25,* 626–639.

Smith, E. E., & Goodchilds, J. D. Characteristics of the witty group member. *American Psychologist*, 1959, *14*, 375–376.

Smith, F. T. *An experiment in modifying attitudes toward the Negro*. New York: Teachers College, Columbia University, 1943. (Cited in Harding, Proshansky, Kutner, & Schein, 1969.)

Smith, M. B. Is psychology relevant to new priorities? *American Psychologist*, 1973, *28*, 463–471.

Smith, M. B., Bruner, J. S., & White, R. W. *Opinions and personality*. New York: Wiley, 1956.

Sommer, R. Studies in personal space. *Sociometry*, 1959, *22*, 247–260.

Sommer, R. Small group ecology. *Psychological Bulletin*, 1967, *67*, 145–152.

Sommer, R. Intimacy ratings in five countries. *International Journal of Psychology*, 1968, *3*, 109–114.

Sommer, R. *Personal space*. Englewood Cliffs, N. J.: Prentice-Hall, 1969.

Sorokin, P. A. *Fads and foibles in modern sociology*. Chicago: Regnery, 1956.

Spanos, N. P. Witchcraft in histories of psychiatry: A critical analysis and an alternative conceptualization. *Psychological Bulletin*, 1978, *85*, 417–439.

Spence, K. W. *Behavior theory and conditioning*. New Haven, Conn.: Yale University Press, 1956.

Spinetta, J. J., & Rigler, D. The child-abusing parent: A psychological review. In R. Kalmar (Ed.), *Child abuse: Perspectives on diagnosis, treatment and prevention*. Dubuque, Iowa: Kendall/Hunt, 1977.

Spinoza, B. *The ethics*. New York: Dover, 1951.

Sroufe, R., Chaikin, A., Cook, R., & Freeman, V. The effects of physical attractiveness on honesty: A socially desirable response. *Personality and Social Psychology Bulletin*, 1977, *3*, 59–62.

Staats, A. W. *Social behaviorism*. Homewood, Ill.: Dorsey, 1975.

Staats, C. K., & Staats, A. W. Meaning established by classical conditioning. *Journal of Experimental Psychology*, 1957, *54*, 74–80.

Stagner, R., & Congdon, C. S. Another failure to demonstrate displacement of aggression. *Journal of Abnormal and Social Psychology*, 1955, *51*, 695–696.

Stalling, R. S. Personality similarity and evaluative meaning as conditioners of attraction. *Journal of Personality and Social Psychology*, 1970, *14*, 77–82.

Stang, D. J. Methodological factors in mere exposure research. *Psychological Bulletin*, 1974, *81*, 1014–1025.

Staub, E. A child in distress: The influence of age and number of witnesses on children's attempts to help. *Journal of Personality and Social Psychology*, 1970, *14*, 130–140.

Staub, E. Helping a distressed person: Social, personality and stimulus determinants. In L. Berkowitz (Ed.), *Advances in experimental social psychology* (Vol. 7). New York: Academic Press, 1974.

Staub, E. *Positive social behavior and morality* (Vol. 1). New York: Academic Press, 1978.

Staub, E., & Feinberg, H. K. Personality, socialization, and the development of prosocial behavior in children. In D. H. Smith & J. Macaulay (Eds.), *Voluntary action research*. San Francisco: Jossey-Bass, 1979.

Staub, E., & Sherk, L. Need approval, children's sharing behavior and reciprocity in sharing. *Child Development*, 1970, *41*, 243–253.

Stech, F. J., McClintock, C. G., Fitzpatrick, N. J., & Babin, C. A. When a cultural prohibition is effective: A field investigation. *Journal of Applied Social Psychology*, 1976, *6*, 211–227.

Steele, B. F., & Pollock, C. B. A psychiatric study of parents who abuse infants and small children. In R. E. Helfer & C. H. Kempe (Eds.), *The battered child*. Chicago: University of Chicago Press, 1968.

Stein, D. D., Hardyck, J. A., & Smith, M. B. Race and belief: An open and shut case. *Journal of Personality and Social Psychology*, 1965, *1*, 281–290.

Steiner, G. A. *The people look at television*. New York: Knopf, 1963.

Steiner, I. D. Perceived freedom. In L. Berkowitz (Ed.), *Advances in experimental social psychology* (Vol. 5). New York: Academic Press, 1970.

Steiner, I. D. *Group process and productivity*. New York: Academic Press, 1972.

Steiner, I. D. What ever happened to the group in social psychology? *Journal of Experimental Social Psychology*, 1974, *10*, 94–108.

Steinman, D. O., Smith, T. H., Jurdem, L. G., & Hammond, K. R. Application of social judgment theory in policy formulation: An example. *Journal of Applied Behavioral Science*, 1977, *13*, 69–88.

Steinzor, B. The spatial factor in face-to-face discussion groups. *Journal of Abnormal and Social Psychology*, 1950, *45*, 552–555.

Stephan, C. Selective characteristics of jurors and litigants: Their influences on juries' verdicts. In R. J. Simon (Ed.), *The jury system in America: A critical overview*. Beverly Hills, Calif.: Sage, 1975.

Stern, P. C. Effect of incentives and education on resource conservation decisions in a simulated commons dilemma. *Journal of Personality and Social Psychology*, 1976, *34*, 1285–1292.

Stogdill, R. M. Personal factors associated with leadership: A survey of the literature. *Journal of Psychology*, 1948, *25*, 35–71.

Stogdill, R. M. Personal factors associated with leadership: A survey of the literature. In C. A. Gibb (Ed.). *Leadership*. Baltimore: Penguin, 1969.

Stokols, D. On the distinction between density and crowding: Some implications for future research. *Psychological Review*, 1972, *79*, 275–277.

Stokols, D. Origins and directions of environment-behavioral research. In D. Stokols (Ed.), *Perspectives on environment and behavior*. New York: Plenum: 1977.

Storms, M. D. Videotape and the attribution process: Reversing actors' and observers' points of view. *Journal of Personality and Social Psychology*, 1973, *27*, 165–175.

Storms, M. D., & Thomas, G. C. Reactions to physical closeness. *Journal of Personality and Social Psychology*, 1977, *35*, 412–418.

Storr, A. *Human aggression*. New York: Antheneum, 1968.

Streufert, S. How applied is applied social psychology? Editorial. *Journal of Applied Social Psychology*, 1973, *3*, 1–5.

Stricker, L. J., Jacobs, P. I., & Kogan, N. Trait interrelations in implicit personality theories and questionnaire data. *Journal of Personality* and *Social Psychology*, 1974, *30*, 198–207.

Strickland, L. H., Aboud, F. E., & Gergen, K. J. *Social psychology in transition*. New York: Plenum, 1976.

Strodtbeck, F. L., & Hook, L. H. The social dimensions of a twelve-man jury table. *Sociometry*, 1961, *24*, 397–415.

Strodtbeck, F. L., James, R. M., & Hawkins, C. Social status in jury deliberations. *America Sociological Review*, 1957, *22*, 713–719.

Suedfeld, P. Sensory deprivation used in the reduction of cigarette smoking: Attitude change experiments in an applied context. *Journal of Applied Social Psychology*, 1973, *3*, 30–38.

Sullivan, H. S. *Conceptions of modern psychiatry*. New York: Norton, 1953.

Suls, J. M. A two-stage model for the appreciation of jokes and cartoons: An information-processing analysis. In J. H. Goldstein & P. E. McGhee (Eds.), *The psychology of humor*. New York: Academic Press, 1972.

Suls, J. M. Misattribution and humor appreciation: A comment on "Enhancement of humor appreciation by transferred excitation." *Journal of Personality and Social Psychology*, 1976, *34*, 960–965.

Suls, J. M., & Miller, R. L. Humor as an attributional index. *Personality and Social Psychology Bulletin*, 1976, *2*, 256–259.

Suls, J. M., & Miller, R. L. *Social comparison theory*. New York: Wiley, 1977.

Sumner, W. G. *Folkways*. New York: Ginn, 1906/1940.

Sundstrom, E., & Altman, I. Field study of territorial behavior and dominance. *Journal of Personality and Social Psychology*, 1974, *30*, 115–124.

Swart, C., & Berkowitz, L. Effects of a stimulus associated with a victim's pain on later aggression. *Journal of Personality and Social Psychology*, 1976, *33*, 623–631.

Swenson, C. H., Jr. *Introduction to interpersonal relations*. Glenview, Ill.: Scott, Foresman, 1973.

Switzer, E. B., Deal, T. E., & Bailey, J. S. The reduction of stealing in second graders using a group contingency. *Journal of Applied Behavior Analysis*, 1977, *10*, 267–272.

Sykes, G. M., & Matza, D. Techniques of neutralization: A theory of delinquency. *American Sociological Review*, 1957, *22*, 664–670.

Szasz, T. *The myth of mental illness*. New York: Harper, 1961.

Szasz, T. *The manufacture of madness*. New York: Harper, 1970.

Tagiuri, R. Person perception. In G. Lindzey & E. Aronson (Eds.), *Handbook of social psychology* (Vol. 3). Reading, Mass.: Addison-Wesley, 1969.

Tajfel, H. Value and the perceptual judgment of magnitude. *Psychological Review*, 1957, *64*, 192–204.

Tajfel, H., Billig, M., Bundy, R., & Flament, M. Social categorization and intergroup behavior. *European Journal of Social Psychology*, 1971, *1*, 149–175.

Taylor, D. M., & Jaggi, V. Ethnocentrism and causal attribution in a South Indian context. *Journal of Cross-Cultural Psychology*, 1974, *5*, 162–171.

Tedeschi, J. T., Schlenker, B., & Bonoma, T. Cognitive dissonance: Private ratiocination or public spectacle? *American Psychologist*, 1971, *26*, 685–695.

Tedeschi, J. T., Smith, R. B., III, & Brown, R. C. A reinterpretation of research on aggression. *Psychological Bulletin*, 1974, *81*, 540–562.

Teichman, Y. Emotional arousal and affiliation. *Journal of Experimental Social Psychology*, 1973, *9*, 591–605.

Teplin, L. A. Preference versus prejudice: A multimethod analysis of children's discrepant racial choices. *Social Science Quarterly*, 1977, *58*, 390–406.

Terborg, J. R., Castore, C., & De-Ninno, J. A. A longitudinal field investigation of the impact of group composition on group performance and cohesion. *Journal of Personality and Social Psychology*, 1976, *34*, 782–790.

Terman, L. M. Are scientists different? *Scientific American*, January, 1955, Scientific American Reprint No. 437.

Tesser, A., & Paulhus, D. L. Toward a causal model of love. *Journal of Personality and Social Psychology*, 1976, *34*, 1095–1105.

Tharp, R. G. Psychological patterning in marriage. *Psychological Bulletin*, 1963, *60*, 97–117.

Thibaut, J. W., & Kelley, H. H. *The social psychology of groups*. New York: Wiley, 1959.

Thibaut, J. W., & Kelley, H. H. *Interpersonal relations*. New York: Wiley, 1978.

Thibaut, J. W., & Riecken, H. W. Some determinants and consequences of the perception of social reality. *Journal of Personality*, 1955, *24*, 113–133.

Thistlethwaite, D. L., & Kamenetzky, J. Attitude change through refutation and elaboration of audience counterarguments. *Journal of Abnormal and Social Psychology*, 1955, *51*, 3–12.

Thorell, T. Selected illnesses and somatic factors in relation to two psychosocial stress indices–A prospective study on middle-aged construction building workers. *Journal of Psychosomatic Research*, 1976, *20*, 7–20.

Thorndike, E. L. *The psychology of learning*. New York: Teachers College, Columbia University, 1913.

Thorndike, E. L. A constant error in psychological ratings. *Journal of Applied Psychology*, 1920, *4*, 25–29.

Thrasher, F. M. *The gang: A study of 1313 gangs in Chicago*. Chicago: University of Chicago Press, 1926.

Thurstone, L. L. Attitudes can be measured. *American Journal of Sociology*, 1928, *33*, 529–554.

Tinbergen, N. *The study of instinct*. London and New York: Oxford University Press (Clarendon), 1951.

Tobach, E., Gianutsos, J., Topoff, H. R., & Gross, C. G. *The four horsemen: Racism, sexism, militarism and social Darwinism*. New York: Behavioral Publications, 1974.

Toch, H. *The social psychology of social movements*. New York: Bobbs-Merrill, 1965.

Tolman, C. W., & Wilson, G. T. Social feeding in domestic chicks. *Animal Behavior*, 1965, *13*, 134–142.

Tolman, E. C. *Purposive behavior in animals and men*. New York: Appleton, 1932.

Tönnies, F. *Fundamental concepts of sociology* (C. F. Loomis, trans.). New York: American Book Co., 1940. (Originally published, 1887).

Totman, R. An approach to cognitive dissonance theory in terms of ordinary language. *Journal for the Theory of Social Behavior*, 1973, *3*, 215–238.

Touhey, J. C. Effects of additional

women professionals on ratings of occupational prestige and desirability. *Journal of Personality and Social Psychology*, 1974, *29*, 86–89.

Travis, L. E. The effect of a small audience upon eye-hand coordination. *Journal of Abnormal and Social Psychology*, 1925, *20*, 142–146.

Triandis, H. C. *Attitude and attitude change*. New York: Wiley, 1971.

Triandis, H. C. *Interpersonal behavior*. Monterey, Calif.: Brooks/Cole, 1977.

Triandis, H. C., & Davis, E. E. Race and belief as determinants of behavior intentions. *Journal of Personality and Social Psychology*, 1965, *2*, 715–725.

Triandis, H. C., & Triandis, L. M. Race, social class, religion, and nationality as determinants of social distance. *Journal of Abnormal and Social Psychology*, 1960, *61*, 110–118.

Triandis, H. C., & Vassiliou, V. Frequency of contact and stereotyping. *Journal of Personality and Social Psychology*, 1967, 7, 316–328.

Triplett, N. The dynamogenic factors in pacemaking and competition. *American Journal of Psychology*, 1897, *9*, 507–533.

Tsukashima, R. T., & Montero, D. The contact hypothesis: Social and economic contact and generational changes in the study of black anti-Semitism. *Social Forces*, 1976, *55*, 149–165.

Tucker, J., & Friedman, S. T. Population density and group size. *American Journal of Sociology*, 1972, 77, 742–749.

Turner, R. H., & Killian, L. M. *Collective behavior*. Englewood Cliffs, N. J.: Prentice-Hall, 1957.

Tyler, T. R., & Sears, D. O. Coming to like obnoxious people when we must live with them. *Journal of Personality and Social Psychology*, 1977, *35*, 200–211.

U. S. Surgeon General's Advisory Committee on Television and Social Behavior. *Television and growing up: The impact of televised violence*. Washington, D.C.: U. S. Government Printing Office, 1972.

Valenti, A. C., & Downing. L. L. Differential effects of jury size on verdicts following deliberation as a function of the apparent guilt of a defendant. *Journal of Personality and Social Psychology*, 1975, *32*, 655–663.

Varela, J. A. *Psychological solutions to social problems: An introduction to social technology*. New York: Academic Press, 1971.

Varela, J. A. Can social psychology be applied? In M. Deutsch & H. A. Hornstein (Eds.), *Applying social psychology*. Hillsdale, N. J.: Lawrence Erlbaum Associates, 1975.

Vaughan, G. M. The social distance attitudes of New Zealand students toward Maoris and fifteen other national groups. *Journal of Social Psychology*, 1962, *57*, 85–92.

Vernon, P. E. Some characteristics of the good judge of personality. *Journal of Social Psychology*, 1933, *4*, 42–58.

Vidmar, N. Effects of decision alternatives on the verdicts and social perceptions of simulated jurors. *Journal of Personality and Social Psychology*, 1972, *22*, 211–218.

Vinokur, A., & Selzer, M. L. Desirable versus undesirable life events: Their relationship to stress and mental disease. *Journal of Personality and Social Psychology*, 1975, *32*, 329–337.

Walden, W. How to know where you

are. *Altantic*, November 1979, p. 87.

Walker, M. *The nature of scientific thought.* Englewood Cliffs, N. J.: Prentice-Hall, 1963.

Walster, E. The effect of self-esteem on romantic liking. *Journal of Experimental Social Psychology*, 1965, *1*, 184–197.

Walster, E. Assignment of responsibility for an accident. *Journal of Personality and Social Psychology*, 1966, *3*, 73–80.

Walster, E., Aronson, E., & Abrahams, D. On increasing the persuasiveness of a low prestige communicator. *Journal of Experimental Social Psychology*, 1966, *2*, 325–342.

Walster, E., Aronson, V., Abrahams, D., & Rottmann, L. Importance of physical attractiveness in dating behavior. *Journal of Personality and Social Psychology*, 1966, *4*, 508–516.

Walster, E., & Piliavin, J. A. Equity and the innocent bystander. *Journal of Social Issues*, 1972, *28*, 165–189.

Walster, E., & Walster, G. W. Effect of expecting to be liked on choice of associates. *Journal of Abnormal and Social Psychology*, 1963, *67*, 402–404.

Walster, E., & Walster, G. W. *A new look at love.* Reading, Mass.: Addison-Wesley, 1978.

Walster, E., Walster, G. W., & Berscheid, E. *Equity: Theory and research.* Boston: Allyn & Bacon, 1978.

Ward, S. H., & Braun, J. Self esteem and racial preference in black children. *American Journal of Orthopsychiatry*, 1972, *42*, 644–647.

Warr, P. B., & Knapper, C. *The perception of people and events.* New York: Wiley, 1968.

Watson, J. B. Psychology as a behaviorist views it. *Psychological Review*, 1913, *20*, 158–177.

Watson, J. B. *Psychology from the standpoint of a behaviorist.* Philadelphia: Lippincott, 1919.

Watson, J. B. *Psychological care of infant and child.* New York: Norton, 1934.

Watson, J., Breed, W., & Posman, H. A study in urban conversation: Sample of 1001 remarks overheard in Manhattan. *Journal of Social Psychology*, 1948, *28*, 121–133.

Watson, R. I., Jr. Investigation into deindividuation using a cross-cultural survey technique. *Journal of Personality and Social Psychology*, 1973, *25*, 342–345.

Webb, E. J., Campbell, D. T., Schwartz, R. D., & Sechrest, L. *Unobtrusive measures: Nonreactive research in the social sciences.* Chicago: Rand McNally, 1966.

Weick, K. E., Gilfillan, D. P., & Keith, T. A. The effect of composer credibility on orchestra performance. *Sociometry*, 1973, *36*, 435–462.

Weiner, B. *Achievement motivation and attribution theory.* Morristown, N. J.: General Learning Press, 1974.

Weiner, B., Frieze, I., Kukla, A., Reed, L., Rest, S., & Rosenbaum, R. M. *Perceiving the causes of success and failure.* Morristown, N. J.: General Learning Press, 1971.

Weiss, R. F., Boyer, J. L., Lombardo, J. P., & Stich, M. H. Altruistic drive and altruistic reinforcement. *Journal of Personality and Social Psychology*, 1973, *25*, 390–400.

Weiss, R. F., & Miller, F. G. The drive theory of social facilitation. *Psychological Review*, 1971, *78*, 44–57.

Weiss, W. Effects of the mass media of communication. In G. Lindzey

& E. Aronson (Eds.), *Handbook of social psychology* (2nd ed., Vol. 5). Reading, Mass.: Addison-Wesley, 1969.

Weitz, S. *Sex roles: Biological, psychological, and social foundations.* London and New York: Oxford University Press, 1977.

Wertheimer, M. Untersuchungen zur Lehre von der Gestalt. *Psychologische Forschung*, 1923, *4*, 301–350.

West, S. G., Whitney, G., & Schnedler, R. Helping a motorist in distress: The effects of sex, race and neighborhood. *Journal of Personality and Social Psychology*, 1975, *31*, 691–698.

Wheeler, L., & Caggiula, A. R. The contagion of aggression. *Journal of Experimental Social Psychology*, 1966, *2*, 1–10.

White, R. K. Misperception in the Arab-Israeli conflict. *Journal of Social Issues*, 1977, *33*(1), 190–221.

White, R. W. Motivation reconsidered: The concept of competence. *Psychological Review*, 1959, *66*, 297–334.

Whiting, J. W. M. Socialization process and personality. In D. R. Price-Williams (Ed.), *Cross-cultural studies*. Baltimore: Penguin, 1969.

Whiting, J. W. M., & Child, I. L. *Child training and personality: A cross-cultural study.* New Haven, Conn.: Yale University Press, 1953.

Whiting, J. W. M., Kluckhohn, R., & Anthony, A. The function of male initiation ceremonies at puberty. In H. Proshansky & B. Seidenberg (Eds.), *Basic studies in social psychology*. New York: Holt, 1965.

Whittaker, J. O. Resolution of the communication discrepancy issue in social psychology. In C. W. Sherif & M. Sherif (Eds.), *Attitude,*

ego-involvement and change. New York: Wiley, 1967.

Whorf, B. L. In J. B. Carroll (Ed.), *Language, thought, and reality.* Cambridge, Mass.: MIT Press, 1956.

Whyte, W. F. *Street corner society.* Chicago: University of Chicago Press, 1943.

Wicker, A. W. Attitudes versus actions: The relationship of verbal and overt behavioral responses to attitude objects. *Journal of Social Issues*, 1969, *25*(4), 41–78.

Wicklund, R. A. *Freedom and reactance.* Hillsdale, N. J.: Lawrence Erlbaum Associates, 1974.

Wicklund, R. A., & Brehm, J. W. *Perspectives on cognitive dissonance.* Hillsdale, N. J. Lawrence Erlbaum Associates, 1976.

Wiesner, J. B. The need for social engineering. In F. F. Korten, S. W. Cook, & J. I. Lacey (Eds.), *Psychology and the problems of society.* Washington, D. C.: American Psychological Association, 1970.

Wiggins, J. S. *Personality and prediction: Principles of assessment.* Reading, Mass.: Addison-Wesley, 1973.

Wiggins, J. S., Wiggins, N., & Conger, J. C. Correlates of heterosexual somatic preference. *Journal of Personality and Social Psychology*, 1968, *10*, 82–90.

Williams, J. E., Giles, H., Edwards, J. R., Best, D. L., & Daws, J. T. Sex-trait stereotypes in England, Ireland and the United States. *British Journal of Social and Clinical Psychology*, 1977, *16*, 303–309.

Willis, R. H., & Hollander, E. P. An experimental study of three response modes in social influence situations. *Journal of Abnormal and Social Psychology*, 1964, *69*, 150–156.

Wilner, D. M., Walkley, R. P., & Cook, S. W. Residential proximity and intergroup relations in public housing projects. *Journal of Social Issues*, 1952, *8*, 45–69.

Wilson, D. W., & Donnerstein, E. Legal and ethical aspects of non-reactive social psychological research: An excursion into the public mind. *American Psychologist*, 1976, *31*, 765–784.

Wilson, E. O. *Sociobiology*. Cambridge, Mass.: Harvard University Press, 1975.

Wilson, G., Nias, D. *Love's mysteries: The psychology of sexual attraction*. London: Open Books, 1976.

Wilson, J. P. Motivation, modeling, and altruism: A person × situation analysis. *Journal of Personality and Social Psychology*, 1976, *34*, 1078–1086.

Winch, R. F. *Mate selection*. New York: Harper, 1958.

Winston, S. Birth control and the sex-ratio at birth. *American Journal of Sociology*, 1932, *38*, 225–231.

Wishner, J. Reanalysis of "impressions of personality." *Psychological Review*, 1960, *67*, 96–112.

Wispé, L. G. Positive forms of social behavior: An overview. *Journal of Social Issues*, 1972, *28*(3), 1–19.

Wispé, L. G., & Freshley, H. B. Race, sex, and sympathetic helping behavior: The broken bag caper. *Journal of Personality and Social Psychology*, 1971, *17*, 59–65.

Wispé, L. G., & Thompson, J. N., Jr. The war between the words: Biological versus social evolution and some related issues. *American Psychologist*, 1976, *31*, 341–384.

Wohlwill, J., & Carson, D. *Environment and the social sciences: Perspectives and application*. Washington, D. C.: American Psychological Association, 1972.

Wolfgang, M. E. *Patterns in criminal homicide*. New York: Wiley, 1958.

Wolfgang, M. E., & Ferracuti, F. *The subculture of violence*. London: Tavistock, 1967.

Woodworth, R. S. *Experimental psychology*. New York: Holt, 1938.

Worchel, S., Andreoli, V. A., & Folger, R. Intergroup cooperation and intergroup attraction: The effect of previous interaction and outcome of combined effort. *Journal of Experimental Social Psychology*, 1977, *13*, 131–140.

Worchel, S., & Teddlie, C. The experience of crowding: A two-factor theory. *Journal of Personality and Social Psychology*, 1976, *34*, 30–40.

Wortman, C. B., Hendricks, M., & Hillis, J. W. Factors affecting participant reactions to random assignment in ameliorative social programs. *Journal of Personality and Social Psychology*, 1976, *33*, 256–266.

Wright, G. O. Projection and displacement: A cross-cultural study of folktale aggression. *Journal of Abnormal and Social Psychology*, 1956, *49*, 523–528.

Wrightsman, L. S. Wallace supporters and adherence to "law and order." *Journal of Personality and Social Psychology*, 1969, *13*, 17–22.

Wynne-Edwards, V. C. *Animal dispersion in relation to social behavior*. London: Oliver & Boyd, 1962.

Young, P. T. Laughing and weeping, cheerfulness and depression: A study of moods among college students. *Journal of Social Psychology*, 1937, *8*, 311–334.

Zajonc, R. B. The process of cognitive tuning in communication. *Journal of Abnormal and Social Psychology*, 1960, *61*, 159–168.

Zajonc, R. B. Social facilitation. *Science*, 1965, *149*, 260–274.

Zajonc, R. B. Attitudinal effects of mere exposure. *Journal of Personality and Social Psychology*, 1968, *9* (part 2), 1–27.

Zajonc, R. B. Family configuration and intelligence. *Science*, 1976, *192*, 227–236.

Zajonc, R. B., & Markus, G. B. *Psychological Review*, 1975, *82*.

Zander, A., & Armstrong, W. Working for group pride in a slipper factory. *Journal of Applied Social Psychology*, 1972, *2*, 326–342.

Zanna, M. P., & Hamilton, D. L. Attribute dimensions and patterns of trait inferences. *Psychonomic Science*, 1972, *27*, 353–354.

Zanna, M. P., Kiesler, C. A., & Pilkonis, P. A. Positive and negative attitudinal affect established by classical conditioning. *Journal of Personality and Social Psychology*, 1970, *14*, 321–328.

Zeigarnik, B. Uber Behalten von erledigten und unerledigten Handlungen. *Psychologische Forschung*, 1927, *9*, 1–85. ("On finished and unfinished tasks.")

Zillmann, D. Excitation transfer in communication-mediated aggressive behavior. *Journal of Experimental Social Psychology*, 1971, *7*, 419–434.

Zillmann, D. *Hostility and aggression.* Hillsdale, N. J.: Lawrence Erlbaum Associates, 1979.

Zillmann, D., & Bryant, J. Effects of residual excitation on the emotional response to provocation and delayed aggressive behavior. *Journal of Personality and Social Psychology*, 1974, *30*, 782–791.

Zillmann, D., Bryant, J., & Sapolsky, B. S. The enjoyment of watching sport contests. In J. H. Goldstein (Ed.), *Sports, games, and play.* Hillsdale, N. J.: Lawrence Erlbaum Associates, 1979.

Zillmann, D., & Cantor, J. R. A disposition theory of humour and mirth. In A. J. Chapman & H. C. Foot (Eds.), *Humour and laughter.* New York: Wiley, 1976.

Zillmann, D., Katcher, A. H., & Milavsky, B. Excitation transfer from physical exercise to subsequent aggressive behavior. *Journal of Experimental Social Psychology*, 1972, *8*, 247–259.

Zimbardo, P. G. The human choice: Individuation, reason and order versus deindividuation, impulse, and chaos. In W. J. Arnold & D. Levine (Eds.), *Nebraska Symposium on Motivation* (Vol. 17). Lincoln: University of Nebraska Press, 1969.

Zimbardo, P. G. *Shyness: What is it, what to do about it.* Reading, Mass.: Addison-Wesley, 1977.

Zimbardo, P. G., Ebbesen, E. B., & Maslach, C. *Influencing attitudes and changing behavior* (2nd ed.). Reading, Mass.: Addison-Wesley, 1977.

Zimbardo, P. G., Snyder, M., Thomas, J., Gold, A., & Gurwitz, S. Modifying the impact of persuasive communications with external distraction. *Journal of Personality and Social Psychology*, 1970, *16*, 669–680.

Zinberg, N. E., & Fellman, G. A. Violence: Biological need and social control. *Social Forces*, 1967, *45*, 533–541.

Zuckerman, H. The sociology of the Nobel Prizes. *Scientific American*, 1967, *217*, 25–33.

Zuniga, R. B. The experimenting society and radical social reform: The role of the social scientist in

Chile's Unidad Popular experience. *American Psychologist*, 1975, *30*, 99–115.

1. Goldstein, J. H., Silverman, A. F., & Anderson, P. K. *A cross-cultural investigation of humour: Appreciation of jokes varying in familiarity and hostility.* Paper presented at 21st meeting of the International Congress of Psychology, Paris, 1976.

2. Levinger, G. *Models of close relationships: Some new directions.* Paper delivered at American Psychological Association, Toronto, Aug. 28, 1978.

3. Goldstein, J. H., Davis, R. W., Kernis, M., & Cohn, E. S. *Retarding the escalation of aggression.* Unpublished manuscript, Temple University, Philadelphia, 1978.

4. Meltzer, L. *Applied, applicable, appealing, and appalling social psychology.* Unpublished manuscript, Cornell University, 1972.

5. Zimbardo, P. G. *Preliminary ideas toward a model of madness.* Unpublished manuscript, Stanford University, May, 1977.

6. Goldstein, J. H., & Kernis, M. *Category-routinized joking: An analysis of letters to "Dear Abby."* Unpublished manuscript, Temple University, 1976.

NAME INDEX

Dillehay, R. C., 106
Dion, K. K., 192, 206, 219
Dion, K. L., 219, 369
Doby, C., 145
Dodge, K. A., 104
Dolan, A. B., 87
Dollard, J., 45, 260, 262, 288
Donnerstein, E., 76, 417
Doob, A. N., 54, 273, 462
Doob, L. W., 45, 260, 262, 376
Douglas, V. I., 109
Downing, L. L., 463
Drewry, B. R., 458
Driscoll, R., 212, 219
Droegemueller, W., 280
Dubin, R., 40
Duncan, O. D., 399, 400
Dunham, H. W., 399
Durkee, A., 46
Duryea, R., 233
Dutton, D. G., 217
Duval, S., 194, 281
Dweck, C. S., 96
Dworkin, R. H., 87

Eagly, A. H., 177, 183
Earn, B. M., 369
Eaton, W. O., 373
Ebbesen, E. B., 183, 282
Eberts, E. H., 385
Edgerly, J., 454
Edney, J. J., 385, 392
Edwards, D. W., 347
Edwards, J. D., 325
Edwards, J. R., 104, 358
Edwards, R. E., 158
Efran, M. G., 392
Eggleston, R. J., 255
Ehrlich, D., 157
Ehrlich, H. J., 360
Ehrlich, H. L., 351
Ehrlich, P. R., 382, 394
Einstein, A., 11, 418
Eisenberger, R., 114
Ekman, P., 127
Elashoff, J. D., 137
Ellis, D. P., 267
Ellsworth, P., 248
Elms, A. C., 159, 284, 473
Emmerich, W., 100
Emswiller, T., 371
English, A. C., 14, 308
English, H. B., 14, 308
Enzie, R. F., 328
Epstein, R., 369
Epstein, Y. M., 369
Erickson, B., 394
Erickson, L. G. W., 429
Eriksen, E. H., 318
Eron, L. D., 458
Ervin, C. R., 192

Ervin-Tripp, S. M., 154
Estes, S. G., 128
Etzioni, A., 294, 435
Evans, R. I., 357

Farber, M. L., 290
Faris, R. E. L., 399
Fatoullah, E., 206
Faucheux, C., 62, 63
Fazio, R. H., 155, 164
Feather, N. T., 371
Feierabend, I. K., 286, 287, 288, 289, 295
Feierabend, R. L., 286, 287, 288, 289, 295
Feinberg, H. K., 243
Feldman, J. M., 374
Feldman, N. S., 143
Feldman, R. E., 247
Feleky, A. M., 125
Fellman, G. A., 258
Fellner, C. H., 248
Fencil-Morse, E., 97, 429
Ferracuti, F., 111
Ferster, C. B., 19
Feshbach, S., 273
Festinger, L., 30, 65, 156, 157, 158, 163, 176, 190, 201, 304, 305, 310, 311, 312, 335, 382
Fiedler, F. E., 320
Fiedler, W. R., 137
Field, P., 154
Fine, G. A., 64, 154, 337
Finney, J., 429
Finney, S., 137
Firestone, I. J., 308, 397
Fishbein, M., 132, 133, 155, 195, 434
Fisher, J. D., 391
Fiske, E. B., 369
Fitzgerald, F., 369
Fitzpatrick, N. J., 331
Flay, B. R., 168
Florman, S. C., 411
Flynn, J. P., 257
Foa, E. B., 22, 37, 105, 219, 309
Foa, U. G., 22, 37, 105, 219, 309
Folger, R., 373
Foltz, W. J., 376
Foot, H. C., 476
Ford, C. S., 63
Forston, R. F., 387
Foucault, M., 445
Fowles, J., 104
Fraas, L. A., 317
Fraisse, P., 382
Framo, J., 219
Fraser, S. C., 278
Frauhauf-Ziegler, C., 107
Freedman, J. L., 158, 169, 384, 393, 394, 395
Freeman, S., 304, 459

Freeman, V., 206
French, J. R. P., 60, 317, 431
Frenkel-Brunswik, E., 355
Freshley, H. B., 243
Freud, A., 70
Freud, S., 65, 88, 92, 256, 257, 258, 289–290, 299, 339, 428, 451, 457
Frey, D., 160
Friedman, P., 243
Friedman, S. T., 397
Friesen, W. V., 127
Frieze, I., 144
Frijda, N. H., 127
Frodi, A., 267
Fromkin, H. L., 273, 274
Fromm, E., 218, 221
Fromson, M. E., 272

Galen, 12
Galileo, 10-11
Galle, O. R., 395
Gallois, C., 153
Gamson, W. A., 55
Garcia-Esteve, J., 63
Gardner, H., 35, 40
Gardner, M., 40
Gardner, R. C., 373
Garfield, E., 21
Garfinkel, H., 34
Gartner, R., 291
Garvey, C., 457
Gaskell, G. D., 248, 269, 295, 457, 459
Gates, M. J., 324
Gaudet, H., 177
Geen, R. G., 264, 265, 266, 269, 295
Geller, J. D., 21
Gell-Mann, M., 13
Gerard, H. B., 331
Gerbasi, K. C., 462
Gerbner, G., 272
Gergen, K. J., 16, 34, 76, 140, 141, 243, 248, 466, 467, 476
Gergen, M., 218
Gergen, M. M., 243
Gewirtz, J. L., 114
Gibb, C. A., 317
Giel, R., 395
Gil, D., 279
Gilbert, G. M., 359
Gilbert, I. A., 239
Giles, H., 104, 358
Gilfillan, D. P., 452
Gillig, P. M., 168
Gilman, A., 154
Gilmore, J., 159
Gladstone, A. I., 181
Glass, D. C., 243, 325, 401, 429
Glass, G. V., 434
Glaudin, V., 107
Gleason, J. M., 144
Glover, E., 258

Godfrey, B. W., 239
Godwin, W. F., 331
Goffman, E., 34, 205, 475
Gold, A., 176
Goldberg, G. N., 390
Goldberg, P. A., 370
Golden, M. P., 78
Goldman, M., 317
Goldschmid, M. L., 379
Goldstein, I. F., 476
Goldstein, M., 476
Good, I. J., 48
Goodale, J. G., 431
Goodchilds, J. D., 321, 454
Goode, W., 259
Goodman, C. C., 120
Goodmonson, C., 107
Goodnow, J., 105
Goodrich, A. J., 453
Goodrich, D. W., 453
Goodstadt, B., 96
Goodstadt, B. E., 317
Goodwin, L., 434
Gordon, C., 34
Goslin, D., 115
Gottesman, I. I., 87
Gottlieb, A., 248
Gottschaldt, K., 107
Gouaux, C., 194
Gould, R. W., 280
Gouldner, A., 246
Gove, W. R., 395
Graen, G., 320
Graham, E., 154
Grahamjun, C. D., 48
Granberg, D., 434
Grant, G., 369, 436
Graziano, W., 141
Green, J. A., 362
Greenberg, C. I., 397
Greene, D., 100
Greenwald, A. G., 47, 155, 160, 164,
     168, 247
Greenwald, H. J., 369, 436
Greenwald, J., 403
Greif, E. B., 108
Greipp, J. R., 37
Griffitt, W., 192, 194, 195, 199, 394
Groff, B. D., 394
Gross, A. E., 54
Gross, L., 272
Gruder, C. L., 168
Gruenberg, E. M., 445
Grusec, J. E., 96, 97
Grush, J. E., 200
Grusky, O., 55
Grzelak, J., 338
Guardo, C. J., 385
Gurr, T. R., 295
Gurwitz, S., 176
Gurwitz, S. B., 104

Guss, A., 234
Guthrie, G. M., 135
Guthrie, R. V., 379
Guttman, I., 157

Hackman, J. R., 335, 431
Haddad, J., 455
Hagen, R., 239
Hagström, W., 465
Halamaj, J., 168
Hall, C. S., 475
Hall, E. T., 383, 385, 386, 407
Hamilton, D. L., 130
Hammond, K. R., 434
Hamsher, J. H., 21, 440
Handel, W. H., 34, 100
Harary, F., 156, 196
Hardin, G., 338, 415
Hardyck, J. A., 312, 358
Harlow, H. F., 114, 187, 323, 453
Harper, L. V., 86
Harpin, R. E., 397
Harrison, G., 369
Harrison, S., 103
Hartley, E. L., 355
Hartmann, G. W., 170
Harvey, O. J., 169, 351
Haskins, J., 172
Hastorf, A. H., 127, 128, 136, 149
Hawkins, C., 462
Hawkins, R. P., 437
Hay, D. F., 100
Hayduk, L. A., 384
Head, K. B., 111
Heider, F., 28, 30, 138, 156, 195, 366
Heller, J. F., 394
Helmreich, R., 419
Helmreich, R. L., 160
Helson, H., 164, 464
Henchy, T., 325
Hendricks, M., 434
Hennigan, K. M., 168
Henry, J., 453
Hensley, V., 194
Herman, D., 234, 281
Herskovits, M. J., 124
Hertel, R. K., 219
Herzog, N., 395
Heshka, S., 395
Heslin, R., 310
Hess, R. D., 82, 105
Hewgill, M., 171
Hill, A. H., 69, 339
Hillary, J. M., 325
Hillis, J. W., 434
Himmelfarb, S., 183
Himmelweit, H. T., 154
Hinkle, S. W., 328
Hippocrates, 12
Hitchcock, J. L., 120
Hjelle, L. A., 317

Hobbes, T., 17, 20, 469, 470
Hochreich, D., 19
Hoffman, D., 429
Hoffman, L. R., 199, 334
Hoffman, M. L., 109
Hoffman, S., 330
Hollander, E. P., 316, 330
Hollingshead, A. B., 445
Holmes, D. S., 55
Holsti, O., 154
Holt, R., 463
Homans, G. C., 22, 23, 335
Hood, W. R., 351
Hook, L. H., 383
Hooten, E. A., 290
Horai, J., 206
Horn, N., 108
Horner, M. S., 370
Hornstein, H. A., 414, 440
Horowitz, I. L., 76, 438
Hough, J. C., Jr., 346
Hovland, C. I., 71, 154, 164, 165, 166,
     167, 169, 177, 179, 340, 361
Hoyt, H., 399
Hoyt, M. F., 160, 308
Hraba, J., 369, 436
Hudson, A. E., 63
Huesmann, L. R., 458
Huff, D., 78
Hughes, G. D., 434
Hull, C. L., 19
Hume, D. 16, 20
Hunt, M. M., 186
Hunt, P. J., 325
Husband, R. W., 323
Huston, T. L., 187, 221
Hyman, H. H., 96

Iliffe, A. H., 204
Inkster, J. A., 160
Insko, C. A., 96, 160, 169, 176, 192,
     357
Irle, M., 160
Isen, A. M., 108, 243
Israel, J., 62, 431, 476
Ivancevich, J. M., 431

Jaccard, J. J., 231, 374
Jacklin, C., 104
Jacklin, C. N., 115
Jackson, D. D., 213
Jacobs, P. I., 135
Jacobs, R. C., 327
Jacobson, L., 137
Jaggi, V., 141
Jahoda, G., 103
Jahoda, M., 355
James, R. M., 462
James, W., 101, 457
Janis, I. L., 154, 159, 179, 181, 334,
     343, 429

Medical view, of deviance, 444
Medicine
    and social psychology, 426–428, 443
    surgery, 427
Medium. See Communication, Mass media
Mental illness
    as attribution, 444–449
    and social class, 443
    as stereotype, 446
    see also Abnormal behavior; Psychopathology
Mere exposure, 202
Methodology. See Research methods
Mind, 27, 102
    in rationalism, 26–27
Model. See Theory
Modeling. See Social learning theory
Moral development, 108–109, 145–146; see also Ethics
Morale, 429
Motivation, 24, 100, 426
    achievement, 429–432
Music, 35, 123, 450; see also Aesthetics
Mutuality, 188

Natural environment, 382
Natural experiment, 62
Nature–nurture controversy, 86–88;
    see also Sociobiology
Need complementarity, 212–215
    dominance–submission, 214–215
    and interpersonal attraction, 212–215
    in marriage, 214
    nurturance–receptivity, 214–215
    types, 214–215
Need for achievement. See Achievement motivation
Negative income tax experiment, 60
Neo-Freudians, 35
Neurosis, and socialization, 97
Nobel Prize, 461
Noise
    and aggression, 267
    effects, 399
Nonadaptive behavior. See Panic
Nonconformity, 329; see also Conformity; Anti-conformity
Norm. See Social norm
Novelty. See Exploratory behavior
Nurturance–receptivity, and need complementarity, 214–215

Obedience, 280–282
    and aggression, 280–282
    see also Conformity
Object perception. See Perception

Observation, nonobjective nature of, 71–72
Observational learning. See Social learning theory
Observational research, 64–65, 77
Oedipus complex, 91, 92–93
Operant conditioning, 19, 95
    of attitudes, 362
    verbal, 96
Opinion leader, 177
Opinionation, 354
Overstimulation. See Stimulation, Stimulus overload

Panic, 336–337
    and arousal, 336
    as collective behavior, 336–337
    and reinforcement, 336
    and threat, 337
Participant observation, 64–65
Peace research. See Aggression; Conflict resolution; International relations
Pearson product–moment correlation coefficient, 52–53, 66–67, 77
Perceived similarity, 192–193
    and friendship, 192–193, 199
Perception, 27, 28, 103, 118–124, 426
    cross-cultural study, 121–122, 124
    and expectation, 121–122, 136–138
    and experience, 121–122, 136–138
    Gestalt principles, 122–124, 130, 132
    and language, 120–121
    see also Person perception
Perceptual constancy, 124
Performance, 320–321, 322, 330–334, 392
    vs. learning, 21, 268, 322
    see also Productivity
Peripheral trait, 130
Person perception, 118, 124–138
    accuracy, 125–129
    cross-cultural study, 134–136
    impression formation, 129–138
    and physical appearance, 205–207
    research methods, 126–128
Person–situation interaction, 111, 241–242
Personal distance, 384
Personal space, 382–390
    cross-cultural study, 384–386, 395
    and crowding, 395
    cultural variations, 384–386, 395
    defined, 382, 388
    sex differences, 389
    and situational variables, 383
    theories, 386–388
    types, 384
    violation, 388–390
Personality, 32, 34, 54, 421, 422, 426

and aesthetics, 449
and aggression, 279, 282
and helping, 227–228, 240–242
and humor, 451
and interpersonal attraction, 205
and leadership, 316–317
and prejudice, 353–355, 358
    structure, 34
Persuasion. See Attitude change
Persuasive communication. See Attitude change
Philosophy, 1–16, 27, 44, 408–411, 412
    vs. science, 44
    see also Empiricism; Rationalism
Physical appearance
    and aggression, 276
    and communicator credibility, 206
    and crowding, 204
    and interpersonal attraction, 203–208
    judgments, 204
    and person perception, 205–207
Physical environment, 378–405
    changes in, 402–403
    and crime, 402–403
    and sports, 323
Physics, 9–11, 13, 28, 464
Physiological arousal. See Arousal
Physiology, and social behavior, 3, 5
Play, 102
Political socialization, 82
Political violence. See Revolution, War
Politics,
    and applied social psychology, 432–434
    voter appeals, 170
    see also Law
Pollution, 380, 435
Population density, 381
    and affiliation, 395
    animal studies, 391–392
    vs. crowding, 391, 393
    emotional effects, 392
Population explosion, 380, 435
Position power, 318
Positive reference group. See Reference group
Post hoc explanations, 72–73, 78
Potlatch, 257
Poverty, 435
Prediction. See Theory
Prejudice, 308, 409, 437, 450
    and belief, 355–357
    defined, 346
    effects, 367
    and humor, 362–367
    learning, 360–362
    and personality, 353–355
    racism vs. belief, 355–357

reducing, 29, 370–374
and law, 370
and social learning theory, 362
and social norms, 367–368
and social psychology, 370–374
and socialization, 353
victims, 367–370
and victim–offender relationship, 367–370
Pretrial publicity, 460
Primary group, 300
Primary process, 88
Privacy. *See* Anonymity
Probability, 14, 67–68
Problem-solving. *See* Decision-making
Productivity, 317, 332, 333, 429–432
Project Camelot, 76, 436–437
Projection, 288, 289, 358
and stereotype, 358
Projective test, 70
Propaganda, 169
defined, 171
techniques, 171–175
see also Attitude change;
Communication; Mass media
Prophecy, 65, 309–310
Propinquity, 201, 302
and affiliation, 302
and emotion, 202
aggression, 202
and friendship, 202
and interpersonal attraction, 201–202
and marriage, 201
Prosocial behavior
defined, 223
and socialization, 107–110
see also Helping
Protestant ethic, 234
Proxemics, 383; *see also* Personal space
Psychiatry, 444; *see also*
Psychoanalysis; Psychopathology
Psychoanalytic theory, 34–35, 39, 70, 88–94, 205, 427
and aesthetics, 449
and aggression, 255–256
and child abuse, 278
cross-cultural study, 92–93
and prejudice, 353–355, 358
psychosexual development, 89–93
and psychotherapy, 34, 444–449
and socialization, 88–94
and society, 34
and war, 287–289
Psychohistory, 315
Psychopathology, 144, 397, 427
labeling theory, 145
Psychophysics, 164
Psychosexual development, 34, 89–93

psychoanalytic theory of, 89–93
Psychosomatic illness, 4
Psychotherapy, 34, 444–449; *see also*
Psychoanalytic theory
Ptolemaic system of universe, 9–10
Public distance, 384
Public policy, and social psychology, 432, 433
Pure science, 409

Quasi experiment, 61–62

Race differences, 345–346
Racial preference studies, 367–370, 432
Racism
aversive, 344
dominative, 344
cultural, 350
see also Prejudice
Radio. *See* Mass media
Randomization, 56, 60, 61
Rape, 237
Rationalism, 26–27
and mind, 26–27
Rationalization, 288, 289
Reactance theory, 180, 328, 425
of resistance to persuasion, 180
Reductionism, 6
Reference group, 302, 330, 368, 427–428, 454
Referant power, 315
Reflexivity, 16
Reification, 297
Reinforcement, 268, 421, 425, 456
and panic, 336
schedules, 19
see also Behaviorism; Learning theory
Reinforcement expectancy, 19–21, 219
Relative deprivation, 284
Relativity theory, 11, 418
Religion, 234
and just-world phenomenon, 234
as social institution, 443
Replication, 47, 63
interpersonal, 163
Research, 8, 42–79
applied, 406–439
and ethics, 74–77, 78, 255
hypothesis-generating, 68–69
hypothesis-testing, 42–67
on real events, 69, 406–439
in relation to theory, 70–71
scientific, 8
Research methods, 29, 32, 42–79
on aesthetics, 450
on aggression, 253
of applied social psychology, 410–411

on authoritarian personality, 353–354
compared, 59
cross-cultural, 62–64
on effects of mass media, 269
in evaluation research, 410–411
on groups, 298, 329
on group structure, 311–313
on humor, 452
on interpersonal attraction, 197–198
on person perception, 126–128
pragmatics, 411
on war, 284
Residual rule-breaking, 446
Resistance, to persuasion, 179–182
inoculation theory, 180–182
and reactance theory, 180
Resource exchange theory, 24; *see also* Social exchange theory
Responsibility
attribution of, 145–147
diffusion of, 226–229
Revolution, 284
and frustration, 285–286
Reward power, 315
Riots, 337–339, 455
and social norms, 337–338
Ritual aggression, 457
Role-taking, 101
Role theory, 34, 435
Romantic attraction. *See*
Interpersonal attraction; Love
Rural–urban differences
in helping, 227–228
in intimacy, 398

Sampling error, 410
Scapegoat, 359–360
Schedules, of reinforcement, 19
Schizophrenia, 447
Science
applied, 408–409
defined, 8
Nobel Prize, 461
vs. philosophy, 44
pure, 409
research, 8
role of theory, 8
social goals, 418–419
social psychology as, 7–9
social psychology of, 461–464
as social system, 443, 463
Secondary group, 300
Selective exposure, to information, 157–158
and cognitive dissonance, 157–158
Self. *See* Personality
Self-esteem, 457, 458
and helping, 241
and sports, 457

see also Arousal; Competence
Stimulation theory, 388
Stimulus overload, and cities, 399
Stress, 426
Structuralism, 35–37, 39
  assumptions, 37
Subjective map. See Cognitive map
Sublimation, 256
Superordinate goal, 371
Supreme Court, 461
Surgery, 427
Surveillance, 402; see also Anonymity
Superego, 89
Symbolic interactionism, 32–34, 39,
    70, 108
  and cognitive theory, 33–34
  and sex roles, 104
  and socialization, 100–103
Symmetry, 196; see also Cognitive
    balance

t-test, 67
T-group, 29
Task-oriented group, 300
Task performance, 330–334; see also
    Productivity
Task structure, 318
Television. See Mass media
Temperament, 12; see also
    Personality
Temperature, 392
Temporal factors, 380
  in achievement, 430
  in aggression, 277–280
  in group interaction, 312–313

Tennis, 458, 459
Tension, 30, 31, 291–292
Territoriality, 383, 390–391
  markers, 389, 390
Thanatos, 88, 255
Theoretical approach, 16
  behaviorism, 16–26
  cognitive, 26–32, 122–124
  psychoanalytic, 34–35, 88–94
  structuralism, 35–37, 39
  symbolic interactionism, 32–34
Theory, 8, 13
  and applied social psychology,
    408–412
  criteria for evaluating, 14
  defined, 14
  functions, 469–470
  heuristic value, 15
  origins, 15–16
  role, 442
  see also specific theories; Research;
    Theoretical approaches
Threat, and panic, 337
Time. See Temporal factors
Trial. See Jury; Law
Two-step flow of communication,
    177–179

Unconditioned response, 18
Unconditioned stimulus, 18
Unconscious, 88, 288; see also
    Psychoanalytic theory
Understanding, as goal of science,
    9–13
Unitary task, 331

Unobtrusive measure, 55
Urbanization. see City
Utilitarianism, 17

Value-added theory, 338–339
Value conflict, 344
Variance, 67
Verbal operant conditioning, 96
Victim–offender relationship, 202
  and prejudice, 367–370
Victimology. See Victim–offender
    relationship; Crime
Violation
  of personal space, 388–390
  of sex roles, 368
Violence. See Aggression; Collective
    behavior
Voir dire (jury selection), 460
Voting, 410, 432
  and communication, 170
  and emotional appeals, 177–178

War, 256, 276, 283–292, 432, 455
  cross-cultural study, 283–287
  and frustration, 283–287
  psychoanalytic theory, 287–289
  research methods, 284
Warm–cold variable, in impression
    formation, 130
Weapons, and aggression, 264–265
Whorfian hypothesis, 121
Wit. See Humor
Witchcraft, 443–444

Xenophobia, 353

CREDITS

Chapter 1 [4] Richard Frear/Photo Researchers [7] Mimi Forsyth/Monkmeyer Press Photo Service [15] Ray Ellis/Photo Researchers [18] Hamlund/Photo Researchers [22] Susan Szasz/Photo Researchers [36] Jim Smith

Chapter 2 [44] Susan Szasz/Photo Researchers [48/49] From I. J. Good, *The scientist speculates*, ©1965, Capricorn Book, Inc. Used by Permission. [54] Paul S. Conklin/ Photo Researchers [59] George Zimbel/Monkmeyer [63] Jim Smith [68] Jim Smith [73] Joe Portogallo/Photo Researchers [74/75] Copyright 1973 by the American Psychological Association. Reprinted by permission.

Chapter 3 [83] Sybil Shelton/Monkmeyer [87] Dieter Grabitzky/Monkmeyer [90] Milton Rogovin/Photo Researchers [95] David S. Strickler/Monkmeyer [99] J. Becker [101] Jim Smith [105] Michael Hayman/Photo Researchers [108] Jim Smith [112/ 113] From *Aggression and crimes of violence* by Jeffrey H. Goldstein. Copyright ©1975 by Oxford University Press, Inc. Used by permission.

Chapter 4 [119] Joel F. Zucker/Photo Researchers [120] By William Walden. Copyright ©1974, by the Atlantic Monthly Company, Boston, Mass. Reprinted with permission. [137] Hella Hammid/Photo Researchers [142] Jim Smith [145] Michael Hayman/Photo Researchers [146] Copyright 1966 by the American Psychological Association. Reprinted with permission.

Chapter 5 [152] Russ Kline/Photo Researchers [161] Michael Kagan/Monkmeyer [169] Margot Granitsas [173] Tom McHugh/Photo Researchers [178] Katrina Thomas/Photo Researchers [181] Jan Lucas/Photo Researchers

Chapter 6 [193] Dan Bernstein/Photo Researchers [203] Les Mahon/Monkmeyer [206] Ray Ellis/Photo Researchers [209] Chester Higgins, Jr./Photo Researchers [215] Adapted from R. F. Winch, *Mate selection*. Copyright ©1958 by R. F. Winch. By permission of Harper & Row. [216] Susan Szasz-Photo Researchers

Chapter 7 [225] Mimi Forsyth/Monkmeyer [229] Amelia Panico [230] Bibb Latane and John M. Darley, *The Unresponsive bystander: Why doesn't he help?* ©1970, p. 115, 117. Adapted by permission of Prentice-Hall, Inc., Englewood Cliffs, N.J. [233] Amelia Panico [236] Jim Smith [241] Jim Smith [239] Copyright 1966 by the American Psychological Association. Reprinted with permission. [249] Jim Smith

Chapter 8 [254] Bruce Roberts/Photo Researchers [259] Bruce Roberts/Photo Researchers [259,279] From *Aggression and crimes of violence* by Jeffrey H. Goldstein. Copyright ©1975 by Oxford University Press, Inc. Used by permission. [261] David Krasnor/Photo Researchers [266] Copyright 1966 by the American Psychological Association. Reprinted with permission. [276] Copyright 1967 by the American Psychological Association. Reprinted with permission. [279] Lynn McLaren/Photo Researchers [280] Jim Smith From pp. 73–74 in S. Milgram, *Obedience to authority*. Copyright ©1974 by Stanley Milgram. By Permission of Harper & Row. [282/283]

Chapter 9 [301] Hays/Monkmeyer [303] Lane/Photo Researchers [306] Mary Thomas [311] Daniels/Photo Researchers [319] Culver Pictures [323] Cranham/Photo Researchers [326] Figure 10.3 (p. 208) in *Social psychology* by Muzafer Sherif and Caroline W. Sherif. Copyright ©1969 by M. Sherif and C. W. Sherif. By permission of Harper & Row. [333] Jim Smith [337] Stanley Milgram/Hans Toch, "Collective Behavior," from G. Lindzey/E. Aronson, Eds., *Handbook of social psychology*, Vol. 4, 2/e, ©1969, Addison-Wesley, Reading Mass., p. 523. Reprinted with permission. [316] Adapted from R. F. Bales, *Interaction process analysis* (1950), University of Chicago Press. Reprinted with permission.

Chapter 10 [*356*] Jim Smith [*359*] Copyright 1969 by the American Psychological Association. Reprinted with permission. [*363*] Suris/Photo Researchers [*371*] Conklin/Monkmeyer [*374*] Jim Smith [ ] From Interpersonal behavior by H. C. Triandis. Copyright ©1977 by Wadsworth, Inc. Reprinted by permission of the publisher, Brooks/Cole Publishing Co., Monterey, California.

Chapter 11 [*385*] Lacey/Photo Researchers [*389*] Reprinted from the December 12, 1977 issue of Business Week by special permission, ©1977 by McGraw-Hill, Inc., New York, N.Y. 10020 [*390*] Robert Sommer, *Personal space: The behavioral basis of design*, ©1969, p. 49. Adapted by permission of Prentice-Hall, Inc., Englewood Cliffs, N.J. [*391*] Copyright 1975 by the American Psychological Association. Reprinted with permission. [*395*] Lacey/Photo Researchers [*396*] Ben-chieh Liu, *Quality of life indicators in U.S. metropolitan areas* (New York: Praeger Publishers, 1976).

Chapter 12 [*413*] Bill Mahan/Photo Researchers [*416*] Paul Conklin/Monkmeyer [*421*] Copyright 1970 by the American Academy for the Advancement of Science. [*423*] Neil Litt [*429*] Reprinted by permission of V. H. Winston and Sons, 7961 Eastern Ave., Silver Spring, MD 20910. [*431*] Bruce Roberts/Photo Researchers [*433*] Copyright 1969 by Macmillan Publishing Co. Reprinted with permission.

Chapter 13 [*447*] Michael Hayman/Photo Researchers [*450*] Lukas/Photo Researchers [*455*] Jim Smith [*456*] David Plowden/Photo Researchers Reprinted by permission of the author and publisher from J. H. Goldstein's *Sports, games, and play*. Hillsdale, N.J.: Erlbaum, 1979. [*465*] Mimi Forsyth/Monkmeyer